# KING OF THE DELTA BLUES

# KING OF THE DELTA BLUES

## The Life and Music of CHARLIE PATTON

*Second Edition*

Gayle Dean Wardlow, Stephen Calt, and Edward Komara

THE CHARLES K. WOLFE MUSIC SERIES

Ted Olson, *Series Editor*

**The University of Tennessee**
*Knoxville*

*The Charles K. Wolfe Music Series was launched in honor of the late Charles K. Wolfe (1943–2006), whose pioneering work in the study of American vernacular music brought a deepened understanding of a wide range of American music to a worldwide audience. In recognition of Dr. Wolfe's approach to music scholarship, the series will include books that investigate genres of folk and popular music as broadly as possible.*

*Second Edition.*

FRONTISPIECE: Charlie Patton, studio portrait for Paramount Records publicity, 1929.
On the brink of national stardom, and knowing it.

**LIBRARY OF CONGRESS CATALOGING-IN-PUBLICATION DATA**

Names: Wardlow, Gayle, author. | Calt, Stephen, 1946–2010, author | Komara, Edward M., 1966- author.

Title: King of the delta blues : the life and music of Charlie Patton / Gayle Dean Wardlow, Stephen Calt, and Edward M. Komara.

Description: Second edition. | Knoxville : The University of Tennessee Press, 2022. | Series: The Charles K. Wolfe music series | Includes bibliographical references and index. | Summary: "Charlie Patton (c. 1891–1934) was born in central Mississippi. By 1908, he had begun his performing career, initially at small house parties, then at barrelhouses and other settings that could accommodate a hundred people or more. Until his death in 1934, Patton was a top draw for the numerous African Americans then living and working in the Delta. In 1929 and 1930, he recorded several hits for Paramount Records, on the basis of which he was sought by the American Record Company in January 1934 for what would be his last recordings. He was immensely influential to other bluesmen, including Tommy Johnson, Kid Bailey, Robert Johnson, and Howlin' Wolf. Since 1991, his collected recordings have been available to the wider public. This book was previously published in 1988 under the authorship of Wardlow (b. 1940) and Calt (1946–2010). Its sole printing of 3,000 paperback copies sold out within seven years, and since 1988 additional recordings of Patton and his associates have been recovered and widely reissued to the public, particularly on Jack White's Third Man Records. Komara (b. 1966) has updated Wardlow and Calt's original edition and has written a new afterword discussing a resurgence of Delta blues–style rock and the continuing influence of Patton and the music genre he helped pioneer"—Provided by publisher.

Identifiers: LCCN 2022017497 (print) | LCCN 2022017498 (ebook) | ISBN 9781621906612 (paperback) | ISBN 9781621906629 (pdf)

Subjects: LCSH: Patton, Charley, 1891–1934. | Blues musicians—Mississippi—Biography.

Classification: LCC ML420.P323 C34 2022 (print) | LCC ML420.P323 (ebook) | DDC 781.643092 [B]—dc23/eng/20220412

LC record available at https://lccn.loc.gov/2022017497

LC ebook record available at https://lccn.loc.gov/2022017498

# Contents

# Illustrations

## PHOTOS

*Following page 200*

## MUSIC EXAMPLES

# Foreword

The text you are now reading is a new edition—painstakingly updated and where necessary rewritten and recontextualized—of *King of the Delta Blues,* a compelling (if in some quarters controversial) 1988 study of Charlie Patton (1891–1934). The book in its original iteration featured twenty years of research conducted in the field and at various archives and libraries by Stephen Calt and Gayle Wardlow, pioneering blues researchers who shared a commitment to illuminating the life and interpreting the music of that legendary musician from the Mississippi Delta. Before Calt and Wardlow's book fleshed out the specter of Patton, the musician was only known among hardcore blues aficionados, who had encountered rare 1920s recordings by Patton on 1960s- and 1970s-era LPs released by companies that specialized in reissues of historical recordings. One of Patton's 78 RPM sides, "Mississippi BoWeavil Blues" (1929), was included on Folkways Records' vaunted 1952 *Anthology of American Folk Music* under the alias The Masked Marvel, but most listeners to that influential album would not have connected such a powerful, hypnotic performance to its real-life creator. Indeed, many of Patton's recordings were released under pseudonyms, and it is hardly surprising that he remained unknown to the general public for many years.

There were other reasons for Patton's obscurity. In reflecting upon the matter, Wardlow observes that Patton's reputation has been mercilessly overshadowed for decades by the hype and hysteria devoted to a younger Mississippi bluesman, Robert Johnson (1911–1938). "I don't think the size of Patton's reputation has changed. But it has seemed smaller when compared to the ballooning reputation of Robert Johnson during the last 60 years, since the appearance of the 1961 Columbia LP *King of the Delta Blues Singers.* Many blues fans have shoved Charlie aside in favor of Johnson, which I think is unfair." The "fame gap" between these two Mississippi legends has been reduced in recent years. Johnson's reputation may continue to soar at ethereal heights, but Patton by the early twenty-first century was entering the limelight in the wake of the multiple Grammy Award-winning boxed set *Screamin' and Hollerin' the Blues: The Worlds of Charley Patton* (Revenant Records, 2001), which utilized Paramount Records' spelling of the bluesman's first name. Accordingly, this new edition of *King of the Delta Blues* is positioned to consolidate Patton's legend and extend the influence of his music among a new generation.

The book originated, Wardlow recalls, during the 1960s blues revival: "Steve and I began corresponding in 1964, and as early as 1968 we began planning a book on Patton and the Mississippi Delta blues. In 1970, we met up in Atlanta, where we embarked on a research trip from there to Mississippi, along the way interviewing Polk Brockman, H. C. Speir, and Joe Rice Dockery. By the end of this trip, we realized that we had enough material on Patton alone to fill a book. Steve began writing in earnest, working hard for 15 years through 1985, and touching up the text until Richard Nevins published it in 1988 through his Rock Chapel Press." The second edition of *King of the Delta Blues* braids together information from the book's first edition with subsequent research conducted by Wardlow (and by Calt through his 2010 death). But this new edition owes its very existence to blues scholar Ed Komara, who took on the daunting task of overseeing extensive revision of an existing and rather complex work. According to Komara:

> Revising the Patton book was my idea. I had helped Gayle Wardlow prepare several of his articles with Stephen Calt for republication in *Chasin' That Devil Music* (San Francisco: Miller Freeman Books, 1998). The tone and syntax of some of their collaborations were remarkably straightforward compared to other writings by Stephen alone. Shortly after Stephen died in 2010, Gayle acquired the Patton book's rights from its publisher Richard Nevins. For the reprint, Gayle initially thought about cutting the passages that were unclear to him. I valued the arguments in the book despite their wording, and I didn't want to see them cut or reduced. I said to him, "Let me try rewriting a few paragraphs. If you can understand them, will you allow me to revise the whole book?" Gayle was pleased enough with my sample revisions to allow me to treat the whole text.

A leading blues music researcher with a keen understanding of the genre's many artists, repertoires, and styles, Komara confesses that his initial interest in the book had much to do with the nature of the collaboration between Calt and Wardlow. "Neither Gayle nor Stephen were ivory-tower academics. During the years of research, Gayle was a journalist for newspapers in Jackson and Meridian, Mississippi. Later he taught journalism on college campuses, but he was a practical teacher of the craft. Stephen was a musician and freelance writer who conducted his literature research in New York City libraries. For the Patton project, they were a well-suited pair: Stephen for his erudition, Gayle for his firsthand knowledge of Mississippi geography and Mississippi people's ways. They were very different from people like me who are instructors at colleges and universities and who write primarily for other academics." Through his editorial effort Komara transformed a text that had been marred by patches of Calt's "turgid writing" (to quote from Chris Smith's April 1989 review of the book in *Blues and Rhythm*), and Wardlow and Komara also saw cause to remove an appendix of the book weakened by Calt's confrontational critique of rival blues scholars. Accordingly, the second edition of *King of the Delta Blues* is leaner and clearer and less mired in momentary scholarly politics.

Calt's reputation may have been tarnished among some of his contemporaries, but Komara believed that Calt—beyond any perceived affectations and aggressions—was a painstaking scholar with a rare and deep understanding of Patton's blues repertoire and style. As Komara conveys, "Stephen Calt studied, identified, and wrote down the musical traits of Patton's style that have not been heard anywhere in the last eighty years—unless the performer is imitating Patton's records. I hope the new edition, with its notated musical examples, will help to improve the understanding of what Stephen wrote about the music. Certainly guitar players will find the revised descriptions useful. Perhaps these republished findings will aid the transcription of Patton's guitar parts. There isn't yet a whole volume of guitar transcriptions from Patton's records, like there have been published for Skip James and Robert Johnson."

In our time, societal conversations about race tend to be based in collective acknowledgment of the complexities in understanding and discussing race. While ostensibly a music biography, this second edition of *King of the Delta Blues*, Komara says, might serve to remind readers of an earlier generation's attitudes toward race relations in pre-civil rights era America:

> I think the new edition reminds us of how bluntly people used to state their opinions about race. Gayle began his interviews in 1963, before the federal legislation in civil rights (1964) and voting rights (1965) were passed. Stephen's interviews were conducted a little later in the 1960s. Most of the interviewees were in their fifties and sixties, so their attitudes were formed, if not hardened, by the start of the 1940s. While smoothing the narrative text, I checked the

> quotes to Gayle's audio interviews whenever possible, and I let them stand as rough as they were. There are a few quotes that disturbed me enough to ask Gayle, "Should we leave them in?" But we retained them. Many recent histories, especially those published by academic presses, don't contain as many quotations as the Patton book, and it is important for the sake of history to keep these quotations and let them bristle.
>
> Gayle and Stephen gleaned many clues from Patton's lyrics about places that no longer exist in the Mississippi Delta, or at least no longer exist in the ways they did a hundred years ago. What Patton called and described as "barrelhouses" were going out of business even at the time he was making his records. The all–African American Delta communities like Mound Bayou in their pre-war primes must have been something for their residents to take pride in. Another Patton scholar, David Evans, titled his study of Patton, *The Conscience of the Delta*. In contrast, Gayle and Stephen study Patton as a valuable "witness of the Delta." On his records, he mentions a lot of people, places, and things that won't be found in the Delta writings of David L. Cohn or in the back files of many Delta newspapers.

The portrayal of Patton provided by this trio of researchers reveals a lively, believable character as well as a master musician, as Komara eloquently relates: "Patton was grand. He attracted and kept his audiences with his music and the way he talked. Memories of him, imperfect as they may have been, suggest a rascal, a rolling stone gathering no moss, and a very smart man who bucked the restrictions of the white-dominated Delta to live very well there on his own terms. In this biography, Patton is a captivating character. There is a joke or an anecdote on every page of Gayle and Stephen's narrative to sustain the reader's interest."

Wardlow, witnessing the reemergence of a book he had co-written decades earlier, maintains that the significance of Patton's music has only increased with the years: "Re-reading the book and helping Ed improve some pages has led me to see Patton as a more dynamic and stronger artist than I had remembered before, if that is possible. He was always "the tops" in Mississippi blues for me. The new edition cements Patton's reputation as one of the earliest practitioners and developers of what became the Delta blues in the early 1900s." Reflecting upon his experience of helping to bring *King of the Delta Blues* back into print, Komara concludes: "I have had much pleasure working with Gayle on this beautiful book."

TED OLSON
East Tennessee State University

# Preface

When Gayle Dean Wardlow and Stephen Calt published their biography *King of the Delta Blues: The Life and Music of Charlie Patton* in 1988, the musician was still of cult interest. Even though the Rock Chapel Press edition of 3000 copies sold out in 7 years, it seemed all of the books were purchased by the faithful flock, and those who were later converted missed out. Patton wasn't mainstream yet.

But then, two events happened to change his standing. One was in 1990, when the 2-CD reissue of Robert Johnson (*The Complete Recordings*, Sony/Columbia Legacy C2K 46222) appeared. It was a greater sales success than expected, which suggested to some reissue labels that there may be consumer interest in CD compilations of blues recorded before 1942. That, arguably, enabled the other event, the complete reissue of Patton's recordings during the 1990s, initially on 3 CDs by Document Records, then with a partial reissue of them on 2 CDs by Yazoo/Shanachie, and most notably in a 7-CD box set with abundant documentation issued in 2001 by John Fahey's Revenant Records. Through these reissues, Patton has achieved the status of classic. He still hasn't overshadowed the other Patton in American culture, General George S. "Blood and Guts" Patton, but perhaps time may change that.

With this increase in awareness of Charlie Patton, the demand for the reappearance of Wardlow and Calt's biography has risen. The 1988 retail price was $15 for the book, which now fetches between $60 and $150 by used book dealers such as those on Abebooks.com. But the content of the 1988 book became outdated. The ongoing recovery of records by Patton and his blues associates yielded several performances that were unknown to the authors in 1988. Also, continuing research by Wardlow, and new findings by younger writers in the 1990s and 2000s, filled in many gaps in Patton's life story. A revision of *King of the Delta Blues* was needed.

*King of the Delta Blues Singers* had a tumultuous history before and even after its 1988 publication. Wardlow had begun his Patton research in 1963 during his research trip with Bernard Klatzko to Dockery Farms and the Mississippi Delta. Wardlow and Calt began collaborating in 1966, their first joint articles appearing in Pete Whelan's *78 Quarterly*. Work on what was to become the Patton biography began in 1970, with a complete draft ready for publishers in 1976. The manuscript, however, was rejected by the University Press of Mississippi on peer advice by David Evans, and suspended at another press when its reviewer Robert Palmer failed to respond or return the reading copy. It is intriguing to note that, at the time, Evans and Palmer were conducting competing research on Patton and his music: Evans with his 1976 doctoral dissertation that was later published as *Big Road Blues* (1982) (with additional Patton research later published as the essay "The Conscience of the Delta" in 1987 in Belgium), and Palmer with *Deep Blues* in 1981. To keep alive their effort to publish the book, Calt and Wardlow made full disclosures about these obstacles to publish in an open letter that was printed simultaneously in 1981 in the magazines *Blues Unlimited* and *Living Blues*.[1]

Finally, in 1986, Nick Perls committed to publishing the book through his Yazoo Records firm. The next year, though, Perls died from AIDS, but not before ensuring that the Patton book publication was a required condition as part of his sale of Yazoo to Richard Nevins at Shanachie Records. Nevins honored that condition by publishing the book in paperback (there was no hardcover edition) through the imprint Rock Chapel Press. The 1988 printed text was considerably different from the 1976 manuscript, with the rewritten text touting Patton above his contemporaries and protégées, the style taking on a new tone that seemed bullying and arcane, and a new appendix "Charlie Patton and the Scholastics" that took severely to task the prevailing publications about Patton, especially those by Evans.

I first read *King of the Delta Blues* in 1993, upon my arrival to the University of Mississippi to direct its Blues Archive and Music Library. The following year I met Gayle Wardlow, and we began a working relationship that produced his book *Chasin' That Devil Music* (1998), contributions to the Revenant set of Patton (2001), various articles for *Blues and Rhythm: The Gospel Truth* and *Living Blues* (see the bibliography under Wardlow's name), and a couple of projects that, if still unpublished, were fun to work on.

Stephen Calt died in October 2010. The following year, Wardlow acquired the rights to the Patton book from Richard Nevins. In 2012, he and I began work towards updating and revising the text. I had never met or spoken with Calt, but the more I worked on the revision, the more my admiration for his work with Gayle increased. "It took Steve 18 years to write this book" Gayle Wardlow told me recently, as his way of saying it was only right of us to have devoted as much time as we did to revive the text, in memory of his co-author, and for the 21st century, too.

The strengths of the 1988 book were Wardlow's research data, especially those that were conveyed through the interview quotes, and Calt's reading of contextual publications, including those published during Patton's lifetime. The hallmarks of their Patton narrative were:

> Patton's life coincided with the rise and fall of barrelhouses in the Mississippi Delta
> The blues likely came to the plantations by way of the barrelhouses, not vice versa
> Patton's blues was a result of the barrelhouse culture
> As a barrelhouse musician, Patton had to be a dance musician
> The necessity of Patton's distinctive musical approach was to ensure that a steady beat was felt if not always heard by the dancers.

To present the last point, Calt wrote some lengthy passages of musical analysis that may be rather dense for the general reader. The payoff for effort to understand those passages is the informed ability to appreciate the musical nature of the personal interactions during the recording sessions, especially those between Patton and Willie Brown during their duet recordings in 1930.

But a thorough overhaul of the text had to be done. The most obvious reason was the overwrought style of the 1988 book, which was written mostly by Calt. Chris Smith, reviewing for the British magazine *Blues and Rhythm: The Gospel Truth* (no. 45 [April 1989] 20–21) identified the problem on appropriate terms as "thesaurus regurgitation," pointing out that it would have been better to write "we don't know how he spent his money" instead of "the trajectory of his . . . income remains unaccountable." What made the revision challenging was that Calt wrote each chapter as a self-sustaining essay; moving even a sentence of text could affect the surrounding page, if not the rest of the chapter. So, as much as possible, Wardlow and I retained Calt's organization at the chapter, paragraph, and sentence levels. But we rendered the wording into standard American-English usage. Comparison of this edition with the 1988 text will show that many pages are translations, in a sense. Some biographical content was moved in accordance with new findings about Patton's life. The only cuts we made to the text were of a table based on a faulty analysis of a Patton song, a couple of passages that made use of an incorrect transcription of Patton's lyrics, and three quotes from sources that we could not verify.

A second reason was the new published information on Patton's last 5 years (1929–1934), especially for his recording sessions, the recording industry at the time, and his last years in and around Holly Ridge, Mississippi. There were also recent biographies of the chief musicians associated with Patton, especially Willie Brown, Son House, and Howlin' Wolf, that provided new details or confirmations for facts in Patton's life.

Thirdly, there was in the 1988 book Calt's contentious third appendix "Charlie Patton and the Scholastics." More than merely exposing the bases—and limits—of the previously published studies of Patton by John Fahey, Robert Palmer, and David Evans, Calt went further to attack the principles of their research, especially those by Evans and Palmer. Wardlow remembered for me that the intent of the appendix was to forestall the criticisms by these writers if they were to review the book for journals and magazines. But the appendix backfired. It made no use of Calt and Wardlow's emphasis of barrelhouse culture in the Delta blues (an aspect that was neglected by the authors' competitors, and that was also not mentioned in Smith's review and, for that matter, in Luc Sante's 1994 review in the *New York Review of Books*). It also made some editors and publishers sympathize less with the authors and more with their rivals. Because the appendix was meant more for 1988 than for the 2020s, Wardlow and I agreed to remove this appendix from the revised edition.

Another appendix in the 1988 book, Calt's glossary of blues terms, has also been removed, this time for reasons of space. For his definitions of words and slang sung by Patton, and for the rest of his blues lexicographical work, see his *Barrelhouse Words: A Blues Dialect Dictionary* (Urbana and Chicago: Univ. of Illinois Press, 2009).

New to the book is the biographical glossary, whose function is to introduce or explain to the reader who was a particular informant or significant person in Patton's life. Since some of the people quoted in the chapters were hardly known until the 1988 edition of this book, the biographical glossary may be of real help to readers who are new to Patton's life and lore.

Improved are the photographs, endnotes, bibliography, and discography. Since neither Calt or Wardlow had received formal training in bibliography, and the production staff preparing the 1988 book for press did not recognize the editorial needs that the submitted text demanded, the scanty documentation of publications and sound recordings was a weakness. To bolster the text for the present revision, the bibliography was updated, and the endnotes were enriched with additional comments and even opposing views in the recent Patton literature. Furthermore, the discography was changed from being a short list of basic reissues to a comprehensive account of releases on 78s, CDs, and LPs.

The 1988 edition of *King of the Delta Blues* contained no musical examples. To illustrate Calt's analytic passages, I prepared over 60 musical examples. One-sixth of them were adapted from previously published notated transcriptions by Stefan Grossman, whose work seemed to have serve as a basis for several paragraphs in the 1988 book; his permission to use in this book is gratefully acknowledged. The rest were transcribed by me from records. For the new transcriptions, I determined the keys from Christopher King's transfers for the Revenant set *Screamin' and Hollerin' the Blues: The Worlds of Charley Patton* (Revenant 212, 2001). These examples are secondary to the recorded music, and they serve primarily to help the reader identify the moments that Calt describes in his analytic passages. Formatting for the music examples was done by my student assistant Ally Jindra; any errors or inconsistencies in notation are mine.

For this revision, I wish to acknowledge the help of many people. Chief among them is Richard Nevins of Shanachie/Yazoo Records who published the first edition in 1988, and from whom Gayle acquired the rights in 2011. Researchers with whom we corresponded early in the project were Randy Meadows, Jesse Lee Yancy, and Lawrence Cohn. Additional colleagues came from Revenant Records and Third Man Records' preparations for their two "cabinets of wonder," *The Rise and Fall of Paramount* (2013–2014), especially the research team leader Alex van der Tuuk, Guido van Rijn, Paul Swinton, and Scott Blackwood. My book reviews editor Jim Farrington for the *Association of Recorded Sound Collections* (*ARSC*) Journal relayed several recent books about Mississippi Delta blues. Jim Swinnich provided me with his then-unpublished research on Dockery Farms, which helped me write the new final chapter on the Patton legacy.

Photographs came from either the collections of the authors, or the public domain. Dean Blackwood of Revenant Records and his graphic artist colleague Susan Archie kindly provided scans for some images that were better than what the authors possessed.

Permission to quote songs, including the notated transcriptions for the music examples, were granted by the Hal Leonard Corporation on behalf of EMI/Longitude. Facilitating the necessary permissions were Jeff Schroedl of Hal Leonard, Dave Rubin, Megan Lanzotti of SonyATV Publishing, Patrick Leblanc and Stefan Grossman.

EDWARD KOMARA

I thank the following persons who since the early 1960s supported the idea of a Patton book which was eventually published in 1988 and is reprinted now. The first is Bernie Klatzko, the New York Patton collector with whom in 1963 I discovered the first factual details about Patton's life, death, and role in the development of Delta blues. Through Bernie I began working with Pete Whelan, initially towards biographical notes for the Origin Jazz Library reissue albums of classic Mississippi Delta blues, then on articles for his magazine *78 Quarterly*. I met John Fahey in Washington, DC, while he was conducting his pioneering research on Patton. Nick Perls and Stephen Calt visited me in 1964, and Henry Vestine in 1965 around the time he joined the blues-rock band Canned Heat; they encouraged and enabled the 1988 Patton book by Calt and me.

Among my many sources, I must acknowledge here the help of Arthur Laibly, formerly of Paramount Records, when I first contacted him in September 1966. Magazine editors who gave vital support included those of *Blues Unlimited* magazine, especially the late Mike Leadbetter, Simon Napier, and Mike Rowe; *Guitar Player* editor Jas Obrecht; and *Living Blues* editors Jim O'Neal and Brett Bonner. Don Kent, Steve LaVere, and guitar designer Jim DeCola were important supporters. My longtime Florida friends Roy Book Binder and Christopher Smith helped, as did Stefan Grossman, who edited the 1988 first edition. Finally, I am deeply thankful to my wife, Janet Swanson Wardlow, who has supported me through many difficult periods and encouraged this publication.

GAYLE DEAN WARDLOW

*Part One*

# THE MAN AND HIS TIMES

I don't reckon nobody
will ever beat him,
in my judgement.
—BOOKER MILLER

*Chapter 1*

# MISTER PATTON

The foreman of Will Dockery's plantation[1] listened dubiously to the neatly attired stranger standing before him. On that spring day in 1929, the man had driven almost a hundred miles on dirt roads into the heart of the Mississippi Delta to Dockery's front entrance. The nearest towns were Cleveland and Ruleville, where lived a combined total of 4000 residents. All that distance traveled just to meet someone for whom the foreman had no use. The visitor did not present a business card, but he introduced himself as Henry C. Speir from the state capital Jackson. Few white men asked to meet Dockery tenants.[2] One of them was the county sheriff from Indianola who sometimes came over, but only at Will Dockery's request. Others were the state policemen who searched the northern rim of the plantation for escapees from the nearby prison known locally as "Parchman Farm." Yet another was a revenue agent who snooped around for hidden stills. The only other outsiders who wanted to speak to Will Dockery's tenants were labor agents representing northern industries or rival plantations. But no labor agent was ever so bold as to make a visit in broad daylight to a plantation like Dockery's. Nor would he seek someone with a bad reputation like Charlie Patton, who once was thrown off Dockery's for being a trouble-maker, but later allowed to return.

To the foreman, Speir explained that he referred black musicians to the record companies. He had received a letter from Patton about hearing him play at Dockery's.[3] Hence how he was engaged in scouting talent for such companies, and why he traveled all that way to Dockery's. Then he drew in his breath. During his three years so far as a freelance "talent broker" as he described himself, the thirty-four year old Speir had grown used to receiving wary glances from white Mississippians whenever he explained his work.

Their initial disbelief at Speir's musical interest would have turned to derision if they ever learned that he was often offered bonuses of fifty or a hundred dollars for each of his recorded discoveries. But those amounts of money were small compared to his retail profits from selling the records made by these and other black musicians and the Victrolas to play them, along with musical instruments and household furniture. They would have also thought little of his desire to promote blues musicians, which was based in his childhood evenings in Sebastopol listening to them sing. They would not have understood his pride in the fact that, unlike the record company executives he knew, he never took a nickel at the expense of the musicians he scouted; he had no official position with any of the companies he worked with, and he was on none of their payrolls. Even so, many of these white Mississippians didn't trust Speir at his word. They drummed him out of the Delta communities of Tutwiler and Marks, thinking that he was a labor agent recruiting their black workers. One time, in Vicksburg, police accused him of selling drugs, and they ordered him out of the city. In Mississippi towns during the late 1920s, dealing drugs in black neighborhoods was more conventional and more believable than scouting blues musicians, and only slightly more disreputable.

In Mississippi, Speir had only one competitor for promoting blues singers to the record labels. He was Ralph Lembo, who traveled outside his hometown Itta Bena to seek and scout musicians.[4] Speir, then, had to travel a little further and wider. He went throughout Mississippi, and beyond to cities like New Orleans, Memphis, Louisville, St. Louis, and even Chicago. The blues singers he sought had no standing as legitimate entertainers in the world of music. Rather, they represented—geographically and socially—the skid row of their profession.

Speir's store was on Farish Street in the black neighborhood of Jackson, where whites frequently came to purchase blues records. Speir sensed, though, that none of his customers thought of bluesmen as plantation minstrels who were worthy of worship. Years later, he tried to explain why. "A man that was singin' the blues, he couldn't intermix with the people too much. He didn't have too much education. He was what we call a 'meat barrel type.' Smell a little bit, you see." Even Speir gagged a few times from the stench of his unwashed blues discoveries.

But there were also class differences among black musicians to which Speir had to be attentive. If he asked the white residents living near Dockery's plantation as to who was their favorite black entertainer, he would have heard W. C. Handy's name mentioned many more times than Charlie Patton's. Even among black residents, Handy was much better known and remembered. Patton's crony Willie Moore admitted that "Handy's more famous among the folks around, he's more up-to-date." In 1927, Handy's orchestra performed at the Bolivar County courthouse in Cleveland, attracting a crowd so large that latecomers could not get within a hundred yards. But if a bluesman like Charlie Patton tried to give a show at the same courthouse, he would have likely drawn a fine for vagrancy. Seeing that his discoveries had unsavory reputations, Speir often had the uneasy feeling that his associations with them could land him in some sort of trouble, whether that brought on by the law, or that created by the artists themselves. He was as wary of all musicians—white and black—as he was of record executives, whom he considered unscrupulous. But he kept an affection for the music that the blues musicians performed.

So, on that spring day at Dockery's plantation, Speir had to use every ounce of persuasion he possessed in order to be allowed to meet Charlie Patton. With the end of the cotton planting season fast approaching, field labor was at a premium. The days of the work week belonged to an overseer who was charged to ensure that the $500 advances given to Dockery's tenants were returned in the form of steady labor. But at the end of each week, "Saturday night belonged to *them*"—the black tenants—as recalled later by Joe Rice Dockery, the son of the plantation's founder. While Patton was not one of the tenants who signed on for the Dockery advances, he was often living with someone who had. Whenever he played music on Saturday nights, he was likely to attract other people who also received Dockery's money. As a businessman, Will Dockery made sure that the money he paid out was spent only or mostly on his plantation. For some years, he even paid in scrip that was good only for purchases at the plantation's store. But he couldn't control where the traveling musicians spent the money that they had received from Dockery's tenants. From a financial perspective, then, the bluesmen were unaccountable to the planters—and hence uncontrollable—but at the same time, they were also viewed as free and independent by the tenants. Perhaps for that reason, the foreman told Speir that while he could visit Patton, he should complete as quickly as possible his business dealings with him.

He then showed Speir how to drive the fifteen miles from Dockery's south entrance to Patton at the northern end. In between, the thousands of acres under cultivation within Dockery's were divided into subplots for tenant families. Each family cabin (or boxcar, as some tenants actually lived in abandoned railway cars) were placed forty or sixty acres apart, in keeping with a scheme introduced before the Civil War to reduce the number of incidents of "immorality" among the then slaves. The shacks Speir passed while driving to Patton's residence housed blacks, Italians, and Mexicans, the last coming to the Delta at the turn of the century and bringing guitars there.[5]

Within this racial diversity in the Delta, Charlie Patton's looks was a frequent cause of wonder about his ancestry. His complexion was as light ("bright" as blacks put it) as a white person's. His hair was brown but beginning to turn gray, yet "good" as blacks of the time and place always described straight hair, which he usually parted and combed down in front. His stature, however, was not imposing or striking. He was frail and short[6]—perhaps 5'7", if that—and he walked with a limp. That he was missing some back teeth was apparent whenever he opened his mouth.

His manner, Speir noticed upon meeting him, was "kinda forward" for a black Mississippian. Patton later said matter-of-factly to him that he considered himself the equal of any Delta blues singer who had yet made records, and that was why he had decided to try his own hand at recording. That claim was nothing compared to what he said to other plantation residents. Will Dockery's cook Sara Garrett remembered him as being insufferably vain and arrogant. "He just thought he was the biggest and best in makin' music, you know, and thought everybody oughta look on him [according] to *who* he was. He just stuck on himself." Who he was, he insisted to his black neighbors, was "Mister Patton."

The letter that Speir had received from Patton was apparently dictated, whether Patton was illiterate or not. But by sending the letter, the musician showed a supreme self-confidence. Anyone else with even a touch of inferiority would not have seriously expected a visit from Speir. Yet Patton's letter succeeded, despite the odds against him. Although Charlie Patton was a household name among Sunflower County's 45,000-odd blacks, and he was renowned in dozens of black neighborhoods throughout Mississippi, the first mention of his name would have meant nothing to the white Speir living in Jackson. All of the blues artists he dealt with so far turned out to have marginal appeal on records, the "off-side" as he put it in the overall context of the national blues recording field, or "out of the mainstream" as we would say today. None of the Delta musicians he scouted to date had made a record that sold ten thousand copies, the number needed to have an unqualified hit in the record industry.

Before considering him as a blues recording prospect, Speir did not ask around about Patton's popularity. Whether or not Patton was known outside Dockery's plantation did not matter to him. He never asked his customers about their tastes in blues, partly because he sensed they didn't have standards, and partly because he "could tell what was gonna sell."[7] Moreover, he thought that hit blues records were due to the emotiveness of the performer, and since he felt that Delta musicians had "incentive" from the prevailing oppressive economic and social conditions to release their emotions by singing, he saw the Delta as a ripe breeding-ground for commercially appealing bluesmen. He, at any rate, was poignantly affected by the Delta bluesmen who had existed, he said, "as long as the Delta's been there." He thought that the blues came from spirituals. His own familiarity with the blues began early in life, practically in his backyard. "Whenever these Negroes would sing, especially late in the evening," he recalled, "it was a lonesome sound. I knew what this Negro singin' was doin', I knew it was good." But that was in the early 1900s. Only in the 1920s did record executives begin to share his long-held belief that this "off-side" music was commercially viable. Quite how the executives reached their conclusion, Speir didn't know. But for himself, he loved Mississippi blues. Yet before entering the record business, he had made a cold calculation that Southern tastes lagged five years behind those of the rest of the country that preferred more sophisticated-sounding music.

This belief in the viability of the blues on records informed Speir's scouting decisions. Although he collected the same fee for a sales flop as for a sales success, he never referred any bluesman who did not impress him as a potential best-seller to a record company, even when he found no fault with the performer's music. He didn't know the standards his employers used to weigh his recommendations, and he came to think that they probably had none at all. The only uncertainty he felt during auditions was how well a voice would sound through the primitive record players of that era. For example, when he heard Tommy Johnson in 1928 near Jackson, Speir doubted the singer's ability to come across on discs. "Tommy Johnson, when you'd hear him play or sing," he remembered years later, "you'd just wonder whether it'd be good or not [on record]. He was just mediocre." One of Johnson's drawbacks as a performer was a speech defect. "You'd be somewhat distracted by the way he kinda hissed, you know, like a snake," Speir described. "You'd notice it and it'd detract from his singin'. It was a nervous habit, and you'd just kinda feel (sorry) for him." But when Speir tested Johnson on his own recording equipment, he found that the microphone didn't capture this mannerism.

To begin his audition, Patton retrieved a Stella guitar from his shack and he braced himself against a nearby tractor. While tuning his instrument, he remarked that his performance would be improved with a little whiskey. When Speir failed to grasp this hint, Patton asked if he had some liquor to offer. Speir had none, but the point registered. Later, whenever Speir traveled to hear Charlie Patton, he made sure to bring along enough corn liquor to keep his pet discovery—and the "gang" of fellow musicians Patton always gathered around him—in the proper spirit of blues-playing. It took two hours of steady drinking and playing, Speir later said, before Patton really hit his stride and got into what Speir called the "swing" of his music.

The overwhelming impression that Charlie Patton in good spirits (alcoholic or otherwise) made upon a listener is illustrated by the reminiscence of Booker "Mr. Pink" Miller, who later in 1929 became Patton's "road buddy."

"I was a guitar-player myself," Miller later remembered, "and I tried to learn everything he played, because I liked it. I *loved* it. In other words, it will carry you: *it'll carry you.* He was the best in *my* book, and it was some real guitar-players had passed through here.[8] He was the champ, and he could sing.

"He had a voice—he had a *voice*! You know what I heard a man tell him one time there in Ruleville, Mississippi? He told him, he said, 'You know, to listen at your records and then come to see you, I thought I'd see a man weighed two hundred and seventy-five pounds! And you! You don't weigh one-fifty!'

"Charlie say, 'I weigh a hundred and thirty five!'"

Likewise, Speir was favorably impressed with the booming baritone voice that came from its pipsqueak possessor. Patton began his audition with his theme song, "Pony Blues." "When I heard Charlie sing," Speir recalled, "I knew that voice would carry (on record). He had a regular ol' Mississippi River voice, that's all there was to it." The rhythmic pulse that propelled his singing struck the scout as sounding different from anything he had ever heard. Had he not been so impressed by Patton's individuality as a singer and guitarist, his enthusiasm for him would have been much less. As he once explained, "My workin' way was to try to get one [song] that was original, [and to record] what he got up himself." And as it so typically happened, most of the bluesmen he had already heard and was to hear in coming years sounded nearly alike to him. Not so with Patton. "Tommy Johnson and Charlie Patton," he said, "was the only ones who had a style that was a little bit different."[9]

During auditions, Speir also listened as much to the guitar work as to the singing. In this respect, he took Patton to be more than exceptional, declaring later "Charlie was *good* with that guitar.[10] I mean, he could handle a guitar *outta this world*!" While he did not bother with the lyrics that his discoveries sang, he considered Patton to be the best blues lyricist he ever encountered. Furthermore, Speir claimed to have no difficulty understanding him, despite the blues singer's sometimes undecipherable diction.

As the audition proceeded, Speir's last remaining criterion for Patton as a recording act was the size and variety of his repertory. That was satisfied when Patton played four or five more pieces. Speir remembered afterward with a little relief, "He really had a lot of songs, and I knew that he was okay." Record companies, Speir had learned, preferred artists who could record at least six titles; those who could produce that number in a single session would earn both Speir and themselves the maximum industry pay-offs for their efforts. In retrospect, Speir stated that Patton's compositional facility exceeded those of the other blues artists he ever dealt with. That included Tommy Johnson, who had developed only two distinctive songs when Speir first auditioned him. "Most singers had only one or two songs," Speir recalled. "Lots of singers could sing other people's songs, but not make up their own." The variety of Patton's repertory impressed him as much as its size. "I'll tell you about Charlie: he just had a *method*—he could play a guitar different on anything he'd sing. A lotta fellas would do the same song (i.e. accompaniment) over and over. Not Charlie."

If Patton was gratified by Speir's immediate enthusiasm for his music, perhaps he also listened cautiously to the latter's recording proposals. After all, he had been approached previously[11] by Ralph Lembo with a recording offer; if they had discussed a recording session, the plans fell through. At any rate, to Speir, he showed little satisfaction with his audition performances. "He told me he'd be better if he'd a had the whiskey," Speir said. As it turned out, Patton likely recorded as sober as when he auditioned. The man who supervised his first sessions, Arthur Laibly at Paramount Records, denied to interviewers that his artists were allowed to drink on the job. "They didn't get a drop while they were recording.[12] You couldn't take a chance. I would give it to them *after* they were done with the recording."

Some weeks after the audition, Patton made his debut for Paramount Records on June 14, 1929. For the rest of that year and the next, he was highly coveted by the other blues recording labels while remaining, as the Memphis record salesman Earl Montgomery put it, "more Speir's nigger than anyone else's." Through his 1934 death, his 78s were marketed to black audiences. Then almost thirty years passed before his recordings elicited new acclaim as by a blues great. What had happened during the meantime, though, was that white record collectors discovered for themselves Patton's 78s in the mid-1940s,[13] and they gradually brought his work to a wider public through LP record reissues.[14] However, they were not the first of their race to recognize his talent. One of Patton's white enthusiasts was Earl Montgomery, who supplied Mississippi retailers with Paramount records. While making his rounds one day, he saw Patton play in the town of Skene. In 1970 he said of him, "That sonofabitch was good." Speir went even further in his praise, declaring before his death in 1972, "He beat 'em all." If as Montgomery said that Patton was "Speir's nigger," then likewise Speir was Patton's honky. With most of his recording talent, he only had perfunctory contact. But for Patton, Speir would entrust his store to an assistant on Thursday or Friday afternoons and make the three-plus hour drive to Dockery's. "I used to go up there and spend half a night, nearly, and then come home," he said. "I'd go up there to see Charlie. Now you're talkin' about havin' fun and really enjoyin' a trip—that would be it!"

What Speir and Booker Miller admired about Charlie Patton's music may be heard in the recordings he made as a result of his Dockery's audition. They suggest that Patton was unique, a blues singer who transcended the blues genre. "It's unfair to label him a Mississippi bluesman," says Woody Mann,[15] a sophisticated jazz guitarist who has transcribed some of his music. "He's like another breed. He's more interesting, more lively and more complex than any

Mississippi bluesman. He's not just someone with a couple of good tunes, or a little bag of clever musical tricks. There's real elegance in his music. He's a real original. He couldn't have basically copied anyone: his music has too much variety, and too few patterns. You just don't see his kind of spontaneity in an imitative musician. He may have been a blues guitarist in name, but in spirit he was a jazz artist."

Yet if many of Patton's blues contemporaries heard Mann's appraisal, they would be inclined to disagree with him. In their reminiscences to the authors, they seldom if ever acknowledged his remarkability, let alone his greatness. Booker Miller may have been the only protégé who suggested to researchers that Patton's music was extraordinary. As for the other men, their grudging remarks may say more about their musical experiences and achievements than about Patton's.

For a start, Mississippi bluesmen tended to speak condescendingly of Patton as a second-rater with a first-rate ability to fool the public. Ishman Bracey of Jackson, who recorded for the Victor and Paramount labels, lumped Patton with the recording stars of the era who he felt played by rote. As he told John Fahey in a 1964 interview,[16] "In those recordin' (days), they mostly keep their style of music, more so than they do now. Now in this commercial time of recordin', they (the record officials) wants different (i.e., varied) tunes, but see people didn't know as much as they do now about those sorts of things, they just had one tune. If his voice would change, you'd know him by his music 'cause he kept that same tune. Blind Lemon, Blind Blake—they had one tune, ol' Charlie Patton had one tune. . . ."[17] Yet, arguably, Bracey himself was less versatile than any of the artists he had named, and on his 1930 Paramount records he would have seemed more limited had he not heeded Arthur Laibly's suggestion that it "was a good idea" (as Bracey put it) to vary his studio accompaniments.

Other blues singers who criticized Patton after his death shared with Bracey a resentment of Patton's popularity. They were especially harsh about the show-off stunts with which he enlivened his performances. "He wasn't all that much a player," said Willie Morris, a Bolton bluesman who saw Patton in such towns as Itta Bena, Moorhead, and Tutwiler, "he was a jiver." On the basis of Patton's "clowning" (showing off), Son House dismissed his music altogether by saying, "He wasn't no musicianer, 'cause he clowned too much." House went on to explain. "You see, blues ain't for no clownin'—lotta guys don't know that, see? Blues ain't for no clownin', man! It's sincere, just like a Christian song. That clownin' part spoil out the blues part, 'cause blues is a sincere, heart-searchin' thing—you really mean what you doin', from the heart, not no 'monkey-junk.'" Speaking in this way, House cast doubt on Patton's abilities, and he removed Patton's music from the realm of what he thought counted as the blues.

Yet House never asked Patton what blues or his other songs actually meant to him. When they met for the first time in 1930, House had been singing blues for three years, whereas Patton had been performing them for at least 20 years. The transformation of blues from Patton's good-time music to House's dour "Christian songs" may have been brought about by the Tin Pan Alley songwriters, whose commercial blues were widely recorded by theatre blues singers of the early 1920s. In 1919, the composer W. C. Handy stated, "The sorrow songs of the slaves we call Jubilee Melodies. The happy-go-lucky songs of the Southern negro we call blues."[18]

But in Mississippi, the blues functioned as party and dance music, and for that purpose Patton tailored his performing style. "He say he always liked the rhythm, what he means 'action,'" Booker Miller said, "he liked the Lindbergh, Charleston, One-Step, Two-Step, he liked that kind of stuff."

Patton generated excitement by providing acrobatic guitar stunts of every description, just like the blues dancer who created lively action through physical gyrations. "What he loved to do was 'clown' with his guitar, just puttin' it all under his legs and back behind him," Sam Chatmon recalled, "takin' his hand and puttin' it all back his head.[19] See, that was doin' the folks more good than just straight playin'; he couldn't do that on a record. Now if they'd a-had picture shows like they got now, he'd a-made him a couple reels [of film performing]. It [the showmanship] a-went over big."

These antics were not just for show. "He said it helps him, it rests him a lot," Booker Miller explained. At a typical dance, Patton had to play for several hours for an audience who for its money expected him to use a tremendous amount of energy and effort, especially when performing his most popular songs. To conserve his voice, he sometimes resorted to his visual clowning. Apparently Patton was clever at pacing himself, because observers did not remember his clowning for what it was, rather more for it fitting well with his flamboyant personality. Nathan (Dick) Bankston met him shortly before World War I, and over fifty years later he remembered the young Patton not only as a colorful musician but as a "clown from his heart" as well. Patton remained so when Frank Howard was his neighbor during the 1920s. Years later as an older man, Howard conveyed his impression of Patton's guitar-playing: "He'd cut monkey-shines with it: put it 'round his head, then change hands with it, play off with his feet and all that kinda stuff." Son House remembered that Patton executed a trick with his hat: while playing guitar, he would play "pitty pat" by alternating hands in a rhythmic motion to knock the hat from one side of his head to the other. "He's just a clownin' guy, that jerk is," House said, but then admitted, "he's good at it, though!"

House insisted that clowning accompanied "near about every one" of the pieces that Patton played when they first met. But when working alone at dances, Patton could not have clowned extensively without disrupting the dancers' "action" that he had been hired to generate. Moreover, had he relied on clowning as much as House claimed, he wouldn't have had the finesse he displayed on his recordings. In all likelihood, House may have paid little attention to Patton's serious music.[20] By attributing Patton's popularity to his show-off antics, House may have shown some resentment about his colleague's success. After all, many lesser musicians resorted to guitar stunts, to no apparent effect on their reputations, good or bad. Also, Patton's records played back only sound and hence they bore no hint of clowning, yet nonetheless they sold "like popcorn" in Mississippi, as his admirer Booker White put it to the authors. If anything, he became a blues celebrity despite his "clowning." Still, some listeners like Bunk Ashford of Skene, Mississippi long remembered that "Charlie carried on too much foolishness." On the other hand, if a fan rated him above other blues performers simply because of his guitar tricks, he or she never said so, then or later, to interviewers.

Even if Patton's guitar stunts made a mixed impression on his audience, the fact that he was a more vibrant performer than a musician like, say, House kindled his celebrity. To Robinsonville's Elizabeth Moore, Patton's musical abilities appeared no greater than those of House, yet she preferred to watch Patton because "he just had a way of actin." Her husband Willie, who played with both musicians, added, "He [Patton] had a way of 'comin' to the people,' you see, would just draw your attention." Likewise, Patton's records have a dynamic appeal that is missing from those by many other Mississippi bluesmen of the era.

Patton's liveliness had an intangible and inimitable quality that raised his performances above the typical house frolic entertainment, and it quite likely made him the singular attraction that people remembered him being. "Oh man, he puts all his-self into it," Booker Miller said of his mentor's performing style. "Sometimes it looks just like he's gonna fall outta his chair."

The records suggest that Patton achieved his intensity by having complete and seemingly effortless command of his material. That intensity is infectious because it is buoyant, never taut. Such is not true of other Mississippi bluesmen who had powerful deliveries, which were necessary for dance-oriented entertainment before the wide availability of portable microphone systems. Lacking Patton's buoyant intensity, other early recorded Mississippi bluesmen sound labored by comparison. Patton's public could and would have been drawn to his kind of intensity, even if they could not put it into words.

Something else that other Mississippi bluesmen lacked was Patton's unpredictable attack. None of them varied his level of intensity during a song. The vocal and instrumental attack of the typical Mississippi bluesman was established during the opening stanza of the blues song and maintained consistently during the rest of the rendition. But by comparison, Patton was forceful. "We just played 'hard' blues, that's what we played," Booker Miller recalled. He added to the vehemence of his playing and singing by using his feet as percussion instruments. "He'd stomp his feet, you know—his feet 'talk,'" Willie Moore said. "I loved to hear him pat his foot and sing. He sure could pat his foot. He'd stomp his foot; keep up a lotta racket, but man, he sure carried on! Tickled me."

When playing while sitting down, Patton sometimes did little dance steps, "look like he's dancin' on his foot," as Johnnie Mack remembered. When he "stomped," he did so with the full weight of his legs, pounding the floor with his heels. To add to the impact of this sound, Booker Miller remembered, he attached metal cleats to the heels of his shoes. This "stomping" may be heard on such records as "Down the Dirt Road Blues" and "High Water Everywhere." He made so much noise, that the operators of the house frolics where he played in Renova between 1910 and 1915 planted pillows beneath his feet,[21] in the fear that he would otherwise awaken neighbors. To Richard "Hacksaw" Harney, Patton's ferocious foot-tapping would "sound like it's five or six people in there stompin'. Folks like it. Racket's all they want!"[22]

It is interesting that Harney said that about Patton. Harney had worked in a Cincinnati jazz band in the early 1920s, and his repertory consisted of guitar instrumentals. To him, Patton's music seemed barbaric. Like other elder bluesmen in the 1960s and 1970s, he showed some envy for Patton's abiding reputation by describing Patton's art as "just playin' on the strings and clownin." Furthermore, he insisted that "Patton couldn't play! Shit, no! He couldn't make no (full) chords or nothin', he couldn't play no chord on no guitar. All he had [was] the mouth and the stompin."

As a blues dance guitarist who accompanied his own singing, Patton didn't have to develop a great prowess with chords. Besides, for their dancing, his black audiences needed only to hear the blues, and they would not have tolerated for very long the pop songs that used more than three chords. Son House liked the World War I era show tune "Goodbye Broadway, Hello France," but his Delta dancers did not. "They didn't want that," House said. "You had to play the real old flat-foot blues. They didn't wanna hear nothin' like that [show tunes], no, man!"

Harney once competed against Eugene Powell in a guitar contest near Hollandale in 1927. Harney won because he accompanied all of Powell's pieces, while Powell could not follow all of Harney's. Any such contest with Patton would have ended in a draw, because Patton used unusual phrasing and accenting patterns, and as Booker Miller pointed out, he "always 'moved out' on the guitar" when he played for dances. The slow tempi for the one-step and the slow-drag dances might have suited such Mississippi bluesmen as Tommy Johnson, Willie Brown, Rube Lacy and Kid Bailey, but not Patton. Instead he preferred playing to such fast dances as the two-step and the shimmy-she-wobble. Johnnie Mack, an associate of Hacksaw Harney, remembered meeting Patton in Longswitch. Since Mack favored "more different chords, fancy chords, pretty chords" like those that Harney used, he had to admit later that at Longswitch dance he couldn't keep up with Patton's combination of speed and intricacy.

Still, Mack agreed with Harney that Patton's "mouth" was his only real asset. "He could whoop and holler and sing and so on," Mack reported. "That's what made him known. Lord God, he could holler. He beat everybody hollerin'. And the people went after him, they like to have a fit." Significantly, the only nickname any of Patton's interviewed acquaintances bestowed on him was "Old Wide Mouth," as Tommy Johnson's brother Ledell called him.

"Charlie Patton, he had a voice one while," David "Honey Boy" Edwards said. "I'm tellin' you, he didn't need no mike. He just stand up with that gross-staggerin' voice he had. He just done somethin' for the people. He broke them country houses down." If he didn't have a tremendous volume as a singer,

Patton would have had a much less lucrative blues career, for no unamplified acoustic guitar could have projected loud enough to provide a dance beat for the noisy audiences who came to the barrelhouses and house frolics.

Although H. C. Speir did not remark to interviewers on the grittiness of Patton's voice, others who heard the singer described it as best as they could. Mandy Whigam heard Patton perform on the streets of Inverness and her native Swiftown. She compared his voiced to those of his associates Willie Brown and Son House. "They rattle off, singin' 'greasy neck,' I call it; just like they got grease in their throat. Charlie's voice came out of his throat. Little Willie (Brown), he tries to come outta his throat, but he really just can't. Charlie didn't have to push, his is just natural." Yet Patton's raucous vocal sound could be said to be mannered, for on the records "Shake It and Break It" and "Runnin' Wild," he sang in an easy crooning fashion.

In every notable respect, Patton's talent was refined rather than raw. That he was Mississippi's most famous blues musician and the Delta's dominant music force during his lifetime may be because he had no musical peer. Rival musicians who craved the recognition that they saw bestowed on him tended to be his harshest critics. But other musicians tried hard to copy him. "I don't care who liked it and who didn't," Eugene Powell said of Patton's music. "He had that country down there. He had that country in his style of playing." Booker Miller felt that Patton had no successful imitators. "Charlie had a style that many guys wanted but couldn't get up to it."

David "Honey Boy" Edwards knew Robert Johnson, Tommy Johnson, and Skip James. But he said to interviewers, "the really best break-down country blues player that I really knowed that drawed the largest crowd was Charlie Patton. He was mostly the leadingest man down through there."

Johnnie Mack recalled, "When you first come in around where he was, everybody went, 'Charlie Patton!' And you couldn't get around in the house for nothin.' 'Charlie Patton!' A man had him to play down there at Longswitch, had him sittin' up on a counter. One night when I first come in, if it wasn't five hundred people, it wasn't one."

"When Charlie Patton's gonna be somewhere," Booker Miller said, "you come there, you'll find the folks. They natural-born loved him."

He was popular enough, Miller recalled, to charge high enough fees to turn away the organizers of the little house frolics held on many Delta plantations. "You just couldn't get a man like Charlie Patton just anywhere. You'd a-had plenty people (who could) raise enough money to pay him, but people was just scared to do it."

Willie Moore agreed that many places were simply too small for Patton to perform. "You never could get Charlie Patton to play in little 'short' places, 'cause wouldn't be no natives to dance—the men wouldn't 'low it. We'd be playin' someplace, man, them men would get them women, carry 'em away from there! 'Cause Charlie Patton, he would start to talkin' them blues and them women'd start to popping their fingers and skippin', man, them niggers turn, say 'Let's get away from here!'

"When he hit that guitar them womens would start to clownin', and that made the mens didn't like Charlie Patton. They'd have to hold them, fling the girls back. 'Get back, honey!' Them niggers don't like it, they go fightin' about every dance we played for. 'Cause you know how them womens go: 'Hey, hey!' 'Child, play it till I get somewhere!' 'Hey, hey child, just play it till I see somebody I ain't seen in years!' You couldn't play for them women, sure couldn't."

David Edwards likewise remembered the hostility that often surrounded Patton at dances. "He had a-lots of womens, you know, and the men'd stand around and look at him and get mad about them old womens."

Patton's contemporaries in the blues were intimidated by his celebrity. "All the musicians was scared of him," Willie Morris noted. Yet Patton relished the challenge of facing bold competition. As Booker Miller reported, "You know, some [blues musicians] you run in on be 'scarey.' You put a hot blues in there, they give up. But some guys just natural-born have the nerve, they wanna go head-on and play. And those was the kind we'se wantin' to meet up with."

Patton was cocky about his ability, yet he wasn't stuck on himself. He listened to other musicians, often giving them more praise than they gave to him. "He wasn't a critic," Miller said. "Charlie was very interested in music, and he seemed to enjoy (other people's) music. I never heard him criticize nobody."

Patton did not snub the nobodies among musicians, even if he insisted that the tenants of Dockery's call him "Mr. Patton." "Charlie was a big shot," declared Miller, "but he'd always come back home and get with us." This willingness to mix with musical also-rans was unusual. Other recording artists that Patton's crony Willie Morris met tended to think of themselves as part of an elite, just because they made records. "All these musicians used to come to Memphis," Morris said. "Every one of 'em what come up North and made records. Some of them was so 'hankty' (stuck up), they wouldn't make theirselves known to you."

By contrast, Patton sought out other musicians. One was Eugene Powell in Tribbet in the late 1920s. "He heard that I could play good and he wanted to hear me play," Powell recalled. "He sent for me, and when I made up my mind to see what he want, I went out there to the place he play at. I went out there Sunday evenin', and he left that mornin'."

In the 1960s, Skip James remembered his blues rivals before 1942 collectively as "a barrel of crabs." But Patton was very helpful to other musicians. When he played his audition for Speir at Dockery's plantation on that spring day in 1929, he mentioned the names of five or six other bluesmen who would be worth recording. During the next four years, he continued to introduce Speir to other musicians; as a direct result of his recommendations, at least six other acts came to record. He freely gave pointers to novices like Booker Miller, who reported, "He'd keep teachin' me and then he get maybe eight, six new pieces, and he'd disappear. And man, in every music store in town, man, you wouldn't hear nothin' whoopin' but Charlie Patton! Then finally he'd come back."

By 1930, Patton stood as Mississippi's only national blues celebrity, and this reputation was all the more impressive to others because his background was so rural. "You take Charlie, he was a plantation man, but he just got famous," Mandy Whigham said. To her ears, Patton sounded like the proverbial "plantation man," while some blues singers did not. One such was Sam Collins, who sang with a clear tenor and relatively smooth diction. Listening to Collins' recordings, she visualized "one of them cornfield men. He raise hogs and corn; he probably had a bunch of kids. He lived on a plantation, but he wouldn't be what you'd call 'Mister Nettlelow's man.' He's not way back (in the country): he's not a way back man. He's got a little more pride. He's a better-class nigger, colored person. You can tell from his singin' and music he was country, but I mean he didn't have the country all in him—not all the way."

But in Patton's records, she discerned "a plantation man. Can't you tell from his singin'? He come way back there on "Mister Nettlelow'—that's just an expression, that means way back on somebody's plantation, it just means he's way back from the country."

Patton's intonation evokes a plantation culture. But in other aspects, his recorded music suggests that early in his career, he stepped out of the small-stakes Delta house frolic scene to become a carnival or medicine-show trouper, or a town- and city-barrelhouse entertainer.

Among Mississippi musicians of the 1920s, tuning a guitar properly was an exceptional skill.[23] Patton knew how, but it is unlikely that he had learned it from someone living on a provincial plantation. Also, he made his guitar notes sound more vibrant and penetrating by tuning the strings above concert pitch. To the authors' knowledge, this trick was used before World War II by one other blues guitarist, Lonnie Johnson, a city musician from of St. Louis and arguably the most sophisticated blues musician of the pre-war era. As for Patton's instrumental phrasing, it had the slapdash quality of the street singer, which was much different than the styles of Mississippi blues as recorded by such frolic-oriented entertainers as William Harris, Rube Lacy, Tommy Johnson, Willie Brown, Memphis Minnie, and Booker White. They played in fixed patterns that were retentions of square dance music and instrumental breakdowns that were still being played on plantations at the turn of the century. Patton's accompaniments, on the other hand, used mixed textures that removed them from the dance-only realm of house frolic music. The unique style that Patton developed served him everywhere, whether as a riff-oriented street player in the city or as a strumming dance entertainer on the plantation. It was largely due to this versatility that Patton's style was not imitated well by his peers, for each one knew either the farm or the city, but not both.

It may have been during his early days as a musician when he gained a wider musical perspective than that of "Mister Nettlelow's man." In his own song lyrics he presented himself as a wanderer who spoke of cities, towns and, for that matter, remote regions that in real life he had probably never seen:

I feel like choppin,' chips flyin' everywhere,
I feel like choppin,' chips flyin' everywhere,
I been to the Nation, oh Lord, but I couldn't stay there.

Some people tell me, "Oversea blues ain't bad,"
(spoken: Why, of course they are)
Some people say, "Oversea blues ain't bad,"
(spoken: What was a-matter with 'em?)
It must not a-been them oversea blues I had.
("Down the Dirt Road Blues")

The "Nation" was the Choctaw Nation or Chickasaw Nation,[24] divisions of Indian Territory in the southern part of what became Oklahoma in 1907. Either Patton was too provincial to know that the Territory no longer existed when he recorded "Down the Dirt Road Blues" in 1929, or for 22 years he kept the habit of singing that lyric even after it became outdated. Nonetheless, he knew the value of presenting himself as a much-traveled man of the world to his plantation audiences:

> Now the water now mama, done took short little town
> Boy they tell me the water, done took short little town
> (spoken: "Boy, I'm goin' to Vicksburg!")
> Well I'm goin' to Vicksburg, over that higher mound.
> (High Water Everywhere Part I)

He sang of Vicksburg, Jackson, Natchez, Clarksdale, Helena, Memphis, Chicago, and St. Louis, yet rarely mentioning what Willie Moore later termed "little short places." Although Patton did play at little frolics, he didn't stay for long on the surrounding plantations that hosted them. Joe Callicott saw him performing in the Hernando, Mississippi area just south of Memphis around 1929. Some forty years later, he remembered that "he come up around Hernando. He didn't tarry; come through here. That guy—this town's too small for him! Wasn't nothin' in it for him!"

Through his hit records, Patton became so famous in the Mississippi Delta, that some of his neighbors had a hard time believing that a Mississippi African American could be as celebrated as any blues star in Chicago or New York City. Richard Harney once described that mistaken attitude, assuming that his interviewer was thinking that Patton came from the north. "He stayed out here on these plantations, I'm tellin' you. Folks have been places out there, and he wouldn't be stayin' ten miles from there out on the place. And they'd think he's from somewhere north, and he's just stayin' out on these plantations."

"I first thought he was a Northern man," laughed Willie "Have Mercy" Young, who met Patton in Merigold in 1929, shortly after his record "Pony Blues" hit the market. "I thought he was from New York!"

Patton as a person amazed nearly everyone who met him, for his personality ran counter to his times, just like his approach to music swam against the musical currents.

Charlie was a hell of a fella;
Charlie was somethin' else.

—DAVID "HONEY BOY" EDWARDS

*Chapter 2*

# PORTRAIT OF THE ARTIST AS A WELL-MEANING WOOFER

"I never knowed him to do nothin' but pick that guitar and crack jokes" said Frank Howard, who for three years was Patton's plantation neighbor. The fuel for Patton's success was whiskey, women, and song. "He just believed in playin' his guitar, havin' a big time with his women, and drinkin' his whiskey," Booker Miller said of him. Aside from chasing, drinking, and performing, Patton was known to fish as a way to relax. But he was all business whenever he arrived to perform at the barrelhouses and house frolics; he did not gamble or dance there, according to Booker Miller.

While performing the blues brought good money to Patton, it was also his means of expressing himself. Few other blues performers in pre-1942 Mississippi conveyed so much of themselves as individuals through their music. Patton's songs exuded a dramatic personality in a way that baffled his peers. "If people just didn't understand him," Booker Miller recalled, "they'd say he was a 'funny' (peculiar) person." Son House couldn't identify what perplexed him: "He had somethin' in him. I don't know what it was."

Facets of Patton's personality came through as his basic performance characteristics. During a single song, he could act out in various moods and roles, like those of the flippant cut-up and the "hard" blues singer whose playing and singing bore a suggestion of nastiness. The memory of that hard singing style led Sam Chatmon to shudder years later. "He just bring his voice out so nasty," Chatmon said, "he could hold it so long, it sound nasty." Something of that vocal manner may be heard on a record like "Down The Dirt Road Blues," during which he pummels his guitar as if he was striking a person, a metaphor that Patton himself made.[1] Yet he would leaven the violence of this musical approach with verbal quips that contributed farcical humor to the performance.

Patton's contradictions as a performer gave real character to all of his songs, even to the flimsy ones. Just as his unexpected flippancy gave a light and zany air to "hard" blues, so also did his boisterousness provide a forceful, lowdown dimension to fluffy material like "Shake It and Break It."

These contrasts during performances reflected his own varied personality. Offstage, he struck Son House as an uncontrollably carefree, happy-go-lucky man who rarely spoke without breaking out into laughter. "He didn't worry about nothin'," House said of him. Yet Patton's lighter side was a mask for a self in turmoil. Asleep, House remembered, he would "fuss all night," tossing and bellowing continually. His waking moments were often no more tranquil. "Patton was kinda . . . you know what I mean; he was evil-tempered," Hayes McMullan said hesitantly of him. "He'd try to boss you around. He was a 'racket' man." Willie Moore agreed, "He wouldn't talk to a man right."

The invective that often dismayed or rankled Patton's acquaintances usually poured forth, House observed, when he was so drunk that "he wouldn't even hardly know he'd done anything." House added, though, that Patton in his reflective moments may have remembered his outbursts and the poor impression they created: "I believe he had enough sense to think about that." He was not deliberately antagonistic towards others, at least when sober. But if he realized that his antics had offended someone, Frank Howard noted, then "he'd beg your pardon, [he'd] tell you he didn't mean any harm whatsoever. He was not a 'imposin' person." With those he liked, he could be a warm, pleasant companion. His protégé Booker Miller was captivated by this side of his personality. "He wasn't on the mean side none, but if you didn't understand him, you'd think he was," said Miller, adding that Patton was "a very nice fella."

One mannerism that could have been mistakenly interpreted as a sign of meanness was his habit of addressing acquaintances by impersonal nouns like "kid," "fella," or "nigger." In return, though, he never received any of the familiar nicknames[2] by which bluesmen were frequently known. "Everybody called him 'Patton,'" Miller remembered. "They didn't call him 'Charlie Patton,' they called him 'Patton,' his friends 'round Ruleville. The rest of 'em, they'd say 'Charlie Patton' straight out." From this and his haughty desire to be addressed as "Mister Patton," it may be supposed that Patton found little in common with his peers, and he may have even kept some distance from them. His nephew Tom Cannon had grown up on Dockery's and lived there for many years, but later to the best of his memory, he recalled for the authors only one person as a close friend of Patton's, a Dockery's farmer named Marshall Turner. Patton liked Booker Miller enough as to give a photograph of himself as a keepsake.[3] Yet they never exchanged visits to each other's home. Rather, they kept in touch by postal mail.

Yet Patton could bask in the company of a crowd, especially in one that marched to the beat of his drum. The steady stream of banter he kept up on the dance floor indicates his easy rapport with his audience. "Oh man, he do all that kinda talkin,' you know, when people be out on the floor dancin,'" Miller said. "He'd be singin' along, an' he'd tell them what to do and all that kinda thing. You've seen people call sets, haven't you? He put it on just like that. Just like you was a good dancer, he'd just as soon call your name; he'd tell you, 'Stop right there and do so-and-so!'"

How impulsive he was is illustrated by his unexplainable habit of stopping the dancing in order to play interludes of church music. "Right there in the middle of a dance," Miller recalled, "it didn't make him no difference, if it hit him, he just go to playin' church songs right there. They'd just back up in a corner and listen, 'cause they couldn't turn him down." With these flights of religious fancy, Patton showed himself as a heretic in a Fundamentalist society that viewed blues-playing and religious feeling as irreconcilable opposites.

In conversations, Patton liked to mention his piety. When he met Frank Howard, he described himself as a former church deacon. Later in life, he upgraded his ecclesiastical claim. "He always said he was a preacher," Miller reported.[4]

Why Patton said that he was involved with a church is curious. In his time, place, and faith, religion was thought to be a matter of deeds, not of words or roles. Neither piety or, at face value, church position were going to impress his religious friends. Baptist elders frowned upon drinking, let alone playing dance music. Frank Howard found Patton so lacking in solemnity, sobriety, and conscience that he considered him as Satan incarnate. "He was a 'devil-right,'" he said long Patton's death. "Was his horn and tail: that's all he lacked for bein' the devil himself."

None of Patton's known blues associates ever saw him behind a pulpit. Then again, few of them attended church. One crony, Willie Morris, cynically allowed that Patton could have succeeded as a religious speaker because "Charlie Patton had a whole lotta mouth, and it takes a big-mouthed man to be a preacher." Son House, on the other hand, thought that Patton was too disreputable to have had a chance to preach. "He couldn'ta [preached] if he'd a-wanted to," he said, "they wouldn't 'low him near a pulpit, nowhere."[5]

Yet Patton himself seemed to have a cheerful attitude about his religious pretensions. "We'd go to talkin' about preachin'," Booker Miller recalled. "I'd say to him, 'Oh hell, man! You know God ain't gonna have nothin' like us!' Ha! It would tickle him to death!"

But with his secular station in life and his spiritual earnestness for religion, Patton was capable of exposing a cleric for hypocrisy, as in his 1930 recording "Elder Greene Blues":

> I like to fuss and fight, I like to fuss and fight,
> Lord and get sloppy drunk off a bottle and ball
> And walk the streets all night

This Patton song promoted a jaded Baptist view of the Church of God in Christ (COGIC),[6] known also as the "Holiness Church." COGIC preachers were known as "elders," and they claimed that converts were immune from sin, in accordance with its doctrine of "sanctification" that the Holy Spirit erases all sin among believers. This claim of sanctification was a target of criticism from Baptists, who in contrast considered themselves tarnished by sin. If the lyrics of "Elder Greene Blues" are indications, Patton may have counted himself as a tarnished Baptist.[7] If so, then the underlying messages of that song were that the Baptist church excluded Holiness elders like Greene for acting like n'er-do-wells, and that "sanctification" was simply an excuse to act freely, even wrongly.

In true Baptist fashion, Patton expressed himself as a deviate of the flesh, yet pure of spirit. On the spiritual "Prayer of Death Part II," he admitted that:

> Ever since my mother been dead
> Ever since my mother been dead

Ever since my mother been dead
Trouble been rollin' all over my head.

In other words, Patton was saying that his mother was a church-goer who had once exerted a restraining influence on him. Charley Jordan depicted the "hellbound boy" in the same way:

Let me tell you boys, don't you have no hard, hard head
If you do you will be hellbound
just as soon as your mother is dead.
(Charley Jordan, "Hellbound Boy," 1932)

In "Screamin' and Hollerin' the Blues," Patton borrowed the concluding lyric chorus of Alberta Hunter's "Down South Blues" (1923) for its childish view of maternal guidance:

If I had listened to my dear old mother
I'd be in my happy home.
But instead I had a hard hard head
So I started out to roam.

When I get back my folks will meet me with outstretched arms
My mother an' father are there to protect me
to keep me from all harm.

My mother's gettin' old an' her hair is turnin' grey
And it would break her heart to see me livin' this a-way.

In "Screamin' and Hollerin' the Blues," Patton presents himself as an unhappy drifter:

Jackson on a high hill mama, Natchez just below,
Jackson on a high hill, mama, Natchez just below,
(spoken: Children, you know where they are)
I ever get back home, I won't be back no more.

'Cause my mama's gettin' old, her head is turnin' gray
For my mama gettin' old, head is turnin' gray
Don't you know it'll break her heart, know, my livin' this-a way?

Although Patton spoke of himself as spiritual if not as religious, he was the very sort of person that Fundamentalist preachers railed against. His dance-floor religious rhapsodies, then, came from a dramatic personality who would loudly scratch any kind of emotional itch. As Sam Chatmon described him, "He always had his feelings sorta on top of his clothes." It was this heart-on-sleeve quality that made Patton a great performer.

But whenever he felt that his sense of decorum was being violated by someone, even in a crude setting like a barrelhouse, Patton would erupt. Willie Moore recalled, "I'll tell you this one thing: if Charlie Patton was sittin' down where women [were] in there, and you know some fellas get drunk and go to 'blackguardin' (cursing) where women were around, that fella [Patton] would get up with a chair or somethin' and try to knock your brains out. He didn't 'low it. And 'playin' the dozens,' I meant, he's against that."

Patton's aversion to cursing is implicit in his 1930 version of "Frankie and Albert." Before killing her cheating boyfriend, Frankie complains:

> Say: "You remember on last Sunday, twenty-fifth day of May
> You 'buked me an' you cursed me, oh baby, all that day."
> "Hey he was my man, but he done me wrong."

"He didn't use nasty language," said Booker Miller, who remembered Patton as a basically wholesome character devoted to "playin' guitar, havin' a good time." But Frank Howard had the opposite view of Patton, recalling him bristling to "The Dozens," the oral game among African American men[8] in which joking, belligerent, and sexual allusions were made to one's mother. "Anytime you get to talkin' some kinda old 'bad' talk and bring his mother in on it, you can look for it (i.e., trouble). I never heard him say nothin' about nobody's mother; nothin' 'bad,' you know."

Son House asserted that Patton "cussed a whole lot," but then again, that may be true only about his behavior around men. Overall, though, House's memory of Patton as a high-handed person was well-founded. "He wanted everything to go the way he wanted it to go," House said. In view of this, and of his combative way of expressing disgruntlement, Patton was much like the roustabouts who worked in the Delta work camps building the levees and roads, and who were known for a rough, kidding style of repartee called "checkin." Many of these laborers were much more boisterous and menacing than Charlie Patton. The musician Skip James as a young man[9] worked at a Ruleville road camp during World War I. He remembered that "those guys on those camps would even get to squabblin' and fightin' at the dinner table. The guys at the table wouldn't say, 'Pass me such and such a thing' if they wanted a big pan of meat or biscuits, or rice and stuff like that. They said, 'Let such-and-such a thing walk up that motherfuckin' table.' If you didn't just pass it right on to him, he'd jump on that table and walk the table to get it. Right over the plates and everything."

Even as a genteel version of the coarse roustabout, Patton still embodied the manners of the Southern frontier society, as W. J. Cash described in his classic book *The Mind of the South*:[10]

"The individualism of the plantation world would be one which, like the backcountry before it, would be far too much concerned with bald, immediate, unsupported assertion of the ego, which placed too great stress on the inviolability of personal whim, and which was full of the chip-on-the-shoulder swagger and brag of a boy—one in brief, of which the essence was the boast, voiced or not, on the part of every Southerner, that he would knock hell out of whoever dared to cross him."

For Patton, too, arguing was a way of life. "He'd scrap in a minute," recalled Hayes McMullan. With either sex, at that; McMullan once saw Patton smashing his guitar over a woman's head. McMullan added that he had never spent a single evening in Patton's company without seeing him argue with another barrelhouser.

Had Patton always been that stormy, he would have been viewed according to what African Americans back then referred to as a "tush hog" or a "wampus cat."[11] But he could also be a tease, as his records suggest. "He could 'play' with you just as good as he could look at you solid," Booker Miller said. He subjected everyone he met to a kind of friendly hazing. Frank Howard reported, "He'd grin at 'im, carry on a lot of foolishness. If he found out you could 'stand' foolishness, he'd carry it on with you."

Often his kidding consisted of barbed quips about a person's appearance. "He'd mostly joke people about their clothes," Howard said. "Tell 'em they are a 'pretty tough-lookin' fellow, don't know whether Death gonna come in by Himself or bring a gun when He come at him, he so 'bad-lookin,' and all such as junk like that."

Patton himself dressed plainly even though, like other blues singers like Skip James, he could have afforded the stylish fashions worn by gamblers and pimps. "He dressed like a plough-hand," Son House recalled. When House knew him in 1930, Patton often wore a pair of farmer's overalls. Yet "he'd put on his other old clothes, pants and things, to go to the ball," House reported.

Patton was fond of hats, sometimes wearing a white cap in the 1920s. Yet the hat that House remembered him wearing during the early 1930s was battered, outdated, and dingy. "He'd buy a hat like this year an' he wouldn't buy another one till two years from now, " House remembered, "He wouldn't care how greasy it got or whatnot." Around the same time in Robinsonville, Elizabeth Moore saw Patton wearing a hat that was crumpled with a torn brim; it may have been the same hat that House described. On other occasions, like the times when guitarist Hayes McMullan saw him perform in the Delta, Patton wore a scarf around his neck. Another item he owned was a billfold. If Booker Miller remembered it as being "nice-lookin," its fresh condition may have been due to Patton seldom opening it. "Now I'd get paid, and he'd get paid," Son House reported. "I'd spend mine, but he wouldn't spend his." Since Patton's needs were few and were often provided by his employers, how he spent his money isn't remembered by his friends and associates.

According to Frank Howard, Patton's spoken foolishness was imitated by his fans. "They'd tried to learn somethin' (from him), and they'd take his words and put it on somebody else." Yet some of Patton's wisecracks came from barrelhouse banter. Willie Moore reported, "I'd hear him sayin' sometimes, (you) say, 'Well, I reckon I will go to Brazil (i.e., the Delta town near Stover).' He'd say, 'Oh man, your head's nappy and your feets is long.Your partner's goin', what you waitin' on?'" These words are similar to what the St. Louis blues pianist Wesley Wallace said in response to Bessie Mae Smith on her her 1929 record "St. Louis Daddy."

Patton also thought of himself as a storyteller, always taking opportunities to entertain his friends with yarns. "Just like you and him was sittin' over there," House reported, "and you had a little snort or somethin' to get him primed up in his line, the rascal! Then: 'Well, now! I'm gonna tell you-all a little story!'—That the way he'd go, like that." The clean versions of Patton's stories that House later retold to interviewers may have been taken from minstrel shows, and they often rhymed. "He used to tell about the dog and the cat, and the squirrel or somethin' like that; the guy that went huntin' and all that kinda stuff, and rhyme it out and it sound good. After he'd tell it and end it, everybody would just laugh it off. One about the turkey, that was a funny one he liked to tell:

> "What did the rooster-turkey say to the little brown hen?'
> "You ain't laid a egg in God knows when!'

"What did the hen say to the rooster?'
"You don't come around as often as you usta!'"

These rhymes[12] bring to mind the opening lyrics of one of Patton's most famous songs, "Banty Rooster Blues," that he would record in 1929.

Sometimes Patton's humor could be quite bawdy. In his old age, House demurred from remembering Patton's favorite jokes, saying merely "They'd all be 'bad,' 'bad' words and things." The women that Patton seduced were favorite targets of his jests. "He thought he was some pigmeat back in those days," House remarked. "Charlie's 'meddlesome' (i.e., given to accost women), that was his trouble," he'd 'meddle' all that time, and then get a big laugh off it." House and Willie Brown preferred hearing the animal rhymes over the sexual boasts. Later on, though, House wondered whether such boasting didn't result in Patton's failures to attract women whenever he was "talking trash" (fabricating affection). "They'd always be tryin' to get rid of 'im,on account of that bullshit," House said of Patton's attempts, "that's what they'd get tired of." One of Patton's blues choruses may suggest such a brush-off:

Aw, that moon has gone down, baby, North Star about to shine,
Aw, the moon goin' down, baby, the North Star about to shine,
Rosetta Henry told me, "Lord, I don't want you hangin' 'round."

In response, Patton in the next chorus implies that the woman is a prostitute who caters to mill-hands:

Oh well, where were you now, baby, Clarksdale mill burned down?
Oh well, where were you now, babe, Clarksdale mill burned down?
(spoken: Boy, you know where I were)
"I was way down Sunflower with my face all fulla frowns."

In view of such low gossip, that Son House seldom if ever confided to Patton is understandable. "He'd tell most anything. I wouldn't trust him, 'cause he get a couple drinks and out it's comin'. He'll tell it if it'll send you to the 'lectric chair."

On his records, Patton routinely mentioned his difficulties with women ("Trouble at home baby, tryin' to blow me down"), yet he was rarely critical of them. Except for maybe one or two instances, his lyrics pass over the specific details about his conflicts. By never making explicit his problems with the opposite sex, Patton seems to suggest that he may be the cause of his troubles at home, as suggested by one of his lyrics:

One of these mornin's, you know it won't be long,
One of these mornin's, baby, know it won't be long,
You're gon' be mistreated and maybe I'll have to leave your home.
("Devil Sent The Rain")

As a traveling blues singer, Patton was in many respects a homeless person, as indicated in one of his tough-bitten lyrics:

No use a-hollerin', no use screamin' and cryin',
No use of hollerin', no use of screamin' and cryin',
For you know you got a home mama, long as I got mine.
("Screamin' and Hollerin' The Blues")

Some blues singers seek to engage the sympathy of their listeners by wallowing in their tales of woe. But Patton mentions not his own misfortunes, but rather those of other people's:

Hard luck is at your front door, blues are in your room,
Hard luck is at your front door, blues are in your room,
Callin' at your back door, "What is gonna become of you?"
("Bird Nest Bound")

On his records, Patton mentioned drinking a few times. But those who remembered him agreed that he craved alcohol as much as he desired women. Hayes McMullan said that the mere sight of a liquor bottle could excite Patton visibly. According to Son House, Patton was willing to try any whiskey. "He'd drink anything if it wasn't poison. All he wanted to know: was people supposed to drink it." House recalled that Patton would frequently "fall out" (pass out) from drinking too much corn liquor, for which he had a low tolerance.

Rather than drinking less during performances, Patton preferred to have a fatty meal beforehand. Miller explained, "He didn't want nothin' but fat meat, you know, sliced off the ham. He said that would keep you from gettin' drunk. He said the whiskey would eat on that, see. If you bring him a lean (slice of ham), he'd send it back and tell 'em to fix it right. And you know, a musician in them days, whatever he asked for, that's what he got."

But there were times when this strategy failed. Henry Austin had performed with Patton at frolics near Itta Bena in the late 1920s. He later remembered that "when he get high, he ain't gonna make much music, [he will] start talking and cussing; and if he know me and you, he's gonna start at us and . . .

just talkin' funny." Likewise, when Hayes McMullan attended parties with Patton, the older man would invariably "fall drunk in a few minutes" and become incapable of performing.

Had Patton taken these pratfalls too often, he would not have thrived in a career in music, or survive for that matter. Many other people remembered him as having a lot of performing stamina. Elizabeth Moore said that "he drank but he never got drunk." Recalling the times when she saw him perform during the late 1920s, she noted, "He could just steady-play. If he started at seven o'clock, why, he'd play till four in the morning."

Booker Miller knew Patton for only the last four years of his life, but he reported that "he could endure, you know what I mean? He didn't get tired and lay his box down and walk out like many musicianers would do, [who would] stand around talkin' about 'I'm tired.' [Rather,] if it took all night, he'd be there with you. If you said, 'Start at seven o'clock,' he'd be there. And you say: 'We goin' till daylight,' he'd be right there. You never would hear nobody comin' in sayin', 'Wonder where he at? Well, what's the matter with the music?' 'Cause it would be goin'. I never did see him get too drunk to play, he'd play anyhow. I don't know how, but he could do it, [he could] keep swayin' and playin.'"

As noted earlier, Patton believed that drinking made him a better performer. But he admitted to Miller that it affected his picking control. "He say that's the reason he didn't use picks. See, when he get kinda liquored up, you know, he hit 'em [his strings] too hard."

Liquor also affected Patton's demeanor to the point where his friends could usually tell when he had been drinking. "The thing about it," House said, "he talked different. That's what I went by. He talked in a way like he wasn't talkin' this mornin' when you saw him. He'd say things different, use his words different, and he had some kinda little old hatred in him."

Hayes McMullan agreed that liquor eroded Patton's temperament. "Now here was Charlie's trouble: Charlie, he was 'whiskey-headed,' and of course when he got to drinkin' whiskey you couldn't tell him too much. He'd argue back." That Patton argued while drunk did not necessarily mean that he began the argument in question. Barrelhouses and house frolics attracted people who liked to pick fights, and in these settings Patton may have felt that with his puniness he had to put up constantly a show of strength.

His foolishness, combativeness, and romantic overtures may be regarded as "woofing," which the folkorist Zora Neale Hurston described as "a sort of aimless talking. A man half seriously flirts with a girl, half seriously threatens to fight or brags of his prowess in love, battle, or financial matters."[13]

"He's a big talker until he thinks somebody's figurin' to fight," House said of him. Johnnie Mack recalled, "Sometimes he would get kinda fractious, make a lotta noise. It was mostly bluff. Everybody's thinkin' he's gonna do somethin', but everybody caught on to him." The only reason Patton's woofing carried any weight in the first place was because of its volume. "He just had a big mouth, and folks didn't know him, they'd think he could chin the moon by the sound of his voice," House said.

But when a fight broke out around him at a house frolic, Patton abandoned his show of strength. Some of his retreats from a barrelhouse scuffle could be comic, like the one near Robinsonville later related by Son House. "Charlie got his guitar and come up the cottonfield to get to the road. Me and Willie Brown was comin' down the road. And we see the cottonstalks and things shakin'. I said: 'Willie, lookey yonder!' Me and him both got scared, [because] we thought it was some kinda animal, you know! So he run to the road, him an' his guitar. And he looked and seen me and Willie, and he went to talkin' to hisself, 'Yeah, them son of a bitches! I'll kill all of them.' I said, 'How in the hell you gonna kill them all, fast as you'se comin' up that cottonfield?' We joked Charlie a long time about that."

Willie Morris described another way how Patton escaped when a brawl over a woman disrupted a frolic at the Red Gum plantation near Leland in the early 1930s. "One of them 'bad' white fellas used to have that, didn't 'low nobody (i.e. the police) on that place and them folks could do what they wanted to and wouldn't get arrested. Me and Charlie was over there playin'; we was gettin' five dollars a night, five dollars apiece. This guy starts shootin' and they all runned out and got in them cottonfields and them cornfields, man, and hid around there. Somebody was standin' at the door with one of them hobtail knives, snappin' everybody comin' out, and they all was hollerin' around there about they was shot, they was shot, but it wasn't nothin' but that guy standin' up there just pickin' 'em over with that knife. He didn't cut 'em bad. Charlie went up the chimney! Them big chimneys, you can get up there apiece. He stayed up there till the war was over."

"When they start fightin' or somethin' like that," Son House said, "he didn't forget that guitar! Him and that guitar were gone, brother! I never heard of him doin' no fightin'." Frank Howard may be the only informant on record who described Patton using his fists. But Howard characterized him, on the whole, as a "peaceful" person who only became "mean" if someone else "got him riled up," and who only fought defensively. "He'd get away if you let him, but now you held him up, he'd try to occupy you for a while," Howard noted.

Yet Patton's sense of entitlement set him constantly at odds with the men in his audience, especially his possessiveness of the women he would see among his rivals. "Little Charlie Patton, he gonna sure squabble, raise a rough-house with anybody—you know what I mean—about a woman," Hayes McMullan said. House concurred, "He'd raise sand in a minute if he think you were foolin' with one of his women."

But in return, Patton considered any woman as fair game for his own attentions. "He called anybody's wife 'honey' and 'sugar,'" reported Willie "Have Mercy" Young. "A real jealous man didn't have no business around Charlie Patton."

According to House, Patton was "quick to meddle" with nearly every woman he saw. David Edwards qualified this judgment, remarking that "Charlie never did 'meddle' nobody. But one thing he would do—he was a heavy drinker—and when he get fulla that stuff, he wants to 'clown' (show off), and be seen. He's just one of them old 'clownish' types, you know, but he wouldn't do it till he's drinkin': 'clown' around with women."[14]

But what to a flirting blues singer was clowning or woofing would seem like meddling to an angry rival, who would be quick to reassert himself by drawing blood. Such a fight between Patton and a jealous man would be ominous for the musician, in view of his puniness and of his lack of weapons (so far as what was remembered about him). How Patton lowered his flirtatiousness when threats were made remains an enigma of his personality. "He say he want the friendship of a person," Frank Howard recalled. "He don't want nobody to be layin' to kill him or shootin' through a window or somethin." Nonetheless, there may have been many nights when, upon arriving, Patton took note of the nearest window for escape. That he was apprehensive about the intentions of others is indicated by Booker Miller's explanation of his customary banter as a way of testing "the friendliness of people, see if they was friendly or unfriendly."

Patton knew what it meant to have enemies in the Delta, for he had created some of them. What more, at least twice, he received disabling wounds from them. When Miller first met him in 1930, he noticed a scar on the side of his forehead that seemed to have been inflicted with a knife or a broken bottle. In or around 1933, Patton's throat was cut seriously enough for him to be taken to a hospital. When the news of Patton's death spread through gossip during 1934, some people refused to believe that he died from natural causes. Their disbelief is understandable in view of Patton's coarse behavior within a rough environment. Yet they should have also wondered at how he lived for as long as he did.

*Part 2*

# THE MAN AND HIS MUSIC

You're never gonna find out much
about these old blues singers.

—J. MAYO WILLIAMS, BLUES RECORDING
PRODUCER AND EXECUTIVE

*Chapter 3*

# THROUGH THE PAST DARKLY (1880s–1900)

Live Patton did, but he became a historical figure with a sparsely documented past. Much about his life remains cloudy and uncertain. Southern blues before World War II was very much part of an oral African American culture. That may explain why it was mostly unnoticed at that time by mainstream America; the few who did notice southern blues mistook it initially as a crude derivative of W. C. Handy's commercial sheet music hits of the 1910s and 1920s. The present-day Patton biographer has to rely mostly on his 1929-1934 commercial 78s and on various recorded interviews with surviving associates conducted during some thirty to forty years after Patton's death. Furthermore, those interviews are piecemeal and often pose problems. If the informal nature of these reminiscences suggest anything, it may be that those who attended Patton's Delta performances had participated with their bodies but not necessarily with their minds.

Consider, for example, Elizabeth Moore's breathless account of how, as a teenage resident of Robinsonville, she reacted to Patton's appearance there in the late 1920s:

> "They tell me they gonna have a new guitar-player up here tonight! And say: 'He come from way down this road!'

"I say, 'Where?'

"'Down on the Dog line, hear?! You-all come out tonight!'

"'All right!' I got there, I been had a little drink of hooch 'fore I got there. When I walked in the door Charlie Patton was down on them 'Backwater Blues.' I said, 'Mmmm!' I looked over there and I said, 'Aw, sho'!' They carried me back home that night."

Likewise, the stories that musicians told about Patton are episodic in form and roguish in character, and they provide few concrete facts for the historian. But sometimes one of their memories can provide a toehold for research. For example, Lake Cormorant's Willie Moore told the authors of how he met Patton, sometime before 1918 in the town of Hollandale:

"A boy say, 'It's some fella down there, man, named Charlie Patton!' An' he say, 'He's in town.'

"I say: 'Oh, I see.'

"He say, 'Yeah, you know what them boys told me?' Say, 'Hot damn, he looks like white folks, almost.' An' say, 'You just ask at the first restaurant.' I say, 'Who runs it?' He say, 'A woman runs the café; he plays for them all the time.' And say, 'Her name is Chris Oliver.'

"I wrote it down on the back of a cigarette butt. When I got down there, he was there. I say, 'That's got to be the fella!' See, he 'bright' (light-skinned), you know, an' his hair just laid back.

"He's just sittin' there, and another fella was there had a mandolin and a solo bass. Them instruments was back there and out, but they wasn't playin'. I walked in, I inquired about him, and I said, 'Dis here is, uh, Mister Patton?'

"'Yeah,' he say, 'Charlie Patton.'

"I say, 'This here's Moore!' I says, 'Look!' I says, 'Where could a man get a little "light" job?'

"He say, 'What can you play?'

"I say, 'Well, I can play most anything.'

"He say, 'Well, I tell you what to do.' He say, 'We got a dance tonight.' And he say, 'We won't start until eight o'clock.' And he say, 'You stay around here and when I go out, I'll carry you with me.' He say, 'We'll run around here (i.e. Oliver's cafe) until about two-thirty then. Then we will run around in the back of the café, with the instruments around there, he say. We'll knock up on a tune or two and see how we get together.'"

Moore's guitar skills proved to be good enough to accompany, and so he spent two nights as a Patton sideman. Then Moore returned to his duties as a troubleshooter for W. C. Handy's Memphis-based dance band. But he kept in touch with Patton, who contacted him by mail whenever he needed him as a sideman again. Yet their dealings were strictly business. For the most part, Moore did not have a social relationship with Patton.

Various reasons why Patton didn't socialize much with other musicians are suggested in other interviews with the authors. Booker Miller was a protégé who assisted Patton on playing dates during the early 1930s. He later remembered that, when on the job, Patton tended to make laconic, impersonal conversation. "We would get ready and go on to the dance. First thing we wanna do is get us a drink or two, and we would be playin.' We never did talk about, you know, too much of people or life. We just playin' and watchin' the folks and talkin' about what they was doin.'"

Another reason was that when Patton mentioned his personal life, his listeners were often turned off by what he said. "He's the biggest liar ever was," Son House claimed, "and he's proud of it. He's a sworn (self-confessed) liar, that guy is: I didn't believe nothin' he said, no kinda way."

Some associates thought that Patton told his story in song. "Whatever events would come in his mind, and wear with him a while, he could play about it," Booker Miller said. "He'd write him a song and play about it." It should be acknowledged that today we may hear many stock blues phrases in the songs that Patton recorded in 1929-1934, yet audiences in the 1910s may have heard those same phrases as new expressions when he first sang most of those same songs. That much said for the songs in general, some of their lyrics may contain autobiographical touches. For example, his 1930 recording "Joe Kirby" is remarkable for mentioning his fleeting romances in throwaway blues lyrics. There is first a swipe at his common-law wife Bertha Lee, and then an indirect mention of a blues pianist named Louise Johnson, whom Patton visited on the Kirby plantation near Robinsonville:

> Say I'll be your monkey baby, sure won't be your dog
> Say I'll be your monkey baby, sure won't be your dog
> Says 'fore I'll stand your doggin' I'll, sleep in a hollow log.
>
> Some people say baby them, Kirby blues ain't bad.
> Some people say baby them, Joe Kirby blues ain't bad.
> An' it must not a-been them, Joe Kirby blues I had.

Well, I'm goin' where, Green River do run down
Well, I'm goin' where, Green River do run down
'Cause the woman I love, Lordie, live in Robinsonville town.

This record could be considered as fluff; a blues of this sort may not be any more meaningful than the affair that inspired it. Its stock phrases would have permitted Patton to refresh it with minor changes, such as where lived a new lover. "Joe Kirby," then, may be listened to as an audio snapshot of Patton's romantic life as it stood during the winter of 1930.

Although Patton might have washed his own dirty laundry on a record like "Joe Kirby," his standoffish manner did not encourage others to ask him personal questions. Thus why Booker Miller, who was intensely interested in his life, did not ask him how his throat had become scarred, or why he had been forced off Dockery's plantation, an event Miller learned of through a rumor. "I often wanted to ask him (about the scar)," Miller said. "I figured down the line somewhere he might would tell me. You know sometime you go to diggin' into things like that, you know; you kinda rile people up." Patton never did tell Miller, even though he was cut some time after the two men first met.

It is ironic, then, that by collecting these kinds of biographical fragments, a researcher may now attain a more comprehensive sense of Patton's life than his peers and neighbors could in the 1930s. Plantation society lacked the stability of the white Southern town, as attested by the Mississippi writer Eudora Welty: "If you grew up in the South when things were relatively stable, when there was a lot of talk and so on, you get a great sense of a person's whole life. This is because you know all of the families. You know several generations because they all live together. You know what happened to So-and-So clear through his life. You get a narrative sense of your next door neighbor."[1] But long-term plantation tenants were rare in Mississippi, where laborers and sharecroppers were noted merely as names in commissary ledgers. When the Mississippi flood inundated the Delta in April 1927, The New York Times admitted that "scores have perished in the flood waters. The exact number may never be known, as there is no possible way to check the families of transient tenant farmers in many sections."[2]

Say what Patton's neighbors may about his behavior—and they did for many years—they were struck dumb by his facial looks and complexion. He lacked a single physical feature with which they could associate to a race to which he could belong. Those who knew him disagreed about his ancestry. Hayes McMullan thought he was part Mexican, as did Will Dockery's cook, Sara Garrett. "I believe he was mixed-up with Indian or somethin'," David Edwards said. Son House also regarded him as part Native American. A neighbor from Ruleville described him from memory as a "kinda Injun-lookin' fella,"[3] but when he was shown the 1929 Paramount Records publicity photo, he asked "That's a white man, ain't it?"

Indeed, many of Patton's acquaintances thought he resembled Caucasians. But while speaking to researchers in the 1960s, they tended to lessen this impression by likening him to an indeterminate ethnicity and saying Mexican. One of the few blues singers who was willing to imply white ancestry for Patton was Ishman Bracey, who described him as "kinda light 'red,' 'red'-lookin' fella, wasn't betwixt an' between 'bright' and dark: he just kinda 'red'-lookin'." In the terms of 1960s Mississippi when that interview was conducted, "red" signified white, a term doubtless brought about into use by the sunburned facial appearance of the white Southerner.

Patton's appearance would have seemed exotic in the acutely complexion-conscious South where blood lines were legally drawn. At the time of his birth, only fifteen percent of the lower South's black population was recorded in the 1890 census as "mulatto"—a catch-all term indicating only that the person so designated appeared to be a racial composite. If New Orleans and its Creole population was removed from consideration, then the percentage of mulattoes in the rest of the Deep South would be much lower.

According to the white ideals of attractiveness[4] that were often adopted by blacks of his generation, Patton was considered handsome. "He was a fine-lookin' fella, I'm a-tell you," Willie Moore said. Other friends, however, made fun of his protruding ears. "His ears sit out, kinda wide," Son House related. "They'se bigger than your ears—bigger than two of 'em: they'd (friends would) just make fun of 'em. Willie Brown, he called him 'a light-eared son-of-a-bitch,' he called him all kinda 'eared' things. But Charlie was better-lookin' than Willie."

Yet, for all his airs of superiority, Patton did not pull rank on those with skin swarthier than his, like House or Brown. The straight or "good" hair that his friends always remarked on did not, according to House, matter that much to him: "He looked like he didn't care nothin' about whether he had it or not." Nor, said House, did Patton have any aversion to dark-featured women—"he's crazy about everything wore a dress"—even though on his 1929 hit record "Pony Blues" he ranked them lower than light-skinned women:

> Ain't a brownskin woman like somethin' fit to eat?
> Brownskin woman is like somethin' fit to eat?
> Oh but a jet black woman, don't put your hand on me.

Even so, Patton perceived others, and was so perceived in return, in the terms of the racial complexion stereotypes that prevailed in his society. He used one such stereotype in his 1930 recording "Mean Black Cat," in which he is victimized by a bedroom intruder that is described only as a "mean black cat." At that time, even in African American cultures, such a phrase likened complexion to character, and in this passage from a 1941 anthropological study:

"It is the black Negro who is regarded as mean, ignorant, primitive, and animal-like. Sometimes the comment of Negroes is very extreme, as in the case of two Negroes overheard discussing 'blackness.' One of them said: 'A black nigguh is the meanes' rascal God evah made!!'"[5]

Many blues songs contain harsh characterizations and biting accusations that are blatant expressions of spite. Aside from what was already noted for "Mean Black Cat Blues" and "Joe Kirby," Patton's songs are unusually mild-mannered for the blues. Their overall civility is enhanced further by the comic flourishes that Son House considered unbecoming to blues singers. It may be that Patton, for all his combativeness, was loathe to act like the typical mean-spirited blues singer, construing such behavior as an unbecoming representation of blackness.

Patton's complexion took after those of his parents, Annie Martin and William Patton (who may or may not have been a stepfather). "His parents was both very 'bright,'" Sara Garrett recalled. "Annie Patton and Bill Patton both was light-skinned people." She likened the proportions that led Son House to describe Charlie as "nothin' but a little runt" to those of his mother. Bill Patton, on the other hand, stood over six feet tall and was a man of considerable girth. If either parent had Native American ancestors, then he or she shared a distinction with less than two percent of Mississippi's "colored population," according to the 1880 census category that then included Native Americans.

The Patton family tree was rooted in Tennessee. Their surname may have been spelled originally as "Patten," as written down in a census entry that included Charlie's grandfather John.[6] Born in 1840, he had settled in or been transported as a slave before the end of the Civil War to Mississippi, where he fathered four children between 1862 and 1875. Bill, the second or third of the brood,[7] was born in March 1864, which would have made him the next to youngest child. Other brothers and sisters may have perished in infancy, for a nine- or ten-year gap separates the ages of the children who remained alive in 1880.

By that year, apparently, John Patten's wife (first name lost to time) was dead, and the care of the children was entrusted to her twenty-five-year-old sister Ether, who had come from Tennessee to live with the family. The Pattens then resided in Coahoma County, one of the first Mississippi Delta regions to be settled, and the probable location of Bill Patton's birth. Some 11,000 blacks—five times the number of resident whites—claimed the county as their own.

With Bill's generation, "Patten" became "Patton." When he grew into adulthood, he did not stay much longer in Coahoma County. In 1884, at age eighteen or twenty, he married Annie Martin, a native of Hinds County[8]; she was at least two years older than him, having been born in January 1862. She was also of a higher social status, it would seem, as she could read and write, but Bill could not. When they married, the bride was at least six months pregnant, so their wedding may have been hasty, perhaps even a shotgun wedding.

During the first sixteen years of their marriage, the Pattons seem to have lived in the hill country of Hinds County, which had been a region of small plantations at the time of Annie's birth and still remained so. All told, the Pattons had seven children, one of whom had died by 1900. The first child, a daughter, Katie (nicknamed Kitty), arrived in March of 1884. Viola, the second born (in January of 1887), proved the hardiest of the lot, surviving until 1969. The third daughter and final family addition, Etha (probably named for Bill's maternal aunt), was born in August of 1899 and appears to have died during childhood. The family was completed[9] with four sons: Charlie; William, whom family would call "Willie" or "Son," born in January 1895; C., born around 1901; and Ed.

Charlie was born sometime around April 1891, according to the 1900 census.[10] At the time, his family was sharecropping on a two or three thousand acre cotton and corn plantation known as Herring's Place, located four miles south of Bolton and four miles north of Raymond in central Mississippi. One of Herring's boundaries was marked by a creek, with the Gaddis and McLaurin Plantation on the other side. "That was wonderful country out there," Sam Chatmon said of the area.

Herring's bore the name of its founder Sam Herring, a one-time slaver[11] that the Chatmon family counted as an ancestor. "He messed[12] with my mother's mother, got mama by her," explained Sam Chatmon, who adopted Herring's Christian name after rejecting his own name Vivian as sissified. "Made her daddy be a white man." Even after the plantation passed into the hands of Herring's sons Willie and Robert around 1906, the Chatmons living next door on Gaddis and McLaurin were extended a special cordiality by the owners. "Anytime we'd be around," Sam recalled, "anybody'd say anything, they'd take it up. They'd say, 'Look, don't talk about those Chatmons, leave 'em alone.' If we got in a fuss or somethin', Herring'd come up and tell 'im, 'You go home, I want the Chatmons to stay on the land.'"

Willie and Robert Herring had bad reputations for being "mean" to both whites and blacks. Across the creek at Gaddis and McLaurin, the future bluesman Walter Vinson as a child was warned by his mother to stay away from Herring's Place. Yet, according to Sam Chatman, the Herring patriarch Sam "was nice to everybody. He just liked colored folks. He'd have places for 'em to gamble, places for 'em to drink, places for 'em to lay in a big shed and sleep there when they got sleepy. It was a jukehouse, and he run a big store, and he'd have music there."

In the early 1890s, when Charlie was still a toddler, his father left the household for a few years[13] under circumstances that are now unknown. Eventually he did return to his wife and family, remaining with them even after they moved to the Delta. That he stayed put with Annie at Dockery's makes one wonder all the more about what caused their separation during the early 1890s. Had Annie been attentive to another man, and had BIll had become jealous? For whatever reason, Bill left, leaving Annie with three children and a sharecropping obligation.

Living on Herring's at the time was a guitarist named Lem Nichols,[14] who was likely in his forties. He may have been the first musician Charlie Patton probably ever heard. He was remembered long afterwards for playing rag ditties like "Spoonful" which Patton would adopt and adapt in his own repertory, and "Pearlee" that Nichols played with a pocket knife.

Horses provided the plantation's favorite forms of entertainment. For children like Patton, there were the hobby horses. "They'd carry you for about five or maybe ten minutes for a nickel," Sam Chatmon said. Older children would have known of Shetland ponies, even if they didn't own one. Patton mentioned Shetlands in his third stanza of the 1929 "Pony Blues" record:

> Got a bran' new Shetland, mare already trained
> Better get you a saddle, tighten up on the rein.

But the chief draw for children and adults at Herring's were its horse races. "The people on his place would raise great, big, fine horses. They'd have them races every Sunday evenin'. It would draw hundreds of folks there, Chatmon remembered. "They had a road run straight out about a mile and a half or two miles. The horses'd be comin' up to it, just flyin'. Man, everybody'd be whoopin' and hollerin'."

With Patton recording in 1929-1934 as part of the first generation of Mississippi bluesmen on 78-rpm records, and his lyrics referring to turn of the century trends like ponies, it is tempting to think that he and the blues came of age at the same time. But even after over 60 years of research, no one knows exactly when and where the first blues were developed, and hence the relevance of Patton's childhood to the early development of the blues is not fully established. For these reasons, a little caution should be taken when discussing Patton's 1929-1930 recordings of his earliest datable songs.

Celebrating Patton as a blues singer is appropriate, but assuming that he was a blues pioneer may be misguided. In blunt terms, Patton may have been part of the first generation of bluesmen on records, but there was an earlier generation of musicians including the first bluesmen who did not have opportunities to make records that Patton would have heard in person. Acclaiming Patton as among the first-ever bluesmen does not take full account of his musical style on the records. From a musical standpoint, Patton's surviving performances are quite sophisticated compared to the basic blues forms he employed—that is to say, his embellishments seem much too skilled and too adept to come from some pioneering player[15] who had formulated the first blues. Had the blues been an entirely new musical world to Patton and his listeners, there would have been little need for his artistic individuality as heard on his records. If Patton was a bluesman of the second generation, then he would have expected his listeners to be already familiar with the conventions of the blues that were set by the first generation, and so he could then concentrate on presenting his innovations, ornaments and embellishments for applause and money.

Much of the current public opinion that Patton was a pioneer of the blues may be due in large part to a misconception about melodic phrasing in the blues. Often a blues song is rendered in music notation as three four-measure lyric phrases in 4/4 meter. W. C. Handy's 1914 "St. Louis Blues" is a classic example.

Here, each measure contains four beats, each phrase contains four mea-

Ex. 1: W. C. Handy, "St. Louis Blues," sheet music publication (1914).

sures having 16 beats, and each blues chorus (or stanza) contains three phrases having 12 measures and 48 beats. The blues chorus is often defined as having 12 measures, no more and no less, and each blues phrase is supposed to be exactly four measures long.

Musicians who use phrases longer or shorter than four measures are often regarded as archaic, primitive, or rustic.[16] Let us take for example Patton's 1929 "Pony Blues" record, whose vocal melody is shown here in a notated transcription:

Ex. 2: Charlie Patton, "Pony Blues" (1929), chorus 1, vocal melody [0:03-0:38].

Note that Patton extends his first phrase by two beats (which in our notation for measure 5 is indicated by necessity with the 2/4 meter), and his third phrase with an extra full measure. Therefore, this first chorus of "Pony Blues" could be described as having 14 measures instead of matching Handy's 12.

For another example, here is the vocal melody of Patton's first chorus of "Down The Dirt Road Blues," also recorded in 1929.

There are two ways of counting the measures in this chorus. One way is by counting the measures in 2/4 meter equally with those in 4/4 meter, in accordance with how the measures are numbered in the notated example. In this manner, this chorus may be said to have 15 measures. Another way is by counting the number of quarter-beat units in the whole chorus: 54, with each

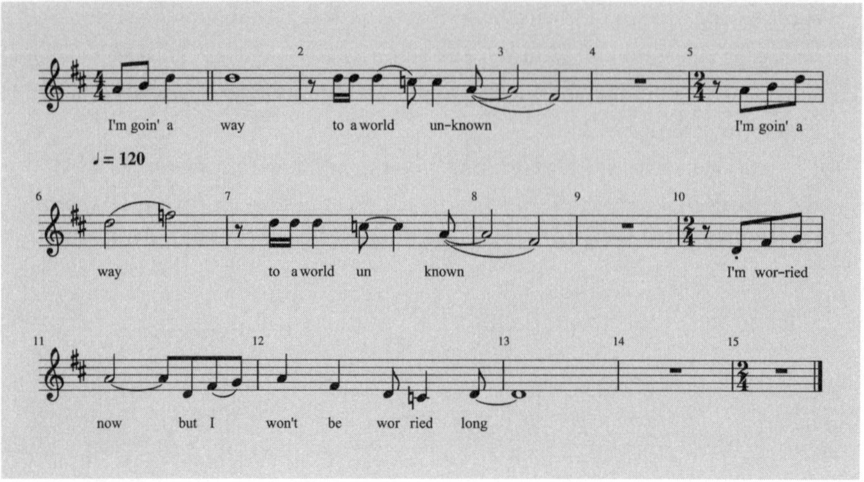


Ex. 3: Charlie Patton, "Down The Dirt Road Blues" (1929), chorus 1, vocal melody [0:02-0:32].

phrase having 18 beats. If those 54 beats were re-organized in four-beat measures, then the opening chorus could be said to occupy 13½ measures. However its measures are counted, the opening chorus of "Down The Dirt Road Blues" does not have the standard lengths for blues phrases and choruses. If this and "Pony Blues" are heard with the expectation that their choruses should be exactly 12 measures, they may be mistaken for early blues expressions that predate Handy's 1910s sheet music hits.

We can explore deeper into blues phrasing by shifting our frame of reference from the blues chorus to the component blues phrase. The two basic parts of a four-measure blues phrase are a vocal lyrical call and an instrumental response. Each call and response may begin at varying points of the melodic scale, but they almost always end on the tonic or root note of that scale (such

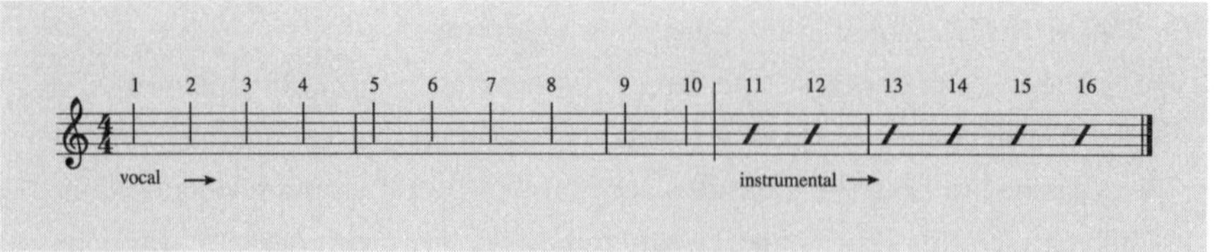


Ex. 4: Division of 16-beat/4-measure phrase into call and response.

as the pitch D in the key of D). But in terms of phrasing, the four-measure phrase in 4/4 meter has 16 quarter-note beats. Classic blues songs will have 10 beats of singing call, and 6 beats of instrumental response: Note that the last two beats of the 6-beat instrumental response (or "fill," as many musicians call it) are often in the tonic chord.

This uneven division of beats for call and response will be called the "ten-six pattern." The ten-beat vocal phrase may be noticed in Handy's "St. Louis Blues," and also on some of Patton's records like "Pea Vine Blues, "Joe Kirby Blues," and "Mean Black Moan":

Ex. 5a: Ten-six pattern in opening 4 measures of W. C. Handy, "St. Louis Blues."

Ex. 5b: Ten-six pattern in opening 4 measures of Charlie Patton, "Pea Vine Blues" (1929) [0:03-0:14].

The beginning of a ten-six pattern is counted on the first beat of the first full transcribed measure, disregarding the "pickup" notes preceding that first measure. In other examples given in this book, the tenth beat is cut short or even omitted if the singer clips his delivery or simply runs out of breath. Although the ten-six pattern may seem to divide unevenly the 16 beats of a phrase, it is a predictable blues characteristic that lends itself well to being played by blues ensembles, even by groups as large as Handy's bands.

In contrast, Patton had his own manner of phrasing the blues. It may be noticed in his phrases of 18 beats, not the standard 16 beats. For example, in his "Down The Dirt Road Blues," he sings the last word of each vocal lyric on the ninth beat, as expected (see Ex. 3, measures 3, 8, and 13); the beginning of each of those words a half-beat before beat 9 is a Patton touch. He extends each of these words past beat 10 to beat 12. That means the usual guitar riffing for the instrumental response could be delayed for 2 beats (beat 13 instead of beat 11 of each phrase). To allow this delay and a brief vocal rest, Patton inserts an extra measure (measures 4, 9, and 14) in each instrumental response. He makes the same insert in measure 13 of the first chorus of "Pony Blues" (Ex. 2), tossing in an extra two beats at the end of that response (m. 14).

There is no logical process of reducing Patton's 18-beat phrases to Handy's 16-beat phrases without losing something of the Patton style. Then again, the ten-six phrasing pattern came about when the eighth-note replaced the quarter-note as the declamatory unit during the transition[17] from 12-measure songs to the blues; the 12-measure songs with lyrics datable to the late 1890s like "Frankie and Albert" and "Railroad Bill" could be said to have thirteen-three phrasing patterns. The widespread use of the ten-six call-and-response phrasing on blues records before 1932 may be due to the musicians playing more by rote than from the experience of creating or mastering the blues form. Of course, Handy and other professional musicians trained in reading sheet music were capable of playing the blues with a full awareness of the form. On the other hand, most if not all southern blues singers of the 1920s on records seemed to take the 12-bar blues for granted, learning how to play it by memorizing the pattern or randomly by chance.

One last characteristic of the 12-measure blues form to be noted here is its lyric scheme. Most of the blues that Patton recorded followed the AAB scheme, that is, one lyric sung as the first vocal call (A) in mm. 1-3, those words repeated as the second call (A) in mm. 5-7, and a rhyming lyric as the concluding phrase (B) in mm. 9-11. A few exceptions to this AAB scheme may be found in Patton's 12-measure repertory. "Going to Move to Alabama" follows a 4+8 verse-and-refrain scheme, in accordance to the song's antecedent recorded previously by Jim Jackson as "Jim Jackson's Kansas City Blues." "Frankie and Albert" as a 12-measure non-blues song of the late 1890s follows an 8+4 ballad scheme, in which the last four measures of each chorus delivers the "done me wrong" refrain.

Complicating attempts to associate the birth of Patton with the birth of the blues is the recollection that Patton himself was uncertain about his age. "That's one thing you couldn't get him to talk about, how old he was," Son House reported, "He never say nothin' about his age." In 1912, Mississippi begin requiring the formal registration of births, by which time Patton was in his early 20s. House was certain that Patton and his playing partner Willie Brown never knew their true ages. "Willie would say, 'Charlie is much older that I is!' I say, 'No kidding!'" House explained. "Well, Willie wasn't no baby. Willie didn't even know how old he was his own self. Both of them was ignorant to things like that."

Other friends and family also didn't know for sure. In 1963, Patton's sister Viola Patton Cannon and one of his ex-wives, Minnie Franklin, stated that he was born in 1887.[18] Sam Chatmon's older sister Josephine Williams remembered Charlie as a child on Herring's plantation, noting: "I'se born in 1886 . . . I was a little older than him." But Dick Bankston, an early Patton imitator who was born in 1897, doubted an interviewer's suggestion that Patton was as much as ten years older than himself. Frank Howard remembered that Patton "told me at the time I got acquainted with him"—in 1921 or 1922—"he was thirty-one years old." A doctor who treated the dying Patton in April 1934 subsequently listed his age as forty-four on the death certificate. As this figure most likely came from Patton, it seems certain that he reckoned his own birthdate as falling between May 1889 and April 1890. But this reckoning was faulty: in 1900, his parents told census officials that he had been born in April of 1891.

That Patton may have thought he was a year older than he actually was suggests some aspects about his life and culture. Many people in Mississippi before World War II, especially the African Americans there, lived almost completely beyond the reach of those government institutions that now require residents to report their birthdates on many forms. It is very likely that Patton was never asked how old he was, aside from registering for the draft during World War I and submitting to an arrest for drunkenness in early 1934. Within the context of his family's poverty, it is easy to imagine that he spent his childhood without celebrating his birthday. Whenever Patton began frequenting barrelhouses—probably during his early teens—it would have been to his social advantage to add a year or two to his age, or as much as would be believable to his older friends. If indeed he was lying about his age early on, he could well have eventually forgotten his actual age. That may explain why he overestimated the number of years to Frank Howard and his physician.

Patton's looks seemed ageless anyway. Only during the last few years of his life, when his hair was turning gray, could his real age be reasonably guessed by his associates and cronies. Ishman Bracey came close to doing so, correctly describing him to interviewers as "close to forty . . . middle-aged" when he (Patton) made his recording debut at age thirty-eight. Son House met Patton him several months afterwards in early 1930. In the 1960s he remembered that "at the time I got acquainted with him, Charlie at least had to have been near about fifty years old. I knowed he was every bit and grain that much, not *under* fifty." Yet to Booker Miller, who knew him during those same years, Patton appeared to be about thirty-five years old. But as appearances were, Hayes McMullan saw no differences between the two surviving photographs of Patton, one a Paramount publicity portrait used in ads during the late 1920s, the other purportedly taken about twenty years earlier when he had not reached twenty. "It's just like him to me," he said upon seeing the earlier portrait. "He never did look old, to my judgment."

Who was Patton's biological father, if not Bill Patton, is another question. It became a matter of doubt[19] when Lonnie and Bo Chatmon returned from a Delta jaunt in the 1920s to their family home on the Gaddis and McLaurin plantation. They told the other Chatmons a story they heard in the Delta that Patton was their half-brother. "His mama must have told Charlie about it, who his daddy was," the Chatmons' sister Josephine Williams later speculated. "The boys would tease Papa about him, but Papa never would say nothin."

"Papa" was Henderson Chatmon (1850-1934), a bearded farmer and square dance fiddler of mixed racial origins. His grandmother, he once claimed, had been captured by slave traders on the Niger River. The planter Sam Herring purchased her as a slave, and then impregnated her; their daughter would later be Henderson's mother. "His mother was the marster's daughter," Josephine reported. "The old marster, when papa's mother was born, he carried her up to his house. And the old missus treated her just like she did one of her own. That was in slavery." As a budding musician during the last years of slavery, Henderson enjoyed the same kind of favoritism at another Big House. After learning fiddle from a planter named Bob Lacy, he became a favorite at Lacy's own dances. "Papa said they worry him so!" said Josephine Williams, "Just walkin' all over the road and hollerin."

Josephine remembered from her childhood that her family lived on Doctor Dupree's plantation, which was located some ten or twelve miles from Herring's where the Pattons lived. It was in the early 1890s, she went on to claim, that her father Henderson had an affair with Annie Patton. "Her husband wasn't with her then," she said, "she was a loose woman." Whether Charlie's birth was a result of their supposed intimacy is unknowable. It is also possible that the rumors of Charlie being a Chatmon half-brother may have arisen from the fact that one of the six sons who had been raised within the Chatmon household[20] was a child of Annie Patton's. Henderson married his wife Eliza in 1875, and she was much younger than him. She not only tolerated his frequent infidelities, but she could also be possessive of his many illegitimate children. At one family reunion, his son Sam claimed, forty or fifty such children were present. One time, while shopping in Bolton, Eliza saw a girl who resembled her husband.[21] She went over to the mother and said, "This baby's just like Chatmon. This is Chatmon's child, won't you let her go home with me and stay some so she can get used to her daddy?"

Sam's own boyhood photograph bears a curious resemblance to Patton's 1929 publicity picture, but the same can't be said for Lonnie and Bo Chatmon. Their sister Josephine claimed that Charlie was an "ugly" baby who "looked real dark, like his mama," darker than herself or her brothers, but lighter than his mother. "When he's little, he was a brownskin. He was a little lighter than his mama. His mama was kinda black. She had 'good' hair, but it wasn't straight, it was pretty nappy. She wasn't no Indian."

If any of Annie Patton's three boys were sons of Henderson Chatmon, then the likely candidate is Willie Patton, who was born on August 9, 1894, within Josephine's recollection of their affair. Willie, or "Son" as he was called, had a lighter complexion but coarser hair than Charlie, as did Henderson Chatmon. Son House remembered seeing Willie Patton. "Now 'Son' Patton, his hair was 'bad' as mine," he remembered "It wasn't near like Charlie's, and I'd say to myself—I wouldn't say it to *them* now: 'Now they brothers: there's somethin' happenin' *some* kinda way.'"

That the "something" resulted in Willie, rather than in Charlie or the remaining brother William (known as "Will C." or simply "C." and born in 1895), is indicated by the fact that Willie was not named by Bill and Annie Patton as one of their five children to the census-takers in 1900. If Bill had done the talking, he may have balked at acknowledging Willie as his son.

If there were blood-ties between any of the Patton children and Henderson Chatmon, the Patton family did not talk about it. When the Pattons arrived to Dockery's plantation, the tenant farming community there regarded Bill Patton as the natural head of the entire household. The death certificates of Charlie, Willie, and Viola all list him as their father. By Sara Garrett's later account to the authors, Bill and Charlie were on good terms.

Henderson left Dupree's for the Gaddis and McLaurin plantation in 1895, at which time he stopped going to Herring's. Shortly afterwards, Bill Patton returned to his wife. It was then, Josephine recalled, that the Pattons "left outta there and went down by Edwards" nine miles west of Bolton.

Although the family lived only briefly in Edwards, Charlie came to be thought by his later friends and musical associates as having been a native of that town. During the 1890s it was known as Edward's Depot because it served as a way station between Vicksburg (eighteen miles westward) and Jackson (twenty-six miles eastward) on the Alabama and Vicksburg train line. It had originally been founded as a consequence of the Vicksburg race riot of December 1874 that witnessed the removal of the town's black sheriff and foreshadowed the end of carpetbag rule in Mississippi. As a journalist reported, "The Vicksburg riot was a severe blow to the prosperity of that town: much of its traffic has gone off to Edward's Station, which has grown in a few months to be a large and busy place. . . . This is what has built up Edward's Station, where the colored men do not hear so much talk about the Caucasian race and the 'damned nigger' as at Vicksburg."[22]

When the Pattons lived there, Edward's Depot showed some promise of developing into a black cultural center. The black newspaper *New Light* was established there in 1888, and its secondary school provided Tuskegee-styled industrial and ministerial training to its pupils. But it is doubtful that Charlie Patton would have stood to benefit from these developments. He never learned to read or write, and supposedly he could spell only a single word—his own first name—by oral recitation.[23] "'C-h-a-r-l-i-e,' that's the way he'd spell it," recalled Son House. "He could spell his own name; that was all he could spell, but he couldn't even write his name after spelling it."

He may never have seen the inside of a schoolhouse.[24] At the turn of the century, nearly half of Mississippi's black residents were officially illiterate. Among black children between the ages of five and eighteen, fewer than sixty per cent of them were even enrolled in school, and fewer yet attended classes on anything approaching a regular basis. Some twenty-two percent of Mississippi children between the ages of ten and fourteen were officially illiterate. By those contemporary standards, nine-year-old Patton's education was very deficient, downright backward.

If he was illiterate, it may have been due to his status in the family as the first-born son. If the Pattons were like other farming families, they would have assigned to young Charlie the task of contributing to the family upkeep. At the turn of the century, it was common to see children as young as six toiling in the cottonfields; Patton being one such child laborer is suggested by the fact that he had yet to enroll in school by the time he reached his ninth birthday. But at the same time, his sisters Viola (then thirteen) and Kitty (then sixteen) were both attending school where they were learning how to read and write.

If Patton had done so much farming as a child, it may explain why he made a point of shunning such hard work as an adult. He flaunted his laziness as a badge of his musical success. On his record "Heart Like Railroad Steel," he made a joking proposal to a woman, offering to perform what were children's plantation tasks on her behalf:

> I will cut your wood, baby, . . .
> Cut your wood, baby, I will make your fire
> I will tote your water, from the boggy bayou

The implication was that he would do no more.

If Patton ever stepped inside a school, it is likely that he would have been shunted aside by the teacher. It was not until 1918 that Mississippi mandated compulsory education for either race; until then, teachers looked askance at the plantation pupil. "They'd always teach the town ones first and let the country children more or less sit on one side," Sam Chatmon recalled. "They'd have they classes and leave us behind. Plenty times the town children warm up by the heater, and they make the country children go back and wait."

Even among the country kids Patton would have cut a humorous and backward figure, thanks to his peculiar pronunciation that he continued using as an adult. "He didn't just speak plain like you and me," said Booker Miller, who during interviews couldn't help but laugh openly at Patton's diction while listening to his mentor's records like "Pea Vine Blues." Miller said he always found Patton's speaking and singing difficult to decipher, admitting of the singing diction that "Sometimes I can understand him and sometimes I can't. See, he got a drag; he got a accent, looks like cuts his speech or somethin." When Miller showed that the opening lyric of "Down The Dirt Road Blues" was "I'm goin' away, to a world unknown," he explained that "you just have to know him. He drags his words; that makes him hard to understand."

As a performer, Patton often reached for his listeners' attentions with his colorful, expressive delivery and his guitar work, rather than with the lyric content of his songs. In a dance setting, the rhythm he provided mattered more than the words he sang, for which reason the lyrics of many of his recorded blues could seem to us workaday in quality.

While Patton was never hired for his abilities as a versifier, he did have a blues sensibility. His songs were not expressions of strife or conflict, but rather they were grounded in another blues aesthetic that dated at least to the turn of the century. Patton's blues are often successions of personal experiences, often dramatized by the singer as recent or imminent actions. This is implicit in his lyrics and in his spoken interjection on Louise Johnson's "Long Ways From Home" (1930): when she sings "I woke up this mornin', blues all around my bed," Patton instructs her to "tell 'em what happened to you!"

Patton's grasp of blues as a set of circumstances with no sentimental overtones has much in common with the Wesleyan doctrine of religion as the idea of "experience." This notion may be found in many nineteenth-century black spirituals and their early twentieth-century successors. Instead of telling a story or affirming faith as such, the spiritual expressed the transport of the revivalist, or it told of the "experience" of the convert[25]:

> Went down to de low groun'; went dere to pray;
> My feet been taken out de miry clary.

Likewise, nearly all of Patton's recorded lyrics referred to events that were plausible if not actual incidents. Some examples relate merely petty experiences:

> I went to the depot, looked up at the board,
> I went to the depot, I looked up at the board,
> An' the train has left where it is now up the road.
> ("Hammer Blues")

By a historical trend[26] in the 1910s, the blues lyric in American sheet music gradually became a depiction of one single experience, that of "having the blues." This narrowing of topics in mainstream blues was completed at and after the beginning of blues recording in 1920, because during the previous year, W. C. Handy characterized blues as "happy-go-lucky songs." Although Patton did sing on his records a few lyrics about depressive strife, he was basically a stranger to that downer attitude. His only full-scale attempt to make a song out of a frown, "Mean Black Moan," appeared to be a presentation of a female's experience.

Within his own blues style, Patton acted out the "experiences" and conflicts of other people. For one example, he portrayed three people in "Banty Rooster Blues," a humorous song suggested by a black farm superstition[27] that the crowing of a rooster heralded the approach of a stranger. With this thought in mind, a farmer is determined to catch out his wife's "back door man" by getting such a bird:

I'm gonna buy me a banty, put him at my backdoor,
I'm gonna buy me a banty, put him at my backdoor,
Know he see a stranger comin,' he'll flap his wings and crow.

His wife ridicules this fancy, prompting a stubborn rejoinder:

"What you want with a rooster? He won't crow 'fore day.
What you want with a rooster? He won't crow 'fore day.
What you want with a man when he won't do nothin' he say?"

When his rival sneers at his possessiveness towards a sexually unresponsive partner, the farmer squelches him with this smart retort:

What you want with a hen won't cackle when she lay?
What you want with a hen won't cackle when she lay?
What you want with a woman when she won't do nothin' I say?

These lyrics may have been adapted from minstrel jokes. Their lack of originality mattered less to Patton than their evocations of experience. In other recorded songs, Patton lifted phrases and verses from various sources ranging from nursery rhymes and Biblical phrases[28] to Stephen Collins Foster's popular song "Oh, Susannah," from which he lifted this verse:

It was late one night, everything was still
It was late one night baby, everything was still

I could see my babe upon a lonesome hill.
("Green River Blues")

Because blues singers shared much the same experiences as traveling musicians, they took lyrics from each other. To their audiences, the blues entertainer represented him- or herself not as an individual, but as a social type and as a member of a professional fraternity. Booker Miller was one such member in the early 1930s. About 35 years later, long after he left the blues for religion, he was reminded of the bluesman's attitude when he heard the opening chorus of Patton's "Down The Dirt Road Blues," quoted below:

I can't go down the dirt road by myself,
I can't go down the dirt road by myself,
(spoken: My God, who you gonna carry?)
I don't carry my rider, gonna carry me someone else.

Booker Miller exclaimed in affirmation, "Oh, man! That was our *slogan*."

Certainly Patton coined some of the most popular slogans of prewar Mississippi blues singers, and he would have taken a few of those sung by others. But only his paraphrases show that he had borrowed, and what. The opening phrase of "Moon Going Down" ("Oh the moon is goin' down baby, North Star a-bound to shine") arose from a spiritual of slave vintage:[29]

The moon run down in purple stream
The sun forbear to shine
An' every star disappear
King Jesus shall be mine.

The second chorus, "Oh where were you now babe, Clarksdale mill burnt down?" was transformed from a song current in Mississippi in 1909:[30]

O where were you when the steamer went down, Captain?
"I was with my honey in the heart of town."

Patton could even make a new song from scraps of his own songs. Booker Miller said, "He had one piece [in which] he used to play a stanza out of every song he ever played, each song: put it together, and make a song out of that."

Patton's illiteracy was not a handicap to his blues versification, but it prevented him from having a first-hand knowledge through reading of the Bible, whose authority he accepted unquestionably. In "Magnolia Blues" he sang:

Got up this mornin' (spoken: "I said my 'fore day prayer")
Got up this mornin'
I didn't have me nobody speakin' Bible here

In order to fully "experience" religion, Patton needed someone to recite the Scripture to him. His recycling of the spirituals he would have heard during his youth ended up as so lyrically jumbled, that Son House took them to be Patton's own inventions. "It was his own make-up," he testified. "He'd have it [a spiritual] all kinda of way—I know that wasn't true. Some of the Christian people hear that, they know it ain't the truth; they know he's lyin." Every so often Patton was given to outbursts of "Bible talk," during which he drew from his mangled memory of other people's sermons. So, he couldn't distinguish between the words of sacred songs and actual Biblical text. To begin his record "Prayer of Death Part II," he mixes the two while reciting a deathbed prayer:

Oh, the Prayer of Death.
Oh Lord, oh Lordy.
I know you been calling him.
Yes, the wages of sin are death,
The gift of God, eternal life.

Mmm, Lordy. He said :
"You're a rock in a weary land,
a shelter in the time of storm"
Mmmm, okay, amen,
Then all of them moaning "Lord have mercy.
Oh, won't you save me, Lord"

What for Patton represented the word of Jesus was actually an 1880s white hymn composed by Ira David Sankey to words by Vernon J. Charlesworth, "A Shelter in the Time of Storm":[31]

Oh Jesus is a rock in a weary land
A shelter in the time of storm.

Patton's spiritual naivety is demonstrated by the Fundamentalist themes he emphasized in song. He sang of the "pie in the sky" aspect, which promised to sweeten the life he described as "trials" in "Some Happy Day" and as "trouble" in "Prayer of Death." During the feverish sermon based on Revelation that he gave during his recording of "You're Gonna Need Somebody When You Die," he equipped paradise with Charlesworth's sheltering rock, even though that had no textual foundation in the Book of Revelations: And the big rock that you can sit behind, the wind can't blow on you no more, and you gon' have the four and twenty elders that you can sit down and talk with and that you can talk about your trouble that you come—the world that you just come "from."

Like many youths in religious families, Patton was probably baptized, regardless of what Son House later said about him and Willie Brown: "Wouldn't nobody dip those guys—them guys [were] scared to death to take a bath!" The Pattons may well have been attracted to the glittering visions and airy promises of the flimsiest Fundamentalism, for earth offered no treasures to them. While Hinds County was Mississippi's most populous and prosperous farm region when the Pattons lived there, its prosperity was well beyond their grasp, and the local conditions yielded bleak lives of unrelenting hardship. Cotton prices between 1891 and 1895 were lower than those of any subsequent period before the Great Depression, and it was thought they were due to overproduction. Ironically, in a farmer's mind, the solution towards making more money would be to increase the crop. That alone may explain why the Pattons looked westward to the Mississippi Delta, despite its reputation as the "Death House." There may have been additional reasons in Edwards to move. A severe drought in 1896 blighted many hill farms. There was a lynching of a black in Edwards in April 1897, and a local yellow fever epidemic[32] that same year. In any event, the Pattons decamped for the Delta in 1900, or soon thereafter.[33] Their departure from the hills may have been provisional at the time, but it proved to be permanent, with few fond memories, if any. Charlie Patton did return to Edwards in the 1920s, but with the intent of "raking up all the money he could get," as the local blues singer Henry Austin witnessed and later attested to the authors.

It was in the Mississippi Delta where Patton developed the skills that enabled him to make money as a musician. If he had not heard the blues as a boy at Herring's or at Edwards, then as a teenager in the Delta he would have heard them for the first time. We have scant knowledge of turn of the century Delta music, but this smattering suggests much. Around 1900, when 78,500 guitars were manufactured,[34] a middle-aged Clarksdale guitarist named Alec

Lee played with a pocket knife[35] a medley of "Poor Boy, Long Ways From Home" and "My Bucket's Got a Hole in It." Whoever created this medley—whether Lee, or the musician he took it from—seems to have set two existing songs to guitar, with no express intention of performing downhearted blues. The result was more likely meant to be a showpiece for audiences who were just becoming familiar with guitar music, at least that played with a fretting implement. The version that Gus Cannon learned from Lee and later recorded in 1927 suggests that nothing fundamental about blues structure in north Mississippi performance practice took place between 1900 and the 1920s.

The first song of this medley as Gus Cannon recorded it was a three-phrase AA'A lyric blues in 4/4 time whose three melodic phrases were cobbled together in a crazy-quilt way. The first phrase may be notated in 6 measures, beginning with an eleven-beat vocal line ("bein' a poor boy, and a long ways from home"), with a ten-beat plucked banjo figure that is followed by a single beat rest, such as would not occur in a dance tune. The second phrase cuts the melody to six beats of singing, with six beats of tonic chord strumming after it. Only the final phrase has the standard four measures with the conventional ten-six call-and-response phrasing.

It seems then that the ten-six phrasing heard in many 1920s blues recordings may go back to the turn of the century blues. But also, going forward in time, it could have been by 1927 such a cliché that Cannon may have been seeking to surprise his record listeners by having it follow the first two phrases of different lengths and phrasings—the regular becoming irregular, perhaps.

If it can—or can't—be proved that "Poor Boy" was the creation of a hoboing street singer, then it could have originated anywhere. In and of itself, it may be considered as a flimsy song, if the vocal lyric call is heard as a mere set-up for the instrumental response that follows. Only in his third chorus did Cannon integrate the vocal and instrumental lines. Also, he sang the lyrics with a skeletal slide accompaniment on banjo, playing only a fleeting V chord in the third phrase. His opening vocal phrase ended awkwardly on a weak beat (on beat 3 in measure 4). For all the apparent spontaneity of the instrumental part, "Poor Boy" was to become a cut-and-dried repertory piece. Fifteen years after Gus Cannon learned it, Eugene Powell learned note-for-note Cannon's rendition from a middle-aged guitarist named Prince Flowers in the Sunflower County town of Lombardy, located 25 miles from Clarksdale. Charlie Patton

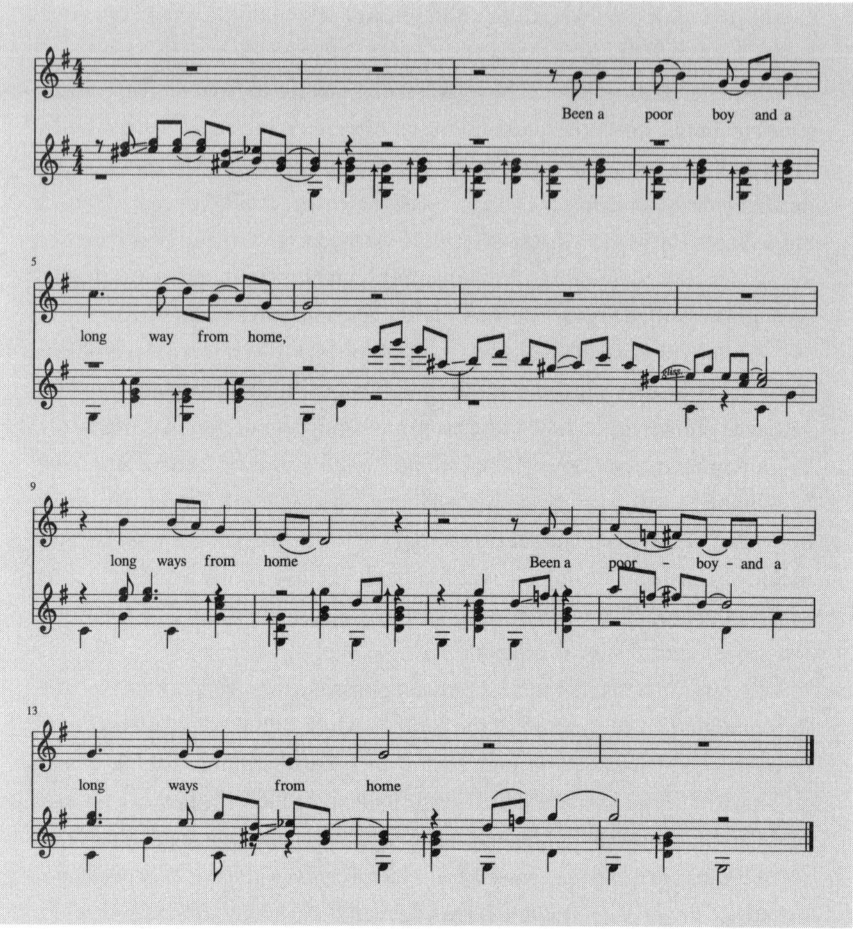


Ex. 6: Gus Cannon, "Poor Boy, Long Ways From Home" (1927), [0:16-0:41] [transcription from Woody Mann, *Bottleneck Blues Guitar* (New York: Oak, 1996), 63–64].

knew this tune's arrangement, for in his 1929 recording "A Spoonful Blues" he would apply one of the "Poor Boy" instrumental glissandos in order to "talk" the titular words of "Spoonful."

The chief importance of Cannon's recording of "Poor Boy" lies in the fact that he was trying to increase the appeal of his music by playing it on banjo in ways that the average guitarist of the period would have found difficult to imitate. By comparison, Cannon's contemporaries playing at plantation dances in Mississippi may have seemed undistinguished.

Of the arrival of blues in the Delta, Booker Miller said, "I think they were here a little before 1900, because my granddaddy was a guitar player. I was born in 1910, and he stopped when I was two." Miller's grandfather Jim Brown was a native of Indianola who played guitar since his boyhood in the 1880s, if not earlier. The songs he continued to play for his own amusement after quitting the house party circuit included W. C. Handy's "Hesitation Blues" and a song that began with a verse Patton would sing in "Pony Blues":

Hello Central, the matter with your line?
Come a storm last night an' tore the wire down.

Despite its title and its twelve-measure form, the widely known "Hesitation Blues"[36] had, strictly speaking, little if any musical kinship with blues. It was a vocal ditty that eschewed the three-phrases and their ten-six call-and-response phrasing for a 4+8 measure verse-and-refrain structure. The Delta repertory pieces of Miller's grandfather's time (1880-1910) seem to have been like "Hesitation Blues" in that they were neither regionally nor individually distinctive, and they placed no emphasis on instrumentation as did the blues. Listening to the 1928 Black Patti recording of "Stack O'Lee" as sung by Papa Harvey Hull and "Long Cleve" Reed, Booker Miller said, "That's way back there in my granddaddy's time. All that stuff was all through the Delta, that was popular then." He likewise said of the duo's "Gang of Brownskin Women," "That sounds kinda like what my granddaddy used to play. *Way* back." That eight-measure melody was a standard repertory tune among blues musicians, and it was recorded by Patton as "Jim Lee Blues" in 1930. W. C. Handy heard the melody performed by vagrants in East St. Louis who called their version "East St. Louis Blues." And so with their melody and title, Handy devised a song of "experience" from their begging as panhandlers:[37]

I walked all the way from old East St. Louis,
And I didn't have but one po' measly dime.[38]

As with "Poor Boy," "East St. Louis Blues" might suggest just how old is the typical blues phrasing pattern. The first two measures have the vocal melody during the first six beats, and rest during the next two beats; this "six-two" phrasing pattern is repeated in measures 3-4. Its second and final phrase (mm.5-8) used the "ten-six" characteristic of the ordinary blues line.

Yet the "six-two" pattern that is heard twice in the first four measures seems

Ex. 7a: "East St. Louis Blues," vocal melody, mm. 1–4.

Ex. 7b: "East St. Louis Blues," vocal melody, mm. 5–8.

to have been used quite often around 1900 by musicians performing Mississippi plantation dance music. "Stack O'Lee" as Hull and Reed recorded it had this phrasing pattern, as did "A Spoonful Blues" as Charlie Patton recorded it in 1929. Patton crony Hayes McMullan, born in 1902, learned it sometime in the early 1910s from Stanford Bennett, a native of Charleston, Mississippi who was then old enough to be McMullan's father. Likewise, around 1906 or 1907, Sam Chatmon heard the tune performed by an adult musician in Bolton named Dave Henderson. The first piece McMullan learned ("as a little bitty boy") was a variant of "Frankie and Albert" called "Hop Joint" that was based on the same musical structure. Numerous such songs, which were sometimes called "rags," appear to have been in vogue around the turn of the century. More melodic but less percussive than blues, rags may have been sung with little expression (if the 1920s recordings of them are any indications), offering few opportunities for an individual performer with a musical personality to spice up his material. As for those performers who lacked musical personalities, they probably had no need to show off their individualities when they played their rags at plantation dances anyway. With this context as a historical backdrop, there is a paradox. On one hand, Patton had the same showy impulse that Gus Cannon had in adapting "Poor Boy" from its likely origins as a street song, and he didn't share the conformity of the plantation performers who sang their kinds of rags. Yet Patton's environment was that of the plantation. "He's a 'planey' boy," Richard Harney said of him.

When Patton's individualism emerged, it needed to be nurtured. In hindsight, his family's move to the Delta may be seen as critical to his development. While there was not enough money in the hills to sustain a professional blues career, the Delta offered a unique opportunity to the musician who was shrewd and talented enough to tap its riches. There were the house frolics that were found everywhere throughout the state. But the Delta offered a kind of performing outlet that was found mostly in the towns like Vicksburg, namely the "barrelhouse" or "jukehouse," which was probably introduced to Mississippi from cities such as Memphis. The barrelhouse was a commercially operated recreation spot[39] that contained several rooms and served as an all-purpose gambling den, dance hall, bar, brothel, and even boarding house. In the Mississippi Delta, such establishments opened Friday evening and remained in continuous operation through Sunday. "They'd stay alla night long," Elizabeth Moore said. "Called 'em 'all-night clubs.'"

By operating around-the-clock and offering many of the same amusements plus prostitution, the barrelhouses resembled the plantation house frolics. Still, there were some differences. The frolic was usually held by a bootlegger as a means of selling his liquor. While the frolic and the barrelhouse were both meant to make money, the frolic catered mostly to the tenants of the plantation on which it was held. On the other hand, the barrelhouse was usually located near a town depot, it was open to the general public, and it was patronized by people from widely scattered settlements. Some Delta clubs even attracted patrons from Memphis. According to the Moores, it was common for someone to travel thirty miles to a Delta barrelhouse, which was often given a formal name and was further distinguished by a green exterior. "You always knew where them jukehouses was because they was green," Elizabeth Moore said. "I don't remember 'em bein' no other color."

Because it admitted outsiders, the Delta barrelhouse could generate enormous profits, chiefly from the gambling that was its commercial reason for being. Elizabeth Moore, speaking from her experiences in operating a barrelhouse in Friar's Point, remembered that a prosperous Delta barrelhouse could garner a Saturday night revenue of approximately $1000,[40] while netting upwards of $1500 for an entire weekend.

These profits were not honest. Since the dice and card games were rigged,[41] most of those who tried their luck at Delta barrelhouses stood no chance of winning. They were pitted against a house gambler who was well-versed in the fine points of cheating, although they sometimes obtained a refund from the management if they saw and complained about the sharp tactics of their house opponent. Willie Moore periodically worked as a house gambler in various Delta barrelhouses, and he remembered that the rare patron who hit the jackpot was then obliged to pay back five percent back to the club.

The blues singers who performed in the barrelhouses functioned as shills; Patton may have been no exception. On his 1930 record "Moon Going Down," he touts the women one could meet in a barrelhouse, who were most likely prostitutes:

> They'se a house over yonder, painted all over green,
> They'se a house over yonder, painted all over green.
> (spoken: Boy, you know I know it's over there!)
> Some of the finest young women, Lord, a man most ever seen.

In what smacks of false naivety on Patton's part, the luckless gambler of "Jim Lee Blues" loses because of a lapse in concentration:

> I was sittin' down, playin' Coon Can,
> I lose all my money but a-one little lousy dime.
>
> Studyin' about my woman, could hardly Coon my hand,
> Studyin' about my woman, could hardly Coon my hand

In addition to being a clip joint, the Delta barrelhouse also helped planters to keep the wages on their properties, not losing them instead to the Beale Street barrelhouse. "They'd be runnin' the barrelhouse for them white folks," Willie Moore said of the black manager who was known as the "house man." "The white man'd put the money up, you see. White man would have a colored man to handle the money and keep things straight." Although this arrangement was a result of the caste system, the cost of establishing a barrelhouse (which Willie Moore estimated at "four-five hundred dollars") needed white investment. Also, the illegal barrelhouse activity needed white protection. According to Elizabeth Moore, the Delta barrelhouse ensured its existence by paying off local sheriffs, who in return might stage an occasional sham raid, but otherwise closed a club for good only if a homicide occurred there.

So, to stay open, preventing violence was a major preoccupation of the house man, who worked as a floorwalker (sometimes with an assistant) and bouncer, and who was always armed. Violence happened often at the plantation house frolics where, as Son House put it, the patrons "wanna see some runnin' done." By contrast, "they'se a little more careful with the jukehouse," he added.

Willie Moore said of barrelhouse managers, "They didn't want no killin' goin' on, 'cause the man couldn't make no money then." An establishment that acquired a reputation for violence not only risked its legal immunity, but it also lost business. Elizabeth Moore knew of Delta establishments that folded for lack of customers after bloodlettings occurred there. The emphasis on security that distinguished the barrelhouse from the house frolic (where patrons were free to carry weapons) served a second purpose: it lessened the risk of a barrelhouse robbery by a patron.[42]

Upon arriving at a barrelhouse, the patron was subjected to a search. He was allowed to check with the house man weapons like guns, razors, knives, and brass knuckles that were forbidden even in the least respectable establishments. One could also check money and valuables with the house, but Willie Moore noted, "That's dangerous. "Cause he'll put the folks on you—then they split the money."

Any patron who became too belligerent in a barrelhouse, Willie Moore said, was "liable to get killed" by the house man. As an intimidator, the house man could eject patrons for fighting with other barrelhousers, or remove cartridges from the offenders' pistols before returning them or, in some instances, withholding the weapons until the following day. Even so, killings as consequences of serious barrelhouse quarrels were merely delayed. Elizabeth Moore said, "They'd tell you about it, then kill you," she said of these patrons. "Say, 'I'm gonna kill you if that is the last thing I do.' If they didn't kill you tonight, don't worry—they was gonna get you." The frequency of these uttered promises led her to regard the average barrelhouser as "crazy." Willie Moore added that patrons lacked "the right understandin,'" explaining, "You take back there, well I say, from 1912 on up, folks kill you; kill another man about a woman."

Troublesome patrons also faced banishment from a barrelhouse for heavy drinking, extreme swearing, and dirty dancing. Extreme drunks were cut off and ejected. House rules posted near the entrance emphasized decorum. "Like 'No Dozens Played'—cussin' you know," Willie Moore said. "They didn't 'low none of that playin' in there, and if they catch you in there playin,' why they make you pay a fine." "They" were the police, who would not permit dances that were considered (in Elizabeth Moore 's term) "scandalous." Such a dance was "that ol' dance they call the shimmy-she-wobble—you know, folks would get way down." It was not the dance per se, Elizabeth noted, but "the way they was doin' it" that prompted police interference. "They'd put you out about that Gator," Willie Moore said, referring to a variation of the Shimmy, the Gator Wobble. "Them gals start them hips rollin', they say 'Come *out!*'"

In addition to being a little safer, the barrelhouse offered some perks not found at the house frolic. While both places were disreputable to the churches, the barrelhouse had a pretense to respectability that the house frolic did not. Some Delta barrelhouses made an outright bid for genteel patronage by requiring Sunday dress. Other barrelhouses offered sexual pleasures that were not found on the plantations. At such establishments, patrons had opportunities to consort with the prostitutes, whose pictures were often displayed on its walls. By contrast, the plantation presented limited opportunities to mix with the opposite sex, and the jealousy shown by local males made it dangerous for other men to tryst while visiting plantations. Such a visitor risked a beating and even death. "They sure will get you now," Willie Moore said, of the jealous male residents. "They catch him over there, that's all she wrote."

Another special attraction of the barrelhouse was its supply of "sealed whiskey," instead of the crude corn liquor sold at house frolics. The catch-all term for commercial alcohol was "bottle in bond,"[43] for which the carousing cleric of Patton's "Elder Greene Blues" had an unhealthy thirst:

> "I like to fuss an' fight, Lord and get sloppy drunk offa bottle in bond . . . "

"That was the whiskey most people, look like, wanted to drink," Booker Miller said of bottle in bond. Properly speaking, "bottled in bond" is a distiller's technical term for 100-proof whiskey that was aged for four years under government supervision. At the time when Patton recorded "Elder Greene Blues" (1930), bottle(d) in bond sold for double the price of corn liquor. "That moonshine whiskey," Elizabeth Moore said, "you got it for twenty five cents (per half a pint). What we call 'bond' whiskey, now—sealed whiskey—it's a whole half a pint of it for fifty cents."

In addition to drink, patrons could buy food prepared by the house man. "They'd have hot fish, any kinda sodawater drink, you know, like Coca-Cola and Pepsi-Cola and stuff like that. Then they'd have cooked these here what they call beef stews; they had plenty a-that goin'." During these segregated times, the barrelhouses in some Delta towns offered the only lodging for blacks for whom there were no hotels. Thanks to its provisions of room and board, a person could spend an entire weekend in a barrelhouse. Barrelhouses were plentiful in the turn of the century Delta. In 1901, a planter complained[44] of the pervasiveness of gambling establishments there: "It is an entirely conservative statement to say that on or near every Delta plantation may be found one to four regularly patronized crap tables, while in every town and village from one to half-dozen Negro crap dives are run."

To Willie Moore, the barrelhouse was a place where "folks shoot the craps, drink whiskey, and dance." Although it is often assumed without evidence that the blues had arisen on plantations, the early existence of barrelhouses makes it as or more likely that the blues were transmitted from town barrelhouses to the plantation frolics, at least in Mississippi, by passing musicians. Turn of the century blues have been reported in New Orleans and St. Louis.[45] Yet plantation-born Mississippi guitarists who came of age during the first decade of the century could not in the 1960s recall blues from the house frolics of their youth. Sam Chatmon admitted that the Bolton guitarists of his 1900s boyhood played mostly "Pearlee" and "My Bucket's Got A Hole In It": "That's all they knowed back in them days. I ain't never heard nobody pick no blues till my brother Bud and Charlie Patton, they'se about the first." Skip James recalled that between 1908-1910 house frolics of his native Bentonia were given over to "Alabama Bound," "Drunken Spree" (a square dance tune based on "six-two" patterns), and a version of "East St. Louis Blues" called "Slidin' Delta," all played with violin as lead instrument. "I hadn't heard of blues then," he noted. "But after a little period of time, I heard my mother and them speak about 'singin' the blues.' I wondered what the blues was then." Richard Harney was the son of a musician who played violin and guitar at frolics, and Richard was weaned on two-chord instrumental "breakdown" tunes like "Old Mule." Breakdown was a name that was applied to unsyncopated dance tunes that were played chordally, with a chord change at the beginning of each measure. About when he first heard the blues in his hometown of Marvel, Arkansas, Harney said, "We'se about eight, nine, ten, somethin' like that. They didn't have no blues 'fore then; nothin' but 'breakdowns.'" Joe Callicott was born in Nesbit in 1900, a year before Harney. The earliest tune he recollected was also a breakdown. Robert Wilkins as a youth in 1900s Hernando heard only what he called "rag" pieces like "Spoonful" and "Make Me A Pallet On The Floor" (the latter another song with six-two vocal phrasing). "They started around Hernando about 1904, something like that," he said of the those rags, which heard played by Delta migrants at his sister's house frolics. Willie Moore, who was born in 1902 and raised in Tunica, likewise recalled no blues from his youth. Gus Cannon had begun learning banjo tunes like "Old John Booker" and "Goin' Round The Mountain" in Clarksdale in 1895. He could not think of any blues besides "Poor Boy" that were performed by Alec Lee, who seems to have not been a plantation resident.[46]

Over time, the blues came to be regarded by researchers as a plantation genre. Yet, as seen in these memories of those who lived during the 1900s, the blues seemed to be mostly absent from the plantations,[47] or at least the earliest blues were not worth remembering. In the face of this observation, we could argue that what are now called the "country blues" were really ruralized blues. That is to say, the first blues heard in the Delta were performed in the barrelhouses by musicians coming from outside the state; those blues were heard by Mississippi Delta plantation frolic performers, who then adapted them into "country blues" dance music. The barrelhouse musicians who were playing guitar songs like "Poor Boy" were common in Clarksdale and the Delta at the turn of the century. W. C. Handy was living in Clarksdale in 1903, and in his 1941 autobiography[48] he recalled that these hoboing singers " . . . were forever coming and going. Some came sauntering down the railroad tracks, others dropped from freight cars. A favorite hangout with them was the railroad station. There, surrounded by crowds of country folks, they would pour out their hearts in song while the audience ate fish and bread, chewed sugar cane, dipped snuff while waiting for trains to carry them down the line."

There itinerants were most certainly heard in barrelhouses near the train depots, that is if their music passed muster with club owners.[49] Of the earliest Delta barrelhouse music, nothing is known or remembered. Willie Moore recalled that player pianos were to be found in some Delta clubs, so it is likely that ragtime music was popular there, as it was in urban barrelhouses. Perhaps it was a shortage of pianists that opened the doors of the Delta barrelhouses to the guitarists who attracted crowds at the railroad depots.

So, once Charlie Patton decided to become a musician, it would have made sense for him to try to perform as often as possible in the relatively safe and lucrative Delta barrelhouses. That meant that he would have to develop an individual sound that was not expected of the house frolic entertainer amusing his neighbors. The lyrics of his songs are filled with many references to barrelhouses, some of them describing the departures of their itinerant musicians.

For one example, he makes Albert of "Frankie and Albert" a barrelhouse habitué:

> Well Frankie went down to Albert's house
> "How late's Albert been here?"
> "Oh Albert's sittin' down some cheap gal's lap, buyin'
> some cheap gal beer."
> "Hey he was my man, but he done me wrong."

He concludes "Jim Lee Blues Part II" with an address to an abandoned bedmate:

> Where were you, oh mama, when the Frisco left the shed?
> "I was way upstairs in my cold iron bed."

That lyric would have likely taken place in a barrelhouse because that type of dwelling had upper floors; plantation housing consisted of single-story shacks. So also this bit of buffoonery at the end of "Jersey Bull Blues" would have been in a barrelhouse:

> An' I remember one mornin', 'tween midnight an' day,
> (spoken: "Aw, sho'")
> An' I remember one mornin', 'tween midnight an' day,
> (spoken: "Boy, I's way upstairs that time")
> I was way upstairs, throwin' myself away.

If from the start the young Patton was preparing himself as a barrelhouse attraction, it may explain why his records are different from the run-of-the-mill Mississippi dance music. His way of using single-string picking to accompany his vocal line (as is done on segments of "Pony Blues" and "Down The Dirt Road Blues") was exotic for frolic dance accompaniment, even for the 1920s. Usually, as Skip James recalled from his 1900s/1910s youth, guitar-playing consisted of "rapped" or strummed accompaniments. The house frolic serenader rapped in order to supply rhythm and volume. Plucking a string diminishes its volume, but Patton was able to compensate by tuning his guitar above concert pitch, giving his notes a piercing quality, if at risk of snapping the strings. According to Booker Miller, Patton broke a string at every performance, for which reason he traveled with two or three sets of replacement strings.

Patton's irregular phrase lengths (like 5 measure [m.]—4 m.—5m. phrases noted earlier for "Pony Blues") stamped him as a soloist like the itinerant musicians on the streets and in the barrelhouses. By comparison, the Mississippi house frolic strummer worked in tandem with another musician. The novelty that Patton brought to such chestnuts as "Spoonful" (in which, as noted earlier, he inserted an ornament shared in common with Gus Cannon's distinctive adaptation of "Poor Boy") marked him as a musician seeking a wider range of audience than the neighbors who went to plantation frolics. To be sure, a performer who played mostly frolics might have been receptive to musical novelty, but he had no need to initiate it. But the barrelhouse entertainer had to do so, because he was in competition with other professionals for tips from appreciative listeners.

During his career, Patton prospered as an entertainer as did no other Mississippi bluesman. "I have known him to make as high as, well, forty-five, fifty dollars, and I heard him say one time he made seventy-five dollars, well that is money [at] one time for one night's playing," Booker Miller recalled. He may well have been the first Mississippi-born bluesman to cultivate a Delta barrelhouse clientele and to approach blues-singing with the ambitious eye of a professional. He did not invent blues, but he did invent "Charlie Patton," a persona that was as equally striking as the blues itself. As "Charlie Patton," he was to captivate listeners in the MIssissippi Delta in some ways that the first person to play blues there did not.

If I could have a wish granted, I would like to come back to earth fifty years from now and see this county, and see the changes.

—WILL DOCKERY, 1936

*Chapter 4*

# THE DELTA (1900–CIRCA 1906)

Ninety-five miles due north of Edwards stands Dockery's, the immense Sunflower County plantation where the Pattons settled after leaving Edwards. Dockery's was established in 1895 at the end of the Yazoo Delta Railroad line's Boyle and Sunflower branch. With such easy railroad access, a family could have moved to Dockery's simply by riding a train there—and some families may have done just that. Some farming families—the Pattons might have been one of them—were hired in advance by labor agents representing Delta plantations. In 1886, when the first influx of Hinds County sharecroppers into the Delta was arriving, these agents were depleting the labor force of the hill farms around Edwards to such an extent that the town formed a thirteen-man vigilante committee to fend them off. The strong-arm tactics used against labor agents during this period are suggested by this turn of the century newspaper account[1] of a gathering of Hinds County farm owners: "More than one gentleman of the number present promised to 'shoot on the spot' the first man found on his premises to decoy away his labor; while others promised to resort to 'tar and feathers.'" If the labor agents were being treated that roughly, then the hill farm sharecroppers were equally at risk of violence from the planters, who sometimes resorted to force to keep the healthy manpower they needed to bring in the crops, especially whenever epidemics of yellow fever struck (like the one in Edwards in 1897).

But despite the threats on labor agents, and the legislation in 1890 that penalized both agents and croppers who left plantations without giving notice, the migration of hill farmers into the Delta was a continual drift during Charlie Patton's lifetime, roughly coinciding with the Delta's rise and decline as a great cotton-producer. Often, some migrants were recruited on a short-term basis to pick cotton in the fall, and then they would stay to crop during the next spring. Some of the Delta's most effective labor recruiters were said to be its tenant sharecroppers, who liked to return to the hill country and impress the farmers there with displays of their comparative wealth. Since the Delta laborer at the turn of the century could earn fifty or seventy-five cents a day for his efforts, the poverty of the hill resident must have been extreme.[2]

The lot of the typical migrant who came to the Delta from the hills and elsewhere around the time the Pattons moved was described by Alfred Stone,[3] who operated a plantation at Dunleith: "The Negroes with whom we started in January of 1899 had absolutely nothing, barring their clothing, bedding, and furniture—all of the scantiest and poorest kind. It would be a most liberal estimate to put their entire belongings at that date at an average value per family of $30. Yet they were an average lot of plantation Negroes."

With its robust cotton strains, larger tracts of farmland, and soil so rich as to require no fertilization, the turn of the century Delta offered to new arrivals at least the prospect of prosperity. Through the 1920s, Delta farm wages stayed higher than those at the hill country farms. H. C. Speir confirmed this to the authors 40 years later: "If he (a farmer) made two or two and a half [dollars] a day [in the Delta], why he'd have to work a whole week out here in the hills to do that." This increase in earning also attracted from the outlying areas into the Delta performing musicians, whose earnings depended on how much money the croppers could spend. Among the traveling bluesmen who came to the Delta and stayed at least a season there working or playing music between 1917 and 1929 were Tommy Johnson, Skip James, Ishman Bracey, Lonnie Chatmon, Bo Carter, Kokomo Arnold, George "Bullet" Williams, and Booker "Bukka" White.

White was a native of Mississippi's northeastern prairie belt who was raised near the Delta town of Brazil. "I always did like the Delta, 'cause of the money," he said. "There was so much money down there. Money wasn't no problem."

The Delta that he likened to a "money tree" yielded its real fruits during the fall harvest season. David Edwards attested to this, saying, "There used to be a lotta money down through that Delta, man, you know when them guys in the fall of the year start pickin' that cotton. They was getting three dollars a hundred (pounds of cotton picked)[4] and some of them guys—some of those guys picked four and five hundred a day." By comparison, the Mississippi hills offered relatively little work for laborers on a day basis. Sam Chatmon recalled, "In the hills you didn't have no work to do at all. If you ain't raised somethin' to get money, you just outta money. Wasn't no work in the day. But now in the Delta, every time you feel up to it you can make a day. They hire you to hoe, plough, just cut, shuck corn, anything you wanted to do, they'd pay you to do it. The man [would] pay you off every Saturday. It wasn't much, but if you could get six bits a day, that's better than nothin."

Some planters complained about the shiftlessness of Mississippi's black laborers. But this inefficiency was very likely brought about by a system that attracted idlers and drifters with the prospect of temporary work. But even the more able croppers realized there was no incentive for them to become committed to the land. "People in the hills always had their own farms," Sam Chatmon said. "But now when you come to the Delta, he (the planter) owned everything." On the typical Delta plantation, the cropper not only rented his home and land from his boss, but his tools and mules as well. Since tenant farmers of every stripe had no lease on their holdings, and since they worked on seasonal contracts, as a whole they formed an unstable population group during any time, whether rich or poor, or fat or lean. Writing in 1901, Stone noted, "No planter among us can tell how many or which of his tenants of to-day will be his tenants of another year."[5] In this respect, Bill and Annie Patton turned out to be exceptional tenants. They remained on Dockery's plantation until their deaths[6] sometime around the early 1920s, and some of their children spent most of their adult lives there.

The Pattons arrived to a Sunflower County that was still sparsely populated. Although its black population had doubled between 1890 and 1900, Sunflower County in 1900 was perhaps the Delta's second most undeveloped region, next to Quitman County. Sunflower County had merely 16,000 residents in 1900, three-quarters of whom were black,[7] nearly all of them tilling on one or another of the county's 2,700 farms. The soil was so lush with nutrients that it yielded one or two bales of cotton per acre, at a time when half a bale was considered a good yield. The intermediate sediment was so fine that a person could drill fifty or sixty feet beneath the topsoil before touching rock. By the 1920s, Sunflower County became one of the state's leading cotton-growing regions, where many of Mississippi's largest plantations were flourishing. By 1930, when Charlie Patton had become famous as a recording musician, the county's population had increased fourfold since 1900, with its percentage of blacks remaining roughly the same. Their population in Sunflower County was nearly two-thirds of the black population then found in such cities as Memphis, St. Louis, and Atlanta. But even then, as the county that was the second most populous in the Delta and the third most populous in the state, Sunflower County lacked a municipality to rival Greenwood, Clarksdale, or Greenville, the only three towns in the Delta with 10,000 people. Only ten of the thirty-odd communities Sunflower County contained in 1930 boasted as many as a hundred residents, and only the county seat Indianola, located twenty miles south of Dockery's, fit within the contemporary definition of an urban community by having a population of 2500. Some four out of every five county residents lived on farms or plantations, and the county's black population contained roughly twice the percentage of ruralites the black race as a whole did. Most of the communities on the Sunflower River, and on that Yazoo and Mississippi Valley railroad that ran parallel to it, served as plantation satellites.

Although the plantation culture in the Delta died out after World War II with the railroad and the riverboat, Sunflower County still retains much of its cloistered, agricultural character of old. As farmland, it is still too good to waste by putting industrial buildings on it. As Joe Rice Dockery predicted to the authors in 1970, the future of the Delta may still lie in raising food products. But even today, one may still feel powerfully what Robert Sherrill described in 1968, that "one can easily stand in the middle of the Delta's streaming sameness[8] and honestly believe that the world goes straight out forever, flat all the way and overripe, and made by a God who in His infinite wisdom gave Adam a cotton allotment."

The Pattons received their cotton allotment from William O. "Will" Dockery (1865-1936), an austere man of Scotch descent and six-foot proportions. He neither smoked nor drank, but he always wore custom-built shoes, a black suit and tie, and a white shirt, even while tending his own commissary. Appearances were deceiving, though, for Dockery was a throwback to the aggressive Southern pioneers that W. J. Cash described in his classic 1941 study *The Mind of the South*.[9] His father was a Confederate colonel who was wounded at Corinth in 1862. Yet three years later the family fortune that was built on slavery was wiped out by the Confederate defeat in the Civil War. After his graduation from the University of Mississippi in 1886, Will Dockery spent two years clerking in his uncle James' store in Memphis. In 1888, he set out on horseback from the family homestead in Hernando. His mission was to get rich in the Mississippi Delta and return home.

Arriving in Cleveland, some 117 miles south of Memphis, he built a wooden store among the five or six commissaries and saloons that then comprised the town's commercial district. In 1888, Cleveland was still a cowtown where hundreds of cattle grazed on the cane ridges lining the outskirts of town, and where the cross ties and pipe staves stood so high alongside the town's railroad tracks that residents could glimpse only the tops of passing trains. Thirty miles to the west, Rosedale was hardly more developed, even though it was a river town. Its sidewalks were two-foot planks, and in 1890 its outdoor lighting facilities were simply coal-oil lamps hung on wooden posts. Years later, for a local newspaper, Dockery remembered the rude character of these surroundings:[10]

> There was a small amount of cleared land then and it was on the bayous, lakes and rivers. The country was covered with blue cane fifteen to twenty feet high and the land was as rich as cream. Woodland was being sold by the Y&MV railroad at $5.00 per acre on long time terms, but it was expensive to clear and lots of people, both white and black, would quit after a year or so and sell out for a small equity.
>
> I remember seeing on forty-acres of land being traded for a cow and another forty acres traded for a Winchester rifle. The only land on large plantations was on the Mississippi River front. Rosedale, Miss. was the county seat and hard to get to as there were no roads worth considering.
>
> To get to Rosedale, you spent three days riding in the mud to make the round trip or went to Greenville or Memphis and took the boat. I remember going to Rosedale in a tall two-wheeled cart with a single horse by way of Merigold. My wheels got stuck and I had to pull the cart out in the cane, and hang the harness in a tree and lead the horse for several miles."

Indeed, the Delta was popularly known as "the Swamp" at the time when Dockery arrived there. Even within Charlie Patton's lifetime, the Delta was not a flat farmland but a swampy timberland, described in 1902 by an engineer[11] who constructed part of the Yazoo Delta Railroad as "a dense wilderness of oak, cypress, elm, ash, hickory . . . " The writer William Faulkner portrayed the Delta as it existed in 1908 as "the vast flat alluvial swamp of cypress and gum and brake and thickets lurked with bear and deer and panthers and snakes, out of which man was still hewing savagely and violently the rich ragged fields in which cotton stalks grew ranker and taller than a man on a horse . . . "[12] To this assortment of lurkers he might have added the wild turkey, the wildcat, the wolf and, that most deadly and prevalent form of Delta wildlife, the mosquito.

Initially, the Delta was valued as a source of white oak rather than as farmland. Its era as a lumbering center began in 1879,[13] when a group of Midwestern millmen, faced with the rapid depletion of Michigan and Wisconsin hardwoods, decided to relocate in Memphis and log from northern Mississippi. Subsequently, lumbering became a substantial industry in the Delta until the 1920s. Now, only occasional clusters of trees on the rivers or planted as property-markers relieve the wide-open look of the Delta landscape. But until the railroads were built, however, lumbering and farming lacked real footholds in the Delta. As a turn of the century observer wrote of the region, "In the rainy season the wagon roads are well-nigh impassable, and a long high haul by wagon through the alluvial mud of this country is, and will continue to be, out of the question."[14]

The town of Cleveland was a bastard child of the railroad. Late in 1884, a team of railroaders for the Louisiana, New Orleans and Texas line laying track southward from Memphis happened to meet in that area the team pushing northwards from Vicksburg. Their meeting place was marked initially by a wooden depot. Then the railroad purchased the adjoining land from the newly formed state levee board at eleven cents an acre, reselling some of its lots to private investors, one of whom decided to name the embryonic town in honor of Grover Cleveland, the nation's first Democratic president since the Civil War. Another offspring of the railroad was Mound Bayou, an all-black town that consisted of thirty or forty thousand acres of plantation land north of Cleveland, and that was established with railway land purchased in 1887 by a former slave of Jefferson Davis.

Eight miles to the east of the rail line on which Mound Bayou had been built flowed the Sunflower River, which during the 19th century was accessible only by riverboat. Back then, distant views of the river were obscured by red gum, sweetgum, and cottonwood trees that grew forty or sixty feet high. In

1888, a local resident predicted to the young Will Dockery that within a decade those trees would be cleared, and then the river could be seen from Cleveland. By 1890, a temporary railroad track to the river had been laid by Cleveland lumber interests, who proceeded to clear the area so thoroughly that the gum and cottonwood trees became virtually extinct in Sunflower County.

As the timber harvesting proceeded, land fever began to quicken the pulses of local settlers, pauper and plutocrat alike. Among them was a black Bolivar County resident, Joe Ousley, whose brother served as the county's circuit clerk. Relying on Will Dockery for collateral towards a series of $2.50 loans, Ousley founded the town of Renova three miles north of Cleveland; it didn't rival Mound Bayou as an all-black town. The same land fever gripped Dockery himself, who also lacked capital, but he could use credit from his Memphis uncle James towards land mortgages. In 1890 he began leasing a 790-acre plantation, only to see cotton prices plummet during the next four years. In 1895, the first year that Sunflower County land had appreciable value, he founded his own plantation, choosing a site on the Sunflower River five miles southeast of Cleveland.

The plantation, which he simply named Dockery's,[15] consisted of nearly ten thousand acres which he drained and cleared himself. Having purchased the land for a price around five dollars an acre,[16] he lived long enough to see its value soar to three hundred dollars an acre, making him a millionaire several times over. To the end of his life, though, he remained a man of rustic pleasures like fishing, hunting, and horseback riding. Finding the title "planter" too pompous for his tastes, he called himself a "merchant and farmer" on his business stationery. He had none of that status consciousness that led other Delta planters to enshrine themselves in Southern Who's Who books. Yet by virtue of sheer wealth, Dockery stood among the cream of the Delta's aristocracy, which valued property rather than ancestry. Like most wealthy planters, he became an absentee owner as soon as he could afford to do so. Deeming the Delta climate too unhealthy for living souls, he presided over his holdings from Memphis.[17]

The scourge of the early Delta was malaria, a disease that decimated the ranks of workers, thus slowing the region's economic development until the late nineteenth century. Malaria was the main reason why the Delta was known in the Mississippi hills as "The Death House." Dread of this disease also hampered efforts to recruit white labor. As a result, most of the brute work by which the Delta was transformed from a canebrake swamp to an inhabitable territory was done by foreign or nonwhite groups who were given no stake in the results. One of the first of these groups was the Chinese who had come to the Delta in 1879, shortly before the passage of the Chinese Exclusion Act, to work on the railroad. For a brief spell, they were seen as a way to revive the plantation system, which was thought to have been ruined by Reconstruction. Although there were only 360 Chinese in the whole state of Mississippi in 1920, they were a familiar sight around Cleveland, where a Chinese mission school was located, and where some Chinese intermarried with blacks. Irish immigrants had constructed the upper Delta's first rude levees in 1884-1885, and the Delta's early plantations were typically cropped not only by blacks but by Italian and Mexican immigrants as well. There were so many Mexicans in Bolivar County that a planter named Matt Dakin arriving there in 1912 learned Spanish in order to carry out his business. The Italians had arrived in the Delta by way of New York and Argentina in the late nineteenth century. Like the Chinese, they could not adapt to the plantation system, but they stayed, even if as social outsiders.

So, the brunt of the Delta's plantation work fell to African Americans, who at the turn of the century outnumbered Delta whites on some farms by as much as eight to one. "A special advantage in having plenty of negro labor," confides Darling, who used blacks as axemen and chainmen while surveying for the Yazoo Delta "Yellow Dog" railroad, "is the fact that the negro is more easily provided, and less liable to sickness from hardships and the unhealthy climate than the white man."[18] The 1888-1892 edition of *Chambers' Encyclopaedia* was even more explicit on this point, claiming that blacks were more resistant to malaria, yellow fever, and even sunstroke than the Southern white. But more important than black durability in the minds of most plantation employers was the question of docility. As a turn of the century observer noted, "The negro is preferred[19] to the native or foreign white hand by a large number of the Southern landowners, especially by those engaged in raising cotton. This class declares that he gives less trouble than a white man because he is content with less comfortable lodgings, with coarser food, and with smaller wages."

Yet even the most pitiless planter had to provide something to his workers. Like many early Delta planters, Dockery needed to establish his plantation as a self-sufficient community, for his property was quite some distance from a business district. In 1896, Dockery's was not directly connected to Cleveland by rail,[20] and Ruleville was not created until 1898. Thus in Dunbar Rowland's *Encyclopedia of Mississippi History* (Madison, WI: S. A. Brant, 1906), Dockery's was classified as a hamlet, and it is even now so described on some of today's maps. Granted, it was a private estate, and so it had no system of government, but it had virtually all the community elements of a small Mississippi town. During its first fifty years of existence, it maintained a government post office, and it minted tokens and paper scrip[21] as a medium of exchange at the plantation's brick commissary and, later on, at Ruleville stores. The commissary once staffed six full-time employees, who dispensed supplies on a monthly basis to tenants who came there from every corner of the plantation, and sometimes to those from other plantations, too. A sawmill and a blacksmith's works were also in full operation. Two churches, Baptist and Methodist (called St. John and True Light), and two elementary schools, both running to the eighth grade (and neither, in the opinion of Dockery's son, very adequate), ministered to the spiritual and educational upbringing of local residents. In death, a Dockery's tenant became a permanent resident by being buried in the plantation's True Light cemetery; Patton's older sister Viola and his younger brother C. are buried there.

Some planters considered the welfare of their tenants only as a matter of business; in other words, their care began and ended at the commissary counter. In contrast, Dockery seems to have been moved by a genuine spirit of paternalism. Upon discovering that the local medical practitioners were bilking his tenants, he hired a white physician to live on his property and to treat patients of either race. To lessen the dependency on an undertaker who charged high fees, Dockery organized a non-profit burial association, and he offered the facilities of the plantation cemetery to anyone who had ever been a Dockery's tenant. More idealistic reforms, such as the renovation of living quarters, were attempted but abandoned in the belief that tenants abused them. Dockery's sense of noblesse oblige is indicated by his close friendship with Leroy Percy, the one-time Mississippi Senator who owned a three-thousand-acre plantation near Greenville and who was the South's most outspoken foe of the Ku Klux Klan. Of the Percys it has been written: "This family has embodied all of the qualities thought desirable by aristocrats and would-be aristocrats. Bound by a tradition of honor, of dignity, of fair-dealing, the family has typified the best of the old Southern aristocracy."[22] To Will Dockery's son Joe, Leroy Percy was a role model.[23]

The charity for which the genteel breed of planter was sometimes noted was selectively given to his favored tenants, so it wasn't offered to every cropper. For the most part, the Delta planter was pragmatic about his labor force, dealing with it in strictly business-like fashion. In some respects, this impersonality shielded Delta blacks from the kind of racial violence that erupted in cities like Memphis, where in 1908 a white man entered a black saloon and randomly shot six patrons to death without suffering legal consequences. As Joe Dockery remarked, Delta planters thought that the killing of blacks was a needless waste of labor. So, as landowners, they looked down on the rabid lynching rhetoric of James Kimble Vardaman, the turn of the century redneck governor who ousted Percy from the Senate; it was Vardaman who said "If it is necessary, every Negro in the state will be lynched; it will be done to maintain white supremacy."[24] Rather than exterminate, the planter manipulated the African American farmers, confident of his ability to handle a tenant he considered as if a child or, as Percy's son William Alexander put it, "a younger brother, not adult, not disciplined, but tragic, pitiful, and lovable."[25] Yet both the planter and the black croppers he hired made a distinction between the "good" and "bad" Negro, according to his submissiveness, productivity, and conformity with prevailing moral standards.

Dockery would have viewed Patton as "bad," simply because he was a musician. The landowner thought music was frivolous, disapproving even his son's wish to take piano lessons. His plantation had no jukehouse. A Dockery's resident who desired headier pleasures than those found at the little frolics or at the plantation's baseball field had to go elsewhere for them. He could leave the plantation easily enough, via Kimball's Ferry (named for a local lake) which provided transportation across the Sunflower River, or a fifty-mile stretch of dirt road that ran from Indianola through Dockery's to Clarksdale. If he planned, he could await the daily arrival of a Yazoo Delta Railroad local called the Pea Vine[26] at the plantation's two-story depot, which had its own station master. This train, which Patton would use as the subject of a 1930 blues record, hauled both passengers and Dockery's cotton harvest, replacing the steamboats that had previously plied the Sunflower River for the same purposes. It originally made three stops and traveled fifteen miles, from Skene to Boyle to Dockery's.

During its pre-World War II heyday, Dockery's work force consisted of some four hundred tenant families, each farming as much as eighty acres.

By the 1960s, when blues historians began researching Charlie Patton, only a handful of tenants remained on the plantation. The story of Dockery's decline as a tenant farm is a familiar one. During the Depression, cotton prices fell to five cents a pound. The plantation began receiving Federal subsidies under the Agricultural Adjustment Administration for reducing the number of acres to be farmed. The need for manual labor was then further lessened by the introduction of tractors, mechanical harvesters, and mechanical pickers. Some of the first tractors used in the Delta were tested experimentally on Dockery's by the firm of McCormack International. After 1950, the plantation's chief crop became rice, a product Dockery's son Joseph promoted on behalf of the National Rice Council of America. When interviewed by the authors in 1970, he had few regrets about the passing of the plantation. And he could offer no memories of the Patton family, even though it was one of the longest-standing tenants on his land.

The Pattons lived on the Lost Lake section of the plantation near Parchman Penitentiary, and it was a tiny village of twenty-three persons when the family arrived there in 1900. The little we know of Bill Patton suggests that he was a hardworking tenant.[27] "He hung around home, he didn't go to no 'suppers' and be rowdy like that," reported his one-time neighbor, Sara Garrett. But she scoffed at the claim by Charlie's sister that Bill was a church elder.[28] "He wasn't so much a churchin' man," she laughed, "he wasn't near about no preacher."

The household he headed consisted of at least seven members, including his brother-in-law Sherman Martin. "Charlie's father had a heap of people stayin' with him," Sara remembered. From Will Dockery's standpoint, this was an asset. As his son said, "The bigger the family, the more desirable they were as tenants." The size of the family would have also made it easy for young Charlie to work less toward his father's crop, for the assistant manager who supervised the tenants measured their productivity in terms of families, rather than the number of the individual members.

Dockery Farms operated according to the usual practices of sharecropping that were prevailing on Mississippi plantations by 1890. The landlord took half of the tenant's fall harvest in exchange for providing him with land, housing, and farm equipment. Advances against living expenses and costs attendant to picking and ginning the cotton were also deducted from the tenant's earnings. In the 1920s, a day laborer could earn a dollar or $1.20 per day there, which was double the wage he might expect for similar work in the hill country. Joe Dockery stated that the total wages paid out by the plantation ran to some $20,000 annually in the 1920s, and that a tenant family could easily clear two or three thousand dollars for their efforts in one season. This figure exceeds the kind of income associated with sharecropping, and it can be only be accounted for on the grounds that Dockery's tenants worked much larger tracts than the fifteen or twenty acres offered elsewhere to Delta tenant families. Such high payouts would certainly have made Dockery's among the most lucrative plantations for tenants, and hence blues guitarists, to work. "They got a fair deal," Joe Dockery said of his father's tenants. "We didn't rob 'em blind like some of them did. I'm not saying that we didn't follow the system—if you tried to buck the system in those days, you woulda been put outta business."

Although this system was feudal in character, during Patton's boyhood the Delta was often seen as a land of golden opportunity for both races. Not all of the African Americans were tillers of the soil; some fulfilled supervisory and civic roles, what with so few whites around. Writing in 1906, Alfred Stone remarked: "Throughout the Delta, there are Negroes filling places of responsibility and trust. In the country the gin crews and engineers are practically all Negroes, and there are Negro foremen, agents, and sub-managers. There are many constables, and there is in my county a Negro justice of the peace. In my own town every mail carrier is a Negro and we have a Negro on the police force. Some are employed by cotton factors and buyers, and earn from $600 to $1000 per annum. . . . One cannot travel through this section without observing Negro landowners everywhere."[29]

The black success stories Patton saw firsthand while growing up may not have persuaded him to a work ethic, and they may have also conveyed the attitude that musicians were hardly the glory of their race, at least in the eyes of most of his neighbors. There was the black aristocracy at Mound Bayou, whose chief financier, Charles Banks, was known as the "J. Pierpont Morgan of this race." Dockery's had the worthy example of Lee Frederick, a tenant who amassed $100,000 over fifteen years by helping Dockery develop Lost Lake. The Pattons would have sometimes worked under black straw bosses, and they would have taken their cotton to black weighing agents. In 1908 Patton would have heard much about Booker T. Washington, who came to Mississippi at Banks' behest and who visited Mound Bayou in a special Pullman car provided by the Illinois Central. After that visit, a Mississippi newspaper editorialized, "No more popular man ever came to the State, and no man ever spoke to larger audiences than he did."[30]

Even so, Patton would have always been reminded that deadly fates were in store for the blacks who did not toe the line as drawn by the prevailing white powers. During the 1900s, his teenage years, Sunflower County compiled a shameful record of terrorism against blacks. In January 1903, the Indianola post office was closed by Theodore Roosevelt in response to the harassment of its black post-mistress. That same year, lynchings occurred at Drew and Cleveland. In February 1904, the year Jim Crow officially came to Mississippi, three blacks were lynched and two others burned alive near Doddsville in retaliation for the killing of the planter James Eastland. Six weeks later, there were two more lynchings at Cleveland. Although Sunflower and Bolivar Counties never again experienced such a high surge of violence, a sociologist could still describe Delta lynching, seven years after Patton's death, as "part of the culture pattern. . . . When the white community quiets down, the Negroes go about their usual occupations. The incident is not forgotten, but the routine of the plantation goes on. The lynching, in fact, is part of the routine."[31]

During Patton's lifetime, the ordeals of the southern African American were not thought as of national concern or popular sympathy. Speaking before the Republican Club of New York in 1905, President Roosevelt declared, "Laziness and shiftlessness, these, and above all, vice and criminality, of every kind, are evils more potent for harm to the black race than all acts of oppression of white men put together." He knew the Delta chiefly as a magnificent hunting ground, where he could enjoy himself in the rough-and-tumble company of planters. One of them, General Wade Hampton of Greenville, took part in the destruction of five hundred black bears, "at least two thirds of them," Roosevelt wrote admiringly, "falling by his own hand."

Lacking influential spokesmen or basic civil rights, the Southern black had to develop his own defense against his own possible extinction. The survival tactic of resignation was learned by every black child of Patton's generation from one's parents. Sam Chatmon cited his father's counsel. "He always told me when a person got a rope around your neck, if you rare back, it'll choke. Just stand still. And what he meant by that: don't argue. If you get in a trap, it's no need of rarin' if you ain't got a loose hand where you can mash the trap to get out; you just have to sit there till the fella let you out."

Charlie Patton was likewise compliant, at least outwardly so. "He was the sort of guy looked like he could 'take' with the boss," David Edwards said of him. "He could talk with 'im, 'Uncle Tom' with 'im." Booker Miller observed that Patton shunned "trouble" with whites, but "didn't act like he was 'scarey' (fearful of them)."

As a professional musician, Patton welcomed his opportunities to play for whites, although his ability to attract them was later ridiculed by Sam Chatmon, who played bass viol in a family string band that catered entirely to whites. "Charlie Patton picked and picked and picked, but he never could be able to play for dances unless it was for colored folks. He couldn't play no fast music. White folks wanted the one-step, foxtrot, and waltz: he couldn't play that. That left him out." However, Chatmon did not know Patton in the Delta, where whites, Booker Miller noted, "wanna dance on everything you play."

Despite Chatmon's skepticism, Patton could play fast music in a way that whites could savor, and his uptempo one-step dance piece "Shake It And Break It" seems to have been tailor-made for white presentation. Joe Rice Dockery knew that song. "That came outta Memphis," he said, "I was raised with that." If transcribed in 2/2 meter,[32] it was a 24-measure song that consisted of a 12-measure verse and a 12-measure chorus, but neither form being a blues. Aside from the skillful guitar picking, Patton's 1929 recording of the song suggests little if anything of black origin: each phrase is in two measures, the vocal melody gives prominence to a major seventh (blues favors minor sevenths), its accompaniment is played chordally, with no attempt to embellish tones by "bending," and its rhythm accents the first beat of every measure, a conventional feature that Patton never used on his recorded blues. Despite its differences from the other songs Patton recorded in 1929-1934, "Shake It And Break It" was once one of the main tunes in his repertory. When Willie Moore met him sometime before 1919, the song was "the biggest thing I heard him play," along with another ditty, "It Ain't Gonna Rain No More." The latter piece became a 1923 pop hit[33] for Wendall Hall and was probably of white origin. Patton's version contained the lines:

> What did the blackbird say to the crow?
> Said: "It rained last night an' the night before
> But it ain't gonna rain no mo."

Another Patton favorite of probable white origin was "Caledonia, The Gal I Love." "He sure played it!" Moore said.

Let us remember that Patton made his records later in his career for black audiences, and so only on a few of them did he play white-oriented material. Another such example may be his sixteen-measure tune "Some Of These Days," which he may have been developed as a take-off on Sophie Tucker's famous 1910 hit. It used diatonic intervals and it had the tonic as its lowest vocal tone, a trait not often heard on Patton's blues and sacred records. Its rhythm pattern emphasized the second beat of each measure (Ex. 8),[34] instead of second *and* fourth beats that Patton favored in blues.

The intricate picking and strumming Patton does in both this piece and "Shake It and Break It" indicates that at some point in his career he had attempted to make a lasting impression on white audiences with his musicianship, perhaps as a medicine show entertainer. It is likely that when he played for white square dances and "sociables," he strummed behind a fiddler and sang tunes in the vein of "Runnin' Wild," with a 16-measure diatonic tune,[35] which repeated the accenting pattern of "Some Of These Days." With a fiddler to play lead, Patton could reel off such tunes indefinitely. Yet it is significant that in 1929 and 1930 when he recorded "Runnin' Wild," "Some Of These Days," and "Shake It and Break It," Patton had a short supply of verses, singing many (for him) repeats of the title verse or chorus. Perhaps by then his days as an entertainer at white functions were mostly behind him.[36] Booker Miller recounted Patton's attitude towards white audiences. "He said they would pay more than colored people, and more easier, but he would rather play for colored people.

Ex. 8: Patton, "Some of These Days," take 1 (1930), beginnings of choruses 1 (*top*) and 2 (*bottom*) [0:03-0:10], [0:31-0:37].

Which I reckon he was right about, 'cause I played for whites, too, but I just woulda hadda sit there. You couldn't 'let go,' you know, you just had to play."

While Patton's blues were created for blacks, his lyrics could often be enjoyed by either race. It is probably no accident, then, that he sang not only of the riverboats and railroads that were part of the Delta's general lore, but also that he singled out by name a white train engineer and white policemen[37] in three separate songs.

But for sheer Americana that can be appreciated by blacks and whites, there is Patton's most famous song, "Pony Blues" with its opening lyric "Hitch up my pony, saddle up my black mare."

The Lynds noted, "In 1890 the possession of a pony was the wildest flight of a Middletown boy's dreams."[38] In 1909, when Patton's song was current and likely new, some two million horse-drawn carriages were manufactured in America, compared to eighty thousand automobiles. In the following year, a Harvard historian who had recently returned from the Delta wrote of Southern blacks, "They are fond of going about the country, and you see them everywhere, on horseback, or in little bull carts, or on foot."[39] According to Sam Chatmon, sharecroppers could not afford riding horses. Rather, they made do with mules, or yearling bulls. The saddle horse was the plaything of the planter, and one of Dockery's proudest possessions was a saddle mare named Alissa Gray for which he had traded almost two hundred acres of land. When Patton sang of owning a saddle mare, he was describing a luxury that a black farming tenant simply could not afford.

Whatever Patton may have thought of the social conditions that made for such disparity, he was not about to use his blues to criticize or to express his disgruntlement. Delta whites were quick to pick up on the social aspects of black songs, even to the point of imagining revolution in lyrics that were sung quite innocently. "In World War I, they sung a song, 'Oh Lord, won't you stop by here?'" Willie Moore recalled. "These white folks was killin' folks about that."[40] Moore himself was once jailed in Robinsonville for an indiscreet song reference to a local sheriff, and years later he opined that Patton was "too smart" to have landed himself in similar trouble with a song. If it ever occurred to Patton or his associates to mention such subjects as lynchings, they quickly suppressed such thoughts. "No sir, they wouldn't bring them up," said the former jukehouse owner, Elizabeth Moore. "I ain't jokin'! They was scared. They wasn't gonna bring it up." Very few lyric references, if any, to racial turmoil may be heard on the pre-1942 commercial 78s by Mississippi bluesmen.[41]

Yet the plantation system itself may have indirectly lent itself to the development of guitar-playing as a diversion, for cotton farming left tenants with a good deal of idle time on their hands. David Edwards thought this was why the Delta had so many musicians. "Mississippi and Arkansas furnished the largest group of musicians," he said categorically, "'cause they didn't have nothin' to do but sit on a stump and sit around and play and drink that 'white whiskey.'" The Delta sharecropper did have long stretches of free time. There was a four- or five-month layoff between the end of each ginning season (usually in October or November) and the onset of the March planting season. There were also shorter periods between the planting, chopping, and picking stages of cotton-growing. Even during the "busy" picking season that began in August, they did not work continuously; one study estimated that bad weather and other factors often resulted in a fifteen-day work month.[42] William Alexander Percy cited one hundred and fifty days as the maximum work year on his Greenville plantation.[43] Joe Dockery remembered that his father's workhands were employed for fewer days than that.

The cotton calendar might have been inefficient, and it might have resulted in much boredom for the croppers. But it did allow a lot of time for some Delta blacks to learn how to play guitar, even if they had no intention of making a career of music. Another local factor that encouraged budding blues careers was the Delta planter's indifferent attitude about how hard his tenants played at the barrelhouses and the house frolics. As Joe Dockery put it, "It was just kinda understood that Saturday night belonged to them." This hands-off approach was a direct carry-over of the Mississippi slave-driver's attitude, which had tolerated slave amusements "so long as they did not affect his working ability."[44]

Planters thought, however, that the social situations in the Delta tended to elicit from blacks a lust for barrelhousing.[45] "The hill people weren't your Saturday night, skin-balling, crap-shooting nigger," one Delta planter recalls. "They'd come to the Delta and pick up bad habits."

Among the bad habits was promiscuity. The hills, where the smaller plantations and family farms were usually a mile or more apart, presented few opportunities for casual sex. But "up in the Delta," Sam Chatmon noted, "shucks, houses just all up on one another." Many Delta plantations, including Dockery's, made a point of hiring women in order to attract male farmers.

As on other plantations, the sexual behavior of Dockery's tenants was considered slack.[46] Some decades later, an aging white resident bluntly remembered the plantation's bygone female tenants as "whores." That may be the culture underlying Patton's womanizing. To Hayes McMullan, Patton appeared to be more "woman crazy" than any man he ever met. In addition to countless girlfriends, Charlie took fourteen known "wives," many of them common-law attachments[47] that often ended as soon as someone else caught his fancy. "Heap of time you'd mostly meet him he'd have a different wife," his nephew Tom Cannon reported. "He'd just put one down, and pick another one out. He could play good music and everything, and they'd fall for him."

Son House said, "Charlie, he didn't stay with no woman too long. He'd always do most of the quittin." House attributed Patton's mobility to lack of respect for his companions. "He'd just figured that there ain't n'ar a one pays him no attention no how. They don't amount to all that much for him to keep interested in."

Patton expressed this attitude in this lyric:

I'm gonna show you common women how I feel
Gonna get me another woman, 'fore I leave.
(Going to Move to Alabama)

Perhaps the kind of woman that the rootless Patton was likely to attract was the type he called "common." His own songs demonstrate little affection for women, and his appreciation of them was avowedly sensual rather than sentimental:

I love my baby an' I
(spoken: "Tell the world I do!")
What made me love her, you will come an' love her, too.
(When Your Way Gets Dark)

He advertised his aversion to marriage in the closing chorus of "Pony Blues":

I got somethin' to tell you when I get the chance
Somethin' to tell you when I get a chance,
I don't wanna marry, just wanna be your man.

He told Son House that except for one time, he took no legitimate wives, but otherwise he often married figuratively by "jumping over the broomstick," a colloquial phrase for cohabitation uttered (according to Partridge) "in reference to the pretence-marriage ceremony performed by both parties jumping over a stick."[48]

Before Patton was out of his teens he had already collected at least four "wives." Of the first, a lady named Gertrude, nothing is known. Between 1904 and 1908 he became involved with a native of Stringtown named Lizzie Taylor (1887–1966). "She was around seventeen, and he was too, when they one met another," her one-time neighbor, Flora Kimball of Sumner, recalled. For several years they intermittently lived together in Yalobusha County, a hill region east of the Delta. "They separate and go back, separate and go back, and eventually, the last time, well, he didn't," Miss Kimball explained.

There is a purported portrait of Patton that, if indeed is him, would date from the time of his relationship with Lizzie Taylor. Compared to the 1929 publicity photo of a gaunt clean-shaven musician, this mid-to-late 1900s studio photograph shows a youthful and robust young man with a mustache. Willie Moore tipped the authors to its existence by telling them about a visit he made in the early 1960s to Taylor on the Mitchener plantation near Sumner, Mississippi, where he saw the picture hanging on the wall.

"I said, 'Look!' I said: 'Miss, where you got that picture from?'" Moore recalled.

"She said, 'That's my husband!'

"I said, 'No! You don't know what you're talkin' about, do you?'

"She said, 'Yeah, I do.' She said, 'What's his name?'

"I said, 'Charlie Patton.'"

Taylor had kept the picture as a romantic keepsake; after her death, her friend Flora Kimball acquired it.[49] "She really loved him," she eulogized to the authors. "She said she never would get over him. She say that's the onliest man she ever loved. She told everybody that. That was her whole talk, all the time."

Patton may not have had yet his cavalier attitude to women during his earliest performing days singing tunes and ditties. But it was a woman, he told Booker Miller, who was responsible for his turning to the blues.

That man was some box-player, man.

—BOOKER MILLER

*Chapter 5*

# THE GREENING OF THE DELTA BLUES (CIRCA 1906–1910)

Charlie Patton's sister Viola Cannon once told her son Tom that her brother learned guitar as a ten or eleven year old and "come up playin'." But Patton himself told his protégé Booker Miller that he began to play guitar around the age of nineteen or twenty. For his birth, let us set aside his census year of 1891, and consider instead 1887 (as his sister reported) or 1890 (as Patton himself reported). Then his account would place the beginning of his career sometime between 1906 and 1910, when he had spent at least five years in the Delta. 1906 and 1907 are plausible starting years, because in 1908 he was already a musician when he met one of his wives, Millie Barnes.[1]

"He told me how he started," Miller related. "Said he sit up all night one night on a doorstep. He was havin' women-troubles then; so he borrowed a guitar. He got as far as his steps, and he sat there all night, and he did learn to tune and kinda learn to play a little bit in that period of time. And after that, then he say he just kept on advancin', he kept on learning, until finally it just got into his blood."

The "women-troubles" that led Patton to take up guitar probably was some sort of drama with a girlfriend or a wife. It is interesting to see him as a young man using a guitar to express or escape romantic turmoil, because eventually through his success as a blues singer he would take women as lovers to be dropped and replaced.

If you don't want me, you oughta been told me so.
For I'll get me a woman, 'fore you leave my door.
(Jim Lee Blues Part Two, 1929)

Certainly Patton was playing some music around 1906 or 1907. If he was playing before then, in the mid-1900s, he may have been trying impress Roxie Gibson, a dark, heavy-set woman he had met around Lula where Will Dockery owned some land. "He was with her quite a while," his nephew Tom Cannon reported. "He kept Roxie longer than he did any woman." "Longer" may mean over four years, the length of his later relationship with Bertha Lee Jones. Roxie herself played the banjo, and she may have been the only one of Patton's many wives who played a musical instrument.

It may have been during his relationship with Roxie that he played with minstrel shows or medicine (or "Doctor") shows.[2] Medicine-show entertainers were hired on a weekly basis by a traveling pitchman to attract customers for quack "patent" medicines.[3] These performing troupes functioned as poor man's vaudeville productions, presenting music and skits by the performers, and windy speeches by the pitchman who purported to be a doctor and touted his goods. Patton's running quips on his "Banty Rooster Blues" record suggest an early association with these shows, as does Millie Barnes' claim that Patton performed with his first wife, Roxie Gibson, before she (Barnes) was to marry him in 1908. A husband-and-wife banjo-and-guitar team would have been unlikely performers at a house frolic, and the banjo had little if any currency as a blues dance instrument. But this combination may be found in descriptions of medicine shows. For example, there was a "Doctor Blackhawk" from Tennessee who posed as a Native American. Whenever he toured the Mississippi Delta, he hired a troupe[4] that included a guitarist and a banjo player, and sometimes a drummer and a trumpet player. Their kind of showmanship was much the same as that for which Patton was noted as early as 1920.

In his porch-step anecdote to Miller, Patton called the tune he wrestled with as "If You Take My Woman, I Won't Get Mad With You." "Now he could play that good," Miller said of Patton's rendition. Miller's 1968 recreation of it to the authors in Spanish (open A) tuning is completely different from the accompaniments Patton recorded in 1930 to that tune. The melody was identical to Furry Lewis' "I Will Turn Your Money Green" (1928), a common blues song that Mississippi hill country musicians Hayes McMullan and Joe Callicott also knew and played.[5] The melody had first appeared on records in 1924 by Georgia's Reese DuPree as part of "Norfolk Blues." It also turned up in Jaybird Coleman's harmonica piece "Trunk Busted—Suitcase Fulla Holes" (1927), as well as in fiddle-guitar duets like Andrew and Jim Baxter's "Bamalong Blues" (1927) and the Alabama Sheiks' "Travelin' Railroad Man Blues" (1931). Considering that Lewis hailed from Memphis, Tennessee, Coleman from Bessemer, Alabama, the Baxter brothers from Calhoun, Georgia, and Patton from Mississippi, the tune may have rivaled "East St. Louis Blues" as a very early, nearly universal, blues standard. Taking into account the various instruments that these musicians played, "If You Take My Woman" may not have been first played on guitar.

The melody associated with "If You Take My Woman" was phrased like a blues, but it did not employ what we now think as characteristic blues intervals. Instead of ending the first vocal phrase on the tonic, its last three pitches (mm. 2-3) descended from the dominant through the subdominant to the mediant (major third).

Ex. 9: Melody of "If You Take My Woman."

If it may be assumed that Furry Lewis' 1928 recording "I Will Turn Your Money Green" could have been typical for the tune some twenty years previous when Patton learned it, then Lewis's performance may offer a valuable glimpse of early Mississippi blues-playing. Lewis' stanzas employed ten-beat vocal lines in an ABC melodic pattern; the melody used the first five degrees of the major diatonic scale, with an occasional addition of a minor third.

The instrumental phrasing of "Turn Your Money Green" was haphazard and jerky in the style of street songs. The first vocal phrase was followed by two identical instrumental "fill" measures.

The first three beats of that fill mimicked the melody and rhythm of the descending vocal cadence (Ex. 10, m.2), and remaining fourth-beats were silent

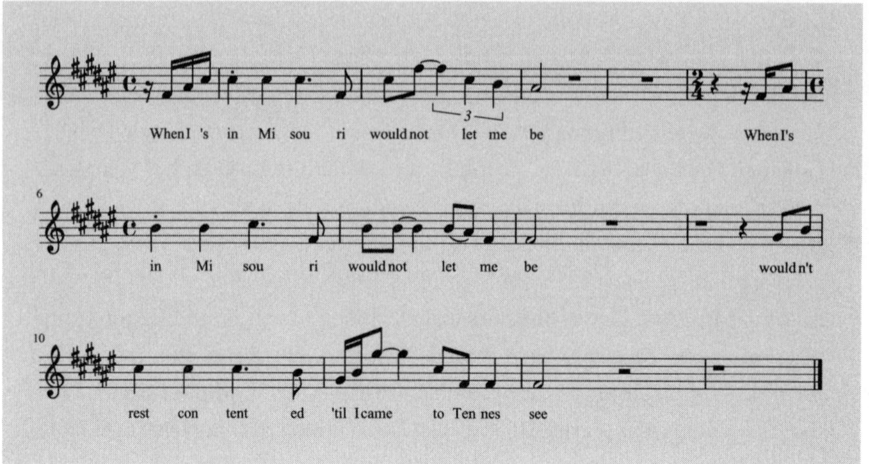


Ex. 10: Furry Lewis, "I Will Turn Your Money Green" (1928), chorus 1 [0:15-0:31].

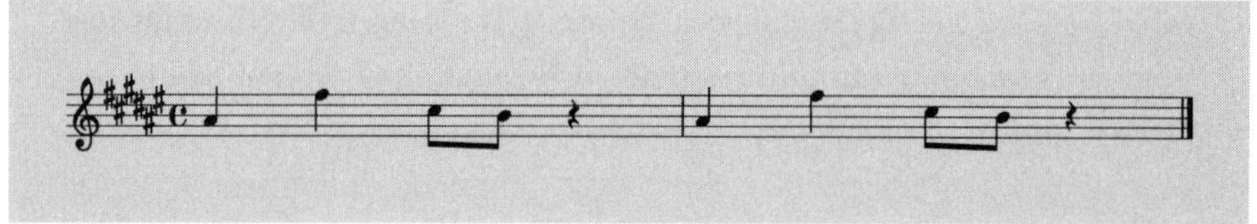

Ex. 11: Furry Lewis, "I Will Turn Your Money Green" (1928), chorus 1, guitar fill [0:20-0:21].

quarter-rests, a feature unusual for dance accompaniments. After the second and third vocal phrases, the guitar fill is not heard, but instead open-string tonic strums. This skeletal accompaniment of the vocal melody had a sing-song quality by virtue of the accented fretted bass note falling on the first beat of the first two measures of each phrase.

Ex. 12: Furry Lewis, "I Will Turn Your Money Green" (1928), chorus 1, mm.1-2 [0:16-0:18].

Patton's distinctive flair as an arranger was demonstrated by his artful conversion of this street-style piece into a dance with a supple beat, "Green River Blues."

Patton's need to convert street-style songs into dances would have come about for his first performances in barrelhouses in towns, cities and rural sawmills. Although the origins of "Green River Blues" (recorded in early 1930) cannot be exactly dated, it is likely that this song was a reflection of his youthful visits to a barrelhouse at a remote sawmill. The place it invoked, a sawmill operated as the Green River Lumber Company,[6] had been founded in 1907 on Plum Street in Memphis by an Indiana lumber family, Addison Boyd Nickey and his sons Samuel Mossman Nickey and W. E. Nickey. Their mill was located in a community known as Green River on the outskirts of Lake Cormorant, which bore a "little old stream" that was also called Green River, as Elizabeth Moore recalled. "They made lumber there all the time, you know," she added, "and they had what I call settlement houses, camp houses."

Sawmill settlements and camp houses were operated by the mill owners[7] as one way of recouping wages from laborers and inducing them to live nearby. These kinds of living quarters were meant more to be inhabited by single men than by women or families. Barrelhouses were often found in sawmill settlements, and they attracted gamblers and urban prostitutes, who vied with the blues singers for the ready money that flowed on paydays. It was in a sawmill barrelhouse that Skip James first encountered a professional blues musician, a piano-playing "sport" named Will Crabtree who was lavishly supported by a clique of prostitutes. "I used to say 'Hot damn!—I ain't gonna be nothin' but a 'sport' like Crabtree,'" recalled James.

Patton's lyrics for "Green River Blues" failed to specify which of the two Green Rivers it invoked, the body of water or the mill. The threefold repetition of the title lyric, "I went up Green River rollin' like a log," may have seemed a bit obsolete when he recorded the song in 1930; its unrhymed, twice-repeated format that was associated with turn-of-the-century black song, and so it is uncharacteristic of the mature Patton of whom Son House said, "he could make his verses rhyme pretty good." But there was nothing outmoded or backward in his musical arrangement, which he played on guitar in the E position (capoed to G, the pitch of Lewis' version) and, for the most part, he rendered in thirteen and a half measure stanzas (41/2—5—4).

To some of the single-measure instrumental fills (as in Ex. 14) after each

Ex. 13: Patton, "Green River Blues" (1930), chorus 1, vocal melody [0:06-0:34] (after Grossman, Grossman, and Calt, *Country Blues Songbook*).

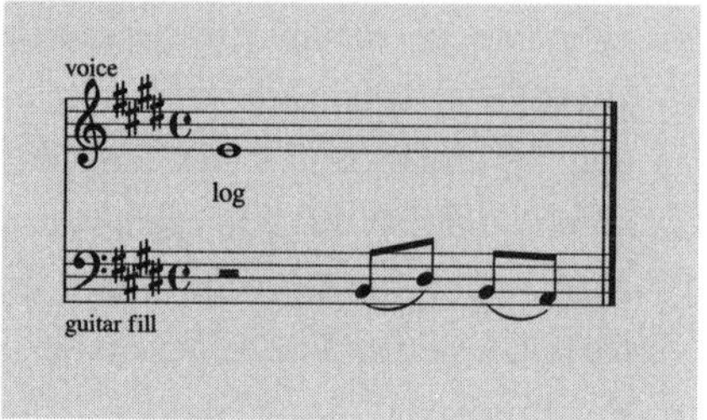


Ex. 14: Patton, "Green River Blues" (1930), single-measure guitar fill example [0:10-0:11].

vocal phrase, Patton would add some percussive taps with each guitar, combining tonal and rhythmic nuances in ways that most guitarists didn't do. His guitar accompaniment thus had a texture distinctive from, say, Lewis' picking version, and his expressive singing had dynamic contrasts to match or complement, such as the diminished volume in the third lyric phrase.

In most of his recorded songs, Patton often began the last word of each phrase on its tenth beat and held it for three beats. But in "Green River Blues" he kept the ten-beat vocal structure intact by beginning his guitar riffs on the eleventh beat, immediately after the end of each phrase's last word. To keep himself to singing 10 beats and not the usual 13, Patton divided each lyric phrase into two distinct sub-phrase snippets. The first two lines (AA) of each AAB lyric stanza were made up of two five-beat clusters:

| Cluster 1 | Cluster 2 |
|---|---|
| Up Green River | rollin' like a log |
| Thought I heard that | Marion whistle blow |
| It was late last night | every thing was still |
| How long | evenin' train been gone? |

Each pair of sub-phrase snippet-clusters had a simple melodic symmetry that was rather unusual for the blues: the ending beats of each cluster of the first line (Ex. 15, measure 1-3, to the words [ri]-ver and log) were sung as major thirds, while the corresponding beats of the second line (mm. 5-7) were sung to the tonic note.

Patton's guitar work was a contrast to the ditty-like quality of the melody. During the first phrase, he played this ringing seven-beat fill:

Ex. 15: Patton, "Green River Blues" (1930), chorus 1, vocal melody and guitar fill, mm. 1-3 [0:06-0:12] (vocal from after Grossman, Grossman, and Calt, *Country Blues Songbook*)

With a similar spontaneity, Patton began the third stanza of "Green River Blues" with an unexpected melodic variation that began high, on the octave above the tonic. So, instead of making his guitar fills identical in the usual manner of Mississippi dance blues, Patton offered two related figures. The result of his tweakings was a rendition that was more subtle and less rigid than the prevailing Mississippi dance blues. Such little triumphs of freedom over formula may be heard in all of Patton's recordings.

In view of that creative approach to the "If You Take My Woman" melody, we may assume that Patton likewise rearranged—or perhaps even composed—

the other song he mentioned to Miller as one of his two earliest pieces. Paramount Records titled the first of Patton's recorded treatments of this other piece as "Screamin' and Hollerin' The Blues," but Miller remembered Patton referring to the tune off-the-record as "Maggie." Whatever the melody was called, and whatever the lyrics that were sung to it, it was the cornerstone of his performing repertory. The underlying guitar arrangement would be used on Patton's records at least seven times, more often than any other of his accompaniments. Oddly, the title word "Maggie" does not turn up in any of Patton's recordings using this melody. Furthermore, its title verse first appeared on records on Tommy Johnson's 1928 classic Victor recording, "Maggie Campbell Blues":

Who's that yonder, comin' down the road?
It walks like Maggie, but she walks too slow.

According to Miller, Patton did sing that lyric in live performances, but when he did, he "turned it off in the last verse—instead a-sayin' 'comin' down the road,' he said, 'Who's that yonder all dressed in red? Walkin' like the children that Moses led.'" Patton certainly popularized the guitar accompaniment for "Maggie." He may have even created it, for when a mutual friend of Patton and Johnson, Nathan Bankston, heard the Johnson recording of "Maggie Campbell," he remarked during the guitar introduction, "That one [will have] Charlie singing that."

The title lyric of "Maggie" may have been developed from that of a nineteenth century spiritual. A song that the Fisk Jubilee Singers featured in concert tours of the 1870s began:

Oh, who is that a coming?
Don't you grieve after me.
It looks like Gabriel
Don't you grieve after me.[8]

Another hymn, "Who Dat Yandah?", began with a similar lyric:

O who's dat yandah?
An' a who's dat yandah?
Say, who's dat yandah?
Looks like a' my Lord comin' in de sky.[9]

But the musical form of "Maggie" is that of a three-phrase blues, not of a two- or four-phrase spiritual. In Patton's various recorded treatments of

"Maggie," he used a free melodic line that amounted to a series of vocal riffs rather than a fixed tune. Whereas melodic variations were incidental in most blues and spirituals, they were fundamental to "Maggie," which on the various Patton performances may be heard as the only genuinely improvisatory blues melody to be heard on records before 1932.

What Paramount titled on records as "Screamin' and Hollerin' the Blues" and Patton called "Maggie" was also remembered by Booker Miller as "Lord Have Mercy On My Wicked Soul," the expression that began the fourth verse of Patton's Paramount record. Patton sang the first phrase in a ten-beat vocal phrase (Ex. 16, mm. 1-3), the sub-phrases consisting of clusters of six and four beats.

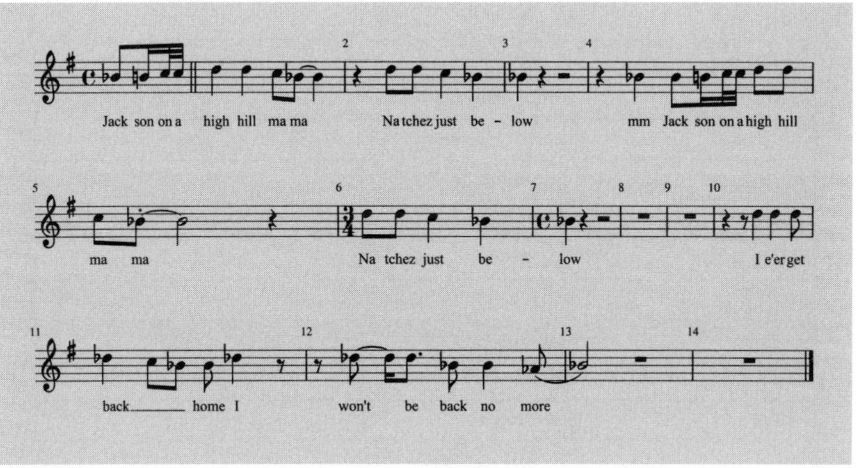


Ex. 16: Patton, "Screamin' and Hollerin' the Blues," (1929), chorus 1 [0:02-0:37] (after Grossman, Grossman, and Calt, *Country Blues Songbook*).

Each lyric phrase ended on the same tone (B-flat as transcribed in Ex.16, measures 3, 7, and 12-13), as did also the first sub-phrases in the first two lyric phrases (see measures 1 and 5).

However, to end the first sub-phrase in the third lyric phrase (Ex. 16, m. 11), Patton sang on D-flat instead of the conventional F pitch according to other musicians' practice. Because of this sub-phrase ending, the melody took on a crude cast, particularly as the same pitch had begun that sub-phrase snippet on the words "I ever get back."

Other than these tonic returns on the sixth and tenth beats, "Screamin' and Hollerin' the Blues" had few redundant notes. Within the eighteen lyric phrases in the six choruses on Patton's 1929 record (see Table 1 below), seven different intervals were used to begin a first phrase, while five different intervals were employed to begin the second sub-phrases. So, instead of singing a theme with variations, Patton produced a unique song having only variations, but no specific theme:

**TABLE 1.**

| | FIRST SUB-PHRASE BEGINNING | SECOND SUB-PHRASE BEGINNING |
|---|---|---|
| | *verse 1* | |
| line 1 | minor seventh | minor 3rd |
| line 2 | tonic | minor 3rd |
| line 3 | minor 3rd | minor 3rd |
| | *verse 2* | |
| line 1 | subdominant | minor 3rd |
| line 2 | subdominant | minor 3rd |
| line 3 | minor 3rd | minor 7th |
| | *verse 3* | |
| line 1 | subdominant | minor 3rd |
| line 2 | minor 3rd | minor 3rd |
| line 3 | supertonic | supertonic |
| | *verse 4* | |
| line 1 | subdominant | minor 3rd |
| line 2 | minor 3rd | minor 3rd |
| line 3 | supertonic | minor 7th |
| | *verse 5* | |
| line 1 | subdominant | dominant |
| line 2 | minor 3rd | augmented 4th |
| line 3 | minor 3rd | minor 7th |
| | *verse 6* | |
| line 1 | minor 3rd | minor 3rd |
| line 2 | subdominant | major 3rd |
| line 3 | augmented 4th | tonic |

Patton sang each of these variations in different volumes, imparting a kind of drama to his words that was not heard in other bluesmen's dance blues. This dynamic expressiveness of Patton's singing, rather than merely the varying melodies by themselves, was what made "Screamin and Hollerin' the Blues" so striking. In this respect, it differed from a ditty like "Turn Your Money Green" that could be simply performed by whistling. One of Patton's expressive devices was to drop an octave on the last beat of the first two lines of a lyric stanza when he sang the tonic note. But by ending the concluding third line of that stanza at a higher pitch than the preceding two line, he could emphasize brilliantly each of his declarations.

Patton's other uses of the "Maggie" theme on records were no less varied than those heard on "Screamin' and Hollerin' the Blues." In "Moon Going Down" (1930), Patton freely substituted major thirds and sixths for minor thirds and sevenths (compare Table 2 to Table 1):

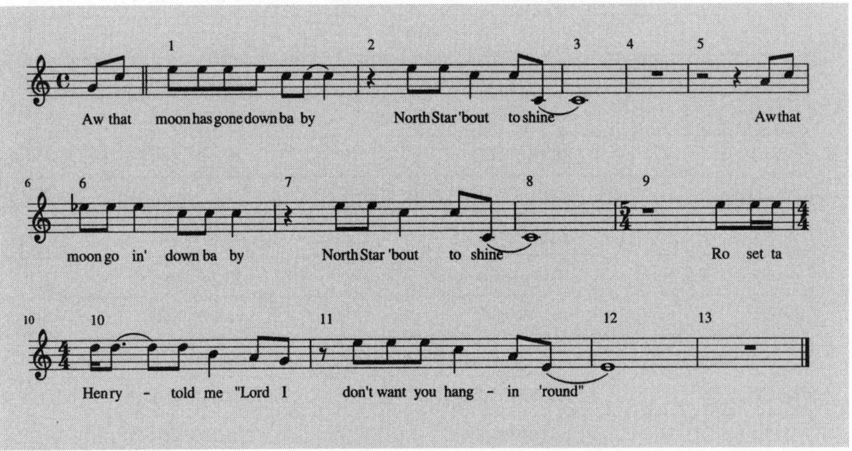


Ex. 17: Charlie Patton, "Moon Going Down" (1930), chorus 1 [0:02-0:38] (after Grossman, Grossman, and Calt, *Country Blues Songbook*).

"Maggie" was also revolutionary for its rhythm. If its varying renditions on Patton's records are any indication, "Maggie" departed from the black dance music of that time for lacking a sustained accenting pattern. Moreover, Patton did not stress equally his accented beats, as was the practice of dance arrangements, black or white; if anything, he sounded more vehement on some of the stressed beats than on the others.

**TABLE 2.**

| | FIRST SUB-PHRASE BEGINNING | SECOND SUB-PHRASE BEGINNING |
|---|---|---|
| | *verse 1* | |
| line 1 | major 6th | minor 3rd |
| line 2 | major 6th | minor 3rd |
| line 3 | major 3rd | minor 3rd |
| | *verse 2* | |
| line 1 | augmented 4th | minor 3rd |
| line 2 | subdominant | minor 3rd |
| line 3 | major 3rd | minor 3rd |
| | *verse 3* | |
| line 1 | major 6th | minor 3rd |
| line 2 | major 6th | minor 3rd |
| line 3 | major 6th | major 3rd |
| | *verse 4* | |
| line 1 | augmented 4th | major 3rd |
| line 2 | dominant | minor 3rd |
| line 3 | major 6th | major 3rd |
| | *verse 5* | |
| line 1 | major 6th | major 3rd |
| line 2 | minor 7th | minor 3rd |
| line 3 | major 6th | major 3rd |
| | *verse 6* | |
| line 1 | minor 3rd | major 3rd |
| line 2 | tonic | minor 3rd |
| line 3 | major 6th | major 3rd |

The rhythms of "Maggie" were determined by the shimmy-she-wobble, a contact dance that was done to both slow and fast songs. It was current at the dawn of Patton's career: in 1907, when "Maggie" would have been a fresh composition, a song called "Shimmy She Wobble" was played in Bolton, Mississippi.[10] When danced to Mississippi blues, the shimmy bore little resemblance to the white version popularized in 1918 by Gilda Gray, Mae West, and

Bea Palmer. If the white shimmy was coyly suggestive, the black shimmy was overtly erotic. "The white folks never did *shimmy*, " Sam Chatmon recalled. "Just to get with a woman and stand like we used to do, and wobblin' upside her, I never did see no white folks doin' that." Its simulation of sex was too much for Chatmon. "One night—I'se about sixteen or seventeen years old—I had to quit dancin' with a girl. She'd shimmy'd so till she got my thing hard and got it on the side and was workin' it so fast, I'se fixin' to do what I had to do in my pants. From then on, I didn't like no shimmy." It is no wonder, then, that barrelhouse police halted couples whenever they caught them dancing it.

The lack of a consistent accent pattern and Patton's varying stresses given to the accented beats of "Maggie" erased the regular beats for a step dance. Instead, Patton's stresses led his dancers to move with their pelvises and hips. Such grinding steps became integral with Patton's execution of shimmy tunes, as in the guitar part to the opening lyric of "Screamin' and Hollerin' the Blues" (Ex. 18):

Ex. 18: Patton, "Screamin' and Hollerin' the Blues," (1929), chorus 1, measures 1-3, [0:02-0:10] with grinding accents in the guitar in m. 1.

Instead of emphasizing equally the accented second and fourth beats, he gave the second beat a harder stress.

The free manner in which Patton sang on his various recorded treatments of "Maggie" was matched by his guitar accompaniment. Although on "Screamin' and Hollerin' the Blues" he used the II-IV-V blues chord progression, on his guitar he played riffs in rhythm with his singing. During any given verse, his accompaniment could be a mosaic of instrumental fills and phrases. In a departure from the common practice of dance blues, Patton used three different guitar lines to accompany the first vocal phrase the six choruses of

"Screamin' and Hollerin." (In other recorded versions of the "Maggie" melody, he played at least three additional guitar lines that were not heard in "Screamin' and Hollerin.") His main accompaniment figure for the "Maggie" songs was a descending one-measure bass phrase involving four or three pitches to the dominant scale pitch, beginning on the second beat and being repeated for two or three measures, and having a 1-2-3-4 beat pattern in 4/4 meter with accent stress on the first beat. Patton used this kind of phrase with the grinding rhythm previously noted to shore up the weak sixth beat of his vocal, which was cast in a 1-2 accenting pattern. By beginning the guitar phrase and its 1-2-3-4 accenting pattern on the second vocal beat, Patton made it mesh with the 1-2-3-4 rhythm pattern of his song:

Ex. 19: Patton, "Screamin' and Hollerin' the Blues," (1929), chorus 1, measures 1-3, [0:02-0:10] with grinding accents in the guitar in m. 1.

This integration of two rhythmic layers, and the use of the guitar to supply an accent where the vocal lagged rhythmically, were necessary innovations for Patton to devise, as through the 1920s his black dancers were dependent rhythmically on a singer's vocal accenting.

Also, Patton added extra percussion by slapping the body of his guitar. He also adjusted skillfully his accompaniment to follow his vocal inflections, particularly while playing a IV7 treble chord during the two measures of the second vocal phrase (mm. 5-8 of a typical 12-measure blues).

But in his guitar phrasing, Patton could be as unpredictable as his accenting and choice of vocal notes. Dance music was supposed to have consistent beats and regular phrases. But in his 1929 recording of "Screamin' and Hollerin' the

Blues," Patton was changing constantly how he sang his phrases.[11] Only two of the six stanzas took the same format, and only the construction of the third phrases of the stanzas were consistent, in order to have the song's distinctive lyric-break midway through (see Ex. 16, mm.11-12, and Ex. 17, m. 11).

One other musical observation should be made, and that is regarding phrasing. On his recordings, Patton did not sing each lyric phrase to four measures each. Rather, he often lengthened them by adding two beats. The result is that notated transcriptions often show a phrase ending with a measure in 6/4 or 5/4 time, instead of in common 4/4 time (see. Ex. 25 "Pony Blues" for one such example). Such changes in transcribed notations are not the result of mixing meters in the manner of classical music composers, but rather the necessity of accommodating a phrase that Patton lengthened in accordance to a dance like the shimmy-she-wobble.[12]

What should be remembered most about "Maggie" was that it was not a set song, but rather that Patton made it and its recorded offshoots as an ever-evolving work of performance. There was no one style of vocal delivery: a lyric might be rendered at a full shout as in "Moon Going Down," or in a softer voice that characterized "Screamin' and Hollerin' the Blues," despite the song's title. The tempo was likewise subject to change according to Patton's whim. The song had no fixed text. Even the standard tonic-note ending of the individual vocal phrases could be dispensed with: some phrases of "Moon Going Down" ended on major thirds and dominants, while some phrases of the related "High Water Everywhere" ended on minor thirds. From the free-wheeling approach that Patton took to what should have been dance music, there were three results. First, the focus of the listener was diverted to Patton the performer, whose material seemed to flow from within him. Second, his lack of repetitiveness discouraged close imitations of his work. Finally, "Maggie" and its descendants seemed to be an expression of mood, or of the moment.

How much more versatile Patton was than his peers may be realized by comparing his versions of "Maggie" with a vocal melody that was its first cousin. This nameless tune was shared among Memphis and Mississippi blues singers. It used three intervals (the tonic, minor third, and minor seventh) during its first two vocal phrases, with an added dominant in the final phrase, as seen in transcription in Son House's "Preaching the Blues":

Ex. 20: Son House, "Preaching the Blues" (1930), ch. 1 mm. 1-3 [0:05-0:11].

This tune may also be heard in Will Weldon's "Turpentine Blues" and "Hitch Me To Your Buggy, Drive Me Like A Mule" (both recorded in 1928), and in Arthur Petties' "Two Time Blues" (1928). Any one of Patton's recorded treatments of "Maggie" has more variation than all of these songs put together.

Although Patton was always fussing with melodies and arrangements, his spontaneity in performance may indicate an exposure to the black church, where extemporaneous preaching and singing were common. Listening to a Patton record, Booker Miller mused, "The blues is kinda like workin' in the church, I guess.[13] Whatever the 'spirit' say do, you do it."

With its one-chord strumming, "Mississippi Bo Weavil Blues" sounds almost archaic when compared to "Green River Blues" and the "Maggie" treatments. Depending partly on pattern strokes and full use of the lower strings (especially the open fifth and fourth strings), "Mississippi Bo Weavil Blues" has a decidedly banjo flavor, much like the cruder and slower playing of Georgia's Julius Daniels on "Ninety Nine Year Blues" (1927). In the form that Patton recorded it in 1929, "Mississippi Bo Weavil Blues" could not be related to any known musical genre, since each of its phrases used a unique 3-1/2 bar vocal phrase, coupled with a 2 ½ (or 3) bar bottleneck riff, and (more or less) two measures of open chord strumming.

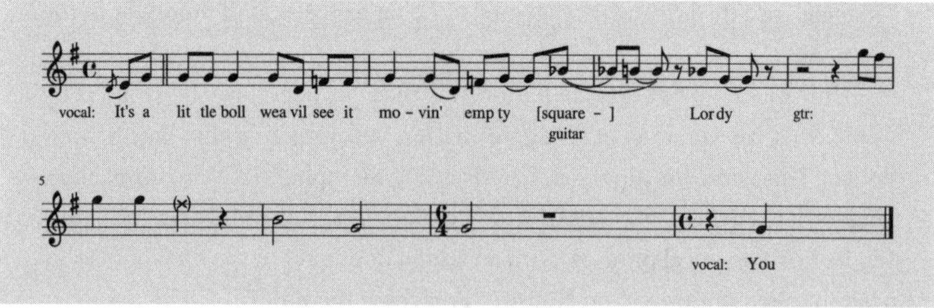


Ex. 21: Charlie Patton, "Mississippi Bo Weavil Blues," (1929), chorus 1, mm. 1-8 [0:04-0:15].

Except for the first phrase of the song, Patton accompanied the first nine beats of singing (involving mostly the tonic) with open string work. The chanting quality of the vocal and the drone-like quality of the open string work permitted Patton to end the phrase with a climactic flourish: for the pitch crossing over from the second to third transcribed measure, he substituted a lyric word with a piercing slide tone, then (m. 3, beats 3-4) he simultaneously sang "Lordy" while executing a descending top string bottleneck riff (involving the minor third, tonic, and minor seventh).

The fill (Ex. 21, mm. 4-5) that followed on the heels of Patton's vocal began with a three-beat tonic lick pitched up, seemingly beyond the normal range of a guitar to that of a violin. The fill concluded with three lower notes (the minor third, and tonic plucked twice) scattered over six beats (mm. 6-7): each was played with a heavy vibrato and allowed to reverberate and fade.

Patton's exquisite treatment of this rough-hewn tune implies a broad exposure to sounds, and an urge to tinker with the music about him.

Such tinkering may also be heard in Patton's 1929 remarkably animated recording of "A Spoonful Blues." It wasn't really a blues, but rather a "rag" ditty that celebrated cocaine addiction. It may have dated to the turn of the century, when the Memphis *Commercial Appeal* newspaper estimated that 80% of the city's African Americans used the drug, buying doses for a nickel or a dime at pharmacies. The song likely originated in black vaudeville. In its flippant, thematic treatment of its subject and the diatonic melody, it was much different from the dance music often heard at Delta frolics and barrelhouses.

Patton imbued his version of "Spoonful" with a new rhythm and a vivid style of presentation. The original song had a downbeat 1-2-3-4 accenting pattern, as may be heard in the recorded versions by Papa Charlie Jackson and Charley Jordan. Patton reset the accenting to a syncopated 1-2 pattern, quickened the tempo, and "talked" the title word of the tune with two different three-beat bottleneck slides. While using a bottleneck technique in an open tuning (E major), Patton accompanied his singing with a facile series of seventh chords. In its opening section (pickup and m.1), the melody descended in a high register (with Patton fretting at the eleventh free fret, assuming that he placed a capo at the first fret while tuned to standard pitch) and involved three chords (I-VII-VI) played on three beats.

This section culminated in a bottleneck glissando (m. 2, beat 3) that began on the third and ended on the second degree of the scale. In the second part

Ex. 22: Patton, "A Spoonful Blues" (1929), chorus 1, mm.1-2 [0:04-0:08] (from Woody Mann, *Bottleneck Blues Guitar*).

Ex. 23: Patton, "A Spoonful Blues" (1929), chorus 1, mm. 3-7 [0:08-0:16].

of the song (mm.4-7), Patton played ascending bottleneck chords (II-IV-V) in a lower register (m.4) and ended with a "spoonful" glissando from the third to the octave tonic note (m.7).

Whereas the usual versions of "Spoonful" like those by Jackson and Jordan amounted to eight bars, Patton's phrase lengths (and the placement of his bottleneck slides) varied accordingly to his lyrics:

> Doctors dyin' (spoken: way in Hot Springs!) just 'bout a . . .
> These women goin' crazy every day in their life 'bout a . . .

(Spoken: "Lookey here, baby, you would slap me?" "Yes I will!") just 'bout a . . .
Hey baby, (spoken: you know I'm a fool a-) 'bout my . . .
"Would you kill a man?" (spoken: "Yes I would, you know I'd kill him") just 'bout a . . .
Most every man (spoken: that you see is) fool 'bout his . . .

Hot Springs was then renowned for its restorative waters, which were supposed to cure "chronic malaria, alcoholism, and drug addictions."[14]

For the spoken asides, which sometimes lasted for a measure and a half, Patton used a variety of voices, some of which were quicker than his preferred style of speech. "He spoke slow," Booker Miller recalled. The way Patton glided effortlessly between speech and song produced an unpredictable effect, and it gave the piece an elastic structure; a verse might involve as many as ten and a half bars, instead of eight. In some stanzas, the opening three chords were instrumentalized; when Patton began a verse with heightened intensity (as in singing "Would you kill a man?"), he added to this effect by playing a succession of high pitches, from the fourth degree of the scale to the second:

Ex. 24: Patton, "A Spoonful Blues" (1929) chorus 4, mm.1-2 [0:40-0:44].

By these devices, Patton thoroughly mastered "A Spoonful Blues," not only by having a triumph over its form, but also by developing a new arrangement that only he could have performed.

The earliest testimony of Patton's career was provided by Ernest Brown, a former musician nicknamed "Whiskey Red" who met him sometime around 1907.[15] Brown was living on Arthur Peerman's plantation, which was located a mile and a half northeast of Cleveland, and about three and a half miles west of Dockery. During the four years Brown cropped there, he witnessed Patton's rise to local celebrity. "He playin' the same kind of music like he did when he put out them records," Brown told Stephen LaVere in a 1974 interview. "When I first knowed him, he wasn't playin' as good as he was after I began to find out who he was."[16] Later, while talking with Patton in Robinsonville in 1926, Brown realized that they shared a musical mentor:

> "I say, 'Who learn you how to play a guitar?'
>
> "He say, 'Earl Harris.'
>
> "I say, 'How come I don't remember you? I learnt from him, too.'"

The answer may be that Patton had moved on by the time Brown became Harris' protégé.

Earl Harris was a tenant on the Peerman plantation, which at the time was better known as C. R. Smith's. "Earl, he's our boss, he's our champ, he's our champ musicianer," Brown recalled. Other Peerman players included Harris' brothers Otis and Jimmy, the latter known as a "one man band," and Patton's future duet partner Willie Brown (I), among others. "There were three or four around there learnin' under Earl," Ernest Brown reported, "one of 'em was named Louie Black." Black was another resident of the plantation, and he may have been—or not—the Lewis Black who in 1927 recorded in Memphis four crudely played blues for Columbia Records.[17] "Lewis Black, he was just a gamblin' man. He'd play music at times. [As] long as he could keep from playin', he'd be in the crap game or somethin'. When you'd find him playin' the guitar, he probably got broke. [As] long as he had money, he drinkin' and gamblin'." Eventually Black fled the area after axing a man during a dispute over a female. As for Earl Harris, Brown said he last saw him in the early 1950s living in Memphis.

Of these Peerman musicians, only Willie Brown would come to have a general musical reputation. Earl Harris himself remained unknown until Stephen LaVere interviewed Ernest Brown, who spoke more about Patton's early fame. "They're always somebody sendin' for him and carryin' him an' bringin' him to dances," Brown said of Patton. Even when Patton brought with him a mandolinist and a fiddler, he was still an attraction in his own right, a genuine musical star. "People just clownin' over him. They'd follow him everywhere they hear tell of where Charlie Patton was; they was there." In Ernest Brown's view, Patton fully merited this acclaim. "He a good songster, he a real singin' man." His playing seemed no less skillful to Brown. "Charlie Patton, he could play 'overhand,'" he remarked, referring to the gimmick of fretting with the palm turned downwards. "B-flat, he could play it from one end of the guitar to the other. He just was—expert."

What exactly Patton learned from Earl Harris remains conjectural. Patton would not have learned for too long according to a school of musicianship, for as we have seen in examining what may have been his earliest pieces, he was much too individual to play in such a generalized manner. Still, he could have learned "If You Take My Woman" from Harris. Maybe he picked up the four-beat vamp (with plucked notes on the first two beats, followed by four tonic strums) that he later used on his recordings of "Pony Blues," "Down The Dirt Road," and "Screamin' and Hollerin' The Blues." Then again, Harris and Patton could have been very different. After all, Ernest Brown did not know of Patton's connection to Harris until Patton remarked on it.

In order for Patton to become Mississippi's first blues celebrity, he had to offer something new to his listening audience beyond what he had learned from Harris. Viola Cannon's statement in 1963[18] that he made up his own singing may imply that he had devised his most popular themes.

"Charlie Patton, he had about two-three pieces everybody loved, white and colored," Ernest Brown recalled. Although Brown did not say what these pieces were, it is certain that "Pony Blues" was one of them. "Pony Blues" was as closely identified with Patton as "Some of these Days" was with Sophie Tucker. Even 30 years after his death, "Pony Blues" was the one song that people who heard Patton readily recalled. It was one of his three signature melodies, along with the "Maggie" tune and "Banty Rooster Blues." While Patton had rearranged extensively the two latter songs, he never quite succeeded in giving "Pony" a distinctive instrumental facelift. Nor did he succeed in making his 1934 re-recording (as "Stone Pony Blues," for Vocalion) as accomplished as his 1929 hit for Paramount.

"Pony Blues" made Patton's blues career. Arguably, it could have done the same for anyone else if one had devised the song before Patton did. Its title verse had the kind of appealing melody that makes for a hit song or an abiding standard. Except for the phrase endings, the placid melody of its title verse was unusual for the blues. Its four notes employed major intervals (the tonic, major third, major fifth, and major sixth) that eliminated the tonal ambiguity heard in most other blues. The prominence of the dominant in all three phrases further removed it from conventional blues melody, which would often lack a dominant in its first two phrases. Instead of treating the dominant as a ceiling tone (in the fashion of "Maggie"), Patton made it a true melody note by sandwiching it between the higher sixth and lower third.

Ex. 25, Patton, "Pony Blues" (1929), chorus 1, vocal melody [0:03-0:38].

While many blues melodies can seem contrived, the first chorus of "Pony Blues" consists of three phrases that seem so closely intertwined as to seem a single basic phrase with two variations.

Whereas the first half of the initial phrase ascends during its first three beats (Ex. 25, pickup and m.1) the last part of the phrase (mm. 2-3) inverts its note sequence (descending from the major sixth to the dominant, the major third [the second may be heard as an ornament], and tonic).

The second phrase (mm. 5-8) begins with the same ascent, and it also repeats the closing cadence of the previous phrase.

The third line resumes the melody of the five beats (mm.9-10), and then (mm.11-12) toys with its three lowest tones for its closing measures.

With this remarkable phrasing, Patton made "Pony Blues" made it far superior to the usual Delta ditty. The structure of his phrasing converted a memorable melody into a masterpiece. During the first two phrases of the titular first verse, he held the final word for four beats while playing a guitar figure. This was symmetrical with the opening sub-phrases of the each lyric phrase (sung each time to the words "Hitch up my pony"), which were also of five beats. The final word of the first stanza was held for four common-time beats—a feat remarkable for blues records.

The vocal accenting of "Pony Blues" may be the most complicated of any dance blues song on pre-1942 records. The unique vocal accenting of the title verse involved a tug-of-war contrast between a 1-2 vocal rhythm and a legato singing style using sustained notes that displaced expected stresses. As in "Screamin' and Hollerin' the Blues," "Pony Blues" had a vocal that had a weak sixth beat (at m. 1, vocal beats marked 4-5 in Ex. 26) that Patton fortified with his guitar accompaniment. Here, he created a complementary rhythm with a non-melodic seven-beat mosaic of eighth notes (mm. 1-2), beginning with a bass note on the first half-beat of m.1 and followed by three beats' worth of damped and bent treble notes. A shorter variation of this phrase began on the first half-beat of m. 2:

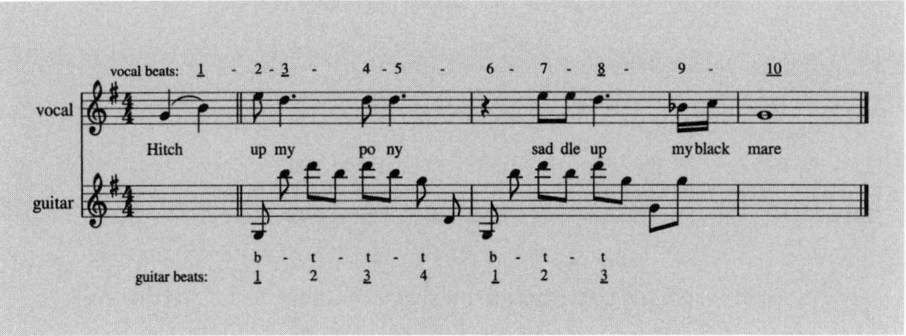


Ex. 26, Patton, "Pony Blues" (1929), ch. 1, mm. 1-4, vocal accenting [0:03-0:14].

Vocal Beats: 1 / 2-3-4-5 / 6-7-8-9 / 10
Guitar Beats: / 1-2-3-4 / 1-2-3
/ b-t- t-t / b-t- t
(b=bass) (t=treble)

Patton may have been the only blues musician who thought in terms of such dual rhythm patterns.

By using these short instrumental figures, Patton not only filled in nearly every vocal beat weak or strong, but also he drew from a variety of tones and instrumental accenting patterns. The bass and treble interplay that formed

Patton's accompaniment punctuations (as notated in Ex. 26) was extremely exotic for Delta blues. His rhythmic punctuations would have sounded unintelligible without the vocal melody they were accompanying.[19] However, Patton's recorded versions of "Maggie" are different in that his guitar work on those songs is phrased mostly in single-measure blocks, generally speaking, in which Patton used a heavy bass to amplify his basic 1-2 vocal beat. But in "Pony Blues," his accompaniment was so full that he almost seemed to be playing two guitars: a bass percussionist, and a lead guitarist who mimicked accents and embroidered the melody with treble work.

By the time Patton recorded "Pony Blues" in 1929, he had been tinkering with it for nearly 20 years. In the six verses heard on that record, each of the three vocal melodies bore a distinctive phrasing pattern and accompaniment features, marking a level of melodic ambition that was otherwise unheard in blues dance music, at least on records. In the 18 phrases, there are six melodic strands; the reiteration of the same line (A") in each couplet gave the strands a cohesiveness not found in, say, a medley performance:

| | |
|---|---|
| verse one | AA'A" |
| verse two | BCA" |
| verse three | BCA" |
| verse four | DEA" |
| verse five | BCA" |
| verse six | DEA" |

These vocal variations contributed towards a dramatic feeling to the song. In the second verse, Patton began by shouting at full voice, but dropping to a lowered volume while delivering the second phrase. In the third verse, he reversed this sequence by singing the first phrase soft and the second one loud. To accompany this third verse, Patton used a technique from his "Maggie" songs of repeating on his guitar a high eighth-note tone for two measures:

Ex. 27: Patton, "Pony Blues" (1929), chorus 3, guitar riff [1:06-1:09].

His rhythmic presentation of the second verse was uniquely creative: after singing the first lyric with a 1-2 accent (Ex. 28, pickup and mm. 1-2), Patton strummed a half-measure fill (m. 3, beats 1-3) and launched the second phrase with an implied, unaccented IV7 chord played for a single beat (m. 3, beat 4). His first measure of singing (Ex. 28, m. 4) then took a 1-2 rhythm pattern, thanks to the accenting of that guitar beat that had preceded it. In other words, that new 1-2 vocal pattern was the result of the guitar transition, not of a vocal imposition.

Ex. 28: Patton, "Pony Blues" (1929), chorus 2, vocal melody with accent indications [0:38-0:54].

Because of these dramatic nuances and percussion, "Pony Blues" demanded an inspired performance, and on his Paramount recording of the piece in 1929, Patton did not—and still does not—disappoint. His timing is a wonder to behold, and he handles his instrument like a toy, producing percussive and timbral contrasts by choking strings for split seconds, muting individual bass notes, and tapping his guitar percussively during the V7 section over the third and fourth beats of the final vocal phrase (as in Ex. 25, m. 8 for the words "a rider."). Guitarist and transcriber Woody Mann calls "Pony Blues" "the most perfect blues recording ever made."[20] It is certainly one whose magic cannot be wholly conveyed through transcribed notation and analysis. It was obviously a song that was dear to Patton, for he played it with sheer love.

Another early signature tune was "Banty Rooster Blues," a slow-drag bottleneck blues that Patton played in "Spanish" open-A tuning. This song was rather conventional as it featured a standard blues three-phrase AAB lyric scheme, and on its 1929 Paramount recording Patton offered only two minor variations of its tightly plotted melodic line.

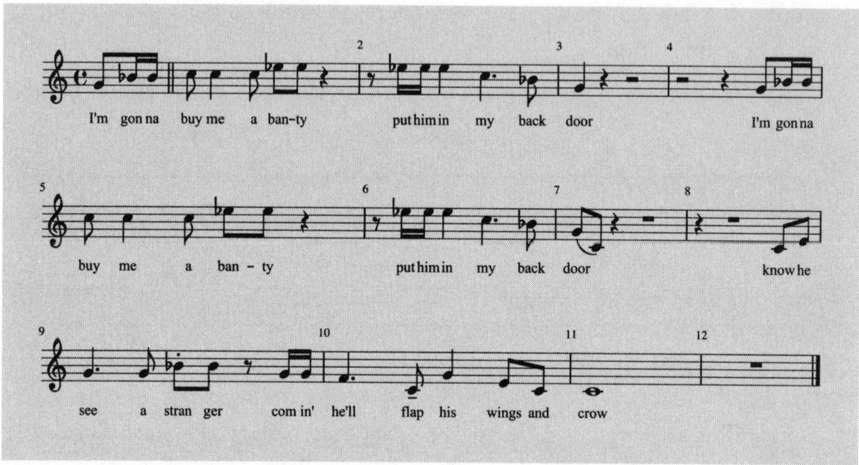


Ex. 29: Patton, "Banty Rooster Blues" (1929) chorus 1, vocal melody [0:02-0:34] (after Grossman, Grossman, and Calt, *Country Blues Songbook*).

Likewise, the phrasing for this song was consistent, which meant the record lacked the variety of surprises that are heard in the "Maggie" treatments and "Pony Blues." Although on the 1929 recording the last word of each phrase of "Banty Rooster Blues" was drawn out, the phrasing pattern began as a "ten/six" phrase model, and it would have been a consistent twelve-bar song except for extra two beat tonic strums added to the end of some stanzas. Unlike most of Patton's tunes, it did not accelerate in tempo.[21] For accompaniment, Patton fretted his guitar with a bottleneck slide implement. He used two chords (I and V), producing a full sound with open-string strumming. While the first two vocal phrases are accompanied with top string slides, the final phrase had a bass-string accompaniment. In terms of finesse and elaborateness, Patton's arrangement may have already seemed rather simple at the time it was recorded in 1929, but its guitar-damping technique could have been a considerable novelty, especially when Patton began using it, probably sometime during the 1910s.

Patton's vocal delivery on "Banty Rooster Blues" is much "bluesier" than his singing of the "Maggie" songs or "Pony Blues." Perhaps in order to convey forlornness, he dramatically lowered his volume at the end of each lyric. (In the first two lines of each stanza, this descent in volume coincided with a melodic dip from the fifth scale step to the tonic, sometimes occurring in the middle of a word.) The low register of his singing added to the mournful quality: the tonic was pitched beneath that of "Pony Blues" (at Bo), and the "Banty Rooster Blues" root-triad fills are heard higher in register than the sung tonic note (to the word "crow").

Ex. 30: Patton, "Banty Rooster Blues" (1929), chorus 1, m.11 [0:31-0:34].

Like "Green River Blues" and "Mississippi Bo Weavil Blues," "Banty Rooster Blues" was infused with a 1-2 vocal accenting pattern. While Patton's use of this pattern often led him to emphasize nonessential words, it worked to underscore the most significant words of "Banty Rooster."

> What you *want* with a *roo*ster? He won't *crow* 'fore *day*-aye.
> What you *want* with a *man* when he *won't* do *nothin'* he *say*-aye.

The predictability of this pattern was offset by Patton's accompaniment and his lack of uniform phrase division. As with "Green River Blues," the punch line paired two five-beat clusters (or 4-and-8 beat clusters, as in Ex. 29), instead of the "four/six" subphrase pairs in each of the first two vocal lines.

The African American slow-drag dance to which "Banty Rooster Blues" was performed was a contact dance that dated to the turn of the century. "All it is is just dry screwin'," Johnny Shines said of the slow drag, which he remembered as the Delta's most popular dance during the 1930s. "Man stands there and just dry screws."[22] Unlike the shimmy, which fell out of fashion during in the 1930s, the slow drag was still popular in 1941, when Arthur "Big Boy" Crudup recorded "If I Get Lucky" for the Bluebird label.

Yet, of all of Patton's bedrock pieces, "Banty Rooster Blues" may have been the one least likely to have been created by him. Its melody resembles "Roll and Tumble Blues," a shimmy-she-wobble bottleneck piece that was recorded first by Hambone Willie Newbern of Brownsville, Tennessee in 1929 for Okeh Records. Before then, Delta guitarists like Patton's friend Hayes McMullan learned it from bluesmen in the hill country east of the Delta in the early 1920s.[23] In the way that Patton sang it on record, this melody was among the least whimsical and most logical of his tunes: its beginning four-note ascent (from the dominant to a minor third) was inverted during the last measure of the phrase. The playfulness of the lyrics as sung by the funereal sound of Patton's voice, and the way he emphasizes important nouns or verbs in a lyric, were not characteristic of his singing of his other songs. The thematic nature of the first three verses is also unusual for Patton, whose other recorded blues had lyrics that lacked a common topic or theme.[24] Patton's guitar accompaniment, moreover, seems to evoke fiddle playing: his root-triad lick (Ex. 30) occurs during the two middle beats (m.11 beat 4, m. 12 beat 1) of his six-beat instrumental fill, the same beats that contain Henry Sims' violin insertions in his various 1930 recorded duets with Patton.[25]

Perhaps the most telling indication that Patton did not create "Banty Rooster Blues" from scratch may be found in his extensive rearrangement of its melody as "Down The Dirt Road," which retains intact the first two vocal phrases. But in other respects, the two songs differ as much from each other as does "Green River Blues" from "If You Take My Woman." "Down the Dirt Road Blues" is a striking synthesis of "Banty Rooster Blues" and "Pony Blues," and it is transposed to the C playing position on the guitar. While taking the basic tune of "Banty Rooster Blues," "Down The Dirt Road" used the symmetrical phrasing pattern of "Pony Blues": each phrase-ending word was held for 4-1/2 beats, complementing the way Patton prolonged the third word of the song ("away") for 4-1/2 beats. The three main lyric phrases also ended in the same diminuendo fashion of "Pony Blues," with Patton embellishing his vocal fade with glissandos between the dominant and the major third beneath it.

The guitar accompaniment of "Down the Dirt Road Blues" shared elements with the "Maggie" songs and "Pony Blues." During the opening lyric of each stanza, Patton played a two-measure descending series of snapped notes on the top string that used the same intervals (tonic, minor seventh, and fifth)

Ex. 31: Patton, "Down the Dirt Road Blues" (1929), chorus 1, vocal melody [0:02-0:32] (after Grossman, Grossman, and Calt, *Country Blues Songbook*).

Ex. 32: Patton, "Down the Dirt Road Blues" (1929), chorus 1, mm. 1-3, vocal melody and guitar riff and snapped descending notes [0:02-0:10].

and timing (eighth notes in 4/4 time) as his accompaniment for the second verse of "Pony Blues."

For the second lyric phrase, Patton strummed a guitar phrase in the fashion of "Maggie," consisting of three full chords: major IV-minor III-I.

The way Patton isolated notes within these chords (like his hand-damped V7 chord during each third lyric phrase) to give nuance to his vocal accents was altogether remarkable.

"Down the Dirt Road Blues" as Patton recorded it in 1929 had some unique characteristics. One was the heavy guitar tapping (involving two taps per beat in 4/4 time) that accompanied its first lyric. Unlike the guitar accompaniments for Patton's other main tunes, the one for "Down the Dirt Road Blues" had a continuous rather than a mosaic quality: each beat of the first two vocal phrases was accompanied with instrumentation. The density of this accompaniment made for a surprising contrast with the last six beats of each verse, which were accompanied only by heavy foot stomping. But during the fifth verse, Patton unexpectedly filled this silent section with a descending single-note phrase that mimicked his singing.

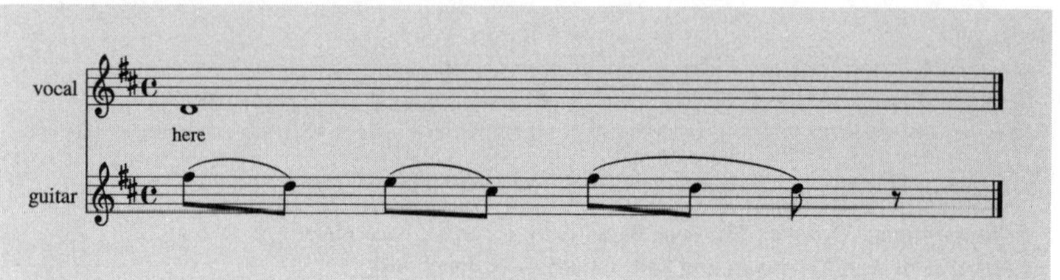


Ex. 33: Patton, "Down the Dirt Road Blues" (1929), chorus 5 (excerpt) [2:17-2:20].

If one believes that Patton had composed "Banty Rooster Blues," then one can then argue that he would not have been tempted to improve it as spectacularly as he had, say, "Down The Dirt Road Blues" or for that matter the "Maggie" songs, on the basis that a musician's creations reflect his own abilities. If he was the sole creator of "Banty Rooster Blues," then he probably wouldn't have tinkered with it as much as he had to "Down The Dirt Road Blues" (which, as will be seen, he played early on in his career). Perhaps, then, "Down The Dirt Road Blues" was his "answer" to a routine blues he learned in the basic form of "Banty Rooster Blues," just as "Green River Blues" was an "answer" to "If You Take My Woman."

I'm goin' away to a world unknown,
I'm worried now, but I won't be worried long.
—"DOWN THE DIRT ROAD BLUES," 1929

*Chapter 6*

# DOWN THE DIRT ROAD BLUES (CIRCA 1906–1910)

Of Patton's initial forays as a teenage blues singer, our knowledge is scant. At first he performed with his first wife Roxie Gibson; they lived near Dockery's sawmill on what was called the "Sixteen Section" of the plantation. For parties off the plantation, he would travel with his uncle Sherman Martin, who may have assisted as a second guitarist.

In 1908 he took his next wife, Millie Barnes, a twenty-one year old resident of Dockery's. In the early 1930s, some 25 years after leaving her, Patton seemed to have some lingering affection for her. "He used to do a whole lot of talk about her," Son House recalled from his conversations with Patton, who freely blamed himself for the demise of their affair. "He claims it was all his fault, wasn't none of Millie's," said House, "He didn't say what the cause (of their separation) was, but he said he was at fault." He further told House—quite falsely if there is no paper documentation about this—that she was the only woman he had ever married legitimately, instead of by "jumping the broomstick." Other neighbors thought by the way Patton treated Millie, he considered her as little more than a broomstick bride. "He didn't ever marry her," Sara Garrett insisted. "He just got a child by her. He never did stay with her." Perhaps claiming marriage was Patton's attempt to maintain an air of respectability for his ex-wife and their daughter. Their child was christened Willie Mae, but as an adult she was called "China Lou"; she was one of Patton's few known offspring.

If early in his career Patton had decided on his professional ambitions, then he needed to travel to hear more music than what was available on and around Dockery's Plantation. For that reason, the youthful Patton roamed a bit, unlike the house-frolic entertainers Dick Bankston and Willie Brown. He certainly traveled to Lula (eight miles from Helena, Arkansas) shortly before 1908. A little later, when he took on more of a musician's lifestyle, he preferred traveling to Dermott, Arkansas with his first cousin "Tee-nicey" Wade to spending time at Dockery's with his wife Millie Barnes. To reach Dermott,[1] Patton would have taken the Kate Adams, a wooden-hulled passenger boat that ran between Memphis and Arkansas City, a river town fifteen miles northeast of Dermott. In 1919, the Kate Adams became stuck on a sandbar near Helena, and there it stayed and became a dance hall for African Americans. Then and afterwards, Patton performed a bawdy song about the Kate and its clientele that, while not recorded, was recited by Willie Moore to Gayle Wardlow in the 1960s:

> The folks said long 'fore the *Kate* was made
> Arkansas City would be that whore's trade.
> The time done come to pass:
> When the *Kate* backs out from the landin',
> She's showin' her 'yas-yas.

"He'd sing it all the time," Moore remembered.[2]

How original was Patton? Or put another way, what had he derived from other musicians? Even his protégées weren't sure. Booker Miller had learned the fundamentals of blues-playing from Patton and James Binnell of Clarksdale. Having borrowed from Patton, Miller took it for granted that Patton as a young bluesman had borrowed in turn from other musicians, explaining years later that "You can go into show business right now. [But] you couldn't just build your show your own way. You'd have to take ideas from him, maybe, if he's a showman in show business, you take an idea, maybe one or two, and put with yours, and maybe you see another one, until you build your own show."

An older Delta bluesman whose "show" may have shaped Patton's general approach to performing was D. Irvin, who lived a few miles southeast of

Dockery's on a plantation between Ruleville and Cottondale. Even in his old age, Irvin was better known than most Delta musicians. "In 1932, I'd put D. Irvin around between sixty-five and seventy," recalled Miller, who met him when Irvin lived in Quito. "He's a old man. I heard him mention that he'd playin' around twenty-five or thirty years." Irvin preferred performing in the key of E, and he sang songs like "Big Kate Adams. " His repertory as a whole, David Edwards reported, consisted of "mostly old-time 'rappin' (strumming) stuff, but he was good." Although Miller observed that Irvin and Patton "played on a different order altogether," he included Irvin in Patton's basic mode as a performer: "D., he made a lotta noise and he clowned a lot. He had what I would call a baritone voice, maybe a bass. It was much lower than Charlie, but he could holler loud." The guitar "slapping" that Patton did on such records as "Screamin' and Hollerin' the Blues" was another of Irvin's own pet mannerisms. An aging Delta resident in the 1960s remembered Irvin as a better guitarist than Patton, describing to the authors the older man's histrionics that Patton became celebrated for. "He'd take his guitar, stand up with it, play it all 'tween his legs, and stick it behind his head, say, 'I'm havin' a fit with it, now!'" Another favorite Irvin aside,"Get down, black cows!," was a directive to dancers. Like Patton, Irvin presented himself as both a blues-player and a preacher.

The stunts that both men did were remnants of nineteenth-century plantation minstrelsy. But they were already considered passé in 1910, when a chronicler noted: "[The] negro minstrel had a manner of performing instrumental music that was peculiarly his own. Trick music, it might be termed, for the banjo and fiddle were played in all sorts of positions, under the leg, behind the back, and over the head." The same writer also thought that such "tricks" had inspired the nineteenth-century white black-faced imitators of plantation banjoists.[3]

Whether or not Patton had taken most of his performing mannerisms from one man, his repertory was varied enough to have likely come from many people. One could have been Earl Harris on the nearby Peerman Plantation, previously mentioned. Another might have been Henry Sloan, an older tenant of Dockery's who would move to Chicago in 1918. Patton's sister Viola stated that during her brother's youth, he was so fascinated by Sloan's playing as to follow him all over the wide plantation to listen to him.[4] She added that Sloan never sang. If that was true, then he may have been a string-band musician, or a performer of the kind of instrumental breakdowns that guitarists Sam Chatmon and Richard Harney remembered from their youths.

Two relatives may have also influenced Patton's guitar style. His maternal uncle, Sherman Martin, was a tall, slender man whose gawky appearance earned him the nickname "Rubberneck." He lived with the Pattons at Dockery's, and he would have been old enough to give young Charlie some early lessons on guitar. David Edwards knew Martin during the 1930s, and years later he said that he thought Martin's skills were minimal. "He never done anything, but he practiced under Charlie all the time. He had kind of a light voice, but he had a good voice." Another relative was Patton's first cousin "Tee-Nicey" Wade, who lived on the adjacent Dave D. Turner plantation near Ruleville; "Tee-Nicey" was a nickname for his small size, and so Wade may have been a first name. It is hard to say now whether Wade had contributed to Patton's development, or instead he was one of Charlie's earliest pupils This uncertainty is because they were the same age and played "near about the same songs," and because the source of that quote was Millie Barnes, one of Patton's early wives who stayed home instead of hearing her young husband perform with Wade.[5] But Booker Miller said that Wade "was very good. [But] he couldn't touch Charlie. Charlie couldn't make him stop playin." Wade moved to the McCloud plantation near Drew sometime during the 1920s, by which time he was seldom performing with Patton, if at all.

Yet another early crony who either borrowed Patton's music or helped him mold it was a brakeman on the Pea Vine train known as "Hobo George." Like Wade, he was around the same age as Patton and who, according to one informant to the authors, played "just like Charlie Patton." Hobo George lived on Dockery's, but later in life he moved to Cleveland, Mississippi, where he was still living, if deaf and infirm, when the authors visited him in 1970.

Even if Patton remembered the music that he heard as a child in Bolton or Edwards, there may have been no one in the surrounding Hinds County who was his model for blues, or who could possibly have given him at least a push in the musical direction that he eventually took. Josie Chatmon Williams, the first Chatmon to take up guitar in Bolton, remembered from the days of Patton's and her own youth only a man named Charlie Harrison, who taught her half-brother Bud to play guitar around 1909, shortly before she moved west to Greenville. When asked to name some songs that were popular among local blacks during the 1900s, she mentioned "After the Ball," an 1892 pop hit that sold five million copies of sheet music and was popularized by John Phillip Sousa; "Maggie," a tearjerker ballad that was unrelated to Patton's like-named blues, and "Careless Love." Such pieces would have been the stuff of Patton's earliest musical heritage.

Our knowledge of the history of the earliest blues is much too vague and sketchy to put Patton at a fixed or meaningful point within it. But it appears that when he took up the blues, the music had yet to have celebrated players, and to take on the connotations of sorrow that the mere label "blues" later suggested. The sentimental association that was attached to blues during the 1910s seems to have been largely fostered by W. C. Handy (1873-1958), whose best-selling sheet music publications[6] impressed the 12-measure form on the nation's entertainment consciousness. Before the publication of Handy's 1914 hit "St. Louis Blues," national appreciation of black vocal music was generally for spirituals and other sacred material.

During the 1910s, Handy was by far the Delta's most famous musician. Even in the 1960s, Patton's friend Willie Moore admitted, "Charlie Patton now, he wasn't 'up' with Handy. Handy's more famous." Yet it was Handy's encounters with musicians of Patton's lowly stripe that gave him the critical ideas towards his own nation-wide success. Upon arriving to Clarksdale in 1903, he organized a nine-piece popular-music orchestra to play at planters' dances, merchant sales, and boat excursions on the Mississippi. He even furnished brothel music. But he "never played for no 'colored,'" Willie Moore reported. "Onliest way the colored folks would get a chance to dance by Handy's music [was that] he play for the white folks until about one o'clock (in the morning), then he play for the colored from one till train time."

Handy first became aware of the commercial possibilities of black music during a dance in Cleveland, Mississippi, when he was upstaged by a local trio performing slow-drag music with a guitar, mandolin, and string bass.[7] Around the same time, while waiting late one night at a Tutwiler depot for a train, Handy heard a ragged guitarist play with a knife on the fretboard an accompaniment to what was apparently a blues song, singing three times a lyric that Patton was to sing on "Green River Blues": Goin' where the Southern cross the Dog.[8] Handy thought that this knife-slide style of accompaniment resembled Hawaiian guitar-playing, which had been developed between 1893 and 1895, and brought to America sometime after the annexation of Hawaii[9] in the wake of the 1898 Spanish-American War.

In 1903, the year of Handy's commercial blues awakening, Patton would have been about 12, and thought by his siblings as no older than 16. But Handy was a man of 30, possessing the kind of opportunism that led him to appraise Delta blues "with the eye of a budding composer."[10] As a trained band musician specializing in the popular white music of the day, he felt that the repetitive slow-drag music he heard in Cleveland by that rustic trio "wanted polishing."[11] The kind of polishing he had in mind may be best examined in his 1914 hit "St. Louis Blues," which used three melodic strains, not just one as in the verse-repeating blues format that may have been suggested by early rustic medleys like "Poor Boy Long Ways From Home." In an attempt to make the blues suitable as a Tin Pan Alley product, Handy recast blues as a song of sentiment.[12] His emphasis on sentimentality was reflected even in the lyrics that he and the rough-hewn blues singers shared in common. Where Patton sang to a jaded audience a smirking complaint about a woman he is about to abandon, Handy sought to woo his genteel audience by nursing a hurt feeling:

> My baby got a heart like a piece of railroad steel
> My baby got a heart like a piece of railroad steel
> After I leave here this mornin' never say, "Daddy how do you feel?"
> (Patton, "Heart Like Railroad Steel," 1929)

> Now if your heart beat like mine it's not made of steel
> And when you learn I left you this is how you'll feel.
> (Handy, Joe Turner Blues, 1915)

The Tin Pan Alley blues composers who imitated Handy[13] likewise coated matter-of-fact or jesting blues lyrics with a layer of mawkishness. In this instance of shared lyrics, the difference between Patton and a city songwriter is striking:

> Some people tell me, "Oversea blues ain't bad,"
> (spoken: Why, of course they are)
> Some people say, "Oversea blues ain't bad,"
> (spoken: What was a-matter with 'em?)
> It must not a-been them oversea blues I had.
> ("Down the Dirt Road Road Blues")

> Was weary lonesome heartbroken and sad
> And yet some people say the weary blues ain't bad.
> (Will Nash, "Goin' Down That Long Long Lonesome Road," 1919)

When 1920s blues records were becoming likely sources for Delta blues lyrics, Patton could lessen, even undo the mawkish renderings:

> Got myself a brand new hammock, placed it underneath a tree
> I hope the wind will blow so hard the tree will fall on me.
> (Spencer Williams, "Mountain Top Blues
> (Blue Mama's Suicide Wail)," 1924)

> Gonna buy me a hammock, carry it underneath through the tree,
> Gonna buy myself a hammock, gonna carry it underneath the tree,
> So when the wind blow, the leaves may fall on me.
> (Patton, "Hammer Blues," recorded 1929)

Whether Patton was the source or the stealer of these lyrics, these examples show that he understood the blues much differently than Handy and his colleagues. For Handy, vocal dance music had little value, and so he thought of dance blues as nothing more than "folk blues"—that is to say, crude products offering merely a rustic sincerity. Handy was too much urbane for the folk blues as he understood them; he left the South in 1918 to launch his publishing firm in New York.

With his training and experience as composer and conductor, Handy seemed to have taken a missionary's attitude about the southern blues singer. As Willie Moore explained, "If Handy got a man like Charlie Patton or me, or anyone, he'd send him to *school*, he'd *learn* them out." During interviews with Gayle Wardlow in the late 1960s, Moore offered himself as a case example of "school." As an eleven-year old orphan, Moore met Handy when the latter played at Tunica's Galton Hotel in September 1909. "He'd said, 'Well look, I tell you what to do: why don't you come and go with me? I'll learn you how to play these horns, and learn you how to sing, and you can make plenty money.'"[14] With Handy's assistance, Moore enrolled at Tuskegee University, where through 1911 he learned to read music and to play trombone. Afterwards, he worked as a caretaker for the band Handy took on from Jim Turner, attending to the musicians' instruments, brushing their hats, and shining their shoes. Later he joined the outfit and helped arrange its bookings in Delta towns like Robinsonville and Webb, coordinating the dates with Handy by telephone. Yet, on occasion he played guitar behind various Delta bluesmen, with whom he became a lifelong peer. From his dual life in early blues, Moore later told a fascinating anecdote about what Patton thought of Handy.

Sometime in the mid-to-late 1910s (exactly when is uncertain), Moore told Handy about meeting Charlie Patton in Hollandale. "He [Handy] asked me, 'Didn't Charlie Patton have a band?' " Moore recalled, " He asked me, 'Can he play?'"

"I said, 'Yeah, he can play when he knows to play.'

"He say, 'What do you think about him?'

"I say, 'Well, I couldn't tell you. One thing I can do is tell you to contact him. I'll tell you what I'll do, say, I'll give him an opening next Saturday night, see how he do.'

"I asked him (Patton) would he come up to a dance, [when] we had a dance at Beulah." (a town south of Rosedale)

Moore had thought that if Patton could already "take with the people" with the music he made "outta hisself," then he (Patton) could playing with such a professional outfit as Handy's. The thought of Patton as a potential Handy band member did not seem at all incongruous to Moore. "He could have joined it, 'cause a whole lotta them blues he's playin' we'se playin'. He played 'em on the guitar and we played 'em on the horns and the guitar, and we'd have . . . a complete thirty-six pieces, from the drum to the piano." So when Moore acted on his telephone call with Handy by inviting Patton to the band's upcoming gig in Beulah, he learned that Patton enjoyed listening to Handy's band, or at least to its guitarist. "Charlie Patton said, 'I hear-ed that band playin' at the depot goin' back to Memphis,'" remembered Moore. "He said, 'Now that fella (the guitarist) played long to suit *me*.'"

Moore said that on a different occasion, he offered him a similar position with another band—"He'd a-got about five dollars out of it"—but Patton turned him down because he knew he would have to read sheet music. "He said he couldn't play nohow 'cause he couldn't read that music from that sheet," Moore recalled. "If you don't understand that, well that's the job. He just said he couldn't play that."

It was probably just as well that Patton didn't play in organized bands, for his kind of blues was incompatible with genteel arrangements like Handy's. Mississippi blues as played in barrelhouses and frolics was a performance music whose dance rhythms were difficult to notate to paper. Handy emphasized rather the vocal melody, to the extent of gaucheness if need be, if that was what his mainstream audience wanted—and that it did. Patton considered himself as excluded from the professional bands because of his musical illiteracy. He also felt that his inability to play an instrument other than a guitar kept him out. Once he ruefully told Moore of his unsuccessful attempts to master the violin. "He said if he could ever learn to play a lead violin, he'd a played with Handy."

If Patton doubted about being hired for an orchestra, at least he devoted his talents to a blues career in which people paid to hear him. H. C. Speir once said of him and Tommy Johnson, "Their blues-singing was brought about, more or less, (by) being poor, and neither one of them didn't love work any too well. If they could drum up something to make somebody listen to them, singing blues would make money, understand."

In his lyrics, Patton presented himself as a mere musician who wandered where the barrelhouse dollars were. On one of his records he sang a reference to the eagles on American coins:

Eagle been here, built a nest an' gone,
Eagle been here, built a nest an' gone,
An' you know by that I ain't gonna be here long.
("Circle Round The Moon," 1929)

"Clowning" was his means of attracting the most listeners and hence the most money. Son House knew that Patton played "for fun and money," but even so he thought that such pandering was demeaning. One time he chided Patton about it. The seasoned musician replied by saying, "Oh man, all I want to do is get paid for it, what's the difference?"

House recalled answering him with "Yeah, but it just sounds so foolish."

"What's the difference, man?" Patton repeated.

If Patton could hear the suggestion made today that the blues may be played for inner satisfaction, he would probably be insulted. During his lifetime, the blues was disreputable, and its singers were thought to be worthless. As Elizabeth Moore reminded the authors, "When I come along, you know, they called 'em 'jukehouse people,' or otherwise they just didn't like 'em. Them there Saturday night folks, good people don't be out with 'em; that's a bad class of people, bad *type* of people . . . bad *character*." If money was the only socially acceptable reason for pursuing a debased trade like playing the blues, then only by becoming a star-quality musician could Patton have earned what social and even family respect that he had. Patton's sister Viola told the story about their father initially discouraging his son's musical efforts with a bullwhip, but later relenting and eventually buying him a guitar. This anecdote may be taken to mean that Bill Patton was impressed by Charlie's earnings as a blues singer.[15]

Yet blues-playing removed young Charlie from his father's cotton patch that everyone in the Patton household would have been expected to cultivate. That much was true a generation later for Robert Johnson (1911-1938), whose situation his former neighbor Elizabeth Moore remembered. "His mama and them was farmin' out there on the place where we was. Stepfather would give him a beatin', you know, make him work. He'd tell him to go out there and work. Well, he'd [Robert Johnson] get that old guitar, and go on off somewhere else. Well, next day the old man would see him, you know, [and say] 'I told you to work. How come you didn't do that like I told you? Son, you can't walk the road. You got to help me work.'

"Well, he [Johnson] didn't *wanna* work. He didn't have that on his mind. And he tell me or anybody else, he say, 'I don't wanna work. I'm tryin' to learn how to make my livin' *without* pickin' cotton.' He say, 'An' I got this here guitar music on my mind and that's what I wanna learn.'

"The old man would beat him. Every time he'd beat him, he'd run off. He'd get him a pretty good-size stick and a switch, all mixed together; he'd give him a good beatin' up. Well, he'd be gone two or three weeks 'fore the old lady would see him again."

Avoiding manual labor was a strong incentive for Patton to improve his musical skills so that he could make a living at blues. "Charlie hated work like God hates sin," Son House remarks. "He just natural-born hated it. It didn't look right to him." On his 1930 record "Rattlesnake Blues," Patton thumbed his nose at labor by singing, "I ain't gonna have no job mama, rollin' through this world." He also put himself above his hardworking neighbors. "Charlie called himself 'smart' 'cause he didn't like to work," House recalled.

Joe Dockery seemed to agree. "If he was smart enough to be a musician," he said to the authors, "he was probably smart enough to get by (on the family plantation) without workin'." David Edwards knew Patton from the 1930s, and he saw for himself how the older musician "got by" with the white landowners. "Now Charlie Patton had a pretty good mind of his own. He lived on the plantation but he didn't do too much work: he stayed 'in' with the boss. He worked a little to stay there, but when he start to recordin', the boss give him a break."

There were times when Patton presented himself as a farmer turned recording artist. Jackson bluesman Ishman Bracey was led to think so. "He farmed. When he *did* farm. After he started puttin' out records, he didn't have time, 'cause he's goin' from town to town. After he started recording, he didn't farm any more. Mighty little."

Of all of Patton's associates, only Richard Harney claimed that Patton was a serious laborer. "He worked mostly at the farm mostly all the time," Harney insisted. "He didn't do much playin'. No! I'm tellin' you what I know, lotta folks don't think and don't believe it—that fella do nothin' but workin' on them farms. Fool wasn't gettin' nothin' out of it—no money . . . "

But no one really knew when and where Patton picked cotton instead of a guitar. His nephew Tom Cannon said, "He picked cotton long in the fall, but long in the former part of the year he'd be here and yonder. He never did settle down for no farmin'." The cotton picker was the bottom rung of the plantation ladder. He was hired by the day, was paid according to how many hundredweights of cotton he picked, and received no food. Sara Garrett knew Patton at Dockery's from her arrival there in 1918 until Patton's expulsion from the plantation eleven years later. In the 1960s she stated to the authors that he never tilled his own crop. "That was his 'thing,' to play music, you know. He would work, but he wasn't steady." She went to explain, "You know some people have different talent; they have to go 'to' that talent, they can't go over and they can't go under. And that's what Charlie was. He was just a kind of sport-like guitar player."

Patton likewise impressed Ernest Brown as a "high sport." On one of his records, "It Won't Be Long," Patton portrayed a "sporting" involvement with a prostitute who made the rounds of sawmill barrelhouses in West Memphis, Arkansas known as "Minglewood":

I believe sweet mama, sure was "kind" to me, baby
I believe sweet mama, sure was "kind" to me, baby
She is up at night, like a police on his beat

Using the same metaphor, the barrelhouse pianist Cow Cow Davenport sang:

They got some 'bad'-lookin' girls on the street
Them gals get a-plenty a money and
Walk the street like a police on his beat.

(Cow Cow Davenport, "That's The Kind
Of Girl I'm Lookin' For," 1930)

Ernest Brown stated bluntly his impression of Patton. "He was just a loafer. Just a loafin' musicianer."

As a budding musicianer, this young loafer moved about during a plantation boom, which meant that he stood to make some real money by performing. But this boom also meant that planters like Will Dockery had difficulty finding and keeping good labor. The Mississippi economy of the 1900s was described by this observer: "During the five years from 1903 to 1907 there was a phenomenal demand for cotton hands, and planters were eager to get anybody that looked like work . . . hence the Negro had the agreeable sensation of seeing people compete for him."[16] This boom ended with the financial panic of 1907 that lowered cotton and timber prices. However, when the boll weevil struck the Delta in 1908, infesting Sunflower County two years later, it inflicted surprisingly little damage. According to one historian, "The Yazoo Delta's favorable dew moisture, vegetation, and soil conditions . . . endowed Delta lands with an inherent resiliency to the boll weevil."[17] Perhaps for that reason, in Patton's "Mississippi Bo Weavil Blues" (recorded in 1929, but may date sometime in 1908-1910), he depicted the insect as waggish instead of destructive, making the rounds like a blues singer:

Bo weevil left Texas, Lord, he bid me "Fare thee well," Lordie!
(spoken: Where you goin' now?)
"I'm goin' down the Mississippi, gonna give Louisiana hell," Lordie!

The gradual spread of the boll weevil from Texas to the other Southern states may have encouraged this lyrical geography lesson. Yet in truth, the insect was a seasonal migrant who liked to stay within a single field,[18] not the roustabout of Patton's portrayal.

Patton's 1929-1930 recordings suggest that, as a developing musician some twenty years earlier, he often performed alone. His idiosyncratic musical structures and his tendency to mix phrasing patterns while performing a song stamp his pieces as developed by one performer for himself. Had Patton worked early on with duet partners, his accompaniments would have been less elaborate and his instrumental timing more consistent. Furthermore, if he had regular duet partners, he would not have developed his penchant for fast tempos as heard in his solo recordings of "Screamin' And Hollerin' the Blues," "Pony Blues,"

"Down The Dirt Road Blues," and "Mississippi Bo Weavil Blues." Even his most celebrated playing partner of later years, Willie Brown (I), once complained to Willie Moore that Patton's fast-paced music demanded too much effort to accompany. "He say when he played with Charlie Patton, Patton played too fast," reported Moore. "[Brown said] Charlie Patton was a good player, but he played too fast, so that'd work you."

That Willie Brown, nicknamed "Little Bill" because of his short size, was among three early associates of Patton to make records, and he was the only one of them who seems to have actually played with him to a great extent. A Patton protégé of sorts, he was nearly ten years Patton's junior and hence too young in 1905-1906 to have taken part in Patton's earliest musical development. Raised on Peerman's plantation near Cleveland, Brown left Sunflower County for northern Mississippi by 1916, settling in the vicinity of Robinsonville. "They stuck together more at Robinsonville than anywhere I knowed," Ernest Brown said of Patton and Brown. They would make records together in 1930.

The fiddler Henry "Son" Sims was another Patton contemporary who may be heard on records. He was raised on Doctor Hall's plantation near Renova, the all-black community three miles north of Cleveland. "They was just about raised up down there together," Sims' sister Roberta Jameson said of the pair. She recalled how Patton would "be wakin' up the folks, playin' that music " late at night in Renova, but adding, "They sure would get up to hear him, though." Yet she didn't remember his ever playing with her brother Henry, who took up guitar as "a young boy" and developed his skills in solitude, perched alongside the local railroad tracks. "I'd hear him sit up many a night . . . just by himself; we'd laugh about it," she recalled. Sims was "about grown," she reported, when he began performing at Renova and Cleveland picnics and house parties with a guitar-playing cousin, Harry Miller, who later moved to Chicago and died there of poisoning. Once Sims took up the fiddle, he played the guitar much less, although he could still play a rendition of "Pony Blues." By 1910 he had moved "all out from Drew." After brief interludes of farming near the towns of Sunflower and Merigold, he settled permanently in Coahoma County. Nonetheless, in 1930 Patton found him and recruited him for a Paramount recording session.

The third 1910s associate who later made records, Tommy Johnson, was one of Mississippi's most imitated bluesmen. In 1928 for the Victor firm, he was the first musician to record some renditions of Patton's songs. Born on a farm west of Terry in the central Mississippi hills around 1896, Johnson learned "common chords" on the guitar from his brother Ledell, who had taken up the instrument in 1900. Tommy eloped with an older woman in 1914, settling in the lower Delta town of Rolling Fork. When he ran off, he didn't even own a guitar. Still, he got to perform often in Sunflower County, according to brother Ledell, playing music "from Rollin' Fork to Boyle, Cleveland, and Drew . . . all around there." Ledell remembered that when Tommy returned home two years later, "he done got pretty good" as he put it, and he was already playing all of the pieces that he would popularize throughout central Mississippi during the next forty years: his theme song "Big Road Blues," "Cool Drink of Water," "Bye Bye Blues," and "Maggie Campbell."

During his 1967 interview with the authors, Ledell thought that Tommy had learned these songs from Nathan "Dick" Bankston, a guitarist who lived near Drew and later moved to Memphis. But Bankston's own recollections seem to suggest that Johnson created "Big Road Blues" and "Cool Drink of Water," while deriving "Bye Bye Blues," and "Maggie Campbell" directly from Charlie Patton or indirectly by hearing Bankston's versions of Patton songs. As a seventeen year old, Bankston first met Johnson in 1914 in Drew, and he met him again seven years later when Johnson lived for a year on a plantation in the vicinity. During the entire time he knew Johnson, Bankston never heard him play "Maggie Campbell Blues" (the Johnson rendition of Patton's "Maggie") or "Bye Bye Blues" (his rendition of "Pony Blues"). During a 1960s interview, while listening to Johnson's 1928 recording of "Bye Bye Blues," he remarked, "That's me"—that is, he credited himself with developing the arrangement of Patton's song that Johnson was playing. Yet Bankston also declared that he neither taught Johnson the piece nor, to the best of his recollection, ever played it in his presence. Perhaps Johnson learned the song by ear from Bankston, but he never told Bankston so. Johnson, Bankston added, was already playing "Big Road Blues" and "Cool Drink Of Water" when he first arrived in Drew in 1914. He had also by then developed the falsetto yodel that was the most distinctive and influential aspect of his singing.

Bankston was Patton's only early imitator who lived long enough to speak to 1960s researchers; Brown had died in 1943, Johnson in 1956, and Sims in 1958. Born in 1897 near Crystal Springs, a town about eight miles south of Terry, he was christened "Nathan" but nicknamed "Dick" by his parents, and he used the names interchangeably. After his father's death in 1907, Bankston and his brother moved with their mother to Lombardy in Sunflower County, or "Lumbard" as he pronounced it. When her death in 1910 left them as orphans, the Bankston brothers moved to a plantation near Drew, which at the time had 278 residents.

Initially a fiddler like his brother, the thirteen-year old Bankston learned guitar from a resident of the plantation near Sumner owned by A. E. Jennings, who was one of Will Dockery's best friends. That musician's name was Willie Brown, but he should not be confused with the diminutive, like-named counterpart in Cleveland;[19] we will note him as Willie Brown (II). When Bankston met this Willie Brown in 1910, the latter was several years older, Bankston later thought, than Charlie Patton (therefore, about twenty five years old) and had a wife named Willie.

Bankston's first encounter with Charlie Patton happened shortly after he took up guitar. The Jennings resident Brown had been describing Patton as a skilled musician to him, and one evening Brown took the opportunity to point out the visiting musician. "I walked into one of the jukehouse somewhere but wheres, I don't know now, it's been so long," Bankston remembered over fifty years later. "Willie pointed him out to me, and Willie was playin' with him before I was."

From Bankston's sketchy memories, we learn chiefly that in 1910, Patton had a sizeable repertory and that he had already developed most of the front-line material that he would feature at his first recording session in 1929. Among these pieces were "Pony Blues," "Screamin' and Hollerin' The Blues," and "Mississippi Bo Weavil Blues." He was even then, in Bankston's words, a "clown from his heart" who would "throw his guitar back his head and everywhere" as he played, a feat he probably had to practice for some while before daring to do it in public. "I couldn't do that," Bankston said of Patton's stunt.

It was from Patton that Bankston learned "Pony Blues," his favorite of all of Patton's pieces and the basis of his own "Bye Bye Blues." Bankston's relatively homey approach to this material is indicated by its one-line title stanza and its unrhymed second verse, which Tommy Johnson's recording preserved:

Bye an' bye, baby bye an' bye
It's bye an' bye, baby won't you bye an' bye?

The Good Book tell you: "Reap just what you sow."
Don't reap it now, baby reap it, bye an' bye.

Between 1910 and 1920, there were many bluesmen performing in and around Drew. Some of these musicians were visitors like Johnson, others were natives like the guitarist Jim Halloway and the fiddler Skeeter Davis. Most of them appear to have been amateurs, or they were at least locals with few if any musical ambitions. "Wasn't nobody up there singin' more [pieces] than my brother," remarked Ledell Johnson about Tommy, who if anything seemed to have made do with perhaps three or four songs,[20] two of them adaptations of Patton songs, as noted previously. Of Patton's songs, Bankston learned only "Pony Blues," but he knew no Tommy Johnson pieces because as he claimed later, "I never did play with Tommy none." The links of influence between Patton, Johnson, and Bankston are thus fleeting and tenuous, and so from the relations among these three men, there is little reason to suppose that any of the musicians who congregated around Drew during the 1910s followed either a regional or collective approach to music.[21]

By World War I, Willie Brown (II) moved east of Dockery's to the Jim Yeager plantation near Drew, taking as wife a female guitarist from Crystal Springs named Josie Gardener. "Him and Charlie traveled around some every which a-way, played a long time together," Tom Cannon reported. Unlike his smaller, like-named counterpart "Little Bill" Brown (I) of Cleveland who worked as Patton's silent accompanist, this Willie Brown (II) "liked to sing himself," reported Josie Johnson. Of his voice, Sara Garrett remarked, "He could sing very good, but not like Charlie." As a performer, Tom Cannon noted, "He could show off good, but not like Charlie."

Although Willie Brown (II) never recorded before his death in Memphis sometime in the 1940s, a few things about his music may be inferred from other musicians' recordings. Listening to the guitar accompaniment of "Little Bill" Brown's (I) 1930 Paramount recording "Future Blues," Bankston remarked, "That doesn't sound like Willie" (II). It would seem then that Willie Brown (II) did not play a version of Patton's "Maggie," particularly as Bankston also likened Tommy Johnson's "Maggie Campbell Blues" to Patton's style. Since Bankston developed "Pony Blues" by listening to Patton, it would seem that the rendition recorded by Brown (I) may have been similarly derivative. "Future Blues" is slower and more sedate than Patton's "Maggie"-based blues, and it is played much in the fashion of Kid Bailey's 1929 recording "Rowdy Blues," which also uses "Maggie." When he heard the Kid Bailey record, Bankston noted, "Me and [big] Willie Brown (II) both played it [in that style]." Ledell

Johnson's wife Mary said of the same record, "Will Brown (II)—it sounds just like him—that's the same way he played. I believe, it *is* him. If he named 'Kid Bailey,' I'm tellin' you, he learnt right from Willie—he sure did!"

Although he was highly regarded in Drew, Willie Brown (II) posed no threat to Patton's general popularity. "Charlie was known throughout this country, more than Willie was," Sara Garrett noted. "He just go along with Charlie and play, you know. The best musician was Charlie, he was better all the way: a singer and a guitar player, too."

How Kid Bailey and Tommy Johnson treated on records some of Patton's songs puts into perspective the local standards of playing the blues, especially when played by Willie Brown (II) and Bankston. Bailey's "Rowdy Blues" may be heard as a typical local rendition of "Pony Blues," but compared to Patton's 1929 record, Bailey seems to be playing by rote. On "Rowdy Blues," Bailey's guitar tone seems bland, and his accompaniment is so spare and sketchy that sometimes it seems subordinate to his second guitarist playing the bass fills. The melody is phrased as a stereotyped twelve-bar blues, squeezing the "Pony Blues" model within the "ten/six" phrasing pattern. The three vocal lines that Baley uses are all but interchangeable, particularly as the same tune fragment (involving a dominant, major sixth, and minor third) appears twice within each lyric phrase. Moreover, Bailey uses identical dynamics in singing each phrase: he boosts his volume at each instance of the major 6th scale step E (in the first vocal chorus [Ex. 34], these instances occur on the syllables "mar," "set," "right," and "this"). These aspects give "Rowdy Blues" a regular sing-song quality. As a singer, Bailey keeps his delivery simple. Whereas Patton's delivery of "Pony Blues" uses seven notes within the span of an octave, Bailey's has four notes within the overall interval of a sixth. Finally, Bailey and his second guitarist play less intricate rhythms than Patton accompanying himself.

Tommy Johnson's adaptations of Patton's material are on the same level of "Rowdy Blues," a circumstance that his rich baritone voice tends to disguise. His 1928 Victor recording of "Bye Bye Blues" is an eleven-bar arrangement of "Pony Blues."[22] During his performance, Johnson performs to a 1-2 square-dance rhythm, which may explain why it seems odd, perhaps amateurish, that he emphasizes some of his vocal syllables on the weak off-beats.[23]

Moreover, Johnson doesn't vary his guitar accompaniment, confining his picking to the top two strings, even though he was working in tandem with Charlie McCoy. The second halves of the last two vocal phrases in each

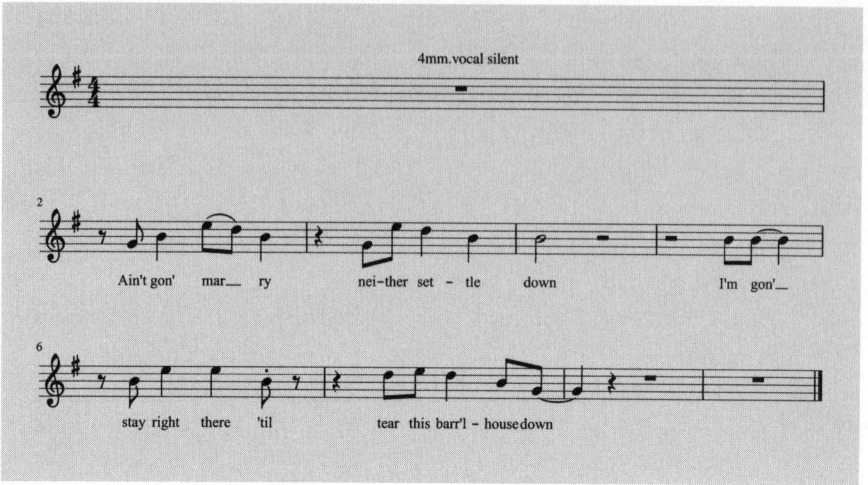


Ex. 34: Kid Bailey, "Rowdy Blues" (1929), chorus 1, vocal melody (Bailey is silent during mm. 1-4) [0:00-0:30].

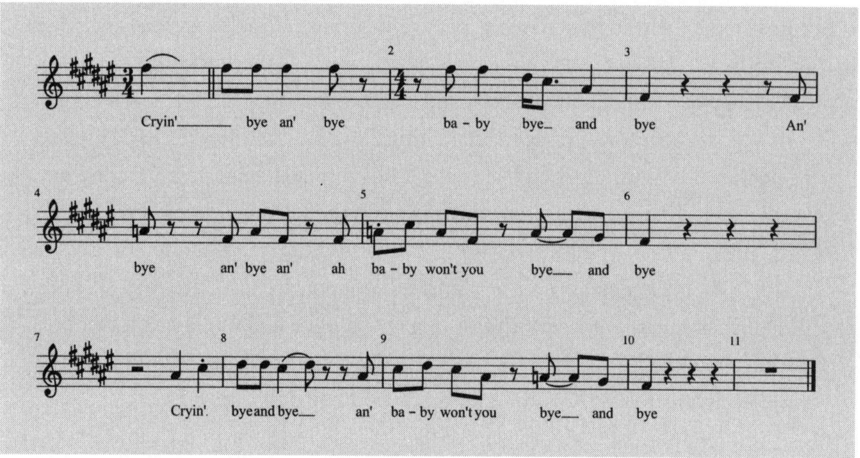


Ex. 35: Tommy Johnson, "Bye Bye Blues" (1928), chorus 1, vocal melody [0:30-0:59].

chorus (in Ex. 35, see m.5 beats 3- 4-m.6 beat 1, and m. 9 beats 3-4—m.10) are melodically and rhythmically identical, resulting in the same sing-song effect of Bailey's rendition. Likewise, Johnson's vocal melody is less rounded than that of the opening chorus of Patton's "Pony Blues." While Patton began his tune by ascending from the tonic through the major 3rd to the major sixth scale tone (see. Ex. 25), Johnson began his treatment by singing immediately at the octave above his tonic. Furthermore, in their respective treatments of the "Pony Blues" melody, Johnson and Bailey can only approximate, but not successfully imitate, the ascending melodic motions of Patton's phrases.[24] It may be possible that on "Bye Bye Blues," Johnson may have been imitating not Charlie Patton, but instead Dick Bankston's imitations of Charlie Patton.

Johnson's transformation of "Maggie" into "Maggie Campbell Blues" resulted in a less resourceful arrangement than Patton's 1929 recorded treatment of that theme as "Screamin' and Hollerin' the Blues." While in the first chorus Johnson is already toying with the vocal melody, ending his first lyric phrase on a minor third and the second phrase on a major sixth, nonetheless he treats the tune as a fixed vocal, venturing none of Patton's variations heard on "Screamin' And Hollerin." The rhythmic banality of Johnson's accompaniment is indicated by its repetition of accenting patterns. For example, the IV chord of the second vocal phrase is accented identically during two measures (where Patton's is not). Also, an eighth-note bass figure (Ex. 36) that is played during Johnson's opening phrase of his first chorus is repeated both in the final vocal measure of that chorus and in the instrumental measure that follows it.

Ex. 36: Tommy Johnson, "Maggie Campbell Blues" (1928), chorus 1, eighth-note guitar figure [0:33-0:36].

So, what distinguishes Patton from musicians like Bailey and Johnson is that the latter two were content to work in terms of rote formulas. Their recorded versions of Patton's songs have a predictability that makes it easy for house frolickers to dance to. But in his audiences, Patton had listeners among the dancers. So he had to play and sing some music to listen to.

"He wanted it set up right."

—BOOKER MILLER ON PATTON'S ATTITUDE TOWARD MUSIC.

*Chapter 7*

# THE ART OF CHARLIE PATTON (1910s–1920s)

Before the 1910s, the Mississippi blues musician appears to have been a semi-anonymous figure: entertaining, but certainly not attracting a following. Ernest Brown said of the Sunflower County bluesmen of his (and Patton's) youth: "There'd be in them times guitar-pickers . . . they wouldn't hardly ever hire (just one). One would play a while; another [would] play a while, an' they just . . . got (paid) a little drink o' whisky. Wasn't nothin' to it." Patton, on the other hand, gathered "people just clownin' all over him; they'd follow everywhere they heard tell of where Patton was."

By becoming the Delta's first blues celebrity, Patton could impose his own repertory upon an audience that, until then, treated and paid performers strictly as request musicians. As Booker Miller recalled, "We'd play whatever the people request. We'd go out and play for a dance, [and] they'd say, 'play something,' 'play this,' 'play that!' Well, see, you're out there for the public, mostly you're requested, see?"

Miller also remembered that even when Patton was at the peak of his popularity in the late 1920s, his audience's tastes ran to three of his tunes: "Pony Blues," "Down The Dirt Road Blues," and "High Water Everywhere." In addition, his "Banty Rooster Blues" and "A Spoonful Blues" were popular. Patton played these songs repeatedly in versions that often lasted, Son House said, "at least ten minutes or better." Whatever else he played in public were filler pieces, or brand-new songs that were either short-lived successes or outright flops.

To cultivate an audience, Patton developed two styles of entertaining, one for day, the other for night. The daytime style was street-singing to promote his next performances at barrelhouses and house frolics to Saturday shoppers. Mandy Whigham remembered seeing Patton work in this capacity, saying years later to the authors that most blues performers sang on the streets only a few songs at a time to let people "know what they could do." Ever the exception, however, Patton was a flamboyant show-off, for as Ernest Brown noted, "he do most of his clownin' with a guitar on a Saturday on the streets, 'cause the people would give him money just to see him clown."

Some of Patton's entertaining stunts were aural rather than visual. "He had the guitar 'sayin' it's prayers' and all that kinda stuff," Frank Howard reported, "say the Lord's Prayer."[1]

His other style, when playing a night dance for eight hours or more, was more boisterous yet less frivolous. The style of "hard blues" for which Booker Miller remembered him emphasized "hard" as defined as "tough, indomitable, given to, or characterized by, violence."[2] His performances were infused with brutality and agitation. When Patton was hitting his guitar, Ernest Brown reported, he would often quip, "This is the way I beat my woman!"

But for the most part, Patton expressed his "hard" blues by playing driving music. According to Willie Moore, he rarely spoke between songs. But whenever he was drinking whiskey during a dance gig, he would then begin to clown. "When he got to drinkin', that's when he'd start to clown," Ernest Brown said.

Whether or not his antics got in the way of his music is a matter of opinion. "Charlie Patton could *play*, but at times he done more clownin' than he did playin'," Brown remarked. Booker Miller was bothered less than Brown about Patton's showmanship. "Talkin' about comical, yes he was, and I liked it, too," he said, adding "When it come down to that, you couldn't beat Charlie."

The foundation of Patton's music and hence his livelihood was his ability to furnish a dance beat. What mattered most were his accenting patterns. Counting for much less were the melodies, phrasing patterns, lyrics, chords, and intervals of his particular songs.[3] His audiences usually didn't care what music he played as long as they could feel (if not hear) and dance to his beats.

"They're for dancin', those blues we were playin' back in them days," Booker Miller reported. "You had to put them in a time when they could dance."

When Patton began his career in the mid-to late 1900s, southern African American dance was still mostly in the 1-2-3-4 pulse, such as what Dick Bankston used for his adaptation of "Pony Blues." This pulse had been used for black square dancing, where it entered from white rural music. It was basic to the recorded music of Henry Thomas ("Ragtime Texas"),[4] a Texas dance musician born in 1874, and it was the beat scheme prevailing in spirituals and in such secular rag ditties as "Careless Love," "Make Me A Pallet On The Floor," ""Stack O'Lee," "Nobody's Business," and "Come On Around To My House, Mama." It was also the beat of non-generic tunes like "Drunken Spree," (a piece Skip James heard between 1907-1909), and of such seemingly early blues as "Old Devil" (Bo Carter's version of the shimmy-she-wobble dance, played at Bolton, Mississippi in 1907), and "That's No Way To Get Along" (a tune that Robert Wilkins of Hernando, Mississippi began featuring around 1912).

Patton appears to have been one of the first, or in the first generation of, guitarists to buck the square-dance trend, change the emphases among the dance beats, and make the 1-2-3-4 pulse a basic component of his music. On his records, virtually all of his secular blues and songs are based on it. He was also skilled at converting existing music from 1-2 to a 1-2 beat,[5] such as "A Spoonful Blues" and the spirituals "Jesus Is A Dyin' Bed-maker" and "You're Gonna Need Somebody When You Die."

Patton's shift from the 1-2 to 1-2 beat may be regarded as revolutionary in dance rhythm. How confusing and difficult this 1-2 beat scheme was for some dance guitarists may be suggested by Frank Stokes' 1927 rendition of "Mr. Crump Don't Like It." Stokes (1888-1955) was a songster who lived and performed in Memphis and recorded for Paramount and Victor in 1927-1929. His "Mr. Crump Don't Like It" is a version of W. C. Handy's composition "Memphis Blues" (1912), which in turn took its sixteen-bar pattern and basic melodic scheme (AABA) from spirituals or "Careless Love." On that record, Stokes and his second guitarist Dan Sane begin with a sixteen-bar instrumental opening with a *1*-2 beat. But when Stokes sings the melody to a 1-2 dance pattern, only one guitarist—likely Sane—is heard playing. Apparently Stokes couldn't adjust his guitar-strumming to match his singing.

The 1-2 pattern enabled Patton to use his many rhythmic gifts, and it has made his music still agreeable for modern listening. Had he favored another beat scheme like the square-dance pattern, to our ears today his music would lack its percussive impact. Of course, the 1-2 pattern is used in Latin dance music including samba and salsa. But the 1-2 pattern has since endured in American music, first through ragtime music, then 1920s stride, later as the basic beat of the 1930s' swing music, and since 1945 it has frequently reappeared in American popular music including rock.

How this 1-2 beat scheme came about remains conjectural. Early nineteenth-century minstrel songs like "Turkey In The Straw" toyed with syncopation for two or four measures. Full-blown syncopated songs were unknown in popular music until the mid-1890s, when a vaudevillian from Louisville named Ben Harney scored successes with "You've Been A Good Old Wagon But You've Done Broke Down" and "Mister Johnson" ( "Turn Me Loose"). However, neither of these two songs were dance tunes, and they seem to have had little effect on popular music. Even during the ragtime era, fully syncopated songs remained a novelty. Only three black vocal tunes before 1910 used the 1-2 pattern: "Poor Boy/My Bucket's Got A Hole In It," the medley that Gus Cannon learned in Clarksdale at the turn of the century; "Hesitation Blues," which Leadbelly dated to around 1907; and "Alabama Bound," an eight-bar ditty that Jelly Roll Morton claimed to have written in 1905 and which was first copyrighted in 1909 by Robert Hoffman of New Orleans, who presented it as a piano instrumental theme and labeled it a "Ragtime Two Step." While each of these three songs were shared and performed by musicians through the 1920s, no one of them could be said to have had a transformative impact on black music.

During Patton's lifetime, dance music played a much smaller role in mainstream American popular music than it would do in the decades after his death. Vocal dance music was virtually nonexistent in the realm of white music, whose conventional dance music of the 1920s used a ponderous 1-2-3-4 beat. The vocal dance music Patton performed with the 1-2 beat lay so far afield from the mainstream dance music of its time that even his later discoverer H. C. Speir was unaware that he and other blues singers intended and arranged their songs for dancing. Speir's opinion was that "you can't hardly dance by old Negro Delta blues."

Of the 40 or so secular titles Patton recorded, only three were not expressly designed for dance presentation. "Mean Black Cat Blues" had a slow tempo and more emphasis than usual on lyrics, and for these reasons the song may have been created by Patton on the spot in the recording studio. "Poor Me" was a simple rendition of a vaudeville song titled "Cryin' Blues" recorded previously by Hound Head Henry. "Frankie and Albert" was a 12-measure "blues-ballad" song from the turn of the century that Patton sang with a dance beat but he accompanied with a light touch on his guitar. If the lack of vocal and instrumental variation in these three performances are any indication, Patton may have played these songs only rarely.

Dance music was so fundamental to Patton's style that he even arranged his spirituals with a heavy 1-2 dance beat. His rousing double-time rendition of "I Shall Not Be Moved" may be more danceable than most secular music using the same beat scheme. Either Patton played sacred music for "sanctified" gatherings where dancing was allowed, or he was so immersed in the dance idiom that nearly everything he played simply became dance music.

Whether Patton categorized his live repertory in his head isn't known, as he had not said anything about it to Booker Miller, Son House, Willie Moore, or anyone else who performed with him. But if he had, he may have grouped his material according to the various dances, rather than giving labels like "blues" or "rag" or "breakdown" which describe their phrasing patterns of intervals. The slow tunes he occasionally performed were all meant for the slow-drag dance. Material like "Rattlesnake Blues" and "Joe Kirby" that he performed at a medium tempo like were for the shimmy and the one-step. The one-step was also known as the "turkey trot," and it was in vogue nationwide between 1910 and 1915 when it was associated with Tin Pan Alley's treatments of "ragtime" songs. The Delta version of the one-step dance alternated forward and backward steps. The uptempo music that Patton performed frequently was for the shimmy and the two-step. What made the two-step different from the one-step was that it alternated two forward steps with two backward steps. The Delta version of the two-step was probably derived from the white two-step, which had become popular when John Philip Sousa's "Washington Post March" became a hit in 1889.

These dances shaped the entire character of Patton's music, to the extent that their steps determined his accenting patterns while singing, even if it meant that his diction was altered to the point of making his lyrics barely intelligible. To make his lyrics scan according to a 1-2 pattern, he would often smother syllables or stress inessential words ("Hitch *up* my pony," "Jackson *on* a high hill," "Just like *a* rattlesnake," "Way down *in* Lula" "Green *Riv*er"), and inessential syllables ("Hello Cen*tral*"), as well as add syllables ("ri/ider" in "Pea Vine") to words. His willingness to maintain an accent pattern during a song, even if clear diction was to be sacrificed, exceeded that of any other Mississippi dance singer, and yet it also contributed to the success of his songs as dance pieces.

The quality of Patton's lyrics was limited by his dance musicianship, because the dancers in his audience cared more about the beats than about the words of his songs. Son House said as much about Delta pianist Louise Johnson. "She'd say anything just so it's something for the guys to dance off and do the old two-step. [It] didn't make no difference to them what she was saying. All they want to hear: the music." For his part, Patton seems to have devised songs with only a memorable opening stanza, or to have sustained a lyrical concept for two initial stanzas, as if assuming that his audience was unlikely to listen to his lyrics for very long.

Like other blues musicians of his era, Patton established his dance accenting patterns with his voice, stressing beats by sudden increases of volume. This approach gives his music an old-fashioned sound. In modern dance music, a singer has more freedom because a band rhythm section bears the burden of establishing accents. Patton's use of rudimentary rhythmic tools imparted a staccato delivery to his singing and required him to establish a loud volume, yet leaving enough for him to raise and lower his voice for dramatic effects.

As a dance blues singer, Patton had no peer. His skill in using his voice as a percussion instrument is such that he makes every accented beat firmly felt; even when he accelerates in tempo, he never blurs an accent. Blues singers like Walter Rhodes who lacked Patton's vocal strength had to sing at higher levels than were comfortable for them in order to make themselves audible to audiences. Because they were extending their voices upward, the words on the beats they stressed lacked distinct articulation.

Yet the most impressive aspect of Patton's artistry as a singer isn't his raw power, but his varied delivery. Other Mississippi singers like Skip James on "Cypress Grove Blues" (1931) or Booker White on "Shake 'Em On Down" (1937) can seem rather tedious because they sing mostly at two volume levels, one for stressed beats and one for unstressed beats. But Patton, within even the restrictions of a recording studio, provides enough variety of attack and dynamic fluidity to make his sound engage the ear and guide the feet.

But Patton's reliance on dance rhythm patterns crimped his expressiveness as a singer. In the first two vocal phrases of "Circle Round The Moon," for example, Patton has the fiddler Henry "Son" Sims assisting him in the accompaniment, and so uncharacteristically he sings without regard to an accenting pattern. He thus achieves a much freer dynamic pattern and more varied vocal attack than he attained on "Green River Blues," which he performed alone and whose melody he sang to a strict accenting pattern.

On his records, Patton used two basic accenting schemes. One was the 1-2 modern dance pattern for a great variety of pieces played at different tempos to different phrasing patterns:

Songs to the 1-2-3-4-1-2-3-4 modern dance pattern

A. Secular Songs

1. "Mississippi Bo Weavil Blues"
2. "Banty Rooster Blues"
3. "It Won't Be Long"
4. "A Spoonful Blues"
5. "Pea Vine Blues"
6. "Tom Rushen Blues"
7. "Going To Move to Alabama"
8. "Green River Blues"
9. "Jim Lee Blues" (Parts One and Two)
10. "High Water Everywhere" (Part One)
11. "Elder Green Blues"
12. "Heart Like Railroad Steel"
13. "Mean Black Moan"
14. "Hammer Blues"
15. "Frankie And Albert"
16. "Dry Well Blues"

B. Spirituals

1. "I'm Goin' Home"
2. "Lord I'm Discouraged"
3. "Jesus Is A Dying Bed-Maker"
4. "You Gonna Need Somebody When You Die"
5. "Troubled About My Mother"

This 1-2 pattern remained current through the 1920s, and it may be heard on such records as Papa Charlie Jackson's 1925 "Shake That Thing" (the first blues dance hit) and Hambone Willie Newbern's "Roll and Tumble Blues." The structure of the 12-measure blues lent itself favorably to the 1-2 pattern, which emphasized the final beat of a standard ten-beat blues vocal phrase, and the fourth beat and sixth beats of the ensuing instrumental riff, which invariably was set to the tonic chord. However, the 1-2 pattern was a demanding pulse to sustain because of the dynamic level increasing during the first two beats of a measure. A small-voiced singer like Papa Charlie Jackson trying this scheme could fade in volume during a measure, weakening the accented fourth enough to give his performances a 1-2-3-4 feel. By contrast, Patton's singing of this pattern is so forceful that his songs often sound as if they are in 2/4 time.

The other basic accenting scheme is an adjustment of the 1-2 pattern in which the second beat is noticeably weakened. This is the result of Patton sustaining notes too long to convey an uninterrupted 1-2 accenting scheme. By holding notes on the fourth or sixth beat, he weakens the sixth or eighth beat of a ten-beat vocal phrase; other songs declaimed with a shouted delivery like "Moon Going Down" and "Bird Nest Bound" contain examples of silent sixth beats. It is notable that "Pony Blues," "Screamin' and Hollerin' the Blues" and "Down The Dirt Road Blues" contain Patton's most percussively ambitious instrumentation, which likely came by the necessity of compensating for the lack of accent during some vocal phrases (as noted in chapter 5).

Songs to the adjusted modern dance pattern 1-2-3-4-1-2-3-4 (or 1-2-3-4-1-rest-3-4):

1. "Screamin' And Hollerin' The Blues"
2. "Down The Dirt Road Blues"
3. "Pony Blues"
4. "When Your Way Gets Dark/Magnolia Blues"
5. "Circle Round The Moon"
6. "Rattlesnake Blues"
7. "Devil Sent the Rain Blues"
8. "Joe Kirby"
9. "Mean Black Cat Blues"
10. "Moon Going Down"
11. "Bird Nest Bound"
12. "Stone Pony Blues"
13. "34 Blues"
14. "Revenue Man Blues"
15. "Jersey Bull Blues"

16. "Love My Stuff"
17. "Poor Me"

Although nearly as numerous than his straightforward 1-2 tunes, these 17 records are based on merely six different vocal themes. Six of them ("Screamin' And Hollerin' The Blues," "Moon Going Down," "Bird Nest Bound," "Revenue Man Blues," "Jersey Bull Blues" and "Love My Stuff") are arrangements of "Maggie," and two others ("Joe Kirby" and "Devil Sent The Rain") are based on the vocal part of "Maggie." Two songs ("Rattlesnake Blues" and "Stone Pony Blues") are versions of "Pony Blues," and the remaining song ("34 Blues") is a remake of "Down the Dirt Road Blues."

Three other accenting schemes that Patton used may be regarded as peripheral:

1-2-3-4 (accenting only the first beat of a measure)

1. "Shake And Break It"

Although a few blues musicians used this scheme in rendering blues material, Patton applied it to this one song, which was an embellished "breakdown" that lent itself well to this pattern because its instrumental accompaniment changed chords at the beginning of each measure.

1-2-3-4 (accenting the first and third beats of a measure)

1. "Hold To God's Unchanging Hand"
   (appearing on "Prayer Of Death, Part Two")
2. "I Shall Not Be Moved"
3. "Hang It On The Wall"

Although Patton did use this square-dance pattern with great forcefulness, he generally avoided it. His only secular recording that had it was "Hang It On The Wall," a re-make of "Shake It And Break It" with more emphatic third beats.

1-2-3-4 (accenting only the second beat of a measure)

1. "Runnin' Wild Blues"
2. "Some Of These Days"
3. "Some Happy Day"
4. "Some Summer Day"
5. "Oh Death"

This pattern may be heard best in the early 1950s blues records by Howlin' Wolf. During Patton's lifetime, though, it was used for white one-step dancing. It was featured in the Mississippi Sheiks' "Sittin' On Top Of The World" (1930), a song for white presentation whose creator Walter Vinson categorized it as a one-step piece. Patton used "Sittin' On Top Of The World" as the basis of his 1930 record "Some Summer Day." The three other songs in this category ("Runnin' Wild Blues," "Some Of These Days" and "Some Happy Day") may be from white origins, all knit from single-measurement phrases.

Patton's vocal accenting also influenced his guitar playing. His guitar accompaniments served three functions. One was to amplify an accented vocal beat, another was to radiate a vocal accenting pattern during a musical "break." The third function was to strengthen a weak vocal beat, especially in the adjusted modern dance pattern (1-2) songs listed in group II above. The guitar fills that Patton inserted between his vocal phrases were often full strumming in order to achieve maximum volume. His picked single-string moments most frequently occur within the vocal line they accompany, except when he is using his bottleneck slide technique. With his guitar, Patton provides a continuous complementary beat of its own on only three recordings—the one-chord "Mississippi Bo Weavil Blues," "Shake It And Break It" (whose first chorus is instrumental) and "Runnin' Wild." None of these three songs are 12-measure blues. As for the blues songs he did record, their unwieldy phrasing all but precluded the use of continuous accompaniments.

Because he lived before the development of electrically amplified guitars, Patton had to feature his voice, not his playing on acoustic guitar. "I don't remember one song that he played instrumental, without vocals at all," Booker Miller said. In most places and with every crowd he attracted, an unamplified acoustic guitar work would not carry well enough to provide dance music. For example, the local house frolics that Skip James played in Bentonia, Mississippi often drew between thirty and fifty people, and they were held not indoors, but outdoors in a hosed-down dirt yard.[6] Memphis barrelhouses would attract between fifteen and seventy-five patrons.

As a dance musician, Patton played with great forcefulness; his plucked treble notes often had the power of strummed chords. The purely percussive nature of his guitar style is indicated by Booker Miller's reminiscence that Patton sometimes dispensed with accompaniment altogether at dances. "I see'd

Charlie got up and when the juice got high enough, I see him just thump his guitar—never touch a string—and they'd jump, man, they'd jump!"

Hayes McMullan also remembered this. "Patton played for dances like I did. There's plenty a' things we'd be playin' for a rest. 'Fore we'd get to playin', to get us started, sometimes we'd be pattin' on the box, you understand?"

What makes Patton a great artist is not his forcefulness in rendering blues dance music, but how he worked above and around the limits and conventions that other early Mississippi bluesmen followed. He is the only recorded blues dance musician who characteristically and deliberately brought elements of drama, surprise, spontaneity and subtly to his work.

More than his improvising peers, Patton thought like a composer and arranger. As noted in the previous chapter, how he combined the contrasting vocal and guitar rhythm patterns in "Pony Blues" and the various blues based on "Maggie" indicate the attention he paid to compositional aspects of his music. Likewise his use of small rhythmic motifs in such songs as "Down The Dirt Road Blues" and "It Won't Be Long." In "Down the Dirt Road Blues," he completes the guitar phrase that follows its first two vocal phrases with several beats of syncopated tonic chord strumming, including the off-beats (Ex. 37, m.4). He transfers this rhythm pattern to the IV chord (Ex. 37, m.5, at the first and second beats of that transcribed measure).

Ex. 37: Patton, "Down the Dirt Road Blues" (1929), ch. 1, mm. 4-5, guitar rhythm patterns [0:10-0:16].

With similar care, he treats another two-beat figure on "It Won't Be Long." This motif, involving two eighth-notes and a quarter-note, is played initially in ascending manner (fretted with a bottleneck on the top string) as successive minor thirds, doubling with the opening lyric phrase (Ex. 38a).

Ex.38a: Patton, "It Won't Be Long" (1929), ch. 1, m.1,
vocal and slide guitar doubling [0:01-0:05].

Ex. 38b: Patton, "It Won't Be Long" (1929), ch. 1, mm. 3-4 (excerpt),
guitar fill figure [0:09-0:12].

The ensuing instrumental fill reiterates this rhythm pattern with bass work, this time in descending manner involving a single minor third to the tonic (Ex.38b):

The subtlety of these manipulations, which as heard on the record may be more likely felt than noticed, may not be found in the pre-1940 recordings of other Mississippi dance blues.

Patton's sense of arrangement is further indicated by his various ways of dismantling or disrupting the standard "ten-six" phrasing pattern, which when overused can make a blues seem banal. He uses three techniques to buck this convention. This first of them could be called a "vocal overlay." It involves holding the final word on the tenth beat of a vocal phrase, so that it leads to the follow-up instrumentation, which then loses its tacked-on quality. While the instrumentation begins on the conventional eleventh beat, it is not anticipated because the vocal phrase appears unfinished when the instrumental fill begins. Patton applies this overlay technique most dramatically in "Pony Blues" (Ex. 39) and "Down The Dirt Road Blues." He uses it modestly in "Green River Blues" and "Banty Rooster Blues," and in "It Won't Be Long" the interpolated word "baby" supplies the extra beats. In singing the each of the stanza-ending phrases of "Jim Lee Blues," his vocal overlays may last for four beats and even six beats.

The second technique could be called a "guitar cut-in" technique.[7] This

Ex. 39: Technique 1: Vocal Overlay - Patton, "Pony Blues" (1929), ch. 1, mm. 3-4 [0:08-0:16].

involves beginning the phrase-ending instrumental fills a beat sooner so that it begins simultaneously with the last vocal beat (or, the final syllable of a vocal phrase). It too obscures the conventional separation between the blues vocal and follow-up guitar phrase to order to hide the tacked-on quality of most blues instrumentation. Patton uses the "cut-in" technique in the first two tenth beats, and lasts five beats, instead of the conventional measure. It also occurs in "It Won't Be Long," where a three-note bottleneck riff begins on the tenth beat, and in "Banty Rooster Blues," where three beats of open-string bass tonics are employed, the first beginning on the tenth beat.

The third way in which Patton breaches the ordinary blues vocal/instrumental barrier is simply by abolishing it, that is, by cutting short or "evicting"

Ex. 40: Technique 2: Guitar Cut-In - Patton, "It Won't Be Long" (1929), ch. 1, mm. 1-4, [0:01-0:13] vocal and fill only.

the vocal melody to make room for the instrumental fill. He may cut off immediately his vocal line with a guitar figure. Or, in another means of "eviction," he may continue playing a guitar figure that was accompanying a vocal phrase beyond the duration of the vocal, as when he played the descending bass riff of "Screamin' and Hollerin' the Blues" for another two or three measures after the vocal it accompanied. "Bird Nest Bound," a 1930 treatment of "Maggie," just about obliterates the conventional call-and-response blues vocal/guitar arrangement. Its first phrase ("Come on, mama . . . ") ends unexpectedly (Ex 41, in m. 2) when it is dislodged by a snapped single string guitar figure that has begun (or heard more prominently four beats previously (in m.1, beginning on beat 3). This guitar figure ends at the beginning of measure 3.

Ex. 41: Technique 3: Eviction - Patton, "Bird Nest Bound" (1930), ch. 1, mm. 1-2 [0:02-0:08].

In the second verse of the same song, he again ends or "evicts" the vocal, this time for a descending bass line that continues for two measures.

Patton applies this "eviction" technique to the second verse of "Pea Vine Blues," creating a two-measure instrumental fill that is virtually the same figure used on "Bird Nest Bound." The technique also occurs during the fourth verse of "Heart Like Railroad Steel," in which his vocal phrase is suddenly cut off at the beginning of the verse's second measure. An impromptu-sounding guitar figure Patton had launched early in measure 1 usurps the next three beats, thus seeming like a two-measure phrase. The same figure is then reiterated for three instrumental measures before Patton plays an I6 chord. He resumes singing, although nearly four measures behind schedule.

Patton appears to have been the only dance musician before 1942 who developed new phrasing patterns, instead of using existing ones by rote. He may have made these alterations to the blues vocal melody because he probably intuitively apprehended its two-part vocal-call/instrumental-response character as a cluster of six and four beats. He would have also recognized that his vocal and guitar component were parts of a single percussive continuum; serving the same functions, the vocal and guitar parts were practically interchangeable.

Most of his phrasing variations were departures from the standard blues phrase. A novel phrase pattern is inherent in the first chorus of "Magnolia Blues" [ Paramount matrix L-48-1].[8] This blues begins with a one-measure instrumental prelude based on a high-register tonic chord. Patton then sings "When your way gets dark, baby" during the first measure, plays a bottleneck-fretted riff in the second measure, speaks "Turn your lights up high" in the third measure, and repeats the guitar riff in the fourth. The second lyric phrase is handled in a similar manner. The result of these alternations is a tune that is almost a new species of blues: half instruments and half speech/song.

Ex. 42: Patton, "Magnolia Blues" [Paramount matrix L-48-1] (1930), ch. 1, mm.1-4 [0:00-0:15].

Another distinguishing aspect of Patton's arrangements was his ability to improvise guitar figures to be heard during his singing. His guitar accompaniments abound in such terse snippets, which meshed flawlessly with his singing. "I've seen him playin' that guitar an' that guitar sounds like it just talkin'," Ernest Brown recalled to Stephen LaVere. "Look like them strings sayin' what he said."

Patton's efforts to make his guitar-playing imitate his vocal accenting[9] gives an underlying unity to such diverse pieces as "Mississippi Bo Weevil Blues," "Shake It And Break It," "Elder Greene Blues," "Some Of These Days" and "Pony Blues," none of which have anything else in common as song types or resemble each other in terms of sound. When making his guitar appear to "talk," Patton does not resort to the easy way by having his singing match an existing prefabricated guitar figure. Rather, he does it in the harder way around, that is, by making his guitar-playing follow his varied vocal inflections. On his records, some of his figures seem completely impromptu. For example, during the second verse of "Joe Kirby," for example, while singing the last two words of the two-beat phrase "Kirby blues ain't bad," Patton begins to emulate his vocal accenting with a guitar roll on the top two strings. Apparently seeing an opportunity to expand this riff, he concludes the verse with a roll that that highlights the words "Joe Kirby." On his recording of the 8-measure choruses of "Elder Greene Blues," Patton concentrates on capturing the rhythmic nuances of the fifth and sixth bars—the second half of the vocal melody and the only measures of the piece that are sung consecutively. During the first few choruses on the record, whenever Patton begins this section, he sounds a little uncertain as to how to proceed with his guitar. By the sixth stanza, however, he follows his singing ("Lord and get sloppy drunk off a bottle in bond / And walk the streets all night") on guitar with rhythmic and melodic exactitude.

Patton's method of accompanying a song in this way would have required a great deal of advance preparation. While the resulting accompaniment could vary within a song, it could be so individualized that it could not be applied to other songs. His ability to mimic his vocal nuances on guitar required an extremely elastic right-hand playing technique. He used no set technique to make his instrument "talk"; he might have played such figures as single-string treble notes within a chord (as in "Shake It And Break It," where Patton isolates notes while playing F, F6 and C7 chord positions), or as a part of a strummed guitar figure (as in "Screamin' And Hollerin' the Blues," in which his open-string work accompanying his descending bass mimics his vocal accenting). For the most part, he "talked" on guitar with unpredictable figures that could last for one, two or three beats.

This ability to make an instrument "talk" was recognized as a mark of black music excellence long before the blues were developed. In 1832, black fiddlers in Maryland were so commended by a slave as "twas jes' de same us ef de fiddles wus er speakin."[10] Although individual blues on records feature this manner of arrangement, only Henry Thomas of Texas and Peg Leg Howell of Georgia appear to have attempts as serious as Patton at developing a "talking" technique. Compared to Patton, though, both musicians played with broad instrumental strokes that didn't always correspond to the finer points of their singing. Patton's mastery of the details of this technique makes his guitar a genuine voice, just as his voice is a genuine musical instrument. This achievement is particularly astonishing when one considers how difficult it must have been for Patton to hear himself in the midst of a noisy dance crowd.

Patton's guitar playing is characterized further by three other distinctive traits. One was that he usually tuned his guitar above concert pitch, often by two or three semitones, whereas most Mississippi blues guitarists tuned below concert pitch. His fondness for piercing tones is further evident by his upper register bottleneck work, especially the eerie high tone he picks while playing the tonic chord of "Mississippi Bo Weevil Blues," the tonic chord he plays during the first two phrases of the first chorus of "When Your Way Gets Dark" (just before and after the spoken interjections), and his slide instrumental introduction of "Jesus Is A Dying Bed-Maker." Sounding these high-register tones would have required him to reach well into the frets on the body of the twelve-fret guitar he played, even if he was tuned in a higher tuning.

Another trait of Patton's guitar-playing is his affinity for accompanying his singing with guitar rolls, which he was able to execute because he picked with three fingers. While guitar rolls are rare in blues-playing, they are heard in abundance in Patton's accompaniments, usually in the form of two- or three-beat treble licks. Remarkably, these rolls do not evoke banjo or mandolin-playing, or flamenco guitar styles. Although he usually plays them at the beginning of the second vocal phrase of a stanza, he has no strict rule for dispensing them; he even climaxes the last vocal phrases of the third and fifth stanzas of "Banty Rooster Blues" with triplet bass rolls. Although he tends to introduce a roll as an accompaniment variation, he makes rolls a regular part of "Banty Rooster Blues" (as treble figures during the second vocal phrase), "It Won't Be Long," "Hammer Blues" and "Tom Rushen Blues." The accompaniment of "Pea Vine Blues" is mostly dependent on treble rolls that move rhythmically and melodically with his voice, such as the second verse that uses three such segments: a three-beat roll beginning in the first measure of the first vocal phrase, and two-beat rolls played in the second measures of the second and third phrases. These rolls make for a unified accompaniment, as the instrument bridge that sets off each vocal phrase contains triplets on the first and third beats. Double-time guitar rolls are fundamental to the presentation of "Some Of These Days," where they occur during the last three beats of the second measure and recur in the sixth vocal measure.

For the most part, Patton seems to have played rolls[11] to enliven the rhythm of his slow and medium-tempo pieces. They also provided a means of fracturing the IV7 chords often heard at the beginning of the second phrase of blues songs, which otherwise can seem rhythmically stagnant if they are played too often as a fixed-chord position.

His third trait was how he slapped his guitar, which his audiences long remembered as one of his musical badges. "Beatin' that box to death—he never stopped beatin' on that box!" Booker Miller said while listening to a Patton recording in 1969. The truth be told, Patton used this gimmick more sparingly than the guitar roll, but he does it on his most popular records like "Down The Dirt Road Blues," "Pony Blues," and the various blues derived from "Maggie." The episodic "box beating" heard on "Pony Blues," "Banty Rooster Blues" "Mean Black Cat Blues" and "Hang It On The Wall" attests to Patton's general fondness for this device. But he makes even this guitar-thumping functional by combining it with string-picking. As Ernest Brown said of his live performances, "He slappin' the guitar, but he be makin' note while he slappin' it."

In order to perform this distinctive feat, he would have had to play the guitar without anchoring his pinky to the box, and not use fingerpicks. By keeping his right hand free, Patton could have a varied touch, much tonal variety, and accents sharply defined with string-snapping and damping (sometimes executed simultaneously). Listening to "Down The Dirt Road Blues" on which Patton damps most of the figures he plays behind his voice, Miller pointed out "And, you don't hear a guitar string, do you? Ha! That guy! You don't hear a *damn* string ring, 'cause he ain't lettin' 'em ring."

For a Delta dance musician, Patton played with remarkable tonal subtlety. In the single-measure riff of "Green River Blues," he could suggest the sound of two guitars by brushing a tonic chord and bending the third string (to sound an augmented fourth) while the chord was still reverberating. Miller explained, "Now you watch, he starts slurrin' them strings; you see, he makes double chords. That's what makes you think it's two boxes."

About Patton's playing overall, Miller said, "I haven't found a musicianer yet or heard of one hardly to imitate that man. That man was different from mostly anybody I heard pick a guitar."

Much of Patton's uniqueness as a guitarist was due to his unmatched intuitive facility for mimicking his voice, and to the fact that he played in no rote, generic style. His playing used many different techniques, textures, and sounds. It is in vain if one listens to his music for a set approach or a specific pattern of picking.[12] The only Patton arrangements that can be called stylized are his performances of spirituals, for which he played the guitar lap-style with a fretting gadget, interspersing fretted notes on the two highest strings with open-string tonic chord strums.[13] But most of his bottleneck-slide songs were played with the guitar upright position, according to Booker Miller. "I ordered a Gibson guitar; they sent me a bar. And so he [Patton] showed me how to play with that bar. But he liked the bottleneck best." The "bottleneck" he employed, Miller said, was really "a piece of brass, you know, like a pipe, and it was cut off just to fit his finger; he'd slip it down on his finger, his little finger."

Even listeners who did not recognize Patton's merits as a guitarist acknowledged that his singing was extraordinary. "That's what helped put him over, too," Willie Morris said, "he sung real good." Sleepy John Estes thought he was the loudest singer he had ever heard.

Other than the mock crooning for "Shake It And Break It," Patton sang with no special devices or gimmicks. Miller said of him "He just flatfoot sing. Now he'd *holler* (shout at full voice), sometimes." His records show that he could sing loud, and even louder. And high and soft, whenever appropriate for the song.

For singing, Patton was probably more concerned with individual pitches to create dramatic feeling, rather than with the intervals between the pitches. One of Patton's most striking vocal traits is his tendency to strive for the highest note he can sing in a given song. In this way, Patton's vocal delivery resembles that of modern soul singers. Patton used heightened pitches to give a sense of urgency or desperation to a lyric.

The highest pitch he sings on a recording is a2 (about a whole-tone above the typical baritone range), a tone that launches three verses of "Spoonful," where it functions as a major third. He hits the same pitch at the beginning of the final verses of "Stone Pony" where it functions as a minor third, and "Revenue Man" where it functions as a minor seventh. On all of these instances,

Ex. 43: Array of Patton's pitches arranged from high to low.

Patton's voice breaks; his difficulty with this pitch leads him to clip his delivery of it. His voice is likewise strained at the a-flat2 just beneath it, which he attempts during the opening verse of "You're Gonna Need Somebody When You Die" as a minor sixth, and which with good sense he avoids trying again for the rest of the performance.

For practical purposes, Patton's high range extends to the g2. He sings this tone at a full shout in two songs pitched an octave beneath it, "Rattlesnake Blues" and "Green River Blues," where it is heard at the beginning of the third verse. He also sings it as the dominant scale-tone on "High Water Everywhere," "When Your Way Gets Dark," "Some Happy Day" and "You're Gonna Need Somebody When You Die," all of whose tonic notes are middle C. Patton takes similar advantage of the next adjacent tone, f#2, which occurs in "Pony Blues," "Shake It And Break It" and "Dry Well Blues" (all anchored at the f#1 tonic an octave beneath it). The same tone occurs as the frequently heard fifth of "Screamin' And Hollerin' The Blues," "Moon Going Down," "Revenue Man Blues" and "Bird Nest Bound," and as the once-heard fifth of "Banty Rooster Blues" (in its third verse). The f#1 is also employed as the augmented fourth in "Mississippi Bo Weevil Blues" and "High Water Everywhere."

In the middle of Patton's vocal range, his voice has less of its strident power when he ventures to b (a step below middle C), but it retains resonance and expressiveness in the octave that runs between middle C (c1) and c2. His voice attains peak mellowness within the octave, which is where he pitches the tonic tones of such songs as "Screamin' And Hollerin' The Blues" (b), "Pony Blues" (f#), and "Down The Dirt Road" (d).

Just as Patton liked to include the highest notes he could reach into his songs, so did he pitch some songs as low as his voice would allow. He thus situated "Banty Rooster" at B (a ninth below middle C) and he used B-flat as the tonic root pitch of "Pea Vine Blues" and "It Won't Be Long." These were tones he could only deliver at diminished volume, and the low register of the three songs gave them a somber and almost funereal sound, while Patton accentuated by drawing out the final note of his phrases. The same dark quality was manifest in "Jesus Is A Dying Bed-Maker," the tonic of which is pitched an octave below middle C (c ).

Patton also liked to mine the depths of this octave while singing tunes with pitches situated at or just beneath middle C, such as "High Water Everywhere" (c1), "Moon Going Down" (b), "Bird Nest Bound" (b), and "Devil Sent The Rain" (b). On these occasions he dropped an octave to sing the last word of a phrase as a variation, the lowered tonic sounding like a grunt, as though Patton were disgusted. He used the same phrase-end octave drop in songs set a fifth beneath middle C (at f) as well: "Joe Kirby," "Mean Black Cat Blues," "Mean Black Moan" and "Frankie And Albert." The G he succeeded in scraping from the very bottom of his register in this fashion had a hollow, speech-like sound.

Patton sometimes employed a similar octave drop while singing dominant scale-tones during the last line of a stanza, at which point he then wriggled his way up to the tonic. The dominant of the last phrase of "Down the Dirt Road Blues" begins as a and ends as A; that of "Move To Alabama" drops from c#1 to c#. These tones, too, have a dry, speech-like quality.

Patton inverted this device to give a climactic sound to some phrase endings. Whereas the verses of "Frankie and Albert" employed G as their tonic, the chorus was completed an octave higher. By avoiding such gyrations in pitch, Patton gave some of his tunes a restful air that suited well their lilting melodies. He avoided his low Bb in "Tom Rushen Blues," which was sung in the key of Bb, and avoided his low grunt-like tonic note in "Green River Blues," "Jim Lee Blues," "Running Wild Blues" and "Some Of These Days." By the same token, Patton generally applied an even instrumental touch to these songs, which at dances probably served as rest pieces.

In Patton's early blues-singing days he had a vibrato, for he uses it fleetingly in Part One of "Jim Lee Blues," at the lyric:

> I lay my head in a feeble woman's arms
> An' she lay her nappy head in mine.

While the Patton who recorded in 1929 was much more advanced a musician than the Patton who played many of the same pieces in 1910, years of shouting had doubtless taken their toll on his voice during the meantime. So, apparently, did smoking. "He smoked a whole lot," Son House said of him, "he just *kept* cigarettes in his mouth." Before beginning "A Spoonful Blues," and after singing the fifth verse of "Jim Lee Blues" (Part One), he can be heard clearing his throat. His voice, whether singing or speaking, had a congested, rheumy sound. "Just like you hear him singin', he had a growl in his voice," Booker Miller said of him. "He just didn't speak clear, 'right.' He just never did cut a word clear." Johnnie Mack knew Patton enough in the early 1930s to hear him speak and sing. He agreed with Miller that "he didn't have a good clear voice." By the time of Patton's last recording session in 1934, his voice had much deteriorated, and he had to strain to reach his high Γ#.

I have been a good provider but I,
believe I've been misled.

—"REVENUE MAN BLUES"

*Chapter 8*

# A SQUABBLIN' SCUTTLEBUB (1914–1924)

The distinctive qualities of Charlie Patton's recorded music as noted in the last two chapters suggest that he had an outstanding blues career, especially during the 1910s when the basic elements of his style were likely to have been established. Even during his later years when he played at the same performing venues as other Mississippi bluesmen, he set himself apart, musically and personally. "He was kinda selfish about playin' with other guys," Son House said of him. "He always liked to play more by himself. That the way Charlie was. He didn't care much about buddies." Whereas the dance blues that were recorded by other Mississippi musicians before World War II lent themselves easily to ensemble performance, most of Patton's front-line pieces were not. Only his "Banty Rooster Blues" was phrased according to Mississippi dance blues conventions and was slow enough for an accompanist to follow. That by 1920 Patton had reworked "Banty Rooster Blues" to develop "Down The Dirt Road Blues" suggests that perhaps he no longer needed the usual house-frolic entertainers. The same may be said also of his "Mississippi Bo Weevil Blues," whose fast tempo would have made the song nearly impossible to accompany on either guitar or violin.

Patton's "way I beat my woman" on his guitar could have been his means of impressing others with his success as a sport who bore the aura of the "big town" blues singer. Big Bill Broonzy once described such a type. "These big town blues players . . . they went out, dressed up every night and some of them had three and four women. One fed him and they other bought his clothes and shoes. One of these sweet back papas had a woman and if she didn't get enough money for him, he'd beat her up."[1]

Patton's general way of ordering people about fit this image. "He was a *squabblin' scuttlebub,*[2]" Hayes McMullan once said of him, "Oh he was a natural squabbler!" So did his propensity for exploiting people, women among them. Son House recalled that Patton "didn't want to buy things he really need; always tryin' to work on somebody else."

He acted this way with his brothers, too. There was one that Son House met in the early 1930s as Son Patton, who was probably the same person that David Edwards recalled as "Ed" Patton, who was tall, stocky, and weighed about 200 pounds. "Ed was kind of a nice fella," Edwards related. "He would drink, but he always would stay off to hisself and look and listen, see what was goin' on. He was kinda quiet. 'Son' and Charlie, they was a devil, used to wanna 'clown.' But Ed, look like he didn't go for that." The brother Edwards recalled as "Son" was probably Willie Patton. The remaining brother, C. Patton, the youngest member of the clan, was to be killed in a gun accident on in 1918. "He and another boy were playin' with a gun," his nephew Tom Cannon reported. "The gun was loaded, and the gun went off."

Charlie had little rapport with Willie. "They couldn't set 'horses,'" House said. "He [Willie] didn't like his ways and Charlie didn't like his much." Tom Cannon agreed. "They didn't go too far together; they'd be arguin' with one another. Charlie could outtalk Son, and Son'd get mad. They didn't get along very good."

Sara Garrett agreed. "They didn't get along too good." She remembered Willie as "Son," and as the family's heavy. "'Son' Patton, he was a big squabbler, and he wanted things to go *his* way. So there it was."

Sometime around 1914 or 1915, Charlie and Willie's relationship had become so bitter that Charlie left Dockery's. It was because he feared killing his brother in an argument, he explained to Sam Chatmon. So he had decided to try living with the Chatmon family on the Gaddis and McCline plantation near Bolton.

Patton's move there may have been facilitated by meeting Ferdinand "Uncle Bud" Chatmon on Dockery's. A bastard son of Henderson Chatmon, Ferdinand was part of the family household until 1910 when he was twenty-five. That year, in a Bolton court trial, he was acquitted from a charge of murder. Despite being declared innocent, he feared repercussions from the victim's brother. So, Ferdinand moved first to Cleveland, MS, then to Dockery's. "I think he went up there 'cause they said it was good huntin' up there," Sam reported. "He always crazy about huntin', and the woods up there, they said, was forty miles wide. He went up there [to Dockery's] and happened up on Charlie Patton there."

It makes sense, then, that it was Ferdinand who suggested to Patton to seek and stay with the Chatmons near Bolton, instead of staying on Dockery's. If so, then Patton apparently preferred acting on this advice to killing Willie. Whether or not he considered himself kin to the Chatmons—probably not, regardless of what Sam Chatmon later claimed to interviewers—he could hardly have presented himself to them without the referral of a Chatmon family member.

Patton spent at least a month with the Chatmons. According to Sam, Charlie was received graciously by both parents. Yet he may not have enjoyed much the company of the man who was reputed among some Chatmon family members as possibly his true father, for Henderson Chatmon was a stern, forbidding figure. "My daddy, he wasn't the sort to make friends with people," Sam noted. "First thing he'd say, 'I don't know him.' My daddy tell you somethin' or other, you better do what he said; he didn't 'play' at all. He'd just as soon hit you with a stick as he'd hit you with a switch." His wife Liza, on the other hand, was admired for her friendly disposition. Charlie became so fond of her that he arranged for his own mother to ship his clothes and belongings to her. "He just thought as much of mama—more I believe—than he did of *his* mama, the way he act. He's just crazy about her, and mama's just crazy about him. Everywhere he'd go, she'd carry him. [She'd] carry all of us. She'd hitch up her wagon, carry us on picnics and all that. As little as I was, I can remember Charlie Patton and a gang of 'em playin' together."

In Bolton, Patton found himself as one of many blues musicians. "I believe there was more around close to Bolton[3] than there was in any town, when I was small," Sam said. "Anywhere you go, you catch five or six in a pile." Perhaps the most highly regarded of the lot was Alec Robinson, an older man who played bottleneck-fretted guitar ditties like "Pearlee." "He's about the best, him and Lem Nichols that I knowed around here in them days," Sam recalled. Both performers served as early mentors to Bo Chatmon, who would become famous on records as Bo Carter.

Patton did not play the kind of waltzes and two-step tunes then in favor with local whites. Sam admitted that "I ain't never heard him try to play n'ar a one of them." Likely for that reason, Patton did not accompany the Chatmons when they appeared as a seven-piece string band at white sociables. But among black audiences of the area, he was quite popular, if only by default. "They liked his pickin' better than they did this Alec Robinson there," Sam opined, "cause he's (Robinson is) pickin' with a pocket knife, and they didn't care much about it (i.e., knife-style pieces) in them days."

Sam Chatmon remembered his brother Bo having no enthusiasm for Patton's playing. Neither, it turned out, did Walter Vinson, who would later form The Mississippi Sheiks with Lonnie Chatmon. Sam supposed in hindsight that Patton's appeal in Bolton was only with the older people of Robinson's generation. "He just played them two songs, 'Pony [Blues]' and 'Banty Rooster [Blues].' That was sufficient for old folks back in them times; I used to like 'em myself 'fore I knew better."[4] If Patton knew of such contempt for his music, he apparently didn't allow it to limit his regard of the records by Bo Carter and the Mississippi Sheiks. In 1930, the Mississippi Sheiks scored a major hit with Okeh Records in "Sittin' On Top Of The World." Seeing its popularity, Patton recorded a robust version of the song, and Paramount released it as "Some Summer Day."

Sam Chatmon noted that in addition to his two pet themes, Patton regaled local audiences with a tune called "Saw A Cow," which was a non-blues piece that began with the lyrics "Mama killed a redbird, and Pap cooked the stew." He also took up a local standard called "Rockin' Chair Blues," which had been featured by Robinson and Nichols as early as 1906, and it was also played by Ferdinand Chatmon. It was a slow-drag version of "East St. Louis Blues," and it contained the lyrics:

> Runnin' down to the river, gonna take me a rocker chair
> If the blues don't take me I'm gonna rock 'em 'way from here.
> The Mississippi's runnin' and the Red River going' dry:
> Sometimes I think my baby oughta be buried alive.

If Patton learned this theme in Bolton if not already in the Delta, then possibly he did so to in order to play a cover of a song by his local competitors. Then, apparently, he stopped singing the "rocker chair" lyrics, using instead (or resuming) the ones about the riverboat Jim Lee. While recording "Jim Lee Blues Parts One and Two" for Paramount Records in 1930, for one chorus he sang this lyric twice:

> Which way, which a-way, do the Red River run?
> Which a-way, do the Red River run?

He had yet another version of this song. "'Slidin' Delta,' that's what he called it," Booker Miller reported.[5]

On the whole, though, there may have been little if any musical swapping between Patton and Bolton's blues musicians. Sam said that Ferdinand Chatmon would sometimes "drum" (tap) his guitar in a manner like Patton's, but also that he knew only a few tunes in open A (Spanish) tuning, "Rockin' Chair Blues," and a waltz in the key of A called "Midnight Serenade." Despite his age, Ferdinand began playing music when his sister Josie left the family household in 1909, and he remained an amateur. "He would no more than play for hisself or play for his woman," Walter Vinson said of him.

Patton might have learned the expression "stone pony" during his stay in Bolton, some twenty years before he recorded "Stone Pony Blues" for Vocalion Records. "They was usin' it around Bolton all the time," Sam reported. "I can recall when my mama and them used to ride cows to parties and I'd hear 'em say 'That's a stone pony!'" He defined the sweeping superlative as "a man that wanna be a 'bad' man, or can play a guitar good, he can do most anything 'ccomplish most anything he started. Anything that was fine or good, they call that a 'stone pony.'" The expression was probably coined shortly after the celebrated 1908 Kentucky Derby upset won by a 24-1 underdog named Stone Street; the racetrack term for a sure winner, "stone blinder,"[6] came into wide use about two years after this victory. In the Mississippi Delta, singers applied the "stone pony" to describe women they desired, as in a once-popular blues lyric "That old stone pony will be my 'fairo' some day"; Willie Moore remarked "All of them was singin' that." In his 1934 reworking of "Pony Blues" as "Stone Pony Blues,"[7] Patton seems to have used the term to boast of a girlfriend: "I got me a stone pony, don't ride Shetlands no more."

However, Patton did not use the term "stone pony" to describe himself. In fact, on his records, only once did he characterize himself, but as a rattlesnake:

Just like a rattlesnake I stay, mama, in a mamlish curl
I say I'm just like a rattlesnake baby I stay in a mamlish curl
I ain't gonna have no job mama, rollin' through this world.
("Rattlesnake Blues")

A "rattlesnake in a curl," Son House said, meant a cheapskate.[8] Patton's tightfistedness was long remembered by his nephew Tom Cannon and House, who remembered him as a poor touch for a loan. "Man, he was *tight* with money," House said. "Whoo, brother, *yeah*. He didn't spend anything much. Charlie sure was 'choicy' about that."

After some weeks, Patton left the hill country of Bolton. It seems that he didn't explain why he left, but some 50 years later Sam Chatmon said, "I figured that he wanna stay up in the Delta, 'cause the folks would have more country suppers on Saturday nights. He'd play somewhere every Friday night and Saturday night, Sunday night." Furthermore, he thought that Patton went to Smedes, a small town twenty-five miles north of Vicksburg that he described as "just a plantation with one little store, a flagstop." There Patton stayed with two of Henderson Chatmon's half-brothers, John and Levi Purvis. For a while, Sam received bulletins about Patton from one of the Purvis children. "I'd get a letter from her and she's talkin' about Charlie Patton was there with them, playin' out every night, and I'd answer the letter sayin' I hope he have success. So finally she wrote me and said he had moved out there between Leland and Greenwood. 'Kellasaw' or somethin' like that was the name of the place. So next time I heard of him he was stayin' out here on Will Dockery's." The town Chatmon could not recall distinctly may have been Kelso, located immediately south of Smedes, in the southeastern region of the Delta.

Patton returned every so often to visit the Chatmon family until 1927, when Henderson and Liza moved to Memphis. Some of these visits may have lasted for up to a month, as Sam recalled. But any of the recollections by Sam are open to doubt, though, especially the ones that Patton had been "raised" by the Chatmons or was considered to be a Chatmon by blood. No one else among Chatmon family and friends claimed to be related by blood to Patton. Sam's sister Josie had no memory of Patton's presence in the household before she left Bolton in 1909, when Patton would have been nearly twenty, and she did not think he had ever been accepted as a genuine family relative. His younger brother Larry, born in 1901, also couldn't recall a Patton visit or any family mention of his kinship with them. Walter Vinson, who met the Chatmon brothers around 1916 and became their closest musical associate, scoffed at the idea that Charlie was related to them. Perhaps the reason why Sam Chatmon claimed Patton as a blood relative was to increase his standing as an elder blues figure during and after the rediscovery era of the 1960s and -70s.

In or by 1916 Willie Moore met Patton, who at the time was living in Hollandale, a town located some forty miles north of Kelso and Smedes. Hollandale was on one of the main stems of the Yazoo Delta "Yellow Dog" railroad, namely a route nicknamed the "Black Dog" that ran from Vicksburg through Cleveland, Leland and Rolling Fork to Clarksdale. It made sense for Patton to move there, as Moore remembered Hollandale as one of the Delta's prime gambling places, and where there was gambling, musicians were often hired. Patton struck Moore as a barrelhouse musician who had outgrown the "little short places" where the house-frolic entertainer performed. Moore's anecdote of Patton being offered a spot in W. C. Handy's band probably took place around this time. It is conceivable that when Patton began returning to visit the Chatmons and their relatives, he was already situated in Hollandale. He seems to have lived there for some time, for J. D. Short, a Clarksdale-based bluesman who took up music in 1919,[9] knew him as a resident of a lumber camp at Mirthy Bow, which was located on the outskirts of Hollandale.

It was during this period that Patton fathered two sons, Johnnie born in 1916, and Will in 1918, with Sallie Hollins of Kentwood, Louisiana. According to David Evans' research,[10] Patton moved her and the boys to the Mississippi Delta at Sunflower Plantation located north of Dockery's, but he did not live with them.

Also, his second daughter, named Rosetta, was born in Renova to Martha Christian on August 10, 1917. According to the birth certificate that had been filed, Christian was 29 and a housewife, and Patton gave his age as 32, and his occupation was supposedly farming. Rosetta Patton lived long enough to meet in the 1990s researchers who knew how famous her father still was.[11] She related that her mother's side of the family owned land at Renova, and that parents were married at the courthouse in Cleveland. While no marriage document has yet to be found, the birth certificate does record the birth as "legitimate." Rosetta admitted that her parents separated by 1919, but she also remembered that Charlie visited her through 1932, bringing on one occasion her half-sister Willie Mae "China Lou."

Yet by 1918 Patton resumed living on Dockery's plantation, according to Sara Garrett, who arrived there that year. It was that year when all of its tenants were examined for malaria by a team of medical researchers from the Rockefeller Foundation; Patton may have been among them. Half of those examined were found to have the disease. Every tenant was then treated with quinine, half of which was paid for by Will Dockery. Also, screened porches and outhouses were built, neither of which were then conventional features of plantation quarters. As a result of the Rockefeller work at Dockery's, an 80% remission of Sunflower County's malaria rate was achieved. The prevalence of malaria until then evidently inspired Willie Brown (I) to use it as a metaphor for blues in a song Willie Moore heard him play around Lake Cormorant:

> The blues ain't nothin' but a lowdown shakin' chill
> If you ain't had 'em, I hope you never will.

Malaria was colloquially known as "chills and fevers."

The state of Patton's health was poor enough to disqualify him from military service. Although he was within the age group targeted for World War I duty[12] under the Selective Service Acts of May, 1917 and August, 1918, he was never drafted, according to Sara Garrett. He later confided to Son House that the doctor who examined him on Dockery's found him unfit for the army. "He couldn't pass for it, he had a bad heart. He said that's what the doctor told him."

Some planters in the Delta who had influence with (or helped administer) local draft boards arranged to have their tenants exempted from service in the interests of keeping their work force intact. This move wasn't merely to help with the home war effort. 1917 and 1918 were boom cotton years during which crop prices soared to 29 cents a pound, double their previous value everywhere else in the country. Some blues musicians managed to avoid the draft by cultivating influential white patrons. Several Chatmon brothers did just that by attracting the patronage of Harold Stovall, a close friend of Will Dockery. He heard them play at a dance in Cleveland around 1917, and he liked what he heard so much, that he hired them as his personal minstrels at his Coahoma County plantation. "He didn't charge 'em a penny for movin' in, and takin' care of 'em all through the winter and settled with 'em better than he would the other hands," their brother Sam recalled. "He'd force the other ones to go and work, but he'd let them sit around, 'cause he wanted to use them playin.'" Such musicians, Joe Rice Dockery said, were known among Delta planters as "white folks' niggers." It is doubtful that Patton could have ever earned that status with Will Dockery, or even merited it. He so infuriated Will Dockery that he was banished from the plantation in the winter of 1921.

Frank Howard, an employee at the nearby Cottondale plantation, came to know Patton well enough to have a remarkable glimpse of Patton's relations with white planters and black women. Howard was originally from Buffalo, New York, but in the early 1920s he was living in the Delta town of Tribbet. During a conversation with Howard shortly after being expelled from Dockery's, Patton quoted the landowner as having ordered him to never return to his plantation because the female sharecroppers "wouldn't half-work, they'd be sleepy all day on account of listenin' to him play at night at different parties." But in light of another altercation with a different planter that Howard witnessed and the sordid circumstances that preceded it, it is more likely that Patton had glibly contrived a harmless, even humorous explanation of his expulsion. Had Patton's popularity indeed posed such a threat to the productivity of Dockery's work force, banishing him would have not been a solution to the problem, for he could have continued to play for the same tenants at places off the plantation. The idea of Dockery suddenly deciding to expel Patton after enduring a decade of his guitar-playing (and presumably, the morning-after yawns of his female workers) seems far-fetched. On the other hand, it is true that the planter had little liking for music, not even hiring Patton for parties. A reasonable question to ask about the expulsion was whether it occurred towards the end of the cotton season, when all hands were expected to be busy. The need for labor would have become more urgent by the postwar price slump of 1920-1921, meaning that Dockery really needed every wisp of cotton that could be gleaned. He had room in his plantation shacks only for tenants who picked cotton, not guitars. Yet another explanation of Patton's expulsion may come from Frank Howard's memories of the musician from 1921-1923.

When he met Patton in December 1921, Howard was working as a chauffeur for George Kirkland, the owner of Cottondale, a 2500-acre plantation that was located about ten miles southwest by rail from Dockery's. Years later, Howard described Cottondale as a "raggedy flagstop[13] between Ruleville and Doddsville on the Yellow Dog railroad." Howard met Patton by chance while buying a box of cigars for his boss at Cottondale's "Chinaman's store" (so-called at the time because the Chinese had formed a merchant class in the Delta and set up grocery stores). Upon entering the store, he saw Patton lounging with a guitar slung over his back. "I got to talkin' with him," Howard recalled, "an' he got in the car with me, went out there to see Mister George."

"Mister George" Kirkland was tending his own commissary when Howard delivered the cigars to him. The first thing about Patton the planter seemed to have noticed was his guitar. "Mister George asked him could he play that box. He told him, well, the peoples *tell* him he could play, and so, he made a couple songs there. Then he asked him where he was livin' at. He told him, well, he kinda lookin' for a location at the present time."

Kirkland saw, and took, the obvious hint directed at him. "Him and 'the man,' Mister Kirkland, went on back in the house. They talk for a while; I didn't hear that." Howard assumed that Kirkland was hoping that Patton would stay on the plantation as his personal minstrel. "That was what he had in view 'cause he liked it [Patton's music] hisself."

Once his deal with Kirkland was agreed to, Patton went outside to the front porch and found Howard. "Charlie come on out. He told me, he say 'Chauffeur there, I think that the boss fella left a message for you.'" The message was that Patton was going to stay on Cottondale in a vacant shack, and that Howard would use Kirkland's old army truck to fetch the belongings that Patton stashed at the "Chinaman's store."

The shack offered to Patton had recently been abandoned by a pair of tenants who had stayed just long enough to weedle an advance against their future crop from Kirkland. "The people had borrowed some money, then went off. The house was already furnished when he moved in there."

Apparently Patton was to earn his keep strictly as a musician. Throughout his stay on Cottondale from December 1921 to the summer or fall of 1923, Patton never touched a plow or any other farm equipment. Nor was he, to Howard's knowledge, ever asked to.

His first performance as a Kirkland musician took place at the end of the week of his arrival. "First Saturday night they had a big time. Mister George himself come down; they had a *great* big time. That was a little bit before Christmas. On Christmas they had a great big time, all during Christmas." The Christmas Day affair took place on the lawn in front of Kirkland's house and lasted an entire day and night, attracting most of the plantation's tenants, who numbered between 75 to 100 at that time.

During the next two years, none of Patton's colleagues from Dockery's, Cleveland, or Drew ever visited him on Kirkland's plantation, nor did Howard recall meeting any of them on the occasions when he accompanied Patton outside Cottondale. The two men went to places like Blaine (just south of Doddsville),[14] "Sunflower City" (officially, Sunflower, about eight miles south of Cottondale), and a "straight-out gambling house" in Ruleville known as Junior Austin's Place. Howard remembered that at Austin's, Patton would sometime "blow a little harp" (harmonica), but "when he got 'round to 'clownin,' he mostly would pick his guitar."[15] He played pieces like "Down The Dirt Road Blues" and "Pea Vine Blues," but mostly his song was, "if he gonna catch up his pony or saddle up his black mare, he goin' out an' find his woman in the world somewhere" (Pony Blues). Another song Patton sang "right smart" (as Howard put it) began with the phrase "Smokestack lightnin,' bell just like gold"; that lyric would be heard on Patton's 1930 record "Moon Going Down."

Most of the time, Patton continued to perform alone. But in 1923 Howard witnessed Patton performing with an eighteen- or twenty-year old guitarist who "frailed 'long behind Charlie" rather than pick an accompaniment. "I and Charlie went to Sunflower City; that's where I got acquainted with him," Howard said of this younger performing partner. The man was named Robert Johnson and told Howard that he hailed from Maud, a town in Tunica County. He was obviously too old to have been the Robert Johnson (1911-1938) of later Delta blues renown, who would have been 12 at that time.

Initially, Patton was cautious of Cottondale, which was prudent of him since trouble was the nature of the places he performed. "He said 'I'm amongst strange people in a strange place, so I won't try to see to get anything, [and I hope it] work out all right. If it don't, I know which a-way to run,'" Howard recalled. He made various pronouncements of his desire to create good will. At first he curbed his drinking in the belief that someone might take advantage of his drunkenness to draw him into a fight or, worse, to poison him, which demonstrates to us how squalid his career was up until then. Once he felt at home at Cottondale, he began to drink frequently or "right smart," as Howard noticed. He tended to drink either a "potion" of moonshine, or a bonded brand named I. W. Harper that Howard described as "hundred proof whiskey."[16]

While Patton kept the peace with his plantation neighbors, he fared less well at the barrelhouses he frequented. Howard saw Patton in two or three fights, all provoked by his opponent. "All of them was fair fights," admitted Howard, who said that he twice intervened to break them up. The two incidents Howard recalled in detail belie the legend of Patton as a cowardly bluffer, and each of them illustrate either his unwillingness to suffer affronts, or his fear of losing face in an unfamiliar environment.

One of the incidents occurred during a Patton performance when "a fella's wife had got drunk, went and sit down on his lap. The fella come up there and jerked the clair out from under him. Then when he (Patton) fell down, the fella kicked him. That's where he had done 'wrong;' he (Patton) got up swinging for him." On this occasion, Patton "done pretty good for hisself" until separated from his adversary.

The other time that Howard remembered was Patton fighting the husband of a drunken woman who had ruined Patton's dinner in a café. "He bought him a fish sandwich. And a woman come up there, get her another drink, says she want another drink. And knock his sandwich out on the floor.

"And he said 'Miss, you done knocked down my supper and that's all I got!'" Howard related, conveying the scene in a plaintive tone as if to suggest that Patton expected the woman to offer to pay for his sandwich.

"The husband told him 'Well, pick it up and eat it, then!' and cussed him."

Patton bristled. "He said 'Well, you done wrong. Mister, I don't cuss *nobody*!'"

But the man took the remark as either a challenge, or a sign of weakness. "The fella throwed another word to him and he shoved him [Patton]. When he shoved him he made a mistake, because Charlie knocked him down, the first lick. He got 'bout half-straight and he [Patton] kicked him, that straightened him out again. And he got 'bout half-straight again. An' when he got kinda half-way up then, he went on crawlin' out the door. He didn't 'study' (contend) with him no more, he had enough."

A little less violent—but not by much—was his marriage to Mandy France. Their formal wedding took place at a "big" Fourth of July picnic in 1922 held on Oss Pepper's plantation, which was between Ruleville and the LeFlore County town of Minter City. After the ceremony officiated by a pastor named Tom Morgan, Patton and Robert Johnson (the one from Maud) serenaded the wedding guests.

Mandy France was a long-time and reliable employee of George Kirkland's. So she was allowed to draw monthly "furnish" money to cover her living expenses during the growing season from March through September, the month when a tenant could expect to begin to recover cottonseed money for a crop. The furnish money Mandy received were advances against the profits she would presumably make when her crop was harvested.

Yet Patton treated his wife as if she was one of the prostitutes who attached themselves to barrelhouse blues singers. During the planting season of 1923, Howard said, Patton began spending her monthly advances. "He take the money, go an' drink it up, an' throw it away, treatin' people—womens and so forth like that. Then he come in and give her a whuppin' about it 'cause she got mad over it." As Patton continued to (in Howard's phrase) "wear her out" by beating her whenever she protested his spending her money, Mandy found herself less able to provide for the bare necessities of life.

Finally she was forced to approach Kirkland with a plea for additional advances. Her explanation why she was seeking this aid prompted Kirkland to declare that he would advance her no more money until her husband made good on her outstanding debts by working in the plantation commissary. Then he delivered the same message to Patton in person. At that point, explained Howard, Patton "got a little bit too smart." He snorted at Kirkland's attempt to involve him in plantation work, and he bragged that he could make the money in less time by playing music. The angry landlord responded by banishing him from his plantation forever.

In terms of Mississippi law at the time, Kirkland let Patton off easy.[17] Anyone who refused to "give service" to a landlord in order to discharge a debt could be fined $100, or be imprisoned for six months in the county jail.

Patton was no lawyer, but he may have been aware of the extent that laws provided protection from predators. Whether he would have counted himself as such a predator is another matter for speculation. At any rate, his aversion to formal marriage arrangements could have been rooted in what he knew about laws. By "jumping the broomstick," he removed himself from legal responsibility for the debts that he saddled his female companions with.

Mandy Patton refused to join her husband in exile, telling Frank Howard and other friends that she "wouldn't go to his bed unless another woman walked with her." She resumed using her maiden name, and she left Cottondale to live with her father Charlie Frank at his home near Ruleville.

In 1930, Patton sang during as his opening stanza of "Magnolia Blues" [Paramount mx. L-48-1]:

When your way gets dark, baby—(spoken: "Hang your lights up high!")
When your way gets dark, baby (spoken: Baby, wonder what's a
matter with 'em!)
When you see my Mandy, come-a easing . . .

It is anyone's guess as to whether Mandy France is the subject of this lyric.

Patton's vicious treatment of Mandy France in 1922-1923 raises the possibility that similar behavior may explain why he was expelled from Dockery's in 1921. Sara Garrett recalled a woman living with him who eventually became fearful of his physical abuse. When the woman decided to leave him, the circumstances were such that Will Dockery went to their shack to retrieve her belongings. "They said he was awful cruel," Garrett reported of Patton. His sister once stated that he kept a bullwhip to punish women with,[18] and Garrett said that his assaultive behavior got him in regular trouble on Dockery's. "When he would mistreat his wife, then the agents would sure get on him—not only him, but any of the men, if they know you doin' it without a cause." The agents' concern was largely due to the fact that women were valued as good workers on Mississippi plantations, often more than men.

Later in his life, during the 1930s, Patton was no longer cutting this sinister figure, either because he changed his behavior, or he had deteriorated physically. Son House said of him, "He'd try (to beat females), but he'd come out behind the eight-ball most of the time. He'd get whupped hisself, 'cause he's so weakly."

Frank Howard remembered that Patton tried returning to Dockery's sometime in 1923, but then Will Dockery learned of his presence. "He found out that he was on the place, and sent him work to get off up there, and don't let him sing. Then he [Patton] went to Helena, Arkansas."

Patton set out for Helena with Frank Howard's sister, a Cottondale cropper named Athie Johnson.[19] She returned alone to the plantation, telling her brother that Patton took a near-fatal gunshot wound at the Hole In The Wall, a well-known barrelhouse on Mississippi Street in Helena. "She said he was in critical condition, [that's] what she told me" remarked Howard. He never saw Patton after his expulsion by Kirkland.

Patton's wounding might account for a limp he walked with for the rest of his life. Hayes McMullan observed that he "kinda hopped" as he walked. Son House thought that Patton was imitating Charlie Chaplin's splay-footed shuffle. Booker Miller said that "he kinda stepped funny on his legs. He kinda dragged one of his legs, he didn't use his left leg like he did his right." He was told by Patton himself that his limp had been caused by a gunshot wound.

With his legs hampered, Patton could no longer pretend that knowing "which a-way to run" would rescue him from trouble. His way of making enemies had caught up with him, and this predicament may which inspired this bleak lyric in "Joe Kirby":

Just like a doggone rabbit, I ain't got no doggone den
Oh I been in trouble Lord, ever since gals been.

In 1924, Patton's next "den" was Merigold, Mississippi, which was located two train stops north of Cleveland. There he took his sixth known "wife," Minnie Franklin, who seems to have been a better conniver than Patton. Viola Cannon recalled that when Minnie deserted him, she took $900 and his .45 pistol, causing Patton to chase her to Vicksburg to recover them. In July 1963, when interviewed in the Vicksburg suburb of Boniva, Minnie cut a convincing figure of respectability.[20] She remembered Patton more for his drinking than for his musicianship, and she opined that he had died of alcoholism rather than heart failure, as she had heard.

But by the end of 1924, Patton somehow managed to persuade Will Dockery to rescind his banishment, for in that year he shacked up on the plantation with a woman named Udy. Her sister named Sudy was married to one of his brothers. Charlie and Udy lived on the northwestern side of Dockery's near Kimball's Ferry, near Merigold where through 1929 Patton was a familiar figure. "He was the only blues singer up in this section of the country. It sure was something having Charlie here," recalled a local companion, Sam Manifield.[21]

Indeed, there were no other blues singers on Dockery's during this time, and it is doubtful that Patton had any regular local associates. His old playing partner "Tee-nicey" Wade moved to Tutwiler in the mid-1920s. Wade may not have been well-known or much remembered in the Delta, but Booker Miller managed to see him perform in Tutwiler and Alligator in the 1930s and thought he was good enough to record. Dick Bankston and a crony from Drew named Jim Halloway played for local house frolics and picnics until 1927, "the year of the high water." Whether either could have been considered as worthy of making records as were Patton and, for that matter, Wade is doubtful. By 1927 Will Brown (II) and his wife Josie had left Drew for Memphis, where both were to die (according to Bankston and Ledell Johnson) around 1940.

As it was, Bankston and Brown (II) didn't travel widely to perform. Patton's nephew Tom Cannon saw Will Brown (II) play with Patton, but he never saw Bankston on Dockery's plantation. Before moving to Lula in 1927, Leroy Willis frequently saw Patton in Drew, Doddsville and Ruleville, but he never saw Bankston, Brown (II) or Halloway.

"A musicianer, he's not got as many men friends as he has women," David Edwards once observed. "The only men friends he has is other musicianers near about." Yet by the end of 1927 if not sooner, Patton seemed to have had no professional musical friendships to speak of. When Son House became met him in 1930, the various musicians Patton had known seemed to matter less than the various women he had met. Sex was just about the only topic he talked about.

"You could hardly get a word in edgeways yourself, not when Charlie's around," House reported. "The whole thing he'd talk about—his women yesterday, the day before yesterday, all what he done to the woman, 'goin' with her and all that. Yeah, he's *good* at that."

House remembered one time when Patton drove Willie Brown (I, "Little Bill") mad with his sexual bragging. "He's be talkin' about the time he's 'with' her, they goin' to bed and how long they can 'stay' and all that.

"It's make Willie so mad! 'God dammit, what in Hell! Shut up, you lapp-eared son-of-a-bitch!'

"I said 'Bill, don't talk about him that way! Let him 'lone.'

House said that Brown spluttered out, "Oh, I get *sick* of that son-of-a-bitch!"

*Chapter 9*

# THE MYTH OF WILLIE BROWN (1920s)

Willie Brown (I) was the sideman to Patton that most informants to the authors during the 1960s remembered. He may have also been Patton's leading Delta blues rival. That may explain why, as early as the late 1910s, Patton liked to put down Brown. "You know Charlie talked loud, that make Brown not devoted to him so much," as Willie Moore described the two during those early times. "Charlie Patton, you know, he's a rough man, if he get mad he go to fightin.' Willie Brown said he wasn't fond of him much because he would argue."

If playing the blues as a congeniality contest was ever held among Delta audiences, Brown would have beaten Patton. "They liked Brown better than they did Patton," Hayes McMullan notes, "cause Patton would argue so." McMullan remembered Brown as a "very nice guy," adding "Willie Brown was a very friendly. I ain't never knowed him to 'clown' (act boisterous)." McMullan's higher esteem for Brown over Patton helps to account for his opinion that Brown was a better guitarist than Patton, whom he did not like. Son House remembered that he and Brown were close "like brothers" during the 1930s, and for that reason he too favored Brown. "Willie Brown could play any piece that Charlie could play and play it better than Charlie," declared House, "He's way better, twice better than Charlie."

These criticisms should be considered with who were the critics. As we shall note later, House was a powerful singer who accompanied himself on guitar with repeated bottleneck-fretted motifs. But as forceful as his best recordings are, none of them have the subtle layering of accents that Patton executed. McMullan was an important source of information about the acoustic Delta blues era to the authors, but he made his living from sharecropping, not from playing music full-time. It may be argued, then, that the limits of their achievements may have prevented them from perceiving in full and appreciating what Patton did. Taken in any other way, their remarks about Patton can seem hypocritical.

House may have shown his support of Brown as musician in order to offset the greater popularity of Patton as showman, a role which Brown, House insisted, refused to play. Yet House's depiction of Brown as a strait-laced performer was a result of a little mythmaking—by Brown himself, it seems. House first met Brown in 1930, so his knowledge of Brown's music-making before that year would have come from him. Brown may have overstated his influence on Patton so much and so often, that House would accept the claims as if gospel truth. During the 1960s, House testified that "Lotta them songs he (Patton) sing, he got from Willie Brown. The one about 'High Water,' he got the song from Willie, the music, the beat of the music. But Charlie, he added the words about 'high water everywhere.' It was the same thing Willie called 'The Jinks,' Willie told me." As Brown was born on February 21, 1897 (according to a recently recovered death certificate),[1] he could not have been more than 13 or 14 years old when Patton first played "Maggie" or some treatment of it, so his "The Jinks" could not have preceded any of Patton's renditions. Certainly he had a little influence on Patton, but it would have been much smaller than Patton's influence on his repertory in return, and Brown seems to have made a determined effort to specialize in playing Patton pieces.

Although he rarely if ever traveled outside the Delta, Brown was an important musical figure in the blues for at least two decades. He was one of the few black guitarists to devote a career to accompaniment, a role to which his weak voice relegated him, and it was this circumstance that wedded him to Charlie Patton. When the two were not feuding, they were exceptionally close. "Them mens just like two sisters or somethin'," Ernest Brown said of them. "Look like they really loved one another."

His full name, Willie Lee Brown, was never used by his acquaintances.

"Instead of 'Willie,' they call him 'Bill,'" Leroy Willis reported, "Everybody called him 'Bill.'" Hayes McMullan said "I called him 'Little Willie' Brown." Mandy Wigman of Swiftown explained this nickname as referring to his short height. "They mostly would call him 'Little Willie' Brown. He was low; Willie was lower than Charlie," she described, "He (Patton) wasn't no size, but 'Little Willie' wasn't big as Charlie."

"He's a little bitty old guy," Willie Young said, "They called him 'Little Bill.'" Frank Howard noted that Brown stood around 5'4" and weighed 135 pounds. His one-time neighbor Elizabeth Moore agreed about the weight, "Willie Brown didn't hardly weigh over 135, 137, that was his size."

Brown's features were as unimpressive as his physique. By the late 1920s, his face had grown so wrinkled that it looked like a maze of "little ditches" to Elizabeth Moore, and his lips were flecked with "'bright' places," probably the mark of a pigmentation deficiency known as vitiligo. His eyes watered constantly from near-sightedness that he never bothered to correct with glasses. His moustache he sported, Son House said, grew "on poor soil." He was dark-complexioned and uncouth, at least in this toast about color he was remembered to have recited: "Your mother was a teddy, an' your sister was a bear, your daddy was a monkey 'cause he had bad hair."

Brown's death certificate lists the birthplace of Perthshire in Bolivar County.[2] He was living on Arthur Peerman's plantation just northeast of Cleveland when Ernest Brown arrived there as a tenant sometime between 1905 and 1907. "Willie learnt in Cleveland," said Ernest who, it should be remembered, learned how to play guitar from Earl Harris, Patton's own acknowledged mentor. He added that "Willie Brown worked on Mister Arthur Peerman's, but when he learned how to play music, he quit workin'." Taking account of his age, this transformation likely occurred no earlier than 1914. It was probably shortly after Willie Brown learned to play that he left Peerman's. "Willie Brown stayed there to my knowin', I reckon about seven-to-eight years," Ernest said. Willie's departure from Peerman's can thus be estimated as having occurred between 1912 and 1915. Although Ernest Brown thought Willie moved from Peerman's to Robinsonville, he might have stopped for an extended time at Dockery's plantation, for he later told Son House that Charlie Patton taught him to play guitar there. That statement can be taken to mean that he learned such pieces as "Jinks Blues" and "Pony Blues" from Patton, and it may also suggest that, until then, he did not know how to pick a guitar accompaniment.

By 1916, however, Brown was coming often to the area around Lake Cormorant (or "Lake Carmen" as pronounced by the locals). There he came to know Willie Moore, then aged 18, who arrived there from Tunica. "He was sixteen when I got 'quainted with him," Moore reported.

The two teenagers became drinking buddies. For Brown, drinking became a full-time occupation. "He say he didn't, you know, drink so much whiskey, but look: he drink it, man, just as sure as you born to die!" said Moore. "And whenever you hear him slappin' that guitar, he been had some, too." Drinking and playing guitar in fact were Brown's abiding life-long pastimes. "He didn't shoot no dice, play no cards, no sir!" said Moore. "There's one thing I know him to do—two things—he drink whiskey and play that guitar. After he had done got that whiskey, he'd go to that guitar, man!"

Over drinks, Brown also tended to become expansive about his past, within the desultory limits of plantation conversation. "Sometimes when we would be drinkin,'" Moore related, "he might say 'Man, I used to live such-and such a place for years!'" He told Moore that he had lived first in Cleveland, and that he had arrived to Bedford by way of Shelby, a Bolivar County town fifteen miles north of Cleveland on the Yellow Dog line which in 1910 had a population of 645. In another conversation, Moore recalled, "he told me he had some fella he used to play with down the road. He told me, "twas a fella stayed down here in Hollandale.' And he said, 'Man, you oughta hear him play!' Said 'Me and him plays together!' He's talkin' about Charlie Patton!"

Since Brown tended to stay put in one place, his association with Patton from 1916 onward was episodic. "All the time I knowed Willie Brown, he lived at Lake Cormorant," said Moore, who lived in the same area until the mid-1940s. Sometimes, Brown would pay brief visits to Cleveland and nearby Boyle around 1920, but afterwards, Moore noted, he "never did go down there after I got acquainted with him." Brown stayed in Robinsonville from 1930 on. For several months in late 1942 / early 1943, he visited Son House in Rochester, New York. Shortly after returning south, on February 23, 1943, Brown entered the Veterans Administration hospital in Memphis,[3] dying there on March 22, 1943 from liver abscess and other ailments.

The town named Lake Cormorant lies about twenty miles south of Memphis, just four railroad stops away. It derived its name from the adjoining four-and-a-half-mile lake. Although it never had as many as a hundred residents or merited incorporation, Lake Cormorant was remembered by Willie Moore as a prime gambling and night-life spot. As we have seen for sawmill barrelhouses, where there was gambling, musicians were hired. That may explain why Willie Brown lived in Lake Cormorant for as long as he did.

The reticent quality that informs our main impression of Brown's character was noticeable during his adolescence. For example, in 1918 he received a notice to report to Hernando for an army physical.[4] "He asked me what I think about it," said Moore, who was likewise summoned. "I told him, I say 'I imagine I wanna go 'cause I ain't never been to France.' He say 'I'll tell you the truth: it's a risk to run.' That's what he said about the war."

They were drafted anyway. With a Bedford mandolinist named Mack Evans, they were duly shipped to Hattiesburg, where Camp Shelby with nearly thirty thousand trainees was one of the army's chief mobilization centers. Brown found the army's inoculations nearly too much for him. "They shot that boy, shot Willie Brown with them 'three c's,' and knocked him out. And we was intendin' to compose a song about it [the army] afterwards, but Willie Brown says 'Damn the song!' 'cause the needles hurt him so bad. He stayed ill around seven, eight days, then he got to feelin' all right." Although Brown and Moore entertained fellow draftees with their music on the Saturday night of their arrival to Camp Shelby, their army careers lasted only two more days. "Both our class cards came on a Friday, and peace declared that Sunday mornin'," Moore said.

During World War I, Brown performed mostly in DeSoto County and Tunica County, with Moore often as his second guitarist. "I played 'second' to Willie Brown all the time," Moore recalled, "Sometime we'd split it half-way: I'd play lead a while and he play lead. Sometimes he'd sing and sometimes I'd sing." Their personal friendship appears to have prompted this partnership. But in a contrasting way, Brown disliked the brother of Mack Evans enough as to not engage him as a support musician. "Willie Brown said him and that boy's [Mack Evans'] brother couldn't get along," remembered Moore. "He was through with him. I forget his brother's name but everybody called him 'Poochie.'"

Brown took Moore along to play dances in Tunica (or, "Tunica City" as Moore knew it then), located twenty miles south of Lake Cormorant with a population of 955 in 1920. They also performed in a jukehouse on the "dog section" between Lake Cormorant and Clack Station (later, Clacks) that was operated by a man named Killraine. "He [Brown] had a woman off this 'dog section,'" Moore said. "In '18 he got that woman there. Jim Smith was goin' with that woman and then Willie Brown married her. She was a nice lookin' brownskin woman. Look like her name was Cora."

Although the musical style Brown would play on his 1930 recordings were already ingrained in him when Moore met him in 1916, most of his early repertory was not recorded. "His main piece was 'Old Cola'" said Moore, who identified the song as Brown's rendition of "Pony Blues." According to Moore, Brown played it in "cross-note" (open E) tuning, the same tuning Son House used in playing the "Pony Blues" that he learned from Brown. "Old Cola" contained the lines:

> Wake up old Cola, with them four white stockin' feet
> The blues ain't nothin' but a low-down shakin' chill.

The title verse may have been suggested by a proverb that said of horses:

> Three white feet, sell him for a friend
> Four white feet, keep him 'till the end.

Another teenage effort, "Red Bell," dealt with what Moore called an "instruction" or "reprobated" woman:

> Heard a mighty rumblin' under the ground
> Lord it was Red Bell, turnin' around.

"Red Bell was a bad woman about killin' the people, just raisin' sand and just slappin' men's bottomsides up," Moore explained. "Couldn't no man do nothin' with her. She's just as 'bad' as a woman could be." Rather than an actual person, she may have been a black fictional descendant of the Bell Witch, a noisy evil spirit whose legend flourished in Mississippi and Tennessee in the early nineteenth and twentieth century.[5] "Rock and Gravel" was another early Brown piece that began with the lyrics "Rocks and gravel, make a solid road"; the melody the words were sung to remains indeterminable.

A fourth early Brown effort was "Make Me a Pallet on the Floor," a square dance "rag" song chestnut that he recorded for the Library of Congress in 1941.[6] Moore first heard the song in 1910 played by a Tunica string band that was led by a middle-aged man named Joe Sercie. "I'll tell you another song he played," Moore said of Brown, "[was] 'Poor Boy Long Ways From Home.'" The presence of this bottleneck-guitar staple in Brown's repertory may be in conflict with Son House's claim that Brown did not play bottleneck style,[7] as may Hayes McMullan's recollection of his 1920s' performances of "Roll and Tumble Blues," another piece often accompanied with slide guitar.

House had described Brown as a deadpan guitarist who disliked Patton's demonstrative and frivolous performing style. But Moore remembered differently, in that Brown took an entertainer's approach to performing. "He stomp his foot, barefooted. He say 'Give me that pony!' Slap that guitar, boy, back there, say 'Set it over yonder!'" Moore's wife Elizabeth recalled Brown's ability to play guitar behind his head, a favorite Patton stunt. Ernest Brown became reacquainted with Willie in Robinsonville in the mid-1920s, and afterwards remembered him as a humorous entertainer who "could think of some of the funniest words look like to sing than anybody I know." Like Patton, Brown made his percussion more emphatic with violent foot-stomping. "His feet sound like two-three feet was dancin'," Ernest Brown said. "He just kept his feet goin' right with the music. He carried so much racket till anybody wanna dance. They sure would dance, 'cause Willie Brown give 'em a dancin' number." He also gave them Pattonesque patter, at least when he accompanied other musicians. "He'd be secondin', and laughin' an' talkin'[8] an' turn his head off (i.e., look elsewhere)" [said Ernest,] "That fella be singin' an' playin', an' Willie Brown be talkin' an' just laughin', laughin' an' talkin' an' complementin', wouldn't miss a note."

Brown mimicked Patton further by adopting "Pony Blues" as his own mainstay song. "The biggest thing I heard Willie Brown sing about [was] old 'Saddle up my pony,'" Moore said. Yet he also did his best to come across as something other than a poor man's Charlie Patton. He did not feature most of Patton's songs, and those he played were not rendered in the Patton way. "He just played his own style all the time," said Moore, speaking from his experiences from accompanying each man as a second guitarist. "If he play with Charlie Patton, why he play his own style."

Despite Brown's dance music orientation, he took pleasure in listening to the vaudeville blues recordings of the early 1920s, and sometimes he took the train to Memphis to hear the them. "He listened to Mamie Smith's records and Kate Smith," Moore recalled. His exposure to records would be reflected in the first two stanzas of his 1930 record "Future Blues," which make use of lyrics from Ma Rainey's "Last Minute Blues" (Paramount Records, 1923).

Memphis Minnie was the most famous female blues singer of the 1930s and 1940s. But in the late 1910s, at age 20, she was newly arrived to the Bedford plantation, where she became Brown's close associate. "They stayed right close," Willie Moore reported. "He'd 'second' behind her. She raised at Lake Cormorant. 'Kid' Douglas her name, but she went out on a record under the name 'Memphis Minnie.'" Even as a "girl, a woman about eighteen years old," Moore noted, "she could make a guitar 'talk,' say 'Fare thee well!!'" When Brown became her neighbor and back-up guitarist, she was about twenty and at least as experienced as he.

Memphis Minnie was born in Algiers, Louisiana in 1897. But she was raised in Walls, Mississippi, five miles (and two train stops) north of Lake Cormorant, where she is believed to have taken up guitar in 1908 at age 11.[9] In 1920 she ran away from home to work as an itinerant musician, traveling as far north as Jackson, Tennessee, where she played on the streets. At Bedford's, Moore said "she learned how play a piano there, after she learned guitar," learning from "a fella that come outta Walls every Friday evenin' to play for a roadhouse; they called him 'Kid' Crackintine." Her main instrument was still the guitar. "She's a guitar king," Moore held.

Her arrival resulted in Moore becoming a third wheel. "When she's playin' with us, she played lead all the time, [Willie played 'second,' and] I'd play 'third.' She do the singin.' When she wouldn't sing, I'd sing, sometime." Often their audiences were white. "Oh man, we played for all them white folks there in Lake Cormorant. Mister Adams what had that big brick house there, when he didn't get Handy's band outta Memphis, if he's given a little light 'sociable' (party) 'round there, we'd play for them. We'd be playin' for all them white folks: Mister Bass and Mister Cox, Mister Blair." They also played for local merchants who hired them to attract black patrons. "We'd be in a store, and the man'd have somethin' to sell. We'd play two, three hours, somethin' like that."

For white audiences, Brown played the role of pop musician. "He's playin' for them white folks mostly about 'You Great Big Beautiful Doll,' said Moore, referring to the 1911 song hit. "The biggest thing them white folks liked was 'Let Me Call You Sweetheart,' that's a waltz." That song had appeared in 1910, selling five million copies of sheet music. Memphis Minnie's favorite pop offering was "What Makes You Do Me Like You Do Do Do?" which was popularized by Gene Austin on a 1924 record. At a 1921 white party on the excursion boat Idlewild, the three musicians boarded at Lake Cormorant and made $119 in tips by the time they stepped off at Biggs, Arkansas. Although Moore found that "some of them white folks liked the blues better than the colored did," the white venues where Brown and Moore performed were not always more lucrative. "I'll tell you one thing: we wouldn't make five dollars that much. We'd get a tip sometimes, sometimes we wouldn't."

Among local black audiences, Moore said, Brown had a larger following than Memphis Minnie, a fact he attributed to her lesser experience. "He's playin' before she was. She wasn't nothin' but a girl, and he'd been playin'." But she was about the same age as Brown, and she was hardly the less experienced guitarist. But Brown had been catering to Lake Cormorant audiences for something like five years when she came to the area, and so he may have had greater recognition by virtue of local seniority. Moore considered her a better instrumentalist than Brown, and he snickered at the authors' suggestion that she could have developed under Brown. "Wasn't nothin' he could teach her. Everything Willie Brown could play, she could play, and then she could play some things he couldn't play."

Although Minnie knew "Pony Blues," she never recorded any material that can be associated with Brown or Charlie Patton. She was the first recorded Mississippi dance guitarist to specialize in fast single-string picking. To boost her sound, she relied on the flatpicked guitar on the bass strings of her common-law husband, Kansas Joe McCoy, whom she met in the late 1920s. The origins of this musical arrangement may perhaps be in her earlier performances with Brown. Nonetheless, Moore reported that Brown was her local duet partner for five or six years, through 1923 or 1924, a span of time that suggests that Brown may have had closer professional ties to Minnie than to Charlie Patton. Despite her frequent travels ("she'd skip around every which a-way"), she lived among Bedford plantation's residents until the late 1920s when, Moore reported, "she went to Memphis." There she began an enormously successful recording career that lasted until the early 1950s. Her departure from Lake Cormorant was welcomed by the women there, who resented her as a competitor for their men. "They didn't like her, and the men didn't like Charlie Patton," Moore reported.

Brown's partnership with Charlie Patton during the 1920s seems to have been mostly for single nights. As he did with Memphis Minnie, he performed as a backup guitarist, adding volume to Patton's music and enabling Patton to coast whenever fatigue or liquor was slowing him down. Brown played the second for so long that, when he met Son House in 1930, he had a solo repertory of "not over five or six pieces," by House's later recollection. "Very seldom would he sing," House said. "He's sing the 'Pony Blues' and the 'Jinks.' But the rest of them, he never did sing much." By the time when Ernest Brown reunited with him in Robinsonville in the mid-1920s, "The Jinks" had replaced "Pony Blues" as the signature tune of Brown's songbag. "That Willie Brown's favorite, the 'Jinks,'" Ernest Brown noted. Because Willie's voice was too weak for house frolics—House compared it to "kinda a rattle"—he relied on his ability to "complement" other performers to be hired for most of his playing dates. Brown's assisting role was what probably encouraged Patton to quarrel often with him, as if Patton considered Brown as expendable.

In his old age, Son House distorted Brown's performing relationship to Patton by presenting Brown's subordination as something he adopted by choice. "Willie would always do the 'complement,' let Charlie lead and he'd do the 'complementing' behind him," described House, "He was a great 'complementer.'" His view of Brown's function was shared by others. Willie Moore said, "Willie Brown was the best 'complement' man. I ain't never heard no one could 'complement' no better." Ernest Brown attested, "Willie Brown could near about make a guitar 'talk,' secondin.'"

But unlike most "complement" guitarists, Brown could play well by himself. Ishman Bracey saw Brown and Patton "up around Indianola" sometime after Patton's 1929 recording debut. In the mid-1960s, he raved on Brown's behalf, "Yes sir, he could play that guitar!" If Patton had any criticism of Brown, he kept it to himself. According to House, whenever Brown played, the older man played the role of appreciative listener and requested his pet piece "The Jinks." "A lot of times we'd be together and Bill—he [Patton] called him 'Bill'—'Bill, you c'mon, play that piece.'" House added, "He didn't act like he was jealous, He act like he loved to hear him [Brown] play."

For the most part, though, Patton and Brown tended to bicker. "They'd squabble all the time, anytime they'se together and playin' and makin' music," House recalled. Musical disagreements often ignited their clashes. Willie Moore noted, "Sometimes they'd get to talkin,' you know, about what was the 'Jelly Roll Blues' played in, or what was the 'Down Home Blues' played in." He remembered their arguments would go like this:

> "Man, I know all about it! It's written in so-and-so!"
> "No!"

"Oh man, such-and-such a thing's written in C!"
"No!"

Although Patton may be thought of as the instigator, he and Brown could be equally argumentative, if what Moore remembered is any indication. But Patton could become abusive whenever he lost his temper, to which Brown kept calm. "Willie knowed how he was and Willie wouldn't pay him no attention," House said. "He did a lot of cussing and raising sand, but Willie knowed he wasn't going to do nothing."

Brown was also less quick than Patton to approach the women. "Runnin' with women and things like that, he never did get into it," Willie Moore said of Brown, "He's careful about that." Mandy Whigam of Swiftown found Patton to be the more forward with women. "Charlie was kinda on the 'quick' side, you know, 'fast,' she remembered, "he [Brown] wasn't as 'far-out' as Charlie. Willie was more quieter than Charlie."

Even so, Brown acted occasionally like a sporting blues singer, like the time when Ernest Brown tried to mock-convert him. "I laughed at him, say 'Willie Brown, I done got saved an' I done got to the preacher. You'se with me when I'se 'wrong.' Now I want you to get with me now. I'm-a pray for you.' He say 'Don't pray for me. I got eleven dozen women. If you pray for me, I don't know what I'd do, [because] I don't wanna quit all the women I got.'"

Despite that flippant remark, Brown appears to have been a generally humorless man. Playing the blues may have been a burden to him, for he was afraid that God would strike him dead with a thunderbolt if he dared to play a spiritual. "Craziness, I'd call it," House said of Brown's belief, "nothin' but silly." But to earn money of his own, he had to play the blues. His illiteracy meant he couldn't read the Bible and become a professional preacher. Unwilling to work at manual labor, he was dependent on his wife and women for their money. He didn't receive an equal share of each performing fee from Patton, who paid him as he found fit. "He's gonna raise sand if if he didn't get the biggest (cut)," House said of Patton. "He could out-count Willie and all, bring up some kind of excuse." The best excuse of all to pay Brown less money was that Brown served a lesser role.

The earliest documented memory of a joint Patton-Brown appearance stems from 1922, when Patton and Frank Howard went to Junior Austin's barrelhouse near Ruleville. When they entered the premises, they saw Brown on the stage. While chomping on a cigar, he sang the piece he called "Jinks" (which eight years later he recorded for Paramount Records, which titled it "Future Blues"). Then he played several duets with Patton. "Oh, he's good," said Howard, although he qualified Brown as "not quite" as good as Patton himself.

Leroy Willis often saw the pair playing near Ruleville between 1924 and 1926. "He was just as good as Charlie Patton," he insisted about Brown. "They'd be together a whole lotta times. I used to have an uncle, he had a jukehouse out there from Ruleville for a long time, down what they called 'Big Field.' They played around there for about a year for my uncle. Charlie there always done the singing." But Willie Young, a guitarist who saw Brown play on a Cleveland, Mississippi street in 1928, thought differently of Brown. "He wasn't as good a musician as Charlie. Charlie was the best. I'd rather hear him anytime than hear Willie Brown."

Hayes McMullan first heard Patton and Brown play in the late 1920s in Tallahatchie County. About 40 years later, to the authors, he remembered Brown as being the better guitarist, on the basis of the assumption that Patton played his guitar mostly in Spanish tuning.[10] "Willie Brown was a better 'note' fella than he (Patton) was. But Charlie Patton was the leadin' man, you see."

Ernest Brown knew Willie Brown better than he did Patton, but he didn't let familiarity color his vision. "He was over Willie Brown," he said of Patton. "Everybody thought that Willie Brown was over Charlie, but he wasn't; Willie Brown couldn't play with Charlie. He's complement him. When Charlie Patton'd get tired a-leadin', he'd let Willie Brown play some, an' he'd 'second' behind him."

While only two of Brown's 1930 Paramount studio recordings survive, comparing them with Patton's records may bring forth some distinctive points about Brown's musicianship. His reputation as a solo bluesman may be considered on the performance that Paramount titled "Future Blues" but what he called "The Jinks." In the 1960s, when Elizabeth Moore heard a copy of the Paramount performance, she exclaimed, "That's Willie Brown's voice, 'cause that's him to a T!" She described its opening bass riff as "draggin' it down" on the guitar. While the piece seems to suggest the opening verse of "Pony Blues," it is really is a slow-drag arrangement of Patton's "Maggie" melody, Brown imitating Patton's fretting positions yet trying to make his treatment sound individual. By snapping each of the four bass notes of the opening riff,

Brown supplies a strong rhythmic pulse that is absent from his singing, whose phrasing usually fits an "eleven-five" call-and-response pattern, compared to Patton's "ten-six."

While listening to the "Future Blues" record, H. C. Speir commented, "There ain't no comparison between him and Charlie," noting that "This is a flat style." A careful scrutiny of Brown's accompaniment suggests that Brown was technically more crude and playing more by rote than Patton. The bass line he uses is much like that of Tommy Johnson's "Maggie Campbell Blues," overlaid with by the snapping effects from the initial verse of Patton's "High Water Everywhere." For much of the performance, Brown's instrumental timing sometimes clashes rhythmically with his singing. For example, during the second lyric phrase of each blues chorus, he plays this single-note bass-string figure:

Ex. 44: Willie Brown, "Future Blues" (1930), mm. 5-6 of each chorus, guitar bass-string figure [chorus 2: 0:42-0:45] (after Grossman).

Patton had used the same figure during the second verse of "Screamin' and Hollerin' the Blues," and also during the third verse of "Heart Like Railroad Steel." Whereas on the latter record Patton's 1-2 dance-blues guitar accenting meshes with his vocal accenting, Brown's accenting is rather even, risking the beat of his song to give way to momentary jumbles. Given the fact that Brown is playing a percussive accompaniment with no real melodic figures, the risk of lapses is quite high for someone whom Son House extolled by saying in 1967, "Charlie could beat him singin', but those beats and things, Willie could beat him in that and he (Charlie) knowed it . . . "[11]

Despite the fact that "Future Blues" was played much slower than Patton's recorded versions of the "Maggie" melody, and that it was the mainstay of Brown's repertory, its recording tends to offer more repetitions than variations. Its IV-chord figure of the second phrase (Ex. 45) is comprised of two identical snippets, although it is a rather understated support for Brown's vocal call.

To render his accompaniment more simple, Brown's instrumental links between stanzas concludes with this snapped-string riff (Ex. 46):

Ex. 45: Willie Brown, "Future Blues" (1930) mm. 5-6 of each chorus, two "snippets" [chorus 2: 0:42-0:45] (after Grossman).

Ex. 46: Willie Brown, "Future Blues" (1930), each chorus, guitar riff leading to next chorus [chorus 1: 0:28-0:32] (after Grossman).

With its irregular timing, and its lack of contrast and variety, Brown's "Future Blues" seems crude compared to Patton's "Heart Like Railroad Steel," whose slow-drag accompaniment is played in Spanish tuning without a bottleneck slide. The two songs have several instrumental touches in common, such as this V chord figure (exs. 47 a and b). Patton plays it during the third vocal line of each stanza, rounding it off with an upward swoop to the dominant chord's root tone (G).

Ex. 47a: Charlie Patton, "Heart Like Railroad Steel," the third lyric phrase of each chorus, guitar V-chord figure, [chorus 1: 0:26-0:30].

Brown also executes the lick during his third lyric phrase of each chorus, but he delays it for a beat, and lets its last tone ring out during the weak fourth beat:

Ex. 47b: Willie Brown, "Future Blues" (1930), the third lyric phrase of each chorus, guitar V-chord figure [chorus 1: 0:23-0:26].

The condition of the surviving copy of Patton's "Heart Like Railroad Steel" is extremely poor, yielding a high volume of surface noise when played. Still, enough music is audible to indicate some differences between his approach and Brown's. Patton's rhythm is much more flowing and vigorous than Brown's. His guitar accompaniment uses two different figures during his initial vocal phrase, is more varied, more spontaneous and more responsive to his vocal accenting. For his guitar touch, he mutes individual bass strings and IV-chord figures, and he makes his strings ring out while he plays the passages for V and I chords involving open strings. Brown's strumming sounds bland by comparison. The many nuances that Patton made while recording "Heart Like Railroad Steel" leads a listener to suppose that he had played it often. However, that may not have been case. Booker Miller told the authors that he never heard Patton perform it at the dances they played between 1929 and 1934.

The other song that Brown recorded in 1930, "M.&O. Blues," was derived from "Pony Blues." Since it is too slow and rhythmically uniform to serve as dance music, it may have been intended for street performing, Although "M.&O. Blues" has the conventional "ten-six" blues phrasing pattern, Brown's instrumental timing is more erratic than that on "Future Blues." He minimizes the accompaniment by using the same guitar figure to accompany that last half of all three vocal phrases. His guitar touch lacks dynamic nuances in various shadings, which may be due to using a pick, and it could be a characteristic of his playing of the period.[12] McMullan and House said that he customarily used a pick on his index finger, House reporting that he "used picks mostly all the time."

The four recordings that Patton and Brown recorded together in the summer of 1930 suggest that there may be some truth to Ernest Brown's observation that Brown was unable to "play" at Patton's level. All of his accompaniments rely on strumming, with simple single-note bass fills put on alternate beats of the second phrase of the blues songs he accompanies. Unfortunately, Paramount's unbalanced setup of its microphones muffles Patton's lead guitar parts, and so it makes it difficult to perceive the effect on Brown. For that reason, Brown's accompaniment abilities may only be broadly described on the basis of his recorded duets with Patton, whose playing often discouraged closely knit accompaniments as noted in earlier chapters.

Willie Brown participated in several non-commercial field recordings for study purposes with the Library of Congress recordings near Lake

Cormorant, Mississippi in 1941. As band recordings, they are supplements to Brown's 1930 Paramount recordings. As such, they convey a vivid sense of the settings that Brown played in. Yet they are frustrating for not providing the kind of sparkling lead guitar work that we today expect of a blues guitar legend. For example, one of the performances is "Uncle Sam Done Called," featuring singer and harmonica player Leroy Williams, with Willie Brown on guitar and Fiddlin' Joe Martin for spoken responses. The recording's five instrumental blues choruses should have provided Brown with plenty of opportunities to display his guitar talents. But his accompaniment with its abrupt changes of chords seems to confuse Williams. Also, there are moments in the song when his playing is perhaps too rote, like when he tries playing the V chord at the start of each third lyric phrase. What Brown is copying is Patton's hand position for fretting thc IV chord that sounds the dominant-scale tone on the E treble string (as may be heard during the second lyric phrases of each chorus on Patton's "Down the Dirt Road Blues"). Brown plays the IV chord, and then moves his fretting-hand up two frets to play the V chord. It all seems convenient, but maybe too much so, since the V chord he plays is lacking the major seventh that is needed to ease the transition to the tonic chord during the chorus turnaround. This suggests, then, that Brown was a position player who was guided more by sights than by sounds. It makes Brown seem primitive when compared to Patton, whose chord voicings are always correct, whether playing blues or popular songs.

Brown's surviving cronies sustained into the 1960s the long-standing legend of Willie Brown, yet they were actually posing a contradiction in terms. Had Brown been capable of real ingenuity as a chord player, he would have thumbed his nose at the blues like a Richard Harney,[13] or he would have reinvented himself as a pop musician like a Charlie McCoy.[14] Instead, one could say cynically that Brown was the most famous and best documented, but he was not necessarily the most accomplished, of the various protégés that Patton groomed as his "complement" guitarists during the course of his career.

To temper that cynicism, and to have a balanced appraisal of Willie Brown (I), it may be good to examine again the music recorded in 1929 by the mysterious Kid Bailey, which was examined in chapter four for any traces of blues practices of the 1910s. This time, it will be considered more for Bailey himself. On his two sides, he sounds as though he could have received training as an understudy from either Patton or Willie Brown (I).[15] He remained so anonymous that Willie Young simply remembered him to the authors as "the other one" who sometimes played at dances with Patton and Brown. Bailey's 1929 recording of "Rowdy Blues" is a duet rendition of "Pony Blues." Listening to a tape copy of this version, Mandy Whigham commented, "That sounds just like Willie (I). I think they kinds copied one another, don't you? Ain't Willie makin' music on there? I think that's Willie makin' music." Son House thought that the vocal and lead guitar was performed by Brown (I) and the bass backing to Patton. Elizabeth Moore responded to the record with the observation, "Him (Willie Brown [I]) and Son both could make that 'introduction' on their music like that. Sounds like that music and that voice—pretty close there, if it ain't him [Brown]." When Bailey's name was mentioned to her, it reminded her. "Him and that Kid Bailey made music together sometime, I know. That fella's been with Willie Brown (I) playin' right here at Lake Cormorant. I see'd him natural, in person. He'd come there with Willie, and I don't know where he lived at: I just knowed they'd been over there to the juke on Saturday night." She then recalled that Brown around 1930 mentioned to her that he had recently recorded with Bailey, a story that for more than 35 years she dismissed as an empty claim.

On his records, Bailey's vocal delivery comes off as sedate when compared to Patton's. But the melody of Bailey's "Mississippi Bottom Blues" is based on the same three intervals (the minor seventh, tonic, and minor third) that Patton had used during the opening verse of his "Screamin' and Hollerin' The Blues."

Perhaps, if such exact vocal openings are indications, Bailey was groomed as an accompanist or intermission performer by Patton or a Patton imitator, but then went into business for himself once he acquired his musical skills. If he was a floater with no fixed base of operations, he enjoyed none of the prestige that came to someone like Willie Brown (I) who could be almost always found in one place. Almost no Delta bluesman of the pre-war era, at least among those who made records, is as obscure as Bailey. None of the authors' informants knew him well enough to learn his proper name or birthplace. Typical of their encounters with a man who seemingly cast no shadow were Booker Miller's sightings of him on the streets of Moorhead and Itta Bena around 1937. Usually, a bluesman promoted his evening performance by busking on the streets during the day. As Miller explained, "You get ready to go in the country at that time, you'd come to town. And you play a piece or two

[to] let the people know which a-way you goin'. Then you take off." But Bailey always seemed to give no hints to his day listeners as to where he "took off" for the evening gigs.

During the time when Miller saw him, Bailey seemed to be mostly around Leland, a town with a population of 2400 that was located between Greenville and Indianola, some twenty-five miles southwest of Dockery's, and ten miles west of Holly Ridge. Aging residents in the 1960s remembered Bailey being in and around Leland between 1932 (when he played with Patton and frequented a café called Ruby's Place) and 1945; a funeral parlor director recalled hearing him perform on a Leland street as late as 1950. In that year, the Bentonia bluesmen Henry Stuckey and Skip James met Bailey playing mandolin in a Moorhead barrelhouse. Another informant heard him play on an Indianola sidewalk in 1958. Two years later, he turned up in Canton, a hill town south of the Delta. There, for a few days, he performed in a beer joint and on the sidewalk in front of the town's black brothel. From that point on, his trail disappears. "They told me he died a natural death," reported Robert Gildart of Leland, who used to engage guitarists for house frolics. "I didn't quiz 'em much about it [because] I wasn't too much interested. I said 'Well, there's another goodtimer gone.'"

Where Bailey came from is more certain than where he went to during the 1960s. Thomas (Niney) Newton was a guitarist from the Sunflower County town of Linn (some fifteen miles southeast of Dockery's) who occasionally accompanied Patton in the 1920s. He stated that Bailey hailed from the 5800-acre Eastland plantation near Doddsville, located five miles south of Ruleville. Another source placed him on McCline's plantation nearby. The aging town constable who patrolled Doddsville in the mid-1960s recalled that Bailey had played on the town's main street for decades, but he did not know anything about him. An occasional local associate was his cousin Ben Wiley Bailey, who died in 1966 at the age of 62. His widow (who lived near Indianola when interviewed in 1967) said that he had played with Kid Bailey in Doddsville sometime before that latter's 1929 recording session. She knew nothing else of Kid Bailey.

Patton visited Doddsville and the Eastland plantation throughout the mid-1920s. In nearby Blaine in the late 1920s, Hayes McMullan frequently met up with Willie Brown (I). Before World War I, the vicinity of Drew, eleven miles north of Doddsville, was the turf of several musicians who borrowed chunks of Patton's material. Although one native of Drew would say that Bailey's "Mississippi Bottom Blues" sounded "just like Drew's Nathan Bankston", Bankston himself never heard of Bailey.

A former Ruleville farmer named Leroy Willis witnessed a number of Bailey's performances in the mid-1920s, and he thought him as Charlie Patton's equal. "I remember the Kid in and around Drew, Ruleville and Tutwiler," he remarked. "He played lots in Tutwiler. He's by hisself all the time." A favorite site of Bailey's performances was Tutwiler's Silver Moon café.

For two years in the late 1920s (probably 1926-1928), Bailey played solo at weekend house frolics organized by a bootlegger named Alfred Davis on the Hollyknoe plantation, which lies about three miles southeast of Leland and forty miles southwest of Doddsville. Davis' wife Julia, who cooked for these weekend affairs, thought that Bailey lived on the plantation but did not farm there. She didn't know what were his weekday activities, and the strong sense of shame she felt about her husband's activities prevented her from taking much notice of Bailey, whom she remembered as a heavy-set "dark brownskin" who stood over six feet tall. Still, she thought that Bailey's voice was superior to Patton's because "he [Bailey] don't 'holler,' singin."

After the Mississippi River flood of 1927, and perhaps following his departure from Hollyknoe, Bailey frequently visited the town of Skene. "He'd come in here, I don't know exactly where he lived at," recalled Bunk Ashford, a former Skene resident. "He'd just go around, different places." Another stop was a jukehouse called Dark Road in Boyle, where Charlie Patton also visited. "It seemed like they was good friends," Ashford said of the pair, adding that Bailey would always "play by hisself. He played guitar, and then he used to play piano a little."

Bailey was also a friend of Tommy Johnson. According to Ishmon Bracey, the two men often played "over there in Rankin County in a juke . . . call it Gold." Johnson claimed to Bracey that he, not Bailey, created "Rowdy Blues." Then again, Johnson had also bragged he had taught "Pony Blues" to Charlie Patton. Bracey took these boasts for what they were, but while listening to Bailey's record he remarked to the authors, "He got that swing from Tommy, but he puts those words in there himself."

Although Bailey worked as a soloist, he is also recalled as a member of a string band that Charlie Patton brought to various Sunflower County barrelhouses in the mid-1920s; it may have been the success of this enterprise that encouraged Bailey's solo career. Its other members were a mandolinist from the Doddsville area named James Hardy, and a violinist who lived between Doddsville and Linn, John Nance. Ishman Bracey saw Hardy play with Patton in Jackson and the Delta and said of him, "He could play and violin and a mandolin and a guitar." Nance was a multi-instrumentalist who also played guitar, as Booker Miller attested, "That man, though, he was a fiddler and a guitar player. That man could play anything, I believe. That fella naturally knowed music: he could make music, but he couldn't sing, he ain't sung one word." By the 1980s, both men were long dead, and the sound they produced with Patton went unrecorded, and also forgotten by those who heard it.

Dockery's Plantation entrance, as may be seen from Mississippi Highway 8. Around 1900, Patton with his family moved there, where he could be found for the most part through the end of 1929. (Wardlow collection.)

Talent broker H. C. Speir as he appeared during the 1920s, when he referred Patton, Tommy Johnson, and a host of other Mississippi Delta bluesmen to the record labels. (Wardlow collection.)

Mississippi Delta landscape, 1940. Tenants lived close to the fields where they worked, yet their shacks were often spaced just far enough apart to discourage much frisky play. (Marion Post Woolcott photograph, Farm Security Administration, Library of Congress / [p.d.].)

Map of northwest and central Mississippi. Edwards and Bolton may be found due west of the state capital, Jackson. Around 1900, the Patton family moved north from Edwards to Dockery Plantation on the northwest border of Sunflower County. (p.d.)

Will Dockery. In 1888 he began wresting cotton farmland from the thick Delta swamp. Despite his success and wealth, his dying wish in 1936 was to return a half-century later to see the changes to his lands. (Wardlow collection.)

Dockery stationery. Unlike other Delta landowners, Will Dockery didn't call himself a planter, but rather a 'merchant and farmer.' (Wardlow collection.)

**WILL DOCKERY**

**MERCHANT AND FARMER**

**Dockery, Miss.,** ................................................ 19

Dockery's plantation commissary, which at one time was run by a staff of six full-time employees. It provided service not only to the residing tenants, but also to those from neighboring plantations. (Wardlow collection.)

The more money that a landowner could keep on his grounds, the less drain on his financial resources. Scrip coins like these from Dockery's (front and back) were one means of regulating the flow of money. Without them, federal currency would have to be used, with a risk to the landowner's economic power. He would have viewed with contempt and suspicion the gamblers and musicians who took federal paper bills and coins from his tenants and spent elsewhere what he regarded as "his" money. (Wardlow collection.)

It is believed that Patton, near the beginning of his musical career, may have performed briefly in a medicine show, which used entertainment to attract customers for quack medicines that were touted as 'good for what ails you.' Here is a photograph of such a show, Dr. Blackhawk's, as taken in Philadelphia, MS, in 1920. (Wardlow collection.)

Clarksdale, Mississippi drugstore, 1909. Certainly a more effective, and more reputable, source for pharmaceuticals than the medicine shows. (Wardlow collection.)

Portrait of the youthful Patton circa 1908, first owned by his early wife Lizzie Taylor. She passed it to her friend Flora Kimball, who then gave it to the author Gayle Wardlow. (Wardlow collection.)

Photographs of frolics, barrelhouses, and juke joints taken before 1942 are rare. The images reproduced here (from Memphis, and from Clarksdale, MS) were taken by Marion Post Woolcott in 1939 as part of the Works Progress Administration Farm Security project. (Marion Post Woolcott photograph, Farm Security Administration, Library of Congress / [p.d.].)

Until the Delta lands were drained, travel was easier by river than by roads. Patton's 1930 record "Jim Lee Blues" was at least nostalgic, if not authentic, for the riverboat era. Lee steamboat line postcard, 1900s. (Public domain.)

"On the Levee, Memphis, Tenn." Another postcard featuring a Lee line steamboat. (Public domain.)

After the forests were lumbered and the swamplands cleared, railroads replaced riverboats as transportation. Shown here is the no. 9 engine on the Yazoo and Mississippi Railroad, which took over the Yazoo-Delta Railroad that was called "the Yellow Dog." (Wardlow collection.)

W. C. Handy in later years. During the 1900s and 1910s, he and his bands were what Mississippi whites and many blacks would have acknowledged as popular blues. Patton, by comparison, would have seemed like a vagrant. (Public domain.)

Willie Moore in 1968. Whether or not he truly was once Handy's valet in the 1910s, Moore thought highly enough of Patton to wish he was in Handy's band. (Wardlow collection.)

Tommy Johnson from a 1928 Victor Records catalog. He learned several of Patton's core songs in the 1910s, and he would make some celebrated renditions of them in his own style on records in 1928 and 1930. (Publicity photograph / public domain.)

Nathan "Dick" Bankston learned from Patton in the early 1910s, and first met Tommy Johnson in 1914. (Wardlow collection.)

The Chatmon family in the mid-to-late 1910s, possibly just after the time that Patton spent with them after fleeing from his brother at Dockery's. Sitting are (*left to right*) Liza and Henderson (mother and father), Josephine, Bo (Carter) wearing cap, and on the far right Lonnie with his hand on Bo's shoulder. Identified among those standing is Sam wearing hat and jacket, between Josephine and Bo. (Wardlow collection.)

Josephine Chatmon Williams, in 1969. (Wardlow collection.)

The plantation house at Cottondale, at which steps Patton met his neighbor Frank Howard. Patton was Cottondale's resident musician from 1921 to 1923. (Wardlow collection.)

Buy War Saving Stamps NOW. Don't delay Let's WIN;

# The Bolivar County D

31 ROSEDALE BOLIVAR COUNTY, MISS. SATURDAY, JUNE 15, 1918.


Bolivar County Democrat
at the Postoffice at Rosedale,
as second-class matter.
SCRIPTION, $1 50.
LINNELL, - - EDITOR
AND LESSE.


AN PROPAGANDA IN THE SENATE.

article in the Saturday g Post of June 8th, David e, a noted writer, has an under the title, "Germany's Thousand Mile Guns," in explained that Germany is using in this war what is hed to guns shooting three ed miles by having agents ere use bombs for destroy- ehouses, ammunition fac- and spreading German pro- da throughout the United

r discussing the German ganda in this country and the that the Government has a checkmate the scoundrels were stirring up strife among borers of this country and g the seeds of discontent g all classes to the extent of ability (which resulted in the ge of the Sabotage law), Mr. erce uses the following lan-

he chief trend of the German ganda at first was an empha- the doctrine that this is a alists war. German agents tri- realist socialist aid in spread- he theory, but with little s."

ly, fortunately, German n did not meet with much s among the socialists of the ry, they found an able spokes- n the United States Senate

riots, strikes and cause discord among the people of the United States and thus aid the Kaiser in his attempts to conquer the world.

We contend that if Vardaman, by his acts above noted, knew that he was attempting to aid the enemy, he should be removed from office; and if he did not realize the fact, he has not got sense enough to represent the people of Mississippi in the United States Senate, and therefore should be defeated at the polls in the August primary.

His recent address to the citizens of our State was merely an attempt to retain his membership in the Senate that he may continue to fight more successfully the battles of the Kaiser than he could if he were a private citizen.

Mississippi cannot afford to have such a man in the Senate. If he should be renominated it would leave a mark of disloyalty on our people that would remain for generations, even though our sons fought ever so valliantly on the battle fields of France.

Evry loyal citizen should think this matter over seriously, and then vote as his conscience dictates.

———W. S. S.———

DODGING THE ISSUE.

Vardaman's personal organ, The Issue, published at Jackson, fails to meet the issue in this campaign —the Junior Senator's record in matters concerning the war—and tries to shift the Senatorial battle to the race question and prohibition. It will find that neither of these issues are "live ones" in this campaign. The negroes are standing by the white people of Mississippi in the prosecution of

LIST OF PERSONS REGISTRING AT ROSEDALE JUNE 5TH.

1 Walter French, Lobdell, col.
2 Jim Campbell, Lobdell, col.
3 Allen Harris, Perthshire, col.
4 Felix Rex Cummings, Gunnison, col.
5 Oliver Richardson, Rosedale, col.
6 Perry Lee Martin, Benoit, col.
7 Will Evans, Benoit, col.
8 John Ellis, Benoit, col.
9 Shelby Slater, Benoit, col.
10 Jesse Kerns, Scott, col.
11 Edward Charles Clork, Rosedale, col.
12 James Porter, Rosedale, col.
13 Johnie Johnson, Deeson, col.
14 Henry Johnson, Dahomey, col.
15 Clarence Watson, Scott, col.
16 Thomas Harris, Gunnison, col.
17 Ambrose Washington, Benoit, col.
18 Joseph Singleton, Deeson, col.
19 Mike Davis, Dahomey, col.
20 Loyd Augusta Chamblin, Beulah, wh.
21 Louis Crawford Crews, Dahomey, wh.
22 Jim Jackson, Round Lake, col.
23 William Parker, Lobdell, col.
24 Jerry Baker, Grapeland, wh.
25 William Parker Scott, Rosedale, wh.
26 Itiliana Pas'asini, Rosedale, wh.
27 Oscar C. Powers, Utica, wh.
28 Hosie Pice, Rosedale, wh.
29 Everett Palmer, Lobdell, wh
30 Clinton Maddox, Pace, wh.
31 John Parks, Symonds, col.
32 Claudius Carlisle Smith, Rosedale, wh.
33 William Walter Butlerworth, Rosedale, wh.
34 William Franklin Young, Rosedale, wh.
35 Nolan Stewart Wren, Stringtown, wh.
36 Robert K. Orr, Benoit, wh.
37 Emmett A. Kindrough, Lamont, wh.
38 Robert Burns, Grapeland, wh.
39 Frank Coon, Grapeland, wh.
40 Arthur A. McDaniel, Rosedale, wh
41 Julius Bossi, Pace, wh.
42 Joe Gosconi, Pace, wh.
43 Tony Pretti, Rosedale, wh.
44 Vinson Ingram, Scott, col.
45 Elijah Benton, Gunnison, col.
46 Paul Barnes, Foote, col.
47 Ernie Ellis, Hillhouse, col.
48 John Owen, Rex, col.
49 Anderson Calvin, Lobdell, col.
50 Henry Mosby, Lobdell, col.
51 Jesse Ward, Perthshire, col.
52 Dennis Wade, Lobdell, col.
53 Willie Wade, Lobdell, col.
54 John Toney, Benoit, col.
55 Henry McEvans, Rosedale, col.

154 Robert Haney, Dahomey, col.
155 Dave Wheeler, Rosedale, col.
156 Solam Martin, Benoit, col.
157 Joe Craig, Benoit, col.
158 Richard Brown, Rosedale, col.
159 Phil Roberson, Benoit, col.
160 Elbert Miles, Benoit, col.
161 James Williams, Gunnison, col.
162 Wil Hays, Gunnison, col.
163 Theo. Bowie, Fall Back, col.
164 William Wright, Stringtown, col.
165 Julius Brooks, Stringotwn, col.
166 Wil Roe, Lamont, col.
167 George Bingham, Fall Back, col.
168 Charlie Webb, Lamont, col.
169 Lee Baker, Rosedale, col.
170 John Gray, Lamont, col.
171 Willie Brown, Round Lae, col.
172 Jones Evans, Round Lake, col.
173 Andrew Weisinger, Benoit, col.
174 John Woodley, Benoit, col.
175 Sylvester Johnson, Gunnison, col.
176 George Singleton, Benoit, col.
177 Shad Buford, Benoit, col.
178 James Banks, Beulah, col.
179 Israel Ball, Beulah, col.
180 Tom Young, Beulah, col.
181 Robert Haney, Lobdell, col.
182 Elijah Junior, Mound City, col.
183 Fred Douglas, Gunnison, col.
184 George Johnson, Gunnison, col.
185 James Johnson, Benoit, col.
186 Robert Garrett, 300 Water st., Helena, Ark., col.
187 Willie Moore, Benoit, col.
188 Joseph Boman, R. F. D. No. 1, Box 87, Shelby, col.
189 William Eugene Neal, Lamont, wh.
190 Sam Brown, Rosedale, col.
191 Eddie Brown, Rosedale, col.
192 Luther Dean, Gunnison, col.
193 Henry Bradley, Gunnison, Col.
194 Grover Ballard, Rosedale; Col.
195 Jacob Carter, Perthshire; Col.

———W. S. S.———

## Red Cross Notes.

This is a summary of the work shipped to the Gulf Division of the American Red Cross by the Riverside Chapter, during the last two weeks of April and the month of May. This chapter is composed of the following towns: Round Lake, Deeson, Perthshire, Gunnison, Malvina, Pace, Rosedale, Beulah, Benoit and Scott.

HOSPITAL GARMENTS.

| | |
|---|---|
| Pajamas | 203 |
| Underware | 76 |
| Socks | 264 |
| Pillow Cases | 106 |



The *Bolivar Country Democrat* (Rosedale MS) newspaper of June 15, 1918, listed Patton associates Willie Brown (no. 171) and Willie Moore (no. 187) among the registrants for World War I service. The armistice came six months later. To Moore, it later seemed that "both our class cards came on a Friday, and peace declared that Sunday mornin'." (Public domain.)

A picture of three workmen, circa 1910s, recently recovered and tentatively identified as (*left to right*) Willie Moore, Willie Brown (l.), and either Billy Dickson or Fiddlin' Joe Martin. If authentic, this may be the only likeness to survive of Brown. Willie Brown may be regarded as either the most enduring, or the most tolerant, of Patton's sidemen, performing with him for about 15 years. Whatever Brown may have felt about Patton then or after Patton's death, Patton made sure to include Brown on his summer 1930 trip to Paramount's recording studio. (Wardlow collection.)

A common sight in Delta towns during the immediate aftermath of the 1927 Mississippi River flood: the waters swamping the streets up to the wheel wells of the cars, while the only dry land was on the levee (*foreground*). (Public domain.)

A shot of another levee just after the 1927 flood, this one at Vicksburg, Mississippi. (Public domain.)

Art Laibly, seen here later in life, was the Paramount Records executive who in late spring 1929 accepted H. C. Speir's recommendation to sign Charlie Patton. (Wardlow collection.)

Although Hayes McMullan was a weekend musician, he was known to the professionals like Patton. In the late 1960s, he claimed to have received second hand an invitation from Patton to travel with him to his first recording session in June 1929. (Wardlow collection.)

The Gennett and Sons recording studio located in Richmond, Indiana. (side and front view). Here in June 1929 Patton made his first recordings, including his hits "Pony Blues" and "Screamin' and Hollerin' the Blues." (Wardlow collection.)

*Chicago Defender* newspaper ad for Patton's "Pony Blues," July 1929. (Publicity / public domain.)

Paramount's *Masked Marvel* promotional contest was held in August 1929, for which Patton's "Screamin' and Hollerin the Blues" was issued as by The Masked Marvel. The contest was successful enough to sell out that initial pressing, and to allow a second run of copies with Patton's name on the labels. (Publicity / public domain.)

"DOWN THE DIRT ROAD BLUES"

by Charley Patton

HE'S had a lot of trouble at home and he's decided to hit the dirty, dusty trail for parts unknown. He wants to forget everything and to go somewhere else, so he sings this novel Blues, as his lazy mule joggles him along the old dirt road. Be sure to ask for Paramount No. 12854, at your dealer's, or send us the coupon.

[ **12854—Down The Dirt Road Blues** and **It Won't Be Long;** Charley Patton; guitar acc. ]

**12851—Hot Lovin'** and **Mama Stayed Out,** Barrel House Five.

**12823—Honey Dripper Blues** and **Nickel's Worth of Liver Blues,** Edith Johnson; piano acc.

**12792—Pony Blues** and **Banty Rooster Blues,** Charley Patton; guitar acc.

**12817—Back To The Woods Blues** and **Good Gal,** Charlie Spand; piano and guitar acc.

**12819—Black And Evil Blues** and **Broadway St. Woman Blues,** Alice Moore; piano-trombone acc.

**12796—Somebody's Been Using That Thing** and **It's All Worn Out,** The Hokum Boys; piano-guitar acc.

**12855—Pitchin' Boogie** and **Just Can't Stay Here,** Piano Solos by Will Ezell.

**12833—Uncle Joe** and **Can I Get Some Of That?**—Coot Grant and Socks Wilson; piano acc

**12825—Twenty First St. Stomp** and **Henry Brown Blues;** Piano Solos by Henry Brown.

**Beautiful Spirituals**

**12834—Paul And Silas** and **I Heard My Mother Call My Name In Prayer,** South Carolina Quartette.

**12815—Way Down In Egyptland** and **I'm Gonna Serve God Till I Die,** Norfolk Jubilee Quartette.

**SEND NO MONEY!** If your dealer is out of the records you want, send us the coupon below. Pay postman 75 cents for each record, plus small C.O.D. fee when he delivers records. *We pay postage on shipments of two or more records.*

**Paramount**

REG. US PAT OFF

*The Popular Race Record*

ELECTRICALLY RECORDED

The New York Recording Laboratories
12 Paramount Bldg.
Port Washington, Wis.

Send me the records checked (✓) below 75 cents each.

( ) 12854 ( ) 12817 ( ) 12833
( ) 12851 ( ) 12819 ( ) 12825
( ) 12823 ( ) 12796 ( ) 12834
( ) 12792 ( ) 12855 ( ) 12818

Name.................................
Address.................................
City........................ State..........

*Chicago Defender* ad for Patton's "Down the Dirt Road Blues," fall 1929. (Publicity / public domain.)

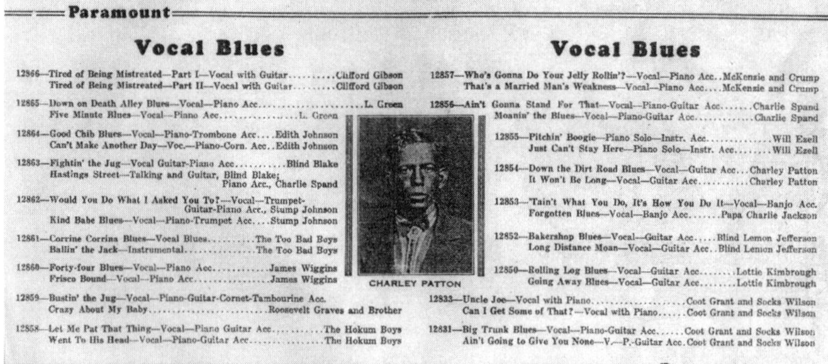

**Paramount**

**Vocal Blues**

12866—Tired of Being Mistreated—Part I—Vocal with Guitar..........Clifford Gibson
Tired of Being Mistreated—Part II—Vocal with Guitar..........Clifford Gibson

12865—Down on Death Alley Blues—Vocal—Piano Acc......................L. Green
Five Minute Blues—Vocal—Piano Acc..................L. Green

12864—Good Chib Blues—Vocal—Piano-Trombone Acc....Edith Johnson
Can't Make Another Day—Voc.—Piano-Corn. Acc..Edith Johnson

12863—Fightin' the Jug—Vocal Guitar-Piano Acc...........Blind Blake
Hastings Street—Talking and Guitar, Blind Blake; Piano Acc., Charlie Spand

12862—Would You Do What I Asked You To?—Vocal—Trumpet-Guitar-Piano Acc., Stump Johnson
Kind Babe Blues—Vocal—Piano-Trumpet Acc....Stump Johnson

12861—Corrine Corrina Blues—Vocal Blues..........The Too Bad Boys
Ballin' the Jack—Instrumental...............The Too Bad Boys

12860—Forty-four Blues—Vocal—Piano Acc............James Wiggins
Frisco Bound—Vocal—Piano Acc.................James Wiggins

12859—Bustin' the Jug—Vocal—Piano-Guitar-Cornet-Tambourine Acc.
Crazy About My Baby..........................Roosevelt Graves and Brother

12858—Let Me Pat That Thing—Vocal—Piano Guitar Acc...........The Hokum Boys
Went To His Head—Vocal—Piano-Guitar Acc.................The Hokum Boys

CHARLEY PATTON

**Vocal Blues**

12857—Who's Gonna Do Your Jelly Rollin'?—Vocal—Piano Acc..McKenzie and Crump
That's a Married Man's Weakness—Vocal—Piano Acc....McKenzie and Crump

12856—Ain't Gonna Stand For That—Vocal—Piano-Guitar Acc.......Charlie Spand
Moanin' the Blues—Vocal—Piano-Guitar Acc.............Charlie Spand

12855—Pitchin' Boogie—Piano Solo—Instr. Acc...............Will Ezell
Just Can't Stay Here—Piano Solo—Instr. Acc.........Will Ezell

12854—Down the Dirt Road Blues—Vocal—Guitar Acc...Charley Patton
It Won't Be Long—Vocal—Guitar Acc...........Charley Patton

12853—'Tain't What You Do, It's How You Do It—Vocal—Banjo Acc.
Forgotten Blues—Vocal—Banjo Acc.......Papa Charlie Jackson

12852—Bakershop Blues—Vocal—Guitar Acc.....Blind Lemon Jefferson
Long Distance Moan—Vocal—Guitar Acc..Blind Lemon Jefferson

12850—Rolling Log Blues—Vocal—Guitar Acc........Lottie Kimbrough
Going Away Blues—Vocal—Guitar Acc........Lottie Kimbrough

12833—Uncle Joe—Vocal with Piano.....................Coot Grant and Socks Wilson
Can I Get Some of That?—Vocal with Piano......Coot Grant and Socks Wilson

12831—Big Trunk Blues—Vocal—Piano-Guitar Acc......Coot Grant and Socks Wilson
Ain't Going to Give You None—V.—P.-Guitar Acc. Coot Grant and Socks Wilson

**Paramount**

Paramount brochure with Patton half-portrait. By the end of 1929, with three hit records in quick succession, Patton was featured by Paramount as its newest star. (Publicity / public domain / Wardlow collection.)

By the time of the *Chicago Defender*'s January 1930 ad for "A Spoonful Blues," Patton's face was deemed recognizable enough to help sell his records. In this song, however, the topic was drugs, not soup. (Publicity / public domain.)

PEA VINE BLUES

by Charley Patton

For some real guitar playing and singing you should hear PEA VINE BLUES by Charley Patton. Get yourself ready for one of the finest records you ever heard — both sides are good and the way the famous artist plays and sings No. 12877 is too good to miss. Hear it at your dealer today or send us the coupon.

[ **12877 — Pea Vine Blues** and **Tom Rushen Blues**, Vocal, guitar-acc., Charley Patton. ]

**12879—Chain 'em Down** and **Louisiana Glide**, Piano Solo, Blind Leroy Garnett.

**12878—My Lovin' Blues** and **Weary Heart Blues**, Vocal, piano acc., James Wiggins

**12872—Bed Springs Blues** and **Yo Yo Blues**, Vocal, guitar acc., Blind Lemon Jefferson.

**12792—Pony Blues** and **Banty Rooster Blues**, Vocal, guitar acc., Charley Patton.

**12860—Forty-Four Blues** and **Frisco Bound**, Vocal, piano acc., James Wiggins.

**12868—Prison Blues** and **My Man Blues**, Vocal, piano-trombone acc., Alice Moore.

**12865—Down on Death Alley Blues** and **Five Minute Blues**, Vocal, piano acc., L. Green

**12852—Bakershop Blues** and **Long Distance Moan**, Vocal-guitar acc., Blind Lemon Jefferson.

**12864—Good Chib Blues**—Vocal, piano-trombone acc. and **Can't Make Another Day**, Vocal, piano-cornet acc., Edith Johnson.

**SPIRITUALS**

**12874—Take Your Burdens To The Lord** and **Telephone To Glory**, Vocal, inst. acc., Blind Arthur Groom and Brother

**12734—He Just Hung His Head and Died** and **Lord I Don't Care Where They Bury My Body**, Vocal, Norfolk Jubilee Quartette.

**SEND NO MONEY!** If your dealer is out of the records you want, send us the coupon below. Pay postman 75 cents for each record, plus small C.O.D. fee when he delivers records. *We pay postage on shipments of two or more records.*

**Paramount**

REG. US PAT OFF

*The Popular Race Record*

ELECTRICALLY RECORDED

The New York Recording Laboratories
12 Paramount Bld, Port Washington, Wi
Send me the records checked (✓) below 75 cents each.

( ) 12877 ( ) 12792 ( ) 1285
( ) 12879 ( ) 12860 ( ) 1286
( ) 12878 ( ) 12868 ( ) 1287
( ) 12872 ( ) 12865 ( ) 1273

Name ............................

Address ............................

City ............................ State ............

*Chicago Defender* ad for Patton's "Pea Vine Blues," February 1930. The title was in reference to the railroad that serviced Dockery Farms, not the vegetable. (Publicity / public domain.)

The Wisconsin Chair Company, the owner of Paramount, had its main factory in Port Washington. In the fall of 1929, it added a recording studio to its Grafton operation. (Public domain.)

Jim Jackson had only one hit, but it was one of the most copied of its time, "Jim Jackson's Kansas City Blues" of 1929. It would be the model for Patton's "Going to Move to Alabama." (Publicity / public domain.)

For someone reputed as being worldly, Patton was remarkably sensitive when arranging and performing sacred music. Hall and Barnett's "Some Day" (shown here from a James Vaughan hymnbook) was the basis for Patton's 1930 recording "Some Happy Day." Patton sang the top treble melody while playing on slide guitar an approximation of the responses of the other three voices. (Public domain.)

Henry Sims, 1920s, some time before he traveled with Patton to Paramount's Grafton studio in the winter of 1930. (Wardlow collection.)

Percy Thomas in later years. From the early 1920s through the mid-1940s, he was Son Sims' guitarist in the Mississippi Cornshuckers, also known as the Son Sims Four. (Wardlow collection.)

Memphis Minnie with Joe McCoy, c. 1929. In 1930 they had a hit record with Bumble Bee, which Patton's last wife Bertha Lee would adapt and sing as Yellow Bee. (Publicity / public domain.)

Everyone who has heard this record says that "HIGH WATER EVERYWHERE" is Charley Patton's best and you know that means it has to be mighty good because he has made some knockouts. You're in for a real treat when you hear this record at your dealer or send us the coupon.

[ **12909—High Water Everywhere,** Part 1 and 2, Vocal, guitar acc., Charley Patton ]

**12915—Honey Dripper Blues No. 2** and **Nickels Worth of Liver Blues No. 2,** Vocal, piano acc., Edith North Johnson.

**12912—Come Back Corrina** and **Farrell Blues,** Vocal, violin-guitar acc., Henry Sims.

**12905—Papa Do Do Do Blues** and **I'll Be Gone Babe,** Vocol, banjo acc., Papa Charlie Jackson.

**12902—Leaving This Morning** and **Runaway Blues,** Vocal, Ma Rainey.

**12888—Police Dog Blues** and **Diddie Wa Diddie,** Vocal, guitar acc., Blind Blake.

**12860—Forty-Four Blues** and **Frisco Bound,** Vocal, piano acc., James Wiggins.

**12899—Southern Woman Blues** and **Mosquito Moan,** Vocal, guitar acc., Blind Lemon Jefferson.

**12872—Bed Springs Blues** and **Yo Yo Blues,** Vocal, guitar acc., Blind Lemon Jefferson.

**12877—Pea Vine Blues** and **Tom Rushen Blues,** Vocal, guitar acc., Charley Patton.

**SACRED**

**12903—Judas and Jesus Walked Together** and **Handwriting on The Wall,** Biddleville Quintette.

**12890—When The Moon Goes Down,** Vocal, Norfolk Jubilee Quartette and **Moanin' in The Land Will Soon Be Over,** Norfolk Jubilee Quartette.

**SEND NO MONEY!** If your dealer is out of the records you want, send us the coupon below. Pay postman 75 cents for each record, plus small C. O. D. fee when he delivers records. *We pay postage on shipments of two or more records.*

**Paramount**

REG. U.S. PAT. OFF.

*The Popular Race Record*

ELECTRICALLY RECORDED

The New York Recording Laboratories
12 Paramount Bldg.
Port Washington, Wis.

Send me the records checked (√) below 75 cents each.

( ) 12909 ( ) 12902 ( ) 12872
( ) 12915 ( ) 12888 ( ) 12877
( ) 12912 ( ) 12860 ( ) 12903
( ) 12905 ( ) 12899 ( ) 12890

Name————
Address————
City———— State————

*Chicago Defender* ad for Patton, "High Water Everywhere," April 1930. This two-sided performance record about the 1927 Mississippi River flood was one of Patton's best discs, and it was his last big hit. (Publicity / public domain.)

*New!*

# Paramount Records

*— Super Electrical Recordings —*

L. JEFFERSON C. PATTON

## Everybody Enjoys These

**12822—Sisco Harmonica Blues**—Instrumental Blues......................Carver Boys
**Wang Wang Harmonica Blues**—Instrumental Blues..............Carver Boys

**12821—Ain't Goin' That Way**—Vocal—Piano-Guitar-Clarinet Acc...The Hokum Boys
**You Can't Get Enough Of That Stuff**—Vocal—Guitar-Piano Acc.

**12819—Black And Evil Blues**—Vocal—Piano and Trombone Acc.........Alice Moore
**Broadway St. Woman Blues**—Vocal—Piano and Guitar Acc......Alice Moore

**12817—Back To The Woods Blues**—Vocal—Piaon and Guitar Acc......Charlie Spand
**Good Gal**—Vocal—Piano and Guitar Acc......................Charlie Spand

**12816—It Hurts So Good**—Trombone Solo—Piano Acc. Henry Brown....Ike Rodgers
**Screenin' The Blues**—Trombone Solo—Piano Acc. Henry Brown..Ike Rodgers

Blind Lemon Jefferson and Patton leaflet from Paramount, January 1930. Note the outtake used for Patton's portrait. By the time this publicity item was issued, Jefferson was found dead in Chicago, and the first effects of the Great Depression were being felt at the label. To make up for these losses, Paramount was increasing its pressure on Laibly to find new star talent in the South. (Publicity / public domain / Wardlow collection.)

Son House ca. 1966 striking a pose as Charlie Patton. In the summer of 1930, Patton brought House with Willie Brown (l.) and Louise Johnson to Grafton. There, House made the records that, 34 years later, inspired three young white men to find him in Rochester, NY. (Calt collection.)

Willie Moore and Elizabeth Glynn Moore, late 1960s. They knew the key bluesmen of the 1910s, 20s, and 30s, from W. C. Handy and Charley Patton through Son House and Robert Johnson. Their interviews with Gayle Wardlow are remarkable for the Delta lore and the explanations of 1930s Mississippi Delta slang. (Wardlow collection.)

Bertha Lee, c. 1963–1964. The last of Patton's wives, she stayed with him from 1930 until his 1934 death. (Klatzko photograph / Wardlow collection.)

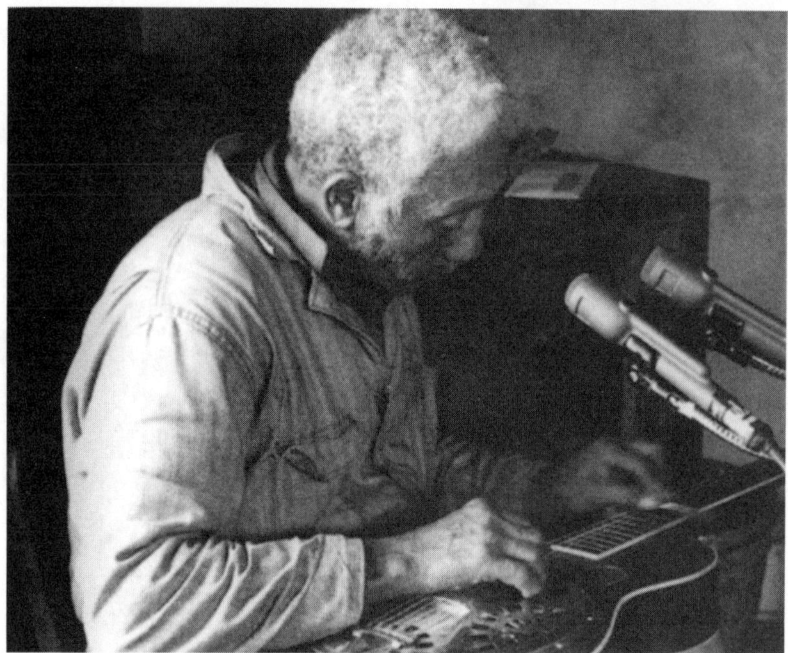

Eugene Powell, Greenville, MS, 1970s, a musician in the mold of the Chatmon brothers. In the early 1930s Powell replaced Patton at a regular frolic gig near Longswitch. (Wardlow collection.)

Johnnie Mack with his wife, 1960s. Mack met Patton in the Longswitch area in the early 1930s. He preferred playing for the genteel white dances rather than the rough frolics, where Patton performed after the Great Depression hit the Delta. (Wardlow collection.)

Speir's Jackson music store in 1929, with H. C. Speir standing at right. Four years later, Patton, Willie Brown, and Son House came there to make demonstration discs for record company consideration. (Wardlow collection.)

W. R. Calaway of the American Record Company sought Patton in January 1934 for new recordings, springing him and Bertha Lee from a Belzoni, MS, jail in order to take them to New York City for the sessions. (Wardlow collection.)

Patton's grave at the New Jerusalem Missionary Baptist Church cemetery, Holly Ridge, MS. The site was unmarked from the 1934 burial until July 1991, when the present stone was placed by Skip Henderson and John Fogerty. (Find-A-Grave website.)

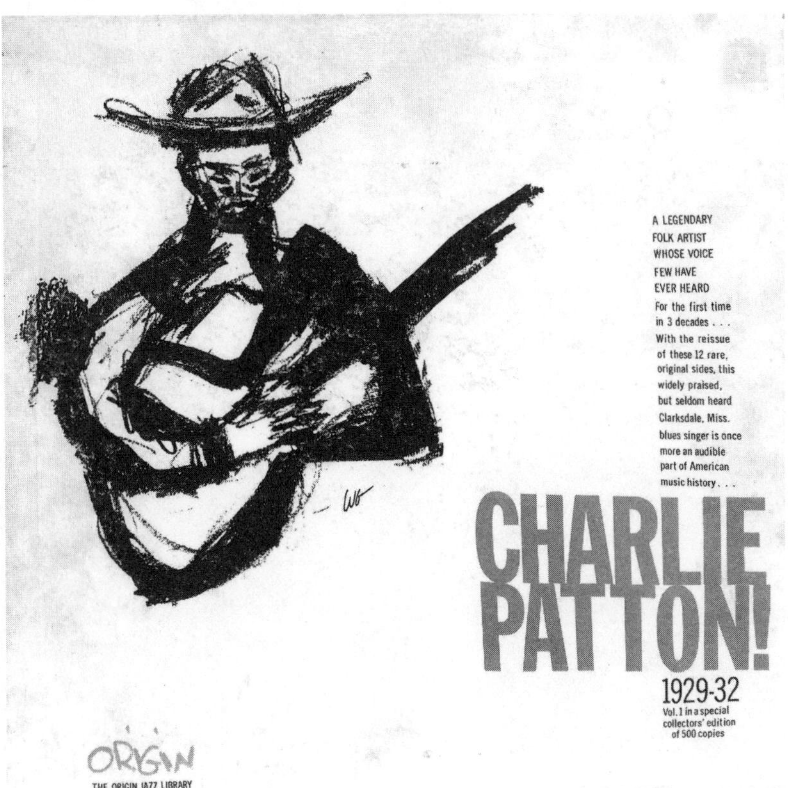


The front cover of the first LP of Charlie Patton's music, *The Immortal Charlie Patton*, Origin Jazz Library OJL-1, 1961. The reissue heralded the rediscovery of Patton's music, and opened the research into his life and times. (Komara collection.)

*Part 3*

# THE MAN AND HIS RECORDS

You don't know, sure don't know my mind

You don't know me, sure don't know my mind

I don't show you my ticket now you,
don't know where I'm goin'.

—PATTON, "DEVIL SENT THE RAIN BLUES"

*Chapter 10*

# FROM RAGS TO RICHMOND (CIRCA 1924–JUNE 1929)

Throughout the 1920s, Charlie Patton appears to have led the life of a footloose blues singer. "These people, they moved from one place to another," H. C. Speir once said of his talent discoveries. "They're not stable, they're in and out."

Because of his travels, Patton was rarely seen by his neighbors. A sharecropper who had moved to Dockery's plantation in the fall of 1921 remembered in the 1960s that "Charlie, he didn't stay in no one place too long. He'd be goin' to different places, makin' music." On weekdays he may drop by his neighbors' cabins, Sara Garrett reported, and "just go play a tune or two. He wouldn't be askin' for no money, and neither no food." On the weekends when he commanded fees for his efforts,[1] he was as likely to be in Arkansas' Delta as in Mississippi's. His contacts with other musicians were sparked by chance, were formed on-the-fly, and were often short-lived. Booker Miller observed that "Charlie, now, he was a man [who had] traveled a lot. Now he would come here, maybe around Greenwood, stay 3, 4 months. First thing, you know, he'd tell you, he's going away. Well, he'd go."

Patton often sang about his rootlessness on his records. His matter-of-fact departures from girlfriends are portrayed in most of his songs:

> Goin' away baby (spoken: Won't be back no more)
> . . .
> I'm goin' away, mama, won't be back no . . .
> (Magnolia Blues, 1929)

On two records, Patton left curious cameos of relationships that were ruptured by his traveling. In "Pea Vine Blues," he abandoned his lover for the flinty reason of "Livin' single, Lord you know I cannot stay."[2] He admits that she could say in response "Yes, you know it, you know it, you know you done done me wrong," to which he would be ready to say "Stop your way of livin', an' you won't have to cry no more."

Another mistress, this time in "Rattlesnake Blues," was but a girl in one of several ports during Patton's random journey:

> When I leave here mama I am goin', further down the road
> I said when I leave here mama I'm goin', further down the road
> And when I leave there I am goin' back to the Gulf of Mexico
>
> I'm gonna shake glad hands mama I say, Lord of your lovin' boy
> I'm gonna shake glad hands I say, with your lovin' boy
> Fixin' to eat my supper in Shelby, Illinois

That he was a substitute for her "lovin' boy" doesn't concern him. After all, he knows that she will cease to care about him once he leaves their meaningless affair:

> An' my baby got a heart like a piece of railroad steel
> Baby got a heart like a piece of railroad steel
> After I leave here this mornin' never say, "Daddy how do you feel?"

None of his songs suggested that he missed a companion, whether on the road or at home. In "Joe Kirby," he described himself as a homeless person by singing "Just like a doggone rabbit, I ain't got no doggone den."[3] In Part One of "Jim Lee Blues," he depicted a Mississippi river roustabout and his promiscuous girlfriend who boasts that she "got a kid, on the wheeler, got a bullcow on the plough, got a plum good man bringin' down the Johnson bayou." Telling this story in the first person from the roustabout's perspective, Patton uses the standard melodramatic clichés of a romantic disappointment and a broken home to account for his character's rambling and womanizing:

I was way up the river, some forty miles or more
I think I heard the big Jim Lee when it blowed.

She blow, so lonesome, like she wasn't gonna blow no more
Hey blow just like my baby gettin' on board.

I'm a poor ol' boy, an' a long way from home
An' she causin' me to leave my plumb good home.

My mama is dead, an' my father went to sea.
I ain't got nobody to love an' care for me.

As for what propelled his own itinerant lifestyle, Patton had nothing to say.

Like his romanticized drifter, the whistle was a stock song prop that Patton used again as the train whistle in "Pea Vine Blues" and the "Marion whistle" in "Moon Going Down." Elizabeth Moore recalled his unrecorded tribute to a boat that shuttled between Memphis and New Orleans and "didn't when she blow." Of these whistles, the Robert Lee Jr. boat of the Lee Line, running between St. Louis and Vicksburg until the late 1920s, had the most renown in the Delta.

By referring to these whistles, Patton played upon Delta romanticism that was expressed by the planter-poet William Alexander Percy: "There is no sound in the world so filled with mystery and longing and unease as the sound at night of a riverboat blowing for the landing—one long, two shorts, one long, two shorts."[4] Moreover, by inserting a name of a boat or train into a lyric, Patton was tapping into the river lore that was later described by Mary Wheeler in *Steamboatin' Days*: "It used to be a point of pride with people who knew and loved the language of the river to be able to recognize the approach of an important boat by the sound of her whistle or bell. Every whistle possessed a tone that could be identified."[5]

Although riverboats were frequently mentioned in Patton's 1929–1930 Paramount recordings, even then they were vanishing into Mississippi's changing landscape.[6] So, too, it seems in hindsight, was the kind of Mississippi barrelhouse where Patton had cut and sharpened his performing teeth. The Mississippi bluesman Skip James associated barrelhouses with sawmill settlements like Banglin and cities like Memphis, and yet for him the basic Mississippi musical outlet in the 1920s was the plantation house frolic. Hayes McMullan said he didn't see barrelhouses in Tallahatchie County, and that he, too, played only at house frolics. It is likely that once Prohibition took effect in 1920 and "bottled in bond" whiskey became unavailable, these barrelhouses attracted much fewer plantation revelers than before. House frolics, on the other hand, served corn whiskey, whose production continued mostly unaffected by Prohibition. Under Mississippi laws of the 1920s that was designed to protect planter interests, state prohibition agents lacked the authority to locate and bust corn alcohol stills on plantation property.

One of Patton's songs commemorated an apparent arrest for drunkenness. "Tom Rushen Blues" (as Paramount Records would misspell the name) is a sedate blues to the tune of Ma Rainey's "Booze and Blues"[7] that smacks of an attempt to curry favor with the deputy sheriff of Merigold, O. T. "Tom" Rushing.[8] He had assumed office in 1928, holding that position for the next four years:

> Laid down last night, hopin' I would have my peace,
> I laid down last night, hopin' I would have my peace,
> But when I woke up, Tom Rushing was shakin' me.

Patton's Merigold crony Willie "Have Mercy" Young remembered Rushing as a "right young law" who "wasn't about twenty five years old" when Patton recorded the song in 1929. Like his brother who worked as the bookkeeper of Dockery's plantation. Rushing was renowned for his athletic prowess, which he used to catch his crooks. "He was a law who wouldn't shoot you for nothin'," Young said appreciatively. "I don't care what you done. If you outrun him, he let you go." As a new arrival in Merigold, Young got into trouble at house frolic when he broke a bowl upon a girlfriend's head. When the towering Rushing arrived, Young thought the white man seemed seven feet tall, and he bolted away. "He caught me. 'Fella, don't you know your legs aren't fast?' I said, 'I just didn't know the town! But if I hadda knew the town, you never woulda got me.' I had three blocks on him. I said, 'What's the fine?' He said, 'Five dollars, and go about your business.'" Patton's song likewise pointed up the uselessness of fleeing Rushing:

> When you get in trouble, it's no use of screamin' and cryin',
> When you gets in trouble, it's no use of screamin' and cryin',
> Tom Rushing will take you, back to the prisonhouse a-flyin'.

In "Tom Rushen Blues," Patton also added three stanzas about Rushing's marshal, a man named Tom Day, who had arrested one of Patton's friends, Seab Holloway[9] for bootlegging, and who was apparently inspired to become sheriff:

It was late one night, Holloway was gone to bed,
It was late one night, Holloway was gone to bed,
Mr. Day brought whiskey taken from under Holloway's head.

I got up this mornin', Tom Day was standin' around,
I got up this mornin', Tom Day was standin' around,
If he lose his office here, he's runnin' from town to town.

Of Day, Young said, "Mister Day was all right, but he wasn't like Tom Rushin'. Mister Rushin' was my man."

If the barrelhouses were fading, then with them was the social context for the happy-go-lucky songs about the "sporting life" like "Spoonful Blues" and "Frankie and Albert." In "Shake It and Break It," Patton portrayed a plantation rube who prowled the town for sex:

I know I been to town, I——I walked around.
I——start leavin' town, I——I fool around.
My jelly, my roll, sweet mama, don't you let it fall

If Delta hayseeds looked forward to their trips to towns, then Patton boasted of his jaunts to cities.[10] At least twice in the 1920s he went to St. Louis, Missouri where, he later told Booker Miller, he performed at "Dago Hill," which was the fifty-block Italian neighborhood on the city's south side (now called "The Hill"). "He had a song about that," Miller recalled, quoting the lyric:

I'm gonna build me a mansion out on "Dago Hill"
Then I won't have to be goin' downtown every mornin', payin' bills

In 1934, he mentioned the section again in "Love My Stuff":

Oh had a , had a notion, Lord I believe I will
(Spoken: "Aw, sho'!")
Oh had a notion, Lord I believe I will
I'm gonna go 'cross the river, stop at Dago Hill

"Dago Hill" was known among blues singers for its resident bootleggers.

From St. Louis, Patton told Miller, he went to Chicago, a city he was to use as the setting for "Mean Black Moan."[11] There, he saw for himself the summer 1922 Railway Shopmen's Strike, which involved over 400,000 employees and brought about the largest rail service stoppage in over 20 years.[12] 8 years later, in "Mean Black Moan," Patton expressed something of the feelings of striking workers:

It's all I can do Lord, ah fight for my life
All I can do Lord to fight for my life
But when the strike is over, Lord I will be all right

Ninety men were laid off, Lord, on the railroad shop
Ninety men were laid off, Lord, in the railroad shop
An' the strike in Chicago, Lord it just won't stop

Patton also spent a week in New Orleans, but told Miller afterward that he disliked "the set-up there." Perhaps on that New Orleans jaunt, or on a separate occasion, he entertained black laborers in the East Green section of nearby Gretna, which was the locale of the then-popular dialect writings of R. Emmett Kennedy.[13]

During the early 1920s, by way of the phonograph, blues entertainers began reaching out to audiences they had never seen.[14] The introduction of cheap portable phonographs as a wartime gimmick around 1918 enabled blacks to become avid record consumers. The free spending habits fostered by decades under the plantation system and the lack of access to banks helps to explain why, despite their acute poverty, they were willing to pay 75 cents for records so poorly pressed that they could be played only a few dozen times. Even so, the phonograph created a generation of blues stars. Through 1925, most of them were women singers in the northern cities and the T.O.B.A. (Theater Owners Booking Association) circuit like Mamie Smith, Gertrude "Ma" Rainey, and Bessie Smith. The first significant southern male musicians on blues records were Blind Lemon Jefferson and Blind Blake, both guitarists whose first records were hits upon release in 1926.

Booker Miller recalled that Patton thought of Blind Lemon Jefferson and Leroy Carr as "big shots," even after he increased his own celebrity with his first records in 1929. This anecdote suggests that Patton saw for himself the power of the emerging blues record industry to make national stars whose levels of fame far exceeded what he achieved after 20 years of performing.

Patton didn't just listen to other artists' records; he also raided them for melodies and lyrics.[15] Many examples turn up on his 1929–1934 recordings. He appropriated the melody and lyrics of Rainey's "Booze and Blues" (Paramount, 1924) to create his own "Tom Rushen Blues" (Paramount, 1929) and "High Sheriff Blues" (ARC/Vocalion, 1934). He paraphrased the lyric of Ardelle (Shelly) Bragg's slow-paced "Bird Nest Blues" (Paramount, 1926) for his "Bird

Nest Bound" (Paramount, 1930). Later, he used Hound Head Henry's buffoonish vaudeville blues "Cryin' Blues" (Vocalion, 1928) as the basis of "Poor Me" (Vocalion, 1934). Booker Miller remembered, "He listened to records. I'll tell you one he kinda liked pretty good, but he never did try to play it. Leroy Carr put out a record, I think it was about in 'twenty-nine; it was 'Prison Bound [Blues].' Now he liked it."[16]

Meanwhile, three of Patton's trademark pieces were being released on records by two Mississippi musicians who were beating him to the recording studio. In 1928 for Victor Records, Tommy Johnson recorded his treatments of "Pony Blues" and "Maggie" (respectively as "Bye Bye Blues" and "Maggie Campbell Blues"). Since the late 1910s, Johnson had a considerable musical influence on other Mississippi bluesmen.[17] But his potential for record sales was relatively low, due to his performing mostly in Jackson, and knowing only a few songs. The talent scout H. C. Speir realized that much about Johnson, but he took a chance on the musician. He recorded Johnson on a recording machine that he maintained on the second floor of his store's building, and he sent the resulting audition disc to Victor's recording director Ralph Peer for consideration. Peer accepted Johnson, but only on the condition that Speir order five hundred copies of each Victor Johnson release to offset the cost of recording them. This was an outsized request, considering that Speir's entire store stock usually had three thousand records.

The willingness of record companies to record Southern bluesmen who, like Johnson, had only regional followings also brought about the December 1927 recording session for Walter "Pat" Rhodes, the first Sunflower County bluesman to appear on records. When, why and how Rhodes learned the song "Banty Rooster Blues" is worth telling at length for the inside look at the way commercial field recording sessions were conducted. Rhodes came from Ruleville, the nearest town east to Dockery's, and he may have been born sometime in the 1860s or the 1870s. He played the accordion, which seems to be an unusual instrument for the Delta,[18] but it was played in communities like Shelby and Shaw by Italians who "whipped the hell out of the 'ccordion," as one planter recalled. Rhodes got his chance to make records from W. H. Buchanon, a thirty-seven year old minister. It came about one day in the fall of 1927, when Buchanon made his regular visit to a Ruleville dry goods store owned by two white brothers, Jake and Oscar Livingston. As Buchanon later recalled, Oscar "knew me well. He wanted me to go up there and preach a sermon or two." After thinking it over for a week, Buchanon accepted the offer. In return, he was handed a train ticket to Memphis, where he was to have his recording session with Columbia Records. A day or so before his scheduled departure, he happened upon Rhodes, whom he had occasionally heard playing what he called "the old country racket" on Ruleville streets and at plantation frolics during the previous six or eight years. He persuaded Rhodes to offer himself to Columbia. In the 1960s, Buchanon admitted later to the authors that he thought little of Rhodes' musicianship, saying "He didn't know music, he didn't know nothin' much." His opinion in 1927 was likely the same. If so, then his invitation may have been to have Rhodes as a traveling companion.

When Buchanon and Rhodes arrived to Memphis, Columbia promptly held auditions with each of them. "They didn't want to accept Pat's manner of singin," Buchanon reports. They didn't want Buchanon, either. Nor did they accept another preacher, the Reverend Frank Cotton of Baird, Mississippi, who eventually succeeded with Paramount Records in August 1928 to become the second Sunflower County resident to appear on shellac. Buchanon remembered one other fellow whose name he couldn't remember. "There's a white fella there from Nashville, and I told him to go home, don't let people make a fool of him. He was a guitar-picker but he couldn't sing, didn't have no voice or nothin'. I said, 'Go on home to your family.' He taken my advice."

After failing his audition, Buchanon then decided to help Rhodes present himself as suitable for recording by giving him some fresh material. So, that night, Buchanon sat up until three or four o'clock in the morning teaching Rhodes a song he knew as "The Crowing Rooster." "I just sit there and I 'studied' a lot of themes, and that's the only one I thought he could sing," Buchanon remembered. When he first recited the lyrics (which he had committed to paper) to Rhodes, he recalled that "it so tickled his fancy, he thought it was somethin' new."

Meanwhile, two guitar-playing brothers from Marvel, Arkansas, Richard and Mylar Harney, had also failed their Columbia auditions. Buchanon thought it was because "these boys made music, but they couldn't sing." Seeing them available, he recruited them as sidemen the day after his all-night session with Rhodes, and rehearsing the three of them for two hours. Then, he presented them successfully to company officials, despite Rhodes being "afraid 'cause they'd seen him do some of them so bad." Rarely if ever was a minister so involved with a secular recording session.

For all of the preparations, and for the 9000 copies that Columbia pressed of the resulting release, "Crowing Rooster Blues" ended up being a wheezing cousin Patton's bottleneck guitar staple "Banty Rooster Blues," which Rhodes sang in the key of D. But while Buchanon during his interview with Wardlow could not recall where or from whom he learned the song, he claimed that he did not derive it from Patton. "I'd see him sometimes playin' in town," he admitted, "but I didn't pay him too much attention." In any event, "Crowing Rooster Blues" was his only issued result in record production. "I didn't pay that much attention to it from that day until now," he reminisced, when interviewed in Moorhead in 1972. As for Rhodes, he didn't gain any new recognition for making a record. If anything, he came to be remembered more in Sunflower County lore for his death from a lightning strike, which was said to have occurred in Alligator, Mississippi sometime in the late 1930s.

The record labels continued to take chances on other seemingly unpromising players from the tank towns of the South. A few musicians succeeded in producing huge hits, especially Jim Jackson. He, for one, created a much greater stir in the Delta than most of its native musicians, and his hit record provided Patton and other Delta bluesmen with a refreshed song motif.

Jim Jackson (1884–1937) was a middle-aged entertainer from the Mississippi hill town of Hernando. For years, from south Missouri to south Mississippi, he performed in medicine shows as a musician, buckdancer, and comedian. "He couldn't play the guitar but a little bit," claimed Richard Harney, who once worked with Jackson, "but he do a whole lotta talkin." When the medicine shows were not touring, he supported himself as a street singer. H. C. Speir first heard Jackson in 1922 in front of various drug stores in the white neighborhoods of Jackson, then noticed him again on Memphis' Beale Avenue in October 1927. Although at that time Speir was just beginning his talent scouting for the record labels, he took a dim view of Jackson. "He was just a bum," Speir remembered, "Nobody ever paid any attention to him." Another liability that Speir noted was Jackson's use of narcotics or "dope" (as Speir called it). Speir referred him to Loren Watson, a wholesaler for Victor Records who was helping the company set up blues recording sessions in Memphis. So, some months later, Speir was doubly startled when he saw Jackson's name on records issued not on Victor but on the rival label Vocalion, for a song called "Kansas City Blues" that he had never heard Jackson perform on the streets.[19] The song's accompaniment used only the tonic (I) and subdominant (IV) chords but not, oddly, the dominant (V) chord, and it was performed to a 1–2 dance pattern. Although "Kansas City Blues" was atypical for Jackson's repertoire and the typical Southern blues, it was a hit that led to more recording sessions for Jackson. While this surprise success had little to do with Speir—he had merely referred Jackson to Watson—it boosted the record dealer's reputation among the companies. It was Watson who recommended Speir to Art Laibly, the recording director for Paramount Records.

During the late 1920s, Paramount's leading blues star was Blind Lemon Jefferson, a guitar-playing street singer from Wortham, Texas. He was placed with the label in 1926 by the Dallas dealer R. J. Ashford as a sales gimmick to attract local shoppers. Jefferson soon became one of the label's leading southern attractions, another being Blind Blake of Jacksonville, Florida, quickly supplanting the female stars of the black vaudeville theaters like Alberta Hunter and Ida Cox who until then prevailed for Paramount. The sales successes of these male blues guitarists in 1926 sparked a record industry demand to the record dealers to discover more talent on their local streets. Jefferson's recordings were copied by nearly every Mississippi bluesman who could mimic them. "Blind Lemon sent out a record about 1928, 1929 (sic) 'Catch my pony, saddle up my black mare,'" Booker Miller said, referring to his "Black Horse Blues" (1926). "Man, you oughta been there! That thing went like wildfire all over the country."

Jefferson's Mississippi sales seemed "just fair" to Speir in his Jackson store, but they impressed his scouting rival, Ralph Lembo (1897–1960) of Itta Bena, Mississippi.[20] Born in Comiso, Sicily, Italy, Lembo emigrated to America in 1910 with his mother and two siblings, landing in New Orleans and proceeding to Itta Bena where his father established himself some six years before.[21] By 1920 Lembo had begun his enterprises in retail with groceries, and five years later he was also owning a theater in Itta Bena, a store in Morgan City, and commercial property in Greenwood.[22] He began scouting talent for record labels in 1927, initially placing Reverend C. T. Thornton, Reverend Frank Cotton, and Rubin Lacy with Columbia Records. The following year, he arranged for Paramount to record Cotton and Lacy.[23]

Meanwhile, Lembo acquired and renovated a new space for his Itta Bena business, and he opened stores in Greenwood and Swiftown. In those places he hosted in-store performing appearances, including Columbia artist Art Gillham at Itta Bena in May 1928, and Jim Jackson in Greenwood that September.[24] The best-known of his in-store promotions was Blind Lemon Jefferson on Friday, October 5, 1928 at Itta Bena. That afternoon he performed at Lembo's store, and in the evening he played a dance at the local Rolling Water High School.[25] David Edwards remembered for the authors that "they had a big dance there and Lemon come in and play, and they was chargin' seventy five cents to come in. That was a lot of money then, and they couldn't get him to play for that seventy five cents."[26] What exactly Edwards meant by "couldn't get him to play" isn't clear, but that evening the matter must have been resolved, as Jefferson was willing to, and later did, return to the Itta Bena area for more performances.[27]

Sometime after these promotional successes, Lembo was visited by Charlie Patton, likely at the Itta Bena store sometime in early 1929. A few years later, Patton mentioned that visit to Booker Miller: "Charlie, he went [to Lembo's store] and he said that he [Lembo] wanted to send him to New Orleans to make some records down there." In view that Patton would make his first records in Richmond, Indiana, and that he had an ongoing relationship with H. C. Speir in Jackson for the next 5 years, it seems that his dealings with Lembo were not as close, if they were ever commenced. Miller was led to believe by Patton that Lembo "was tricky, and I think Charlie must have kinda got wind of that."

Whether such a "tricky" reputation was warranted isn't confirmed by the surviving documents about Lembo, who sustained his scouting through the early 1930s, his record retail activities through the end of that decade, and his real estate ventures through the 1950s. If anything in 1929 could have made prospective recording artists hesitate about Lembo, it may have been his early failures to get his first talents on records. In April and December 1927, during two sets of recording dates, Reverend C. F. Thornton recorded four sides, two of which were issued by Columbia Records; but Reverend Frank Cotton and bluesman Rube Lacy, each recording four sides, failed to see any of them released. In 1928, Paramount did better by Lembo, releasing four sides by Cotton, and two sides by Lacy in a well-regarded, nationally advertised release.[28]

If the Itta Bena businessman missed out on Patton in 1929, he would in 1930 secure the young bluesman Booker T. Washington "Bukka" White for his debut discs on Victor. His most successful signing, it turned out, was the Mississippi Sheiks, who would record for Okeh one of the best-selling and most influential blues records of the 1930s, "Sitting on Top of the World." When the record industry shrank in size in 1931–33, Lembo was not receiving his due royalties and finder's fees from the firms. By mid-decade he had ceased scouting, turning his musical interests to performing as drummer and leader of a local music ensemble.[29]

How Patton heard of H. C. Speir in the spring of 1929 cannot be ascertained. He might have learned about him from one of Speir's discoveries like Jim Jackson, with whom he reportedly played in Friar's Point. After his successful audition at Dockery Farms, Patton became Speir's best guide to blues talent, freely recommending rival artists without demanding payment for himself. In addition to the side musicians that he later brought to Paramount, he also introduced Speir to several blues singers in Helena, Arkansas, of whom the scout remembered that "they were good." Other Patton recommendations were much less impressive, such as the women singers, probably girlfriends, that Patton brought to Speir's store and accompanied their auditions on the guitar. "I didn't think much of the women," Speir recalled, but he would oblige them and Patton by making vanity records of their singing for free, a generous act since he normally charged five dollars to paying customers.

With each successful audition at his store, H. C. Speir recorded multiple discs on his vanity record machine, send them at the same time to the record companies with whom he had working contacts, and accept the offer from the first label who responded. In his older age, he had a vague recollection of making tests of Patton. This would have meant that after his audition at Dockery's, Patton traveled to Jackson sometime in April or May to make the sample discs on Speir's machine. Speir also remembered that one of the discs was sent to Victor, the industry's largest record firm. If so, then Victor either had sent a rejection slip, or it responded too late. As it was, the Paramount label signed Patton on the basis of Speir's verbal recommendation, resulting in something like a $150 commission for the scout.[30]

Paramount Records was established in 1917 as a mainstream popular music label by the owner of a desk and school furniture manufacturer, the Wisconsin Chair Company of Port Washington, Wisconsin.[31] As an early advertisement stated, Paramount featured "artists the record buyers know—Billy Murray, Henry Burr, Arthur Fields, Helen Clark . . . " But during the first few years, Paramount was unprofitable due to a combination of circumstances: the inexperience of Paramount's executives, who knew chairs, desks and furniture but not records; the lack of money to sign bona fide recording attractions; the steep competition from over 150 rival labels for the same marginal markets that Paramount was selling to; the emergence of radio, which in the early 1920s began displacing the Victrola as a favorite item of home listening; and an economic slump that had followed World War I. Then, contrary to the established record industry wisdom, Paramount recording director Maurice Supper abruptly changed the label's music orientation to African American music without conducting what would be called today "market research." Once the company entered the "race record" field for African American music in 1922, its losses began shrinking immediately. As the company's former president Otto Moeser later said, "Race records put us over."

Despite Paramount's position as the only solvent record label of its day that basically catered to African Americans, it was neither the best-selling "race" label nor the most discriminating in regards to musical talent. It maintained distributors in nearly every large city east of the Rockies, from Detroit to Dallas, but by the mid-1920s, its most lucrative markets were concentrated in Mississippi and Arkansas. In 1930, the combined black farm population of these largely rural states was over a million persons. The region was singlehandedly serviced (and developed mostly) by Earl Montgomery, a Memphis-based employee of Paramount's largest distributor, the Artophone Corporation of St. Louis.

During Patton's lifetime, there were few record stores in the South. That meant Montgomery had to sell Paramounts, OKehs and Vocalions not only to the furniture and drug stores which in the time and culture counted as the most important retail outlets, but also to plantation commissaries. Thus Paramount 78s were readily available for purchase even in Mississippi's most remote areas. Sometimes, enterprising town dealers visited outlying plantations and sold the records door to door.

Montgomery didn't know the blues or what made some musicians better than others. Yet this unfamiliarity with the music actually helped him get his job around 1925. During his interview with the president of Artophone, Montgomery blurted out that he couldn't "tell one fuckin' note from another one." His future employer approved of this admission, saying "I could tell that the minute we sat down. That's the reason I'm hiring you. These guys who know all about music can't sell doodley-shit."

Yet Artophone's executives had few principles to guide them when they ordered new releases from Paramount. "We never had a theory," recounted the firm's former vice-president Herb Schiele. "We would spend a long time listening (to sample records) and trying to . . . judge the hits against the duds." For a few years, Paramount itself relied on the cocksure opinions of a Birmingham record salesman named Harry Charles to identify and weed out the sales duds. Charles was hired in the early 1920s to evaluate Paramount's weekly releases for commercial sales potential. The downside of Charles' advice to his employer was that his own talent-scouting finds were often duds. He was let go by 1929. During a 1970 interview with Wardlow, Charles listened to Charlie Patton's "Pony Blues," making comments that showed the thinking of a 1920s "race records" advisor. Patton's song impressed him "not much," he said, adding that "there's a lot better." Had he been consulted in 1929, he would have advised Paramount to reject Patton because the singer's diction would have been unintelligible to black recordbuyers.

Fortunately for Patton, it was Arthur Laibly, not Harry Charles, who was selecting the artists for Paramount in 1929. Formerly a lumber salesman, the 35-year old Laibly rose within Paramount's executive ranks by recommending the signing of Blind Lemon Jefferson. His five main scouts of blues talent were H. C. Speir, Harry Charles, Ashford, Watson, and W. R. Calaway of Virginia. Laibly relied so much on Speir's recommendations that he accepted them without requesting an audition record. Then again, as Speir observed of his record contacts especially at Paramount, "a lot of them didn't" need audition records, as a scout's suggestion was often enough to place a new artist with a label. After accepting Patton, Laibly mailed to Speir a train ticket for the musician to use for the 750-mile ride from Jackson, Mississippi to Richmond, Indiana, a city of 32,000 located fifty-five miles northwest of Cincinnati. Not having yet its own recording studio, Paramount was using the facilities of Gennett Records, which stood off Main Street on Richmond's west side, paying Gennett a fee of $80 per wax master. Recording artists often arrived at the C&O

Railroad depot a few blocks from the studio, which had to begin its recording takes between train arrivals so as not to pick up whistle noises.

Patton's first recording session was scheduled to begin on June 14, 1929. So it would have been during early June when Patton invited another Delta guitarist, Hayes McMullan, to travel along. At that time, McMullan was 27, living in plantation quarters near Tippo, Mississippi. One Saturday morning, while he and his wife were walking to town, a Model T Ford with four or five black passengers pulled up beside them. "They wanted me to go make records with Charlie Patton," he reported.

McMullan was born in 1902 in Charlestown in the hill country east of the Mississippi Delta. He had been playing guitar since childhood, as did also his brother John Thomas. Over time he had learned (by his count) nearly a hundred songs, including a version of Patton's "Maggie" around 1920–1921, from players in Tallahatchie County hamlets including Oakland and Charlestown. "I was famous from about 1920 to '36, from this side of Oakland over near around Drew," he says. Oddly, he never owned a guitar. So when he was introduced to Patton as a fellow musician in 1928 at a dance near Indianola, he demurred from showing his skills on Patton's guitar, because "I never asked a man to let me play his guitar." Nonetheless, he served as Patton's sideman at a few dances, with the "biggest time I seen him was between Ruleville and Cleveland," he remembered. He learned Patton's "Banty Rooster Blues," "Pony Blues," and "Down the Dirt Road Blues," adapting them to his own way of playing, and resetting the latter two pieces to Spanish tuning.

Before being approached to record with Patton, the last few times when McMullan had seen him were the Saturday night suppers "out from Glendora" where Patton and "Little Willie" Brown were playing. However, on that June day in 1929, something about the prospect of recording blues and about the record business led him to refuse, and afterwards he never mentioned the offer with Patton. Some forty years later, to the authors, he justified his decision by explaining that "At that time, see, I just didn't want my voice all over the world, you know. I thought it was too bad, playing blues for the world like that, you know. And they didn't offer me but five dollars for every record I put out. It wasn't much. The five dollars mighta been all right, but see, they take one record and they could make a thousand records from it, you know, and look at the money they'd be makin' if they didn't sell 'em for but fifty cents apiece, see?"

At first, McMullan's claim that Patton tried recruiting him as a backing guitarist for the Richmond session seems odd, if not wrong. But five dollars per side was the standard fee that H. C. Speir offered blues accompanists, so McMullan's story may well be true. But still, this invitation to McMullan is curious because Patton had no musical need for accompanists, as noted earlier about the development of his musical style. He could not have chosen a less likely sideman for recording than McMullan, who preferred listening to Patton to performing with him. "When I'd meet up with [Patton and Willie Brown], I wasn't goin' to play with them folks. I'd just be out, at the ball." Brown, for his part, was willing to have McMullan as his second, of which McMullan remained proud for many years. "I don't care where I was," he stated with pride, "he wanted to play with me." But for the Paramount recording session about to take place in Richmond, it would have made much more sense for Patton to take Brown with him. But as near as Son House guessed in the 1960s, Patton and Brown may have been in a period of "a fallin' out. They couldn't get along together no kinda way."

It is possible, then, that Patton turned to McMullan to spite Brown. As it so happened, McMullan's refusal to record with Patton was a blessing for posterity. McMullan had the habit of tuning his top guitar string flat, and he played mostly in the slow tempo suitable for dancing the shimmy-she-wobble. On records, he would have sounded sluggish and incompatible with Patton's piercing string tones and fast tempi.

At the Gennett studio in Richmond, Patton shared session time with Walter "Buddy Boy" Hawkins. Since Hawkins was from Birmingham, Alabama, from which the Southern Railroad connected to Jackson, Mississippi and points west, it is conceivable that Patton and Hawkins proceeded north from Jackson together. Hawkins had recorded twice before, in 1927, when Harry Charles arranged for him a Paramount contract. "I found him here in Birmingham singin' on the streets," Charles explained. But Hawkins' recording debut in April 1927 in Chicago didn't go well, or so Charles claimed afterward. Supposedly Hawkins was so intimidated that he kept recoiling from the microphone, spoiling numerous takes in the process.[32] "I had the hardest time recordin' him I did anybody," Charles said. In order to keep Hawkins still, Charles gave him a pair of headphones and directed him from the control booth. "Every time he started to move I say, 'Stand still! Stand up there!'" In the studio, Charles needed Hawkins' cooperation more than his talent, and by the end of the day, Charles came to look at him with contempt as a nuisance. "He'd look at you just like a monkey. He didn't have a speck of sense. He didn't even have brains enough to get back to the train (after recording). You couldn't tell what he's gonna do." Nonetheless, the records sold well enough that summer for Paramount to invite Hawkins to return to Chicago to make more records. Those too were selling respectably through 1928 and into 1929 to lead to one more recording date. At Richmond, without Charles there screaming at him, Hawkins probably had an easier time, performing acceptable takes for what would be his last two record releases.

Even though Patton was making his record debut, his composure is attested to by his gargantuan studio output. In a single session held on June 14, 1929, he spun out fourteen sides, more than any blues recording act had ever produced in one sitting. His knack for producing perfect sides on the first takes may have amazed Laibly. By comparison, the previous Paramount recording director, Mayo Williams, had considered a day's session complete if a recording artist made anywhere from 6 to 16 takes, from which master takes were selected to release three or four usable titles; those masters were then pressed back-to-back to produce two 78-rpm disc releases. In other words, Patton used the same number of takes to yield 7 new Paramount discs, as other artists needed to have two.

Patton's efficiency was all the more impressive when one considers the tuning adjustments he would have had to make between songs. He used three tunings (standard, open A and open E) set at various pitches. Recording all of his songs on a single instrument would have required him to retune his guitar five times during the course of his session. He may have eased this process by using a studio model in addition to his own. Patton's guitar was a Stella that Booker Miller described as looking "like it was made out of cypress. Tan, with a lotta fancy trimming around it."[33] "He kept a Stella all the time; that was his favorite box," added Miller, who maintained that a Stella "picked easier" than a Gibson, which he conceded as "the best guitar you could buy in those days." Stellas were cheap, too. Patton's deluxe model cost about thirty dollars, compared to the $47 Gibson that Miller regarded as the most expensive instrument then available. More significant than the Stella's decorations was the fact that Patton seems to have tuned it at least a step above concert pitch.

The penetrating guitar sound he thereby attained was ideal for the Paramount label, whose pressings were even then notorious among dealers for their poor sound quality.

Thanks to his productivity, Patton stood to earn something more than the flat $50 per side that Speir usually negotiated for his finds. "If a man that was makin' the record didn't have but two songs," Speir noted, "he didn't get much. If you come up with six songs, he got pretty good pay."

That Patton was permitted to record enough material for seven double-sided records shows that Laibly as producer recognized his superior sales potential as a recording act. Let us say that Patton received $50 per side (although he could have received as much as $75 per side), and that Speir received a finder's fee. Then that first session would have cost at least $1,970 for Laibly to produce. To earn back that investment, plus the cost of record manufacture and the expense money for Speir (whom Paramount reimbursed ten cents a mile for all travelling done on behalf of accepted discoveries) and Patton (which would amount to the cost of his train ticket, and meal money), the company would have had to sell an average of 1300 copies of each Patton release, or about 9100 copies of the 7 releases combined. Although this total seems trifling today, it exceeded the 500 copies that the race-record companies represented to Speir as the break-even sale for single blues records. Such outlays in expenses and production were particularly extravagant for a company who was so tight-fisted, that the return of a hundred unsold records from a distributor was an occasion for executive grumbling.

A full day's schedule at a recording studio was said to consist of four or five recording sessions, resulting in the creation of eighteen or twenty sides. The 18 masters that Patton and Buddy Boy Hawkins waxed probably took nearly an entire working day. When heard in matrix number order (and hence may be in chronological order), the collected recordings suggest that the session proceeded casually and unstructured.

Patton went first, warming up with his slide-guitar piece "Mississippi Bo Weavil Blues." He laid down 11 lyric choruses about the boll weevil's travels to where "there is cotton and corn." Then he took a short break, likely to retune his guitar for "Pony Blues." During the meantime, Buddy Boy Hawkins recorded two songs. The first was "A Rag Blues," which wasn't really a blues, but a rag with an ABACDEFEA succession of 16-measure themes. His second was "How Come Mama Blues," a 16-measure hokum tune based on the popular song "How Come You Do Me Like You Do" by Gene Austin and Roy Bergere.

Returning to the microphone, Patton was ready to erupt in full roar. He proceeded with his signature blues "Maggie," including the lyric about waking "up in the mornin,' jinx all around your bed"; Paramount would release it not as "Maggie" or "The Jinx," but as "Screamin' and Hollerin' the Blues." Then he went next to another trademark tune, "Down the Dirt Road Blues," feeling loose enough to sing the World War I era lyric about the "overseas blues" not being bad.[34] In full swing now, he then performed "Pony Blues," endowing the performance with the multi-layered guitar arrangement that he had been using for at least 15 years. The last side before his second session break was "Banty Rooster Blues." After using up his three lyric choruses about the rooster and the hen, Patton then sang a stanza about the barrelhouse Jackson's Wall, and another using images from fishing. The last chorus, about the barking watchdog, serves as a frame to the opening lyric about the crowing rooster.

During this torrential series of takes, Patton recorded his top four pieces in a row. It is hard to say that he did so because Laibly was an indulgent producer, or if Laibly made himself so unobtrusive as to seem like a visiting assistant at Gennett's studio. If Mayo Williams was still with Paramount and supervising Patton and Hawkins, he would have exercised more restraint than Laibly by making sure that they recorded some unpromising material along with the potential hits. The rationale was, as Williams admitted some years later to researchers, "we would throw anything on the B-side, we didn't want two hits on a record." But on that day in June 1929, Patton seemed to make everything sound like a hit.

Hawkins resumed his share of the recording session with "Snatch It and Grab It," which had a 16-measure verse and a 16-measure refrain. Midway through the first singing of the refrain, another voice—perhaps Patton resting in the studio—may be heard saying "Say you do." His remaining song was "Voice Throwin' Blues," a novelty reworking of Handy's 12-measure "Hesitation Blues" with a simulation of ventriloquism used to sing the words at the end of each chorus. From the sound of the issued recordings, Hawkins performed well enough, certainly much better than what the scout Harry Charles reported of Hawkins' 1927 studio debut.

But Patton's B-material came off on records as better than Hawkins' best. "It Won't Be Long" was the melody of "Banty Rooster Blues" sung to new words mentioning Memphis, the sawmill town Minglewood, and a woman who prefers Patton to her pimp and other men. This was the only one of the nine blues that Patton recorded at Richmond that did not belong to his usual repertory and so, according to Williams' criterion, it may be deemed as an appropriate B-side to "Down The Dirt Road Blues."

Back to full voice, Patton laid down two of his recent blues and two more of his standards. "Pea Vine Blues" referred to the Yazoo and Mississippi Valley Railroad spur that provided service to Dockery plantation. For the melody, Patton used the 12-measure tune that was known among pianists as "Forty Four Blues" (as recorded by Lee Green and Roosevelt Sykes) or "Vicksburg Blues" (as made famous by Eurreal "Little Brother" Montgomery). Patton added an updated touch by including a lyric about the "levee sinkin," which likely referred to the 1927 Mississippi River flood. Then he performed his new ode about deputy sheriff Tom Rushing, whose name was later misspelled by Paramount as "Rushen" for the 78-rpm release. With those two stately blues done, he turned to two brisk display pieces. "A Spoonful Blues" was his trusty fast number about addictions, whether for drugs or for sex. Despite dating back to the beginning of his career, the references to Parchman Penitentiary and to the Hot Springs spas were still timely. His spoken asides that are embedded within many of the sung lyrics could be said to have a greater ventriloquist effect than Hawkins' refrains in "Voice Throwin' Blues." "Shake It and Break It (But Don't Let It Fall Mama)" is entirely different than Hawkins' "Snatch It and Grab It," despite the similar titles. Patton's choruses in his song are 8 measures, using two melodic strains in a rag-like manner. For a man in his late 30s, he performs as if he is still confident of attracting women in their 20s.

Patton ended his recording day with four sacred songs. Even if his sister Viola scoffed then and later at the mention of Charlie being a religious man, he instilled an inner, functional sense of spirituality in his recordings of spirituals and early gospel songs. "Prayer of Death" Parts I and II may have been the product of some studio puttering, but it is still an astonishing tour-de-force. Part I begins with chiming imitations of a death bell, followed by a slide guitar instrumental on "Nearer My God To Thee" (Sarah Adams—Lowell Mason), and then with Patton singing 7 choruses of the 8-measure spiritual "Take a Stand." For Part II, Patton begins with a free introduction combining guitar responses to his vocal affirmations of faith, then he sings five choruses of another spiritual, this one in 16 measures, "Hold to God's Unchanging Hand." Considering how fervent both sides are, one wonders why Laibly had Patton record two more sacred tunes. A plausible answer may be that the producer thought that the "Prayer of Death" could sell very well, in which case a second sacred disc by Patton should be pressed for release. "Lord I'm Discouraged" was better known as the spiritual "There'll Be Glory." "I'm Goin' Home" was another recording of "Take A Stand," but without the prelude heard on "Prayer of Death" Part I. While the performances of these last two spirituals sound straightforward on shellac, in the studio they must have been compelling enough for personnel to stay, despite what may have a been a late hour; at the end of the third verse of "I'm Goin' Home," a second singer (unknown, but certainly not Hawkins) may be faintly heard singing with Patton.

How Laibly understood and assessed the sides while and just after Patton recorded them may be gleaned from the way he coupled sides and scheduled their releases. Songs containing sexual innuendo was sure to have commercial value, but Laibly misunderstood the intent of "Shake It and Break It" by issuing it as the B-side of "A Spoonful Blues." Also put on the B-sides were titles with proper names like "Tom Rushen Blues," "Elder Greene Blues," and "Jim Lee Blues," on the apparent grounds that the national unfamiliarity with these people lowered their commercial appeal. "Joe Kirby" was issued as an A-side, but it was belatedly issued over a year after it was recorded. Four songs that were not strictly blues ("Mississippi Bo Weavil Blues," "A Spoonful Blues," "Runnin' Wild Blues," and "Elder Greene Blues") would be labeled as such on the apparent belief that the label "Blues" enhanced their sales appeal.

It seems that Laibly may not have asked from Patton, or made sure with him, what were to be the titles for the songs. "Maggie," for a leading example, was released with the title "Screamin' and Hollerin' The Blues." Other titles were transcribed phonetically; "Tom Rushing Blues" was spelled on the paper Paramount labels as "Tom Rushen." Composer credits were routinely ascribed to Patton, regardless of what material he recorded, but this act was a formality: in keeping with company practice in 1929, none of the songs was copyrighted.

Considering that Patton was paid only a flat fee for each accepted take, the inspired quality of his performing makes his records seem fresh. It is all the more so when one realizes how old much of Patton's material was. If he played, let's say, "Pony Blues" only three times a week since 1910, he would have performed it nearly three thousand times by the time he made the record in Richmond. Yet he brought an air of immediacy and unpredictability to this song and the other staples of his repertory.

However dated Patton's material, to all intents and purposes he brought a new dimension of artistry to dance music as it existed on records in 1929. Of all the bluesmen of the pre-war era who reached the recording studio, he was the only singer-guitarist capable of embellishing his voice while he played, and the only dance guitarist who executed improvisatory figures. As "A Spoonful Blues" demonstrated, he was seemingly the only blues guitarist of his time and place who could completely rearrange material. As noted previously (in chapter 4), he recorded the only blues song ("Screamin' and Hollerin' the Blues") with a basically improvisatory melody, the only dance blues ("Pony Blues") without a constantly repeating melody, and the only dance song ("Screamin' and Hollerin' the Blues" with its three bass lines) that had appreciable instrumental variations. These devices and his versatile singing imparted a dramatic impact that made his recorded music much different from the usual Mississippi dance music.

Yet the nuances that made Patton's music special was unnoticed by his record producers. "Any of those people didn't know a thing except from sales," H. C. Speir said of the day's race recording directors. "If it didn't sell, they knew that. If it made money, then they knew that, too." Laibly was among them. When he was interviewed in 1966, he declined to single out any Paramount artist as a talented guitarist. The mere suggestion that his label had presented any musicians of stature exasperated him. "These people," he said of the musicians on his blues roster, "were simple people. They sang the way they lived and thought."

Charlie had so many crazy pieces,
you couldn't count 'em.

—SON HOUSE

*Chapter 11*

# A SESSION WITH SON SIMS (JULY 1929–FEBRUARY 1930)

During the months after his Richmond trip, Patton visited H. C. Speir's record store in Jackson to purchase copies of his new releases; he continued this practice after each of his other recording sessions. He resold the records to his Dockery's neighbors, probably for more money per copy than Paramount's 75-cent retail price. "Everybody on the place wanted 'em," his nephew Tom Cannon recalled.[1] Promoting himself with an élan that other bluesmen often lacked, he kept Speir informed about his availability for more recording opportunities. To listeners hearing him perform on the street, he passed out cards bearing his photograph and handwritten details of forthcoming engagements.

Patton may have also provided his photograph to Art Laibly. As a rule during this time, Paramount did not arrange to have publicity photographs taken of its recording artists. However the way it was provided, the company used his photograph on the front page of a four-page sales catalogue it sent to dealers during the fall of 1929. If the youthful portrait that Lizzie Taylor claimed was Patton is viewed as doubtful, then the publicity photograph is the only authenticated picture of him. Compared to Taylor's portrait, the 1929 photograph shows Patton looking gaunt and emaciated.

As a promotional contest, Paramount advertised "Mississippi Bo Weavil" in *The Chicago Defender* as by the "Masked Marvel," offering a free record to anyone who could identify its performer. On another release, the company put on the same record two of Patton's best-known songs, "Pony Blues" and "Banty Rooster Blues," thus having one hit record with two good songs, squandering its opportunity to have two hit records with each good song on the A sides. The "Pony Blues"/"Banty Rooster Blues" disc was issued in July 1929, becoming a Paramount best-seller despite what was an untimely appearance. As Speir explained to the authors, blues records tended to sell best in Mississippi during the fall harvest season, while the discs released in other seasons languished on the shelves, especially during the winter when farmers lacked income. This unexpected summer success may have been welcomed by Art Laibly, who since becoming Paramount's recording director in 1927 had not turned up a hitmaker.

As with the other popular artists on "race" records, Patton's choice for flat fees instead of royalties proved costly to him. Let us say his royalty could have been the standard rate of 2.5 cents per side, but the recording fee he opted to take was $75 per side. Then with the sale of a mere 3000 records, his royalties would have begun exceeding the $1050 in total fees that Patton had received in Richmond. The irony of Paramount's self-serving rate structure was that it may have allowed the company to preserve by issuing and disseminating much if not most of Patton's repertory for posterity, in the hope that one of the resulting records might become a hit.

While there are no sales records for "Pony Blues," it very likely sold more than the 10,000 copies needed for Paramount executives to declare a "hit" and, during Mayo Williams' tenure, served as the minimum sales figure for an artist to be invited by the company for a second set of sessions. The record may even have sold 50,000 copies, which was half the number that Paramount sold of its biggest "race" hits by artists who enjoyed general Southern racial popularity like Blind Lemon Jefferson and Ma Rainey. Most of its purchasers were probably Mississippians who had already heard Patton or knew of him by reputation, which was enough for Paramount to tout him in its *Defender* ads as "one of the best-known artists in the South."

Patton's success was noticed by other record companies. Speir remembered that they pursued him "like a swarm of bees" in the wake of his successful recording debut. This interest in Patton did not tempt Speir to place him with another label, as he was adverse to the contract-jumping that was then rife in the blues field. Had he suspected back then that Paramount contracts were of dubious validity, Speir might not have been so faithful to the company. For in 1924, before Speir began working with it, Paramount had forfeited its corporate status by claiming that it was defunct, apparently to avoid paying taxes.[2]

Patton spent the summer of 1929 in the Bolivar County town of Merigold, located two Yazoo Delta Railroad stops north of Cleveland. At the time, Merigold numbered 800 people, including a contingent of Belgians, deputy sheriff Tom Rushing, and a 23-year old fledgling guitarist recently arrived from Arcola, Willie "Have Mercy" Young. "The first time I seen him," Young recalled of Patton, "he's on the streets playin' that box about: 'Saddle up my pony, catchin' up my black mare!' Ha—I never will forget that old piece." Young learned the Spanish guitar tuning and a rudimentary version of "Pony Blues" from Patton. In 1967, to interviewers he claimed to have accompanied Patton at local house parties, and he played guitar for his own amusement on the back porch of his home in Leland, his style still sounding as if unchanged since 1929.

Another protégé Patton befriended at this time was Booker "Mister Pink" Miller of Swiftown. As a 19-year old, he first encountered Patton on a Ruleville sidewalk shortly after Paramount's release of "Down The Dirt Road Blues" in November 1929. "He was playin' at a place at Ruleville, and I come by, and I was playin' a few notes on the box there," Miller later recalled. "He came to me. We began to talk to each other, and he found out that I was interested in music, and he musta liked me because I liked him, I admired his records. So he taken a big interest in me and he began to teach me different things that he thought I ought to know." During the next five years, Miller not only received general blues pointers from Patton, but also demonstrations of the first pieces his idol had ever played on the guitar. A week after their first encounter, they performed together at a dance on Eastland's plantation near Doddsville. Then, for a time afterwards, Miller learned from another experienced bluesman, James Binnel of Clarksdale. "Now he was good," Miller said of Binnel. "He wasn't as good as Charlie was, but looked like to me I could do better on the James [pieces] than on Charlie's, because Charlie fussed a lot. If you didn't do it right, now, he [Charlie] just don't harbor with you."

Patton's bedmates still outnumbered his musical cronies. While living in Merigold, he had assorted so-called "wives" known today only through their first names Udy (whose sister Sudy had married his brother "Son" Patton), Polly, and Bessie. Then he took interest in a Dockery's tenant named Katie

Williams, to the chagrin of her husband Floyd. When Patton and she left the plantation together, Williams as a long-time Dockery's tenant complained about Patton's behavior to Will Dockery's foreman, Herman G. Jett. This incident marked at least the second time Patton had broken a Dockery's household by cuckolding one of the wage hands.

Upon hearing Williams' account, Jett apparently chose to favor the man who was more productive to the farm. "When he (Patton) come back," his nephew Tom Cannon recalled, "Mister Jett told him if he couldn't do no better than that, he'd rather for him to leave." In short, Jett warned Patton to leave the plantation.[3]

Patton accepted his expulsion without protest, even though at that time some black tenants were willing to raise their fists against Dockery's white employees. "He said he'd rather went," Booker Miller recalled. "He didn't hunt trouble." A little over four years later, Patton sang of his banishment, if half-intelligibly, on a blues recording:

> I ain't gonna tell nobody, "Thirty-Four!" have done for me
> Christmas rolled up, I was broke as I could be.
>
> They run me from Will Dockery . . .
> . . . told papa Charlie: "Don't want you hangin' round
> on my job no more."
> (Thirty-Four Blues)

In contemporary slang, "Thirty-four" meant "Get away."[4]

As it turned out, Patton's fling with Katie Williams lasted only two or three months. Although he was still prohibited from living on Dockery's, he was allowed to visit family for extended stays. His nephew Tom Cannon remembered that "he'd come in here anytime he got ready to see his sister. He'd come in and stay a whole week. Mister Jett didn't bother him." For other visits in the area, Patton would stay on the adjoining D. D. Turner plantation near Ruleville.

For the rest of 1929, Patton appears to have had no fixed address. He spent a brief period on the Anderson plantation near Cleveland. His next residence was probably the R. M. Dakin plantation near Skene, four miles southwest of Cleveland, where his daughter Willie Mae lived. Over the next few years, he was seen so often in Skene that Earl Montgomery, the salesman who supplied its plantation commissary with Paramounts, mistakenly thought he was living there. Willie Young reported that Patton lived in Pace, located between Skene and Rosedale, during in the latter part of 1929; a local fan named Willie Jackson would chauffeur him in a car to parties at such places as Leland. During the same time, Patton also joined what Young called "a little old nigger minstrel show" that operated out of Nashville. He appeared with it in Memphis, "all out there to Drews, Tutwiley (Tutwiler), Lamose (Lambert), Blaimes (Blaine), all right down to Cleveland, Shaw, Rolling Fork . . . "[5] Hooking up with Patton again in Skene at this time was Kid Bailey. A local resident who saw Bailey and Patton perform in Skene remembered years later that "He (Bailey) didn't sing Charlie's songs, he'd always sing different."

By the end of 1929, Paramount had issued at least four records from his debut session, all excellent sellers. Sometime in January 1930, Speir received a telegram from Arthur Laibly directing him to arrange for Patton's return to the recording studio.[6] Finding Patton proved to be no easy task.

Going first to Dockery Farms, Speir was told there that Patton had left for Cleveland. Proceeding to there, he learned that Patton had since moved to Jefferies, a Coahoma County plantation large enough, like Dockery's, to be rendered as a town on contemporary maps. There Speir finally found him. On hearing of the invitation to record again, Patton proposed to bring with him a second musician. He had in mind his old friend Henry Sims, who was living 25 miles away on Will Borden's plantation near Farrell. He was now 39 years old and the leader of a local string band called the Mississippi Corn Shuckers. Speir seems to have accepted Patton's suggestion without feeling a need to hold an audition with Sims.

The two musicians subsequently traveled by train from Memphis to Paramount's front offices in Grafton, Wisconsin, a small town near Port Washington. There was a new studio on Falls Road that an English sound engineer had designed free of charge for Paramount. Tommy Johnson and Ishman Bracey would make records there a few months after Patton's visit, and Johnson likened the dwarfish structure as a "chicken coop."[7] Still, it was a studio that Paramount owned and could use to record at any time, allowing for multi-day recording sessions with musicians visiting from outside Wisconsin.

On this first visit to the Grafton studio, Patton recorded a series of sixteen titles in either one or two days, then returned the next day to wax nine more tunes, and finally, on either the third or fourth day, he led one more recording.[8] Sims provided fiddle accompaniment on twelve of these sides.

None of Patton's records from these sessions list Sims as his fiddle partner, and all but one of them were labelled as featuring only guitar accompaniment. These omissions may be called a typical Paramount oversight, but then again, Sims didn't have as lengthy an affiliation with Patton as, say, Willie Brown had. Perhaps Sims' presence on Patton's records was due to the fact that "they had been playin' music a long time, they was good friends on the music, they was all right with one another," as Sims' sister Roberta Jameson put it.

Henry Sims was born on August 22, 1890 as the only son in a family of six children, in the Mississippi Delta town of Anguilla, which then had 175 residents.[9] His boyhood was spent near Cleveland at the all-black town of Renova, where his mother Mary gave him what was to be his lifelong nickname, "Son." His first musical efforts were on the piano, which his parents initially disapproved, sharing with their fellow churchgoers the prevailing attitude about secular music. Yet they also believed that his "nature" should be allowed to assert itself, and so they permitted him to pursue music without interference. Eventually Sims learned how to play piano, guitar, bass viol, violin, and mandolin. He learned the violin from his maternal grandfather Warren Scott in Renova, who had been raised as a slave in Maryland, and would later move to Eudora, Arkansas, where he died sometime during the 1910s. Sometime around 1910, his sister later thought, Sims met Patton for the first time, but it is uncertain whether if the pair performed together then.

During World War I, Sims served in the army, but as another sister, Lilly Hester, recalled later, he stayed in the U.S. Otherwise, his life was placid, if insular. During the 1920s, he spent most of his time in and around two Coahoma County towns, Farrell and Clarksdale, the one numbering 250 and the other 10,000 residents in 1930. His career as a string band musician began in 1919 or 1922, when he walked into a Clarksdale barrelhouse and buttonholed a local guitarist named Percy Thomas (1897–1968) with the proposal that they join forces.

During their first practice sessions, Sims frequently chided Thomas for making musical errors. After three weeks, however, he pronounced them ready for professional engagements and sought out additional musicians. In Stovall, the nearest town north of Farrell, he recruited a mandolin-playing friend, Louis Ford, who was three years older than himself. Then he visited Greenville and procured a local bass player known only as "Pitty Pat," the nickname describing the percussion that his bare feet provided. This group remained intact for the next twenty-five years, with Sims serving as its violinist and eventual namesake: christened the Mississippi Corn Shuckers, it gradually became known as the Son Sims Four.

On weekends the Corn Shuckers played music that appealed to whites, and their most lucrative bookings were the square dances given by a Clarksdale social club on the first Friday of each month. Although Sims made no secret of his dislike of plantation labor, he worked as a sharecropper anyway. During the winter lay-off seasons, though, he liked to spend time in a section of Clarksdale called "The Brickyards." It was there, or in Farrell, where Patton found Sims, forming a musical association for recording that lasted only a week or so, or so Percy Thomas later supposed. This association was unheralded and unpublicized. Sims never introduced the other Corn Shuckers to Patton, nor did he mention the recordings that they had made for Paramount. Why he never mentioned his trip with Patton may be due to either avoiding his colleagues' jealousy, or to knowing their capability to upstage him. Besides, he depended on them in order to land those good-paying weekend gigs at white parties.

Sims' manner resembled more that of the clergy than of his fellow Delta bluesmen; this may have been shaped by a childhood religious conversion. Most of his income went towards food and clothes. The pastor preaching at his funeral at Clarksdale's Bell Grove Baptist Church in 1958 declared that Sims had set a better Christian example than most of the congregation's regular members. He met and married Lizzie Smith, even though she was twelve years older than him, and she would outlive him by six years. They enjoyed an enduring marriage, and Sims addressed her deferentially as "Miss Lizzie." Like many couples, they had occasional domestic spats. After each such fight, Sims would take refuge either with Percy Thomas or with his sister Roberta Sims in Memphis, where he would work as a houseboy until prodded by her suggestions that he return to his wife.[10] Although he was fond of alcohol, drinking made him pious and drowsy. "He drank but he didn't 'clown,' you know," Roberta said. "He'd get somewhere, talk all that 'deacon' talk, and he'd go to sleep." The single occasion when Percy Thomas remembered him losing his temper was in 1922, while the band was traveling to a picnic, when he became heated during an argument with a man called "Sparkplug." The matter ended suddenly when Sparkplug cold-cocked Sims on the nose with a brass-knuckled fist. All told, there was probably no musician in the Delta who less resembled that "squabblin' scuttlebub" Patton than Son Sims, who stood an inch or so shy of six feet, weighed 160-odd pounds, and was recognizable by the flabby pouches of flesh protruding beneath his deep-set eyes.

The sounds of their recorded duets would not have resembled what has been described about Patton's live solo performances. As noted earlier, Patton's style never really needed a second instrumentalist, and it never occurred to H. C. Speir to suggest a recording partner for Patton. As he later explained, "Charlie was good with that guitar." Furthermore, the fiddle was not Sims' favorite instrument. "He liked that mandolin best," his sister reported. Nor was it Patton's preferred accompanying instrument. "He said he'd rather play with two guitars than play with a fiddle," Booker Miller noted. When Sims returned home from their Paramount session, he was carrying a mandolin, not a fiddle. Perhaps he intended to back Patton on mandolin, but then he may have been directed to play violin by Art Laibly, who had once played that instrument in a West Virginia pop orchestra.

Having played his front-line repertory at his first session, Patton had to dig deep into his career songbag for his winter session at Grafton. For that reason, those records are much different from those he made at Richmond. Booker Miller had just met Patton the previous fall, and "in the time me and him was together"—the next four years—"I heard him play every piece he knew." But he was completely unfamiliar with "Going to Move to Alabama," "Elder Greene Blues," and "Mean Black Moan," the first two and last songs from this session with Sims.

Patton may not have had to delve so deeply into his repertory had he been willing, or been allowed, to record the sexual material that was a mainstay of his live performances. "He sing more of them than he did blues," Son House said of songs in the mode of "Shake It and Break It," of which Miller said, "Back there in the thirties and twenties like that, stuff like that was popular." The risqué songs he knew included "Jelly Roll King" and "Mama Can't You Keep It Clean," the latter of which House said, "Charlie had so many dirty verses to it. He'd sing it often, you know, at them Saturday night balls." Willie Moore recalled "Jelly Roll King" as a Patton favorite, its opening lyrics were:

> Jelly roll, jelly roll is so hard to find
> It killed the old man and run the young one blind.

Another bawdy song that House heard Patton perform began:

Don't sell nothing, don't give a thing away
Save it all for your daddy, I'll be back some day.

"There was one, he got me to singing it directly," House added. "Charlie had me singin' that mess, 'Up the hickory, down the pine, I bust my britches right behind.'"[11] In addition to these songs, Patton performed the 1928 hokum hit "Tight Like That" and standards like "Salty Dog," "Four O'Clock Blues," and "Make Me A Pallet On Your Floor." After listening to Willie Brown's 1941 Library of Congress recording of the last piece, Hayes McMullan noted, "Charlie Patton used to play them kinda pieces, too."

One type of material that Patton knew and made use of at this winter session were songs from mainstream popular music. When Mayo Williams supervised Paramount recording sessions from 1922 through 1927, he discouraged his black artists from recording white or popular material; Laibly seems to have continued this practice. But somehow Patton sneaked in three tunes that would have appealed to whites and blacks alike, if not to Laibly: "Frankie and Albert" and "Some of these Days," were the last Patton titles that Paramount issued, and "Runnin' Wild" would be issued as a "B" side.

Yet at his recording sessions, Patton apparently preferred to record lesser-known tunes, or works of his own devising. "Here's what Patton could do," said Hayes McMullan, by way of pointing up what he thought was Patton's most remarkable gift. "Charlie Patton could make up a song outta anything." Every time McMullan heard Patton, the artist had at least one new piece to offer his audience.

The first two songs of Patton and Sims' recording visit, "Going To Move To Alabama" and "Elder Greene Blues," sound particularly practiced as true musical duets. "Going to Move to Alabama," Patton's reworking of Jim Jackson's recent hit "Kansas City Blues," looks due east from Mississippi instead of northwest. It was uptempo, and it had a conventional accompaniment that provided a smooth platform for Patton's remarkably animated singing. During the 7th chorus, he lets slip "Louisiana" instead of Alabama, which may suggest that he sang the song as "Going to Move to Louisiana" a number of times. "Elder Greene Blues" gave a hard blues twist to the placid "Alabama Bound," an eight-bar rag that was also known during the previous 20 years as "Don't You Leave Me Here." Sims knew the tune, as his sister later reported. The impetus for Patton's rearrangement was probably Charlie Jackson's "I'm Alabama Bound" (Paramount 12289, 1925), which included the lyric "Elder

Green's in town, and he's going around / And he's telling all the sister and the brothers he meets, he's Alabama bound." Blind Lemon Jefferson recorded "Elder Green's In Town" for Okeh in 1927, but it was not issued, and it may now be lost. The title name "Elder Green" was a recurring but enigmatic allusion in black song. It is likely that he was a fictional type personifying all preachers, as the phrase "lady green" had been a late 19th century slang term for a clergyman.[12] Two takes survive of Patton's "Elder Greene Blues," the first one used as the released master. A listen to the second take suggests it may have been rejected for Patton's repeats of three stanzas. In the master takes for "Going To Move To Alabama" and "Elder Greene Blues," Sims achieved a full accompaniment by emulating Patton's vocal melody. Yet Laibly issued both of them as "B" sides, which suggests that he wasn't very impressed by them.

Sims' inexperience as a fiddle accompanist begins to show in "Circle Round The Moon" and "Devil Sent The Rain." On these performances, he merely matched Patton's tonic chord strums and riffs with his own phrases, often supplying only three or four beats of accompaniment while Patton is playing a six-beat fill. Both songs were based on common models. "Circle Round The Moon" used the same tune that Patton as a teenager played on his porch-step as "If You Take My Woman, I Won't Get Mad At You." "Devil Sent The Rain Blues" was a new version of "Maggie"/"Screamin' and Hollerin' the Blues." That Sims comes off less well than on the first two titles of the session suggests that he and Patton lacked the time to prepare and practice individual arrangements for these and other songs that they recorded later during their visit. If so, that may explain why Patton performed the next four songs alone.

"Mean Black Cat Blues" was a simple blues to begin Patton's solo part of the first session, its accompaniment using just one chord. Its style was based on the music of Blind Lemon Jefferson, whose 1928 Paramount disc "Long Lastin' Lovin'" was apparently the source inspiration for Patton's last two choruses. For "Frankie and Albert," Patton concentrated on telling the lyric narrative, limiting his guitar accompaniment to a simple strumming pattern. In 1899 in St. Louis, Frankie Baker shot and killed her lover Al Britt. It was a sensational crime that was told in various lyrics to a 12-measure pre-blues song. But in Patton's retelling, Frankie catches him cheating on her, but he escapes her wrath. Later Albert kills a man, for which he is duly tried in court (with Frankie in attendance) and dies in jail.

A sublime session curiosity was "Some of These Days," a sentimental song that belonged to the realm of white music. Shelton Brooks published "Some of These Days" in 1910, which that same year Sophie Tucker made a famous recording; that song may have been adapted from "Some o' Dese Days" composed by Frank Williams. In addition to Patton's master take, a safety take survives; both are quite alike. The song's structure was 16 measures, although in a few instances Patton adds another 4 measures by repeating a lyric. He sings to a single phrasing pattern and the major-scale melody, ending phrases with cadences to major thirds and fourths. Patton's syncopated one-step rhythm won't be found in the Brooks and Williams antecedents, and for that reason, white audiences of Patton's time would not have much appreciated the rollicking rhythm that, on the record, elevates it above the status of a simple ditty for us today.

Rounding out this nostalgic part of the session was "Green River Blues," Patton's youthful blues about either Green River or the lumber mill named after it. Compared to the simple guitar parts for the previous three songs, this performance of "Green River Blues" had a surprisingly intricate accompaniment, using long instrumental fills and a variety of ornaments and licks.

No session logbook or other written documentation survives of Paramount's Grafton recording operation. So, it can't be said for sure whether and at which song Patton and Sims stopped recording at the end of the first day. But if the surviving alternate takes for "Elder Greene Blues" and "Some of These Days" suggest anything, it may be that Laibly had at least two takes recorded of each song. So, from "Going to Move to Alabama" through "Green River Blues," possibly 16 to 20 takes were waxed of eight songs. Such a number of takes would equal what Mayo Williams said was a full day's recording load. The next two songs in the Grafton matrix number series are duets featuring Sims as vocalist. It is plausible, then, that after "Green River Blues," recording ended for that day, and Patton spent that evening rehearsing with Sims.

Laibly's hands-off approach as a recording director is suggested by his willingness to go along with Patton's studio whims, and by his allowing Sims to sing despite his inexperience. The fiddler's sister Roberta never heard him sing any of the four titles he recorded for Paramount, or many songs at all. "He didn't do much singin," she reported. Percy Thomas agreed. "He always say he couldn't sing," he attested, "that's the reason he didn't sing no more than he did."

Sims' singing is characterized by his thin, timorous, baritone delivery. Yet he also seems to have adopted some of Patton's vocal wares and airs. The two vocal sides he made to lead off his second duet session with Patton, "Farrell Blues" and "Come Back Corrina," were melodically akin to the first two vocal phrases of Patton's "Green River Blues." His lyrics was on the level of doggerel, such as "Farrell blues, mama, sure don't worry me / It's all I want just to, see what a poor man do." On the other hand, Sims' way of marshalling tones indicate a lack of vocal development and possibly some detachment from the milieu of black singing. While singing, he restricted himself to within a single octave, often using the tonic as his lowest tone. Patton, by comparison, hit the tonic notes as part within the middle range of his songs, with the dominant below it serving as the lowest tone; exceptions to this practice did occur when Patton growled at the bottom of his voice.

For these two sides, and the other two performances with Sims singing, there should be noted three guitar ornaments that Patton often played in succession, usually during the middle four bars of each chorus: the descending run during Sim's vocal (m.6 of Ex. 48), the two-step lick (m.7, beats 1–3), and the upbeat lick (see m.7, beat 4—m.8, beat 1).

For the rest of this day of recording, Patton performed alone, making some of his most laconic records on which his guitar seems to be doing the singing. The second of the two surviving takes of "Hammer Blues" seems to have been selected for having more completely sung phrases than the first take. It was based on Spencer Williams' "Mountain Top Blues," which Bessie Smith recorded for Columbia in 1924. Williams' song lyrics were suicidal in feeling, including wishing for death by a falling tree, while Patton sang of sleeping under the same tree. His low-key singing gave an appropriate reposeful feeling to the melody, even though his indistinct diction led the Paramount staff

Ex. 48: Son Sims, "Tell Me Man" (1930), second vocal chorus, mm.5-8 [0:52-0:57].

to mistranscribe its title "Hammock Blues" as "Hammer Blues." His leisurely slide guitar accompaniment was far removed from the modern stereotype of Delta blues-playing, although it was arranged with a dance accent.

The next few performances had surprisingly intricate accompaniments, considering that the songs had new or negligible places in his performing repertory. "Magnolia Blues" was a uniquely phrased slide-guitar tune, in which the middle four measures of each 12-bar chorus was played instrumentally, not sung. For some reason—probably inexperience by the staff—the second take was treated as a separate piece, being assigned a new matrix number and a new title, "When Your Way Gets Dark," and released by Paramount on 78 six months after "Magnolia Blues." "Heart Like Railroad Steel" was the "Maggie" tune performed at a much slower tempo than, say, "Screamin' and Hollerin' the Blues," but Patton nonetheless turned in a nuanced performance with no slackness in rhythm.

As he did in Richmond the previous year, Patton ended the recording day with spirituals. "Some Happy Day" was a stately but fervent rendition of the hymn "Some Day" by J. Graydon Hall and H. E. Barnett. The printed hymn arrangement (such as that published by Stamps and included in the photo section) directs the choir or congregation to sing the chorus antiphonally in two separate groups. Performing alone, Patton arranged his guitar accompaniment in such a way that his slide-fretted tones serve as the answering group to his Baptist-style vocal singing.

Since recording the two songs with Henry Sims earlier that day, Patton sounded leisurely, perhaps a little too much at ease for a Delta bluesman. But for "You're Gone Need Somebody When You Die," Patton rouses himself to perform in the manner of the Church of God in Christ. The song itself was a 16-measure spiritual that was patterned closely after "You Better Get Somebody On Your Bond," which enjoyed wide circulation at the time. Blind Willie Johnson recorded what was to be a famous performance for Columbia Records on December 11, 1929. If it was released before Patton and Sims traveled to Grafton, then its success would have lent urgency for a Patton version. Patton began his record by singing the chorus twice. Then he gave a brief sermon, paraphrasing these four verses from the Book of Revelations, in this order:

> (1:14–15) But his head and his hair were white as white wool, and as snow, and his eyes were as a flame of fire, and his feet were like fine brass, as in a glowing furnace, and his voice like the voice of many waters.

> (22:2) In the midst of the city street, on both sides of the river, was the tree of life, bearing twelve fruits, yielding its fruit according to each month, and the leaves for the healing of the nations.
>
> (4:4) And round the throne are twenty-four seats; and upon the seats twenty-four elders sitting, clothed in white garments, and on their heads crowns of gold.

Somehow, hearing Patton expound on these verses in his indistinct way, is believing. His resumption in singing the sacred tune sustains this white-hot momentum for the rest of the record.

The next four numbers in the Grafton studio's matrix number series were assigned to a white dance music session led by Lynn Howe and Bill Carlsen. If it was held on the morning after Patton's sermon performance, then Patton and Sims returned to the studio for another long and productive session either early that afternoon, or the following morning.

Patton continued recording by himself. His main piece for that day was the blues about the 1927 Mississippi River flood, but with its fast tempo, it was best to warm up first with a moderate-paced blues, "Jim Lee Blues." It used the melody of what was known as either "Slidin' Delta" or "East St. Louis Blues," and its lyrics conveyed a nostalgia for the 1890s and 1900s—when Patton was a boy—when passenger boats chugged between the Delta communities. Then Patton tore into his 1927 flood blues, "High Water Everywhere," describing first the break and torrent, then the destruction in its wake. Since the artistic impact of "High Water Everywhere" was felt most upon its hit release in April 1930, it and "Jim Lee Blues" will be discussed in that context in the following chapter.

After the exhausting work on the two-part flood blues, Patton relaxed with two more spirituals. "Jesus Is a Dying Bed Maker" is first deftly played instrumentally with a slide, then sung to collection of lyrics, the first few about the Gospel of John story (4:4–26) of the Samaritan woman meeting Jesus by chance at a well. Patton begins the performance deliberately slow, then he speeds it up as if performing for a Church of God in Christ occasion. "I Shall Not Be Moved" was a widely known Southern sacred tune, sharing an antecedent melody with "Oh Mary Don't You Weep Don't You Moan." Two takes survive, but the sole copy of take one has "rim bite" damage that loses the first line of the first vocal chorus. The first take is steady and slow throughout. During the second take, Patton gradually speeds up the tempo, making that performance the preferred one for Paramount release.

With "Rattlesnake Blues," Sims returns to join Patton at the microphone. For the remainder of that day, they would record five more duets, two of them towards a second Paramount 78 featuring Sims as singer. By this point in the recording visit, Patton performed towards 22 masters for release. If Laibly and the Paramount recording staff were recording at least two takes per title, Patton may have recorded at least 44 takes, or as many as 50, during the course of 2 or 3 days in the studio, with another 7 titles yet to do before he left Grafton. This recording marathon would have required Patton to pace himself in the same way whenever he played an all-night dance. In that kind of setting, the presence of any instrumentalist who could mount a few leads could allow Patton to coast with undemanding "complement" guitar, such as the 1–2 boom-chuck pattern he strummed on "Runnin' Wild,"[13] the song he and Sims played after "Rattlesnake Blues." If, before taking this trip, Patton was planning to record as much as he did, conserving himself may explain why he asked Sims to go with him. It may also explain why during the visit he took in stride Sims' limited capabilities, especially in the group of takes from "Rattlesnake Blues" through "Joe Kirby Blues" at this time during their sessions.

Patton's adaptation of "Pony Blues" into "Rattlesnake Blues" showed his ingenuity in remolding his own material.[14] While retaining the accompaniment of the title verse almost whole, Patton recast its overall sound by changing his vocal attack to a boisterous bawling delivery, and altering the melody by replacing major thirds and sixths with minor thirds and sevenths. He also made unexpected dynamic contrasts with his guitar by muting treble figures while he shouted notes on the third beats of his vocal phrases (as in chorus 2 for the word "leave," as in "when I leave here mama I am goin'"). Another dynamic contrast may be noticed at the fourth beat of the second transcribed measure of his vocal opening (or, at the tenth beat of his lyric phrase), when he created gasping guitar sounds by damping the bass slides to and from the tonic:

Ex. 49: Patton, "Rattlesnake Blues" (1930), ch. 1, mm. 1-3, vocal melody, with "gasping" guitar bass-string downward slide on the tenth beat [0:06-0:15].

A distinctive lyric is in the third chorus, "Fixin' to eat my supper in Shelby, Illinois," which may refer to the 1922 shop workers strike, about which Patton sings in greater detail in "Mean Black Moan."

"Runnin' Wild Blues" was a diatonic ditty (not a blues) that struck Hayes McMullan, upon hearing Patton's record in the 1960s, as sounding "like a church song"—which it was, originally. The 16-measure melody went back to the 1855 tune "Oh Happy Day" by Philip Doddridge and E. F. Rimbault. It gained renewed currency during the Prohibition era with the words "How Dry I Am," and in 1923 on Broadway with James P. Johnson and Cecil Mack's hit "Runnin' Wild." In May 1930, the early country music group The Carter Family used the melody for their Victor record "When The World's on Fire." Today it is most often heard as the melodic basis of Woody Guthrie's "This Land Is Your Land." On his "Runnin' Wild," Patton sings conventionally, even taking Sims' manner of singing his lowest notes on the tonic.

The next two songs featured Sims singing "Tell Me Man Blues" and "Be True Be True Blues." "Tell Me Man Blues" used the same melody that Sims sang previously on "Farrell Blues" and "Come Back Corrina," but with each third lyric phrase modified with the same descent from minor 7th to 5th that Patton had used in rendering "Mean Black Cat."

"Be True Be True" was different from Sims' other songs, in that it was a sung rendition of "Careless Love" (which in turn was an antecedent shared in common with Patton's "You're Gonna Need Somebody When You Die," Blind Willie Johnson's "You're Gonna Need Somebody on Your Bond," and Blind Lemon Jefferson's 1927 "See That My Grave Is Kept Clean"). For his guitar accompaniment, Patton plays to the *1*–2 square dance accenting pattern. While Sims' melodies were similar to those Patton sang earlier in their sessions, the guitarist provided mostly run-of-the-mill bass strumming behind Sims's singing. Maybe Patton thought it was bad form to intrude upon Sims' show; the strict time-keeping role he performed on Sims's featured sides was probably his typical style in accompanying other singers. If Patton thought of playing fancy behind Sims, he restrained himself to the same guitar licks he had played a day or two before on "Farrell Blues" and "Come Back Corrina."

Still, some positive historical interest could be taken in Sims' musicianship for its likely link to nineteenth-century idioms by way of his grandfather's fiddle playing. His terse filler phrases are nearly devoid of blues tones. In "Devil Sent The Rain Blues," for example, he contributed the tonic, second, third, and dominant notes from the major scale, while his fills on "Rattlesnake Blues" pitted major thirds against Patton's minor thirds. He played "Elder Greene Blues" with the pentatonic intervals of "Alabama Bound," while Patton was performing it to the blues scale degrees of the minor third, minor seventh, and major fourth. This dissonant clash in scales is aggravated by Sims' imprecise intonation and his apparent failure to use rosin on his bow, giving his tone a shrill, grating quality. "He'd come 'cross (i.e., sound) kinda like a saw," a sister said of his playing, "I'd be listenin' at the music. I didn't have time to ask him about the roughness (of his sound); I'd be enjoyin' the music."

The last record of this part of the session was "Joe Kirby." It was not a spiritual, but an updated treatment of Patton's "Maggie" theme. Resuming the singing duties, Patton mentions explicitly the plantation owner near Robinsonville, Joe Kirby, and the store "Clack's Crossroad" in Robinsonville. Implicitly, he seems to allude to Louise Johnson, the blues pianist in and around Kirby's plantation and Robinsonville who was also having a romance with Patton at the time of this session.

It appears, from the Grafton studio's matrix number series, that Patton and Sims stayed for one more day. Booked for a session was Edith North Johnson, a 27-year old singer and pianist from St. Louis. Her husband was Jesse Johnson, a local entrepreneur who, among his activities, referred talent to Paramount and other record labels. Like Patton, Johnson made her Paramount debut in Gennett's Richmond studios. Two of the sides she made there, "Honey Dripper Blues" backed with "Nickel's Worth of Liver Blues," sold well enough to have Paramount invite her to Grafton. Years later, she remembered the new studio not as a chicken coop, but rather "a great big barn place."[15] She recorded at least 6 known sides, including the "no. 2" versions of "Nickel's Worth of Liver Blues" and "Honey Dripper Blues."

A third side that Johnson made at Grafton was "That's My Man," a 12-measure verse and refrain (4+8) blues, on which an uncredited guitarist sits in. During the third lyric phrase of each chorus, the guitarist plays this set of licks (Ex. 50):

Comparison of this example to that for the Sims/Patton sides (Ex. 48) lends credence to the identification of Patton as the guitarist. Acceptance of this side as a genuine Patton performance[16] may help one to have a good idea of how he performed in the cities including St. Louis, whose Dago Hill section he mentioned in two of his recorded songs.

Ex. 50: Edith North Johnson, "That's My Man" (1930), chorus 3, mm. 9-12 [1:26-1:33].

Shortly after Johnson's last take, Patton and Sims entered the studio and made one more recording, "Mean Black Moan," Patton's 1922 blues about the railroad shop-workers strike in Chicago. Patton sings his lyrics to the melody of "Maggie"/"Screamin' and Hollerin' the Blues," but he plays the guitar accompaniment for "Circle Round The Moon"/"If You Take My Woman." Meanwhile, Sims' fiddle accompaniment seems tailored for this song, including some remarkable flourishes of mandolin-like rolls; perhaps his contribution can be safely reckoned as the product of several days of Grafton tinkering. Patton may have revived "Mean Black Moan" just for this Grafton visit, as he seems not to have played it live afterwards, not even after the record's release in July 1930. Booker Miller didn't even know of the song until he heard Patton's record in 1968. "That's a new one on me," he admitted, "but that sure is him."

However, "Mean Black Moan" has an unfinished quality, as do three other Patton recordings from this trip, "Mean Black Cat Blues," "Devil Sent The Rain Blues," and "Joe Kirby."[17] Their lack of detailed arrangements may indicate something about Patton's method of assembling his blues accompaniments and coordinating them to his singing. All four of these songs are conventional twelve-bar blues with the stereotyped 10–6 vocal phrase/instrumental phrase divisions. While recording them, Patton seems primarily concerned with establishing an expressive vocal attack. His instrumental accompaniment embroiders his vocal line with guitar snippets; the vocal phrases are followed by simple tonic strums rather than with the intricate riffs of his more ambitious blues that he recorded at Richmond in 1929. None of these four songs use his "overlay" technique of holding a phrase-ending word beyond the tenth beat of a line. It was probably only with the material that Patton was fully at ease when he lengthened the vocal phrases, and when he embroidered tonic strums with plucked guitar figures.

Shortly after leaving Grafton, Sims sent his sister Roberta a letter from Detroit. It is very likely that Patton and Sims went there with Charlie Spand, a Detroit blues pianist who recorded three sides at Grafton before they began their session. On the morning after Sims' letter was delivered to his sister, the musicians themselves arrived at her home on Exchange Street in Memphis, carrying copies (likely test-pressings) of some of their records. She refused to listen to them in the belief that blues were sinful.

Sims spoke to his sister of receiving $75 a side for his work. If Patton received the same rate per master, he would have pocketed $1800 for his winter 1930 recordings. The total in fees he likely received for his first two recording trips would have been $2850, which was more than 5 times the gross earnings ($510) of the average Mississippi wage-earner for the same year. It would also have been well above the median American income for 1929 ($1760), and only two hundred dollars less than what the average American college professor earned that year.

After parting company, the musicians resumed their individual careers. A few months later, Patton met Son House. When asked in a 1966 interview if Patton had ever mentioned Sims, House replied, "Not as I knows of."[18] He never learned that the two had ever played together, and he remarked, "Charlie didn't play with nobody too much."

SIMS TOOK ONE more opportunity to record, if for posterity than for profit. While toiling on the Belmont plantation near Stovall in the summer of 1942, Sims and Percy Thomas were summoned by their foreman, a "Captain Holt," to the shack rented by Muddy Waters, another tenant on the plantation. There, joined by Louis Ford and "Pitty Pat," they were recorded by the Library of Congress. In 1946 Ford died in Rosedale from complications of untreated syphilis, and the Son Sims Four became three. The death of "Pitty Pat" soon after brought about the end of the group. Sims continued playing for at least another decade, "mostly for white people" his sister remarked. Thomas, a portly man Sims addressed as "Chief," was such a trusted friend that Sims gave him his pocket watch before undergoing a series of medical operations in the 1950s. A kidney stone condition required several operations at the Memphis Veterans Hospital. Apparently left unattended after undergoing a biopsy, he choked to death in his hospital bed on December 23, 1958. He was buried in an unmarked grave, and he left no descendants.

> Old Charlie Patton, I liked them blues he play
> about he goin' down this old Jackson Road . . .
> You know, the Backwater Blues. An' he say:
> "Water's backin' all up."
>
> —ELIZABETH MOORE

*Chapter 12*

# HIGH WATER (JANUARY–FEBRUARY 1930)

Henry Sims' two Paramount discs as featured artist with Patton assisting, and Kid Bailey's Brunswick 78 with a cover of a Patton song, were both released in 1930. All three releases were commercial flops. Which went to show that Charlie Patton's celebrity didn't rub off on others by association or imitation. Even when Patton set up recording opportunities for his friends and also for some foes, they made records that just did not sell.

His first recorded imitator of the 1930s, Mattie Doyle, was no exception. When she recorded in 1930, Doyle was a newcomer to secular music, even though she was 25. She was raised in the southeast fringe of the Delta between Howard and Tchula, two small towns located halfway between Greenwood and Yazoo City. Her home was marked by death, first of her mother, then of her older sister to gangrene brought on by untreated cut on her leg from a thorn. Her first experiences in music were as a choir singer in a Baptist congregation. She began playing guitar at age 22, sometime around 1927, the year of the "high water." "About three months after she started, she runned off, went to Memphis," her first cousin Lilly Berry recalled. "Her mother was dead [by] then, and [there] wasn't nobody but her daddy." Himself a church member, Doyle's father was stricken by her defection from home and church. He and his other children "couldn't find out, they went everywhere, looking for her," Lily said, "he never could find her." Perhaps to continue eluding him, she took the pseudonym of Mattie Delaney when she recorded two sides in Memphis for the Brunswick label in February 1930.[1]

She may have been street singing in Memphis, for she took the persona of the hobo street singer in "Down The Big Road Blues":

> My mother said six months 'fore I was born:
> She was gonna have a girl-child wouldn't never stay at home.
>
> I feel like cryin', ain't got no tears to spare
> I had a happy home, an' I wouldn't stay there.

Perhaps Mattie may have met Charlie Patton, for her song was a treatment of his "Down The Dirt Road Blues" that was issued just three months before her session. Like other contemporary renditions of Patton's material, it comes off—compared to Patton—as relatively conventional and somewhat bland. She adjusted the guitar accompaniment by transferring the fretting position from a C to G position (and placing the capo on the second fret to play in the key of A). There is no doubt of Patton as her model, for she sustains the word "the" in the title lyric "the big road" for four beats, as does Patton in for the equivalent lyric on "Down The Dirt Road Blues." But the melody of her song stressed major thirds, where Patton had sung minor thirds. Her phrasing followed the "ten-six" vocal/fill blues pattern, altered only by the omission of two-beat tonic strums (at the conclusion of the first and last vocalized verses) and the addition of two extra beats to the second line of the fourth vocal verse. Whereas Patton held the final word of each of his "Down the Dirt Road Blues" phrases for six beats, Doyle did so for only two.

As for her "Tallahatchie River Blues," she played the guitar accompaniment in the D position, and she sang according to the "ten/six" beat scheme for each of her lyric phrases. For pitches, she relied on the same intervals Patton used to create the first stanza of "Screamin' and Hollerin'," namely the tonic, minor third, and minor seventh. However, she sang within a relatively restricted range (d2-g2), and without the embellishments Patton brought to the melody.

Her lyrics, however, were more thematic than those of most dance blues:

> Tallahatchie River risin', Lord it's mighty bad
> Some peoples on Tallahatchie done, lost everything they had.

The people in the Delta are wonderin' what to do
They don't build some levees I don't know what become of you.

High water risin', got me troubled in mind
I got to stay here an' leave my daddy behind.

"Tallahatchie River Blues" was part of a lingering record industry trend for blues about floods,[2] especially about the 1927 Mississippi River flood. Delaney sang about the January 1930 flood affecting Greene and Mississippi Counties, Arkansas, portions of Missouri, and Tallahatchie and Quitman Counties, Mississippi. What made the 1930 flood different—and worse in some ways—than the 1927 Mississippi River flood was the extreme cold that froze the floodwaters into ice sheets, trapping victims inside—and in some instances on top of—their homes for over a week until help arrived.[3]

Patton's "High Water Everywhere" used the melody of "Maggie," and its popularity with audiences quickly rivaled that of his signature song "Pony Blues." "When he'd be playin' that piece," Willie Moore recalled, "they'd have to fling the girls *back*!" The success of the record's release in April 1930 also kept his star status with Paramount executives. More than any other Patton disc, "High Water Everywhere" displayed his tremendous vocal power and heavy guitar beating for which he was noted in live performance. "Just to see him in action with that record!" remembered Booker Miller in awe. "He just put so much in it!"

On "High Water Everywhere," its first part especially, Patton pushed himself like perhaps no other blues singer on records had done before, or arguably has done since. Maybe on "Pony Blues" did he succeed as thoroughly in imposing his personality upon the song and in subordinating its blues structure to self-expression. In "Pony Blues," Patton seems to be a musical magician who floats on air rather than who treads along the narrow idiom of the blues. But in "High Water Everywhere," he renders that idiom as transparent with his full-voiced delivery, banter, heavy guitar-slapping, foot-stomping, and spontaneity. One does not think of the "High Water Everywhere" recording as a blues at all, but rather as Charlie Patton "in action." It resembles "A Spoonful Blues" as barrelhouse theater. In both songs, he mimics a variety of voices with such finesse that his own voice is lost in the process. But if "A Spoonful Blues" is playful, then "High Water" is dramatic, and Patton's delivery has the tumultuousness of the flood itself.

The topic of the 1927 Mississippi River flood was tailor-made for

Patton, as it gave him an extended opportunity to mention the place names that he frequently used to convey bits of realism into his lyrics or to make them more memorable to listeners. While constructing its verses, Patton was less concerned with plotting a plausible story than with cramming as many place names as possible into the song. The resulting narrative serves as a pretext for Patton's grand tour, which unfolds along different paths than the actual flood.

The Mississippi Delta was created by alluvial flooding over the river's banks. After the levees were built in the 19th century, overflooding and breaching were recurring dangers. It is likely, then, that early in his career Patton had sung a topical blues about a minor flood, from which he drawn and revived to create "High Water Everywhere." His mentions of Tallahatchie River towns may be heard as timely updates from the January 1930 flood. It could even be argued that "High Water Everywhere," especially its second part, was a studio creation. For Patton had not performed it among the fourteen songs he had recorded on the first working day of his Paramount visit with Son Sims, and it is difficult to imagine him devising the entire two-part song without drawing from years of experience and many lyrics about floods.

Before setting down "High Water Everywhere" on wax, Patton warmed up by recording a two-part "Jim Lee Blues" that presented him at his most traditional and least flamboyant. It, too, was a river song, but one in a turn of the century style:

> The other day, Jim Lee keep a-backin' up an' down,
> She sandbar stuck, man if you're water bound.
>
> The Jim Lee, up the river, Stack in Arkansas,
> An' the sidewheel knockin', "Lord I'm water bound."

The James Lee II and the Stacker Lee were among the fourteen steamboats operated by the Lee Line of Memphis, all named after the various sons of owner Robert Edward Lee. Songs about his boats had probably sprung up into existence with the inception of his fleet in 1890, which ran between Memphis and Friar's Point, then later extended southward to Vicksburg. In 1924, the Lee Line merged with the Rosedale Packet Company. By the time of Patton's Paramount sessions, it was out of business, and Patton may have turned to the song out of nostalgia. The 8-measure melody is the same as those of "East St. Louis Blues" and "Slidin' Delta." He embroiders what was a conventional guitar accompaniment with small, effortless tricks, strumming at different dynamic levels and altering each closing cadence of the first vocal phrase per chorus, ending either on the subdominant scale tone or the major second. With these devices, he seemed to give a taste of what counted as musical individuality in Mississippi in the days before such showstoppers as "High Water Everywhere."

The chaotic effect of "High Water Everywhere Part I" is enhanced by the way Patton stages the song as a desperate scramble for survival during the flood's first thirty-six hours, when no part of the Delta promised a safe refuge:

> The backwater done rose all around Sumner now,
>     drove me down the line
> Backwater done rose at Sumner drove poor Charlie down the line
> An' no tellin' what the water done to through this town.
>
> Lord the whole 'round country, Lord, river has overflowed
> Lord, the whole round country man is overflowed
> (spoken: "You know I can't be stayin' here, I'm—gotta go
>     where it's high, boy!")
> I was goin' to the hilly country, 'fore they got me barred.

Son House recalled that Patton once mentioned being at Rolling Fork when the "high water" broke.[4] He was certainly nowhere near the Tallahatchie River town of Sumner in the eastern Delta, for if he had been, he would have known that the flooding never reached that area. House thought that Patton's reference to being "barred" from the hill country meant that he was drafted for levee or rescue work in the flooded Delta regions, as were many plantation hands.[5]

Most of the flood victims were those who stayed at their homes, taking shelter on what rooftops, treetops, and even Indian burial mounds when the river waters arrived and rose. Those like Patton who did leave the area were later derided by the planter William Alexander Percy as "nonresidents from the hills who regarded the river hysterically . . . and the usual run of rabbit folk who absent themselves in every emergency."[6]

Patton's third verse made as little historical sense as the first:

> Now looka here now at Leland, river was risin' high
> Lookey here boys around Leland tell me, river was raisin' high
> (spoken: "Boy it's risin' over there, y'hear?")
> I'm gonna move over to Greenville, 'fore I bid "goodbye."

Greenville was submerged in as much as twelve feet of water, and it was flooded before Leland ten miles away to the east. It was the midnight collapse of the twenty-foot high levee at Stop's Landing eight miles north of Greenville on April 21, 1927 that flooded the Delta.[7] Eventually the water covered an area extending seventy-five miles north and south of Greenville, and fifty miles east of it. In the immediate wake of the Stop's Landing catastrophe, 75,000 Delta residents became homeless and a hundred blacks died. An attempt was made to sandbag the levee near Leland,[8] but the effort proved futile when four or five feet of water subsequently overran the bulwark. Leland's 2500 residents and some 4000 refugees from outlying areas then took shelter in the center of town, which the flood did not touch.

At face value, the third verse of "High Water Everywhere Part I" poses the unlikely picture of a refugee who flees dry Leland and heads into the flood. Patton could hardly have envisioned Greenville serving as a flood haven, so perhaps instead he could have been thinking of its three-mile long levee as the main gathering place for blacks who were displaced by the flood. Some twelve thousand such refugees did camp on the forty-foot wide embankment there for six weeks in tents provided by the War Department and Red Cross, sharing the space with cattle almost as numerous as themselves.[9]

Evacuation to Greenville ended the peril faced by most of the flood survivors, and it would have served as the climax of a realistic "high water" account. But in his flood blues, though, Patton continued:

> Lookey here the water now Lordie done broke, rose most everywhere
> The water at Greenville—and Leland! Know it done rose everywhere
> (spoken: "Boy, you can't never stay here!")
> I would go down to Rosedale, but they tell me water there

The river town of Rosedale was located twenty-five miles northeast of Dockery's Plantation and nearby Cleveland. Patton may have mentioned Rosedale because Will Dockery, unaffected by the flood, had volunteered one of his straw bosses and a hundred of his tenants to assist in levee work there.[10] Although the flooding extended from Rosedale to Vicksburg, Patton envisioned the latter town as a sanctuary:

> Now the water now mama, done took short little town
> Boy they tell me the water, done took short little town

(spoken: "Boy, I'm goin' to Vicksburg!")
Well I'm goin' to Vicksburg, over that higher mound.[11]

The basis of these lyrics was probably the evacuation of a thousand refugees from the Greenville levee to the one at Vicksburg on April 24. This ended up being a bad move when Vicksburg was overrun by water on April 30. Most of these transferred refugees were white; a group of Red Cross steamers intended for the removal of blacks was prevented from leaving Greenville by influential planters who feared that their tenants would never return.[12]

The garbled sixth verse involved a return to the area of Sumner:

I am goin' out of that water where lands don't never flow
Well I'm goin' over the hill where water, oh it don't never flow
(spoken: "Boy, Sharkey County an' everything was down in Stover")
Bolivar County was inchin,' over that Tallahatchie skid.[13]
(spoken: "Boy went in Tallahatchie to find it over there!")

Stover lies about seven miles northeast of Sumner, far removed from the flood scene. The concluding stanza, whose reference to "old Jackson road" may be to Highway 49, had no basis in fact:

Lord the water done rushed all-a, down old Jackson road
Lord, the water done raise-ed, over the Jackson road
(spoken: "Boy, it starched my clothes!")
I'm goin' back to the hilly country, won't be worried no more.

As a treatment of "Maggie," Patton's accompaniment is notable for its fast tempo and distinctive guitar-slapping. Thanks to its surging pace, the guitar part for Part I of "High Water Everywhere" was less fluid and responsive to his vocal than that for "Screamin' and Hollerin' the Blues." The final measure of each stanza-ending vocal phrase was accompanied only with foot-tapping. Where "Screamin' and Hollerin' the Blues" used three different instrumental figures to accompany the initial vocal phrase of its various stanzas, Part I of "High Water Everywhere" used just two. During the first chorus, Patton played an embellishment of the descending bass that Willie Brown (I) would later record on "Future Blues," slapping the guitar as well as snapping the low E string in Brown's fashion. The first vocal phrases of the other choruses of this recorded side used similar slaps to accompany repeated treble tonic notes (probably played on the B string) that cascaded into strummed tonic chords. Whereas the "Screamin' and Hollerin' the Blues" bass is a full measure, Patton's equivalent "High Water Everywhere" figure is a repeated two-beat riff, beginning on Patton's second sung beat and extending two beats after the vocal it accompanies.

The filler riff that set off the second and third vocal phrases was spread over to two measures (Ex. 52) rather than the three measures that the corresponding riff in "Screamin' and Hollerin' the Blues" needed.

Ex. 51: Patton, "High Water Everywhere Part I" (1930), chorus 2, mm. 1-3 [0:29-0:37].

Ex. 52: Patton, "High Water Everywhere Part I" (1930), chorus 2, mm. 7-8 [0:44-0:48].

The guitar figure he used during the stanza-ending vocal phrases, consisting of a strummed V chord beginning on the second beat and of bass eighth-notes just before and on the sixth beat [Ex. 53] was copied whole from "Heart Like Railroad Steel," which Patton had recorded the previous day.

Perhaps because he was singing some lyrics that, until then, he had never sung live to an audience, Patton's vocal phrasing made several slapdash departures from its usual ten-beat length. The opening phrase of the song, as a starting example, consisted of three vocal measures while eleven- and nine-beat phrases variously opened the fourth and sixth verses [Ex. 54].

Ex. 53: Patton, "High Water Everywhere Part I" (1930), chorus 1, mm. 9-11 [0:50-0:55].

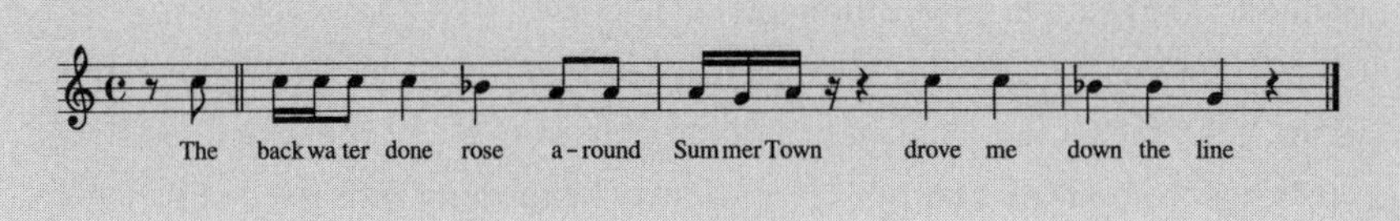


Ex. 54: Patton, "High Water Everywhere Part I" (1930), chorus 1, mm. 1-3, vocal melody [0:02—0:10].

But the real freedom in Patton's performance lies in the breadth of its vocal melody rather than the lengths of its phrasing. His relatively set accompaniment on guitar allowed him to sing with real abandon. While "Screamin' and Hollerin' the Blues" ranged an octave, "High Water Everywhere" ranged an additional fifth (from $c^1$ to $g^2$).

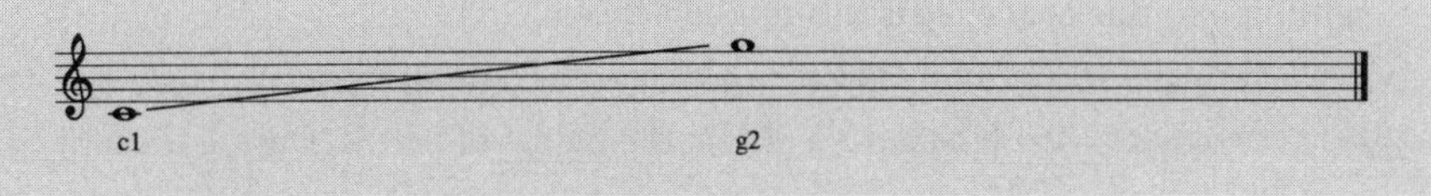


Ex. 55: Vocal range of Patton, "High Water Everywhere."

The first and second vocal phrases of "Screamin' and Hollerin' the Blues" are frequently identical. But in "High Water Everywhere Part I," if an opening phrase of a stanza begins on an augmented fourth, the second phrase often begins a half-tone lower. Whereas all of the vocal phrases of "Screamin' and Hollerin' the Blues" have phrases ending on the tonic, some phrases of "High Water Everywhere" end on minor thirds. The first phrase of its fourth stanza ends on a major third, while the second phrase of the final stanza ends on a dominant.

When Paramount advertised the "High Water Everywhere" disc in the *Chicago Defender*, it asserted that "everyone who has heard this record says that 'High Water Everywhere' is Charlie Patton's best piece and you know that means it has to be mighty good because he has made some knockouts." If Laibly was enthusiastic in the recording studio for the song after Patton had just performed it, this may explain why a second part was done. Booker Miller never heard Patton sing the lyrics of "High Water Everywhere Part II" or play its arrangement. "That's a new one," he said of the record. "I never heard him him play it that slow. You know, he always 'moved out' on the guitar." Miller added, "That sure is music, though!"

"High Water Everywhere Part II" may seem anti-climactic when heard after Part I. But if Part II is listened to as a separate work about the 1930 flood,[14] its remarkable qualities may be noticed. It may be the least rehearsed of Patton's recordings, with the possible exception of "Prayer of Death" at the Richmond session the previous fall. While performing and recording most of his repertory, Patton used spontaneity as a spice, and the general ingredients of his performances were tried and tested. But in the second part of "High Water Everywhere," one senses that Patton had no idea how he was going to proceed after the opening verse. If that was the case, then the result is a unique event in recorded blues history: a completely spur-of-the-moment dance accompaniment. It may be the initial uncertainty for the song that led Patton to begin it at a slow tempo, and the way he gains momentum into spontaneity while settling into this new song is thrilling to behold.

Although for continuity Patton makes use of some elements of "High Water Everywhere" Part I, he has no plan at the outset of Part II. During the first two verses, he accompanies each initial vocal phrase with a bass segment he had used in the second, third, and fifth choruses of "Heart Like Railroad Steel," involving a bass tonic note plucked with a heavy vibrato on every other beat, and extended for three measures after the end of the vocal phrase it accompanied (Ex. 56).

During the third verse, Patton accompanies the same phrase with a series of muted sixth string snaps (alternating between a minor seventh and major sixth) sounded on each beat (Ex. 57)

In the fourth and sixth verses, he grafts the initial accompaniment phrases of "High Water Everywhere" Part I, but he extends those phrases (for four and three beats respectively) beyond the conclusion of the vocal phrase. His

Ex. 56: Patton, "High Water Everywhere Part II" (1930), ch. 1, mm.1-5 [0:03-0:10].

Ex. 57: Patton, "High Water Everywhere Part II" (1930), ch. 3, mm.1-3 [1:06-1:13].

treatment of the IV and V chords that accompany the second and third vocal phrases of each verse is likewise unscripted. For example, he plays the V chord of the first stanza as a high-treble repeating strum (Ex. 58):

In the fourth stanza, the IV chord is played as a descending triad lick on the phrase's the sixth beat (Ex. 59).

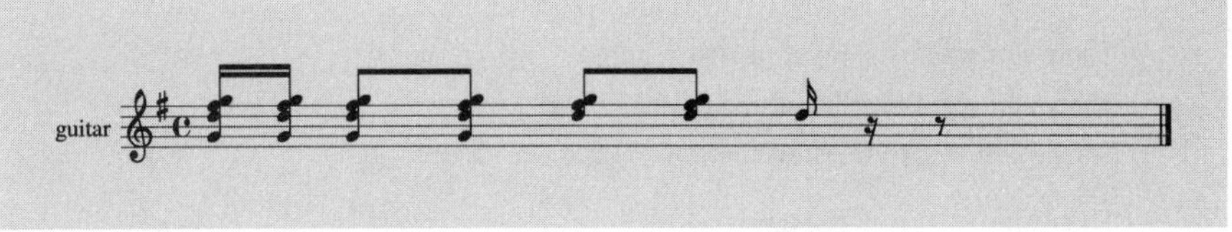


Ex. 58: Patton, "High Water Everywhere Part II" (1930), ch. 1, m.9 [0:26] (after Grossman, *Delta Blues Guitar*).

Ex. 59: Patton, "High Water Everywhere Part II" (1930), ch. 4, m.6 [1:53-1:54].

Yet while providing this arresting view of himself as an impromptu performer, Patton sounds fatigued, obviously from his stupendous exertions for "High Water Everywhere" Part I. Yet Patton seems to make positive use of this fatigue by incorporating it into his performance of Part II. At the end of the second phrase of the fourth verse he gasps, adding a vivid sound effect to his portrayal of a terrified flood victim:

Oh I hear the roar! Water up on my door!
(spoken: You know what I mean? Same here)
I hear the ice, Lord, went sinkin' down (gasp)
I couldn't get no local, Marion City gone down.[15]

Patton's generally wooly sound on this part of the record prompted H. C. Speir to comment that "He's about drunk now. You can hear it." While it is true that on various occasions liquor did get Patton "pretty well tongue-tied," as Speir remembered, here it is uncertain that it was a factor. He was probably improvising not only his accompaniment but his lyrics as well, and under these circumstances he could hardly have devised a smooth delivery. Most of his lyrics are held together by the bare thread of rhyme:

Backwater at Blytheville, doctor weren't around
Backwater at Blytheville, done took Joiner town
It were fifty families and children, come to sink and drown.

The water was risin' up at my front door
The water were risin', up at my friend's door
Some men says to these womenfolk, "Lord, we's better go."

The water was risin', got up in my bed
Lord the water it rollin', got up to my bed
I thought I would take a trip Lord, out on a big ice sled.[16]

Oh I hear the roar! Water up on my door!
(spoken: You know what I mean? Same here)
I hear the ice, Lord, went sinkin' down
I couldn't get no local, Marion City gone down.

So high the water risin', I been sinkin' down
Then the water was risin', at places all around
(spoken: Boy, they'se all *around*)
It was fifty men and children come to sink and drown.

Oh Lordie! Women an' grown men down.
Oh! Women an' children sinkin' down
(spoken: "Lord have mercy!")
I couldn't see nobody home well, was no one to be found.

Blytheville, Joiner, and the surrounding Mississippi County were surrounded by ice that was too thin to walk on, yet too thick to break with small boat prow. After the ice melted and the waters receded, Blytheville served as one of several camps where refugees were brought to live in railroad boxcars and tents. As David Evans has written to sum up his valuable account of the January 1930 flood, "There is no accurate accounting of the damage and the number of lives lost." [17]

The dramatic character of Patton's performance gives it an aura that is unlike that of any other blues song. For the most part, blues is testimony, not playacting, and for that reason it tends to be even and consistent in manner once the style of singing is chosen and begun. Often a singer will stick to a set delivery that may correspond little to his lyrics. But not Patton in Part II of "High Water Everywhere." Each of his verses has an individual vocal interpretation of the lyrics it poses, even if the last two verses are compromised a little by Patton's buffoonish vocal asides. But in the fourth verse ("Oh I hear the roar! Water up on my door!"), when Patton suddenly shifts to the present tense, his intensified delivery makes the narrator sound like a living figure who is terrified by the threat of imminent extinction.

PATTON'S DRAMATIC DELIVERY of "High Water Everywhere Part II" may be the most refined example of Mississippi blues singing ever recorded. It can't be explained as the product of the same noisy dance setting that Mattie Doyle and other blues-players of the time catered to, where musicians were judged mostly for their ability to be felt, if not heard, by a whole crowd.

Son House, he got his pattern from Patton and Brown;
when he come along I had done quit it.

—HAYES MCMULLAN

*Chapter 13*

# GRAFTON (SPRING–FALL 1930)

The Coahoma County river town of Lula was two train stops southeast of Jeffries Plantation and eight miles southwest of Helena, Arkansas. Patton moved there shortly after his Paramount recording trip with Son Sims. At the time, Lula had no paved streets, and some 35 years later it was remembered by Son House as "nothin' but a little flagstop—wasn't nothin' to it." But in 1930, its population was 450, considerably fair-sized for a hamlet when compared to Jeffries' 100. Patton was long familiar with the Lula area, as he occasionally stayed on the outlying plantations. "He stayed up there around Lula two [or] three times," his nephew Tom Cannon reported. In the spring of 1930, he was living on a neighboring plantation in a shack that House said was located "four [or] five miles outta town, way out next to that levee there, way out next to the water."

Lula was where lived his latest common-law wife, a twenty-eight year old woman named Bertha Lee Jones (born Pate).[1] "We all called her 'Bert,' she was nice-lookin,' too" David Edwards said of her, adding that "Patton had every nice-lookin' woman." Before moving in with Bert in Lula, Patton had left another "nice lookin' tall woman" as David Edwards described a woman now known only as Bessie living in Merigold.

"Bert" Jones was originally from Flora, Mississippi. In 1907, at age five, she moved with her family to Lula, where Patton in his teens happened to be romancing Roxie Gibson. Roxie and Charlie then moved to Dockery's, where she stayed there long after they separated. The last that is known of Roxie is that she left Dockery's around 1930,[2] coincidentally the same year when when Patton moved to Lula. Bertha Lee grew up on a plantation between Lula and nearby Dundee. "She was livin' there with her auntie," her former neighbor Elizabeth Moore recalled, "her auntie raised her." In the mid-1920s, she was singing in the choir of Lula's First Baptist Church. But by the time she met Patton, probably in the spring of 1930, she had become in Elizabeth's eyes a "pretty rough" person who "shot the dice Saturday nights, you know; keep up with them jukes." Son House thought of her as a "high stepper." But if the lyrics she sang on her 1934 record "Mind Reader Blues" indicate anything, Bertha Lee thought of herself as a low stepper compared to her common-law husband:

> An' I remember the days when I was livin' in Lula town
> My man done so many wrong things till I had to leave the town.

Patton and Bertha Lee stayed together for four years. Their relationship, however, was remembered by other musicians not for the tenderness but by their fights. "All they done was fight all the time. Charlie was a hell-raiser," David Edwards reported. Their bouts probably didn't affect one way or another Patton's overall feelings for her, because throughout his life his rambling ways resulted in clashes with all of his lovers anyway. According to House, Patton "made a dunce outta her" during their days in Lula. "He wasn't that crazy about her," he said.

House thought, if anything, Patton declared his affections for her in order to mooch free meals from the plantation house kitchen where she worked as a cook.[3] "He wouldn't even give Bertha no money much. He wouldn't even buy food half the time. He'd wait on her to come from the white folks' kitchen and bring him his food," he reported, "that's the way he ate, out the white folks' kitchen." To the authors in 1970, Joe Rice Dockery admitted that he long knew of this kind of ploy, describing it as a "basket habit," and he shrugged it off simply as "part of the plantation game."

The act of stealing food from plantation kitchens had, for the cooks like Bertha Lee who did it, other risks than being caught by their employers. The early 1930s was a time of drought, Depression, and hunger for many people, and no cook would have ever wanted to see a flock of poor folks coming and returning to her kitchen stoop. Patton seems to have done his best to cover for Bertha Lee by leading their Lula acquaintances to believe that she was stingy with food, even with him. "She's starvin' me, she's killin' me," he complained[4] with such great feeling to one local resident who, in an interview with the authors in the mid-1960s, held Bertha Lee responsible for Patton's death from starvation. Yet for someone so scrawny, Patton had a huge appetite, which Bertha did her best to satisfy. "Man, he'd eat a cow and a half and a bull and a half!" House marveled. "Every time Bertha'd get ready to kill a chicken or somethin', wasn't no use of goin' out to get one; she always had to come back with nothin' under two. He crazy about guineas."

Coincidentally, Paramount illustrated his zest for food by promoting his cocaine record "A Spoonful Blues" as a song about soup with an advertisement in the January 11, 1930 issue of the *Chicago Defender* depicting Patton in a restaurant waiting for service. The next Patton ad in the *Defender*, on February 1, for "Pea Vine Blues" showed not a train but a cluster of peas. It seems, then, that Paramount was less concerned with presenting the content of Patton's songs than with conveying his status as "a famous artist," a phrase that recurs in these advertisements.

With his fame throughout and outside the Mississippi Delta, Patton was in Lula a big frog in a small pond, so to speak. Its local barrelhouses presented few musicians, none of whom were either remarkable or rivals to Patton. There was a female blues pianist known as "Piano Playin' Willie," and a family band featuring guitar and bass fiddle. Previously, through 1917, a blues guitarist named Rennis Glisson lived there. But people remembered him less for his music and more for his arrest in 1917. "He had a wife named Doug," Willie Moore said, "an' he cut her head off, and they sent him to Parchman for life."

More significant in Lula was the a capella gospel group, the Delta Big Four. "First Baptist Church in Lula, that's where they demonstrated all the time," recalls Elizabeth Moore, who also heard them sing with a local restaurant owner, Sara Knights. Even though they specialized in sacred material, the four men impressed Patton enough that spring to take them to H. C. Speir's music store to make an audition record. The quartet's leader and senior member, thirty-five-year-old Wheeler Ford, owned a Buick automobile and came to be a crony of Patton's. The Delta Big Four failed an audition for Okeh Records, but through Speir they were accepted at Paramount.

Sometime in late April or early May 1930, H. C. Speir used his car to round up and drive everyone to the recording session. First he went from Jackson to Anguilla, where he hoped to find Bo Chatmon and have him come with them, but he failed to find him there. So he proceeded to Lula and picked up the Delta Big Four. They traveled to Grafton by way of Rockport, Illinois in order to avoid the heavy traffic in Chicago. Five men, several of them unwashed, in close quarters in early spring made for uncomfortable travel. Speir remembered nearly forty years later how the smell of the men lingered in his car for a month after the trip.

Their Paramount recording session was jointly supervised by Laibly and H. C. Speir, who recorded two spoken monologues for the amusement of his friends.[5] He also took the time during his visit to help Laibly renovate the studio, the acoustics of which vexed the company. "You couldn't do nothin' with that old building," Speir said. "Man, that building. It was an old rock building, big rooms, all square and everything like that. You had dampness in there all the time. You can't have dampness when you're recording. That dampness, even it if wasn't but just a small degree, it'd throw the sound off a little, you see." One change was adding sliding panels to reduce the size of the recording room.

The sound on the resulting eight recordings by the Delta Big Four turned out rather well, with the adjusted space minimizing any boxy resonance that it may have had previously. The performances were quite respectable, too, although coming from a Baptist group, they were going to seem sedate compared to, say, a sanctified Holiness group. Their lead numbers, "We All Gonna Face The Rising Sun" (or, "Four and Twenty Elders" as Son House remembered it) and "Moaner Let's Go Down in the Valley" sound well-rehearsed, sonorous, and majestic. Less so was "I Know My Time Ain't Long," whose mid-phrase rests and long phrase-ending notes nearly make the performance seem stodgy:

Ex. 60: Delta Big Four, "I Know My Time Ain't Long" (1930), chorus 1, mm. 1-4 [0:00-0:09].

Yet the members were hip enough to permit themselves a "shave and a haircut, two bits" rhythm during the middle of each chorus of "Jesus Got His Arms Around Me."

Ex. 61: Delta Big Four, "Jesus Got His Arms Around Me" (1930), internal phrase [chorus 1: 0:48-0:55].

Meanwhile, the chief executives of the Wisconsin Chair Company (probably with Otto Moeser among them) were talking with Speir about buying Paramount. It made sense to approach him, as he may well have been its leading retailer. It was one, if not the main, reason why Speir made this visit. "They were gonna liquidate," Speir recalled. He was told for an explanation that Paramount's northern location made it too expensive to record Southern musical talent.

But soon after returning home, his attempts to purchase Paramount were impeded by his failure to obtain backing from Jackson's Chamber of Commerce. "I couldn't get no one down here to even help me move the company," he said. Had Speir taken over Paramount, the Depression-era fortunes of Charlie Patton and numerous other Mississippi bluesmen might have been raised.

In early 1930, the Great Depression was already stifling the record business; "in '29 it stopped right quick," Laibly later remembered. But two new acts pointed up Mississippi as still a good place to go prospecting for blues. On the day before Mattie Delaney recorded for Brunswick in Memphis, Memphis Minnie appeared in the same makeshift studio and recorded the best-selling "Bumble Bee," a slow-paced ode to sex that was sung without a strong dance pulse.

Three days before "Bumble Bee" was recorded, an unheralded duo produced an even bigger hit at a commercial field recording session. The musicians, Walter Vinson and violinist Lonnie Chatmon, were playing exclusively for white dances in Mississippi. While practicing for one such dance in Itta

Bena, Vinson began puttering with a nine-bar ditty, "Sittin' on Top of the World," causing his partner to wonder aloud, "What kind of song is that?"

Soon discovered by Ralph Lembo in Itta Bena, they were dispatched to Shreveport, Louisiana where Polk Brockman was supervising at a field recording site for OKeh Records. His main reason for being there was to make a celebrity recording of William Kennon "W. K." Henderson, Jr., who was the owner of Shreveport radio station KWKH, a blistering on-air speaker, and a crony of Governor Huey Long.[6] Brockman remembered that Henderson was so popular at the time, "he was harder to get to than the president of the United States was." While Brockman was setting up the recording equipment on the roof of a local hotel, he met Vinson and Chatmon. "They just came in, unannounced and everything," said Brockman, who noted the addition of violin that distinguished them from "the same old guitar and singing deal." He proceeded to record the two men in a lengthy session that included that tune "Sittin' on Top of the World." Afterwards, he worked with Henderson in a spoken-word side that was later titled as "Hello World." For release on the custom label Hello World Doggone 001, the speech was coupled with a "Hello World Song" sung by Andrew Jenkins under the pseudonym Blind Andy. Despite its meticulous preparation and custom release, "Hello World" was a flop for Okeh. But "Sittin' on Top of the World" by Vinson and Chatman as the Mississippi Sheiks was a hit.

For many years, Brockman remained thankful for the Mississippi Sheiks. "If it hadn't been for them, I'd a-lost my shirt on that 'Hello, World' deal," he later recalled. Despite its incongruity with the times ("Wasn't nobody sittin' on top of the world in those days," Brockman snorted), Vinson's ditty became one of the most popular race recordings of the era. Reflecting afterwards on this success, Brockman said, "I've always said it wasn't the things you planned in recording. The biggest things were accidents, somethin' that just strayed along." Laibly would have agreed with him. He owed his position at Paramount to the mention of Blind Lemon Jefferson by one of his dealers. But since then, he was running a catch-can operation. "The only thing Laibly was doin'," Speir said, "was tryin' to stay in business, hopin' that somethin' was gonna happen." That may explain why he took chances on so many musicians, even those brought unannounced by other artists.

By the spring of 1930 Patton had become one of Paramount's few remaining stars, thanks to the death of Blind Lemon Jefferson the previous December. Laibly was desperate for appealing talent,[7] and this situation may explain his willingness to approve in advance Patton's scouting suggestions. So far that year he had gotten few results from the recommendations of Speir, the only dealer who was then regularly providing him with talent. In February, Speir had furnished Laibly with a Lake Providence, Louisiana street singer who recorded as Blind Joe Reynolds, who would provide Paramount with a classic blues, "Outside Woman Blues."[8] Speir later admitted that he felt sorry for him, which may explain why he arranged a session for Reynolds with Victor later that same year. In March, Speir had sent the label two Victor cast-offs, Tommy Johnson and Ishmon Bracey. Johnson, Speir noted, "was pretty hard to keep sober," a fact Laibly discovered when he saw the musician spend his Grafton visit in a state of such drunkenness that he could record only a half-dozen tunes.[9] Laibly issued the first of Johnson's Paramount releases, the appropriately titled "Alcohol and Jake Blues," that July, a delay of some four months that suggests that he had low expectations for retail sales.

It was a newly released Parchman prisoner who provided Patton with professional companionship in Lula. Eddie "Son" House Jr. had little performing experience when he met Patton in 1930,[10] but his recent disillusionments with menial labor and religion,[11] and a newly acquired taste for corn liquor, led him to professional blues-singing. He was born in 1902 to Eddie and Maggie House in Lyon near Clarksdale, Mississippi. His religious upbringing led him initially to hold the blues in contempt. "I didn't like no guitar when I first heard it; oh gee, I couldn't stand a guy playin' a guitar. . . . I didn't like none of it." But in 1926, while attending a house frolic in Lyon,[12] he changed his mind about the music, and before long he began singing and playing the blues on guitar. In keeping with the popular axiom that blues-singing boded "trouble," House sometime in 1928 or 1929 shot a man at a Saturday night frolic in Lyon, and he was duly sentenced and sent to Parchman. Due to the lobbying of his relatives,[13] his sentence was terminated after two years, either in late 1929 or early 1930. The judge who declared him free also warned him never to set foot in Clarksdale again. "I told him I could cover as much territory as a red fox if he turned me loose," House recalled, "so I walked to Jonestown and caught a ride to Lula. Then I run up on this woman, Sara Knights. She heard me playing over there at the train station. She wanted me to come over to her place and play some to draw a crowd. That's the way 'that' started."

"That," House explains, was his "talking trash" (feigning affection) to

Knights in the manner of Charlie Patton, in the hope of spending some of her profits from selling bootleg whiskey. "She run a little restaurant not far from this train station. I'm playin' Charlie Patton now with her. She's running a restaurant and I sure want to get in with her."

House had been more eager to "play Charlie Patton" than to meet Patton. But the two men soon met at the Lula depot, Patton "clowning and running his mouth and talking as usual, telling funny lies and things like that." Although Patton seemed to pay no attention when House performed at the depot, seeing the crowd that House later attracted to the porch of Sara Knight's cafe evidently led Patton to think that they might do business together. "He looked over and saw me playin' over there, and he come over, and that's what got us teamed up. Then he wanted me to play with him for Big Sis."

"Big Sis" was a three-hundred pound woman who went by the last names of Brock and Williams, and she operated a jukehouse near the levee at Powell, a town between Lula and Jefferies. Patton was performing there often by the time he met House.

At this point in House's telling, his association with Patton becomes a little hazy. As the first of Patton's associates to be interviewed by researchers, House was asked more questions about Patton than about himself. In 1966 he stated, "Near about ever Saturday night me and him would play together." But in a 1969 interview, he noted that he had never played for dance audiences in Lyon or Lula, and he recalled that when in Lula, Patton played primarily for white audiences. "They liked him for his clownin', they like-ted that. He could dish that out, man!" Moreover, the style of House's 1930 recordings as a solo performer are considerably different from Patton's, making it abundantly clear that House and Patton never teamed up at a Lula jukehouse.

For one reason why, Patton engaged many of his accompanists for one night at a time, often after an audition. One was Willie Moore, who with Willie Brown came upon Patton one time in the late 1920s in Hollandale. Moore recalled of that meeting, "He says, 'Fella,' says, 'if I could get you all down here tonight, I could make some good money. Then I'd come up the next time, help you if it would be possible.'" While it was Moore who first approached Patton sometime before 1918 to assist on a gig, this time Patton auditioned Moore before pronouncing him satisfactory.

Another reason was that when dance blues singers pooled their talents at jukehouses and house frolics, their roles were cut-and-dried. One musician sang and accompanied himself as though a soloist, and the other supplied "complement" guitar. In neither role could House and Patton have meshed. House's three chief two-sided recordings from 1930 ("My Black Mama," "Preaching The Blues," and "Dry Spell Blues") were one-chord bottleneck pieces without the usual blues phrasing patterns and dance accents. It is doubtful that Patton could have complemented these pieces, and in return House was too inexperienced as a guitarist to accompany Patton. At Big Sis's jukehouse, House likely played solo between Patton's sets.[14]

Since House was a musician more for listeners than for dancers, he tended to assess Patton's songs in terms of their lyrics. "He'd take all them foolish songs and things. Some of them would sound all right. Some of them had a meaning to them, some didn't. That's the way he played. He'd just say anything, the first thing he could think of: 'Hey baby,' and all that old kind of funny stuff." Without the experience of playing for dancers, House didn't realize, then or later, that Patton's lyrics scanned according to rhythm patterns (as noted earlier).

While they had less in common musically than House originally let on, they did have more in common socially than House later admitted, even though the two made an unlikely pair. While Patton was an incurable kidder who "didn't believe in what he's sayin' his-self," House was a relatively gloomy man who was guilt-ridden about singing blues. But they passed a considerable time as drinking companions, and House later stated to interviewers that he liked Patton for his generosity with a liquor bottle. "He wouldn't hide that from me. No, he wanted me to have that." House even poked a bit of fun at Patton's expense. "In the run of the night, Charlie couldn't just say drink corn liquor," he claimed, "he couldn't drink much of that."

House's anecdotes about Patton should be taken with some caution. After he was hailed in 1964 as a blues rediscovery, during his interviews he sometimes bit the bluesman's hand that once fed him, so to speak. Although his reminiscences of Patton have real historical value, some of them can be resentful, especially those in which he called Patton a "jerk" and a "shit-ass." From these instances, it could be inferred that perhaps Patton found House's company objectionable on some level. If that was the case, then House never recovered from this slight. His comments concerning Patton's cheapness, for example, may be the complaints of an unsuccessful borrower who, from Patton's perspective, may have been a sponge. If House in 1930 expected their acquaintance to blossom into a professional association, then he learned the hard way what Booker Miller said he learned about the same time as Patton's understudy: "If you didn't do it right now, he just don't harbor with you." That House craved more of Patton's attention is indicated by his claim, "I never did hear him act like he's interested in other guys' playin'. Charlie, he was the most self-conceited guy. He liked his-self, the way he played. But somebody else; he wouldn't hardly look around at him." Of his songs "My Black Mama," "Preachin' the Blues," and "Dry Spell Blues," House said that Patton "never would play none of them."

At any rate, during the 1960s, House was reserved in his statements about Patton's music. Of "High Water Everywhere," he said, "that is the onliest one I liked for myself," but professing to find only its lyrics appealing. However, he used a crude version of its guitar accompaniment to play his renditions of "Pony Blues," "Pea Vine Blues," and "Banty Rooster Blues," using lyrics borrowed from Willie Brown. House's silence about the rest of Patton's songs may be due either to his inability to play them in the Patton way, or to Patton being unwilling to teach them to him. For whatever reasons, his learning Patton's songs in the Willie Brown way, and not in the Patton way, prevented him from deriving in full the musical lessons from the characteristics of Patton's songs. While he prided himself on having a better voice than Patton, his singing remained relatively undisciplined. His "Preachin' the Blues," for one example, had much the same hollering sound as Patton's "Maggie," but it used three repetitive tones.

Yet one fact remains clear: Son House became, is, and will continue to be, renowned for the records he made for Paramount on Patton's recommendation, regardless of the supposed personal slights that House later claimed to have received from him.

One day in the summer of 1930,[15] an afternoon's tedium at the Lula depot was broken by the appearance of a white stranger in a business suit. Stepping momentarily off a Texas-bound train, the man held a brief conversation with Patton. "After he left, Charlie come on 'cross there (i.e., the main street of town) and told me what he said." This news was another recording session for Patton, House learned. "Charlie told him about me. So he told Charlie then he wanted me to come with him. I said, 'What?' He say, 'Yeah, he want you to come with me.' I say, 'Yeah, sho' I go, man.'"

The white man with the recording invitation was Arthur Laibly, the Paramount Records executive whom House mistook for Patton's "manager."[16] The first release from Patton's second session, "High Water Everywhere Parts I and II," sold well enough for Laibly to ask H. C. Speir to help him arrange for Patton's return to Grafton.[17] But at that moment, Speir had other business commitments that prevented him from driving to Lula. Laibly was about to travel to Texas to scout new talent, so he took the opportunity to renew personal contact with Patton along the way. It is likely that, to make sure the musician was at the Lula station during his brief stop, Laibly may have sent a telegram to Patton in advance. In addition to giving Patton the details for the next session, Laibly granted him his blanket approval to recruit other musicians for the forthcoming session, handing him (as House recalled) a hundred dollars for their combined travel expenses.

It may seem odd that in mid-summer 1930 Laibly was still willing to record any artists that Patton brought or recommended, since none so far had produced any hits. Henry Sims, for one, did not sell, nor did the Delta Big Four. Also as curious was Laibly's haste in arranging another session with the Mississippi bluesman. After all, Paramount still had a backlog of at least seventeen sides from the previous Patton session. But the one-year contract that Patton would have signed on the day of his recording debut (June 14, 1929) may have just expired or was soon to do so, so retaining the new star on Paramount's roster must have figured prominently in Laibly's plans. It is likely, then, that he wished to offer Patton a new contract for 1930–1931, to prevent the musician from taking one of the offers from other labels that Speir had fielded since the previous fall. This may explain why Patton on this third recording trip recorded only four known titles, taking a studio backseat to House, who recorded at least twice as many.

Some three days later after Laibly's appearance at Lula, Patton and House went to the Frank Harbart plantation near Robinsonville, where Willie Brown was living with a heavy-set woman named Susie. "We set up all that night," recalled House, who was introduced to Brown that night, "drinking and practicing, you know; playing together."[18]

During the late 1920s, Ernest Brown reported, Patton and Brown were performing frequently together, playing "from Robinsonville plum to Walls." But then, as Brown observed, "a woman, I think, split 'em up. They told me, Charlie Patton just got crazy about that woman an' he was just followin' her, and him and Willie Brown kinda split up." Perhaps "that woman" in question was Bertha Lee, which is plausible in view of Patton's moving to Lula to live with her. By thinking of Willie Brown for this session, Patton may have wanted to make sure that something of their music got on records.

After rehearsing all night, the three musicians were met up by Wheeler Ford, who was going to drive them in his Buick. Son House recalled that "he [Ford] knowed the way and directions," most likely because his memories of his own trip to Grafton with the Delta Big Four earlier that spring were still fresh. They packed their Stella guitars in the car and set out for Grafton. At the Joe Kirby plantation north of Robinsonville, Ford made a short stop, evidently at Patton's request because the young woman who emerged from her dwelling stepped into the front seat beside Patton. "We circled 'round there and went by there and picked her up and kept a-goin'," House said.

The new passenger, House discovered, was Louise Johnson, Patton's "side track" girlfriend. Later in time, House came to think that Patton was involved with her before moving in with Bertha Lee. If that was the case, then he may have met her through Willie Brown, who used to live on Kirby. "He [Brown] lived there on Mister Kirby's plantation an' he used to tell us, 'I'm makin' this song up on this Joe Kirby,'" Willie Moore recounted. "We said, 'Man, better not let some people 'round here—better not let that white man hear you, 'fore you be in jail!" Patton's own Kirby blues had been used to express his infatuation with Louise Johnson:

> I'm goin' where Green River do run down
> 'Cause the one I love mama, live in Robinsonville town.

House said she was a "nice-lookin' old gal," despite the fact that "her hair was short, you know: look like she been had a man's haircut in them days." He thought that at the time "she wasn't 'bout twenty-three, twenty-four years old. She's kinda young."

The car had not gone much further past the Mississippi/Tennessee border when it made another stop. As House recalls, "After we left Memphis, Tennessee, we stopped at another place just north of Memphis and we bought some liquor. We all drinkin' except Wheeler Ford; he didn't drink none."

While taking a rest break in Cairo, Illinois, Patton and House visited a music store and bought new Stella guitars at 12 dollars apiece. Back on the road, the musicians resumed drinking, and then they got to arguing. According to House, Patton started three fights, the first two of them with Willie Brown.[19] During the first one, Patton became so heated that he opened his passenger door, and thank heavens House prevented him from leaving because Ford was driving at full speed. But Patton didn't simmer down, and he resumed his arguing with Brown. This time, he ordered Ford to park on the side of the road so that he and Willie Brown could settle their differences with their fists. According to House, Brown jumped out first, then after him was Patton all hot and stumbling drunk—and then falling on the new Stella he had bought in Cairo. House described the guitar becoming "as flat as a patty cake right alongside the road. He didn't even get to play one piece on it. And man, he cussed and swore!"

With Patton returning to the car in this foul mood, it wasn't long before he got into an argument with Louise Johnson. When he slapped her, she moved to the back seat and sat next to House. "That's when 'it' went to happen," House recalled.

"It" happened between snorts of liquor. "I got a-snortin,' she'd take one. Charlie, he mad, he's sittin' in the front. I commended to leaning over, 'talkin' trash' to her. I say, 'I really kinda like you, gal,' and we take another big swallow. And so when we got to Grafton, Charlie didn't know I had done 'made' her."

Nor did House, at first. The group stopped in Kankakee, Illinois to visit a guitarist friend of Wheeler Ford's. Finally they reached Grafton, where they checked into a boarding house where Paramount lodged its artists, near the recording studio. "We all stayed in the same hotel. When I come upstairs, say, 'Where's the man have my key?'

> Louise says to me, "Say, I got our key!"
>
> I say, "Our?" What you mean, "our?"
>
> She says, "Yours, you jerk you!"
>
> I say, "Oh! 'Scuse me, honey!" I say, "All right! Okie-doak!" I say, "Oh, brother! It's my old pal's used-to-be woman." Well, I didn't know how that was comin' out.

The next morning, House was a little apprehensive about what his "old pal" of about three months thought of Johnson taking up with him. But before the first of their recording sessions began, Patton took him aside.

> I said, "Now Charlie—what you want (i.e., a fight) I ain't for it right now, I ain't ready for that kinda stuff."
>
> "Oh come here, nigger! I ain't thinkin' about that little old 'tight-haired' (i.e., short-haired) woman!"

> I said, "Oh well ain'tcha? Now listen, Charlie. I don't like it; you'll have to excuse me, look over (i.e., overlook ) me for that.
>
> "Listen, listen, fella! I didn't want her in the first place! Now you keep her now and I'll treat you as good as I ever is! Go on and just act like there ain't nothin' happenin'."

Despite being musicians who often performed at night, they did all their recording in the morning. "We'd go down to the studio at nine o'clock in the morning, and 'round about twelve we'd come back," House recalls.

Due to the dampness and the studio alterations, relatively little recording took place in proportion to the amount of time the musicians spent in Grafton. Over a period of four to six days, the four blues acts produced twenty-one known titles. Each performer took two turns, with the apparent exception of Patton, who ended the session with four duets with Brown. Louise Johnson recorded four titles, as did Brown, whose voice, House said, did not impress Laibly. House recorded nine sides, which amounted to six actual songs, as three of his works were two-part blues for back-to-back release on 78s.[20]

The musicians used themselves as an audience.[21] "We'd all be in the same big room," House recalls. "While one was in front of the mike the other one was sittin' over there, lookin' at him and listenin'." Instead of auditioning their material for Laibly, the musicians would simply begin recording it. If Laibly decided to reject the piece in question, he would tell the performer to stop playing after a verse or two. In such an event, he would not explain why he was rejecting the song, but instead he would request a new piece. "He always liked Charlie's records," House recalls. Once a song had been recorded, Laibly played back a brief excerpt of it over a loudspeaker. "He wanted to know how it sound to us."

Louise Johnson recorded first. A free spirit like Patton, she "didn't do nothin' but drink and play music; she didn't work for nobody" as House later described her. On her Paramount 78s, she sounded as though she had either taken singing lessons from Patton, or she had absorbed his approach by accompanying some of his local performances. The first two songs she performed at Grafton, "All Night Long Blues" and "Long Ways From Home," were simplified vocal renditions of "Maggie." The records, when played at 78 revolutions per minute, play back in the key of to F# major, an odd key which indicates either Johnson played mostly on the black keys of the piano, or the recording turntable was off-speed.[22] On two verses of these songs, she emulated Patton by beginning the second phrase of a stanza with a sudden rise from the augmented fourth to dominant, which imposed a real strain on her voice. Her tendency to yank notes from the top of her register (which ranged from c#$^{2}$ to c#$^{3}$ on her recordings) and to imbue her delivery with a semblance of a growl also seemed to reflect Patton's influence, which for her was not necessarily effective as she did not have a particularly suitable voice to copy his singing. Nonetheless, House thought she was a better singer than Bertha Lee. Of her playing, he said, "She could eat a piano up." Although her left hand on the bass keys was not always well coordinated with her right hand treble work, she mimicked on the piano a "talking" style of her vocal accenting, a practice that was done more often by blues guitarists than by pianists.

The two takes of "All Night Long Blues" and the one surviving take of "Long Ways From Home" are distinguished by the boisterous studio chatter from Patton, House and Brown. On "Long Way From Home," she seems to be overwhelmed by their distractions, sputtering out after playing a twelve-bar instrumental after the fourth verse. House later explained to interviewers that they did this to soothe her studio jitters. It is especially interesting to hear House as a young man shouting with glee on these records, because during his old age he declared that "blues ain't for no clownin." But the ways that the men kept interrupting her singing and interjecting with flip comments may lead the casual or first-time listener of these sides to think that they may have had a low opinion of her playing. It must have required considerable poise on her part to complete acceptable takes of these pieces. With this chaos captured on wax, it is a wonder that Paramount issued the master takes of "All Night Long Blues" and "Long Ways From Home," let alone pairing them as the first blues release from the session.

Yet by recording this pure mayhem, Laibly captured a unique document of Charlie Patton's style of barrelhouse commentary. According to Booker Miller, his vocal responses on Johnson's records was how he usually behaved among other blues singers. "He'd talk all the time when he go to gettin' 'heavy,' you know, drinkin'. And [when] that dance go to gettin' good, over in the night, man, he could put on a good show, then."

On the first take of "All Night Long Blues," Patton starts the show, as may be heard during the record's first vocal chorus (after the opening piano solo):[23]

CP: "Do it a long time, baby!"
LJ: I woke up this mornin,' blues all 'round my bed
I woke up this mornin,' blues all 'round my bed
WB: "Do it a long time; good and wild; good and wild!"
LJ: I never had no good man, I mean, to ease my achin' head
SH: "Lord, let's have a meeting here now."
CP: "Aw, sho,' now!"

The three men sustain this midnight Delta barrelhouse atmosphere during Johnson's next record, "Long Ways From Home," even though the take was probably done around noon in that damp Wisconsin building, as in its first chorus:

CP: "Play 'em a long time, baby!"
LJ: Lord I woke up this mornin,' blues all 'round my bed
WB: "Play 'em all night long!"
LJ: Lord I woke up this mornin,' blues all 'round my bed
SH: "Good and wild, good and wild!"
CP: "Tell 'em what happened to you!"
LJ: I never had no good man, I mean, to ease my worried head
SH: "Lord, what a shame!"
WB: "Get right, get right!"

If indeed the recording turntable was running off-speed and needed repairs, that may be why the session ended after Johnson's "Long Ways From Home."

It was likely during the afternoon of the first recording day that the musicians learned (probably from Laibly) that Blind Lemon Jefferson had died.[24] By that time, Jefferson had been dead for about 7 or 8 months. But meanwhile, Paramount kept releasing and advertising new Jefferson records as though he were still alive,[25] as if thinking that sales would drop if the news of his death became widespread. Even as late as March 29, 1930, Paramount ran an ad in the *Chicago Defender* referring to Jefferson in the present tense: "Blind Lemon Jefferson says 'Southern Women are hard to beat' and he ought to know." The remaining Jefferson discs from his last session appeared the following May and June. These spring releases bought Laibly some time to make some trips to Texas to try to find a new Jefferson; his brief stop in Lula to meet Patton was part of one such trip. But Laibly's searches proved to be fruitless. To make the most of an irreplaceable loss, then, he began asking his recording artists to make tribute discs in Jefferson's memory. That March, he had John Byrd and Washboard Walter record "Wasn't It Sad About Lemon?" for release on (Paramount 12945). Hence why he asked his Mississippi visitors if any of them knew any Jefferson songs and be willing to record them as a tribute.

Son House, for one, understood why Laibly wanted to capitalize on the death of Blind Lemon Jefferson, especially if his classic "See That My Grave Is Kept Clean" (1927) could be used in some way. "See, they made a lotta money outta that piece," House remembered in 1966. He recalled from that afternoon that "me and Charlie and Louise say, 'Don't know whether I can do it.'

"Willie and Charlie, couldn't none of them do it! They tried, but they couldn't, 'cause of that beat that Lemon had. I didn't go to bed until finally at a while I hit it. This gal Louise, she say, 'Oh, you got it, you got it!'"

The second day of recording was begun by House, towards making that tribute disc for Jefferson. He remembered Laibly's reaction to what House had worked up.

> So when we went down to the (recording) laboratory at nine o'clock,[26] I hit it, I say, "Mister Laibly! See how this sound to you."
>
> I put one verse on it. He say, "Stop it, stop it!"
>
> I say, "What's the matter; what's wrong?"
>
> He say, "That's it, that's it!"

"Mississippi County Farm Blues" was made to order for Laibly, making use of the melody Jefferson's "See That My Grave Is Kept Clean," which in turn had been developed from the turn of the century standard "Careless Love."[27] House's baritone singing is deep and rich, and his guitar playing is spiky, especially with the imitation of "that big bell" near the end of the recorded side. His lyrics drew not from Jefferson's life but from his own, describing his recent term at the county prison farm (it should be noted that Parchman Penitentiary was a state prison farm) for killing a man that House names in the song as Leroy Lee.

This may be a good point in this chapter to mention the so-called "Walking Blues" test pressing of a performance that House recorded at Grafton.[28] This long-lost performance follows the melody and many lyrics of Blind Lemon Jefferson's "Lonesome House Blues" (Paramount 12593, 1927), which in turn uses Jefferson's popular "Black Snake Moan" melody. For accompaniment, House played slide guitar licks while a second guitarist (likely Willie Brown) strummed chords in common 4/4 time. His last stanza, beginning with "Good morning blues, blues how do you you?" seems to be taken from Bessie Smith's "Jail House Blues" (which Smith co-wrote with Spencer Williams). The only control number for this recording is 9/2 #1, which isn't a matrix number, but more likely a test pressing number, so for that reason it isn't known before which songs "Walking Blues" was recorded. But its use of Jefferson melodies and lyrics suggest that House may have recorded it as his intended B-side to "Mississippi County Farm Blues."

Laibly's show of enthusiasm for "Mississippi County Farm Blues" was either feigned or short-lived. That side was not issued until 1931, and then coupled not with "Walking Blues," but with another song that House recorded, "Clarksdale Moan." That record, Paramount 13096, sold in such meager quantities that only one copy survives. In any event, even after four years, Jefferson's song was too dated to have much commercial value in the form of a cover, let alone one with provincial lyrics.

At this point in the surviving matrix number series, a recording session by Baker's Music Masters and the "Broadway Military Band" was held. Afterwards, perhaps in the mid or late afternoon, House resumed recording. "Clarksdale Moan" seems to have been given its title on the basis of the 12-measure blues moaning that House performs midway during the performance. Throughout the song, House mentions Clarksdale, but in the third lyric chorus (following the moaned one), he sings of going to the Midtown Drug store to buy snuff and Alcorub rubbing alcohol.[29] The guitar accompaniment has a _1–_2-_3–_4 bass beat, and it has several elements that House would later apply to his renditions of "Pony Blues."[30]

"My Black Mama Parts 1 and 2" and "Preachin' The Blues Parts 1 and 2" were House's core blues, both of them using melodies that House later acknowledged learning in Lyon, Mississippi from James McCoy, an unrecorded musician. The melody of "My Black Mama" would become known throughout the Delta as the "walking blues" theme,[31] to be recorded by Robert Johnson, Muddy Waters, and other younger bluesmen. Its lyric scheme may be said to be AA' (4+8), in which the complete lyric is sung in measures 1–4, then it is repeated during the course of the remaining 8 measures. House's majestic singing and his gleaming guitar tone from his bottleneck slide make this two-sided performance a classic. Some lyrics, however, were of the era: the "death letter" concept was on records since Ida Cox's in "Death Letter Blues" (Paramount,

1924); the "worry blues" stanza comes from "Mama's Got The Blues" (1922, composed by Sara Martin and Clarence Williams, and also recorded by Bessie Smith in 1923); and the words "Fold my arms and walked away" came from Hambone Willie Newbern's "Roll and Tumble Blues" (Okeh, 1929). "Preachin' The Blues Parts 1 and 2" was a cynical take on organized religion, especially on the Baptist Church. Most of the lyrics may be his own, but the one about a "heaven of my own" very likely comes from Bessie Smith's 1924 record "Work House Blues." His fairly simple motif for bottleneck-fretted guitar would be developed into a fearsome descending run by Robert Johnson for his 1936 cover "Preaching Blues" for ARC/Vocalion.

One aspect of these two blues, and of "Dry Spell Blues" recorded after them, is the vocal phrasing. In notated transcriptions (such as Ex. 20 for "Preaching the Blues"), the first beat or half-beat of each (or most) measure(s) in a vocal phrase is occupied with a rest. Such a vocal break on each metrical downbeat occurs in work chants such as ax-songs. This kind of phrasing may be regarded as reflective of House's previous experience as a laborer.[32] His kind of mid-phrase breaks are different in nature and purpose from Patton's signature mid-phrase vocal break in the third phrases of his "Maggie" songs (as noted in chapter 5 for "Screamin' and Hollerin' the Blues" and "Moon Going Down.")

At this point in the scant Paramount documentation, there is a long stretch of matrix numbers for which nearly nothing has been known or recovered, except for the two surviving Willie Brown sides as featured performer and Louise Johnson's last two performances. Also known for Brown, but only by titles, are "Kicking in My Sleep Blues" and "Window Blues" (which were advertised as having been released on Paramount 13099, but no copy has yet been found), and "Grandma Blues," which is known from another label's file card.[33] Brown may have recorded more sides, but none were saved, not even as test pressings. Still, it may be certain that he took one turn at recording by himself, between House and Louise Johnson's second turn. While the two surviving performances have been examined in depth in Chapter 8 for their style, they are worth mentioning again for the context they provide in this least-documented part of this recording trip.

"M & O Blues" was Brown's treatment of "Pony Blues." It is puzzling as to why Brown sang about taking the "M&O"—the Mobile and Ohio Railroad—because it evaded the Delta by running north from Mobile, Alabama, through Meridian and Tupelo, Mississippi, to St. Louis, Missouri.[34] The title of "Future

Blues" came from Brown's borrowing the lyric "Can't tell my future an' I can't tell my past" and another stanza from Thomas A. Dorsey's 1923 "Last Minute Blues" (which Brown would have likely heard from Ma Rainey's Paramount record). But he sings those lyrics to Patton's "Maggie" melody. To begin the performance, Brown follows the Delta practice of playing instrumentally the first line of the first chorus, then beginning to sing at the second line. While playing that first line, he gives a textbook example of how to punch out on the guitar's bass strings the "Jinks" descending motif.

That a break in recording was taken before Louise Johnson's second turn makes sense, if to reposition the recording equipment for the piano. Patton was present while she performed her two remaining masters, as he may be heard making comments during "On The Wall." That song was based on the melody and accompaniment of Cow Cow Davenport's "Cow Cow Blues," which was a standard 12-bar blues for southern pianists at that time. In her lyrics, she mentioned Jim Kinnane's Monarch saloon on Beale Street in Memphis. The Monarch had a rough reputation for crime, even for Beale Street. In 1938, Jelly Roll Morton claimed that "nothing went into that place but pimps, robbers, gamblers, and whores."[35] Her last side, "By The Moon and Stars," was based on the melody known to pianists as "Vicksburg Blues" or "44 Blues" and to Patton as "Pea Vine Blues."

The end of the recording visit kicked off with two blues about the Great Drought then occurring as the worst in the nation's history.[36] The crisis affected not only the Deltas of Mississippi and Arkansas, but also 28 other states from Pennsylvania to Montana. Although less dramatic than the 1927 "high water" flood, the effects of this drought were more widespread. In most areas, the "high water" had only disrupted farming temporarily, for when the water receded, the crops were "muddied in." But while the drought's heat broke in early September 1930, its aftereffects lingered into the following year, dealing crippling blows to countless farmers who were already staggered by the Depression.[37] When Son House and Charlie Patton recorded their songs,[38] the drought was still accompanied by a suffocating heat wave. In Arkansas, wrote one observer, "the thermometer reached or exceeded 100 degrees for 42 of 43 consecutive days; rainfall for 100 days was not enough 'to wet a man's shirt.'"[39]

That Son House had some difficulty recording his "Dry Spell Blues Parts 1 and 2" is suggested by the high take numbers in the matrix numbers: 4 takes for part 1, and 2 for part 2. This blues may be original to House, who most likely composed it shortly before the recording session. His account of the drought is very serious: the crops are parched, prices of meat are rising, and the farmers are helplessly idle.

Patton may have conceived "Dry Well Blues" during that summer to follow the successful "High Water Everywhere" as another natural disaster blues. The lyrics were sung to Patton's one-step treatment of his "Pony Blues" melody. Even if the song was a recording studio creation, he did play it afterwards as part of his live repertory. Like House, Patton shouted his words with a seriousness that is remarkable even for him.

> Way down in Lula, hundred an' ten heat
> Way down in Lula, hundred an' ten heat
> Lord the drought come an' caught us an' parched up all the trees.
>
> Lord, the cities around Lula, all, was doin' very well,
> Cities around Lula, all was doin' very well,
> Now they're in hard luck together 'cause, rain don't flow nowhere.
>
> Boy, they tell me the country, Lord, it'll make you cry,
> Told me, country, Lord, it'll make you cry,
> Most anybody, Lord, hasn't any water in the bayou.

For this and the other three blues Patton recorded on this trip, he had Willie Brown accompany him as a second guitarist. The microphone balance on their duet records favors Brown more than Patton, which suggests that Brown was sitting in front. Those who remembered Patton's live performances of "Dry Well Blues" were surprised at the tempo of this recording. Booker Miller remarked upon hearing it in 1968, "Now that one kinda surprised me. I never did hear him [Patton] play that slow; he always was fast on it." This slowness may be due to Brown. "You know Willie Brown didn't like to play fast," Willie Moore commented on his music-making in general. "He liked to play it slow, and if you played it any faster, he'd say that was wearin' him out."

Although "Dry Well Blues" was recorded while the drought was still happening, it was not issued for nearly a year, and only then to serve as the flip side of "Bird Nest Bound." But this performance is worth studying as a demonstration of Patton's ability to reshape his own material. It employs a "hollering" vocal style that Patton had not used on "Pony Blues." Instead of fading out at the end of its phrases as he does on "Pony Blues," Patton often ended the "Dry Well Blues" phrases with an increase in volume. His vocal phrasing was more conventional than that of "Pony Blues." Instead of holding the final word of a phrase for six beats, he held words for four or two beats (a measure or half measure of transcribed music), sometimes for no beats. The quarter-note beats were sung to a consistent 1–2 accenting pattern, and the ten-beat vocal melodies consisted of two phrase snippets divided in the usual manner of six and four beats. This would have been easier for a second guitarist to accompany than the unusual evenly divided "five-five" vocal snippets Patton sometimes used in his 1929 recording of "Pony Blues."

By the time of the summer Paramount trip, the Mississippi Sheiks' "Sittin' On Top Of The World" had become all the blues rage. Risking the commercially fatal course of imitation, Patton dabbed the now-widespread hit with some Mississippi Delta color. His uptempo bottleneck version, "Some Summer Day," recycled many of the verses from the Sheiks' record, but its refrain lyrics were changed to depict a lover assuring Patton not to worry about her man in prison:[40]

> "It was in the spring, one summer day,
> Oh, when he left here, he's goin' to stay,
> But now Harry's gone, Charlie don't you worry,
> 'Cause he's still at Camp no. 3."
> "Some got a month, some got a year,
> Tell me, Charlie, got lifetime here
> But now he's gone, don't you worry,
> Because he's still at Camp no. 3."

When Patton isn't shouting the lyrics to the melody of "Sittin' On Top Of The World," he takes two unusual breaks on his guitar, one that may be transcribed in five measures and the other in five-and-a-half. Brown strums his guitar to the same complementing pattern that Patton had previously used behind Henry Sims' fiddle playing on "Runnin' Wild," which too was phrased in single measures and had the same accenting pattern (1–2-3–4 / 1–2-3–4).

"Moon Going Down" and "Bird Nest Bound" were renditions of "Maggie" that have Patton playing his guitar in Spanish tuning and Brown in standard tuning and fretting at the A position. The success of these performances is due to Patton's full-voiced singing and his spurring Brown to take fast tempi. Although Patton makes the records exciting, as duets they have some bumpy moments. Consider the opening four measures of "Moon Going Down." Ex. 60 is how the record should have started:

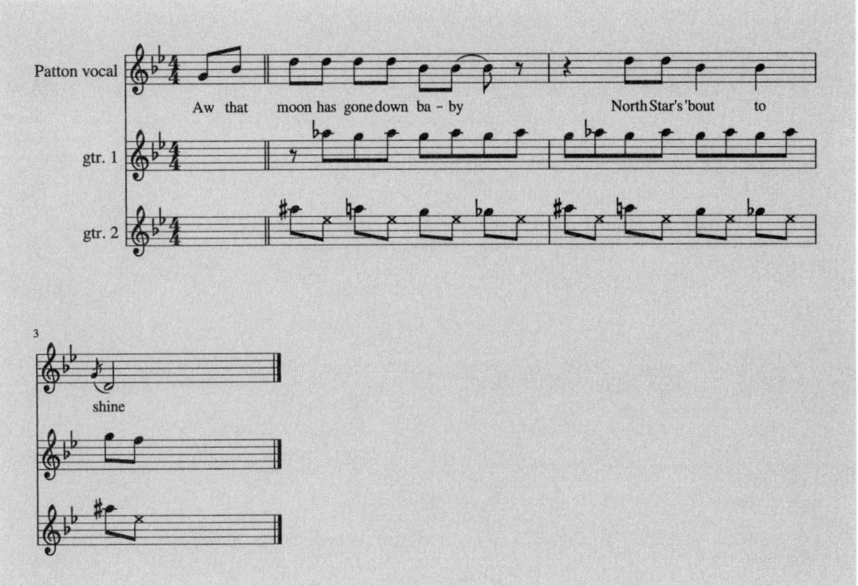


Ex. 62: Patton with Brown, "Moon Going Down" (1930), ch. 1 mm.1-3, conjectural correct start.

The phrasing of Brown's accompaniment (guitar 1 in Ex. 62) was probably inspired by the similar descending bass that Patton used on some of his "Maggie" treatments. Patton's guitar bass part (guitar 2 in Ex. 62) begins when he sings the word "moon" (m.1), continuing to create an "overlay" effect by starting a third time on the same beat of the word "shine" (m.3). In the same passage, when Patton sings "has" (m.1), Brown was to start his treble phrase (distinguished by his dominant sevenths); but instead of recurring as the vocal phrase ended (like Patton's), Brown's guitar phrase was supposed to end at the same time as the vocal word "shine." But on the record, this beginning didn't quite go as planned (Ex. 63):

Patton muffs the first line by singing "baby" a half-beat too long (m.1), then adds an extra quarter-beat rest (m. 2) in which he starts over his guitar bass part. Meanwhile (m.2), Brown had begun a repeat of his riff. Both men were in danger of ending their guitar riffs a beat sooner (m.3, beat 4) than Patton's vocal (m.4, beat 1). From the condition of the source record, it is hard to tell whether Patton is playing his full part or just thumping his guitar during mm. 3–4. But Brown covers Patton's blunder in measure 1 by adding an extra strum

Ex. 63: Patton with Brown, "Moon Going Down" (1930), ch. 1 mm.1-4, actual vocal start [0:02-0:13].

at Patton's word "shine" (m.4, beat 1) before resuming the riff. The smoothness with which he saved himself and Patton indicates that he was no stranger to such lapses on Patton's part. In the ensuing second verse, during its first vocal phrase, Brown used two more such "fake" strums to balance more lapses in Patton's singing.

However, during the fourth chorus of "Moon Going Down," what seem to be more vocal lapses during the first lyric phrase are intended as set-ups for three iterations of the words "Helena whistle" (in a style Booker Miller termed "doublin' back"). This extended variation literally caught Brown and his "down the staff" guitar technique short, by two beats. So, in the fifth chorus, as if adjusting to Brown, Patton modified his "doubling back" pattern so that Brown could play four of his figures within his singing. In this way, this fifth stanza contained the only true guitar interplay between two musicians, with Patton punctuating Brown's accompaniment with snapped bass slides on each beat.

The rollicking tempo of the "Moon Going Down" more than makes up for the awkwardness of its phrasing. The spoken banter following the second line of stanza 4 conveys the impression that Patton and Brown are having a lark, even if they were straining with their phrasing. Their show of casualness may have been why people long remembered the Patton-Brown duo, even if on record their musical coordination seems a little disorganized.

Brown's contribution to "Moon Going Down" was as ambitious as many lead guitar parts, but Paramount gave him no acknowledgement for it; the label credits on the 78-rpm release indicates the presence of only one guitar. When Booker Miller listened to the record some thirty-five years later, he scoffed at the mention of an accompanist. "See, you never heard him play," Miller said of Patton. "Ain't but one (guitar) there—he'll make you think it's two. That man's just the king."

There is one more note to be made. The lyric "the smokestack is black and the bell it shine like gold" had appeared earlier that year on another hit record by the Mississippi Sheiks, "Stop and Listen Blues" (Okeh, 1930). Howlin' Wolf would use it in contracted form on his 1956 hit single "Smokestack Lightning" (Chess Records).

The title "Bird Nest Bound" and some of its lyrics came from Ardelle "Shelly" Bragg's 1926 "Bird Nest Blues."[41] During the opening of the second verse Patton's record, another bumpy moment ensemble for Patton and Brown occurs. After singing "If I was a bird, mama" (mm. 1–2), Patton unexpectedly falls silent, and when (mm. 3–4) he should be completing the vocal phrase with "I would start a nest in the heart of town," only one guitar is audible; most of measure 4 may be heard as an attempt at regrouping before Patton sings the second vocal phrase in full.

Ten of the eighteen guitar response-fills of "Bird Nest Bound" are two measures long; most of them take up Patton's usual six beats, but after the first line of the final chorus there is one that lasts seven beats, perhaps unintentionally. Yet unusual two-measure patterns may be heard during "Moon Going Down," appearing often after the second and third lines of each stanza, accounting for half of the guitar responses on the record. With such freedom and sometimes haphazardness of Patton's vocal phrasing, these two blues are exceptionally difficult to arrange and execute as duets, even with the assistance of Willie Brown, whatever one thinks of his musicianship.

What Laibly thought of the group's collective work is suggested by the masters he selected for issue between the summer and fall of 1930. Six of the thirteen sides he placed on the market were Charlie Patton pieces, the first five of which he selected from Patton's previous sessions.

During the course of a year as a Paramount mainstay, from June 1929 through the summer of 1930, Charlie Patton was recorded more intensively than any blues singer before him. He had produced at least 42 sides, enough music to fill over three long-play albums, or two compact discs. He had used the recording studio more creatively than any blues singer of his time, rearranging his own material, recording songs of passing fancy, preaching, playing the role of show-off spectator, and drafting his own studio musicians. It may also be argued that he acted as his own producer, if all that Laibly did was sit and watch.

While drawing from over 20 years of repertory to record his unique musical self-portrait, Patton produced three hits, namely "Pony Blues," "Down the Dirt Road Blues," and "High Water Everywhere." But as noted earlier, his own Mississippi audiences remembered him for four songs. So, it is reasonable to think that even if the Depression had not interrupted his recording career, Patton's association with Paramount would not have lasted much longer than the end of his second contract in mid-1931 anyway.

Upon their return from Grafton, Patton, Brown, Louise Johnson, and House all held court in a barrelhouse on the Kirby plantation. The venue's owner, a woman name Lonnie Armstrong, lived in Memphis. "She wouldn't hardly tell Charlie 'Good mornin','" House says of Armstrong, "she just wanted that clown to draw people for her to make money."

After that homecoming night at Kirby's, House saw Louise Johnson only once, and later he said he thought she drifted to Helena, Arkansas. For a time in the 1930s, she lived on the King and Anderson plantation near Clarksdale. Leroy Willis remembered her for "playin' long back in the '30s at a little old place they call Rich." He also recalled that she commuted from Rich to Lula to perform with its local pianist Piano-Playin' Willie.

During the Grafton trip, House bonded with Willie Brown. He moved from Lula to Lake Cormorant, where he was Brown's neighbor and best friend into the 1940s. Brown groomed House as his vocalist, and he taught him guitar pieces including some of Patton's songs. Perhaps as a result of Brown's training, House came to share the regional opinion that Brown was a better musician than Charlie Patton.

After the session, Patton and Bertha Lee left Lula to live in Robinsonville. "I don't know why he left Lula," House says. "He took Bertha with him. The folks lost a cook when he left." At any rate, Patton befriended a farmer named Richard Baker. "Thing about it, he wasn't so crazy about Richard," House reports, "it was Richard's old lady, but Richard didn't know it."

SO, PATTON AND BERTHA LEE'S stay in Robinsonville was brief. "They didn't stay in there over two months," Elizabeth Moore said. "Then he kinda went back and forth there to make music."

We was increasin', Charlie was decreasin'

—BOOKER MILLER

*Chapter 14*

# LATER YEARS (FALL 1930–FALL 1933)

Someone who undoubtedly attended Patton's Robinsonville performances in 1930 was Robert Johnson (1911–1938). He was only 18 years old, with only 8 years left to live, but he would succeed Patton as the Delta's most influential bluesman. Within three years after Patton's 1934 death, Johnson's boogie-bass arrangements gripped the Delta blues.[1] "Boy, it spread all over the Delta," Booker Miller recalled. "Most everywhere you heard it." Johnson began his career in the late 1920s with a repertory of standards like "Make Me A Pallet on the Floor," "East St. Louis Blues," and "Casey Jones."[2] In addition to Patton, Johnson also learned music from Son House and Willie Brown. In 1930 he went to Hazlehurst, Mississippi, where he developed his guitar skills further with Ike Zimmerman,[3] and in the following year he hit the road as a traveling bluesman. In 1931 or 1932 Johnson was based in Hattiesburg, hoboing to Jackson to play there on Friday nights, then moving on to Saturday night engagements in the Delta town of Sunflower. During his railroad stopovers in Jackson, he taught his boogie style to Johnnie Temple, who knew him as "R. L."[4]

Willie Moore knew the youthful Johnson in Robinsonville; he once heard him disparage Patton by saying that "Charlie Patton stomped both his feet and keeped up too much-a noise" for him. During the next two years, though,

Johnson changed his mind enough to be regarded by Temple as a Patton imitator, both vocally and instrumentally. When Johnny Shines met Johnson in Arkansas in 1935, "Pony Blues" and "Banty Rooster Blues" were in his playing repertory. Shines recalled that Johnson frequently spoke of Patton as an inspiration.

Eventually he outgrew his identity as a Patton imitator to the extent of not recording any direct covers of Patton's records. Yet the records he made in 1936 and 1937 showed that he had full command of Patton's musical style. The bottleneck damping Johnson used on works like "Traveling Riverside Blues" was reminiscent of similar damping Patton executed on "Banty Rooster Blues." The mid-phrase bass slides Patton that featured during each third lyric phrase per stanza in several of his "Maggie" treatments (like "Screamin' and Hollerin' the Blues," first chorus, third phrase, after the second instance of the word "I" [see 64 b]) may be heard in Johnson's "Terraplane Blues" (at the corresponding moment after the word "Terraplane" [see 64 a]) and "Stones In My Passway":

It should also be recognized that Johnson adapted and updated some Patton techniques in accordance to the latest 1930s blues trends. The bottleneck bass riff that set off verses of Johnson's "Come On In My Kitchen" was clearly based on the piano riff that Roosevelt Sykes' played on St. Louis Jimmy

Ex. 64a: Mid-phrase bass slide in Robert Johnson, "Terraplane Blues" (1936), ch. 1, third phrase [0:25-0:30] (from Komara, The Road to Robert Johnson, fig. 7a).

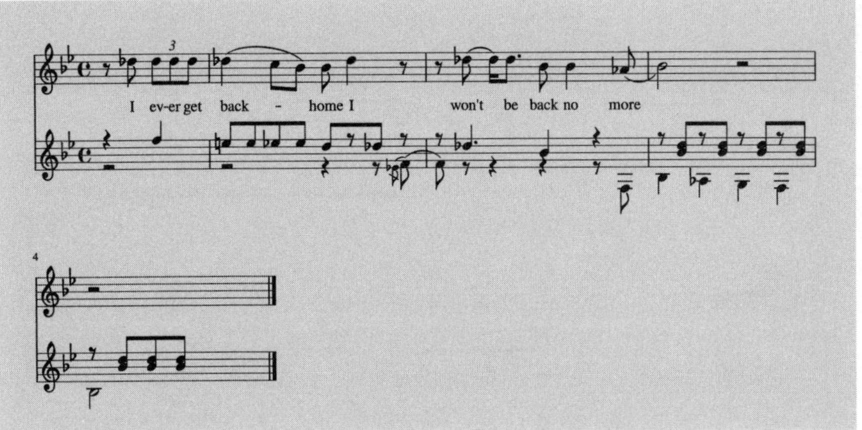


Ex. 64b: Mid-phrase bass slide in Charlie Patton, "Screamin' and Hollerin' the Blues" (1929), ch. 1, third phrase [0:27-0:37] (from Komara, The Road to Robert Johnson, fig. 7b).

Oden's "Six Feet in the Ground,"[5] but in Johnson's song the riff could be said to have functioned for Mississippi listeners in a similar manner as Patton's bass riff of "Pea Vine Blues." Moreover, the repeating one-measure bass figure of the "Maggie" songs provided the spadework for the boogie phrases Johnson would play in "When You Got A Good Friend," "Sweet Home Chicago," and "I Believe I'll Dust My Broom." Although Johnson employed in "I Believe I'll Dust My Broom" (Ex. 65) two bass figures in a V-I harmonic sequence in contrast to Patton's single descending line, he did follow Patton's method of arranging the phrase within a vocal line, launching it on the second beat (on the first syllable of "lovin'") so that the third measure would coincide with his last vocal beat (the last beat of "room").

Johnson's appropriations of Patton were also at the melodic level. Willie Moore remembered that Johnson used to perform Patton's "Banty Rooster Blues." This is borne out in Johnson's 1937 recording of "Traveling Riverside Blues."[6] During the first 8 measures of each chorus (the AA lyric phrases), Johnson sings much to the contours of Patton's song, including the downward drawl on each of those phrases' last words. However, for the remaining 4 measures (the B lyric phrases), Johnson switches to the corresponding part of the melody from Hambone Willie Newbern's "Roll and Tumble Blues" (which Johnson makes more use of for the melody of his "If I Had Possession Over Judgement Day").

Ex. 65: Robert Johnson, "I Believe I'll Dust My Broom" (1936), ch. 1, mm. 8-11 [0:19-0:32] (from Robert Johnson, *The New Transcriptions* [Milwaukee: Hal Leonard, 1999], 14).

But for his 1936 recording "The Last Fair Deal Gone Down," Johnson sounds very much like Patton, arguably to the extent of imitation.[7] The song's melody shares with Patton's "You Gone Need Somebody When You Die" the antecedents of "Careless Love" and "You Gone Need King Jesus on Your Bond." Also, Johnson's slide guitar part is much like Patton's. And in his fifth chorus, Johnson sings in a near indecipherable manner:

The words are phonetically (and, for that reason, well) rendered in Stephen LaVere's lyric transcription:

> Take camp tain he and see
> Camp ain't he and see
> At scal ain't be at seen, good Lord
> On this Gulfport Island Road[8]

Ex. 66: Robert Johnson, "The Last Fair Deal Gone Down," ch. 5, mm. 1-8 [1:25-1:35] (from Komara, The Road to Robert Johnson).

In Johnson's other surviving recordings, he doesn't indulge in this sort of word-play. What he sang here could be regarded as nonsense. But if the affinities of the performance with Patton's "You Gone Need Somebody When You Die" are taken into account, one may speculate that Johnson was singing in Patton's manner what he had sung clearly during the fourth chorus:

> My captain's so mean on me
> My captain's so mean on me
> My captain's so mean on m'-mmm, good Lord
> On this Gulfport Island Road

The first few years of the 1930s were lean times for bluesmen. "Most musicianers then, talkin' about back in 1931 and 1932," Booker Miller said, "if you was gettin' three or four dollars or five dollars for playin', you was gettin' good pay. There wasn't much money out." Such were the discouraging conditions that faced Patton in the twilight of his own career. Sure, he still held his popularity as a top Delta attraction. But his records became increasingly difficult to find.

"High Water Everywhere" ended up being Patton's last great commercial success. "Pea Vine Blues" was issued in February 1930 to respectable sales, if the ten or so copies of the record extant today are indications.[9] Ten copies also exist of "Rattlesnake Blues," which was issued in May 1930. However, after that month, Patton's record sales dropped off. Between July and December 1930, Paramount issued seven Patton records, more or less to a monthly release schedule. Again, if the number of surviving copies suggest sales, "Jesus Is A Dyin' Bed Maker" in October and "Moon Going Down" may have earned back the cost of their production, but the other five Patton releases of that summer and fall sold so poorly that no more than three copies remain of each of them.

Paramount 78s still cost seventy-five cents each, but because of the Depression, Mississippians could no longer afford them. Other forces were also working to grind Patton's sales to a halt. Shortly after "High Water Everywhere" appeared, Paramount stopped advertising in the *Chicago Defender*, apparently to cut costs, and so the rest of Patton's Paramount releases received no newspaper publicity of any kind.[10] In the same period, the company was dealt a devastating blow when its largest distributor, the Artophone Corporation, decided to leave the record business.[11] Its defection left Paramount with no supply wholesale lines to Mississippi retailers. While some dealers like H. C. Speir had to now order Paramounts directly from the company, it is doubtful that many others did so. The most likely reason why was that retailers were already shunning the label, according to Speir: "Dealers cut 'em off. Quit handlin' their records." What turned off dealers, Speir explained, was the poor sound quality of Paramount discs due to the substandard pressing compounds.[12] The irony is that Paramount had begun its race program partly because the pop records were not selling due to their inferior sound quality.

By the end of 1930, Paramount began reducing its record production in accordance with the shrinking market. If the printing orders for labels are any indication, Paramount cut back by fifty percent or more. During the 1920s, the company would order 3000 items for each release, but in 1930–1931 it ordered 750 sets of labels for Patton's "Circle Round The Moon," and the same amount for another title (Kaydee Short's "Doubtful Mama") that was given the same release number (Paramount 13040). 750 may have been the sales figure that Paramount expected each of its 1930 releases to attain. As a consequence, its three-man pressing department was now working only part-time. "We worked about three days a week, five hours a day, at the end," said one of the pressers, Alfred Schultz.

Around this time, Patton's importance in the company's catalogue began to wane, most likely because of Paramount's loss of Mississippi's distribution. Seven of the company's one hundred-plus offerings between the summer and close of 1930 were Patton records. "Circle Round The Moon" was a low seller, of which two copies remain among collectors. Paramount then issued twenty-nine race records before its next Patton release, "Bird Nest Bound," in the spring of 1931. That item, along with "Some Summer Day" issued soon afterwards, were the only Patton releases for 1931.

Sometime during the spring or summer of 1931, Arthur Laibly was fired by Wisconsin Chair's chief executive, Otto Moeser. Laibly later portrayed himself as a casualty of industry "conditions."[13] Of the men in the record industry who supervised recording sessions with African American artists before 1941, Laibly did not stay in in the record business. After a stint as a salesman of busts of George Washington, he became an insurance agent for Boars and Wausau.

With Laibly's departure, the operation of the label was directed perfunctorily by Henry Stephany, a chair company draftsman and engineer. Early in 1932 the company released its last Patton masters, "Frankie and Albert" backed with "Some of These Days," and "Joe Kirby" backed with "Jim Lee Blues Part II," all of which were recorded during Patton's visit with Son Sims two years before. Of these issues, the twentieth and twenty-first Patton records, only a single copy of each survive. At the time of their original releases, Paramount would hold only one more recording session and release some twenty more discs before ceasing operations. In view of the decline in Paramount's pressing runs and of the halt in sales distribution in Mississippi, it is doubtful that Patton himself may have seen and heard most of the 78s released from his second and third sessions.

According to Otto Moeser, the label was still breaking even when he decided to pull Paramount from the record business in mid-1932. Paramount's tiny production costs were what enabled the firm to avoid losses. But its owners were not interested in merely staying afloat. They wanted sizable profits, which were simply not forthcoming during the depth of the Depression.

The dismantling of Paramount resulted in the swift destruction of much blues history.[14] The company executives sold as scrap metal the nickel stampers from which they pressed the records, and they disposed of their remaining stock. The Grafton production plant and recording studio were simply abandoned, and eventually the company's recording machine crashed through the rotting studio floorboards to the cellar below.

Shortly after Paramount ended, folklorists began recording African American music including the blues not for profit, but for study. Chief among the institutions engaged in this activity was the Library of Congress, the first non-profit organization to try to document black Southern music. The Library's Archive of American Folk Song's early field recording trips were undertaken by John Lomax (1867–1948), a Mississippi-born folklorist who sought especially field hollers and work songs. In August 1933, he spent four days at Parchman Farm, where he recorded forty-plus a cappella prison songs.[15] Had Lomax been more of a musicologist and less of a folklorist, he could have worked with H. C. Speir, who had knowledge broad enough to guide Lomax to other musicians in Mississippi, and with Charlie Patton, whose recollections alone would have complemented and enhanced these prison recordings.

Another folklorist of sorts who scoured the Delta for material during the Depression was the New Orleans newspaperman Roark Bradford (1896–1949). A popular dialect writer, his book *Ol' Man Adam An' His Chillun* (New York: Harper and Brothers, 1928) had been adapted by Marc Connelly for the hit Broadway play *The Green Pastures* (1930). Bradford became a friend of Joe Rice Dockery, and sometimes he came to Dockery's plantation where he would solicit material from the resident cook. Later, with Joe Dockery's assistance, Bradford visited Parchman Farm to collect prisoner lore. Bradford's early Delta diggings were apparently used in his dialect fable *John Henry* (New York: Harper and Brothers, 1931), which became a national Literary Guild selection in 1934 and a Broadway musical in 1940.[16]

In his book *John Henry*, Bradford depicted the legendary steel-driving man as a plantation and levee roustabout, and he used him to make broad generalizations about African Americans. This version of John Henry makes for a notable contrast with Charlie Patton, the Delta's only flesh and blood legend of the age. Bradford's John Henry is impulsive, footloose, readily provoked to immense rage, and beats up men and women alike. The captive of child-like emotion, Henry goes from one random adventure to another. As seen by the white planters, Henry seems like a simple laborer who is driven by his own appetites.

What would have Bradford made of Patton? The musician made professional calls at Parchman, but not to gather song material. Rather, as a black policeman from Indianola recalled to the authors, Patton came and performed at the prison on a few Fourth of July holidays, when convicts received cash presents from their relatives and had money to spend on entertainment.

Patton did have to watch out for the sort of men that Bradford described as his John Henry. During the early 1930s, many barrelhouses closed. That left on many plantations the small house frolics. With fewer people around, Patton stood out, making him a target for flirting women and their jealous men. "A lotta mens didn't like him at the time 'cause a lotta womens fool over him," David Edwards said. Even if Patton did nothing to spark their interest, it brought trouble to him. Skip James noted that at frolics, "Some old 'clowny' woman come up to you. She get a drink or two in her head, she just wanna show herself. She had never seed you before sometimes, but she wanna make people think you done fell for her. Quite naturally their boyfriends or their husbands wouldn't like that. Boyfriend or husband or somethin' say, 'Get rid of that nigger; kill him.'"

Willie Morris spoke frankly of Delta men. "Shit man, them guys down there, if they see you around their woman and they caught up with you, they'd kill you. They'd go out there and get them cottonfield women, you know: if one quit 'em, they couldn't get another one; they'd kill you."

Men who were valued as steady workers on their plantations could kill a bluesman for any reason—or none at all—with little or no retaliation from the law. "They could kill you down there," Sam Chatmon noted, "and they say, 'That nigger he killed wasn't no 'count. Turn him loose. That's a good worker.' They'd turn him loose." David Edwards echoed this statement. "You wouldn't go nowhere if you killed somebody and was a good worker: you'd just go back and work some more." Son House agreed, "Wasn't no law botherin' you. Not if you'se a good worker. If you'se a good worker for Mister so-and-so, that settled it."

Ever since the 1910s, when Ernest Brown saw him as a young "high sport," Patton walked on a dangerous tightrope. Now living in his 40s, he was more liable than ever to lose his footing—and be killed, literally. At a house frolic around 1930 in or around Moorhead (or Itta Bena 13 miles away), Willie Morris saw a man attack Patton because his wife was indiscreet with her glances to the musician. Another attempt in 1930 on Patton's life occurred at a frolic in Sunflower, where a man named Snuff Gibson came so close to succeeding, that town residents long thought into the 1960s that Patton had died from gunshot wounds.

The most serious known attempt occurred in 1933, in which Patton nearly died at a Holly Ridge house frolic when his throat was slit.[17] The wound damaged his vocal cords and impaired his singing ability. "One of those old guys cut him," David Edwards recalls. "It was a deep cut in his vein, a bad cut." Edwards had gone to the frolic in the hope of accompanying Patton, only to learn upon arriving that Patton had just been taken to the King Dawson Hospital in Greenville, twenty miles west of Holly Ridge.

Willie Young wasn't at that frolic, but he heard afterwards that Patton was killed there, not maimed. While the truth wasn't as bad as Patton's friends feared and his enemies wished, the story that Young heard may contain some true details. As Young told the story years later, Patton was killed on the Hollyknoe plantation, a few miles southwest of Holly Ridge. "This woman went got up on Charlie's lap (during a performance), but Charlie, he didn't make the woman get on his lap. She wanna come kinda easily. And the guy (i.e., either her husband or lover) was a jealous guy, you understand. The guy come in and found her in his lap. Just let out on him with a knife."

Afterwards Patton bore a long, jagged scar across his throat. Still, he maintained his happy-go-lucky exterior. "Wasn't either of us thinkin' about death," Booker Miller recounted. "We was here to stay, we reckoned." In all likelihood, Patton took such an assault as an occupational hazard. "If you get to be a good musician, you'se accused of all the women," Miller said. "They gonna chase you, but they turn around and say you chasin' them. That's the way that go."

That was what the professional blues singer had to endure. Patton didn't help his situation much with his flirting, but both Miller and Edwards attributed that behavior to his drinking. But at a deeper level in his personality, Patton may have been possessive of any and all of the women he desired, which would account his contempt for the jealous plantation men. As he sang in 1934 on his record "Stone Pony Blues":

Well I didn't come here to steal nobody's brown
Didn't come here, steal nobody's brown
I just stopped by here, well to, keep you from stealing mine.

But some of the women he called "mine" were married, a status that did not deter him in the least. He thought that the husbands were in his way. In "Circle Round The Moon," he sang two stanzas lamenting about languishing in prison while there were women were to be had:

Out on the road, servin' out my time,
Out on the road, servin' out my time,
An' the Delta women were tryin'-a run me down.

How long, great God, how long?
How long, great God, how long
Shall I be here rollin' when your man is gone?

Prison time was lost time, in Patton's view, because it deprived him of occasions to visit his mistresses while their men were away working their farm jobs.

Although Patton sang to and about married women, some people in the Delta spread a rumor that it was his common-law wife Bertha Lee, not a jealous husband, who gave him that scar across his throat. The rumor was that Bertha Lee cut his throat with a butcher knife in Cleveland, either killing him or nearly killing him in the process. In truth, she was Patton's provider. "She took good care of him," Miller said of their relationship. While Patton cavorted freely about the countryside, David Edwards reports, "his wife stayed there and worked all the time" at their plantation residences. There were even times in the early 1930s when she was pulling a plough instead of cooking for him.

Bertha Lee came to resent Patton's loose lifestyle, though. Son House saw this for himself when he visited them in late 1933. When the two musicians returned from an all-night house frolic, Patton entered his bedroom, from where he was soon calling House for help. House entered to find Bertha Lee pinning Patton to the floor, flailing at him with her fists. Patton implored House to "pull her offa me 'fore she gets hurt," but the sound of his voice coming from underneath her made House laugh. Yet on her side of the relationship, Bertha was pathetic as a love-struck creature whom Patton didn't always desire. When she made records with Patton in 1934, she used "Mind Reader Blues" as a song of rebuke, presenting herself as the one steadfast companion remaining to him after everyone else has shunned him as a scoundrel:

Baby I can see, just what's on your mind
you got a long black woman with her gold teeth in her face.

I take a long look right smack down in your mind
And what I see on your mind you would not have no friends.

I take a long look right smack down in your mind
An' I see poor papa come a-hobblin' down the line.

Aw don't kid your mama you ain't foolin' nobody but yourself
An' what I see on your mind you would not have no friends.

I caught the riverside, my man got the transfer boat
An' the next time I seen him he had a girl way up the road.

The last stanza suggests that Patton might have left her in Lula for another woman. If so, the song itself may have been inspired by his episode. Then, in that case, he responded by including these lyrics in "Poor Me":

> Don't the moon look pretty shinin' down through the tree?
> Oh, I can see Bertha Lee, Lord, but she can't see me.
>
> You may go, you may stay, but she'll come back some sweet day,
> By and by, sweet mama, baby won't you, by and by?

However much she clung to Patton, their relationship, Son House snorted, "didn't amount to nothin." So it would have also seemed to Patton. In 1932 or 1933, he formally married the daughter of a black plantation overseer[18] on a farm near Morgan City, a hamlet in southern LeFlore County with 150 residents.[19] In attendance was Henry Stuckey (1897–1966), recently arrived from Sartartia, MIssissippi and an admirer of Patton's. A dozen years earlier, while living in Bentonia, Stuckey taught Skip James the fundamentals of playing guitar in the D minor tuning. During that wedding, Stuckey did not know that Patton was still living with Bertha Lee on a plantation twenty miles away. Morgan City did not have a railroad stop, so its isolation would have made it easy for Patton to deceive both women. The Morgan City marriage was brief, which suggests that the wives learned about each other, and Bertha Lee may have been the one who ended Patton's juggling act.

Regardless of his romances on the side, Patton continued staying with Bertha Lee. During the nearly four years that remained of his life after leaving Robinsonville in the summer of 1930, they lived in three adjacent plantation communities between Leland and Indianola: Longswitch, Holly Ridge, and Heathman (also called "Heathman-Dedham" for the plantation that gave the town its identity), none of them having 100 residents in 1930. Perhaps because Holly Ridge was the most familiar of the three communities, Patton was generally thought of as one of its residents by associates who did not live in the area. "I don't know why he didn't record it," Booker Miller said, "but he sung a very beautiful song about Holly Ridge."

Patton seems to have spent most of the early 1930s on the Heathman-Dedham plantation. The plantation could readily be construed as part of Holly Ridge, even though the farm lies two miles west of it.[20] During the early 1890s, Heathman was one of Sunflower County's eight existing communities, serving as a way station on the Georgia Pacific railroad line and having its own postal and express office.[21] But at the time when Patton arrived there, Heathman had become, like Longswitch and Holly Ridge, a mere flagstop on the Southern line. David Edwards remembered the single train that provided service for that part of the railroad. "That little thing had about two coaches on it," he described, "had a stripe in front, look like a doodlebug." For that reason, the local residents nicknamed the train as the "Doodlebug line." Patton made it the subject of one of his last songs, "Southern Whistle Blues."

Patton's move with Bertha Lee to Heathman-Dedham might have been brought about by his uncle Sherman Martin, who lived with them on the plantation.[22] Like he did in the late 1900s, Martin chauffeured his nephew to the house frolics, this time in an automobile.[23] One reason why Patton remained in the area may have been his declining health. "His wife said that when he came to Holly Ridge and settled down, she say she figured then that he was nearin' the end," Booker Miller remembered. Ishman Bracey often saw Patton during this time in nearby Indianola; some thirty years later, he remembered the slow physical decline. "They say he had been all and around sickly a good little while before he died," Bracey told John Fahey. "Some say he had somethin' like the double pneumonia. He did used to have kidney trouble."[24]

One circumstance that limited his travel to dances was the reduction of Mississippi railway service due to the Depression. In 1932, the Illinois Central Railroad, owner of the rails serviced previously by the Yazoo Delta Railroad (later the Yazoo Mississippi Valley Railroad), suspended its passenger service on all but its Moorhead branch that ran from Belzoni to Clarksdale.

Patton mentioned this event in his later recording, "34 Blues":

> Fella down the country, it almost make you cry
> Fella down in country, it almost make you cry
> (spoken: My God, children!)
> Women and children flaggin' freight trains for rides

As for himself, Patton used other forms of transportation. "Most of the times he'd get in a car and go [to a dance] or catch a Greyhound bus, besides the train, you know," Booker Miller reported.

The "Dog" Yazoo Delta Railroad had once brought people from many Delta towns to the barrelhouses. But where rail service had stopped, blues activities dropped. The suspension of rail service in the Mississippi Delta and the relative infrequency of buses made the barrelhouses all but impossible to operate. With this situation prevailing in the early 1930s, Patton had little choice but to travel widely, for it is doubtful that the performing fees offered by house frolics across the Delta ever matched those previously offered by the barrelhouses.

During the early 1930s, Patton trained Bertha Lee as a singer and had her sing with him, perhaps to compensate for his decline in stamina. One place near Holly Ridge where they often performed were the plantation frolics held by Lonnie Hodges. On one occasion, Patton threw a temper tantrum and smashed his guitar, which led Hodges to think that he was unbalanced. Another place was a general store whose white owner, John Allen, sometimes sat in on fiddle during their duets.[25] One song that Bertha sang was "Bo Weavil Blues"—more likely Ma Rainey's 1924 hit than Patton's 1929 record. She was remembered better for her rendition of Memphis Minnie's "Bumble Bee" as "Yellow Bee." "She could sing pretty good at that time," David Edwards opines. "I thought she was a good songster," Booker Miller agreed, but added that "didn't look to me, though, she could sing like Charlie could. I'd rather hear Charlie than hear her anytime." According to Son House, Patton thought little of her vocal abilities. "Charlie, he didn't think Bertha could sing good enough. No, he didn't think that." But during Patton's 1934 session, she made a pair of recordings that were good enough to be released. On them, she comes off as a contralto with a persistent vibrato and showing little variety in her vocalism during each song. Still, she was a competent singer, certainly better than most of the others who sang at the same frolics. When men showed their appreciation for her singing, Patton readily became indignant. "He was jealous of her," reported Johnnie Mack, who attended some of their appearances. "He sure was. He'd have a fit sometime. He get mad, and get up, and walk out [of the frolic]."

Rejoining Patton at this time was Kid Bailey. Robert Gildart hired Patton to play at his frolics on Will Thompson's plantation near Longswitch in the early 1930s. Like everyone else who recalled Bailey for the interviewers in the 1960s, Gildart had a shadowy memory of him, thinking that his first name was John. But he did remember that Bailey "come out to Holly Ridge and lived for a while. Him and Patton was out there together together. They played on a jukehouse on the side of the road goin' towards Indianola. He'd play 'second' sometimes, and then again he'd play lead and Charlie Patton would 'second' him." But Bailey soon set his eye on greener pastures. "He'd mention all the time that he was gonna leave here and make him some money." When not with Patton, Bailey was to be found in Leland, nearly ten miles southwest of Holly Ridge. "After Charlie Patton died, Bailey he left there," Gildart reported. "Bailey left [Leland] and I heard he went out there around Morgan City."

Sometime in 1931 or 1932, Patton lived on the Hancock plantation close by Longswitch. There several Depression musicians vied for the local grubstakes. These included Bo Weavil Jackson, the accordion player Walter Rhodes, and a Leland bluesman named Tom Toy who was noted for "Catfish Blues."[26] Also among them was Johnnie Mack (born 1896), a guitarist and mandolinist who loved listening to Blind Blake's records. Mack had begun playing music in 1924, and he considered himself the most capable musician in Longswitch. His musical partner was Lewis Nichols of Greenville, who like Mack played mandolin and guitar. So they were not inclined to yield their turf to Patton. Then again, to Mack's ears, Patton "played so funny till I couldn't hardly catch on to it: have a bottleneck and all that kinda mess, and hollerin', and whoopin.'" Mack and Nichols were often hired by white planters who paid them seven or eight dollars per performance to play pop and ragtime standards like "Five Foot Two" and "Darktown Strutter's Ball." Their favored status with whites, and their indifference to Patton's music (which Mack dismissed as "junk") created friction with Patton, or so Mack would later claim.

Mack told to the authors one story about how he and Nichols supposedly upstaged Patton at a black frolic in Longswitch. "Me and Lewis was just standin' outside," Mack related, "and Lewis say, 'Let's 'run' that guy away from here!' And sure enough, that house rocked. He quit, boy. He sit down there a while and a woman come in. 'Oh Charlie, play!' 'I ain't gonna play here . . . ' And 'fore we knew one more thing, he's gone!" But this anecdote, not by what happened but by the way it was later told, may tell more about Mack than about Patton. Mack did not play black dance music, and by telling this story he showed how little he knew or remembered the ways of black frolics. There, musicians were paid at the end of each night. Walking out abruptly as Mack claimed would be implausible for what we know about Patton, because that would have meant giving up his fee.

During this time, Patton was giving in more to his advancing alcoholism than to his musical rivals. Robert Gildart saw this for himself when the artist accepted his offer of five dollars, free food and free drinks to perform at his Longswitch frolics. "Charlie Patton would drink as long as you give it to him till he get so drunk he couldn't walk," Gildart recalled. Booker Miller said that Patton cradled a crock of moonshine at his feet while performing. A song that Patton recorded in 1934, but left unreleased, was called "Whiskey Distillery," about what could happen from his drinking. "He often sang it," Booker Miller recalled, reciting some of the lyrics as:

> Some love they gin,
> but give me my Rockin Rye
> If I don't quit drinkin' this moonshine whiskey,
> Lord I soon will die.

Some of Patton's cronies thought that alcohol was particularly deadly to persons with social diseases, and so whenever he drank to excess, his philandering should have given him some cause for alarm. "Much whiskey as he drank, man, if he had syphilis or gonorrhea or anything like that, man, he'd have been dead before he was," Booker Miller said, "'cause he drink that stuff every day." Patton's drinking and his flirtations with other men's women were invitations to a death scenario more lurid than venereal disease. "I really believe someone gave Charlie a dose of poison whiskey," Willie Morris said, echoing what many Delta people supposed about his death.

But Patton lived on, long enough to begin outliving his popularity. By the early 1930s, the novelty of his popular pieces had faded, and younger if inexperienced musicians were hired by some employers because their sounds seemed new. For example, his regular five-dollar gig at a frolic held between Bellewood and Tribbet (a town five miles south of Longswitch) was given over to Eugene Powell of Hollandale, a guitarist twenty years his junior who was among his admirers. "Charlie had played there so much till his music had done got common, that's all," Powell recalled. "They done hear-ed it, know how it sound and everything. Mine's all new to 'em. So I got his place. I didn't try to 'roll' him (i.e., steal his job). They just said they'd rather have me."

That Patton's sound was so prevalent and familiar may have limited Patton's influence on the younger Delta bluesmen of the 1930s. This may explain why Robert Johnson treated it indirectly on his own recordings. As Powell explained for himself, "That's how come I never did learn none of Charlie Patton's pickin'. Because I played out in there where he played, and I wanted somethin' different." During his youth, Patton himself had assessed the most popular musicians of the day, and likewise the musicians who copied him two decades later were most likely beginners who were just starting to build repertories of their own.

Among those who adopted Patton as their base was Chester Burnett (1910–1976), who as Howlin' Wolf became in the 1950s one of the last commercially successful blues singers.[27] At age 13 in 1923 he had moved from east Mississippi to the Young and Morrow plantation near Ruleville to live with his father. There, around 1928, he first laid eyes on the famous musician. "I was plowin'—plowin' four mules on the plantation. And a man come through there pickin' a guitar called Charlie Patton, and I liked his sound," the Wolf remembered expansively during a 1967 recording session. "So I always did want to play a guitar, so I got him to show me a few chords, you know."[28] One of the first songs he learned was "Pony Blues." In 1931, Wolf was playing wherever he could, including barrelhouses and frolics that couldn't hire anyone else. Whenever he could, he visited Patton for more lessons and musical pointers. Bertha Lee remembered how one day in Cleveland "Charlie worried with him all day before that man would leave him alone."[29] Johnny Shines was an early admirer, saying later in life that "Wolf played a whole lotta Patton's pieces" back then. Booker Miller, on the other hand, was much less impressed. "He was came through Greenwood about in 1932, and man, he was terrible!"

Another younger musician was Toomer Wilson, who lived on Wood's plantation near Hollandale and in Estill, a town twenty miles southeast of Holly Ridge. His imitations of Patton bordered on impersonation, not only mimicking the foot-stomping, guitar-slapping and vocal asides, but also the cater-cornered sitting position that Patton often took when he played. "Every time I'd see him play, I'd think about Charlie Patton," Sam Chatmon recalled. "His singin' and pickin' was just like Charlie Patton. He'd bring his voice out—'Aaugh!'—just the same way Charlie Patton did."[30] No matter how amateurish Wilson may have seemed, he may have played often in his native Washington County, for Patton rarely appeared there during the 1930s.

Other later Patton imitators are now known only by name. "I could name you two or three who tried to play like him," said Booker Miller. "This boy they called Elijah Jones, he tried it: he failed. Never could get it down. We had another one down here, he didn't last too long, we call him T. L. Little, and another one down there called Joe Donnelly." All three players were from Swiftown, about eight miles southeast of Morgan City. The best of Patton's assorted imitators, Miller believed, was an Itta Bena bluesman dubbed "Bo

Diddley" after the children's game, and not to be confused with Ellas McDaniel who took the name in the 1950s. Miller remembered the Itta Bena Bo Diddley. "Now he was a pretty good musicianer," he opined. This Bo Diddley died in the late 1930s. "He got cut to death in Tutwiler. A woman cut him to death."

Patton's influence on the Mississippi blues of the era is strikingly demonstrated in the first records made by Big Joe Williams, the itinerant blues singer from Crawford, an eastern Mississippi town near Alabama. Williams met Patton in Hollandale in the late 1920s, and he later saw him in Holly Ridge. On February 25, 1935, WIlliams recorded 6 pieces during his debut session for RCA Bluebird, one of which was a free treatment of Patton's "Pony Blues" as "My Grey Pony." Williams made Patton's manner of snapping the bass strings a general feature of his recordings that day, and he also seems to have shared Patton's liking for high-pitched bottleneck slides by capoing his guitar as high as the tenth fret, producing eerie tones that lay within the register of a violin. But unlike Patton, Williams worked within a narrow style that was based on one-chord accompaniments with the guitar in Spanish tuning.

Another protégé was David Edwards of Greenwood, who occasionally assisted Patton in Holly Ridge in the early 1930s. Edwards was good enough to become Booker Miller's favorite guitarist besides Patton. Moreover, Edwards shared Miller's high regard for their mentor. "It's a thousand musicians down there," Edwards was to say, "Robert Johnson and Charlie Patton was the best." For the Library of Congress field recording team led by Alan Lomax on July 20, 1942, Edwards played "Water Coast Blues" (played with G fretting handshapes), in a performance that virtually summarized what Delta musicianship through that time had to offer, including little touches from Patton songs during a few of the guitar fills. The achievement he made in "Water Coast Blues" makes all the more regrettable that he did not play for Lomax that week his versions of "Pony Blues" or "Jersey Bull Blues," which he would record only much later as an elder blues rediscovery.

A faint retention of Patton's music may be heard in the recordings made by Booker "Bukka" White, another native of eastern Mississippi. His "Aberdeen Mississippi Blues" (1940) used the off-beat device that Patton had featured in "Pony Blues," that while singing the second vocal phrase of its stanzas, he makes a melodic and rhythmic variation by heavily emphasizing every other beat during the first six beats of the line. Otto Virgial of Columbus, Mississippi used the same device during the extended first phrase of each stanza to his two-chord dance piece, "Little Girl in Rome" (for RCA Bluebird, October 31,1935).

But of these partners and imitators, the one who was most involved during Patton's late career was Booker Miller. He was a short, light-complexioned farmer nicknamed "Mister Pink," and he lived on the Bear Ridge plantation between Swiftown and Pugh City. In 1929, he became Patton's regular sidekick, closest protégé, and most ardent admirer. In a set of interviews with Wardlow in 1968 and 1969, Miller provided a vivid view of Patton, conveying this long-gone blues great as a person. His reminiscences unexpectedly showed Patton as a wholesome, industrious man, and not as unsavory as Son House and Hayes McMullan spoke of him. Miller was fascinated by Patton, whom he respected, remembered, and revered as a father figure.

"I was a loner till I met Charlie," Miller recalled. "If I hadn't never met him, I don't think I would have taken it up, the guitar, you know. I mighta learned to play maybe one record or one song, to suit my fancy. But he told me, 'Say, man! You oughta go head-on out there and just—just pick!"

Between 1930 and 1934, Miller was virtually Patton's only sideman. "If we wasn't playin' together, he was playin' by himself," he declared. Patton would notify him by mail of their upcoming appearances. "He'd write me, tell me where he was gonna be, he say, 'Kid, I want you to be there.' If he sent for me, brother I'se goin." For one trip, he reported, "the furthest point that I traveled away from home with Charlie was up here near Memphis, a place they call Tunica, Mississippi." From there, Miller returned home to work, but Patton would continue traveling towards Memphis, and possibly to points north of there.

In addition to musical assistance, Miller provided Patton with protection from strangers, carrying on him a .38 pistol for that purpose ("I carried one everywhere I went"). Even a modest journey of 15 miles, such as from Itta Bena to Sunflower, could present some dangers. Miller recounted an incident in the early 1930s when Patton raised his voice to a bootlegger named Hollins at a rural jukehouse. "One [Patton] said he paid; one [Hollins] said he didn't pay," Miller remembered. "He [Patton] didn't wanna settle for it, he said he wasn't gonna pay twice. We [Miller and another friend] didn't know how many we'd have to fight. We didn't want him to get hurt. In them days, you'd get to arguin' with one man, and another man would [come up and] knock your brains out."

They settled the argument without bloodshed. But afterward, "he spoke one time, that same day. He said, 'You-all oughta let me 'had' (fight) him.' I told him, 'No, man!' I said, 'You don't know these fellas!' He be fightin' one man, another man walk up there and knock him in the head. Well, I woulda had to shoot somebody to keep him from him [Patton]."

As Patton's assistant, Miller got to hear his favorite musician often, never tiring of hearing his songs ("I loved to hear him play"). He also took the opportunity to improve his guitar skills with Patton's help. He had begun learning to play late in 1929 when Patton had promised him that "if you listen to me, I learn you how to pick a guitar." At first Miller was a slow learner, becoming so frustrated in his efforts to learn Patton's music that he turned to a Clarksdale musician named James Binell for pointers. "Now he was good," Miller said of Binell, "but he wasn't as good as Charlie. That boy was good with a guitar, but he wasn't my ideal to worship. You know some people is 'sumptious with what they got, and you have to coax 'em, and to beg 'em, persuade 'em (to part with it), and that was the part about him [Binell] I didn't like."

Although Patton "fussed" a lot as Miller's teacher, he showed more patience than his pupil. "I used to tell him all the time, I said, 'My fingers is too big to get in there!'

"He say, 'They ain't no bigger than mine! They get in there.'"

Eventually Miller became proficient in playing Patton's basic repertory, including "Pea Vine Blues" and "Banty Rooster Blues." "I got to the place where I thought, I reckon I'se as good as he was." Even so, he recognized, and respected, the wide difference between their talents. "He played a lot of songs I couldn't play. He lost me on 'em—I just couldn't produce 'em like he could. I'd learn 'em after he played 'em."

His recognition that Patton's talent was greater than his demonstrates an interesting protocol that was practiced among professional blues singers. Miller learned some of Patton's songs by watching him play. Yet he saw that Patton still had a proprietary need for the songs that earned him his living. For that reason, Miller did not perform his versions of Patton pieces in front of his mentor. "I played like him when he wasn't around, but I didn't try to imitate him when he's around. I just played *with* him."

In 1932, Miller felt confident enough with his music to try to make records. He went to Itta Bena and presented himself to Ralph Lembo as a recording prospect. During his audition, Miller avoided playing his favorite Patton pieces, "Pony Blues" and "Down The Dirt Road Blues," for the reason that

Patton "was too famous with 'em, and I didn't wanna try 'em." Still, Lembo liked what he heard, and he encouraged Miller. "He told me that I could go over the top, just for a little practice." With Itta Bena's Bo Diddley, Rube Lacy, Reverend C. F. Thornton and Lembo, Miller traveled to New Orleans. There he made four test recordings, probably for the Victor label. One song was called "Katy at the Landing," which was Patton's "Maggie" sung to lyrics that Patton didn't use on his records. Another was "Crow Jane," a song that "he'd help me sing it," Miller said of Patton, "but he never did take that for his own song." Lembo was impressed enough with Miller's audition recordings (which have not survived) to offer a commercial recording session for seventy-five dollars. Miller consulted with Patton, who said, "Don't bother with it, isn't nothin' to it." Miller decided to turn down the offer.[31]

As an artist, Patton set new standards, yet as a teacher he appreciated what Miller was achieving for himself. When the Delta flooded in 1932, they updated "High Water Everywhere." "Man, we had some water here in 1932. He sung about it," Miller said. Miller contributed a new stanza:

> It's water here an' it's water everywhere
> I would go to Greenwood, but the water's taken Baptist Town[32]

That led Patton to praise him. "Kid, you're finally learnin', ain't you?"

Of Patton's later songs, only one appeared to take real hold with his audience. It was played on the order of "Maggie" and it was called "Black Cow Blues." "Oh Lord, I remember that one," Miller said. "Brother Lord; yes-yes! 'If you see my black cow, drive that heifer home; I ain't had no milk since my cow been gone.' Old Charlie could sing that, too! Now you talkin' about a comedy act, now, he put one on with that, and people—oh man, they had him playin' it everywhere."

Towards the end of 1933, Patton decided to revive his recording career, perhaps on the grounds that he had enough new material for an extended session. But he didn't call on Miller for help, even though he had advised the younger man on the Lembo offer the previous year. Instead, he looked up two of his companions from his last Paramount trip, Willie Brown and Son House.

During the 1930s House was a full-fledged bluesman, even though Willie Brown wondered if House shouldn't have been a preacher. "He said if Son House couldn't make enough money playin' the guitar, he gonna pick up a [church] collection," Willie Moore quoting what Brown told him. "He'd preach a year, somethin' like that six months again. He could preach, you know." Those who heard House preach in Hernando and at the Morning Star Baptist Church between Banks and Robinsonville shared this opinion. "If you was a Christian or said you was one, and hear him preach and sing one them 'Doctor Watt' (i.e., a hymn)," reported Elizabeth Moore, "you'd just know that Reverend was right. He really could sing and he really could preach."

But Willie Brown, with his weak singing voice, needed House as his singer to continue earning a living through music. Willie Moore recalled that "Willie Brown would go to the church where Son House was pastorin'. He'd tell him, say, 'Well, I sho need you.' Willie Brown would swear he [House] done quit [music]. Next time Willie would hear him, he would be playin'." Unluckily for House, others heard him, too. "He went to carryin' on so bad," said Elizabeth Moore in continuing her husband's story, "until the church folks didn't want him. They got rid of him an' he run back, then back." Running from the devil and Willie Brown, House landed a pulpit at Commerce, but his reputation caught up with him, and "the members up there put him outta business," Elizabeth noted. Then, in the fall of 1933, Patton tried putting House back in the music business, but as a gospel singer.

House recalled in 1966[33] that Patton "got somebody to write a letter to Willie and tell us about H.C Speirs (sic) was wantin' us to come down with him and make some records." House thought Speir operated a commercial record label, a mistake that is understandable when it is remembered that for the 1930 Paramount session House had dealt only with Patton, not with Speir. From what happened next, it appears that Patton decided early on to play a little joke on Speir. After gathering House and Brown in Skene, Patton rehearsed them as a gospel group. Using the name of a bluff set beyond nearby Boyle, Patton christened them the Locust Ridge Saints. He coached them in singing "I Had A Dream Last Night Troubled Me," the text of which caused House to growl, "That's not religion." Nonetheless, House went along with Patton.

Then they traveled to Speir's store in Jackson, even though Speir had not solicited an audition nor expected them. House remembered how that audition went. "We'se just with Charlie, see, and let Charlie do all the leading and singing, we'd just complement along with him." But from the other side of the store counter, Speir had a different view. While House and Brown sang for Speir, Patton stood behind them and sang with a hat pulled down across his forehead. "He was dressed up like a Sunday preacher," recalled Speir. "I almost bust my gut laughin.' I pretended I didn't know who he was. And when I asked Charlie if he knew any blues, he laughed himself."

Having successfully played his joke to Speir's delight, Patton began the task he had come to do, which was making some blues demonstration records for Speir's use. What exactly he played is forgotten, but House later said they were "a lot of little foolish songs. Charlie, he'd try to make a record out of anything, you know, 'cause he loved to 'clown.'" All told, the unholy three spent about two days in Jackson recording for Speir. After returning home to Lake Cormorant, House asked Speir for copies of some of the demonstration records. The samples he received "went all haywire" after a few days. As Speir tended to send such records to commercial companies as audition material, his willingness to send some of them to House suggests that he didn't expect to place House and Brown with a record label.

After their Jackson trip, Patton, Brown and House spent a week performing around Boyle, where they stayed as house guests to Patton's ex-wife Millie Barnes and her current husband Cliff Toy.[34] Their cordiality to Patton came as a real surprise to House. "He knowed Charlie used to be his old lady's old man, but yet and still he didn't act like he was jealous. Whole lotta guys won't do that. But Cliff, he treated him just like a brother." Patton's daughter China Lou had taken her stepfather's surname Toy, and she was now in her mid-20s. House remembered that she had "nice hair" and "pretty brown skin," but he was also startled by her open contempt of her wayward father. "She liked her mother better than she did her father, because he didn't wanna do nothin' but run all over the country and play guitars and pick up with every woman he see and have 'em cook for some white folks and slip him out some bread, and she just didn't have the confidence in him that she had in her mother. She wouldn't pay him no attention, just like he wasn't her daddy. She wasn't fond of him much—his own daughter."[35] Charlie's brother Willie "Son" Patton—the one that David Edwards remembered as Ed—was a good friend of the Toys, and he came to visit that week. House saw that Willie Mae acted less aloof with her uncle. House figured it was because "he wouldn't play music and he wasn't a drinker and he just had better ways. See, he didn't do all this ramblin' and drinkin' this corn whiskey and 'kickin' up heels' and things."

BUT DURING THAT same week in Boyle, Patton resumed his quarreling with Willie Brown. One morning after a performance, Patton saw that a ten-dollar bill was missing, and he suspected Brown of taking it. "He said Willie got it. He laid it on Willie," attested House. "They didn't do no fightin'; just argue and trick one another. Willie didn't have it. Somebody else got it, but he [Patton] put it on Willie 'cause they slept in the same room that night." At the end of that week, Brown and House went their way, and Patton went his. They never saw him again.

All I ask you to do for me:
come an' lay me on the coolin' board

—PATTON, "JESUS IS A DYIN' BEDMAKER," 1930

# *Chapter 15* LAST SESSION (JANUARY–APRIL 1934)

Twice in January 1934, Patton found himself in the Humphreys County courthouse in Belzoni, Mississippi. One time was for a minor disturbance he caused when he got a little too drunk while playing a house frolic in Belzoni. Deputy K. Carlos Webb was summoned to remove the musician. "He got drunk, he told me," David Edwards recalled, "and the police 'rested him and carried him to jail." Booker Miller, who also heard of the incident, remarked, "That's all they coulda got him for (i.e., drunkenness), 'cause he didn't bother nobody." In his cell, Patton was probably safer there than at the house frolic. "They was pretty rough down in there then," Booker Miller said of the frolics, without exaggerating.

The other time, though, was for a much more serious incident that Bertha Lee remembered, to which Patton and Bertha Lee were merely witnesses.[1] While they were performing at a frolic, James Manuel killed Henry Freeman. Deputy Webb would have been the officer to have been called in, and he would have taken Manuel, the frolic host, the Pattons, and the various eyewitnesses to the Humphreys County courthouse, holding them briefly in the cells until all of the information was gathered. The next grand jury was not scheduled to meet until early March, so Patton and Bertha Lee did not receive their subpoenas to serve as state witnesses until March 10.

Patton told Edwards that it was while sitting in jail when he had "made up a song" about Deputy Webb and his superior, Sheriff John D. Purvis, by updating his Paramount record "Tom Rushen Blues" as "High Sheriff Blues":

Get in trouble in Belzoni, it ain't no use of screamin' and cryin',
Get in trouble in Belzoni, it ain't no use of screamin' and cryin',
Mr. Webb will take you, back to Belzoni jailhouse flyin'.
Lay there late one evenin', Mr. Purvis was standin' 'round,
Lay there late one evenin', Mr. Purvis was standin' 'round,
Mr. Purvis told Mr. Webb to let poor Charlie down.
It takes boozey booze, Lord, to cure these blues,
Takes boozey booze, Lord, to cure these blues,
But each day seems like years in a jailhouse where there is no booze.
Oh, Lord, in trouble, ain't no use to screamin'...
When I was in prison it ain't no use of screamin' an' cryin',
Mr. Purvis' the onliest manager can, ease that pain of mine.

Patton had derived several of these rhymes from Ma Rainey's 1924 Paramount record "Booze An' Blues" (credited on the paper labels to T. Guy Suddoth). But he had no inkling that the fourth stanza was itself a paraphrase, derived from Oscar Wilde's famous *Ballad of Reading Gaol*:

. . . each day is like a year,
A year whose days are long.

While Patton was thinking up material in his cell, a recording representative was conducting a manhunt for him. W. R. Calaway of Florida was once a Paramount dealer, but he was now the sales manager for the American Record Company (ARC). He had received Patton's audition records from H. C. Speir, and he wanted to add the musician to ARC's blues roster.

Calaway first went to Speir's store in Jackson. Since Calaway also visited ARC's distributor in Memphis, Earl Montgomery, his arrival at Speir's store might have been received as a routine sales call. But then Calaway announced that he wanted to find Patton and bring him to ARC's New York City studio. What he proposed was unusual, on two counts. For one, his usual practice was to send a train ticket to Speir for Patton's use, like the Paramount executives did five years earlier. And for the other, white record executives normally didn't travel with black artists unless it was necessary. It may be possible, then, that Calaway on his own tried to contact Patton, perhaps making a second effort through Montgomery, and when those attempts failed, he came to Speir in Jackson.

Speir had dealt with Calaway before, when they scouted talent in 1932 for ARC. With each of the potential artists they identified, Speir made test recordings and duly sent them along, only to learn that the commercial labels had not approved the artists. Then he saw those same discoveries inexplicably turn up on releases by the same commercial labels, who cut him out of finder's fees—a move that Speir suspected that Calaway had something to do with. There were other times when Speir delivered an artist to a company, only to find himself frozen out of future dealings with the singer, while Calaway gave himself a sales royalty as the latter's "manager." As a result, he thought of Calaway as the least principled person in the recording industry.[2] Despite his wary reservations, Speir grudgingly gave Patton's address to Calaway.

Upon leaving Jackson, Calaway likely went first to Holly Ridge or nearby Heathman, and if the record man didn't find him there, then he would have learned that Patton was detained in Belzoni, where as a white man he could secure Patton's release. A record man could be trusted.[3] Speir had acted similarly before, by writing at Patton's request a character reference on his behalf. "I never got what Charlie got into, mighta been a debt or somethin," Speir said of the earlier incident.

If Patton had intended to record again with Willie Brown and Son House, Calaway's unexpected arrival scuttled that plan, as fetching them at Lake Cormorant would have involved a detour of one hundred and twenty-five miles. Their inaccessible location may have opened a studio door for Bertha Lee, who probably wouldn't have passed an audition for H. C. Speir (that is, if he still "didn't think much" of the women singers Patton had been bringing to him for consideration).

When Son House learned during a 1964 interview that Bertha Lee recorded with Patton, he was puzzled by her participation. "She wasn't interested in singing," House said of her. Elizabeth Moore knew her since the mid-1920s, and she too was a little surprised. "I never heard her sing no blues, but I heard her sing some church songs," she said. Patton may have needed her with him in the recording studio, for his voice had been damaged when his throat had been slashed the previous year. "He still had his voice, but he had a kinda hoarseness in it," David Edwards reported.

They prepared eight religious duets and four blues vocal duets, one of the latter being "Whiskey Distillery." Only two of their duets were to be released on records, "Oh Death" and "Troubled 'Bout My Mother." On both of them, Bertha sings lead, with Patton providing some vocal pepper. Bertha would have known "Oh Death" from the services at the First Baptist Church in Lula, either singing it as a choir member, or by hearing the church's resident group The Delta Big Four perform it. There was also the Delta Big Four's recording that Paramount released as "I Know My Time Ain't Long."

Reportedly, ARC sent letters to House and Brown to join the Pattons in New York City. If so, they may have been sent at Patton's request if he was expecting Calaway to include them. However, the letters did not contain train tickets, so at best they were sent as "fair attempts" by Calaway and ARC with no expectation of seeing House or Brown.

Patton, Bertha and Calaway departed for New York City on the Southern Railroad by way of Meridian. About thirty years later, Bertha told Bernard Klatzko that during their train ride north, Calaway wrote down on paper the lyrics of the songs that Patton planned to record them.[4] This suggests strongly that Calaway intended to copyright them. Patton traveled with a new guitar, a Gibson with a black top. "I don't think he lost it," Booker Miller said of the Stella he had previously used. "I just think he beat the sound out of it, 'cause Charlie was rough on boxes. It took a Gibson to stand up to him."

When they arrived at Grand Central Station, New York was in the middle of a harsh winter, which may have caused considerable discomfort to Parton, who was suffering a cold. The couple from Mississippi then checked in at the Hotel Theresa at 125th Street and Seventh Avenue. While they stayed there, when not recording, Patton performed at the hotel and on Harlem streets.

On each of the three days of recording, Calaway escorted them to the ARC studio. It was located with various music firms and the American Academy of Music in the Lazarus Building at Broadway and 57th Street. Supervising ARC's recording activities was Arthur Satherly, who in the 1920s had worked at Paramount and QRS; he may have been present in the studio with Calaway, Patton and Bertha.

But the budget at ARC was not at the same level of QRS, or even of Paramount. The Tennessee bluesman Yank Rachell recorded for ARC at the same New York City studio the week after the Patton sessions. He remembered ARC as "the cheapest company I ever worked for." As a subsidiary of the Pennsylvania-based Scranton Button Company, ARC was controlled by Herbert Yates (1880–1961), an English businessman who soon took over Republic Pictures.[5] Yates was noted for his crassness within the crass industries of records and motion pictures. Of his film company it was written, "the studio was devoted to money rather than to movie-making. No A-budget pictures were produced—most films were made for less than $100,000 . . . most writers called it 'Repulsive' Studios and spoke of it as a prison."[6]

In the record industry, ARC was likewise run as a low-budget firm. Its records were priced at thirty-five cents apiece, or three for a dollar. "The big business was on the Victor label and the Brunswick label, and they were higher priced," recalled J. B. Long, a North Carolina dealer.[7] Although ARC also operated Brunswick, it placed Patton on the cheaper Vocalion label, whose releases were mostly of rustic music. In 1933, ARC had recorded nearly two hundred blues and gospel titles, a phenomenal total considering the near-death condition of the industry. It was, therefore, a logical and appropriate firm for Charlie Patton in 1934.

When Patton recorded for ARC, the company was still building up a catalog in the hopes of becoming a credible label to dealers. It sold its records directly to retailers, permitting them to order one copy, if need be. Because ARC lacked a force of salesmen to promote its releases, dealers like J. B. Long did not receive sample records to help them make selections for their store stocks. Rather, they ordered only the records by artists whose names they already knew. Meanwhile, in 1934, in the state of Mississippi, ARC had few dealers in retail stores, aside from H. C. Speir in Jackson. With these circumstances viewed in hindsight, Patton's sales potential may have seemed rather low, if not unpromising.

The company's intensive recording procedures were different from the practice of the previous decade. In the 1920s, when a company first worked with an unknown African American artist, it recorded between two and six titles and issue them as "race records," and only in the event of sales success would they invite the musician to return to the studio. But ARC, on the other hand, during the first and only session it may have with a new artist, "they milked 'dry, got everything they [the musicians] had," as Earl Montgomery said. ARC recording totals were astronomical. Each session it held during the early 1930s often ran for two or three days, during which were recorded as many as twenty-five titles, the figure rarely falling below ten. By following this procedure, the company thus had a backlog of material available for release if the artist's first release happened to be a hit. Instead of having to raise recording fees for return sessions as did companies in the 1920s, ARC drew from their backlogs of its artists' complete repertories without having to pay additional fees.

In that way, ARC could afford its marathon sessions by paying its artists practically nothing. The popular country and western singer Roy Acuff, as a leading example, received a total of $250 from ARC for recording twenty sides in 1936.[8] Blues acts earned even less. Earl Montgomery thought that the company customarily paid blues singers forty or fifty dollars per session, which, if the artist recorded 20 or 25 songs, may average out to a mere two dollars per master side. Whereas the typical firm of the 1920s like Paramount tried to earn back its high investment by issuing its stockpile of recordings, ARC's policy was to junk all remaining unreleased masters by an artist whose initial releases did not turn out to be hits.

But ARC's indiscriminate recording approach increased the chances of commercial flops. With large quantities of material to choose from, the white ARC executives were unlikely to distinguish the front-line repertory pieces from the secondary songs that also were recorded during the company's milking process. ARC's first Patton release, "Poor Me," for example, illustrates the inadequacies of this approach and the limitations of Arthur Satherly as its guiding executive. A song whose basic chorus was in 16 measures, "Poor Me" was the twenty-third piece Patton had recorded during his visit. It was neither a dance tune nor a blues, and since Booker Miller never heard him play it, it may not have belonged to Patton's performing repertory. With Patton persistently going off-key while singing the phrase-ending tonic note of each chorus of "Poor Me," Satherly's approval of the first take for release is baffling unless he thought naively that this song was as good as any other.

Even so, from ARC's perspective, Patton's productivity in the studio would have made him seem like the ideal recording artist. During his late January 1934 visit in New York, he recorded more sides than any ARC artist before him had produced in an ongoing session. During the course of a three-day session beginning on January 30th, he completed twenty-six sides, plus another three sides as Bertha Lee's accompanist, despite a heavy cough that often threatened to disrupt several recording takes. However, since the first few releases did not sell well, ARC issued only 10 of the 26 masters, junking the rest. The five record releases were Patton's final legacy, documenting his decline as a bluesman. Recording at last for a label whose records sounded well during playback, Patton was no longer the spectacular performer of yore. He was a dying man.

Still, Patton's ARC performances are remarkable, in view of the fact that at the time of the sessions, he lived for only eighty-eight more days. But several questions may be asked about the circumstances of the visit. With his declining health, was he mindful of being remembered only as a blues singer? If so, was that one reason why he planned to record more sacred material than usual for him? If he was padding his repertory with spirituals and gospel songs, does that indicate possible misgivings about ARC's recording rates?

Thinking of Patton's 1929–1930 sacred recordings for Paramount, Booker Miller said, "After his death, I figured that's why he would 'cross over,' you know, and record those church songs. I figured he might have been thinkin' about it (dying), but he didn't discuss it with me. Some things'd be on your mind, you know; you don't mention it." Any unspoken thoughts about death may explain why Patton recorded six blues during the first ARC session on January 30, but at least four of the eleven titles he produced the following day were spirituals, as were the first three of nine songs recorded on February 1.

Whether Patton was disgruntled by his recording fees is suggested by his failure to record more new versions of his Paramount songs, like his remake of "Shake It and Break It" that ARC released as "Hang It On The Wall." From what Booker Miller told his interviewer about Patton's 1930–1934 repertory, a glaring omission is the 1932 update of Patton's last Paramount hit, "High Water Everywhere." Nor did he bother to remake "Banty Rooster Blues," which still counted as one of his theme songs. In 1968, when Booker MIller heard some of Patton's 1934 recordings, he thought that they fell below the caliber of live performance that he remembered Patton was playing even during his last weeks.

Since his previous session in 1930, Patton as a singer had lost wind and volume. He no longer had the ability to sustain phrases that he had used to impart a unique sound to "Pony Blues" and "Down The Dirt Road Blues." In the first stanza of "Stone Pony Blues," a remake of "Pony Blues," he variously held phrase-ending words for two, three, and five beats, without employing the diminuendo "fade-out" effect that had marked his eight-measure sustains in "Pony Blues." In "34 Blues," a slow treatment of "Down The Dirt Road Blues," he generally held the final word of a phrase for one four-beat measure instead of six beats, as he had done in the earlier performance. Yet even this clipped delivery apparently strained him, for he consistently gave himself an extra breath by strumming through the midpoint of the first phrase of each stanza. He similarly conserved his waning vocal resources during "Revenue Man Blues," an adaptation of "Maggie." Among its first phrases, he shifted his mid-phrase rest between the fifth and eighth beats of the melody (Ex. 67), but when singing the second phrase of the second, third, and fourth verses, he took a break-rest on the sixth beat (or, the first beat of the second full transcribed measure).

While in his ARC sides Patton managed to interject these pauses so gracefully as to make them practically unnoticeable, in his Paramount discs he didn't need to take vocal rests in mid-phrase. The overall effect of these phrasing problems on the listener was and is a feeling of sluggishness.

For that reason of lackluster energy on these last recordings, Miller wondered if Patton was sober in the recording studio. "You see, we had our juice with us then," he said of their live appearances. "A man can kinda 'come up' when he got that." Yet Patton during his Paramount sessions might have been sober, too. In the midwestern towns like Richmond, Indiana and Grafton, Wisconsin during the height of Prohibition, a black stranger was unlikely to be permitted by local bootleggers to buy liquor, particularly on the weekdays when recording sessions were often held. But when Patton recorded for ARC in January 1934, Prohibition had just been repealed. It may be naive to suppose that Patton arrived at his sessions without having bought legally some kind of liquor in a 125th Street store in Harlem.[9]

Whether sober or not, the Patton who recorded for ARC was still a masterful guitarist, as may be heard in the precision with which he accompanied the nuances of his singing on "High Sheriff Blues" and "Poor Me." He remained a dynamic entertainer, as his inspired comedic performance of "Hang It on the Wall" indicated. He was capable of new surprises, such as the fleeting falsetto he interjected in single stanzas of "High Sheriff Blues" and "Jersey Bull Blues," and the unexpected measure of double-time he played in the coda of "34 Blues." Yet these moments of artistry appeared now in small spurts, not in a stream as before.

Patton's ARC recordings appear to have been a mixture of current repertory and of new songs prepared for the session. Miller said that Patton did perform live "Revenue Man," "Whiskey Distillery" ("I remember it too many

Ex. 67: Patton's lyric openings for "Revenue Man Blues."

times!"), "Till the Day Is Done" ("That was a good one, all right"), "Southern Whistle," and "Move Your Trunk." He never heard Patton play "The Delta Murder," "Charley Bradley's 1066 Blues," "My Man Blues," or such spirituals as "Stoop Down" and "Oh Lord I'm In Your Hands."

To begin the first day of recording, Patton performed "Jersey Bull Blues" to the tune of "Maggie." Who knows whether he took the concept of "Jersey Bull Blues" from Bill Broonzy's 1932 recording of "Bull Cow Blues," or, less likely, Broonzy took it from Patton by hearing him live. In his song, Patton presented the attitudes of both husband and wife about philandering:

> If you got a good bullcow you oughta, feed your bull good at home
> If you got a good bullcow you oughta, feed your bull good at home
> (spoken: "Boy, feed him good at home")
> It may come along a young heifer an' just, tow your bull from home.
>
> Oh, my bull's in a pasture be, Lord where there's no grass
> An' my bull's in a pasture, Lord where there's no grass
> (spoken: "Boy it ain't no grass in this pasture!")
> I swear every minute it seems, like it's gonna be my last.

While Patton tried to sing in his "hollering" style for "Jersey Bull Blues" and "Love My Stuff," his voice lacked its former volume. By casting "Jersey Bull Blues" in the key of B-flat, a half or full step lower than his other "Maggie" songs, he should have been able to sing with relatively little strain on his voice. Yet whereas the usual top scale tone of "Maggie" was a perfect fifth above the tonic, in "Jersey Bull Blues" he seldom ventured above the interval of a minor third.

"Charley Bradley's Ten Sixty-Six Blues" is lost, but Booker Miller remembered that Patton did perform this at dances and that the song was not a reworking of his previous railroad record, "Pea Vine Blues." To pick up Bertha for the session, Patton and Calaway would have gone from Belzoni to Heathman on the Moorhead branch of the Yazoo Delta Railroad. The engineer of this route, whose locomotive was designated engine number 1066, was a man named Charley Bradley, whose dark features led Delta blacks to consider him an Italian. Renowned for his whistleblowing, he was the subject of a local topical blues by Patton, "Charley Bradley's Ten Sixty Six Blues." "That man was 'bad' about that engine, an' he was a clowner, too," Booker Miller fondly recalled. David Edwards was less amused by Bradley, remarking, "He was a kinda mean guy. He'd get there an' blow that whistle and if you didn't get off that track, he'd run over you. I know he killed a lot of people."

The next two songs also referred to Delta topics. "High Sheriff Blues" was Patton's new Belzoni jail reworking of his "Tom Rushen Blues"; the recording may be its first-ever performance. "Southern Whistle Blues" is unissued and lost, but reportedly it was about the section of the Southern Railroad running between Greenville and Morehead ("where the Southern cross the Dog," as the classic blues lyric went.)

It is likely that "Stone Pony Blues" and "34 Blues" were composed for the recording sessions, as Patton was still playing the original versions of those songs to his audiences in the South. The expression "Stone Pony" was explained by Booker Miller as "a man hard—do things in a big way." That blues seems to mention a girlfriend in Rayville, Louisiana:

I got me a stone pony and I don't ride Shetlands no more
I got me a stone pony, don't ride Shetlands no more
You can find my stone pony, hooked to my rider's door.

Vicksburg's my pony, Rayville is my grey mare
Vicksburg's my pony, Rayville Lord is my grey mare
You can find my stone pony, down in Louisiana tied somewhere.

Rayville is a small town across the Mississippi River from Vicksburg. Patton had performed there in the 1920s with a fiddler, possibly John Nance. They had traveled there "out from Bolton, over there to Brownsville," according to Ishman Bracey. "Vicksburg—that's the both of 'ems home," Bracey surmised. "Right across the river from Vicksburg."

Likewise, Patton's fingers seemed no longer able to sustain such powerful music. Aside from the renditions of "Maggie," his thumb work on other surviving ARC sides was unaccountably minimal and weak. Whereas the rhythmic impact of "Pony Blues" depended partly upon forceful bass interjections, "Stone Pony Blues" had little bass work to speak of; in the first phrase of its first chorus, only a single beat (the sixth) featured prominent bass notes.

Patton banished his care and sorrow with the aid of women and alcohol, both of which were plentiful to blues singers. "There's three things wasn't no object: that's womens, whiskey, and food," Booker Miller said. "You didn't have to worry about nothin' like that." In the process of becoming a blues singer, however, Patton wound up with a bad reputation that often made him an outcast. As he sang on "Stone Pony Blues":

Vicksburg on a high hill and Natchez just below
Vicksburg on a high hill, Natchez just below
And I can't feel welcome, rider nowhere I go

The first day of recording ended with "My Man Blues" with Bertha Lee co-singing, which was not released and now lost. Before they entered the studio for their second day of work, during the meantime two other acts recorded:

the guitar duo Carl Kress and Dick McDonough cut two masters, and the accordionist Norm Zeller cut four.

Patton and Bertha Lee resumed from where they left off by continuing to make duet records. "Yellow Bee" was her cover of Memphis Minnie's 1930 hit "Bumble Bee." At first Bertha Lee seems a bit coy if not innocent with her lyrics, replacing Minnie's "stinger" with "honey" and "stung" with "buzz," but her last stanza begins with the explicit "stinger as long as my arm." "Mind Reader Blues" was her answer to infidelity, whether Patton's or anyone else's, to the melody of Walter Davis' "M. and O. Blues." Both of these performances were issued on Vocalion 78s. The next song, "You're Gonna Miss Me Honey," was not released, and it may be presumed lost. From its title, one could suppose that it was a re-recording of Patton's "Some of These Days," but the documentation says Patton performed it with Bertha Lee, so they may have performed a different song that was better suited for a duet.

Bertha Lee then sat out, and Patton handled two songs by himself. Patton's "Stoop Down" was unissued, but this lost performance was very likely of the 16-measure spiritual that began with "Everybody's got to stoop down, stoop down, stoop on down and drink and live."[10] "34 Blues" dwelt not with the new year, but rather on Patton's expulsion from Dockery Plantation in 1929, to the melody of "Down the Dirt Road Blues." At the end of the record, the prediction for the coming year that ends "34 Blues,"

And it may bring sorrow, Lord it may bring tears
It may bring sorrow Lord and it may bring tears
Oh Lord, oh Lord, let me see a brand new year.

paraphrased Proverbs 27:1, which advised "Boast not of tomorrow, for thou knowest not what a day may bring forth."

Bertha rejoined Patton at the microphone for four sacred songs, all of which were left unissued and now unknown. "I've Got a Mother Up in Kingdom," if it matched a printed version then circulating[11] would have been an 8-measure tune to the words "I've got a mother up in Kingdom, outshines the sun, outshines the sun, outshines the sun.". "Ananaias" was likely the sacred song whose refrain had the words "Ananias, Ananias Ananias, Ananias, tell me / What kind of man Jesus is."[12] Of "Listen What She Said" and "Till The Day Is Done," nothing is known or may be speculated.

Patton and Bertha Lee then turned to their secular material. "Black Cow

Blues" is lost, but Booker Miller learned the song from hearing Patton at their joint appearances and, some 35 years later, recited to one of the authors the lyrics that he still remembered. It was a 12-measure AAB lyric blues that had the "Maggie" melody. The title stanza was "If you see my black cow, drive her home / I ain't had no milk since my cow been gone," sharing a lyric concordance with Son House's "My Black Mama" recording for Paramount in 1930. Miller also said that the guitar accompaniment featured a snapped bass-string run as may be heard on "High Water Everywhere." "Dog Train Blues" is also lost, but this was Bertha Lee's third and final side as featured solo singer, the title referring to the Yazoo and Mississippi Valley "Yellow Dog" train.

Most of what was released from Patton and Bertha Lee's second day of recording was recorded near the end. "Love My Stuff" (or "stuffie" as Patton sang on the record) was another treatment of Patton's "Maggie" melody. Midway through the performance, he mentioned the Devil:

> Oh the lights burnin' dim in the levee (blast) camp again
> It must be the devil, a-strikin' terror again.

The belief that "lights burnin' dim" heralded the approach of unseen spirits was an ancient superstition. William Shakespeare, in Act IV, scene 3 of his play *Julius Caesar*, used it to signal the visit of the murdered Julius Caesar to Brutus' tent, causing the latter to rave, "How ill this taper burns!—Ha! who comes here? . . . Some god, some angel, or some devil / That makest my blood run cold, and hair to stare?" Whether Patton was staging the same scene out of fear or for laughs is anyone's guess. As for the encounter with the evil spirit, it may have been a figment of Fundamentalist rhetoric. As a blues singer, Patton would have been perceived as an enemy of God, who was thought to have an eternity for hellfire in store for musicians who had provided sinful dance music for revelers. It was no wonder that Patton and his Fundamentalist peers numbed their tortured souls by getting drunk.

> Oh I'm gonna leave Mississippi nappy, 'fore it be too late
> It may be like '27 highwater, swear it just won't wait.

"Nappy means fast," Booker Miller said, who added to the term a secondary meaning of "disagreeable."

"Revenue Man Blues" was the tenth song of the second day's session. By then, Patton may have been feeling somewhat spent. But somehow he returned to his energetic form of 1929 and 1930, summoning up a rousing "Maggie" that rivaled the intensity of "High Water Everywhere Part I" and "Moon Going Down." Among its lyrics were the first stanza of his 1930 Paramount record "Bird Nest Bound" and the classic line "jinx all 'round my bed." Arguably, "Revenue Man Blues" deserved to be released first, but it was on the fifth and final disc to be drawn from the ARC sessions. The masters with provocative titles like "Black Cow Blues," "Bed Bugs and Snakes," "The Delta Murder," "Whiskey Distillery," and his final recording "Move Your Trunk" were not released and now lost. But their fate does not necessarily mean that they were bad. They may have been even as good as "Revenue Man Blues," but their merits could have been simply unrecognized by ARC executives who just didn't know Patton's style.

Patton and Bertha Lee wrapped up the second day with "Oh Lord I'm In Your Hands" (unissued and lost) and "Oh Death." The latter is Patton's deft rearrangement of what the Delta Big Four recorded in 1930 as "I Know My Time Ain't Long." Little differences between the two recordings suggest that Patton and Bertha Lee were remembering the Delta Big Four's performances in Lula than working directly from the group's Paramount disc. Two significant lyrics in the Pattons' version that were not in the Delta Big Four's were "Oh hush, oh hush, Oh hush, oh hush, somebody's calling me" (which in Bertha Lee's accent sounds very affecting) and "Oh move my pillow, then turn my bed around." While Patton and Bertha Lee could have thought up these additional lyrics, it is more likely that they were remembering lyrics that the Delta Big Four sang in church but could not fit on the three-minute record side.

Also notable on the Patton disc were several musical features. One was Patton's interweaving his and Bertha's voices during the first phrase of each chorus, to give some flexibility to their phrasing (Ex. 68).

Ex. 68: Patton and Lee, "Oh Death" (1934), chorus 1, mm. 1-3 [0:02-0:07].

Another was Patton's inserting the word "Lordy" in eighth-notes in the manner of the Delta Big Four's bass Archie Smith, which on the Delta Big Four's records he may be heard doing that on "Jesus Got His Arms Around Me" but not on "I Know My Time Ain't Long." A third was Patton's slide guitar accompaniment that follows the singing as if it was a third voice, while he plays with his thumb an alternating bass pattern to keep the tempo even. And finally, midway through the final chorus, Bertha Lee replaces "me" with "you":

> Oh hush, oh hush, oh hush, oh hush, somebody is calling me,
>     good Lordie now
> Oh hush, oh hush, somebody is calling you
> Oh hush, good Lordie I'll, oh hush, somebody is calling you
> Lord I know, Lord I know my time ain't long

She may have been teasing Patton, although to us today her changed lyric seems like a prediction of Patton's imminent death.

To begin their third and final day of recording, Patton and Bertha Lee took up "Troubled 'Bout My Mother." This spiritual had a few antecedents on records, the most pertinent of which were Frank Palmes' "Troubled 'Bout My Soul" and the Thankful Quartette's "I'm Troubled, Lord I'm Troubled." Patton accompanied their singing with a one-chord guitar part that was fretted with a bottleneck slide. To fill up a three-minute recording side, the Pattons had to sing through the 8-measure form 11 times, using lyrics involving both parents (the mother three times), a sister, King David, and the prophet Daniel. It is interesting to note that "Troubled 'Bout My Mother" used the same four intervals of "Maggie's" variously named melodic cousins. The spiritual's simple repetitive cadences from the minor third to tonic were also characteristic of "Maggie," while its dip from the minor seventh to dominant half way through the first line (at the seventh beat) was a standard blues cadence used in the final line of a stanza.

Ex. 69: Patton and Lee, "Troubled 'Bout My Mother" (1934) chorus 1, mm. 1-4 [0:01-0:10].

The next three songs—"God's Word Will Never Pass Away," "Bed Bugs and Snakes," and "The Delta Murder" do not survive on disc or in memory. By its title alone, "The Delta Murder" may have commemorated any number of plantation bloodlettings by violent patrons. There was the one the previous fall at Will Richards' plantation near Iverness that had brought pandemonium to a frolic where Patton was playing; Mandy Whigman described years later to one of the authors what had happened. Enraged by a man's advances to her young daughter, a woman hacked him to death with an axe, whereupon her son killed a second person in the same way. There was also the murder of a gambler known as "Quicksilver" at Four Mile Lake sometime in the early 1930s, which Big Joe Williams later claimed to have witnessed with Patton.[13] These axe murders appear to have been part of the latest trend in house frolic homicides, bringing a new element of slaughter to an already bloody setting.

Of Patton's last four recorded songs, "Whiskey Distillery" and "Move Your Trunk" are lost and irretrievable. So, the end of Patton's surviving legacy are "Poor Me" and "Hang It On the Wall." "Poor Me" is unusual for Patton's repertory in that it was a 16-measure non-blues song. It was previously recorded in 1928 for Vocalion as "Cryin' Blues" by Hound Head Henry with the pianist Cow Cow Davenport, two recording artists who were far outside Patton's circle of musicians. Patton enhanced their lyrics by adding the couplet "Don't the moon look pretty shinin' down through the tree? / Oh, I can see Bertha Lee, but she can't see me." "Hang It On The Wall" was a remake of his 1929 record "Shake It and Break It," which had a skewed balance favoring the treble tones. As much as Patton tries, he can't quite match the spirited performance that he gave Paramount. Certainly his long-term decline in health accounts for the markedly lackluster performances for "Poor Me" and "Hang It On The Wall." But they were also performed at the end of three long and busy winter days in a northern city by a musician who was weighed down with a cold.

On the weekend of April 8, 1934, Patton and Booker Miller were providing Saturday night entertainment at a dance on Strickland's plantation near Greenwood, a favorite Patton watering-spot. Patton had arrived at the frolic with a woman named Willie, whose light complexion caused Miller to take her for a Creole Louisianan of French or Spanish descent. To Miller, Patton appeared carefree and healthy. Then again, "I never heard him complain about nothin' much," he said of Patton's health. At Strickland's plantation, "he didn't act like he was sick. When a man's breath go to tanglin' with him, it stops him from singin' a lot."

The night started out well. "Oh man, we'se knockin' 'em out there," Miller recalled. But towards morning, a couple began quarreling outside the premises, where a double-bit axe was kept. "This man aimed to go out that gate and that lady hit him with that axe," Miller said. "He was dead when we left there and we left there as quick as we could get ready." Patton turned to Miller and shouted "I'm gettin' outta here!" then fled into the night. Miller never saw him again.

Yet Patton had come to the end of his physical resources, and he was sustaining himself on willpower alone. In short order, Tom Cannon recalls, "he lost his breath, couldn't lay down." On January 27 Patton had consulted a doctor in Indianola, presumably about whether his condition would prevent him from making the trip to New York. Bertha Lee remembered Patton suffering this shortness of breath upon returning home after his last performance, a white dance in early April;[14] that night, he had to open the windows to get the breezy air. These symptoms of heart failure became severe enough for the Indianola doctor to be called on April 17th and 20th.[15]

EIGHT DAYS LATER, on April 28th, Patton died on the Heathman-Dedham plantation. The vital statistics information on the death certificate that was duly filed[16] was provided not by Bertha Lee, but by a man named Willie Calvin, a neighbor.[17] Patton had just reached or was about to reach his forty-third birthday. Despite the lack of a newspaper obituary, the news of his death spread quickly. "It went out over the country like wildfire when he died," Miller said. "And when I heard it, I woulda rather heard anything than heard that."

He was just a man could pick a guitar, and I loved it.
I loved to be around him and with him.

—BOOKER MILLER

*Chapter 16*

# AFTERMATH (MAY 1934–1970)

Word of Patton's death spread through the Delta in fits and starts, providing ample time and opportunity for little fictions to develop into legends. Within a few days of his passing, the news traveled thirty miles southeast of Heathman to Sam Chatmon in Hollandale. "Somebody come in, say, 'Is Charlie Patton your brother?'" Sam recalled. "I say, 'Yeah.' Say, 'He's dead; they buried him yesterday.'" As was noted earlier, Chatmon's kinship with Patton was doubtful at best, and his familiarity with him was casual at most. But in the 1970s he used his association with Patton promote himself to blues enthusiasts, which went to show that Patton's name still had a magical effect.

During the first week of May, 1934, David Edwards was making his way towards Holly Ridge in hopes of picking up work as Patton's accompanist.[1] But he arrived too late. "They told me when I come to Indianola—that was about twelve miles from Holly Ridge—they said, 'Charlie Patton died last week.' I said, 'No!' So I went on by there: a little old gravel road through the country. Before I got to his house, there's a cemetery right 'side the gravel road, and I looked around and seen the fresh grave there; they had just buried him. I went to his peoples' house and stayed up all night with them."

Willie—either one from Patton's last days—was not among these "people." But there were Bertha Lee, his uncle Sherman Martin, and the latter's wife Aida. The Willie that Booker Miller saw with Patton at Strickland's, or Bertha Lee for that matter, were likely never seen by the Willie Calvin of Heathman who had served as the informant for Patton's death certificate, which may explain the ambiguous notation there about his marital status. Although the document included the county of Patton's birth and the names of his parents, the entry for the name of his wife was completed with the phrase "d.k.," an abbreviation of "don't know." It may be that Willie Calvin was reluctant to recognize Bertha Lee as wife, whose name must have been familiar about Heathman, or it may be that he simply didn't know.

How Bertha Lee and Viola Cannon really felt about Patton at the time of his death is suggested by how they buried his body. Patton was entitled to free burial beside his parents and brother Will C. on Dockery's Plantation, where Viola and his brother Willie "Son" were still living. But he was taken a short distance to a Holly Ridge graveyard that, by the early 1960s, had been neglected to become a patch of weeds.[2] Patton had sung in "Troubled 'Bout My Mother" of joining his mother in the "kingdom." But in real life, he might have been thought unworthy to be buried near her, even though in her former hometown Bolton she was the subject of gossip among the Chatmans and their neighbors.

Tom Cannon remembered that a "world of people" attended Patton's funeral in Holly Ridge.[3] But this world did not include Patton's daughter Willie Mae or any blues singers. Son House and Willie Brown were in Lake Cormorant when a telegram from Bertha Lee informed them of Patton's death. Apparently she didn't mention the cause of death, because House later said he thought Patton died from mumps. Although House and Brown accepted the opportunities Patton gave them in 1930 and 1933 to make some records, neither came to his funeral.

Meanwhile, at the funeral in Holly Ridge, Viola Cannon, speaking to her son Tom, regarded her late brother as having "lived a fast life, and it carried him down." She very likely had based her opinion from the sermons of contemporary preachers, who reasoned (in the words of one recorded sermon at the time) that the "little habit of drinkin' moonshine carried thousands of men and women, boys and girls, to a disgraceful life an' to an untimely death."[4]

Yet what ended Patton's life had nothing to do with his lifestyle. The doctor who examined him less than two weeks before his death diagnosed him as a mitral heart valve case, a then-incurable disorder that ranked among the most common forms of heart disease.[5] Except in congenital cases, the disease is a sequela arising from rheumatic fever, which during Patton's lifetime was untreatable. The initial bout of rheumatic fever would have struck Patton either in early childhood (between 1894–1896) or early puberty (1902–1904). The resulting scar tissue constricted his heart valve and, some ten or fifteen years later, produced symptoms of mitral valve malfunction including shortness of breath and chronic fatigue (due to lung congestion which forces the heart to overwork). In addition, the disease would have produced a heart murmur to disqualify Patton from military service in World War I.

Although the severity of the symptoms and the rapidity of their onset can vary among individuals, Patton's physical condition may have been noticeably subnormal at some point between 1904 and 1919. It is certain, then, that the Patton who made some unsurpassed blues recordings in 1929 was already contending with a handicap that could have impaired his ability to sing and play. During the last six months of his life, his deteriorating condition would have taken a severe toll. Yet Patton concealed his condition from his associates, perhaps thinking it was due to drink or to God's displeasure with his calling.

Regardless of what Patton may have believed about his health, he was a casualty not of fast living, but of poor living, for rheumatic fever is associated with poverty. As one medical textbook states, "Like many diseases, rheumatic fever appears most frequently in population groups receiving a low income. Crowding, dampness, and poor nutrition are common in such populations."[6]

For flouting the morals of his society, Patton in death continued to pay a price. One of his ex-wives, Udy of Merigold, told Hayes McMullan a lurid tale about his demise. "He was gettin' ready to go—he had done dressed, you know—to go make music at a picnic," McMullan reports. "And Udy said it wasn't even cloudy. Sittin' on his porch practicin' with his guitar. And lightnin' struck him. That's what Udy said. She said she was his wife at that time." Such must have been the retribution Udy wished on Patton, for it was a common rural black belief that God, in Zeus fashion, destroyed "mean" people with thunderbolts.[7]

Despite the admonition that Viola Cannon gave her son Tom at her brother's funeral, she later heaped posthumous glory to his memory.[8] She even told Tom that the American Record Company had built a monument to Patton for his gravesite. But no one else, including Tom, ever saw it. In all likelihood, ARC never built one.[9] The company did not care that much about Patton. It didn't even bother to copyright Patton's material, even though Calaway had transcribed them to paper just before the session. If its executives did learn of his death, they were apparently little impressed, if the fact that they issued no tribute records is any indication.[10] The company quietly released "Love My Stuff" some four months after Patton died, on September 1, 1934. The next and last Patton release, "Hang It On The Wall," appeared nearly a year after his death, on April 15, 1935. With that, ARC wrote Patton off. In 1938, ARC was acquired by Columbia Records. Sometime in the 1960s, a record collector consulted Columbia for file copies of Patton's unissued sides, only to learn that the metal parts had been destroyed.[11]

The opportunity from ARC to record showed that Patton's musical style was still viable commercially just before his death. Yet that style died with him. He was simply too skilled and too unorthodox to inspire anything more than crude and rote imitations. While some of Patton's ambitious innovations, like his use of two or three accompaniment lines for a single vocal phrase, should have had an impact on subsequent blues-playing, they did not.

In the end, Patton's musical imagination proved to be too much for the Delta, a confined area of both space and thought. He was remembered not as an accomplished musician, but rather more as a personal presence, a symbol of frivolity in an age of sober religion, and as an embodiment of all that was boisterous and excessive about the culture that supported him. To his associates, his baffling personality overshadowed over his performing skills, and the happy squabbler that was one aspect of the man dominated their other memories of him. The owner of the Cottondale plantation, George Kirkland, had hired Patton in 1921 because he naively mistook Patton's musical ability for good character, only to fire him in 1924 for bad behavior. In 1969, Patton's Cottondale friend Frank Howard remembered him as a person, but not as a musician. "Sometime I think of words I heard him say, and jokin,' carryin' on with folks," he said.

Patton had used his music to get women, whisky and food. But he had also understood, as did few of his peers, that the best way to amass a public following though music was to offer a new and distinctive sound, a seductive dance beat, and an captivating stage personality. To these ends, he succeeded superbly. To announce his presence on noisy streets and saloons, his bellowing voice and bouncing guitar were peerless. But at the end of his life, however, the invention of the jukebox was making Patton seem like a figure from a rapidly vanishing era.

During the early 1930s, the jukebox began displacing live entertainers in Mississippi cafes and roadhouses. Some of the singers on the jukeboxes crooned, not bellowed, and so by comparison they could often seem bland. The acoustic guitar was also becoming obsolete as an instrument for solo music, falling into disuse until the folk music revival in the late 1950s and early 1960s. The last Delta bluesman to become a hit-maker with an acoustic guitar, Arthur "Big Boy" Crudup (1905–1974), was in the 1940s an anomaly as a self-accompanied musician.

"By '40 they begin to use bands," H. C. Speir observed of Mississippi blues singers. "The guitar and a couple of trumpets . . . and that begin to take over; when they put these records on the jukebox, you understand . . . that would create more attention than it would when a Negro was playin' a regular old blues. The big fish was eatin' up the little fish."[12]

The little fish who swam against this musical tide still had the problem of contending with female fans and their jealous men. Now alone, Booker Miller continued to play the music he had learned from Patton. "I haven't found but one man I could play with, and that was Charlie," he was to say. "I like-ted Charlie's style, and that's the only way I played." At a cafe in Moss Island in 1937, he was performing Patton tunes and Delta standards. Returning from an intermission break, he found his seat occupied by a woman he didn't know.

"It ain't but one chair in the room, and she had the box across her lap," he recalled. "I didn't know her—I don't bother with women, you know, 'cause I don't know who their men are." Before Miller had figured out a way to deal with this situation, her escort appeared on the scene. "He said [to her], 'Get up!' say, 'You can't pick it; give it to him and let him pick it, and if he don't wanna pick it I'll throw it outdoors.'"

"I say, 'No, you better give me the box, 'cause if you throw this box outdoors, I'm afraid you're goin' out there behind it." And I bent my head down to tune a string, and that fella hit at my head with a dog-iron outta the fireplace.

"I didn't want him to swing a second: I hit him. Well, he staggered back and drawed back [the iron] and this buddy of mine took it out of his hand.

"It was many places like that. That's the reason I wouldn't want my kids to know nothin' [first hand] of that. I didn't want none of 'em to go out like that."

To avoid a violent death, and to set an example to his children, Miller ended his career at age twenty-seven, sold his guitar to David Edwards, and entered the Baptist ministry. The only regret he expressed for spending so much time with Charlie Patton came during a moment of reflection. "Sometimes when I get to thinkin' about it now," he admitted in 1967, "I think we done a little too much of some things and not enough of another. But that's all in life. You got to learn to live it, what to live it for." By Miller's standards, Patton lived a well-spent life, not only because he mastered what for Miller was an arduous undertaking, but because he enriched Miller's own life. Reverend Miller died of lung cancer in 1969. Of all of Patton's companions who were interviewed in the 1960s and 1970s, only Miller said, "I loved him, I really loved him."

Patton's last wife Bertha Lee eventually moved to Chicago, where she ran a small thrift shop. She told the researcher Bernard Klatzko[13] that she remembered Patton because he loved her. She also claimed that Patton died in her arms, saying that among his last words were "You're gonna have it tough from now on." She died in Chicago in 1975.

In 1940 Patton's brother "Son" left Dockery's for Gary, Indiana, where he died of a stroke at age sixty-three on September 3, 1957. Reputedly a bootlegger on Dockery, he might have been even more disreputable after moving north, for his widow didn't say on his death certificate what was his occupation.

Viola Cannon died in Greenville on August 8, 1969 at the age of eighty-two. The last of the Patton's siblings, she was buried in Dockery's True Light cemetery.

Willie Mae, or "China Lou," lived with her mother Millie Barnes until she married Johnnie Money sometime in the mid- or late-1930s. Although Patton's former wife Millie Barnes stated that their daughter Willie Mae died in 1950 at Mound Bayou under the name Willie Mae Money,[14] the state of Mississippi has no contemporary record of her death.

Patton's other daughter, Rosetta, lived her adulthood in Clarksdale, Mississippi.[15] For a time, she worked as a cook and cleaner for Guy Malvezzi. The nephew of her employer was James Mathus, later a rock musician as Jimbo Mathus. He came to realize who exactly she was, and she told him about her father, including that "he mostly sang gospel songs when he was around her. And you know how weird his voice is when he sings, she said when he talked he just talked like a normal guy." In 1997, she suffered a stroke, and to help raise money to pay her medical bills, Mathus recorded and released a CD titled *Songs for Rosetta*. That same year, she copyrighted her father's recorded songs.[16] She died in Clarksdale in 2014.

Of the two sons that Patton had with Sallie Hollins in 1916 and 1918, the younger son Will was interviewed by David Evans in 1989 in Cleveland, Mississippi.[17] Hollins had married Frank Williams, and her two sons adopted his surname. They then moved to Meltonia, where in 1933 they were visited by Patton. Williams told Evans that he was aware of Patton having moved another of his wives and 11 children to Sunflower Plantation; none of their names are yet known or recovered. Furthermore, from Patton's nephew Tom Cannon, Evans learned of a wife, Bertha [Burtha] Reed, whom Patton took in 1926, and they reportedly had two children.[18]

"Some summer day" in 1970,[19] an enfeebled dying man in his eighties was discharged from a hospital in Cleveland, Mississippi. During his youth, he had been a brakeman on the Pea Vine railroad that provided service to Dockery's, and he was a weekend frailer on guitar. Feeling his mortality, he decided to see the old plantation one last time. There he found, sitting on their porches, three or four tenant families who knew him by his nickname, "Hobo George."

Walking up to them, he began talking in garbled and feverish fashion about his old friend Charlie Patton, the one-time dandy of Dockery's and the demon of the Delta. The name was barely familiar to them as a relic from another time. Politely, they waited for him to change the subject. But either Hobo George knew no other subject to talk about, or he thought that no other subject would be interesting to Dockery's residents. Despite their blank stares, he continued droning on about Patton. Because of his deafness, it was impossible for them to tell him that they had no idea of who he was talking about and nor did they care. All they could do was wait for the old man to run out of steam and leave, which he eventually did, to their relief.

The only difference between a saint
and a sinner is that every saint has a past,
and every sinner has a future.

—OSCAR WILDE,
*A WOMAN OF NO IMPORTANCE*, ACT III

*Chapter 17*

# THE LEGACY OF CHARLIE PATTON (1970–2020)

Fifty years have passed since Hobo George's valedictory visit to Dockery Farms. Would anyone there now recognize the name of Charlie Patton?

The obvious answer is yes, due to the signs placed near Dockery's front entrance in 1999 by the Mississippi Department of Archives and History, and later by the Mississippi Blues Commission, both of which include Patton's name.[1] Whether Patton is truly still a household name on Dockery's depends on how aware the residents have been of his life and music. For the life, the very first book was a short monograph, *Charley Patton*, by the guitarist John Fahey that appeared in England in 1970.[2] The first edition of the present biography was published in 1988 through Rock Chapel Press, a subsidiary of Shanachie Records in New York.[3] A volume of proceedings of a conference in Belgium in 1984 to mark the 50th anniversary of Patton's death was issued in 1987 in Lieges, then reissued in 2018 by the University Press of Mississippi.[4] Reissues of Patton's recordings have been in print in one album or another since 1961, initially on vinyl LPs, then on compact discs, and most recently as digital downloads and through YouTube.[5]

But the answer could also be no, using the same evidence that was just cited for yes. The three books documenting and celebrating Patton were printed in small quantities; none of them were published by the commercial publishers who have placed their latest books for purchase in Mississippi retail stores.[6] Likewise for the record labels. Origin Jazz Library, Yazoo, Herwin, Document, Revenant, and Third Man have been small firms who have had as much—or more—sales through mail-order than through retail stores. When Patton's music is played on the radio, it is more likely on a show hosted by a blues fan on a community- or college broadcast station, than on a playlist on a commercial station. Furthermore, there have been no bio-pic films of Patton as the leading character for the movie theaters, or documentaries about his life and times for prime-time PBS shows such as *American Masters.*

Of the legendary Delta bluesmen, it has been Robert Johnson who has garnered the national record sales, blues fan attention, press ink, and movie deals lucrative enough to attract the noticc of today's Delta resident. The irony is that Johnson died just four years after Patton, having performed music for merely 9 years to Patton's 25. The factors that made Johnson's music more commercially viable than Patton's are small, beyond anyone's control, yet significant. For one, Johnson recorded solely for the American Recording Company (ARC), not for Paramount Records. ARC's recording conditions were hardly better than Paramount's, but it pressed its 78s on less noisy shellac and it later kept the metal stampers. In 1938, ARC was purchased by Columbia Records, which received and retained the metal parts including Johnson's; meanwhile, Wisconsin Chair was selling its Paramount metals for scrap. The result was that in 1961, for the first LP reissues of Johnson and Patton, Columbia presented clear-sounding Johnson performances newly processed from the ARC stampers, while Origin Jazz Library had to work mostly with Patton Paramount 78s that yielded a surface sizzle through which a listener had to strain to hear the music. This difference of surviving recording sources for Johnson and Patton, and the difference they make for listeners, has continued to the present day of compact discs and digital files.

Another difference has been the accessibility and availability of Johnson and Patton reissues. At the time Columbia acquired the Johnson masters in 1938, it was one of the three major recording firms in the U.S. (the other two being RCA Victor and Decca). Through the subsequent years and changes in firm ownership (now with Sony Music Group), Columbia was a leader in record retail, which meant that its two Johnson LP reissues *King of the Delta Blues Singers* vols. 1 and 2 were easily found, or ordered, in record shops.[7]

That has been not necessarily so with the small independent firms that have reissued Patton, as previously noted. That meant that Johnson's music in the early 1960s could be found and purchased in urban record stores, whether in New York by Greenwich Village folk singer-guitarists, or in London by white blues enthusiasts between club sets at the Marquee and the Crawdaddy. That John Fahey possessed several Patton 78s by 1960 and researched his music during the height of the folk-music boom says more about Fahey's singularity as a musician and his tenacity as a researcher than for Patton's appeal.

Availability of the music during the 1960s leads to a third difference, that of influence on mainstream rock and popular music. When both the American folkies and the British bluesologists turned to rock in the mid-1960s, they were more likely to cover Johnson's songs, or at least play in his style, than to perform Patton's songs in the manner analyzed in this book. As Speir put it in the previous chapter, "the big fish" that were eating up the little fish were the 1930s/1940s swing bands and the postwar rhythm and blues bands with trumpets (and implicitly a piano-bass-drum rhythm section). They evolved during the 1950s and 1960s into rock bands with electrically amplified instruments and a bass-drum rhythm section. Some of Robert Johnson's songs like "Ramblin' on My Mind" and "I Believe I'll Dust My Broom" were imitations of this emerging swing band sound,[8] which later were well suited for adaptations by rock bands in the 1960s. As a result, Johnson has since been regarded as a forerunner of rock.[9] Patton was at least 20 years older than Johnson; perhaps for that reason he has come to be thought of a pioneer of the blues, a characterization that the present book tries to deconstruct. Nonetheless, his brand of blues is detached enough from the elements of rock as to have little influence on the white bands of blues-rock of the 1960s and 1970s.[10]

Yet one more difference between Johnson and Patton are the places associated with each of them. For Patton, Dockery Farms is an undisputed historical site, still standing, and easily found on Route 8 just west of the intersection with Highway 49 West. On the other hand, Johnson's "Cross Road Blues" as a song has been transmuted into "crossroad" folklore. The tale is still told often, especially among white fans of blues and rock, that at a crossroad a bluesman would sell his soul to the devil in exchange for superlative performing skills on the guitar. Whenever and wherever the tale began—whether before World War II in African American communities, or after World War II among white rock fans—it has served as a convenient blues predecessor to the rock bands of the

1970s who were reputed to have practiced witchcraft (or who encouraged that reputation). By comparison, the stories of Patton getting evicted off Dockery Farms are bland. Travelers on their way to Dockery's have printed maps and roadside signs to guide them. If the Dockery's foreman on that spring day in 1929 scarcely knew what to make of H. C. Speir, residents of Clarksdale during the 1990s and 2000s were just as bemused by visitors asking for directions to Johnson's "crossroad."[11]

Charlie Patton has not been featured on the covers of mainstream magazines like *Time* or *Newsweek*. Occasionally he may be seen inside the covers of small magazines, despite—or perhaps because of—his times during the long-past pre-1942 era of Mississippi. A survey of the magazine articles about him since 1960[12] suggest a subtle turn of audience. Nearly all of the journals and magazines mentioning him have been written by white writers and editors for a mostly white readership. Aside from the Paramount advertisements in the *Chicago Defender* in 1929–1930, Patton's name has been unlikely to appear in an African American serial such as *Ebony* or *Jet*. Rather, during the 1960s, it cropped up in articles about Delta blues history written by and for white blues enthusiasts in *Blues Unlimited* (England) and in *78 Quarterly*, whether about Patton himself, or in association with Son House, who returned to public performance after his "rediscovery" in 1964. These early publications sketched the broad outlines of Patton's life and music, but the question of whether Patton was truly a national figure, or merely a regional favorite who happened to hit it lucky with "Pony Blues" in 1929, was unanswered. Peter Guralnick in his 1971 book *Feel Like Going Home*[13] conveyed this question as it stood then: "What is perhaps most surprising about Charley Patton is that he got a chance to record as much as he did. . . . That he [Patton] was the most powerful of performers is borne out by the fact that he still retains this ability to move us today, that there remains this intensity and force even across so wide a gulf of years and culture. When you listen to Charley Patton today [1971] you can't help but conjure up not only the commanding presence of the man himself but the strong suggestion of a world that has all but passed."

What that world was—not just the people, but also the places—was yet to be researched. When the number of periodicals for blues and American folk music declined in the 1970s and 1980s, the number of other publications reviewing books about or mentioning Patton[14] slowly began to expand: general music (*Notes: The Journal of the Music Library Association*), folk (*Sing Out,*

*Folk Roots, Ethnomusicology*), and jazz (*Downbeat, Coda*). When John Fahey and Dean Blackwood reissued Patton's recordings in a 7-CD box set, nearly all of these magazines reviewed it; even rock critic Dave Marsh mentioned it in *Playboy*.[15] Upon the blues revival of the 1990s, the leading blues magazine in America, *Living Blues*, began featuring more historical articles along with the current profiles, as did the early issues of *Blues Revue*. Meanwhile the British magazines *Blues and Rhythm* and *Juke Blues* came to the fore after *Blues Unlimited* published its last issue in 1988. Oddly, for a leading figure in the blues, a genre that is regarded by popular music critics as the roots of rock, Patton is rarely written about in the rock magazines. An exception is Robert Palmer's review of the Yazoo Records' Patton CD reissues in *Rolling Stone* in 1990,[16] notable because of Palmer's standing as a leading critic of rock and for his chapter on Patton in his 1984 book *Deep Blues*.

But there have been new perspectives on Patton, his blues, and his times to be found in other magazines. The academic approach has been rather in the folklore manner in articles and books by Harry Oster, William Ferris, David Evans, and their students, which have overlapped only slightly with the history pieces in the magazines mentioned previously. A literary approach has lately been taken for the blues in general for the journal *Southern Cultures* (University of North Carolina Press) and the book series *Southern Literary Studies* (Louisiana State University). For many years, the value of Patton's rare discs was in terms not of dollars, but of corresponding rare records in trade (as seen in *78 Quarterly*, especially its "Rare Records" column). When in the 1990s the public auction and sale of rare blues 78s were taking place, the collector's magazine *Goldmine* took notice, especially for Patton discs.[17] Most notably, perhaps for future trends to be seen later, is the "hands-on" approach in the guitar magazines, especially in *Guitar Player* in the 1980s and 1990s by Jas Obrecht and, a little later, Dave Rubin. A more decidedly acoustic approach, if not a purist one, may be read in the recent issues of *Acoustic Guitar* magazine, perhaps suggesting a return for Patton's reputation from rock to the roots, whatever they were.

Then again, would anyone at Dockery's would want to recognize the name of Charlie Patton? Is Patton respectable? Before answering those two questions, we should ask who is there now at Dockery's.

The farm's subsequent history has been researched by James W. Swinnich, whose information is the basis of the next few paragraphs.[18] Mechanization of cotton picking and other field tasks led to a drop in demand for farm labor during and after World War II. From 1940 to 1980, the work force in Sunflower County (containing Dockery and Cleveland) dropped by half, from 43,477 workers to 21, 591).[19] Joe Rice Dockery tried diversifying his crops; a September 27,1962 article in the *Enterprise-Tocsin* (Indianola) newspaper depicted him trying to grow coastal Bermuda grass (80 acres at that time of writing, but hoping to expand to 1000 acres) and 506 head of cattle. The remaining labor needed for cotton through the 1960s was retained on sharecropping terms, if not under the same work conditions 30 years before. In November 1980, the US Post Office at Dockery's was closed; mail was then forwarded to Cleveland. The general merchandise store, nearly 70 years standing, burned down on April 19, 1976.[20]

When Dockery Farms began to be mentioned with Charlie Patton in articles and LP notes as early as 1964, Joe Rice Dockery and his wife Keith Somerville Dockery began receiving letters of inquiry from early white blues fans. They hosted interview visits with Gayle Dean Wardlow and Stephen Calt in 1970, and with Robert Palmer in 1979, among other researchers. Keith Dockery to Palmer admitted that "None of us really gave much thought to this blues thing until a few years ago. . . . In other words, we never heard these people sing. We were never the type of plantation owners who invited their help to come in and sing for parties. I wish we had realized that these people were so important."[21]

Joe Rice Dockery died on July 2, 1982 at the Baptist Memorial Hospital in Memphis, Tennessee; his body was cremated, and his ashes were spread at Dockery Farms. For the next twelve years, his widow supervised the crops for cotton, rice and soybeans. In 1985, she married George Hite McLean, continuing to live at Dockery's.[22] On April 23, 2006, at age 91, she passed away in Cleveland.[23] By long then, no farming families remained at Dockery's.

Meanwhile, a new and curious trend of blues tourism began to emerge in Mississippi.[24] From the late 1950s through the late 1970s, there were a few visitors to Mississippi, not so much tourists as "drifters," as blues tourism historian Stephen A. King terms them. Just about all of them were in their 20s or 30s, white, and male. Some were looking for the men who made the music, such as Tom Hoskins for John Hurt in 1963, Dick Waterman, Nick Perls and Phil Spiro for Son House in 1964, and John Fahey, Mike Stewart and Bill Barth for Skip James also in 1964.[25] Others were conducting interviews and making field tapes of performances in African American cultures, such as Paul Oliver, David Evans and William Ferris. Some of them were viewed with distrust by white Mississippians as "foreign agents"—just as the Dockery's foreman viewed Speir or any other white visitor to the farm—who were there not for the music, but for labor, the Communist Party, or desegregation.[26]

In 1978, the Mississippi Delta Blues Festival was held for the first time by the Mississippi Action for Community Education (MACE) at a site near Greenville. Also that same year, Bentonia hosted a blues festival and, in 1980, Rust College of Holly Springs began an annual blues festival through the early 1990s. Of these early festivals, the Mississippi Delta Blues Festival (later the Mississippi Delta Blues and Heritage Festival) has survived to become one of today's major blues festivals, along with the Sunflower River Blues Festival in Clarksdale (established 1988) and the King Biscuit Blues Festival across the Mississippi River in Helena, Arkansas.[27] Research institutions for the study of the blues were established, especially the Delta Blues Museum in Clarksdale in 1979, and the Blues Archive at the University of Mississippi in 1984. These festivals and collections became destinations for a new kind of blues visitor to Mississippi, namely the blues tourist,[28] for whom the classic blues was the 1930s recordings by Robert Johnson that were reissued on compact discs in 1990. For these tourists, Johnson and the Mississippi Delta blues are the roots of rock music, and the roots of the blues are somewhere in the Mississippi Delta. They have come in increasing numbers to see for themselves what Alan Lomax titled his book *The Land Where the Blues Began*.[29] This romantic notion is at odds with what the authors of this book argued in chapter 3, that the blues came to the plantations from the barrelhouses, in turn from the roads, rivers and by-ways from outside the state. Even so, it is the romantic notions, not always the researched truth, that sings the sirens' calls.

In Swinnich's estimation, it was with Keith Dockery McLean's efforts in the 1990s and 2000s that the claim that Dockery Farms was "the birthplace of the blues came into focus."[30] During the late 1990s, a proposal to widen Route 8 on its northern side (it runs east-west) threatened to remove the surviving buildings, including the main barn displaying Dockery Farms and the names of Will Dockery and Joe Rice Dockery. If McLean hadn't realized during the 1970s the relevance of the blues to her farm, at the end of the 1990s she was beginning to make others realize that for themselves. Whether during the meantime she had recognized the treasure of the blues, or she recognized the usefulness of blues history towards saving the farm buildings, or both, is open to question. Either way, in 2000 she succeeded with the help of William Lester to lead the Department of Transportation to decide to widen Route 8 on the south side, away from the farm buildings.

In 2004, the Dockery Farms Foundation was created, to which the parent Dockery Farms LLC transferred the eight farm buildings and six acres of land. Since then, Dockery's has been maintained as a farm museum and destination of blues fans.[31] It was added to the National Register of Historic Places in 2006, and declared by the Mississippi Department of Archives and History as a "Mississippi Landmark" in 2017, a designation that "offers the fullest protection against changes that might alter a property's historic character."[32] If the residents of Dockery's in 1970 were puzzled by the mention of Charlie Patton's name, the present-day non-resident guides of the farm museum recognize it, respect it, and celebrate it.

In his lyrics, Patton mentioned Dockery Farms and its managers, and about two dozen additional place names, including 17 municipalities, three counties, three railroads and three rivers.[33] Some of them may be visited today, not just Dockery, but also the state capital Jackson, Vicksburg, Natchez, Greenville, Clarksdale and Belzoni; Parchman Penitentiary, with its signs forbidding drivers not to stop, is best viewed while passing by on Highway 49 West. But other places may be forgotten were it not for Patton, such as Green River, Joe Kirby plantation, and Lula. If Patton's musical legacy is faintly felt due to the "big fish" changes in blues and American music that H. C. Speir had described, his other legacy, the geographical legacy, endures for today's blues visitors to visit. If for no other reason than Patton's mentions, they may drive to and discover these places for themselves, if to the occasional amazement of local onlookers.

One of the first people to follow that Patton legacy—not as a drifter, or as a tourist—was Gayle Dean Wardlow for what was to become the research basis for this book. Born in Texas, he was raised and educated in Meridian, Mississippi. In 1962 he was living in Jackson, where he began acquiring and trading for 78-rpm records.[34] Seeking Patton 78s, he had to travel to the neighborhoods where older African American lived and kept their old records, as no more unsold store stock was available. Coincidentally, he found his first two Patton records in the musician's birth town, Edwards, "Pony Blues" backed with "Banty Rooster Blues," and the two-part "High Water Everywhere." A little later, he began working as a sports reporter for the newspapers in Jackson and Meridian. Volunteering to cover the out-of-town games for local high school football teams, Wardlow often arrived early to each town, going to the African American neighborhoods first, knocking on doors for "old Victrola records" and for conversation towards research leads. A few rarities turned up where Patton or his recording associates lived, such as a copy of the Delta Big Four's "I Know My Time Ain't Long" in their hometown of Lula. For other discs, Wardlow's travels had to proceed beyond Jackson and the Delta, going to Port Gibson in south Mississippi, and across the Mississippi River to Rayville (which Patton mentions in "Stone Pony Blues") and the Louisiana Delta.

By 1970, the Patton generation of Delta residents had moved or died. To find more of the Patton records listed by John Godrich and Robert M. W. Dixon in the 1968 (2nd) edition of their discography *Blues Records 1902–1942*,[35] Wardlow had to trade with collectors in other states. North Carolina was an obvious area, where the blues record customers in the early 1930s had jobs in the apple orchards and tobacco fields. But he also traded with private collectors around the country in Kentucky, Georgia, Missouri, Texas, Virginia, and New Jersey. The crowning trade was in the late 1980s when he acquired Patton's "Some Summer Day," which had not yet been reissued on LP or the emerging compact disc. That item was held by John Steiner, who in the 1940s purchased the remaining assets of Paramount Records, and since then was seeking to add to the Paramount properties.

All the while, Wardlow was finding people. His first finds were in Jackson, meeting Tommy Johnson's surviving associate Ishman Bracey and the "talent broker" H. C. Speir. In 1963, he hosted Bernard Klatzko, an accountant and early collector of Patton records, on a research trip to Dockery Farms and the Delta. There they met and interviewed Patton's sister Viola Cannon and his early wife Mille Barnes Toy, among others.[36] In 1967–1968, Wardlow took the roads that Patton less traveled on—and did not sing about on records—towards Cottondale to meet his 1920s neighbor Frank Howard, and to Sumner for Hayes McMullan. That aging guitarist introduced Wardlow to Willie and Elizabeth Moore, who provided valuable information about Patton's times. In 1968, Wardlow met and interviewed Patton's protégé Booker Miller several times before his death from cancer. An important tour of meetings and interviews was taken in 1970 when Wardlow's co-author Stephen Calt came to Mississippi; together they interviewed the landowners Joe Rice Dockery and

Matt Dakin, the Dockery's cook Sara Garrett, and Henry Sims' sisters Nellie Hester and Roberta Jameson.[37]

By crisscrossing Mississippi to locations mentioned by Patton on records, even during the most dangerous times of racial unrest and violence in the 1960s, Wardlow found places where he would have never thought of going to as a newspaper reporter. As a guide for his colleagues including Bernard Klatzko, Nick Perls and Stephen Calt, he showed where memories of Patton were still abiding.

During Patton's lifetime, the Mississippi Delta was dominated by landowners who intended to make money. Everything and everyone—land, equipment, men, and mules, in that order of priority—were systematically exploited to that purpose. If Will Dockery is granted his wish to see Sunflower County now, he will see that the vast expanses of his fields are unchanged. But upon learning from the current employees there that the best-known resident of Dockery Farms is not him or a descendant, but a black man, he may become puzzled. That the man did not work at farming, he may show some dismay: worn lands, broken equipment, old mules and unproductive men were undesirable in a financial enterprise, and they were invariably cast off. That the man is Charlie Patton may displease him, for Dockery evicted him twice off his farms. That the names of Dockery, Joe Kirby and Cottondale's George Kirkland are inscribed not in stone, but in this biography about a black man who merely sang the blues, may be the supreme insult to their earthly power and financial fortunes.

Charlie Patton lived free of these men by singing the blues. He may not be surprised to hear that his records are still played. But he may be amazed to learn that people today come to Mississippi to visit not their family and friends, but to see *his* places: Jackson "on a high hill," Natchez "just below," Highway 61 north, Lula, Clarksdale, Highway 49 West south, Dockery's, Holly Ridge.

# *Discography*

There is much to be much to be enjoyed in the records that Charlie Patton made. There is also a great deal to be learned from them. Patton was a performer, not a composer notating music on paper. Furthermore, he made his records before the development of magnetic tape. Therefore, the shellac 78-rpm records are the primary sources of the reissues on vinyl LPs, compact discs, and digital files. The present appendix is in five sections:

Patton's 78-rpm releases
Patton as sideman on other 78s
CD reissues of Patton
LP reissues of Patton
Additional recordings

The ideal copies are the 78-rpm discs whose stampers are negative derivations of the direct-to-disc wax masters cut during Patton's recording sessions. But, as related in the biography, the stampers were later scrapped by the recording companies, who also didn't keep clean copies of the pressed 78s on file. The copies from which all transfers for LP and CD have made were, until they were acquired in the 1960s by record collectors, were played and replayed—sometimes nearly to the other side of the disc—by the people who bought the records. They didn't have audiophile equipment, but rather they often could afford only hand-wound gramophones, with heavy tonearms that were fitted at various times with sharp needles, or worn needles, and occasionally with a rock or some other weight on the tonearm to ensure that the already worn record played all the way through. That is how many of the copies of Patton's 78s survived—often barely—in the battered conditions in which they are found today.

## PATTON'S 78s

Here are Patton's 78s, in the order they were released by Paramount and ARC (on its Vocalion subsidiary), in matrix number order, with dates of public release included:

1. Paramount 12792. Charley Patton. A: "Pony Blues" [15216]/B: "Banty Rooster Blues" [15217]. July 1929.
2. Paramount 12799. Elder J. J. Hadley [Charlie Patton]. A: "Prayer of Death—Part I" [15225]/B: "Prayer of Death—Part II" [15225-A]. August 1929.
3. Paramount 12805. The Masked Marvel [Charlie Patton]. A: "Screamin' and Hollerin' the Blues" [15214]/B: "Mississippi Bo Weavil Blues" [15211]. September 1929.
4. Paramount 12854. Charley Patton. A: "Down The Dirt Road Blues" [15215]/B: "It Won't Be Long" [15220]. November 1929.
5. Paramount 12969. Charley Patton. A: "Shake It and Break It But (Don't Let It Fall Mama)" [15224]/B: "A Spoonful Blues" [15223]. January 1930.
6. Paramount 12877. Charley Patton. A: "Pea Vine Blues" [15221A]/B: "Tom Rushen Blues" [15222A]. February 1930.
7. Paramount 12883. Charley Patton. A: "Lord I'm Discouraged" [15226]/B: "I'm Goin' Home" [15227]. March 1930.
8. Paramount 12909. Charley Patton. A: "High Water Everywhere—Part I" [L-59–1]/B: "High Water Everywhere—Part II" [L-60–2]. April 1930.
9. Paramount 12924. Charley Patton. A: "Rattlesnake Blues" [L-63–2]/B: "Running Wild Blues" [L-64–1]. May 1930.
10. Paramount 12943. Charley Patton. A: "Mean Black Cat Blues" [L-41–1]/B: "Magnolia Blues" [L-48–1]. June 1930.
11. Paramount 12953. Charley Patton. A: "Mean Black Moan" [L-77–1]/B: "Heart Like Railroad Steel" [L-50–1]. July 1930.
12. Paramount 12972. Charley Patton. A: "Green River Blues" [L-44–3]/B: "Elder Greene Blues" [L-38–1]. [September 1930.]
13. Paramount 12986. Charley Patton. A: "Jesue Is A Dying-Bed Maker" [L-61–1]/B: "I Shall Not Be Moved" [L-62–2]. October 1930.
14. Paramount 12998. Charley Patton. A: "Hammer Blues" [L-47–2]/B: "When Your Ways Gets Dark" [L-49–1]. [November/December 1930.]
15. Paramount 13014. Charley Patton. A: "Moon Going Down" [L-423–1]/B: "Going To Move To Alabama" [L-37–1]. [January/February 1931.]
16. Paramount 13031. Charley Patton. A: "Some Happy Day" [L-51–1]/B: "You Gone Need Somebody When You Die" [L-52–1]. [February/March 1931.]
17. Paramount 13040. Charley Patton. A: "Circle Round The Moon" [L-39–1]/B: "Devil Sent The Rain" [L-40–1]. [March/April 1931.]

18. Paramount 13070. Charley Patton. A: "Bird Nest Bound" [L-433–1]/B: "Dry Well Blues" [L-429–2]. [June 1931.]
19. Paramount 13080. Charley Patton. A: "Jim Lee Blues—Part I" [L-57–2]/B: "Some Summer Day" [L-431–1]. [June/July 1931.]
20. Paramount 13110. Charley Patton. A: "Frankie and Albert" [L-42–1]/B: "Some of These Days" [L-43–2]. [January 1932.]
21. Paramount 13133. Charley Patton. A: "Jim Lee Blues—Part II" [L-58–1]/B: "Joe Kirby Blues" [L-67–2]. [March 1932.]
22. Vocalion 02651. Charlie Patton. A: "Poor Me" [14757–1]/B: "34 Blues" [14739–1]. [March 1934.]
23. Vocalion 02680. Charlie Patton. "High Sheriff Blues" [14725–2]/B: "Stone Pony Blues" [14727–1]. [April 1934.]
24. Vocalion 02782. Charlie Patton. "Jersey Bull Blues" [14723–1]/B: "Love My Stuff" [14746–1]. [September 1934.]
25. Vocalion 02904. Patton and Lee. "Oh Death" [14749–3]/"Troubled 'Bout My Mother" [14752–1]. [March 1935.]
26. Vocalion 02931. Charlie Patton. "Hang It On The Wall" [14758–1]/"Revenue Man Blues" [14747]. [April 1935.]

There are also these alternate takes that were recovered from unique test pressings:

Charlie Patton, "Elder Greene Blues" [L-38–2]
Charlie Patton, "Some These Days I'll Be Gone" [L-43–1]
Charlie Patton, "Hammer [Hammock] Blues" [L-47–1]
Charlie Patton, "I Shall Not Be Moved" [L-62–1]

## PATTON AS SIDEMAN ON OTHER 78s

Sometimes taken for granted are the records that Patton participated in as a sideman. As noted in the biography, Patton lent his support to Henry Sims, Louise Johnson, and Bertha Lee because he had brought each of them with him to the sessions. As for the sides by Buddy Boy Hawkins and Edith North Johnson, he happened to be in the studio, waiting for his next turn to record. Although his contributions are not intrusive, they are identifiable to him, and for that reason, it is always delightful to recognize him.

1. Paramount 12814. Buddy Boy Hawkins. A: "Snatch It and Grab It" [15218]/B: "A Rag Blues" [15212]. October 1929. Patton contributes vocal interjections on "Snatch It and Grab It."

2. Paramount 12912. Henry Sims. A: "Farrell Blues" [L-45–1]/"Come Back Corrina" [L-45–2]. April 1930. Patton provides guitar accompaniment on both sides.
3. Paramount 12939. Edith North Johnson. A: "Eight Hour Woman" [L-74–2]/B: "That's My Man" [L-73–2, -3]. June 1930. Patton provides guitar accompaniment on "That's My Man."
4. Paramount 12940. Henry Sims. A: "Tell Me Man Blues" [L-65–1]/"Be True Be True Blues" [L-66–2]. June 1930. Patton provides guitar accompaniment on both sides.
5. Paramount 12992. Louise Johnson. A: "All Night Long Blues" [L-398–1]/B: "Long Ways From Home" [L-399–2]. [November 1930.] Patton contributes vocal interjections on both sides with Son House and Willie Brown.
6. Surviving alternate take of Louise Johnson. "All Night Long Blues" [L-398–2]. Patton adds interjections on this side with House and Brown.
7. Vocalion 02650. Bertha Lee. "Yellow Bee" [14735–2]/"Mind Reader Blues" [14736–1]. [March 1934.] Patton provides guitar accompaniment on both sides.

## COMPACT DISC ISSUES OF PATTON

Presentations of Patton's 78s on compact discs vary widely. Some CDs have his complete recordings, others have selections. Some may offer audio transfers with a minimum of shellac surface noise but with the high tones compromised, others may have the appropriate piercing high tones (especially for Patton's guitar work) but with a maximum of surface noise. The keys in which individual performances play back vary among the CDs. Many listeners may be happy enough with one or two CDs of Patton's music, but those who can't get enough may (or should) have a few different transfers.

Revenant Records' 2001 7-CD box set *Screamin' and Hollerin' the Blues: The Worlds of Charley Patton* (Revenant 212) is the king of Patton collections. Envisioned and funded by John Fahey, and executed by Dean Blackwood, *Screamin' and Hollerin'* provides Patton's complete recording sessions, not only the sides that he performed as featured artist or as sideman, but also those that were recorded by other artists while he was taking breaks. So the set also includes the 1929 sides by Buddy Boy Hawkins, the 1930 sides featuring Son Sims and Edith North Johnson, and the complete Grafton road trip recordings by Louise Johnson and Willie Brown with the 7 then-known sides by Son House (for the two others by House, see in the Yazoo section below). Also included are the spring 1930 recordings by the Delta Big Four and H. C. Speir. Everything that is referred to in chapters 10–15 of this book may be found here. Additional recordings by Patton's cronies and protégés round out the audio selections, including the first publication of excerpts of Booker Miller's conversations with Gayle Wardlow. Enhancing the set to research value are the printed materials. Some are reprints of classic but long-unavailable studies, such as Bernard Klatzko's 1964 essay (with Wardlow's assistance) for Origin Jazz Library's second Patton LP reissue (see LP section below), Fahey's 1970 Studio Vista book *Charley Patton*, and David Evans' 1988 "Conscience of the Delta" study. Others were new studies by Fahey (among his very last writings before his 2001 death), Richard Spottswood and Edward Komara. Spottswood also transcribed new lyrics transcriptions from all of the music on the set, and Komara provided a thematic catalogue of the recording sessions and a bibliography. As a bonus, a sticker set of the labels of all of Patton's Paramount and Vocalion 78-rpm releases are bound in. The run of 10,000 copies sold out within 5 years. The original purchase price was $150, so readers considering buying used copies should take price inflation and collector demand into account. Many libraries did purchase this set, so readers aware of a copy accessible near them should consult it. Christopher King made all new transfers from 78-rpm copies, including many provided by Wardlow. His results are different from those issued previously by Yazoo, Document, and the Buck Foundation, and for that reason they may not be to the tastes of casual listeners. Still, while preparing the music examples for this revised edition, I found that many characteristics described in the text by Calt and Wardlow are most noticeable in King's transfers.

Many serious Patton listeners will have the Shanachie/Yazoo CDs as their preferred reissues. Since Shanachie owns the 78-rpm disc collections of legendary Patton collectors Nick Perls and Bernard Klatzko, its transfers of Patton are made mostly, if not only, from the excellent specimens that it holds. Its two current reissues are *The Best of Charlie Patton* (Yazoo 2069, released 2003) and Patton, *Primeval Blues, Rags and Gospel Songs* (Yazoo 2074, released 2005). They replace Yazoo's previous Patton reissues, Charlie Patton, *King of the Delta Blues: The Music of Charlie Patton* (Yazoo 2001, 1991), and Charlie Patton, *Founder of the Delta Blues 1929–34* (Yazoo 2010, 1995), which are still worth having if one finds them by chance.

Document's three-volume Patton series (Charlie Patton, *Complete Recorded Works in Chronological Order* volumes 1–3, Document DOCD 5009, 5010, and 5011, 1990) was the first presentation of Patton's records in chronological order. In addition to his featured sides, the series also included the ones by Son Sims and Bertha Lee. Document's founder Johnny Parth, working in Vienna, Austria, whose copyright laws at the time were considerably different from American ones, used as his audio sources many of the reissues from the LP era (1960–1988, see below). Yet to his credit, in this series, he did present the first issues anywhere of "Jim Lee Blues Part I" and "Some Summer Day," receiving both tracks from Gayle Wardlow, who had recently located and acquired their source 78, Paramount 13080. The finest presentation of Parth's edition is not on the Document CDs, but rather on the Japanese set that Pea-Vine issued by arrangement with Document, because of the notes and lyric transcriptions by Jim O'Neal (Pea Vine PCD-2255/6/7, Charley Patton, *The Complete Recorded Works,* 3 CD set, 1993).

The least known CD reissue of Patton, but one worth seeking out, is *The Voice of the Delta: The Complete Paramount Recordings of Charley Patton* (Black Swan BSCD 21/22, 1994, 2 CDs). Since 1970, the George H. Buck Foundation has owned the remaining assets of Paramount Records, which Buck purchased from John Steiner, who in turn had acquired from the Wisconsin Chair Company in 1948. The Buck Foundation is a non-profit organization that offers reissues of classic jazz and blues, with discounts to purchasers who register as members for five dollars. *The Voice of the Delta* covers only Patton's 1929–1930 Paramount masters as featured artist. While the producers of this set had to rely on many of the same rare sources as other CD reissuers, they distinguish their efforts by pitching many of their sides in different keys than those adopted on Yazoo and Document. As of this writing (2022), this 2-CD set is still available from the Foundation's Jazzology website (http://www.jazzology.com).

## LP REISSUES OF PATTON

What made the CD reissues possible, and arguably what led to the rediscovery of Patton as a historical figure in the 1960s, were the vinyl LP issues from 1961 through 1988. All of them were labors of love by the collectors who recovered the 78-rpm discs mostly from home collections that were stashed under beds and in closets, and sometimes from unsold store stocks and through trades from jazz record collectors. Aside from pressing materials and playing duration, what made the LP reissues different from the 78s was that they were marketed not to African Americans, but to a small segment of the young white Americans who were discovering acoustic guitar blues during the 1959–1965 folk music revival. The pressings were low-budget, the printing of text and notes were minimal, and the transfers were crude. But this was how the first two generations of white record collectors first heard Patton's music. While these record albums cannot match the transfers and documentation of the Revenant box and the Yazoo CD transfers, they are still highly desired collector's items. (For a visual discography on the web, see Stefan Wirz, "Charley Patton," http://www.wirz.de/music/pattofrm.htm, accessed 13 May 2022.)

It was Pete Whelan and Bill Givens who compiled the first reissues of Patton's music in 1961. (Eight years previously, Harry Smith had included "Mississippi BoWeavil Blues" on the first volume of the *Anthology of American Folk Music*, but for credit he gave not Patton's name but the ascription on the original Paramount 12805 release label, The Masked Marvel.) On five LPs issued from 1961 through 1966, Whelan and Givens issued approximately half of the Patton legacy. The bulk of their Patton efforts were on their first release, Origin Jazz Library OJL-1 *The Immortal Charlie Patton* (1961), and its followup OJL-7 *The Immortal Charlie Patton* vol. 2 (1964), the latter including the pioneering biography and research account by Bernard Klatzko with Gayle Wardlow. Other issues with Patton tracks were OJL-2 *Really! The Country Blues* (1962), OJL-11 *Mississippi Blues no. 2: The Delta, 1929–32* (1965), OJL-12 and –13 *In the Spirit* vols. 1 and 2 (1966). Whelan left the label in 1966 to begin the journal *78 Quarterly*, but Givens continued with several more issues, among them OJL-17 *Mississippi Blues vol. 3: The Transition 1926–1936* that had the first reissue of Bertha Lee's "Mind Reader Blues."

Picking up where Givens and Whelan left off was Nick Perls, the son of art dealers who was rapidly acquiring a top collection of pre-1942 blues on 78s. In 1968, he founded Belzona Records, then soon renamed it Yazoo Records. Three of the LP reissues he released before his 1986 death are of particular interest to Patton collectors on LP. Belzona L-1001 (later pressings are as Yazoo L-1001) *Mississippi Blues 1927–1941* reissued "Pea Vine Blues," "Mean Black Moan," "Hang It On The Wall" and Henry Sims' "Be True Be True Blues," and Yazoo L-1009 (1968) *Mississippi Moaners 1927–1942* gave "Devil Sent The Rain Blues." But the most important Patton package from Yazoo was L-1020,

*Founder of the Delta Blues*, a 2-LP set that kept in circulation those performances that were previously issued on Origin Jazz Library. What helped this 1970 set supersede the OJL albums was the attached gatefold booklet with notes and lyric transcripts by Stephen Calt, Jerry Epstein, John Fahey, Don Kent, Nick Perls, Michael Stewart and Alan Wilson. Vinyl collectors should be aware that repressings of this double album in the 1980s and 2011 lack the interior booklet. One of Perls' unreleased projects, but mentioned in the 1988 edition of this book, was a Patton anthology to have been titled *The Last Legacy* (Yazoo 1075), to have contained of recently discovered sources including three outtakes that Perls had lately purchased from collector Michael Kirsling.

Two minor LPs issued by leading Patton experts of the 1970s are worth picking up if they are seen in used vinyl bins. One is *Mississippi Bottom Blues* issued around 1972 on the Mamlish (S-3802) label owned by the late Don Kent, containing Patton's "Jersey Bull Blues" and "Love My Stuff." Kent would later assist Richard Nevins on the Yazoo/Shanachie CD releases in the 1990s. The other was *Patton, Sims, and Bertha Lee* on Herwin 213 in 1977. The LP incarnation of Herwin was owned by Bernard Klatzko, whose other issues included the complete reissues of Henry Thomas (with notes by Mack McCormick) and Gus Cannon (with notes by Bengt Olsson). *Patton, Sims, and Bertha Lee* was curated by Klatzko with notes written by Don Kent, reissuing for the first time on LP four of the rarest Patton Paramounts ("Mean Black Cat," "Farrell Blues," "Magnolia Blues," "Jim Lee Blues II," and "Joe Kirby"), with Patton's sideman recordings to Henry Sims and Bertha Lee.

European fans will know the name of Johnny Parth, who ran the Roots reissue label in the 1960s and 1970s, collaborated with the Wolf label in the 1980s, and founded and operated Document Records from the 1980s until his sale to Gary Atkinson in the 2000s. The two volumes of *Mississippi Blues* (Roots RL-302 and -303, both 1967) gave a total of 8 Patton sides, half of them featuring his sacred material. Charley Patton, *1929–34: The Remaining Titles* (Wolf WSE 103, 1982) had the first reissue anywhere of "Circle Round The Moon." Among his more important Document LPs was *Delta Blues* vol.1 (Document DLP 532, 1988), for which Parth somehow acquired transfers of the three Patton outtakes intended for Yazoo's unreleased *Last Legacy* LP and additional dubs from the discs in Kirsling's Paramount find.

Collectors seeking vinyl issues of all of Patton's music should note three of his performances ("Jim Lee Blues I," "Some Summer Day" and "I Shall Not

Be Moved" take 1) never appeared on LPs before 1990, their first issues being in the Document DOCD 5000 CD series (specifically, DOCD 5009–5011, Charlie Patton, *Complete Recorded Works in Chronological Order*, and Document DOCD 5276 *Too Late Too Late Blues vol. 3*). In order to have absolutely everything on vinyl, one should purchase Third Man Records' pressings by arrangement with Document Records (Charlie Patton, *Complete Recorded Works in Chronological Order*, Third Man Records TMR 154, 172, 180 and 189), or in Europe, Monk Records's box *Charley Patton: You're Gonna Need Somebody When You Die—The Recorded Works* (Monk MK300QLP; individual LPs available on serial numbers Monk 304, 307, 308, and 311), which seem to also make up of Document's sources.

## ADDITIONAL RECORDINGS

As told in the biography, Patton was influential to other musicians, and he was influenced in return. A selection of records by his contemporaries and protégés is worth hearing. Anyone who owns or has access to the Revenant Patton box will find many of the recordings mentioned in this biography, especially on the sixth disc that is titled "Charley's Orbit." A smaller selection based on Patton's closest colleagues including Son House, Willie Brown, Kid Bailey, and Bertha Lee is *Masters of the Delta Blues: The Friends of Charlie Patton* (Yazoo CD 2002, 1991).

All of the surviving recordings by pre-1942 blues artists mentioned in this section of the discography may be found in Document Records' *Complete Recordings in Chronological Order* series of reissues. The compact discs are still in print, but students and faculty at colleges and universities may have convenient streaming access to the Document collection via the Alexander Street Press service American Song. For many of the artists discussed immediately below, their only reissue may be in the Document series, and the respective issues will be indicated with the serial numbers (prefixed with either DOCD or BDCD).

Of all of Patton's colleagues, **Son House** (1902–1988) was the one who was accorded by most 1960s listeners the status of elder statesman. All but two of his 1930 Paramount recordings may easily be obtained as part of the Revenant Patton box, Yazoo's *Masters of the Delta Blues*, or on Document's House CD (DOCD 5002), with the recently recovered Paramount disc 13096 ("Mississippi

County Farm Blues" backed with "Clarksdale Moan") easily available as part of Yazoo's 2006 anthology *The Stuff Dreams Are Made Of* (Yazoo YAZ CD 2202). Memories of House as a performer during the 1930s are of him performing with a group including Willie Brown. Among the most astounding discs, then, in the field recordings made by Alan Lomax in 1941 in Mississippi are those of House, Brown, Leroy Williams on harmonica, and Fiddlin' Joe Martin (playing mandolin, not fiddle) performing then-current (now historical) pre-war Delta blues. Those are available on CD with the 1942 solo sides by House for Lomax on the Biograph CD Son House, *Delta Blues: The Original Library of Congress Sessions From Field Recordings 1941–1942* (Biograph BCD 118, 1991). The recordings on Paramount and for Lomax were what spurred the location of House in Rochester NY by Dick Waterman, Nick Perls and Phil Spiro in June 1964. House and Waterman then embarked on a distinguished Indian-summer performing career that, for all intents and purposes, ended with his 1970 tour of England. Many recordings abound from House's rediscovery period, the most important of which are his 1965 Columbia Records LP *The Legendary Son House: Father of the Folk Blue*s (Columbia CL 2417; reissued on CD with additional takes as House, *Father of the Delta Blues: The Complete 1965 Sessions*, Columbia/Legacy C2K 48867, 2 CDs, 1992), and the 1965 Oberlin College concert (best available as part of *Son House Revisited*, initially on Varese Sarabande CD 061249 (2002) and recently on Fuel 2000 (2006). A complete visual discography is offered on the web by Stefan Wirz, "Son House: Discography," http://www.wirz.de/music//housefrm.htm, accessed 13 May 2022.

**Louise Johnson** and **Bertha Lee** made no more records after their sessions with Patton. All of Johnson's surviving sides including one alternate take are in the Revenant Patton box and also Document CD 5157. Bertha Lee's two featured Vocalion sides are most often found in the complete Patton reissues. **The Delta Big Four**'s lone session, their 1930 recordings, may be found in the Revenant Patton box and also Document CD 5538, although only the Revenant box will have the two spoken sides that Mississippi talent broker **H. C. Speir** recorded while the Delta Big Four were taking a session break. **Willie Brown** made several recordings with Lomax for the Library of Congress in 1941, most of them the previously mentioned performances with House, but also a solo performance of "Make Me A Pallet On The Floor" that was first issued on LPs, and later included in the Revenant Patton box (and also on a rather hard-to-find CD multiple-artist anthology *Mississippi Blues: Library of Congress Re-*

*cordings 1940–1942*, Travelin' Man TMCD07, 1996). **Henry Sims** also made recordings for Lomax, in 1941 and 1942 with his string band including Percy Thomas and a young Muddy Waters. Those performances are available complete on CD as Muddy Waters, *The Complete Plantation Recordings* (MCA/ Chess CHD9344, CD, 1993)

While the complete recordings of Tommy Johnson, Ishman Bracey, Kid Bailey, Mattie Delaney, Garfield Akers, Joe Callicott, Blind Joe Reynolds and Otto Virgial may be found in the Document reissue series, most of their sides may be heard in better transfers on other labels, especially on Yazoo. Those of **Kid Bailey**, and some of those by **Tommy Johnson** and **Ishman Bracey**, may be found on the Yazoo *Masters of the Delta Blues* CD mentioned previously regarding House. Among the CD reissues of Johnson and Bracey's 1928 Victor recordings is *Canned Heat Blues: Masters of the Delta Blues* (RCA / BMG CD 61047–2, 1992), which, although out of print, is cheap to purchase from used CD dealers. In recent years, a few more of Johnson's Paramount recordings have been found, filling in some discographical gaps; a complete reconstruction of the Grafton road trip taken in early 1930 by Johnson, Bracey, Charley Thomas and Kid Thomas can now, and should, be compiled into one reissue. Yazoo's *Mississippi Masters: Early American Blues Classics 1927–35* (Yazoo 2007) has excellent transfers of the two Brunswick performances by **Mattie Delaney**, and of the best sides made by **Garfield Akers** with **Joe Callicott**, **Otto Virgial**, and **Blind Joe Reynolds**.

As Patton's friends admitted in interviews during the 1960s, **W. C. Handy** was much more popular than Patton, even among Delta African Americans. A sample of his earliest band recordings (1917–1923) may be had on *W. C. Handy's Memphis Blues Band* (Memphis Archives, 1994). To today's blues ears, Handy's performances may seem much too slick and genteel for someone dubbed "The Father of the Blues," but that is the kind of music that was asked for by the Mississippians who avoided the barrelhouses and frolics where Patton played. Also in much mainstream demand was **Sophie Tucker**, whose earliest recordings including her 1911 rendition of "Some of These Days" are collected on Tucker, *Origins of the Red Hot Mama 1910–1922* (Archeophone 5010, 2009).

Musicians, especially men, from the rural South did not have opportunities to make records until 1925. Despite their belated arrivals to the recording studios, a few guitarists from Memphis and Mississippi managed to record some music that they had been playing since the 1910s, perhaps back to the 1900s. **Gus Cannon**'s "Poor Boy Long Ways From Home" is most easily available on the first of the two Document CDs of his complete early recordings (Document DOCD 5032–5033). **Furry Lewis's** "I Will Turn Your Money Green" is on the RCA/BMG *Canned Heat Blues* CD mentioned previously for Tommy Johnson and Ishman Bracey, but Document in recent years has improved the sound of its Lewis CD (Document DOCD 5004). The Lewis Black who recorded for Columbia Records in 1927 (Document DOCD 5169) may (or may not be) the same **Louie Black** who was part of the Earl Harris circle of musicians at Peerman Plantation, but either way, the crude accompaniment on the Black recordings give food for thought as to what was primitive if workaday guitar playing in the 1910s Delta. **Sam Collins** lived some distance south of Charlie Patton, living in a culture that seemed to be based more corn than cotton, but his recording of "Hesitation Blues" is a good indication of the impact that W. C. Handy's printed sheet-music blues had in Mississippi in the 1910s. The Document CD (DOCD 5034) has all of Collins' surviving sides, but the out-of-print Yazoo CD of selected sides (Crying Sam Collins, *Jail House Blues*, Yazoo CD 1079, 1990) is worth seeking for its improved transfers.

The first blues records were released to the public in 1920. The height of the initial commercial trends of blues women was attained with the first sessions for Bessie Smith and Ma Rainey. To have **Bessie Smith**'s performance of Spencer Williams' "Mountain Top Blues" that Patton reshaped into "Hammock [Hammer] Blues," one is going to have to resort to one of the volumes of her complete recordings, as it will be absent from any of the "Best of" collections. As the present owner of Smith's label Columbia, Sony/BMG's reissues should be given first consideration, whether the 1991–1996 five-volume *Complete Recordings* series (Columbia/Legacy C2K -47091, -47471, -47474, -52838, 57546), or the collected 2012 single-box *Complete Columbia Recordings* (Sony Music 88725403102). Collectors value more the Frog label reissues of Smith (8 volumes) for their superior transfers and playback sound; volume 3 (Frog DGF42) has "Mountain Top Blues." There are two reissues of **Ma Rainey**'s 1923–1928 Paramount recordings. Easier to obtain are the Document "Complete Recordings in Chronological Order" series (Document DOCD 5581, -2, -3, -4, 5186) and the JSP 5-CD box *Mother of the Blues* (JSP JSP7793, 2007). The Buck Foundation issued a Ma Rainey series, *The Paramounts Chronologically* (Black Swan BSCD 1 through 5), but as of this writing, only volumes 2 and 5 are available. Once male bluesmen made it to records in the mid-1920s, bits of their songs began turning up in Mississippi blues. **Papa Charlie Jackson**, as one of the first men, recorded several of the first renditions of widespread repertory (Document DOCD 5087, -88, -89), including "I'm Alabama Bound" and "All I Want Is A Spoonful." **Jim Jackson**, not of Kansas City but Hernando, Mississippi, scored a national, and influential, hit in 1927 with "Jim Jackson's Kansas City Blues" (which is much anthologized, but it may be found on the first disc of Document's 2-CD collected edition [DOCD 5114–5115]). All male stars in the blues, even Blind Blake, were outshone by **Blind Lemon Jefferson** of Texas (1893–1929), each of whose releases were sales events for Paramount Records. The main reissue is Document's four volumes (DOCD 5017–5020), although American readers may find it more convenient to purchase the JSP 4-CD box Blind Lemon Jefferson, *The Complete 94 Classic Sides Remastered* (JSP JSP7706, 2003). Jefferson's sudden death in Chicago at the end of 1929 was a blow to Paramount, who found itself with a small pile of unreleased masters from his last session. Once it issued them, it requested its other artists (like Son House) to make some tribute records. One of the best was Paramount 12945, which paired "Wasn't It Sad About Lemon" by **Washboard Walter and John Byrd** (found on *Rare Country Blues Vol 2 1929—1943* [Document DOCD 5641) with **Rev. Emmet Dickinson**'s "Death of Blind Lemon" (Document DOCD 5441, with Dickinson's 1931 sides on DOCD 5490).

There are some melodic similarities of Patton's "Banty Rooster Blues" with "Rollin' and Tumblin," whose early treatments on records were made by musicians active in west Tennessee north of Memphis. **Hambone Willie Newbern**'s "Roll and Tumble Blues" (1929, Okeh) is much anthologized, and its Document reissue may be found on the 3-CD compilation of songsters on records (Document DOCD 5678) *Never Let The Same Bee Sting You Twice*. **Sleepy John Estes** recorded the tune in 1929 to the title "The Girl I Love, She Got Long Curly Hair" (found on the first volume of Document's Estes reissue, DOCD 5015–5016). Assisting Estes on that performance was mandolinist **James "Yank" Rachell**, who five years later recorded in ARC's New York City studio a week after the Pattons; that surviving session may be heard on the Wolf label's first volume of Rachell's "complete recorded works" (Wolf WBCD-006, -007, now out of print).

**Walter Rhodes**' 1927 go at "Banty Rooster Blues," retitled by Columbia Records as "The Crowing Rooster," may be heard on Revenant's Patton box or on Document's *Memphis Blues vol.* 2 (1927–1938) (Document DOCD 5159), the latter also containing **Pearl Dickson**'s sides from the same Memphis recording visit. The brothers Maylon Harney and **Richard "Hacksaw" Harney** were credited as "Pet and Can" on the original Columbia labels of the Rhodes and Dickson 78s, but their playing was recorded much too faint. For a later and wide-ranging demonstration of Hacksaw Harney's musical skills, see Adelphi/Genes' invaluable CD Harney, *Sweet Man* (Adelphi Genes 9909, 1996). **Rube Lacy** was another musician who recorded for Columbia in Memphis that week, but none of his sides were released. His disc debut "Mississippi Jail House Groan" and "Ham Hound Crave" was for Paramount in 1928; as one of the first 78s by a Mississippi Delta bluesman, it has been included on many samplers on LP and CD, including as filler on Document's Son House CD (DOCD 5002).

In 1930, new recording artists from Mississippi joined Patton as national stars. **Memphis Minnie** with her then-husband Joe McCoy established her recording career with the hit "Bumble Bee." That song appears on the first volume of Document's current edition of her records through 1941 (DOCD 6008—6012), and on many of the "best of" anthologies of her career. **The Mississippi Sheiks**' "Sitting on Top of the World" was a massive hit, helping Okeh records stay solvent during the early part of the Depression, and becoming a standard repertory song for bluesmen ever after. Their complete February 1930 Shreveport session may be heard on volume 1 of their Document series (DOCD 5083–5086), but a better transfer of "Sitting on Top of the World" may be heard on Yazoo's Sheiks anthology *Stop and Listen Blues* (Yazoo 2006, 2002). The members of the Sheiks, Lonnie Chatman and Walter Vincson, continued recording, often with Lonnie's brother Bo Carter. In October 1936 the brothers recorded with **Eugene Powell** for RCA Bluebird. The collected recordings from that day are now available on *St. Charles Blues* (Nehi Records 03, 2014). Although Powell, recording as Sonny Boy Nelson, did record a song released as "Pony Blues," it was in the styles of the Chatmans and Leroy Carr than in Patton's. Lesser known in their day, but rewarding now, are the records by Blind Roosevelt Graves and Skip James. **The Graves brothers Roosevelt and Uaroy** were from south Mississippi, but once H. C. Speir heard them, he made sure that Paramount recorded them in 1929. They recorded both early boogie blues (in the manner of Pine Top Smith) and sacred songs (with a sanctified feel). Their collected sides (which also includes performances for ARC in 1936) on Document DOCD 5105 are a must-have for Mississippi music collectors. **Skip James** was a man apart, more a composer and arranger than a performer. He lived on the southeast rim of the Delta and, at the beginning of the early 1930s, tried to establish himself in Jackson, hence why he came to Speir for a record audition. His 1931 Paramount recordings of blues and spirituals are perhaps the most artful examples of pre-1942 Mississippi music. The best transfer of these rare sides (some surviving in one copy) is *The Complete Early Recordings of Skip James 1930* (sic) on Yazoo 2009.

**Robert Johnson** was just about the same age as those of the Graves brothers, but his kind of boogie was that of Leroy Carr and Roosevelt Sykes. Yet he still retained his Mississippi Delta origins; "The Last Fair Deal Gone Down" sounds as if indebted to Patton's "You Gone Need Somebody When You Die." The current (and best) audio restoration of Johnson's 1936–37 ARC sessions is *The Centennial Collection* (Sony/Columbia/Legacy 88697 85907 2, 2 compact discs, 2011). **Johnnie Temple** worked closely with Skip James in 1930–31, and sometime in 1931–1932 he swapped songs with a musician he knew as "R. L." who very likely was Johnson. Temple would later move to Chicago where he enjoyed a respectably long run of recording sessions with Decca (Document DOCD 5238–5240). But his 1935 debut for Vocalion (on Document DOCD 5238) has his Mississippi-based repertory, which has echoes of Son House (via "R. L."/Johnson) and Skip James. **Big Joe Williams**' 1935 RCA Bluebird session, including his "My Grey Pony" and an astounding "49 Highway Blues," may be found complete on the first of two Document CDs devoted to his output through 1949 (Document BDCD 6003–6004). **David "Honey Boy" Edwards** knew Patton, Robert Johnson and Big Joe Williams, so his "Water Coast Blues" seems like a grand summation of pre-1942 Delta styles. That performance was part of a 1942 field recording session for the Library of Congress, and the most reliable and accessible edition of those performances is on Edwards, *Delta Bluesman*, Earwig CD 4922, 1992.

Eugene Powell, Big Joe Williams, and Honey Boy Edwards continued performing after World War II. But the bluesman who best retained the memory and musical style of Charlie Patton through the postwar Chicago era was **Howlin' Wolf**. Of the many reissues of his music, the one most pertinent to Patton is Howlin' Wolf, *The Chess Box* (MCA/Chess CHD3–9332, 3 CDs, 1991), an excellent career overview that includes the Wolf's spoken reminiscence of his mentor. **Booker "Bukka" White** was a great Mississippi bluesman of the

1930s—his 1940 sides for Vocalion may be equal in achievement to Robert Johnson's recordings. Among his 1963 "rediscovery" recordings for John Fahey, White's spoken "Remembrance of Charlie Patton" (currently available on White, *The Historic Recordings that Marked the Rediscovery of a Great Bluesman* [Sonet/Universal 0602498692462, 2005]) is less a memory and more a fanciful tribute, but for nearly four minutes he spins a good tale. **Charlie Booker**'s 1951 Blues and Rhythm 78, "Greenville Smokin," with its guitar nod to Patton, may be most easily found on the CD included in Gayle Wardlow's book *Chasin' That Devil Music* (San Francisco: Miller Freeman Books, 1998). Other last glimmers of Patton's style may be gleaned from the early recordings of **Arthur "Big Boy" Crudup**, whose "Dirt Road Blues" (most easily available on Document's first volume of his collected early recordings [Document DOCD 5201–5204) have some lyrical traces of Patton's record of the similar name, even if the music sounds like a prototype for Crudup's later and more influential "That's All Right, Mama."

**Paramount Records** was the label that recorded most of the Mississippi musicians before 1942. "Race records," made by and for African Americans, was the main part of its catalogue, but there were also releases in jazz, old-time music (early country music), mainstream popular music, even a Spanish series. Beginning collectors who want to begin sampling the Paramount legacy could start with the three 4-CD box sets issued by JSP Records, *The Paramount Masters* (JSP 7723, 2004), *Paramount Old-Time Recordings* (JSP 7774, 2006), and *Paramount Jazz* (JSP 960, 2009). Additional collections should be the Black Swan CDs that have been issued by the George Buck Foundation, the current owner of Paramount's assets. All of its available CDs are best purchased through the Foundation's website Jazzology (http://www.jazzology.com, accessed 13 May 2022). What the Foundation has reissued to date has been of the early jazz and southern blues releases (including Patton's Paramounts), but as of this writing, only half of its 40 or so CDs are in print. If one want to immerse oneself into the whole Paramount experience, there are the two deluxe sets collectively titled *The Rise and Fall of Paramount Records* (2013, 2014). Jointly prepared by Revenant Records and Third Man Records with arrangements with the Buck Foundation, the two sets tell the whole history of Paramount in words and sound. Each set contains 6 LPs, a USB drive containing 800 songs, and two books. The first set covers the history from 1917 through 1927, the second from 1928 through 1932. While there is nothing quite like these two sets, they are not for casual purchase. Each set costs $400 apiece, and they are best bought through the Third Man Records retail sales website (http://thirdmanstore.com, accessed 12 April 2016) which offers a combined price of $650 for both sets. Some copies have been purchased by research libraries, so readers should ask their local librarians as to what library near them has the sets for consultation.

One resource that every reader of this book should avail themselves are the interviews conducted by **Gayle Dean Wardlow** from the late 1960s through the early 1970s that are now accessible for listening on the Center for Popular Music Archives Collection website, Middle Tennessee State University, (http://popmusic.mtsu.edu/archives/Inventory/Wardlow.htm), accessed 13 May 2022. The original tape reels are at the Blues Archive, the University of Mississippi, but in 1994 the reels were loaned at Wardlow's request to the Center for digitized transfers and audio log-keeping. Many of these interviews were used by the authors for the Patton biography (Calt may be heard on a few tapes), the others served as the bases for articles in *Blues Unlimited* and in Wardlow's book *Chasin' That Devil Music*. They should be heard—even enjoyed—for the character of each informant's voice as for the stories and information they relate.

# Biographical Glossary

Bunk Ashford (interviewed 1970): Long-time resident of Skene MS who heard in person Patton and Kid Bailey during the mid-to-late 1920s.

Henry Austin (born 1897; interviewed 1968): Delta resident who spoke to the authors of hearing on separate occasions Patton and Mattie Delaney.

Lilly Berry (interviewed 1968): Friend, and primary source of information, of Mattie Delaney.

Nathan "Dick" Bankston (1897 or 1899-after 1970?): Learned guitar from Patton and Willie Brown in the 1910s in and around Drew, MS. Later formed a string band with his brother Ben. Did not make records. Interviewed by researchers in the 1960s, including the authors in Memphis TN, 1967.

Millie Barnes Toy [Bonds, Torrey] (died 1968): One of Patton's early wives, 1908. Located in 1963 by Bernard Klatzko and Gayle Wardlow.

Willa Mae "China Lou" Barnes (later Money) (c.1909: 1950 or 1962): daughter of Millie Barnes and Patton.

Charlie Booker (1925–1989): Early postwar Mississippi bluesman who learned guitar from family members and studied early blues records including those of Patton. Made records of his own in 1952. Later moved to Indiana.

Ishman Bracey (1901–1970): Bluesman from central Mississippi who recorded for the labels Victor and Paramount in 1928–1930. Often associated with Tommy Johnson, with whom he traveled and performed from the mid-1920s until the mid-1930s. Located by Wardlow in Jackson, MS in 1963 and interviewed several times through 1969.

Ernest "Whiskey Red" Brown (interviewed 1972–74): Associate of Charlie Patton and Willie Brown (1), initially at Peerman Plantation (circa 1907–1915), then in Robinsonville (circa 1925–1929). Learned guitar from Patton.

Rosetta Patton Brown (1917–2014): Patton's only certified descendant living after 1962.

Willie Brown (1) (1900–1943): Nicknamed "Little Willie" by some friends for his small size and weight. Learned guitar from Patton in the 1910s, and was a frequent performing partner with Patton in the north Delta through 1929.

Recorded for Paramount in 1930 and the Library of Congress in 1941. From 1930 through 1942 he performed with Son House.

Willie Brown (2) (born circa 1890s): Guitarist active around Drew, MS. Remembered by Dick Bankston and eight other informants as tall and heavyset (like about 6 feet tall and about 210 pounds). Did not make records.

Reverend W. H. Buchanon (born 1890; interviewed 1972): Delta preacher who assisted with Walter Rhodes's 1927 Columbia Records session in Memphis.

Joe Callicott (c.1900–1969): north Mississippi musician (mostly around Hernando) who played in the 1920s Memphis style. Recorded with Garfield Akers in 1930. Interviewed by Wardlow in the 1960s, and made recordings for LP on Arhoolie and other labels.

Gus Cannon (1883–1979): Important early performer of blues and antecedent styles. Born in north Mississippi, and eventually settled in Memphis. Made some of the most important jug band records for Paramount and Victor in 1927–1930. Also composed "Walk Right In," which became a pop hit in 1963 in a recording made by the Rooftop Singers. Was one of the chief "rediscovered" talents in Memphis during the 1960s and 1970s.

Tom Cannon (interviewed 1970): nephew of Patton, son of Patton's sister Viola Patton Cannon. Lived on Dockery Farms through the 1970s. An important source of Patton family lore to researchers, including the authors. Also interviewed by David Evans in 1967 and 1986.

Viola Cannon (1887–1969): born Viola Patton, sister to Charley Patton. First interviewed by Wardlow and Bernard Klatzko at Dockery Farms in 1963. Interviewed several times by other researchers until her death, including David Evans in 1967.

Harry Charles (1900–1973): Talent scout for record labels who was based in Birmingham, Alabama. Did not handle Patton. Provided Wardlow with much contextual information about the record industry during interviews conducted in 1968–1970.

Bo Chatmon (1893–1964): Born in the Bolton MS area, brother to Lonnie and Sam Chatmon. Recorded as Bo Carter from 1928–1936 for Okeh and RCA Bluebird labels. Last years were spent in blindness and poverty in Memphis.

Larry Chatmon (born 1901; Interviewed in 1970): Brother to Bo, Lonnie and Sam Chatmon in the Bolton MS area. Interviewed by the authors in Bolton in 1970.

Lonnie Chatmon (1888 or 1890–1942 or 1943): Brother to Bo, Larry and Sam Chatmon in the Bolton MS area. Part of the Mississippi Sheiks and other 1930s recording acts.

Sam Chatmon: (birth year variously listed as 1897, 1899, or 1900: 1983): Brother to Bo, Larry and Lonnie Chatmon in the Bolton MS area. Performed mostly as sideman on commercial recordings through 1943, including those by his brothers. Located in 1960, when he resumed performing. Claimed Patton as his half-brother.

Jack Cooper (born 1910; interviewed 1967): Nephew of central Mississippi bluesman Tommy Johnson, resided in Terry MS.

Matt Dakin (interviewed 1970): Mississippi Delta landowner with property near Pace MS. Interviewed by the authors.

Joe Rice Dockery (1906–1982): Son of Will Dockery. Inherited Dockery Plantation in 1936. Interviewed by the authors in 1970.

Will Dockery (1865–1936): Landowner. Established in 1895 Dockery Plantation, where Charley Patton's family moved in the 1900s.

David "Honey Boy" Edwards (1915–2011): Singer and guitairst. Born in Shaw, MS. In or by 1932 he began performing at picnics and juke joints in the Delta. Patton was one of the earliest bluesmen he met. Also worked with Big Joe Williams, Tommy McClennan, Robert Petway, and Robert Johnson (including the night Johnson was poisoned). Moved to Chicago in 1956. Continued performing in the pre-1942 style through the 2000s.

Sleepy John Estes (1899–1977): Singer and guitarist. Born in Ripley, TN and moved to nearby Brownsville. Formed musical associations with Willie Newbern, Yank Rachell, and Hammie Nixon. First recorded commercially for Victor in 1929. Continued performing and recording until his death in 1977.

Mandy France: Married Patton at Osa Pepper's plantation, 1922; marriage lasted two years.

Minnie Franklin: Patton's wife, married 1924.

Sara Garrett (interviewed 1970): Will Dockery's cook at Dockery Plantation. Knew Patton personally through 1929.

Roxie Gibson: One of Patton's early wives, circa 1907.

Shirley Griffith (interviewed 1971): former resident of Brandon, MS who heard Patton perform during the 1920s.

W. C. Handy (1873–1958): Composer, arranger and dance bandleader. In 1903, he first noticed the blues as a popular song style. During the 15 years, he wrote some of the most popular blues of the time, especially "St. Louis Blues." During Patton's lifetime, Handy was arguably the prevailing force in the blues in the Delta, where his bands attracted white and black crowds alike.

Richard Harney (1902–1973): Guitarist and pianist. In 1927, with his brother Mylar, he performed with singer/accordionist Walter Rhodes during a Columbia Records field session in Memphis. Located in 1972.

Earl Harris (active 1900s–1920s): Guitarist at Peerman Plantation. According to Ernest Brown, Patton acknowledged Harris as a guitar teacher. Did not make records. Brown reported seeing Harris last in Memphis in the 1950s.

Nellie Hester (interviewed 1969–1970): one of two sisters of Henry "Son" Sims and a primary source of information about Patton and Sims' Paramount trip in winter 1930.

George Hobo [Hobo George] (circa 1890–1970): Brakeman on the Pea Vine Railroad. Lived on Dockery Plantation, later moved to Cleveland, MS. Reputed to have played recreational guitar in the manner of Patton.

Lonnie Hodges (interviewed 1970): operator of house frolics in and around Holly Ridge, for which he occasionally engaged Patton in the early 1930s. Later moved to Leland MS.

Eddie "Son" House (1902–1988): Singer and guitarist. One of Patton's better known talent discoveries. Scouted in Lula, MS in 1930 by Patton, who brought him to Paramount's recording studios for a session. Also recorded for the Library of Congress in 1941 and 1942. Moved to Rochester in 1943, where he was located in 1964. His rediscovery career (mostly 1964–1970), managed by Dick Waterman, was one of the more distinguished "Indian summer" careers among elder bluesmen in the 1960s.

Howlin' Wolf (Chester Burnett) (1910–1976): Singer and guitarist. A dynamic performer who began his blues career in 1929, receiving early encouragement from Patton. Made a successful transition to electrically amplified blues, and in 1953 moved to Chicago, where he recorded for Chess Records through 1973.

Frank Howard (born 1899; interviewed 1967): Patton's neighbor at Cottondale MS in 1921–1922. Later entered the ministry.

Nehemiah "Skip" James (1902–1969): Composer, singer, and guitarist. The most artful of a group of bluesmen in Bentonia MS who played in minor-key guitar tunings. After a successful audition for H. C. Speir, James recorded for Paramount Records in 1931. After spending over 30 years outside of music, in 1964 he revived his performing career. Best known today as the composer of "I'm So Glad," which was recorded by the British rock group Cream in 1966.

Roberta Jameson (interviewed 1969–1970): one of two sisters of Henry "Son" Sims and a primary source of information about Patton and Sims' Paramount trip in winter 1930.

Blind Lemon Jefferson (1893: 1929): Singer and guitarist. Texas bluesman who during the late 1920s was Paramount Records' greatest star. Among his hits were "Matchbox Blues" and "See That My Grave Is Kept Clean."

Ledell Johnson (born 1892; interviewed 1967): Brother of Tommy Johnson and a primary source of information about him. Interviewed by Wardlow in south Jackson, MS.

Robert Johnson (1911–1938): With Patton, one of the best known Mississippi Delta bluesmen active before 1942. Began career in 1929 in northwest Mississippi, eventually performing throughout the state and in east Arkansas. Recorded for the American Recording Company in 1936 and 1937. Stricken at a juke joint near Greenwood, MS in August 1938 and dying soon after under mysterious circumstances.

Tommy Johnson (ca. 1896: 1956): One of the most-loved figures in pre-1942 Mississippi blues. While living in and around the Delta region of Drew, MS in the mid-to-late 1910s, Johnson learned several blues from Patton. In the 1920s he settled in Jackson, MS. Recorded for Victor in 1928 and Paramount in 1930.

Flora Bates Kimball [Kimble] (interviewed 1968): friend of Patton's early wife Lizzie Taylor. Source of purported studio photograph of Patton taken in Yalobusha County in the mid-1900s.

Rubin "Rube" Lacy [Lacey] (1901–1969): One of the first Mississippi Delta performers to make records, first with an unissued session for Columbia in 1927, and then with one issued 78 for Paramount in 1928. Became a Baptist preacher in 1932, and lived his later life in California.

Arthur Laibly (1894–1971): Paramount executive who came to prominence in 1926 for having discovered the year before Blind Lemon Jefferson through a Texas dealer. Supervised Patton's 1929–1930 recording sessions. Fired from Paramount in 1931. Later career was as an insurance agent for Boars and Wausau.

Leadbelly [Huddie Ledbetter] (1888–1949): Texas singer and songster who accompanied himself on the 12-string guitar. Discovered in prison in 1933 by John Lomax, who arranged pardon and release the next year. Made many recordings, some of them commercial, the others as field recordings for study and transcription.

Lee, Alec (active 1900s): Turn of the century African American performer in north Mississippi who was an influence on Gus Cannon.

Ralph Lembo (1898–1960): Itta Bena, MS entrepreneur who scouted talent for the record labels from the mid-1920s through 1932. Most notable discovery were the Mississippi Sheiks, who on his recommendation were signed by Okeh Records, and who then recorded the massive 1930 hit "Sitting on Top of the World."

Hayes McMullan (1902–1986; interviewed 1967–1971): Weekend Delta guitarist who was well versed in African American music in the Delta through 1930. Did not record during the 78-rpm era. Recorded an LP album's worth of material in studio sessions produced by Wardlow in 1967. Claimed to know Patton well enough, and vice versa, to have turned down Patton's invitation to travel with him to Richmond, IN in June 1929 for what would have been Patton's first recording session.

Booker Miller (1910–1969): Patton protégé from 1929 through 1934. Did not record commercially, although he received from Ralph Lembo an invitation to do so, but Patton cautioned him not to take it from Lembo. Left music in 1939. During his 1968–1968 interviews with Wardlow in Greenwood MS, Miller was a valuable source of information and memories about Patton as man and musician.

Earl Montgomery (interviewed 1970): Memphis-based dealer and wholesaler of 78-rpm records issued by Paramount, Okeh, Vocalion, and the American Record Company.

Elizabeth Peterson Glynn Moore (born 1910; interviewed 1967–1971): Knew Charlie Patton, Son House, and Willie Brown (1). Was also neighbor to the mother of Robert Johnson 1929–1938. First husband was a laborer known as "Hard Rock" Glynn; second husband was Willie Moore (see below). Owned and operated a juke joint during the 1930s.

Willie Moore (Moses Alexander) (born 1902; interviewed 1967–1971): Mentored by W. C. Handy during the 1910s. Later became a professional gambler in Mississippi Delta barrelhouses. Occasionally assisted Patton as second guitarist. Wardlow's interviews with Willie and Elizabeth Moore are remarkable for the information on African American slang and on Delta lore.

Willie Morris (interviewed 1971–2): Bolton MS guitarist who heard Patton in several towns across the central Mississippi Delta in the 1920s. Did not record commercially.

"Hambone" Willie Newbern (flourished 1920s-1940s): Medicine show performer in Tennessee, Arkansas and Mississippi. Best known for being the first performer to record the blues standard "Roll and Tumble Blues."

Bertha Lee Pate (1902–1975): The last of Patton's wives, from 1930 until Patton's death in 1934. Assisted him as second singer during his January 1934 American Recording Company sessions. Located by researcher Bernard Klatzko in 1963.

Eugene Powell (1908–1998): Mississippi Delta singer and guitarist with strong associations with the Chatmon brothers. With Bo Carter's sponsorship, Powell recorded for RCA Bluebird in 1936 under the pseudonym Sonny Boy Nelson. Was musically inactive from the mid-1950s through the 1960s, but he revived his performing career in 1972.

James "Yank" Rachell (1906–1997): Singer, mandolinist, guitarist born in Brownsville, TN. Began recording in 1929, and participated as sideman in sessions for Sleepy John Estes and John Lee "Sonny Boy" Williamson, in addition to his own dates. His February 1934 session was for the American Recording Co. Stayed active as a performer until his death at age 91.

Alfred Schultz (interviewed 1968): Paramount pressman at Grafton, WI plant during 1920–1932.

Mrs. Paul Sauers (interviewed 1969): Widow of Ralph Lembo, residing in Itta Bena, MS. See Ralph Lembo above.

Henry "Son" Sims (1890–1958): Multi-instrumentalist in the Mississippi Delta who is best now known for his recordings as fiddler. Assisted Charley Patton during their winter 1930 recording session for Paramount. Also formed a string band, known often as the Son Sims Four, whose members included Percy Thomas and Muddy Waters; that group recorded for the Library of Congress in 1941 and 1942.

Henry Sloan (active 1900s-1910s): Guitarist at Dockery's Plantation during Patton's youth. Acknowledged by Patton's family as a teacher. Moved to Chicago in 1918.

H. C. [Henry C.] Speir (1895–1972): Furniture dealer and record store owner in Jackson, MS during the 1920s. Also acted as a talent scout for Paramount, Okeh, American Recording Company, Victor and other labels through the end of the 1930s. In that role, he discovered Patton in 1929 and referred him to Paramount, and in 1933–34 to ARC. Left the record business in the early 1940s for other commercial ventures. Located in 1964 by Gayle Wardlow, and granted informative interviews about the southern recording industry in the 1920s and 1930s.

Henry Stuckey (1896 or 1897 -1966): Chiefly noted for introducing minor-key guitar tunings to Bentonia, MS guitarists, especially to Nehemiah "Skip" James. Also claimed to the authors to have witnessed a Charlie Patton wedding in Morgan City in 1933.

Lizzie Taylor (1887–1966): Originally from Stringtown, MS. Patton common-law wife between 1904 and 1908, living with him in Yalobusha County. Kept a mid-1900s photograph purportedly of Patton until before her death, gave it to Flora Kimball, who in turn in 1968 gave it to Wardlow.

Percy Thomas (1897–1968): Guitarist and singer who performed with Henry "Son" Sims and Muddy Waters in the Son Sims Four, including the group's recordings for the Library of Congress in 1941 and 1942.

Bessie Turner (interviewed 1960s-1970s)—niece of Patton, daughter of Patton's sister Viola Patton Cannon. Interviewed by David Evans in 1967 and 1979.

Walter Vincson [Vinson] (1901–1975): Guitarist and, with Lonnie Chatmon, a core member of the Mississippi Sheiks.

Mandy Whigham (interviewed 1972): Delta resident (including Swiftown and Moorhead MS) who heard Patton as a street musician during the 1920s.

Booker "Bukka" White (1906–1977): Mississippi bluesman who performed regularly in the Delta in the 1930s. After serving time in prison for murder (1937–1940), White moved to Memphis. One of the great bluesmen on records, especially for his 1937 hit "Shake 'Em on Down" and his 1940 post-prison session for Vocalion. Located in 1963 by John Fahey, for whom he recorded a colorful "Remembrance of Charley Patton" that may be not be true. Enjoyed a revived musical career through 1976.

J. Mayo Williams (1894–1980): One of the few African American music executives in the record industry before 1950, in the roles of talent scout and session producer. After working for Paramount (1923–1927), Williams ran the short-lived label Black Patti (1927). Through 1940, he was associated with Jack Kapp, first for the Brunswick and Vocalion labels (1928–1931), then for Decca (1934–mid-1940s). After World War II, he ran a number of small recording firms.

Josephine Chatmon Williams (born circa 1890; interviewed 1969): Born in Bolton, MS, as the sister of Chatmon brothers Bo, Lonnie, Larry, and Sam. Learned in Bolton how to play guitar. Moved to Greenville in 1909. Was living in Jackson MS during her 1969 interview with the authors.

Leroy Willis (interviewed 1968): Farmer, who heard Patton, Willie Brown and Kid Bailey on various and separate occasions, especially in Ruleville, MS during 1924–1926. Moved to Lula in 1927, where he later heard Patton and also Louise Johnson.

Willie "Have Mercy" Young (interviewed 1967): Guitarist and friend of Patton, meeting him in Merigold, MS in 1929. Did not make commercial records.

### *Patton's Known Children*

Willa Mae "China Lou" Barnes Toy (later Money) (born c. 1909: 1950 or 1962): mother was Millie Barnes Toy [Bonds, Torrey]

Rosetta Patton Brown (1917–2014): mother was Martha Christian (1888-?)

Johnnie Williams (born 1916) and Will Williams (born1918): mother was Sadie Hollins

Two children (1920s; genders unspecified): mother as Bertha Read

Several children—unidentified mother—reported by Will Williams (4.) to researcher David Evans.

# Notes

### Preface

1. Stephen Calt and Gayle Wardlow, "Bitchin' Boogie: An Open Letter to Blues Fans," *Blues Unlimited* no. 140 (Spring 1981), 39. Also published as "An Open Letter to Blues Fans," *Living Blues* no. 50 (Spring 1981), 5.

### Chapter 1

1. The narrative about Patton's audition is an expansion of Henry C. Speir's account to Wardlow, taped interview, May 18, 1968.
2. Joe Rice Dockery, Calt and Wardlow, interview, 1970.
3. Speir to Wardlow, May 18, 1968.
4. For a comprehensive profile of Ralph Lembo, see T. DeWayne Moore, "Revisiting Ralph Lembo: Complicating Charley Patton, the 1920s Race Record Industry, and the Italian-American Experience in the Mississippi Delta," *Association of Recorded Sound Collections [ARSC] Journal* 49, no. 2 (Fall 2018): 153–184.
5. Matt Dakin, a Delta planter in Pace, MS, in interview with Calt and Wardlow, 1970. Dakin said that by 1912 he hired so many Mexicans for his plantation, that he learned Spanish in order to communicate with them better; he also recalled their early guitar-playing. Another source of guitars to the Delta at the turn of the century were the mail-order services of retailers like Sears, Roebuck.
6. Patton's 1934 death certificate is the chief document of his vital statistics. It was initially published in Gayle Dean Wardlow and Jacques Roche [Stephen Calt], "Patton's Murder: Whitewash? Or Hogwash?" *78 Quarterly* no. 1 (Autumn 1967), 10–17, and reprinted in Wardlow, *Chasin' That Devil Music* (San Francisco: Miller Freeman Books, 1998), 94–100. Son House to David Evans ("An Early Interview with Son House," *Frog Blues and Jazz Annual* no.5 [2017], 36) remembered Patton's height at 5' 2" and weight around 150 pounds.
7. Stephen Calt typed notes of his and Gayle Wardlow interview with H. C. Speir, Jackson, MS, 1970.

8. While living near Itta Bena in the the 1920s and 1930s, Booker Miller saw such blues-players as Blind Lemon Jefferson, Rube Lacy, Tommy Johnson, Robert Johnson, and Willie Brown. He also heard Blind Blake in Chicago.
9. On records, Patton had his murky growl, and Johnson had a distinctive falsetto yodel.
10. It is quite likely that Speir's enthusiasm was caught by the executives at Paramount Records, the company that recorded Patton. Although its recording director Arthur Laibly was not taken by the abilities of the blues guitarists he recorded, its July 1929 advertisement in the *Chicago Defender* newspaper for Patton's "Pony Blues" would praise his guitar expertise, stating "What he can't do with a guitar ain't worth mentioning." None of the company's other artists received comparable advertising hype.
11. Booker Miller to Wardlow, taped interview, 1968. For more, see Chapter 10.
12. See Gayle Wardlow's comments about Arthur Laibly in Ishman Bracey, "Got Four, Five Puppies, One Little Shaggy Hound," *Blues Unlimited* no. 142 (1982), 4–11 (reprinted in Wardlow, *Chasin' That Devil Music*, 45–60. Also, Bracey and Skip James (Stephen Calt, *I'd Rather Be The Devil: Skip James and the Blues* [New York: Da Capo Books, 1995]) both reported that Laibly gave them a single drink prior to the beginning of their 1930 and 1931 sessions. It may be that sometime in the fall of 1929 or the winter of 1930 that Laibly began allowing musicians to drink during their recording sessions.
13. One of the earliest white collectors of Patton, if not the earliest, was James McKune of New York City, whose letters were saved and later published by Henry Renard ("Letters from McKune," *78 Quarterly* no. 3 [1988]: 54–62). In addition to Renard, McKune introduced Patton's recordings to Bernard Klatzko and Pete Whelan.
14. Pete Whelan and Bill Givens issued two LPs of Patton, *The Immortal Charley Patton* (Origin Jazz Library OJL-1, 1961), and *Immortal Charley Patton volume 2* (Origin Jazz Library OJL-7, 1964). A key reissue was *Founder of the Delta Blues* on Nick Perls's label Yazoo in 1970 (Yazoo L-1020, 2 LPs). Bernard Klatzko's Herwin LP issues in the 1980s reissued many of the last remaining commercial Patton 78s.
15. Calt interview for the 1988 edition of Calt and Wardlow, *King of the Delta Blues*.
16. Ishman Bracey, interview with John Fahey, Jackson MS, June 1964.
17. When the authors followed up on this statement Bracey added, "Charlie Patton had two-three . . . "
18. W. C. Handy, "The Significance of the Blues," *Talking Machine Journal* (August 1919), 50. For a recent study of the transition of blues from good-time music to somber, see Peter C. Muir, *Long Lost Blues: Popular Blues in America, 1850–1920* (Urbana; Chicago: University of Illinois Press, 2010).
19. As Sam Chatmon demonstrated this gesture to Calt in 1972, Patton would cup his ear with his left hand while singing in a simulated posture of woe.

20. Such is indicated by House's report that Patton played "Down the Dirt Road" (one of his most popular pieces) with a flatpick, a technical impossibility.
21. Lilly Hester to Wardlow, taped interview in Memphis, TN, 1969–1970.
22. For additional remarks on Patton's foot-stomping, see David Evans, "An Early Interview with Son House" parts I and II, *Frog Blues and Jazz Annual* no. 5 (2017), 35.
23. Speir interview with Wardlow.
24. The topic of whether Native American culture has some relevance to early blues has reoccurred in conference proceedings and occasional writings since the 1990s. The most developed printed presentation to date is Joe Gioia, *The Guitar and the New World: A Fugitive History* (Albany: State University of New York Press, 2013).

### Chapter 2

1. Booker Miller to Wardlow, 1968.
2. "Mostly you'll find nicknames for people," Booker Miller remarked, in regards to blues singers. For an anthropological discussion of nicknames in African American blues culture, see William Ferris, *Blues from the Delta*, second edition (New Haven: Yale University Press, 1978), 13.
3. "Charlie took a good picture," Booker Miller recalled. To his great regret, the photograph was destroyed in a house fire.
4. Yet Patton family members remembered Charlie sometimes preaching in churches, including one in Renova (David Evans, "Conscience of the Delta," in Robert Sacre, *Charley Patton: Voice of the Mississippi Delta* [Jackson, MS: University Press of Mississippi, 2018], 48–52; previous appearances of Evans' essay were in Robert Sacre, editor, *The Voice of the Delta* [Liege: Presses Universitaires de Liege, 1987], and in the notes accompanying *Screamin' and Hollerin' the Blues: The Worlds of Charley Patton* [Revenant 212, 7 CD set, 2001], 6–34), 1987, 138). His nephew Tom Cannon told Evans that Patton tended to preach in the Mississippi hill country and other places where he wasn't known as a blues singer.
5. Although Patton reacted favorably to Son House's account of his career as a pastor, he never mentioned to House that he himself had done any preaching. Perhaps the reason why he was silent about it was his lack of real credentials for this role, which House would have readily discerned; House thought Patton was an ignoramus in regards to religious scripture. Booker Miller was a preacher later in his life, but at the time when he met Patton, he wasn't attending church. Even so, Miller was prepared to believe that Patton had been a preacher because "he acted like one," even though he was a carousing blues singer most of the time.
6. A recent history of the Church of God in Christ is Calvin White Jr., *The Rise to Respectability: Race, Religion, and the Church of God in Christ* (Fayetteville: University of Arkansas Press, 2012).
7. Yet, according to Son House, Patton was attracted to "sanctified" music "'cause

there's a whole lotta jumpin' in it," and he imparted a "sanctified" twist to his spirituals by playing them with a dance beat.

8. See Paul Garon, "The Dirty Dozens," *Living Blues* no. 97 (May/June 1991): 33–35; and Elijah Wald, *The Dozens: A History of Rap's Mama* (New York: Oxford University Press, 2012).
9. Calt, *I'd Rather Be the Devil*, 56–72.
10. W. J. Cash, *The Mind of the South* (1941; reprint, New York: Vintage, 1960, 44). This passage refers to the Southern white.
11. Calt gleaned these meanings from Sam Chatmon during their interview. In *Barrelhouse Words: A Blues Dictionary* (Urbana and Chicago: University of Illinois Press, 2009), 256, Calt states that "tush hog" and "wampus cat" are synonymous terms in African American culture for "a quarrelsome, pugnacious person." Calt also states that "tush hog" originally meant a wild hog. "Wampus cat" is thought to refer to a kind of cougar. Both terms have occurred in blues music: Bo Carter recorded a "Tush Hog Blues" in 1940, and Oscar Woods recorded with a group called the Wampus Cats in 1937.
12. Bo Carter reported, "I worked on doctor shows, I used to play for doctors one time. I'd say, 'What did the rooster say to the hen?' Ask the doctor that." Paul Oliver, *Conversation with the Blues* (New York: Horizon Press, 1965), 84.
13. Zora Neale Hurston, *Mules and Men* (1935; reprint, New York: Harper and Row, 1970, 305).
14. "Any a-us would 'clown,' you know, (when) we got far enough out there in the booze," Miller said to Wardlow. "You start cuttin' up with the people you know."

## *Chapter 3*

1. Eudora Welty, in discussion with William F. Buckley and Walker Percy, *Firing Line*, PBS television, taped December 12, 1972. Transcript first published as "Eudora Welty and Walker Percy: The Southern Imagination," *Mississippi Quarterly* 26 (Fall 1973), 493–516.
2. "7 More Die in Flood Along Mississippi," *New York Times*, 16 April 1927; "Fight Great Flood in Mississippi Area," *New York Times*, 15 April 1927.
3. A neighbor from Ruleville described him from memory to the authors as a "kinda Injun-lookin' fella."
4. The term "bright" includes an obsolete meaning of "beautiful." *Oxford English Dictionary*, 2nd edition, s.v. "bright".
5. Allison Davis, Burliegh B. Gardner, and Mary R. Gardner, *Deep South: A Social Anthropological Study of Caste and Class* (Chicago: University of Chicago Press, 1941), 41.
6. According to David Evans' research ("Conscience of the Delta," 2018, 34–35), this paternal grandfather's name was Bill, whom Evans refers to as "elder Bill Patton," and who took as wife a woman named Rose.
7. The others were Anderson (b. 1862), Rosa (b. 1865), and Marriah Patten (b. 1875).

The March 1864 birthdate for Bill Patton is from Evans, ("Conscience of the Delta," 2018, 34); Calt and Wardlow in the 1988 edition thought either thought 1864 or 1866, the later birthdate being more likely.

8. Evans, "Conscience of the Delta," 2018, 34, relays Tom Cannon's statement that Annie Martin's father was Grandeville Martin; Evans also says that she had two brothers, Jim and Sherman, the latter a half-brother.
9. The birth data of Patton and his siblings (except for Ed Patton) is confirmed in Evans, "Conscience of the Delta," 2018, 32–33; in the 1987 version of the essay, 125–128, Evans expressed doubts about who was Ed Patton.
10. The 1900 census entry for the Patton family was provided to Calt and Wardlow by Stephen LaVere. That data was reproduced in Jim O'Neal, "Revisiting the Worlds of Charley Patton, " *Living Blues* (December 2017): 64–70. O'Neal notes that Viola Cannon stated to interviewers David Evans, Bernard Klatzko and Gayle Wardlow that her brother Charlie was older than her, yet in the 1900 census he is listed as younger than her; O'Neal wonders if the census birth year for Charlie as 1891 is not the result of a mistransposition by the census taker, and that the birth for Charlie was in 1887 and Viola in 1891. See note 18 below for more remarks on this matter.
11. In the 1988 edition of this book, Herring's name was rendered as Heron. The correction to Herring was provided by Jim O'Neal, "Revisiting," 66. At the eve of the Civil War, a third of the county's farmers owned fewer than ten slaves. Frank Lawrence Owsley, Jr., *Plain Folk of the Old South* (Baton Rouge: Louisiana State University: 1949), 14.
12. During his interview with Stephen Calt, David Edwards generalized what was then a continuing situation regarding interracial sex in Mississippi. "In them hills out there, them old colored women'd slip off," he said, "You don't catch nothin' but them old half-white boys and half-white girls out there. There's more of that in the hills than in the Delta." Sam Chatmon admitted to Calt that his grandmother "Creasie" Hammond was herself "half-Indian and half-white."
13. Sam Chatmon to Stephen Calt.
14. Sam Chatmon to Stephen Calt.
15. Consider the recordings made by Texas songster Henry Thomas ("Ragtime Texas") for Vocalion in 1927–1929. To be sure, Thomas did not invent the blues, but he was one of the early performers of blues: some of his lyrics and melodies are datable to the late 1890s, and they include references to locations and people in East Texas and St. Louis, Missouri. His guitar accompaniments are rudimentary, but whether that is due to his limited performing abilities, or to the accompaniments remaining set for up to 30 years, is an open question. But certainly his accompaniments lack the embellishments and ornaments that Patton brought to his recorded performances. The best study of Thomas' recordings is Mack McCormick's notes for *"Ragtime Texas" Henry Thomas: Complete Recorded Works, 1927–1929, in Chronological Order*, Herwin H 209, 1975, 2 LP set.
16. The assumption that Patton's irregular phrasing is archaic underlies, and

arguably muddies, Robert Palmer's presentation of Patton in *Deep Blues* (New York: Viking, 1981), 65.

17. See Edward Komara and Dave Rubin, *12-Bar Blues* (Milwaukee: Hal Leonard, 2000). In the 1988 book, Calt opined that there was no logical process underlying the 12-measure blues "ten-six" phrasing pattern, but without explaining why.
18. The 1887 birth year was given by Viola Cannon and Minnie Franklin during separate interviews in August 1963 to Bernard Klatzko and Gayle Wardlow. The two researchers cited this month and year in their essay accompanying the LP record *The Immortal Charlie Patton 1887–1934 no.* 2, Origin Jazz Library OJL-7, 1964. During an interview conducted by David Evans on August 22, 1967, Cannon gave 1881 as her brother's birth year. This may explain why Evans asserted in his book *Big Roads Blues: Tradition and Creativity in the Folk Blues* (Berkeley: University of California Press, 1982) that "Patton was living on Dockery's plantation in 1903 and was already an accomplished musician" (p.175). 1885 was given by Patton himself on his U.S. draft registration card on September 18, 1918; the authors thanks Randy Meadows for providing this information.
19. Lonnie Chatmon is said to have been born in June 1888, and Armenta (Armenter) "Bo" Chatmon on March 21, 1893 or in January 1894. Lonnie was to become famous as one of the Mississippi Sheiks, and Bo was a bestselling recording artist in the 1930s as Bo Carter.
20. In addition to Lonnie and Bo, the other Chatmon siblings were Ferdinand (b. 1885), Laurie (b. 1888), Fred (b. 1890), Willie Edgar (b. 1895), Lamar (b. 1897), and Sam (1899–1983).
21. Sam Chatmon to Stephen Calt.
22. Charles Nordhoff, *The Cotton States in the Spring and Summer of 1875* (New York: D. Appleton and Company, 1876), 81.
23. "Charlie" is the form of Christian name that is used in this book. The spelling "Charlie" was used by the American Record Company on Patton's 1934 recordings. Also, David Evans, "Conscience of the Delta," 2018, 32–33, acknowledges that "Charlie" is the form of name used on many of the surviving public documents pertaining to the musician. Paramount Records used the form "Charley" on the 78-rpm record labels and advertising, which is the lead reason why that is used in many publications about the musician.
24. However, David Evans, "Conscience of the Delta," 2018, 48, relays the Patton family's claims that Charlie was educated to the ninth grade, and could read and write. Asked by Evans (2018, 135, n.41) as to why Patton marked an "X" by his name on a 1908 marriage license in the manner of an illiterate, Tom Cannon thought that Patton was probably "pulling somebody's leg."
25. Newman Ivey White, *American Negro Folk-Songs* (Cambridge, MA: Harvard University Press, 1928; reprinted Hatboro, PA: Folklore Associates, 1965), 70.
26. See Peter Muir, *Long Lost Blues: Popular Blues in America, 1850–1920* (Urbana; Chicago: University of Illinois Press, 2010.

27. Newbell Niles Puckett, *Folk Beliefs of the Southern Negro* (Chapel Hill: The University of North Carolina Press, 1926; reprinted New York: Dover, 1969), 485.
28. Stephen Calt, "The Country Blues as Meaning," in Stefan Grossman, Stephen Calt, and Hal Grossman, *Country Blues Songbook* (New York: Oak; London: Music Sales, 1973): 16, 23.
29. Howard Odum and Guy Johnson, *The Negro and His Songs: a Study of Typical Negro Songs in the South* (Chapel Hill, NC: University of North Carolina Press, 1925; reprinted Hatboro, PA: Folklore Associates, 1964): 69.
30. E. C. Perrow, "Songs and Rhymes from the South," *The Journal of American Folklore* 26, issue no. 100 (April-June 1913), 123.
31. Ira David Sankey, "A Shelter in Time of Storm," to words by Vernon J. Charlesworth. First published in Sankey, *Sacred Songs and Solos* and *Gospel Hymns No. 5*, London: Morgan and Scott [circa 1890s]. Also published as text only as hymn no. 539 in Sankey, *Sacred Songs and Solos: Twelve Hundred Hymns* (London: Marshall, Morgan and Scott, 1921) [unpaginated]. In the 1988 edition, Calt cited the inclusion of this hymn in words and music in George Stebbins, editor, *Northfield Hymnal* (New York; Chicago: Biglow and Main Company, 1904), hymn no. 152.
32. By the fall of 1897 fear of yellow fever had acted to disperse the population of Edwards to such an extent that the Delta town of Rosedale issued a proclamation forbidding anyone from Edwards to enter community limits without obtaining a health certificate.
33. Before leaving Edwards, the family was counted in Hinds County for the 1900 census.
34. "Music Trades," in W. L. Hubbard, editor, *History of American Music* (*American History and Encyclopedia of Music*, volume 8; New York: Irving Squire, 1910), page 334.
35. Bengt Olsson, notes accompanying Gus Cannon, *Cannon's Jug Stompers: The Complete Works in Chronological Order 1927–1930 including Gus Cannon as Banjo Joe*, Herwin LP 208, [1974] 2 LP records.
36. Leadbelly in 1948 recalled its popularity in Louisiana "around 1910, 1909, 1908, and -7" (Leadbelly, *Leadbelly's Last Sessions volume one*, Folkways FA 2942, 1953, 2 LP set). W. C. Handy made a national hit of it in 1916, after learning it from "a wandering musician who said he had it from a hymn." (Handy, *A Treasury of the Blues* [New York: Charles Boni, 1926, 1949], 243–244.)
37. In his 1926 version for his *Blues: An Anthology: Complete Words and Music of 53 Great Songs* (New York: Charles Boni, 1926), p. 53, Handy adds vocal pitches to fill in the rests in measures 2 and 4, and he extends the final note (m.7) from a half-note to whole note. So the result is considerably different from other treatments of the "East St. Louis Blues" melody including Patton's "Jim Lee Blues" parts 1 and 2 and, for that matter, the authors' discussion of the base form of "East St. Louis Blues" in the following paragraphs.
38. W. C. Handy, *Father of the Blues* (New York: Macmillan, 1941), 142.

39. The barrelhouse is a distinctive element in the present biography of Patton. By contrast, David Evans, in his essay "Conscience of the Delta," 2018, 57, mentions cafes and juke houses, stores, house parties, wedding and birthday parties, picnics, and medicine shows, but not barrelhouses.
40. One Delta club only admitted patrons who flashed a $100 gambling stake, Willie Moore recalled to Gayle Wardlow.
41. Willie Moore said, "They play Skin, and they play Blackjack, too, and Five Up, and Cotch . . . Eight a-Kings—that was poker, too."
42. Barrelhouse robberies were nonetheless chronic, often staged by gangs of five or six who overwhelmed the floorwalker and created chaos by knocking over the kerosene lamps that illuminated the establishment.
43. This phrase is given as "and get sloppy drunk off a bottle and ball." But Patton also pronounces with the long vowel "o" (as in bone) the word "bond" on "You're Gonna Need Somebody When You Die." So for "Elder Greene Blues," "bottle in bond" is a reasonable transcription.
44. Cited in Alfred Holt Stone, *Studies in the American Race Problem* (New York: Doubleday, Page and Co., 1908), 107.
45. See Alan Lomax, *Mister Jelly Roll* (New York: Grossett and Dunlap, 1950), 20–21, and Paul Oliver, *Conversation with the Blues* (New York: Horizon, 1965), 94–97.
46. Olsson, notes accompanying Gus Cannon, *Cannon's Jug Stompers.*
47. The earliest such blues in Mississippi that Calt and Wardlow could trace back using their resources was a shimmy-she-wobble dance that Walter Vinson heard around 1907 being performed by a middle-aged Bolton guitarist, P. G. Hodges, which in 1938 was used by Bo Carter as the basis for his commercial recording "Old Devil" (RCA Victor Bluebird B8093).
48. Handy, *Father of the Blues*, 87.
49. Elizabeth Moore during an interview with Wardlow said that was how the barrelhouse owner auditioned prospective performers. "You'd wanna hear how his music sounded . . . see if it could 'take' with the people."

## Chapter 4

1. Cited in Vernon Lane Wharton, *The Negro in Mississippi, 1895–1890* (Chapel Hill, NC: University of North Carolina Press,1947), 111.
2. For a capsule account of black farmer migration from the hill country to the Delta, see James C. Cobb, *The Most Southern Place on Earth: The Mississippi Delta and the Roots of Regional Identity* (New York; London: Oxford University Press, 1992), chapter 4 "Conquering the Plantation Frontier," 69–97, especially 82–83. Calt and Wardlow in the 1988 Patton book cite unattributed what a post-World War II Delta planter said of his ancestors as ruthless recruiters of black labor: "They used to love to get hill niggers into the Delta, because money was an unknown quantity to them."
3. Stone, *Studies in the American Race Problem*, 121.

4. That this was a superior wage is shown in the Southern Tenant Farmer's Union unsuccessful demand in 1936 for a standard wage of $1.25 per hundred pounds.
5. Stone, 109–110
6. David Evans, in his essay "Conscience of the Delta," gives a few specific notes about Patton family members buried at Dockery's. Charlie Patton's younger brother C. was killed in 1918 in a hunting accident. His older sister Viola married John Cannon in 1904 and they continued residing on Dockery's, where she died in 1969. As for Patton's parents, Evans learned from Tom Cannon that Bill Patton died in 1927 or 1928 in Vicksburg, and he relays family information that Annie Patton died sometime in the early 1930s and her body was transported to Bolton for burial.
7. The Pattons' native Hinds County numbered 39,500 blacks in 1900, while Bolivar County, which adjoined Sunflower County and was at that time Mississippi's greatest cotton-producing region, had 31,000.
8. Robert Sherrill, *Gothic Politics in the Deep South* (New York: Grossman, 1968), 187.
9. W[ilbur]. J. Cash, *The Mind of the South,* especially chapter 2, "Of The Man at the Center."
10. *The Rosedale Democrat,* centennial issue, June 1936. Joe Rice Dockery showed Calt and Wardlow a copy of the Dockery article from this issue.
11. J. N. Darling, "The Yazoo Delta of Mississippi, and Location and Construction of its Railroads," *Journal of the Western Society of Engineers* 7, no. 6 (November-December 1902), 560–573.
12. William Faulkner, *The Mansion* (New York: Random House, 1955), 48. Recalling his days in Cleveland, Dockery wrote, "Venison was common food on the tables then. I asked Austin Thomas, a negro who lived on the Quiver River and who traded with me, why I sold him no meat and lard, and he replied that he had sufficient bear bacon and bear lard to last him three years."
13. A short overall history of Mississippi lumbering, including the move south by northern lumbermen, may be found on Tony Howe, "Growth of the Lumber Industry (1840–1930)," Mississippi History Now, <http://mshistorynow.mdah.state.ms.us/articles/171/growth-of-the-lumber-industry-1840-to-1930>, accessed 30 April 2020.
14. Darling, "The Yazoo Delta of Mississippi, and Location and Construction of its Railroads."
15. After Will Dockery's death in 1936, the plantation was passed into the hands of his son Joe Rice Dockery, who renamed it Dockery Farms.
16. By law, private plantation holdings were limited to ten thousand acres.
17. The daily operations of the plantation were left to the assistant manager, who was the "rider" for the absent landowner.
18. Darling, "The Yazoo Delta of Mississippi, and Location and Construction of its Railroads."
19. Phillip Bruce, *The Rise of the New South* (Philadelphia: George Barrie and Sons, 1905), 27.
20. In other respects, the present outlines of Sunflower County were largely drawn

after Dockery's was founded. Doddsville, five miles to the south of Ruleville, came into being in the 1890s as a 5000-acre plantation. Drew, six miles north of Ruleville, was incorporated in 1897. Moorhead was established in 1898. Boyle, five miles south of Cleveland, in 1905.

21. Scrip was commonly used by plantations, railroads, and mining firms in order to ensure that the wages of employees were returned to them in the form of commerce. In the plantation system, it also acted as a check on tenants who the planters feared might move secretly and suddenly from the farm with the advances they had drawn from their annual settlements in order to subsist.
22. V. O. Key, Jr, *Southern Politics in State and Nation* (New York: Random House, 1949), 238. Leroy Percy's son William Alexander Percy, the poet and author of *Lanterns on the Levee* (New York: Knopf, 1941), was to form a close friendship with Dockery's son, as did David Cohn, the author of *God Shakes Creation* (New York; London: Harper and Brothers, 1935).
23. Cobb, 135–136.
24. James Kimble Vardaman, speech at Poplarville, Mississippi, April 1907. Quoted in Ray Stannard Baker, *Following the Color Line* (New York: Doubleday and Page, 1908), 216.
25. Percy, *Lanterns on the Levee*, 309.
26. The nickname Pea Vine was used previously for the Rosedale and Mississippi Central Railroad that ran in the 1880s from Rosedale to Bogue. Melanie Young ("Where the Southern Cross' the Dog: Mississippi Blues and the Railroad," *Living Blues* 45 no. 5 (no. 233) (October 2014), 36–37) calls this stretch of railroad "the Kimball Line branch."
27. David Evans, "Conscience of the Delta," 2018, 45, agrees with this description, relaying Tom Cannon's claim that his grandfather came to be, over time, a "big farmer at Dockery's."
28. David Evans, "Conscience of the Delta," 2018, 48, takes seriously the claim of Bill Patton as a church elder, through whom (Evans argues) Charlie would have acquired a basic religious upbringing.
29. Stone, 112.
30. Emmett Scott, *Booker T. Washington: Builder of Civilization* (New York: Doubleday, 1916), 130–131. After this visit, many African American babies born in Mississippi were named with Booker T. Washington's full or partial name. The christening of Booker White (b. 1909) and Booker Miller (b. 1910) were part of this naming trend.
31. Charles S. Johnson, *Growing Up in the Black Belt* (Washington DC: American Council of Education, 1941), 318.
32. See the transcription published in Stefan Grossman, Stephen Calt and Hal Grossman, *Country Blues Songbook*, 54.
33. Mott Willis, a central Mississippi guitarist who moved to Drew in 1919, derived a version of this song (which he termed a "rag" and fretted in the C position on the guitar) from Patton. See David Evans, *Big Road Blues: Tradition and Creativity in the Folk Blues*, 201–202.

34. In "Some of These Days," that second beat was emphasized with an anticipatory eighth-note syllable on the same tone, as on "ne-(ver)" and "man" in take 1, chorus 2, phrase 1 (transcribed in Ex. 8 b).
35. John Fahey, in his incipit catalogue of the Patton recordings in his book *Charley Patton* (London: Studio Vista, 1970), transcribes the song in 16 measures (see p. 95). The melody on Patton's 1930 Paramount record is that of "Oh Happy Day," an 1855 hymn composed by Philip Doddridge and E. F. Rimbault. This tune is better known today as a basis of Woody Guthrie's "This Land Is Your Land."
36. David Evans, "Conscience of the Delta," 2018, 70–71, relays claims from Patton's family and his last wife Bertha Lee that he continued playing for whites on up to his last performances in 1934.
37. For Paramount in 1929, Patton sang of deputy Tom Rushing, and in remaking the song in 1934 for Vocalion as "High Sheriff Blues," he sang of deputy John D. Purvis. The engineer was Charley Bradley who ran locomotive no. 1066 on the Yazoo-Delta Railroad, about whom was Patton's unreleased and now lost 1934 Vocalion recording "Charley Bradley's Ten Sixty Six Blues." Each of these three songs will be discussed later in the book in their respective recording sessions.
38. Robert Staughton Lynd and Helen Merrell Lynd, *Middletown: A Study in American Culture* (New York: Harcourt, Brace and World, 1929), 251.
39. Albert Bushnell Hart, *The Southern South* (New York: Appleton and Co., 1910), 117.
40. Willie Moore attributed the song to a Tunica pastor who led his congregation in singing it: " . . . they wanted everybody to go in prayer."
41. During his 1941–42 field recording trips to Mississippi for the Library of Congress, Alan Lomax encouraged bluesmen to sing blues and songs on racial topics. For Lomax's later account and rationale for encouraging such material from bluesmen, see his memoir *The Land Where the Blues* Began (New York: Pantheon, 1993).
42. Henry Bates Brown, *Cotton* (New York: McGraw Hill, 1938), 380.
43. Percy, *Lanterns on the Levee*, 279.
44. Newbell Niles Puckett, *Folk Beliefs of the Southern Negro*, 10.
45. According to Stone, *Studies in the American Race Problem,* the Delta furnished seven times as many state convicts to the prison population of 1900 as the hills. While fewer than half the black hill residents then in prison had been convicted of violent felonies, three-quarters of the Delta-drawn convicts were serving time for murder, attempted murder, or manslaughter, all crimes associated with barrelhousing.
46. Hart relayed "a stock statement, a thousand times repeated, is that there is no such thing as a virtuous negro woman" (Hart, *The Southern South*, 134).
47. Calt and Wardlow in this book on one hand, and David Evans ("Conscience of the Delta," 2018, 77) agree on the number of "wives" Patton was said to have taken, but their lists differ. A combined list of wives (formal or common-law) names these women: Lizzie Taylor (circa 1904–1908), Roxie Gibson (mid-1900s), Gertrude Lewis (1908; marriage certificate granted but ceremony not carried out), Millie Bonds (or Barnes, 1908), Dela Scott (1913), Roxie Morrow (1918), Minnie

Franklin (1922), Mattie Parker (1924), Bertha [Burtha] Reed (1926), and Bertha Lee Pate (1930–1934). There were also three women who bore him children: Sallie Hollins (two boys in 1916 and 1918), Martha Christian (1917), and a woman around Merigold, MS named Sudy (circa 1924–1930). Others were another woman in Merigold named Udy, and a woman now unknown whom Calt and Wardlow said had filed for a marriage certificate with Patton in 1933. Each of these wives and lovers will be mentioned at longer length where appropriate in this book.

48. Eric Partridge, *A Dictionary of Slang and Unconventional English*, 7th edition (New York: Macmillan, 1970), s.v. "broomstick, jump (over) the." The phrase derives from an actual wedding ceremony once performed by European gypsies and peasants, and a military variant was practiced in eighteenth century England by jumping over crossed swords to the rhyme, "Leap rogue and jump whore, and then you are married for ever more."
49. Taylor's photograph portrait of young Patton is now owned by Gayle Dean Wardlow. Its first publication was as the frontispiece to the 1988 book.

## Chapter 5

1. Millie Barnes was also known to researchers as Millie Toy and as Millie Torry. The earliest documentation of her was a mention of a 1963 interview meeting in the essay insert by Bernard Klatzko (with Gayle Dean Wardlow) accompanying *The Immortal Charlie Patton no.* 2, Origin Jazz Library OJL-7, 1964, LP record. She also granted a 1967 interview to David Evans with Marina Bokelman (Evans, *Big Road Blues*, 176).
2. David Evans ("Conscience of the Delta," 2018, 62) relayed Viola Cannon's memory that Patton performed in some medicine shows.
3. Unlike the minstrel show, the medicine show charged no admission. For a general history of medicine shows, see Brooks McNamara, *Step Right Up* (Garden City, NY: Doubleday, 1976). Matt Dakin of Skene, MS noted to Calt and Wardlow that instead of selling medicine (which was often an alcoholic "medicinal spirit"), the pitchman would sometimes sell certificates for it that could be redeemed at a local drug store.
4. Matt Dakin to Calt and Wardlow. For a photograph of the Dr. Blackhawk medicine show, see the photograph section.
5. McMullan interviews with Wardlow, 1967–1968. Joe Callicott recorded the melody to the words "Hoist Your Window and Let Your Curtain Down," in a studio session on July 21, 1968 for Callicott's LP *Presenting the Country Blues*, Blue Horizon 7-63227.
6. C. P. J. Mooney, editor, *The Mid-South and Its Builders* (Memphis, TN: Mid-South Biographic and Historical Association., 1920), 163.
7. By the 1910s, though, the sawmills declined as lands were cleared and the demand for timber was dropped. See Evans, "Conscience of the Delta," 2018, 55.

8. "Don't You Grieve After Me," included in J. B. T. Marsh, editor, T*he Story of the Fisk Jubilee Singers With Their Songs*, 7th edition, London: Hodder and Stoughton, 1877.
9. An early printing is in William E. Barton [editor] *Old Plantation Hymns: A Collection of Hitherto Unpublished Melodies of the Slave and the Freedman, with Historical and Descriptive Notes* (Boston; New York; London: Lamson, Wolfe and Company, 1899).
10. Sam Chatmon to Calt. It is not known if this song, which began "If you can't Shimmy, you got no business here" was actually designed for the dance of the name.
11. A table showing these changes in the 1988 edition has been removed from this point in the text, because of Calt's counting of the first chorus appears to be wrong.
12. Woody Mann in his remarks preceding his notated transcription of Patton's "Screamin' and Hollerin' the Blues" (*Sing Out!* 46 no. 2 [Summer 2002], 53–57) notes the "consistency of an uneven beat schematic such as three bars of 4/4, one bar of 6/4" and accounts for it as "probably due to the fact that he was playing in and around a certain dance step."
13. See the two passages in Chapter 14 regarding Frank Palmes' "Troubled 'Bout My Soul" and Patton's "Troubled 'Bout My Mother."
14. William Marion Reedy, *The Hot Springs of Arkansas*, Missouri Pacific brochure, c. 1916, p. 15. Congress declared Hot Springs as a reservation in 1832, and as a national park in 1921.
15. The date is inexact because Brown was unsure if he was born in 1891 or 1893, and he dated events in terms of his age. He moved from his native Utica to Shaw at ten or twelve (i.e. in 1901–1905) and moved to Skene a year or so later, where he spent three years before coming to Cleveland. While this chronology dates his arrival in Cleveland to 1905–1910, he recalled meeting Willie Brown there at age twelve or thirteen, which would indicate that he was ten when he moved to Shaw, and came to Cleveland no later than 1907.
16. All of our information derived from Ernest Brown was generously supplied to the authors by Stephen LaVere, who located him in Memphis.
17. Miniscule resemblances between the recordings made by Black and Patton encourage the possibility that the two men had mutual associates. Both musicians play two-beat tonic chord strums and a two-note riff on the top two strings (a dominant and minor third) as part of an E position accompaniment. Black's insertion of part of a bridge figure within the last two vocal beats of "Rock Island Blues" is a mannerism that Patton used on such songs as "Banty Rooster Blues."
18. Klatzko with Wardlow, essay insert accompanying *The Immortal Charlie Patton* no. 2, 1964.
19. In this respect, the arrangement for "Pony Blues" was much like the 1970s soul and disco records, in that both used percussive phrase-snippets.
20. Woody Mann remark to Calt during the preparations of the 1988 edition of this book.

21. The opening verse of "Banty Rooster Blues," consisting of twelve bars, consumes nearly 35 seconds, while the closing verse (eleven bars) takes ten seconds less.
22. Johnny Shines interview with Stephen Calt, circa 1964–1971. For a fuller definition from Calt of "slow drag," consult his *Barrelhouse Words: A Blues Dialect Dictionary*.
23. McMullan interviews with Wardlow, 1967–1969. Also, Sleepy John Estes of western Tennessee learned the song from Hambone Willie Newbern sometime during the 1910s; in 1929 for Victor Estes recorded the melody as "The Girl I Love, She Got Long Curly Hair." As for Newbern's Okeh recording "Roll and Tumble Blues," it begins with the same three-note ascent (dominant-minor seventh-keynote) as Patton's "Banty Rooster Blues." Yet the concluding vocal phrases of each song are dissimilar, and "Roll and Tumble Blues" does not employ the major second of "Banty Rooster Blues" as an interval.
24. Son House's blues lyrics were as thematic as Patton's. Even so, House took him to task for this trait. In the 1960s to Calt he remembered that "Charlie, he'd sing a lot of monkey-junk in a record and I didn't believe in it. Let's say you wanna make 'The Cigarette Blues.' The next few verses he'd be singin' about 'the flower.' I say 'uh, uh, that don't work.' Charlie'd put anything in his verses."
25. Patton uses this root-triad phrase also on two other recordings, "Tom Rushen Blues" and "Hammer Blues."

## Chapter 6

1. David Evans, *Big Road Blues*, 176. Evans had conducted his own interview with Millie Barnes [Toy/Torrey] in Boyle, MS in 1967.
2. A chaste version of the first two lines was collected by Mary Wheeler and included in her book *Steamboatin' Days: Folk Songs of the River Packet Era* (Baton Rouge: Louisiana State University Press, 1944), 12.
3. W. L. Hubbard, *The American History and Encyclopedia of Music* (New York: Irving Square, 1910), 64.
4. A Patton family tradition, relayed by his niece Bessie Turner to Evans, "Conscience of the Delta," 2018, 53–55, had it that Charlie was playing as early as age 7 or 10 years old. Part of that tradition also had it that he had learned from Dockery's plantation musicians—but the Pattons did not move to there until Patton was 10. Perhaps his youthfulness was exaggerated by his family to show how prodigious he was with the guitar once he took it up.
5. Interview with Bernard Klatzko and Gayle Wardlow, August 1963, Boyle, MS.
6. Handy's chief blues publications are examined by Peter C. Muir in his book *Long Lost Blues: Popular Blues in America, 1850–1920*.
7. Handy, pp. 76–77.
8. Handy, 74. At that time, the first rail stop south of Tutwiler was the newly incorporated town of Moorhead, forty miles away, which was then the only point of

intersection between the "Dog" and the "Southern," which ran east to west. The "Dog" itself was a new arrival to the Delta, running through undeveloped wilderness. "They tell me many years ago," Elizabeth Moore said, "when they opened it up, it was so muddy in here, you know, comin' down that 'Dog,' that they named it 'The Mud-Line.'" Patton and Brown applied the latter name to one of their favorite duets, Willie Moore said, "That's just what they'd say, Let's play 'The Mud-Line.'"

9. Helen H. Roberts, *Ancient Hawaiian Music* (Honolulu: Bernice P. Bishop Museum, 1926), 10. For a presentation for guitar players of Delta slide guitar styles with an emphasis on Hawaii, see Michael Messner, "Slide Blues Roots," *FRoots* [Folk Roots] 35 no. 6 (December 2013): 54–57.
10. Handy, 75.
11. Handy, 76–77.
12. In his book *Long Lost Blues*, Peter C. Muir delves in chapter 3 ("Curing the Blues with the Blues") "the notion that music dispels blues," with which findings he carries over into chapter 4 ("The Blues of W. C. Handy").
13. The Handy, Nash, and Williams songs appear in full in Handy, *A Treasury of the Blues* (New York: Charles Boni, 1949), 93, 119, 158.
14. At the time, Willie Moore recalled to Wardlow, "Handy didn't have no band. When he picked me up, he playin' for Jim Turner. It was Jim Turner's band that Handy was handlin." According to Moore, Handy inherited the outfit upon the death of Turner. This differs from Handy's view in his memoirs *Father of the Blues* of Turner as his subordinate.
15. Robert Palmer, *Deep Blues*, 50–51.
16. A. B. Hart, *The Southern South* (New York: D. Appleton, 1908), 266.
17. Robert L. Brandfon, *Cotton Kingdom of the New South* (Cambridge, MA: Harvard University Press, 1967), 123–4.
18. H. B. Brown, *Cotton* (New York and London: McGraw-Hill, 1938), 345.
19. Whereas Cleveland's Brown was even shorter than Patton, Sumner's/Jennings' Brown was a man of hulking proportions. Bankston indicated that he stood six feet tall and weighed in the neighborhood of two hundred pounds. Ledell Johnson, his Mary Johnson, and Sara Garrett all produced nearly identical physical descriptions of Brown, whom Tom Cannon described as a "pretty good size guy" who stood at least half a foot taller than Patton. However, in a contrasting opinion, David Evans (*Big Road Blues*, 176) takes Jennings' Brown as having been born in Drew or in Shaw, and to be the same man who recorded with Patton in 1930. For additional notes from Wardow and Calt towards distinguishing the two Willie Browns, see their sidebar "The Two Browns," as part of their article "Can't Tell My Future: The Mystery of Willie Brown," *Blues Unlimited* no. 147 (Spring 1986), 6–9 (reprinted in Wardlow, *Chasin' That Devil Music*, 181–190, especially 186–190).
20. In Wardlow's article "Ledell Johnson Remembers His Brother, Tommy" (*78 Quarterly* no. 1 [1967]: 63–65), Ledell remembers more names of his brother's ex-wives than titles of his brother's songs.

21. For that matter, it is impossible to distinguish meaningfully musicians of Drew from those of adjoining Tallahatchie County; the six-foot tall Willie Brown lived there as a tenant of the Jennings Plantation, as did both "Tee-Nicey" Wade and Dick Bankston in the 1920s, when both settled in Tutwiler.
22. The song would be a regular twelve bar blues, except that one measure is cut from the end of the first line.
23. In the first phrase of the song, Johnson disrupts this pattern by accenting the sixth beat (-by [of the word "baby"]) instead of the fifth ("ba-"). The first piece Skip James learned, "Drunken Spree," was a square dance that was accented according to a 1–2 pattern. Likewise, Leadbelly's Library of Congress demonstration of a square dance pattern, "Poor Howard," was given 1–2 accenting.
24. Patton tends to use the major third scale step to ease his ascending melodic motions, whereas Johnson and Bailey often eschews it, often leading to awkward-sounding results.

## Chapter 7

1. Examples of Patton's mimicry on guitar may be heard on the two parts of "Prayer of Death," especially on Part I during which he imitates on guitar a singing of "Nearer, My God, To Thee."
2. Mitford Macleod Mathews, *A Dictionary of Americanisms on Historical Principles* (Chicago: University of Chicago Press, 1951), s.v. "hard."
3. Patton's material was for the most part standard blues fare in terms of its melodies, intervals, accompaniment harmonies, and guitar keys. His most unusual melody besides "Pony Blues" was "Hammer Blues," which was his adaptation of Spencer Williams' 1924 composition "Mountain Top Blues." The two phrases of the first chorus of Patton's version end not on the tonic but on the major third scale step, which in the second phrase also served as the lowest tone in the song (which is unusual of many blues). Overall though, in his recorded songs, Patton's only unusual scale degrees are his augmented fourths. His harmonic treatment of chords involves a common Mississippi blues device of implying a dominant seventh by omitting its major third (and sometimes even its root), which Patton used to advantage to sing and play with great melodic and rhythmic freedom. His basic guitar positions were the key of E and open A ("Spanish") tuning.
4. Henry Thomas is thought to be the oldest black musician whose work is available on records. He recorded 23 issued sides for the Vocalion label in 1927–1929. While he may not have been as accomplished a musician in his place and culture as Patton was in his, Thomas did preserve on his records a number of African American songs of the late 1890s and 1900s and some of the earliest datable blues. The most extensive examination of Thomas' life, music and lyrics is Mack McCormick's essay and transcripts accompanying the 2-LP set *"Ragtime Texas" Henry Thomas: Complete Recorded Works 1927–1929 in Chronological Order,* Herwin 209, 1975.

5. For comparison examples in the square-dance 1–2–3–4 pattern, consult Blind Willie Johnson's recordings for Columbia Records of "Jesus Make Up My Dying Bed" (1927) and "You're Gonna Need Somebody on Your Bond" (1930).
6. Booker White explained to Calt that "the people wouldn't dance in the house [because] most [of] the time they'd break the houses down, be so many people."
7. The "cut-in" technique was employed on a few other Mississippi blues, such as William Harris' "Kansas City Blues" (1927), Skip James' "Devil Got My Woman" (1931), and Robert Johnson's "I Believe I'll Dust My Broom" (1936).
8. As will be noted in the chapter "A Session with Son Sims," Patton recorded two takes of the blues whose first lyric is "When Your Way Gets Dark." For some reason, the Paramount recording engineer numbered the takes as L-48–1 and L-49–1, instead of L-48–1 and L-48–2. L-48–1 was released as "Magnolia Blues," and L-49–1 as "When Your Way Gets Dark." In the 1988 edition of this book, although describing the beginning of the take issued as "Magnolia Blues," Calt mistakenly gives the title as "When Your Way Gets Dark." It was probably this song that Miller (who could not remember its title) counted as his favorite Patton piece. "It was slow, and people didn't dance by it," Miller said of the song, which he relished so much that Patton always included it in their outings together. "He'd say, 'Well kid, I reckon I better play your piece now, and get you off my back.'"
9. Patton's only accompaniments that lack a "talking" component are "Runnin' Wild," where he defers to a fiddler, and "High Water Everywhere, Part One."
10. Eileen Southern, editor, *Readings in Black American Music* (New York: W. W. Norton, 1971), 81.
11. Patton's rolls typically stand separate from whatever guitar figures that follow them. But during the second chorus of "Rattlesnake Blues," he does a striking job of linking a roll with a follow-up riff. What he does is begin a three-beat bass roll on the second beat of the second vocal phrase, then fuse it with a snapped treble string tone on the fifth beat (which happens to be the minor seventh of the implied IV chord) and the bass eighth-notes on the sixth beat to lead to a treble riff that he borrowed from "Pony Blues."
12. The nearest he comes to establishing a set guitar pattern are the tonic bass-fills that he inserts during the last vocal phrases of "Green River" and "Jim Lee." While the fills are heard on these records on every other beat in a 1–2 pattern, sometimes they are omitted.
13. Son House, during an interview conducted by David Evans, remembered Patton playing slide guitar lap-style and fretting with a knife. David Evans, "An Early Interview with Son House," 35.

## Chapter 8

1. William Broonzy, *Big Bill Blues: William Broonzy's Story* (1955; revised edition, New York: Oak Publications, 1964, 48–49).

2. In the 1920s "scuttle" was a perjorative term for an African American person. Harold Wentworth and Stuart Berg Flexner, editors, *Dictionary of American Slang* (New York: Thomas Y. Crowell and Company, 1960), s.v. "scuttle."
3. Bob Eagle and Eric S. Leblanc, in their geographical blues directory *Blues: A Regional Experience* (Santa Barbara, CA: Praeger, 2013), list 16 musicians as having been born in or around the Bolton/Edwards area. However, it should be noted that some of them in the list did not make records, and many of them are Chatmon family members. But even with that quantity adjusted, Calt's assertion in the 1988 edition of this Patton biography that "Bolton furnished more recorded bluesmen than any other Mississippi town" may hold true, at least for bluesmen per person living there.
4. Vinson's bias was shared by Willie Moore, who said of Patton in 1972, "I'll tell you what made him popular: 'The Crowing Rooster Blues' (sic), 'The Pony Blues.' They wasn't all that good, but at that time the people didn't know too much about music. Music wasn't as 'classical' as it is now, and it wasn't as hard to do it as it is now."
5. The "Sliding Delta" was the name of a train that ran between the Mississippi towns Greenwood and Grenada. Tommy Johnson's "Slidin' Delta" for Paramount Records in 1930 is of a different melody, in a 12-measure three-phrase form instead of in Patton's 8-measure form in "Jim Lee Blues."
6. Partridge, *A Dictionary of Slang and Unconventional English* (New York: Macmillan, 1953), s.v. "stone blinder."
7. Origin Jazz Library's first reissue LP of Patton, *The Immortal Charlie Patton* (OJL-1, 1961) contained "Stone Pony Blues." In a 1968 interview ("Gypsy Eyes," *Cleveland Scene*, November 1968), singer Linda Ronstadt acknowledged that the name of her band The Stone Poneys (sic) was taken from Patton's song. Given the rarity of the 1934 Vocalion 78, it may have been from the OJL reissue LP where they got this name.
8. House used the expression in his own "Dry Spell Blues" (Paramount Records, 1930) to describe the "money men" (the planters) of Lula.
9. Samuel Charters, notes accompanying Son House and J. D. (Jaydee) Short, *Blues From The Mississippi Delta*, Folkways LP FA 2467, LP record, 1963. Short's claim that Patton was "haulin' logs" at the camp is unlikely.
10. Evans, "Conscience of the Delta," 2018, 64, 79.
11. Clarksdale MS blues historian Robert Birdsong happened to meet Rosetta Patton Brown in April 1991. Jim O'Neal acknowledged her and Birdsong in his 1993 booklet essay for Charley Patton, *The Complete Recorded Works*, Peavine PCD 2255/6/7, and David Evans includes her among Patton's known children in the 2001 and 2018 versions of his "Conscience of the Delta" essay.
12. In 2012, Randy Meadows located Patton's draft registration card dated September 18, 1918. On that document, Patton gives his birthdate as July 12, 1885.

13. Cottondale was founded shortly after the Civil War. In 1968, the plantation was acquired by L. D. McCoy, Jr. As of 1988, it was still in operation.
14. Bessie Turner told David Evans ("Conscience of the Delta," 2018, 70–71) how at Blaine in 1921 that whites and blacks literally fought with each other to have Patton to play at their parties.
15. Golden Kelly, who in 1968 was Cottondale's last remaining resident who lived there when Patton did, remembered him for his mandolin work, which he liked better than his guitar playing. There are no other reports that Patton played this instrument.
16. During his interview with Wardlow, Frank Howard says the bottled in bond whiskey was "Doug Harper." Checking sites on the history of American whiskey and bourbon, there is no brand named Doug Harper, but there is I. W. Harper, in business since 1872, which was bottling in bond 100 proof rye whiskey in 1932 (see Whiskey ID, https://whiskeyid.com/i-w-harper-rye-bonded-pint-1917–1932/, accessed 30 April 2020).
17. Charles H. McCord, *The American Negro as a Dependent, Defective, and Delinquent* (Nashville: Benson Printing Co., 1920), 262.
18. David Evans, "Blues on Dockery's Plantation: 1895 to 1967," in Mike Leadbitter, editor, *Nothing But The Blues: An Illustrated Documentary* (London: Hanover Books, 1971), 129–132.
19. At one time, Howard said during his 1967 interview with Wardlow, his sister Athie Johnson owned three snapshots of Patton, one displaying him with his arm around a girlfriend's neck. When she was contacted at her home on the Beauty plantation near Forest City, Arkansas in 1972, she said that she no longer possessed them, and that she had no interest in discussing Patton.
20. Minnie Franklin interview with Wardlow, Bovina, MS, July 1963, unpublished notes, but information cited in Klatzko and Wardlow, "The Immortal Charlie Patton," and Stephen Calt and Gayle Wardlow, "Patton's Murder: Whitewash, or Hogwash?"
21. Klatzko with Wardlow, "The Immortal Charlie Patton."

## Chapter 9

1. For many years, it was believed that Willie Brown (I) lived from 1900 to 1952, based on a death certificate recovered by Wardlow in 1965. This revised biography of Patton makes use of a death certificate that was recovered by Randy Meadows in 2011; see Wardlow and Meadows, "Searching for Willie Brown," *Living Blues* no. 229 (February 2014), 66–69. This document was examined with other data by Bob Eagle, "Willie Brown Revisited," *Frog Blues and Jazz Annual* no. 4 (2015), 135–139. A third death certificate should also be be noted, for a Will Brown (ca.1897 - March 6, 1951, Memphis, TN) retrieved by Alex van der Tuuk (reported in his article "Son House: How Paramount's Elusive Artist Became A Blues Icon," *Frog Blues and Jazz Annual* no. 4 (2015), 125–134).

2. Wardlow and Meadows, 66–69.
3. Wardlow and Meadows, 66–69.
4. See Wardlow and Meadows, 66–69, and Eagle, 135–139. A partial confirmation of Moore's World War I account may be seen in the newspaper article "List of Persons Registering at Rosedale June 5th," *Bolivar County Democrat*, 15 June 1918, which includes the names of Willie Brown (no. 171) and Willie Moore (no. 187).
5. For accounts of the Bell Witch, see Arthur Palmer Hudson, *Specimens of Mississippi Folk-Lore* (Ann Arbor, MI: Edwards Brothers, 1928), and Andrew Tackaberry, *Famous Ghosts, Phantoms, and Poltergeists for the Millions* (New York: Bell Press, 1952).
6. With one exception, blues experts agree that the Willie Brown who recorded "Make Me a Pallet on the Floor" in 1941 was the same man who recorded for Paramount in 1930 and performed with Son House through the 1940s. Oddly, the lone disagreement came from the man who supervised the Library's recordings, Alan Lomax who, writing some 50 years afterward (in *The Land Where The Blues Began* [New York: Pantheon Books, 1993], p. 494, ch. 1 note 2), "believe[d]" that a William Brown that he had recorded earlier in Arkansas "was the same William Brown who recorded later . . . with Son House and earlier with Charley Patton." As much as one wishes to believe Lomax because he was there, one is led by the recordings to think that Lomax was mistaken or writing without notes or review of the recordings.
7. On records, Patton's bottleneck technique sounds more fluid than Son House's. Still, in 1966, House claimed to Calt and Nick Perls that Patton "never could use them (bottleneck) and neither could Willie Brown. They didn't understand how to use them, because if you just take the bottleneck just like you take your naked finger, you know, and chord like that, it sound like the devil. You got to keep your hand moving (i.e., laterally, to produce a vibrator). And they never could get that hand so they could play."
8. An instance on records, however indistinct, of Brown and Patton laughing and talking may be heard just after the second lyric phrase of the fourth chorus of Patton's "Moon Going Down" for the lyric "Lord I think I heard that Helena whistle." (Thanks to the late R. R. Macleod for pointing out this moment in his transcription of this song's lyrics in his book *Yazoo 1–20* [Edinburgh, Scotland: PAT Publications, 1988].) From his memories, though, House maintained to Calt and Perls, "He never would barely talk. He didn't talk much."
9. Mike Leadbitter, "My Girlish Days," *Blues Unlimited* no. 78 (December 1970), 8–9. Paul and Beth Garon, in their book *Woman With Guitar: Memphis Minnie's Blues* ([Boston]: Da Capo Press, 1992), p. 14, state that Memphis Minnie received her first guitar as a Christmas present in 1905.
10. "You'll notice that Charlie Patton plays everything he play in one tunin' mostly, in 'Spanish,'" McMullan said. "Little Willie didn't do that." Less than half of the thirty-two blues recordings Patton produced during the time McMullan knew him were played in "Spanish" tuning.

11. In his favoring Brown over Patton, House went so far as to assert that Brown was more consistent in maintaining the rhythm of the accompaniment than Patton. "Charlie used to 'break time' in lots of pieces. You take 'High Water [Everywhere],' he breaks a little time if you notice it right careful. Charlie played (it) the way Willie Brown (played) 'The Jinks.' But Charlie he makes two beats, then he change right over there, but Willie he keeps over to the third verse and then he change."
12. When Ernest Brown knew him, Willie Brown played without picks.
13. Although Richard "Hacksaw" Harney (1902–1973) recorded very little, he was highly prized as a musician in the Delta. *Living Blues* magazine ran his obituary (no. 17 [Summer 1974], 7) and in the next issue of that magazine, Stephen LaVere published a profile ("Hacksaw Harney," *Living Blues* no. 18 [Autumn 1974], 7). His only recordings on 78s are as sideman to Pearl Dickson and Walter Rhodes for Columbia in 1927, which will be examined in Chapter 9. The most substantial documentation of Harney's musicianship are the recordings issued on Harney, *Sweet Man* (Adelphi/Genes GCD 9909) with the booklet notes by Larry Hoffman and Denise Tapp.
14. Charlie McCoy (1909–1950) was born in Jackson, Mississippi and died in Chicago, Illinois. Although he made a number of records as leader or featured artist, he also contributed as a sideman to other recordings. Among his earliest recordings are his assistance to Tommy Johnson and Ishman Bracey during their 1928 Victor sessions. After moving to Chicago in 1934, he made a successful transition to swing music, and among his recording sessions were those by the Harlem Hamfats for Decca. While his sessions as leader are collected by Document Records (Charlie McCoy, *Complete 1928–1932 Recordings*, Document BDCD 6018, and T*he McCoy Brothers* volumes 1 and 2, Document BDCD 6019 and 6020), samples of his versatile sideman work may be heard on Charlie McCoy, *Jackson Stomp: The Charlie McCoy Story* (Nehi Records NEH02, 2013, with essay by Russell Beecher).
15. For thoughts on the Kid Bailey recordings in addition to those given here by the authors, see David Evans, ". . . Ramblin'," *Blues Revue Quarterly* no. 8 (Spring 1993), 14–17.

## *Chapter 10*

1. Shirley Griffith, who formerly resided in Brandon, Mississippi, reported that Patton played frequently in Jackson during the 1920s, traveling there by way of Hattiesburg (interview conducted by Calt, Indianapolis, Indiana, 1971). During his 1965–1969 interviews with Calt, Skip James told of Patton's appearances in the late 1920s in his home town of Bentonia, a hill town north of Jackson.
2. The transcription of "Pea Vine Blues" for the *Country Blues Songbook* by Stefan Grossman, Hal Grossman and Stephen Calt (New York: Oak, 1973, p. 164), renders that stanza as:

> Well, the levee sinkin,' you know I, baby . . .
> (spoken: Baby, you know I *can't* stay!)

The levee is sinkin,' Lord, you know I cannot . . .
I'm goin' up the country, mama, in a few more days.

3. Southern speech is laced with Biblical quotes, and Patton's lyrics are no exception. This simile involving rabbits and dens may be likened to Jesus' saying "The foxes have holes, and the birds of the air have nests; but the Son of Man hath not where to lay his head" (Matthew 8:20).
4. Percy, *Lanterns on the Levee*, 14.
5. Mary Wheeler, *Steamboatin' Days* (Baton Rouge: Louisiana State University Press, 1944), 5.
6. Two early African American assessments of the Delta's passing river culture were written in the early 1940s by Lewis Wade Jones and Samuel C. Adams, Jr. as studies resulting from the 1941–1942 joint research in the Delta undertaken by the Library of Congress (represented by Alan Lomax) and Fisk University. Jones' and Adams' contributions were published with John W. Work's research as *Lost Delta Found: Rediscovering the Fisk University-Library of Congress Coahoma County Study, 1941–1942* (Nashville: Vanderbilt University Press, 2005).
7. In his lyrics transcription and notes for "Tom Rushen Blues" in the 2001 Revenant set *Screamin' and Hollerin the Blues* (p.59), Dick Spottswood affirms Gertrude "Ma" Rainey's 1924 Paramount recording "Booze and Blues" as a chief antecedent for the lyrics and music, and he mentions Jelly Roll Morton's 1924 "Tom Cat Blues" (aka "Midnight Mama") sharing the same melody. In a set of emails to Edward Komara (10–14 April 2020), Spottswood pointed out additional publications and recordings from 1920 through 1952. A chief antecedent is Alex Valentine's "Four O'Clock Blues" published in 1920, (Memphis, TN: Bluff City Music), which pre-dates the 1921 events behind the lyrics "Betty and Dupree" that were adapted and widely sung by professional and vernacular musicians to the tune (see Richard Polenberg, *Hear My Sad Story: The True Tales That Inspired "Stagolee," "John Henry," and Other Traditional American Folk Songs* [Ithaca, NY: Cornell University Press, 2015], 137–148).
8. For more about Rushing, including a short firsthand account, see Evans, "Conscience," 2018, 60, 98–102; see also Evans, " . . . Ramblin," *Blues Revue Quarterly* no. 6 (Winter 1993), 10–12; and Jim O'Neal's "Tom Rushen Blues" section of "Revisiting the Worlds of Charley Patton," 66–70..
9. Jim O'Neal, "Charley Patton: Paradigm and Paradox," booklet accompanying Charley Patton, *The Complete Recorded Works*, Peavine PCD-2255/6/7, 1993. One of O'Neal's informants for Patton lore was Seab Holloway's son Osborn "Rooster" Holloway.
10. According to Evans, "Conscience of the Delta," 2018, 64–65, Patton often left the South to play for blacks who had moved to the northern cities.
11. Richard Spottswood, lyric transcription and notes for Patton, "Mean Black Moan," in the notes accompanying Patton, *Screamin' and Hollerin' the Blues* (Revenant 212, 7 CDs, 2001), p. 66.

12. Colin J. Davis, *Power at Odds: The 1922 National Railroad Shopmen's Strike.* Urbana: University of Illinois Press, 1997.
13. Not Robert Edward Kennedy as mistaken in the 1988 edition. Of Irish descent, Robert Emmett Kennedy (1877–1941) was born in Gretna, Louisiana. In 1923 he moved to New York City, where with his pen name R. Emmett Kennedy he began writing books, a few of which were steeped in the African American culture of the East Green section of Gretna, especially *Black Cameos* (New York: A. and C. Boni, 1924), *Gritny People* (New York: Dodd, Mead and Co., 1927), and *Red Bean Row* (New York: Dodd, Mead and Co.,1929).
14. The early history of commercial blues recordings is told by Robert M. W. Dixon and John Godrich, *Recording the Blues* (London: Studio Vista, 1970), which was later reprinted as part of *Yonder Come the Blues* (Cambridge: Cambridge University Press, 2001). Dixon and Godrich were also the compilers of the standard discography of pre-World War II "prewar" blues records, now in its fourth edition as *Blues and Gospel Records 1890–1943*, compiled by Robert M. W. Dixon, John Godrich, and Howard Rye (Oxford; New York: Oxford University Press, 1997).
15. Other records that Patton made use for his studio recording sessions were: "Vicksburg Blues" by Little Brother Montgomery; "Jim Jackson's Kansas City Blues" by Jim Jackson; "Mountain Top Blues" by Bessie Smith; "Sittin' On Top of the World" by the Mississippi Sheiks; "Bumble Bee" by Memphis Minnie; "M. & O. BLues" by Walter Davis; and "Troubled 'Bout My Soul" by Frank Palmes. How Patton treated these songs will be discussed where appropriate in the remaining chapters.
16. The record Miller remembered Patton liking was Leroy Carr with Scrapper Blackwell, "Prison Bound Blues" issued on 78 as the reverse of "How Long How Long Blues no. 2" (Vocalion 1241). Both performances were recorded in Chicago in December 1928, and released early the following year.
17. The extent of Tommy Johnson's influence may be assessed in two chapters from David Evans' *Big Road Blues*, "The Local Tradition" (pp. 167–264) and "The Traditional Blues Song" (pp. 265–311).
18. For an overall history of African American accordion playing in Mississippi, including Walter Rhodes' place in it, see Jared M. Snyder's excellent and timely article "Squeezebox: The Legacy of Afro-Mississippi Accordionists," *Black Music Research Journal* 17, no. 1 (Spring 1997): 37–57.
19. The relationship of Jim Jackson's "Kansas City Blues" (1927) to Blind Blake's "Diddie Wa Diddie" (1929) is not very clear. Both records have a similar melody, share the 4+8 verse and refrain blues structure, and feature phonetic imitation on the rhyming sounds of "city" and "diddie." From the recording dates and the high sales of the Jackson record, it would seem that Blake is derivative of Jackson. In the 1988 edition of this book, Calt thought mistakenly that the Blake record was made in 1926 and, presumably supposing that Booker Miller heard Blake in person at the same time (per Miller's interviews with Wardlow), argued

for Blake as the ultimate source of "Kansas City Blues." This argument should be balanced with the fact that Blake did not record with this melody in 1926–1927, before Jackson recorded "Kansas City Blues."

20. The section about Ralph Lembo is indebted to T. DeWayne Moore's article, "Revisiting Ralph Lembo," 153–184.
21. Moore, 155–156.
22. Moore, 157.
23. Moore, 159–161. Lacy was one of the earliest Mississippi Delta musicians to make commercial records. The Columbia sides were never released and are presumably lost. The two Paramount sides, "Mississippi Jail House Groan" and "Ham Hound Crave" were issued back-to-back on Paramount 12629.
24. Moore, 163–165.
25. Moore, 165.
26. Quote from Edwards interview with Calt, 1971. See also Edwards' later retelling of the Jefferson performance in his autobiography (with Janis Martinson and Michael Robert Frank) *The World Don't Owe Me Nothing: The Life and Times of David 'Honeyboy' Edwards* (Chicago: Chicago Review Press, 2000), 90.
27. Moore, 166.
28. Recording data for Cotton, Lacy and Thornton may be found in respective entries in Robert M. W. Dixon, John Godrich, and Howard Rye, *Blues and Gospel Records 1890–1942.*, fourth edition (New York: Oxford University Press, 1997). Lacy's "Mississippi Jail House Groan"/"Ham Hound Crave" (Paramount 12629) was promoted by Paramount in a picture advertisement in the *Chicago Defender* newspaper, 2 June 1928.
29. Moore, 171–172.
30. Speir received this communication after each of Patton's sessions.
31. Calt and Wardlow published their Paramount research in five articles for *78 Quarterly*, as follows: "Anatomy of a 'Race' Label, pt. 1" *78 Quarterly* no. 3 (1988), 9–23; "Pt. 2," *78 Quarterly* no. 4 (1989), 9–30; "Pt. 3: The Buying and Selling of Paramounts," *78 Quarterly* no. 5 (1990), 7–24; "Pt. 4: The Advent of Arthur Laibly," *78 Quarterly* no. 6 (1991), 8–26; "Pt. 5: Paramount's Decline and Fall," *78 Quarterly* no. 7 (1992), 7–29. Since then, a flood of CD reissues, books, discographies and other resources have been produced. Alex van der Tuuk's *Paramount's Rise and Fall* (Denver: Mainspring Press, 2003; revised and expanded edition, 2012) looks at the history of the label from the perspective of its parent firm, The Wisconsin Chair Company. Since 1971, Max Vreede's *Paramount 12000/13000 Series* (London: Storyville, 1971) has been the chief discography of the label's African American recordings, but research since 1990 has made it somewhat outdated. To give an update about the surviving blues and black sacred issues, and to widen scope to include Paramount's white artists, Alex van der Tuuk and Guido van Rijn published five volumes of their *New York Recording Laboratories Series* (Overveen, The Netherlands: Agram Blues Books, 2011–2015). Reissues of

Paramount music may be sampled on disc and audiostream services, especially on the CD labels Document and Yazoo. The most elaborate presentations of Paramount history to date are the two volumes of *The Rise and Fall of Paramount Records*, issued jointly by Revenant Records and Third Man Records in 2013 and 2014, each set containing two books, a pouch of facsimile documents, 6 LPs, and a USB drive containing 800 audio music tracks and related advertising artwork.

32. Yet the session's entry under Hawkins' name in Dixon, Godrich and Rye, *Blues Records 1890–1943* 4th edition show that none of the issued sides have take numbers higher than two. Either Paramount numbered only those takes that were acceptable for release and the respective alternates in case of damage to the preferred takes, or Hawkins' was more efficient in the recording studio than Charles claimed.
33. House remembered it for its inlays, saying to Calt and Perls, "His'n was a little more fancy than me and Willie's [Brown's] . . . The neck of it was made a little different . . . it had fancy coils in it." Also, Tom Cannon told David Evans ("Conscience," 2018, 66) that Patton kept three guitars, one of them with "gold pieces plastered all on it."
34. As notated in the Gennett recording ledger page, the take for "Screamin' and Hollerin' the Blues" was titled "Overseas Blues" by the attending engineer.

### *Chapter 11*

1. According to David Evans, "Conscience," 2018, 68, a Clarksdale record dealer named Joe Lavene sold Patton 78s in large quantities at the picnics where Patton was playing.
2. Calt and Wardlow, "The Anatomy of a 'Race' Label, Part II: The Mayo Williams Era," *78 Quarterly* no. 4 (1989), 29. See also Van der Tuuk, *Paramount's Rise and Fall*, second edition, 105.
3. Tom Cannon told David Evans ("Conscience," 2018, 126–128) that it was Jett's idea, not Will Dockery's, to expel Patton. Evans also believes that the expulsion occurred in late 1933 or early 1934, not in 1929.
4. Wentworth and Flexner, *Dictionary of American Slang*, q.v. "Thirty-four." The fact that Patton recorded his "34 Blues" with its lyric "Christmas rolled up, I was broke as I could be" in January 1934, not that December, confirms that Patton's use of the phrase "Thirty-four" was figurative.
5. Evans, "Conscience," 2018, 62, heard the Patton family story that Patton had lived briefly in the Orange Mound section of Memphis and offered guitar lessons there. Evans supposed (135, n. 49) that, if true if not verifiable (he didn't find Patton listed in the Memphis directories for 1924–1934), Patton would have been there briefly.
6. Following up his success in providing Patton, Speir had sent Paramount the team of Blind Roosevelt and Uaroy Graves, whom he heard in a church in McComb, a town that normally "wasn't any good" for talent. A native of Rose Hill, Graves toured

Delta towns like Helena and Greenwood and once mentioned meeting Patton to a traveling companion. For a complete biography, see Gayle Wardlow, "Blind Roosevelt Graves (1909–1962)," in Wardlow, *Chasin' That Devil Music*, 191–195.

7. Bracey interview with Wardlow.
8. Three masters from this session remain untraced. The date of the session is uncertain. The fourth edition of Dixon, Godrich and Rye's *Blues and Gospel Records 1890–1943* (1997) dates it to October 1929. Recent research and redating by Alex van der Tuuk and Guido van Rijn, *New York Recording Laboratories volume 1: L Matrix Series*, second edition (Overveen, Netherlands: Agram Blues Books, 2015) posit a new range of late January/early February 1930, which brings it close to the distinct memory of Sims' sister Roberta Jameson as occurring in the spring of 1930. It was Laibly's policy to have Grafton artists record three takes of each potentially issuable song. He would then review the takes with a recording engineer (usually Walter Klopp) and decide which of the three to issue. In 1985, unissued takes of three Patton songs ("Elder Green Blues," "Hammer Blues," and "Some of These Days") were recovered by Michael Kirsling from the attic of a Waukegan, Illinois house; see Bob Hilbert, "Paramounts in the Belfry," *78 Quarterly* no. 4 (1989), 71–76.
9. Most of what is known about Sims, especially his family life, comes from two interviews conducted in 1969–1970 in Memphis by the authors with Sims' sisters Roberta Jameson and Lilly Hester. An updated biography of Sims was published by Wardlow alone as "Henry 'Son' Sims: 'Farrell Blues Mama, Sho' Don't Worry 'Bout Me,'" *78 Quarterly* no. 9 [1995], 11–20.
10. Their longest separation lasted two years in the mid-1920s, during which time Sims lived with Percy Thomas on Wall's plantation near Farrell. On that time, peace was made when his wife appeared at Thomas' doorstep to return Sims' clothes.
11. To accompany this song, Patton played "just most anything what fits, you know," Son House said. "Something like 'Shake It and Break It'. . . . The guys (in the audience) they didn't know no better nohow; they didn't care—they're interested in the words."
12. See John Stephen Farmer and William Ernest Henley, *Slang and its Analogues Past and Present* ([London:] for subscribers only, 1890–1904, 7 volumes), q.v. "lady green." During the 17th and 18th centuries, "green-apron" was a slang term for a lay preacher.
13. During some measures on this record, such as the last measure of the first chorus and the first measure of the next chorus, Patton may strum some variants to his "complement" pattern like three or four treble beats in a row.
14. Although the vocal extensions that end each lyric phrase of "Rattlesnake Blues" involve relatively short durations of two or four beats, the guitar phrasing is identical with that of the title verse of "Pony Blues," except for the omission of half-bar strums from each phrase. The accompaniment takes a repeating pattern of 12 ½ bar verses (in which the beats of each phrase are arranged in the lyric-fill patterns of 10–6, 10–6, 10–8 pattern, so the extra ½ measure per chorus is in the turn-

around fill leading to the next vocal chorus) until the final verse. The main difference that "Rattlesnake Blues" has from the "Pony Blues" title verse accompaniment is in having the subdominant-7th (IV7) rolls during each second lyric phrase.

15. Charles O'Brien, telephone interview with Edith North Johnson, St. Louis, 19 April 1980. Cited in Guido van Rijn, Cor von Sliedregt, and Hans Vergeer, booklet accompanying *Edith Johnson 1903–1988: Honey Dripper Blues*, Agram Blues AB 2016, 1991.
16. In his Edith North Johnson reissue *Honey Dripper Blues*, Guido van Rijn argued that the guitarist was Charlie Patton, whose matrix numbers for his Paramount session with Son Sims occur before and after those of these Johnson masters. In the same notes, Van Rijn was also the first writer to point out that the guitar licks may also be heard in Patton's accompaniments to Sims' "Farrell Blues" and "Come Back Corrina." In my notes for the 2001 Revenant set on Charley Patton, I agreed with van Rijn's identification, adding Sims' "Tell Me Man" as a third example. Oddly, in the same set, David Evans weighed in with his opinion that the guitarist was Smoky Harrison of North Carolina, who recorded after Patton and Johnson. If so according to Evans, then Harrison, not Patton, would have been the guitarist on Sim's four singing sides, an unlikely and, at bottom, absurd circumstance in view of the various times during the recording visit when Sims sang on his sides.
17. But even in these song sketches, Patton's singularity is manifest in the off-beat touches he freely added. Damping and percussive guitar tapping mark "Mean Black Cat," primarily a vehicle for lyrics. Unorthodox damped tonic bass slides herald the end of each vocal phrase of "Devil Sent the Rain," which had an affecting contrast between a torpid tempo and a turbulent vocal delivery. In "Joe Kirby," he simultaneously snapped and damped a sixth beat bass fill.
18. Son House interview with Calt and Perls, 1966.

### Chapter 12

1. David Evans in "High Water Everywhere: Blues and Gospel Commentary on the 1927 Mississippi River Flood" (in Robert Springer, editor, *Nobody Knows Where the Blues Comes From: Lyrics and History* [Jackson, MS: University Press of Mississippi, 2006], 3–75), doubts the authors' ascription of Mattie Doyle as the recording artist Mattie Delaney. Instead, he cites a federal census report taken on April 5, 1930 in Glendora, MS for a Mattie Delaney, age 25, married, but having no occupation, and living with a blacksmith grandfather. He states that "almost certainly" this Mattie Delaney is the one who recorded "Tallahatchie River Blues," which he says is about the January 1930 Tallahatchie River flood, not about the broader spring 1927 Mississippi River flood.
2. For a basic list of commercial records made during and shortly after the 1927 flood, see Keith Briggs, "High water everywhere: blues and the Mississippi flood

of 1927," *Living Blues* no. 87 (July 1989), 26–29. For lyric transcripts and commentary about many of these records, see David Evans, "High Water Everywhere: Blues and Gospel Commentary on the 1927 Mississippi River Flood." The flood itself was brought on by three weeks of steady rainfall, after eight months of abnormally frequent rain had swollen the Mississippi and softened its dirt levees.The standard narrative about this event is John M. Barry, *Rising Tide: The Great Mississippi Flood and How It Changed America* (New York: Touchstone/Simon and Schuster, 1997). For a photographic survey, see Pete Daniel, *Deep'n As It Come* (New York: Oxford University Press, 1977). When Calt and Wardlow wrote this chapter for the 1988 edition, there were only the Daniel book and few, if any other, monographs about the flood, so much of their research and presentation were done from the primary sources accessible to them. The references to Barry's book are for the reader to look up for additional reading, not as indications of what sources Calt and Wardlow had used for the 1988 edition.

3. Evans, "Conscience of the Delta," 2018, 109.
4. Patton's nephew Tom Cannon thought his uncle was at Gunnison near the river, while his niece Bessie Turner thought he was at the town of Shelby, some ten miles east of of the river. See Evans, "Conscience," 2018, 106.
5. For examples of forced labor by plantation hands on the levees, see Barry, pp. 184, and 192–196.
6. Percy, *Lanterns on the Levee*, 249.
7. Barry includes this collapse as part of the larger collapse that same day, April 21, 1927, at Mound's Landing; see his book *Rising Tide*, 196–206, for an overall depiction of this break, and page 201 for his mention of Stop's Landing.
8. Barry, 204, includes an eyewitness account of the flood coming into Leland in waves that were "five or six feet deep and just rolling and rolling."
9. See Barry, 306 and 312, for his initial descriptions.
10. Joe Rice Dockery interview with Wardlow and Calt, 1970.
11. Booker Miller deciphered this phrase for the authors. Apparently "higher mound" means an Indian burial mound.
12. Percy, *Lanterns*, 258, wrote that "the dispersal of our labor was a longer evil to the Delta than a flood."
13. The meaning of "skid" is obscure. Patton may refer to a skid-road, i.e., a plank road upon which logs were hauled.
14. The revision of this chapter's explication of "High Water Everywhere" Part II is indebted to David Evans's convincing presentation of it as about the January 1930 flood, first presented in the 2018 version of "Conscience of the Delta," 109–112.
15. Will Dockery owned a plantation in Marion City. Patton's reference to a Marion whistle in "Green River Blues" indicates his familiarity with the area. An alternate rendering of this lyric chorus is offered by Evans, "Conscience," 2018, 111, as:

> "Oh, I hear the horn blow, blowin' up on my shore.
> (spoken: Blowin'; couldn't hear it.)

I heard the iceboat, Lord, was sinking down.
I couldn't get no boat, so I let 'em sink on down."

Evans' replacement of "ice, Lord" with "iceboat" in accordance with the 1930 flood may ease the deciphering of that lyric line, if not of the whole chorus.

16. Ice boats were used for rescue purposes during the flood, and Patton is apparently referring to one here. Evans, "Conscience," 2018,111, also renders this line as "I thought I would take a trip, Lord, out on the big ice sled."
17. Evans, "Conscience of the Delta," 2018, 109.

## *Chapter 13*

1. David Evans, in the 1987 version of his "Conscience" essay,167, thought Bertha Lee Jones was born in 1917, and that she began living with Patton in 1933 at age 16. For the 2018 update, 82, he agrees with the authors that she was born in 1902, and adds that she had been previously married to Cleveland Harper and had a son by him.
2. Tom Cannon interview with Calt and Wardlow, 1970.
3. The musician who worked this routine was known as a "sweet back papa" and his girlfriend, a "sweet mama." For other examples in literature about blues and early jazz, see Alan Lomax, *Mister Jelly Roll*, 19–20, and William Broonzy, *Big Bill Blues*, 48–49. In his 1908 book *Following the Color Line* (New York: Doubleday and Page), Ray Stannard Baker wrote that (p. 60) "a woman who works as a cook in a white family will often take enough from the to feed a worthless vagabond," illustrating his point with a lyric from a "Negro song" (but not a blues) in which the male singer brags that "I doan has to work so ha'd / I's got a gal in the white folks' ya'd."
4. This quote was initially published at the end of Calt and Wardlow's article "Patton's Murder - Whitewash or Hogwash," 10–17.
5. These consisted of excerpts from editorials of the April 12th and April 19th editions of the Puckett, Mississippi newspaper. Laibly had the company press a hundred copies of each monologue, and gave them to Speir free of charge. Before his 1973 death, Speir gave his last remaining copy to Gayle Wardlow, who in 1995 sold it to the Blues Archive, the University of Mississippi. The monologues were issued on Charley Patton, *Screamin' and Hollerin' the Blues* (Revenant 212), 7 CDs, 2001.
6. For a complete account and transfers of both sides of Henderson's "Hello World" disc, see R. Connor Montgomery, "Hello World! (Doggone Ya)," Old-Time Blues Electrically Recorded weblog, http://oldtimeblues.net/2015/05/27/hello-world/, accessed 30 April 2020.
7. Beaumont, 57, believes that Laibly was making frequent trips to the Lone Star state to find blues successors to Blind Lemon Jefferson, the Texas star for Paramount who died in Chicago in December 1929.

8. For a comprehensive profile, see Calt and Wardlow, "He's a Devil of a Joe," *Blues Unlimited* no. 146 (Autumn/Winter 1984): 16–20 (reprinted in Wardlow, *Chasin' That Devil Music*, 170–180).
9. For more about the Paramount recording trip that Tommy Johnson took with Ishman Bracey, see Gayle Wardlow, "Got Four, Five Puppies, One Little Shaggy Hound."
10. As acknowledged earlier, Calt and Wardlow drew from Calt and Nick Perls' 1966 interview with House in New York as the main source of his quotes about his life and about Patton. David Evans' interview with House has been recently published ("An Early Interview with Son House," *Frog Blues and Jazz Annual* no. 5 [2017]: 28–44, 176–194). For the present revision, Daniel Beaumont's *Preachin' The Blues: The Life and Times of Son House* (New York: Oxford University Press, 2011) has been valuable for checking and confirming House's anecdotes.
11. Beaumont, 36–38.
12. 1926 is the year that House gave to Alan Lomax during an interview conducted during a Library of Congress field recording session in 1941. The alternate year, 1927, was given to Julius Lester, who reports it in the published interview with House as "I Can Make My Own Songs: An Interview with Son House," *Sing Out!* 15, no. 3 (July 1965): 38–47.
13. In *Preachin' The Blues*, 49, Beaumont believes that a planter for whom House's father and uncles worked may have interceded with a Clarksdale judge to reconsider House's case.
14. That House very likely performed solo between Patton's sets may explain the fact that he learned all of his versions of Patton pieces not from Patton, but from Willie Brown during the 1930s. Since what he learned was through Brown, he would have then heard and remembered Patton's music in Brown's way, not in Patton's, which may explain why House in later interviews seemed to miss the finer points of Patton's craft. Elijah Wald (*Escaping the Delta: Robert Johnson and the Invention of the Blues*, New York: Amistad, 2004, 158) and Beaumont (*Preachin' the Blues*, 54) agree with Calt and Wardlow that House likely played solo during Patton's set breaks, although Beaumont also thinks plausible that Patton could have "comped" or strummed along with House's bottleneck-fretted blues.
15. The Patton/House road trip story is one of the most cherished in Delta blues lore. It is the subject of two lengthy articles, one by Jas Obrecht for guitarists ("Deep Down in the Delta," *Guitar Player* 26, no 8 (August 1992), 66–70+), the other by Edward Komara for bibliographers ("Blues in the Round," *Black Music Research Journal* 17, no. 1 (Spring 1997), 3–36). For the present account, the version of events related by Son House to Nick Perls and Stephen Calt in 1966 (partially published in transcription as "Son House Interview Part One," *78 Quarterly* no. 1 (1967), 59–61; "part two" was never published) will be followed, with sources of additional details acknowledged in these notes.
16. Son House to Julius Lester, "I Can Make My Own Songs," *Sing Out!* 15, no. 3 (July 1965): 40.

17. Laibly asked Speir in Grafton when the Jackson businessman escorted the sacred group the Delta Big Four there at or shortly after the end of April, per Gayle Dean Wardlow, "The Talent Scouts: H. C. Speir (1895–1972)," *78 Quarterly* no. 8 (1993), 25.
18. In his 8-part 1965 serial "Son House" for the Boston folk magazine *Broadside* 4, nos. 3–10 (March 31 through July 7; later collected as *Blues Unlimited Collectors Classics* no. 14 [October 1966]), based on his 1964 interviews with the musician, Al Wilson reported that Patton had fetched Louise Johnson and brought her to Lula to meet House and Brown during the night before they departed north. In view that Wheeler Ford was to be the trip driver, and that Johnson was living on the Kirby plantation just north of the Harbart plantation where Brown was, the present narrative follows the version in which Johnson joined the others on the first morning of the trip.
19. The details of Patton's two car fights with Brown come from an interview with House conducted by John Fahey, Barrett Hansen, and Mark Levine on May 7, 1965, tape now housed at the Southern Folklife Collection, the University of North Carolina at Chapel Hill, and cited by Beaumont, 61.
20. One of these sides, "Walking Blues," was unissued at the time. A test pressing of this performance was among the discs recovered by Mike Kirsling (Hilbert, "Paramounts in the Belfry"). It has since been issued on the labels Yazoo, Document, Pea-Vine, among others.
21. This makes sense for the Johnson sides and Patton/Brown duets. But it is also plausible for the solo sides, too. Between the second and third phrases of he fifth chorus of House's "Preachin' the Blues Part I," a muffled background noise may be heard. The lyrics transcriber R. R. Macleod, for *Document Blues -1* (Edinburgh: PAT Publications, 1994), 26–27, rendered the sound as "Wait for it. Follow me," and noted "The quiet speech (by another?) suggests more than solo v[ocal]/g[uitar]." In citing this note in his article "Blues in the Round," Komara opines that only House was performing, and that the noise was made by a witness.
22. Johnson's other two sides, "On the Wall" and "By The Moon and Stars," play back in the key of B-flat. In their 1975 article "A Handful of Keys: Louise Johnson Again!" (*Blues Unlimited* no. 115 [September/October 1975], 21–22), Bob Hall and Richard Noblett noted the playback keys in F# for the first two Johnson titles, and they suggested that the session was stopped so that repairs to the equipment could be made. If so, then Johnson may have played her first two songs in the key of F, then had to quit recording when the mechanism problems were realized.
23. In his lyric transcripts for the Patton box set *Screamin' and Hollerin' the Blues* (Revenant 212), Dick Spottswood renders the complete audible barrelhouse banter on the Louise Johnson sides, and he also identifies which voice belongs to whom. In this revision of the present book, some of Calt's partial transcripts of the banter are retained, but Louise Johnson's lyrics are restored to the context, and Spottwood's voice identifications are adopted.

24. House recounted to Alan Wilson (1966, 5).
25. Komara, "Blues in the Round," 15–16.
26. The recently recovered copy of House's "Mississippi County Farm Blues," which uses the melody of Jefferson's "See That My Grave Is Kept Clean," bears the matrix number L-401. Louise Johnson's "All Night Long Blues" has L-399, and it is unknown what was on matrix L-400. (The latest matrix number listing for Paramount's Grafton studio is Guido van Rijn and Alex van der Tuuk, *New York Recording Laboratories Matrix Series vol. 1: The L Matrix Series [1929–1932]*, revised second edition, Overveen, The Netherlands: Agram Blues Books, 2015.) Assuming that repairs had to be made to the recording equipment and they took up all of the preceding afternoon, House's claim of recording his blues based on "See That My Grave Is Kept Clean" early on another day of recording is plausible for the second day. Then, according to the studio's matrix number series, House's "Mississippi County Farm Blues" was followed immediately by four sides recorded by a brass band (released on Broadway 78s as either by the Baker's Music Masters or the Broadway Military Band.
27. The Paramount 78-rpm release of House's "Mississippi County Farm Blues" was long known about, but only in 2005 was a copy found, duly reissued on CD the next year. Until then, blues fans settled for House's 1942 rendition known as "County Farm Blues" for Alan Lomax and the Library of Congress. This later performance is different, in that the tempo is slower, the guitar playing is smoother, House's singing seems a little strained and tight, and he doesn't mention the name of Leroy Lee.
28. Although this performance was titled "Walkin' Blues" for its first issue on a Document LP (Delta Blues - Vol. 1, Document DLP 532, 1988), its melody and lyrics are not those of House's "My Black Mama" or Robert Johnson's "Walking Blues" (ARC/Vocalion, recorded 1936). The House test recording was not issued on commercial 78s, but it survived on a test pressing that was found in 1985 by Michael Kirsling (for more about this find, see Hilbert, "Paramounts in the Belfry").
29. According to Stephen Calt, *Barrelhouse Words*, Alcorub was an isopropyl rubbing alcohol that was made by the same company that produced Sterno ("canned heat"). Although rubbing alcohol is toxic, Calt thought that severe alcoholics resorted to it nonetheless when nothing else was available or affordable.
30. See especially "The Pony Blues" that he recorded for Alan Lomax and the Library of Congress on July 17, 1942.
31. John Cowley, "Really the 'Walking Blues': Son House, Muddy Waters, Robert Johnson and the development of a traditional blues," *Popular Music* 1 (1981), 57–72; reprinted in its entirety in *Juke Blues*, no.1 (July 1985), 8–14.
32. Komara, *Road to Robert Johnson*, 7. For more about work songs, the most helpful demonstrations in print form are those in Bruce Jackson, *Wake Up Dead Man: Afro-American Worksongs From Texas Prisons* (Cambridge, MA: Harvard University Press, 1972).

33. See Max Vreede and Guido van Rijn, "The Paramount L Master Series," *78 Quarterly* no. 9 (1995), 67–87, esp. 73.
34. Apparently Brown had never been to St. Louis, as apparently he mistakenly sings "Decatur Hill" instead of "Dago Hill," as Spottwood believes in his transcription for Revenant 212, Charley Patton, *Screamin' and Hollerin' the Blues*. Spottswood and Gayle Wardlow agree that its initial sales and its 1935 reissue on the Decca's Champion subsidiary is likely due to executives confusing Brown's "M&O" with Walter Davis' "M&O Blues" which was a hit record and steady seller for Victor to the 1940s.
35. Alan Lomax, *Mr. Jelly Roll*, 137
36. The 1930 drought and the blues about it have not been as well researched as as the 1927 Mississippi River flood and those songs. When Calt and Wardlow were preparing the 1988 Patton book, Nan Elizabeth Woodruff's book A*s Rare as Rain : Federal Relief in the Great Southern Drought of 1930–31* (Urbanan: University of Illinois Press, 1985) had just appeared. Edward Komara's unpublished study "No Water Anywhere: The Drought Blues of Charlie Patton, Son House, and Skip James" was read at the Delta Studies Symposium "The Blues II," Arkansas State University, Jonesboro (April 19, 1996), for which his primary sources were the 1931 American National Red Cross report *Relief work in the drought of 1930–31; official report of operations* (Washington, DC: American National Red Cross [1931]) and the *Memphis Commercial Appeal* newspaper from April through September 1930; David Evans was in attendance. In a printed response in 2001, as a new footnote in his revision for the Revenant Patton *Screamin and Hollerin'* box set of the his 1987 "Conscience of the Delta" essay, Evans made use of the summer 1930 issues of the *Clarksdale Daily Register* newspaper. His latest presentation of the 1930 drought is in "Conscience," 2018, 115–118.
37. Komara, "No Water Anywhere." There are three recorded blues that deal explicitly with the drought: Son House's "Dry Spell Blues," Patton's "Dry Well Blues," and Spider Carter's "Dry Spell Blues" for Brunswick recorded on September 13, 1930. A fourth blues could be included, Skip James' "Hard Time Killing Floor Blues," recorded for Paramount in February 1931, if what James described in his lyrics could be taken as consequences of the drought the previous summer.
38. Dating the Patton/House/Brown/Johnson recording trip was a longstanding problem. The nearest hard evidence towards a date was a test pressing of Irene Scruggs' Paramount performance of "You've Got What I Want" [matrix L-348–2] whose label bore a handwritten date of May 28, 1930. It should be noted that House, during his 1964 interviews that became the basis for Alan Wilson's *Broadside* serial, said that August was when the session took place. The discographers Robert Dixon and John Godrich in the first (1963) edition of their *Blues and Gospel Records 1902–1942* supposed reasonably that the Patton, House, Brown and Johnson sides were recorded "c. July 1930," but in their subsequent editions (1969, 1982 and [with Howard Rye] 1997) they moved the dates back to on or around

May 28, 1930. In the 1987 version of his "Conscience of the Delta" essay, Evans used the timeframe "late May 1930," and in the 1988 edition of this book, Calt and Wardlow say April or May 1930, during the immediate success of Patton's "High Water Everywhere" release. In his essay "Blues in the Round," Komara reopened the matter of dating this session, cautiously positing a range of late May/mid-June 1930, but encouraging conjectures through August 1930. His unpublished 1995 essay "No Water Anywhere" was undertaken in order to support such a recording month of August. In 2001, for the new endnote toward the Revenant republication of the "Voice of the Delta" essay, Evans verified House's memory that August was the month of the trip by using drought reportage from the Clarksdale newspaper. Beaumont in the "My Black Mama" chapter of his House biography *Preachin' the Blues* makes use of the mid-summer range instead of late May.

39. Harris Warren, *Herbert Hoover and the Great Depression* (New York: Norton and Co., 1967), 178–179.
40. In the 1988 book, Calt had supposed that for the lyrics for "Some Summer Day," Patton was inspired by a local woman named Johnnie whose man was at Parchman Penitentiary. Dick Spottwood's 2001 lyric transcription for the Revenant Patton box set has "Charlie" in place of "Johnnie," shifting the utterance of lyrics from Patton to Patton's lover. After reviewing Spottwood's trancription and the Revenant transfer of the recorded performance, it was decided to follow Spottswood's suggestion and revise this passage accordingly.
41. [Chris Smith,] "Words Words Words," *Blues and Rhythm: The Gospel Truth* no. 208 (April 2006), 24, is the source of the fresh interpretation of Ardelle "Shelly" Bragg's "Bird Nest Bound" as referring not to home but to a club or juke joint.

## Chapter 14

1. In his book *The Road to Robert Johnson* (Milwaukee, WI: Hal Leonard, 2007), Edward Komara showed that Johnson borrowed much from the early 1930s piano styles of St. Louis and Indianapolis for his guitar boogie-bass songs.
2. Willie Moore interview with Gayle Wardlow, 1968, as quoted in transcription in Stephen Calt and Gayle Dean Wardlow, "Robert Johnson," *78 Quarterly* no. 4 (1989), 44. Moore assisted Johnson as a sideman in and around Robinsonville in 1929–1930.
3. For a recent article about Zimmerman (Zinnerman in early articles), see Bruce Michael, "Ike Zimmerman: The X in Robert Johnson's Crossroads," *Living Blues* 39, no. 1 (February 2008), 68–73.
4. Johnnie Temple interview with Gayle Wardlow, Jackson, MS, circa 1967–1968.
5. Edward Komara, *The Road to Robert Johnson* (Milwaukee, WI: Hal Leonard, 2007), 49.
6. Willie Moore interview with Gayle Wardlow, in Calt and Wardlow, "Robert Johnson," 44, and Komara, *Road*, 16.

7. Komara, *Road*, 30–32. For a notated music transcription of Patton's "You Gonna Need Someone When You Die," see Dave Rubin, *Acoustic Country Blues Guitar: Delta Blues Before Robert Johnson* (Milwaukee, WI: Hal Leonard, 2000).
8. Stephen LaVere, note and lyric transcriptions accompanying Robert Johnson, *The Complete Recordings*, Sony/Columbia Legacy C2K 46222, 1990.
9. Two informal censuses of Patton 78s held among record collectors have been published. One is the "O-P-Q" installment of "The Rarest 78s," *78 Quarterly* no. 9 [1995], 21–36. The other is Gayle Wardlow with Edward Komara, "Collecting Patton 78s," published as appendix 4 in the documentation accompanying Patton, *Screamin' and Hollerin' the Blues*, Revenant 212, 2001.
10. Most, if not all, of the visual advertisements for Patton's releases during and after the summer of 1930 survive in advertising brochures distributed by the mail-order retailer F. W. Boerner.
11. Calt and Wardlow, "Paramount's Decline and Fall (Part 5)," *78 Quarterly* no. 7, 9.
12. Stephen Calt and Gayle Dean Wardlow, "Pt. 3: The Buying and Selling of Paramounts" (*78 Quarterly* no. 5 [1990]), 8; and Alex van der Tuuk, *Paramount's Rise and Fall: A History of the Wisconsin Chair Company and its Recording Activities*, revised and expanded edition (Denver: Mainspring Press, 2012), 36–37, 179. 20% of the mixture for Paramount's 78s was shellac (not 30% as were those made by other firms), and the other ingredients were china clay, mineral-black or lamp-black, cotton flock, rotten stone (limestone mixed with silica), and gynsonium (which had an asphalt-like base that deteriorated chemically).
13. Arthur Laibly, letter to Calt, July 23, 1970. In the 1988 edition, Calt and Wardlow that a likely reason for Laibley's dismissal may have been his failure to obtain a new distributor to replace Artophone. Alex van der Tuuk (*Paramount's Rise and Fall*, 2012 edition, 179) thought the reasons were more general, namely that the record business was not profitable and that layoffs had begun taking place in the Grafton record pressing plant.
14. Calt and Wardlow, "Paramount's Decline and Fall (Part 5)," 24–25; Van der Tuuk, 2012, 189–190.
15. A selection of John Lomax's 1933 recordings at Parchman are included on the CD *Jail House Bound: John Lomax's First Southern Prison Recordings, 1933* (West Virginia University Press, 2012, 1 CD).
16. Joe Rice Dockery related his anecdotes about Bradford's visits during his 1970 interview with the authors. For a scholarly consideration of Bradford's sources, see the introduction and scholarly materials in Steven C. Tracy, editor, *John Henry: Roark Bradford's Novel and Play* (New York: Oxford University Press, 2008).
17. Patton's niece Bessie Turner told David Evans ("Conscience of the Delta," 2018, 75–76) that the razor attack took place in 1929 in Mound Bayou, committed by a man named Garf Tucker, and that Patton was brought to Cleveland for medical attention. Perhaps Patton suffered two such attacks, four years apart?
18. Henry Stuckey interview with the authors, Sartartia, Mississippi, July 1965. The

Stuckey interview has been the only source about this marriage, as no marriage license or other document has been retrieved, and David Evans in his versions of the "Conscience of the Delta" essay does not include this marriage in his listing of Patton's wives.

19. According to Booker Miller, the local Morgan City bluesmen of the period included an aging D. Irvin, who arrived there in 1933 by way of Itta Bena and later settled settled in Quito; Bo Weavil Jackson (a different man from the Paramount blues artist), who worked as a log hauler on the nearby Mayday plantation and who taught Miller "Shake 'Em on Down" in 1932; and a string band consisting of Stuckey, guitarist Arthur Casey, mandolinist Walter Howard, and a violinist, "Old Man" Johnnie Adams. "All them mens was old men back in them days," Miller said of Stuckey's colleagues.
20. Much of the basis of revision of this and the following chapters is Terry Barkley, "In Search of Charley Patton: Revisiting Holly Ridge and Longswitch," *Living Blues* no. 209 (October 2010), 72–75.
21. B. B. King (1925–2015) spent the first five years of his life in the area surrounding Heathman including Itta Bena and Indianola. A lesser-known postwar bluesman, Charlie Booker (1925–1989), was born on a plantation in the same region, but around Moorhead and Sunflower. Booker as a child heard Patton in person, and in 1952 he recorded for the Blues and Rhythm label a tune called "No Special Rider" that he learned from his uncle, the tonic riff of which borrows a guitar figure from Patton's "Green River Blues." For more about Booker, see Gayle Wardlow, "Greenville Smokin'," *Blues Unlimited* no. 99 (February/March 1973), 12 (reprinted in Wardlow, *Chasin' That Devil Music*, 73–74), and Stephen LaVere's obituary for Booker, *Living Blues* no. 89 (November/December 1989), 38–39.
22. In his autobiography, *The World Don't Owe Me Nothing: The Life and Times of Delta Bluesman Honeyboy Edwards* (Chicago: Chicago Review Press, 1997), 92–93, remembered Sherman Martin as a bootlegger running a juke joint in Holly Ridge.
23. Tom Cannon told David Evans ("Conscience," 2018, 66) that Patton owned and drove cars, at first Ford Model T's, then Chevrolets.
24. Ishman Bracey interview with John Fahey, 1964.
25. According to Barkley, "In Search of Charley Patton," that store's structure has long vanished, and it is not to be confused with the general store currently standing in Holly Ridge.
26. The musical and lyric antecedents for the Delta standard "Catfish Blues" may be heard on records made as early as 1927. Yet the first rendition of "Catfish Blues" was made by Robert Petway for RCA Bluebird in 1941. For an overall history of this song, see Edward Komara's entry in the *Encyclopedia of the Blues* (New York: Routledge, 2006), q.v. "Catfish Blues." Tom Toy's standing regarding this song in the context of the present book is vague. But it is likely that Toy was active musically since the 1930s and had taken up in the early 1940s "Catfish Blues,"

for which he was long remembered even if he did not create it or had no opportunity to make a record of it.

27. For his biography, see James Segrest and Mark Hoffman, *Moanin' at Midnight: The Life and Times of Howlin' Wolf* (New York: Pantheon Books, 2004).
28. This recorded reminiscence was first issued on Howlin Wolf, *The Chess Box*, MCA/Chess Records, 1991, 3 CD set.
29. Samuel Charters, *The Bluesmen* (New York: Oak Publications, 1967), 53.
30. Toomer Wilson, of whom Sam Chatmon said that, did not make records. None of the singers who did record renditions of Patton's tunes borrowed that mannerism of drawing out the last word of a phrase.
31. Booker Miller initially told Gayle Wardlow of his 1932 recording trip with Lembo during a 1968 interview (Wardlow Collection, Center for Popular Music, Middle Tennessee State University [MTSU], tape 0182ll). The following year, Wardlow made sure with Miller, who told it twice during the course of MTSU tapes 0182mm1 and 0182mm2, the latter the basis for the account given in this book's text. Curiously, both Miller and W. H. Buchanon claimed that Rev. Thornton sued Lembo, purportedly over royalties, but differing over when: Buchanon thought in the late 1920s after Columbia released two of the four sides that Thornton recorded in 1927 (the remaining two sides left unreleased), Miller after the 1932 trip. The legal proceeding or any written account about it is yet to be found. Another legal matter, this time with Thornton as defendant, his arrest in 1929 for passing bad checks, has been verified by Moore, 163.
32. Baptist Town was a black neighborhood in north Greenwood, Mississippi. Bluesman Tommy McClennan lived there during the mid-1930s.
33. House's account of his Jackson visit with Patton to Speir's store is taken from the interviews with Nick Perls and Stephen Calt, 1965–1966. A second account from House has been recently published by David Evans, "An Early Interview with Son House," *Frog Blues and Jazz Annual no. 5* (2017): see especially pages 36–37 and 189–190.
34. Millie Barnes Toy [Torry] was still living in Boyle, MS when she was interviewed by Wardlow and Bernard Klatzko in 1963 and in 1970, and by David Evans with Marina Bokelman in 1967.
35. Patton's niece Bessie Turner told David Evans ("Conscience," 2018, 79) a different story, that China Lou admired her father Charlie and kept several of his records.

## Chapter 15

1. The initial report, based on an interview with Bertha Lee, was in Fahey, 26. For more about this incident, see David Evans, "Conscience," 2018, 119–120 and 123–126, and the same author's " . . . Ramblin," *Blues Revue Quarterly* no.7 (Winter 1993), 14–15; in both writings, Evans refers to a set of documents that he found in the circuit court clerk's office.

2. On January 15, 1934, only a week or ten days before leaving New York City to find Patton, Calaway supervised an ARC recording session with Louis Washington aka "Tallahassee Tight." The first song Washington recorded was "Had A Dream That Troubled Me." Patton's audition records for Speir made the previous November included "I Had a Dream Last Night Troubled Me." It is possible, then, that Calaway gave the song to Washington but pocketed the composing royalty when the performance was released on Vocalion 02634.
3. David Evans, ("Conscience," 2018, 126, and ". . . Ramblin," *Blues Revue Quarterly* no.7 [Winter 1993], 15) figures that Calaway, during or shortly after Patton's detention, assured Sheriff Purvis that he would ensure Patton's return to Mississippi.
4. Bertha Lee Pate interview with Bernard Klatzko, Chicago, 1964. Other information relating to Patton's trip to New York was supplied to the authors by Don Kent.
5. For a detailed account of the origins of ARC and its gradual coalescence of labels, see Geoff Wheeler, *Jazz By Mail: Record Clubs and Record Labels, 1936–1958* (Manassas, VA: Hillbrook Press, 1999), 293–294. For a parallel account for blues researchers, see Robert M. W. Dixon, John Godrich, and Howard Rye, "The A.R.C. Labels," *Blues and Gospel Records 1890–1943*, fourth edition (Oxford; New York: Oxford University Press, 1997), xxxii–xxxv.
6. Jay Martin, *Nathaniel West: The Art of His Life* (New York: Farrar, Strauss and Giroux, 1970), 276.
7. J. B. Long interview with Kip Lornell, Elon, North Carolina. See also Lornell, "Living Blues Interview: J. B. Long," *Living Blues* no. 24 (September/October 1976), 13–22.
8. Acuff to Gayle Wardlow, various conversations, 1960s, Nashville, Tennessee.
9. In an interview quoted by Samuel Charters in *The Bluesmen* (New York: Oak, 1967), 54, Bertha Lee remembered whiskey bottles were furnished for consumption during each day's session, even afterwards when Patton played dance music for Calaway and other present ARC personnel.
10. "Stoop Down" was current enough to 1930s Mississippi as to be recorded commercially by the Gold Star Quartette in 1936 during an ARC session in Hattiesburg.
11. R. Nathaniel Dett, editor, *Religious Folk Songs of the Negro as sung at Hampton Institute* (Hampton, VA: Hampton Institute Press, 1927), 123.
12. The function and recording history of "Ananaias" are somewhat obscure. The name is mentioned for three men in the Bible, all in the Book of Acts: one who attempted to cheat the apostle Paul (Acts 5:1–5), one who opposed Paul (Acts 23:2, 24:1), and the most plausible one being who aided the blinded Paul (Acts 9:10–17, 22:12). The only other performance of a piece titled "Ananaias" listed in Dixon and Godrich's discography of pre-1943 blues and gospel is a 1936 Library of Congress field recording at the Raiford (FL) state farm of Beulah MacIntyre singing it. There is also a version collected in Alabama by Ruby Pickens Tartt in 1936, published by Olivia and Jack Solomon, editors, *"Honey in the Rock": The Ruby Pickens*

*Tartt Collection of Religious Folk Songs from Sumter County, Alabama* (Mercer University Press, 1991, 127). The concept, if not the exact song that Patton could have sung, continued into in the 1950s with recordings made by the Chosen Gospel Singers ("Ananais," [sic], Specialty Records, 1952) and Big Bill Broonzy.

13. Big Joe Williams, "Big Joe Talking," *Piney Woods Blues*, Delmark DL 602, LP, 1958. As part of his speech, Williams claimed that Patton wrote a blues about the murder they witnessed, including the lyrics "I know poor Quicksilver gonna hear Gabriel when he sound / He gonna raise up in the grave, but the poor boy got to lay back down." Not all of Williams' various claims to interviewers have turned out to be true, and this one about Patton is as subject to doubt as any other of Williams' tales. Even so, David Evans, in his "Conscience of the Delta," 2018, 119–120, believes that Williams may be telling a true story, and that the song lyrics he recited may be from Patton's "The Delta Murder."
14. Charters, *The Bluesmen*, 56.
15. Evans, "Conscience," 2018, 84. In the 1987 version of this essay, 170, Evans thought the consulting doctor was the same as the doctor who signed the death certificate, D. W. Compton.
16. For its reproduction and full interpretation, see Calt and Wardlow, "Patton's Murder." Terry Barkley, "In Search of Charley Patton," 7, notes that the address was written on the certificate as "350 Heathman," but the number was written in a different handwriting than the plantation name, suggesting that "350" isn't for a house number at all.
17. In the 1988 edition of this book, Willie Calvin was thought by the authors to be the same person as the woman who Booker Miller saw with Patton at the frolic on April 8. But Terry Barkley, "In Search of Charley Patton," 75, states that Calvin was a man, citing a World War I draft card for Willie Calvin, and saying he was a Heathman plantation resident and employee.

### Chapter 16

1. Quotes from Calt's interview with Edwards, 1971. In *The World Don't Owe Me Nothing*, 93–94, Edwards remembered seeing a small cross and a paper wreath on Patton's grave.
2. However quickly that Patton's grave may have been overgrown by weeds, it was occasionally visited by those who knew him. For example, Howlin' Wolf and Fiddlin' Joe Martin made a pilgrimage to Holly Ridge shortly after World War II (James Segrest and Mark Hoffman, *Moanin' at Midnight: The Life and Times of Howlin' Wolf* (New York: Pantheon, 2004), 58. Terry Barkley, "In Search of Charley Patton," 72, raises the tradition that Patton was buried not in Holly Ridge, but at the Union Cemetery in nearby Longswitch. While noting that Calt and Wardlow (in the 1988 and present editions of their biography) and David Evans (in his "Conscience of the Delta" essay) agree that Patton was buried at Holly

Ridge, Barkley admits to having a "gut feeling" that Patton may be buried at Longswitch.

3. According to David Evans, "Conscience," 2018, 86, the funeral was held by the Central Burial Association of Indianola, which suggests to Evans that Patton had an insurance policy.
4. Reverend A. W. Nix, "That Little Thing May Kill You Yet" (Vocalion 1431, released 1929).
5. Calt and Wardlow, "Patton's Murder - Hogwash, or Whitewash."
6. Harrison, Tinsley Randolph, editor [et al.] *Principles of Internal Medicine*, 2nd edition, (New York: Blakiston, 1954), 876.
7. Melville J. Herskovits, *The Myth of the Negro Past*, (New York: Harper and Brothers, 1941), 205. The author relates this belief to West African religion.
8. Some decades later, Viola Cannon's daughter Bessie Turner sanctified her uncle's last days by claiming to David Evans ("Conscience," 2018, 85), that he had spent his last week of life preaching and singing spirituals.
9. The present gravestone for Patton at the New Jerusalem Missionary Baptist cemetery in Holly Ridge was placed on July 20, 1991 by guitar dealer Skip Henderson and rock musician John Fogerty.
10. Then again, tribute issues were rare. Paramount's tribute discs in 1930 for Blind Lemon Jefferson were of songs performed by other artists, not re-pressings of the performances by Jefferson now of historical, not commercial, interest. The first noteworthy repackaging of a blues singer's records as a memorial issue was Columbia Records four-disc album for Bessie Smith in 1938, shortly after her gruesome death in a car accident while on tour in Mississippi.
11. Letter from Bernard Klatzko to Wardlow, 28 September 1963. Later on, Wardlow learned that the control numbers from Patton's 1934 session were reassigned to recordings of Chinese music.
12. The introduction of brass and reed instruments as soloists, and of a homophonic rhythm section consisting of piano, bass and drums, were critical towards the development of swing in jazz music during the mid-to-late 1920s. Swing came to be adopted by bluesmen in the early to mid 1930s; Robert Johnson's 1936–37 recordings are important performances of the transition in blues to swing and the big beat. For a detailed account of this transition, see Komara, *The Road to Robert Johnson*.
13. Bertha Lee Pate interview with Bernard Klatzko, Chicago,1964.
14. Evans, "Conscience," 2018, 79, states that Willie Mae died in 1962 from a stroke.
15. Jimbo Mathus, "Rosetta and Me," *Oxford American* no. 16 (Spring 1997): 46. See also Mike Jordan and Hal Horowitz, "Charley's Daughter," http://www.charleypatton.4t.com/photo3.html, accessed 24 May 2016.
16. The list of titles copyrighted by Rosetta Patton Brown may be retrieved online at the U.S. Copyright Office, Public Catalog, https://cocatalog.loc.gov, accessed 30 April 2020. The document number to be entered in the search box is v3412d404. Rosetta Brown's descendents include her daughter Martha Brown and grand-

daughter Kechia Brown. See T. DeWayne Moore, "Charley Patton's Grave: More Than a Memorial in Holly Ridge," http://www.mississippifolklife.org/articles/charley-pattons-grave-more-than-a-memorial-in-holly-ridge, 3 April 2018, accessed 31 December 2021

17. Evans, "Conscience of the Delta," 2018, 78–79. Researcher Jim O'Neal learned of Will Williams from Tom Cannon (Jim O'Neal, "Charley Patton: Paradigm and Paradox," 41), but it was Evans who has shown that Williams was the son of Patton and Hollins.
18. Evans, "Conscience of the Delta," 2018, 81. In the 1987 version, 167, Evans reported hearing from Tom Cannon that Patton and Bertha Reed had two children, but in the 2018 revision, Evans has considered that the two children may have been confused with the two sons Patton had with Sallie Hollins.
19. These closing paragraphs are an expansion of an interview the authors conducted with Hobo George in Cleveland, MS in 1970.

*Chapter 17*

1. For more about the Mississippi Blues Trail markers placed by the Mississippi Blues Commission, see Richard Grant, "Selling the Blues: To Draw Tourists, the Mississippi Delta Plays on its Musical Heritage," http://projects.aljazeera.com/2015/04/mississippi-blues/, accessed 30 April 2020.
2. John Fahey, *Charley Patton*. London: Studio Vista, 1970. It was a publication of Fahey's 1966 M.A. thesis at the University of California, Los Angeles, titled "A Textual and Musicological Analysis of the Repertoire of Charley Patton."
3. Stephen Calt and Gayle Dean Wardlow, *Charlie Patton: King of the Delta Blues Singers*. Newton, NJ: Rock Chapel Press, 1988.
4. Robert Sacré , editor, *The Voice of the Delta: Charley Patton and the Mississippi Blues Traditions, Influences, and Comparison: An International Symposium*. Liège, Belgium : Presses Universitaires de Liège, 1987. An updated edition was published as Sacré, editor, *Charley Patton: Voice of the Mississippi Delta*, Jackson: University Press of Mississippi, 2018.
5. A survey of Patton issues on 78s, LPs, CDs and digital files is offered in the back matter in this book.
6. For the present revision, Komara and Wardlow inquired among commercial or "trade" publishers for their interest. Finding none, they turned to their academic press contacts including the University of Tennessee Press in 2019.
7. Robert Johnson, *King of the Delta Blues Singers* (Columbia CL 1654, 1961, LP record), and *King of the Delta Blues Singers*, Volume II (Columbia 30034, 1970, LP record).
8. Robert Palmer, *Deep Blues* (New York: Viking, 1981), 117. See also Komara, *Road to Robert Johnson*, especially pp. 42–52.
9. "Robert Johnson: The Father of Rock and Roll," cover headline, *Musician* (January 1991).

10. Canned Heat was one of the few rock bands of the 1960s and 1970s to adapt Charlie Patton songs. Then again, the band had researcher-musicians Alan Wilson, Henry Vestine and Bob Hite. On their early albums through 1970, they recorded their arrangements of Patton's "Pony Blues" and "Shake It and Break It," Henry Sims' "Tell Me Man Blues," and Willie Brown's "Future Blues."
11. Adam Gussow, *Beyond the Crossroads: The Devil and the Blues Tradition* (Chapel Hill: University of North Carolina Press, 2017), 279–283.
12. Citations of magazine articles about Patton were gathered using the indexes *Music Index* and *RILM Abstracts.*
13. Peter Guralnick, *Feel Like Going Home: Portraits in Blues and Rock 'n' Roll* (New York: Outerbridge and Dienstfrey, 1971), 48–50.
14. In addition to the previously cited books by Fahey, Sacré, and Calt and Wardlow, there were also David Evans' *Big Road Blues: Tradition and Creativity in the Folk Blues* (Berkeley: University of California Press, 1982), and Francis Davis' *History of the Blues: The Roots, the Music, the People from Charley Patton to Robert Cray* (New York: Hyperion, 1995).
15. D. M. [Dave Marsh], review of Charley Patton, *Screamin' and Hollerin' the Blues* (Revenant 212), *Playboy* 49, no. 2 (February 2002), 28.
16. Robert Palmer, "Deeper into the Blues: Before Robert Johnson, There Was Charley Patton," *Rolling Stone* no. 625 (5 March 1992), 63.
17. See especially the columns by Susan Silwicki in *Goldmine* 36, no. 23 (May 2010), 38–45; *Goldmine* 37 no. 1 (14 January 2011), 98; and *Goldmine* 38, no. 6 (May 2012), 12.
18. James W. Swinnich, *Living and Playing the Blues on Dockery Plantation—Farms,* (Parker, CO: Outskirts Press, 2021).
19. Swinnich cites J. Todd Moye, *Let the People Decide: Black Freedom and White Resistance Movements in Sunflower County, Mississippi, 1945–1986* (Chapel Hill: University of North Carolina Press, 2004), 31, and Department of Commerce, County Data Book, 222 and Census of the Population, 26–11, 26–24).
20. *Bolivar Commercial* (Cleveland, MS), April 20, 1976.
21. Palmer, *Deep Blues*, 55.
22. Swinnich cites Keith Somerville Dockery Mclean's memoir, *Wanderer from the Delta* (Xlibris Corporation, 2002), 125 and 127.
23. Keith Somerville Dockery McLean, https://www.legacy.com/obituaries/name/keith-mclean-obituary?pid=17302463 (accessed 30 April 2020).
24. For this account of blues tourism, I rely on Stephen A. King's *I'm Feeling The Blues Right Now: Blues Tourism and the Mississippi Delta* (Jackson: University Press of Mississippi, 2011), especially Chapter 2, "The History of Blues Tourism in the Mississippi Delta," pp. 54–77.
25. Eddie Dean, "Skip James' Hard Time Killing Floor Blues," Washington (DC) City Paper, 25 November 1994. Accessible online at https://www.washingtoncity

paper.com/news/article/13009741/skip-james-hard-time-killing-floor-blues (accessed 30 April 2020).

26. King, *I'm Feeling The Blues Right Now*, 55
27. King, *I'm Feeling The Blues Right Now*, 56–65.
28. King, *I'm Feeling The Blues Right Now*, 56.
29. Alan Lomax, *The Land Where the Blues Began*, New York: Pantheon, 1993. Lomax had earlier used the title for a film on Mississippi blues for the PBS television series *American Patchwork*.
30. Swinnich, *Living and Playing the Blues*, 137.
31. Dockery Farms Foundation website, http://www.dockeryfarms.org/, accessed 30 April 2020.
32. "Blues Site Named a Mississippi Landmark," http://www.mdah.ms.gov/new/news/iconic-blues-site-named-a-mississippi-landmark, accessed 30 April 2020.
33. See the map of locations mentioned in Patton lyrics by Paul Mitchell for the Revenant set *Screamin' and Hollerin' The Blues*, p. 37.
34. The account of Wardlow's travels for records and research is based on Gayle Dean Wardlow with Edward Komara, "Collecting Patton's 78s," in book accompanying Patton, *Screamin' and Hollerin' the Blues*, pp. 122–124. Additional information about his interviews may be found in the article introductions for the contents of Gayle Wardlow, *Chasin' That Devil Music* (San Francisco: Miller Freeman Books, 1998).
35. John Godrich and Robert M. W. Dixon, *Blues Records 1902–1942*, second edition, Chigwell, England: Storyville, 1969. This standard discography of pre-1943 blues is now in its 4th edition (New York: Oxford University Press, 1997).
36. Klatzko and Wardlow's account of their 1963 research trip is the basis of the short Patton biography included in the second LP of Origin Jazz Library's Patton reissue, *The Immortal Charlie Patton* vol. 2, Origin Jazz Library OJL-7, LP record, 1964. Viola Cannon's great grandson Kenny Cannon appeared in the 2017 PBS television film series *American Epic* and in the accompanying book, Bernard MacMahon and Allison McGourty with Elijah Wald, *American Epic: The First Time America Heard Itself* (New York: Atria), 2017.
37. Wardlow's surviving tapes of his interviews are now held at the Blues Archive, John D. Williams Library, the University of Mississippi. Digitizations are accessible for listening at the website for the Wardlow Collection, the Center for Popular Music, Middle Tennessee State University, http://popmusic.mtsu.edu/archives/inventory/wardlow.htm, accessed 30 April 2020.

# Bibliography

## Biographical Resources with Lyric and/or Music Transcriptions


Ainslie, Scott. "Standing at the Crossroads." *Acoustic Guitar* 20, no. 5 (November 2009): 43–51.

Barkley, Terry. "In Search of Charley Patton: Revisiting Holly Ridge and Longswitch." *Living Blues* 41, no. 5 (October 2010): 72–75.

Barton, William E. [editor] *Old Plantation Hymns: A Collection of Hitherto Unpublished Melodies of the Slave and the Freedman, with Historical and Descriptive Notes.* Boston; New York; London: Lamson, Wolfe and Company, 1899.

Basiuk, Bo. "Eddie "Son" House—Delta Bluesman." *Blues Magazine* 2, no. 5 (October 1976): 40–55.

"Blue n' Rhythm." *Blues and Rhythm: The Gospel Truth* no. 305 (December 2015): 22

Bracey, Ishman. "Got Four, Five Puppies, One Little Shaggy Hound." *Blues Unlimited* no. 142 (1982): 4–11.

Briggs, Keith, and Alex van der Tuuk. Notes accompanying *The Definitive Charley Patton.* Catfish Records KAT CD 180. 3 CD set. 2001.

Calt, Stephen. *I'd Rather Be the Devil: Skip James and the Blues.* New York: Da Capo Books, 1995.

———. "Unholy Trinity." *Guitar World* 27 no. 2 (February 2006): 56–57.

Calt, Stephen, Jerry Epstein, John Fahey, Don Kent, Nick Perls, Michael Stewart, and Alan Wilson. Notes and lyric transcriptions for Charley Patton, *Founder of the Delta Blues.* Yazoo L-1020. 3 LP set. [1969]

Calt, Stephen, and Don Kent. Notes accompanying Charley Patton, *King of the Delta Blues.* Yazoo L-2001. 1991. 1 CD.

Calt, Stephen and Gayle Dean Wardlow, "Bitchin' Boogie: An Open Letter to Blues Fans," *Blues Unlimited* no. 140 (Spring 1981), 39. Also published as "An Open Letter to Blues Fans," *Living Blues* no. 50 (Spring 1981), 5.

———. *King of the Delta Blues: The Life and Music of Charlie Patton.* Newton, NJ: Rock Chapel Press, 1988.

Cash, W[ilbur]. J. *The Mind of the South.* New York: Knopf, 1941.

Charters, Samuel. Notes accompanying Son House and J. D. (Jaydee) Short, *Blues from the Mississippi Delta*, Folkways LP FA 2467. LP record. 1963.

Charters, Samuel. *Poetry of the Blues.* New York: Oak, 1963.

Charters, Samuel. *The Bluesmen.* New York: Oak, 1967.

Davis, Francis. *The History of the Blues.* New York: Hyperion, 1995.

Evans, David. *Big Road Blues: Tradition and Creativity in the Folk Blues.* Berkeley: University of California, 1982.

Evans, David. "Charley Patton: The Conscience of the Delta." In Sacré, Robert, editor, *The Voice Of The Delta* (Liege: Presses Universitaires, 1987): 109–214. Republished with updates in the book accompanying Screamin' and Hollerin' the Blues: The Worlds of Charley Patton, Revenant 212, 7 CDs, 2001. Revised with new material in Sacré, Robert, editor, *Charley Patton: Voice of the Mississippi Delta* (Jackson: University Press of Mississippi, 2018): 23–137.

Evans, David. "High Water Everywhere: Blues and Gospel Commentary on the 1927 Mississippi River Flood." In Robert Springer, *Nobody Knows Where the Blues Comes From: Lyrics and History* (Jackson, MS: University Press of Mississippi, 2006): 3–75.

Fahey, John. *Charley Patton.* London: Studio Vista, 1970. A published revision of his *A Textual and Musicological Analysis of the Repertoire of Charley Patton* (M.A. Thesis, University College of California, 1966).

Garon, Paul. *Blues and the Poetic Spirit.* London: Eddison Press, 1975.

Givens, Bill, and David Evans. Lyric transcriptions accompanying later pressings of *Really! The Country Blues.* Origin Jazz Library-2. LP originally released in 1962.

Givens, Bill, and David Evans. Lyric transcriptions accompanying later pressings of *The Mississippi Blues no. 2: The Delta 1929–1932.* Origin Jazz Library-11. LP originally released in 1965.

Groom, Bob, editor. *Blues World Booklet no. 2: Charlie Patton.* Knutsford, Cheshire: Blues World, 1969.

Groom, Bob. "Lyric transcript no. 3: My Black Mama." *Blues World* no. 14 (May 1967): 19–20.

Groom, Bob, Alan Grainger, and Ted Griffiths. "Dry Spell Blues." *Blues World* no. 8 (May 1966): 22–23.

Grossman, Stefan. *Delta Blues Guitar.* New York: Oak, 1969.

Grossman, Stefan. "'Mississippi County Farm Blues' by Son House." *Guitar Player* 15, no. 7 (July 1981): 146.

Grossman, Stefan, Hal Grossman and Stephen Calt. *Country Blues Songbook.* New York: Oak Publications, 1973.

Grossman, Stefan, and Woody Mann. *The Roots of Robert Johnson.* Pacific, MO: Mel Bay, 1993.

Kent, Don. Lyric transcriptions and essay for *Patton, Sims, and Lee.* Herwin Records 213. LP record, 1977.

——. Notes accompanying *Master of the Delta Blues: The Friends of Charlie Patton.* Yazoo L-2002. 1991. 1 CD.

LaVere, Stephen. Notes and lyric transcriptions accompanying Robert Johnson, *The Complete Recordings*. Sony/Columbia Legacy C2K 46222, 1990. 2 CD set.

Macleod, R. R. *Yazoo 1–20*. Edinburgh, Scotland: PAT Publications, 1988.

——. *Yazoo 21–83*. Edinburgh, Scotland: PAT Publications, 1992.

——. *Document Blues-1*. Edinburgh, Scotland: PAT Publications, 1994.

——. *Document Blues-4*. Edinburgh, Scotland: PAT Publications, 1996.

——. *Document Blues-6*. Edinburgh, Scotland: PAT Publications, 1996

MacMahon, Bernard, and Allison McGourty with Elijah Wald. *American Epic: The First Time America Heard Itself* (New York: Atria), 2017.

Mann, Woody. "'Screamin' and Hollerin' the Blues': The Guitar Style of Charley Patton." *Sing Out* 46 (Summer 2002): 53–57.

Marsh, J. B. T., editor. *The Story of the Fisk Jubilee Singers with Their Songs.* 7th edition. London: Hodder and Stoughton,1877.

Messer, Michael. "Slide Blues Roots." *FRoots* (*Folk Roots*) 35 no. 6 (December 2013): 54.

Monge, Luigi. *La Lingua Inglese dei Negri d'America e i Blues: Analisi Critica di Alcuni Testi.* Degree thesis, University of Genoa, 1985.

——. "Preachin' the Blues: A Textual Linguistic Analysis of Son House's "Dry Spell Blues." in David Evans, editor, *Ramblin' on My Mind: New Perspectives on the Blues* (Urbana, Champaign, Chicago: University of Illinois Press, 2008): 222–257.

Oakley, Giles. *The Devil's Music.* London: BBC, 1976.

Oliver, Paul. *Screening the Blues: Aspects of the Blues Tradition*. London, Cassell, 1968.

Oliver, Paul. *The Story of the Blues*. London: Barrie and Rockcliff, 1969.

Oliver, Paul. *Songsters and Saints: Vocal Traditions on Race Records*. Cambridge: Cambridge University Press, 1984.

O'Neal, Jim. Booklet notes and lyric transcriptions to Charley Patton, *The Complete Recorded Works*. Tokyo: Pea VinePCD-2255/6/7. Three CD set. 1993

Palmer, Robert. *Deep Blues*. New York: Viking Press, 1982.

——. *Blues and Chaos: The Music Writing of Robert Palmer*. New York: Scribner, 2011.

——. "Deeper into the Blues: Before Robert Johnson, There Was Charley Patton." *Rolling Stone* no. 625 (5 March 1992), 63.

Patton, Phil. "Blues for Cousin Charlie." *Esquire* 114, no. 4 (October 1990): 54–56.

Paulus, George. "Charley Patton Publicity Photo—That's All, That's All . . . , " *Blues and Rhythm* no. 171 (August 2002): 13.

Polenberg, Richard. *Hear My Sad Story: The True Tales That Inspired "Stagolee," "John Henry," and Other Traditional American Folk Songs.* Ithaca, NY: Cornell University Press, 2015.

Raim, Ethel, transcriber. "Preachin' the Blues." *Sing Out!* 15, no. 3 (July 1965): 46–47.

Rubin, Dave. *Acoustic Country Blues Guitar: Delta Blues before Robert Johnson.* Milwaukee: Hal Leonard, 2000.

———. "Charley Patton." *Guitar Player* 40 no. 8 (August 2006): 64–68.

Rye, Howard. "Charley Patton." *Collectors Items* no. 14 (October 1982): 20–21.

———. "Charley Patton (Revised)." *Collectors Items* no. 69 (Spring 1995): 12–14.

Sackheim, Eric. *The Blues Line: A Collection of Blues Lyrics.* New York: Grossman, 1969.

Sacre, Robert, editor. *The Voice of the Delta: Charley Patton and the Mississippi Blues Tradition.* Lieges: Presses Universitaires, 1987. Includes the first version of David Evans' essay "Charley Patton: The Conscience of the Delta."

———. *Charley Patton: Voice of the Mississippi Delta.* Jackson: University Press of Mississipp, 2018. Includes the third version of David Evans' essay "Charley Patton: The Conscience of the Delta."

*Screamin' and Hollerin' the Blues: The Worlds of Charley Patton.* Revenant 212, 7 CD set, 2001. With contributions from John Fahey, Dick Spottswood, Edward Komara, Gayle Wardlow, and the second version of David Evans' essay "Charley Patton: The Conscience of the Delta."

Sherrill, Robert. *Gothic Politics in the Deep South.* New York: Grossman, 1968.

Silwicki, Susan. Columns regarding auctions of Patton recordings in *Goldmine* 36, no. 23 (May 2010), 38–45; *Goldmine* 37 no. 1 (14 January 2011), 98; and *Goldmine* 38, no. 6 (May 2012), 12

Smith, Chris. "Words Words Words." Blues and Rhythm: The Gospel Truth no. 208 (April 2006): 24–25.

Snyder, Jared M. "Squeezebox: The Legacy of Afro-Mississippi Accordionists." *Black Music Research Journal* 17, no. 1 (Spring 1997): 37–57.

Taft, Michael. *Blues Lyric Poetry: An Anthology*. New York and London: Garland, 1983.

———. *Talkin' To Myself: Blues Lyrics, 1921–1942*. New York: Routledge, 2005.

Titon, Jeff Todd. *Early Downhome Blues*. Urbana: University of Illinois, 1977.

———. *Early Downhome Blues*. Second edition. Chapel Hill: University of North Carolina, 1994.

Uncredited. Lyric transcriptions accompanying *The Mississippi Blues: 1927–1940*. Origin Jazz Library OJL-7. LP [1963–1964]

Uncredited. Lyric transcriptions accompanying *Country Blues Encores.* Origin Jazz Library-8. LP, 1964.

Uncredited. Lyric transcriptions for *Son House-Blind Lemon Jefferson*. Biograph 12040. LP record, 1972.

Van Rijn, Guido et al. Notes and essay for Edith North Johnson, *Honey Dripper Blues*. Agram 2016. CD, 1992.

Wardlow, Gayle Dean. "Ledell Johnson Remembers His Brother, Tommy." *78 Quarterly* no. 1 [1967]: 63–65.

White, Jack. "Founding Father: Charley Patton." *The Observer Magazine Music Monthly* no. 3 (16 November 2003): 25.

Wyatt, Keith. "The Ax Museum: Charlie Patton." *Guitar World* 21 (October 2001): 91–94.

Wynne, Ben. *In Tune: Charley Patton, Jimmie Rodgers, and the Roots of American Music.* Baton Rouge: Louisiana State University Press, 2014.

*Additional Biographical Resources*

Barnie, John: "Charley Patton's Jailhouse Blues." *Blues Unlimited* no. 124 (March/June 1977): 22–23.

Berkowitz, Kenny. "Making It Count." *Acoustic Guitar* 26 no. 7 (January 2016): 16.

Beaumont, Daniel. *Preachin' The Blues: The Life and Times of Son House.* New York: Oxford University Press, 2011.

Briggs, Keith. "High Water Everywhere: Blues and the Mississippi Flood of 1927." *Living Blues* no.87 (July/August 1989): 26–29.

———. "Down the Dirt Road: The Life and Music of Charlie Patton." *Blues and Rhythm: The Gospel Truth* no. 104 (November 1995): 15.

Briggs, Keith, and Tony Burke. "'We Called It The Walking Blues.'" *Blues and Rhythm: The Gospel Truth*, no.37 (June/July 1988): 4–5.

Buenger, Kathy. "Port Chair Company makes music history." *Ozaukee County Guide* 30, no.11 (24 November-1 December 1987): 1–3.

———. "Grafton was part of early record industry." *Ozaukee County Guide* 30, no.12 (2–8 December 1987): section 2, pp. 1–3.

Charters, Samuel. "Charlie Patton: A review and some new information on the singer." *Record Research* no. 40 (January 1962): 2, 20.

———. *The Blues Makers.* New York: Da Capo, 1991. Reprints *The Bluesmen* and *Sweet As Showers of Rain*, retaining the original pagination of each book, with a new preface by Charters.

Cohn, Lawrence, "The Blues Didn't Die With Charlie Patton's Last Record!" *78 Quarterly* no. 1 (1967): 46–48.

Cowley, John. "Really the 'Walking Blues': Son House, Muddy Waters, Robert Johnson and the development of a traditional blues." *Popular Music* 1 (1981): 57–72. Reprinted in its entirety in *Juke Blues*, no.1 (July 1985): 8–14.

———. "Son House 1902–1988: An Historical Appreciation." *Blues and Rhythm: The Gospel Truth*, no.41 (December 1988): 8–10.

Crumb, Robert. "Patton." *Zap*, no.11 (1984): 3–14.

Eagle, Bob. "Willie Brown Revisited." *Frog Blues and Jazz Annual* no. 4 (2015): 135–139

Edwards, David "Honeyboy," as told to Janis Martinson and Michael Robert Frank. *The World Don't Owe Me Nothing: The Life and Times of Delta Bluesman Honeyboy Edwards.* Chicago: Chicago Review Press, 1997.

Evans, David. "Son House-Some Further Comments." *Blues Unlimited*, no.43 (May 1967): 8–10.

———. "Charley Patton: His Life and Music." *Blues World* no. 33 (Autumn 1970): 11–15.

———. *Big Road Blues: Tradition and Creativity in the Folk Blues.* Berkeley: University of California Press, 1982.

———. "Ramblin," *Blues Revue Quarterly* no. 6 (Winter 1993): 10–12.

———. "Ramblin." *Blues Revue Quarterly* no.7 (Winter 1993): 14–15

———. "Ramblin." *Blues Revue Quarterly* no.8 (Spring 1993): 14–17.

——. "An Early Interview with Son House" Parts I and II. *Frog Blues and Jazz Annual* no. 5 (2017): 29–44, 176–194.

Garon, Paul, and Beth Garon. *Woman With Guitar: Memphis Minnie's Blues.* [Boston]: Da Capo Press, 1992.

Groom, Bob. "An Interview with Son House." *Blues World* no.18 (January 1968): 5–8.

——. "Blues Forum." *Blues World* no. 32 (July 1970): 18–19.

Hall, Bob and Richard Noblett. "A Handful of Keys." *Blues Unlimited* no.112 (March/April 1975): 18, 23.

——. "A Handful of Keys: The Apocryphal Clarence Lofton." *Blues Unlimited* no. 113 (May/June 1975): 14–16.

——. "A Handful of Keys: Louise Johnson Again!" *Blues Unlimited* no. 115 (September/October 1975): 21–22.

——. "A Handful of Keys: I'm Sorry I'll Read That Again." *Blues Unlimited* no. 116 (November/December 1975): 20–21.

Handy, W. C. "The Significance of the Blues." *Talking Machine Journal* (August 1919): 50.

——. *Blues: An Anthology: Complete Words and Music of 53 Great Songs.* New York: Charles Boni, 1926.

——. *Father of the Blues.* New York: Macmillan, 1941.

——. *A Treasury of the Blues.* New York: Charles Boni, 1949.

Heath, Rob. "The Louise Johnson Controversy." *Blues World* no. 29 (April 1970): 14–15.

Hoffman, Larry, and Denise Tapp. Notes accompanying Richard "Hacksaw" Harney, *Sweet Man.* Adelphi/Genes GCD 9909. 1 CD.

House, Son, as told to Julius Lester. "I Can Make My Own Songs." *Sing Out!* 15, no.3 (July 1965): 38–45.

Johnson, Orville. "The Delta Blues." *Acoustic Guitar* 22 no. 6 (December 2011): 50–51.

Klatzko, Bernard. "Finding Son House." *Blues Unlimited* no. 15 (September 1964): 8–9.

——. "Willie Brown Fare Thee Well." *78 Quarterly* no.2 (1968): 47–50.

Klatzko, Bernard [and Gayle Dean Wardlow]. "The Immortal Charlie Patton." Essay accompanying the LP *The Immortal Charlie Patton 1887–1934* no. 2, 1964.

Komara, Edward. "Blues in the Round." *Black Music Research Journal* 17, no. 1 (1997): 3–36.

——. "Son House's 'Clarksdale Moan' Considered." *Tri-State Blues* 2, no. 1 (September/October 1997): 16–17.

——. *The Road to Robert Johnson.* Milwaukee: Hal Leonard, 2007.

LaVere, Stephen. "Hacksaw Harney." *Living Blues* no. 18 (autumn 1974): 7.

——. Obituary for Charley Booker. *Living Blues* no. 89 (November/December 1989): 38–39.

Leadbitter, Mike. "My Girlish Days." *Blues Unlimited* no. 78 (December 1970): 8–9.

Lester, Julius. "I Can Make My Own Songs: An Interview with Son House." *Sing Out!* 15, no. 3 (July 1965): 38–47.

"Looking For The Blues." *Newsweek* 64 (13 July 1964): 82–83.

Marsh, Dave [signed D. M.] review of Charley Patton, *Screamin' and Hollerin' the Blues* (Revenant 212), *Playboy* 49, no. 2 (February 2002), 28.

———. "Charley Patton's Grave: More Than a Memorial in Holly Ridge." http://www.mississippifolklife.org/articles/charley-pattons-grave-more-than-a-memorial-in-holly-ridge. 3 April 2018. Accessed 31 December 2021.

Mathus, Jimbo. "Rosetta and Me." *Oxford American* no. 16 (Spring 1997): 46

Michael, Bruce. "Ike Zimmerman: The X in Robert Johnson's Crossroads." *Living Blues* 39, no. 1 (February 2008): 68–73.

Moore, T. DeWayne. "Revisiting Ralph Lembo: Complicating Charley Patton, the 1920s Race Record Industry, and the Italian-American Experience in the Mississippi Delta." *Association for Recorded Sound Collections [ARSC] Journal* 49, no. 2 (Fall 2018): 153–184.

Napier, Simon A. "Eddie 'Son' House." *Blues Unlimited* no.14 (August 1964): 6, 11.

Obrecht, Jas. "A Major Delta Blues Discovery." *Guitar Player* 22, no.8 (August 1988): 14.

———. "Deep Down in the Delta." *Guitar Player* 26, no.8: (August 1992): 66–70, 72, 74, 76, 78–81, 98.

Oliver, Paul. *Conversation with the Blues.* New York: Horizon Press, 1965.

Olsson, Bengt. Notes accompanying Gus Cannon, *Cannon's Jug Stompers: The Complete Works in Chronological Order 1927–1930 including Gus Cannon as Banjo Joe.* Herwin LP 208, [1974]. 2 LP records.

O'Neal, Jim. "Revisiting the Worlds of Charley Patton," Living Blues no. 252 (December 2017): 64–70.

Perls, Nick. "Son House Interview-Part One." *78 Quarterly* no.1 (1967): 59–61.

Roberts, Helen H. *Ancient Hawaiian Music.* Honolulu: Bernice P. Bishop Museum, 1926.

Rubin, Dave and Edward Komara, *12-Bar Blues*. Milwaukee: Hal Leonard, 2000.

Sante, Luc. "The Genius of Blues." *The New York Review of Blues* (11 August 1994).

Segrest, James, and Mark Hoffman. *Moanin' at Midnight: The Life and Times of Howlin' Wolf.* New York: Pantheon Books, 2004.

Sliwicki, Susan. "Dive In To 'Some Summer Day': The Ain't-Broke Blues of Charley Patton." Goldmine 37, no. 1 (14 January 2011): 98.

Smith, Chris. "Charlie's Angles." *Blues and Rhythm: The Gospel Truth*, no. 45 (April 1989): 20–21.

Spiro, Phil. "How We Found Son House." *Broadside* (of Boston) 3, no. 11 (24 June 1964): 2, 4.

Stewart, Milton. "Structure and Style in Country Blues: General Characteristics of Country Blues." *Musikethnologische Sammelbande* 8 (1986): 103–125.

Stolie, Roger. "Reverend Peyton." *Blues Revue* no. 130 (July/August 2011): 33–34.

Titon, Jeff Todd. "Living Blues Interview: Son House." *Living Blues*, no. 31 (March/April 1977): 14–22.

Tottenham, John. "Charley Patton—The Voice of the Delta." *Jazzbeat*, no. 6 (16 August 1994): 7–10.

Uncredited. Obituary for Richard "Hacksaw" Harney. *Living Blues* no. 17 (summer 1974), 7.

Van der Tuuk, Alex. "Son House: How Paramount's Elusive Artist Became A Blues Icon." *Frog Blues and Jazz Annual* no. 4 (2015): 125–134.

Wardlow, Gayle. "Son House (Collectors Classics 14) Comments and Additions." *Blues Unlimited* no.42 (March-April 1967): 7–8.

———. "Greenville Smokin." *Blues Unlimited* no. 99 (February/March 1973), 12.

———. "Got Four, Five Puppies, One Little Shaggy Hound." *Blues Unlimited* no. 142 (1982): 4–11.

———. "Can't Tell My Future: The Mystery of Willie Brown." *Blues Unlimited* no. 146 (Spring 1986): 6–9.

———. "The Talent Scouts: H. C. Speir (1895–1972)." *78 Quarterly* no. 8 (1993): 25.

———. "Henry 'Son' Sims: 'Farrell Blues Mama: Sho' Don't Worry Me." *78 Quarterly* no. 9 (1995): 11–20.

———. "Blues Today: Where Were You Forty Years Ago? The Summer of 1963 (Charley Patton's Dark Past." Living Blues no. 169 (September/October 2003): 16–17.

Wardlow, Gayle. *Chasin' That Devil Music.* Edited with an introduction by Edward Komara. San Francisco: Miller Freeman, 1998.

Wardlow, Gayle, and Stephen Calt. "Patton's Murder—Whitewash? Or Hogwash?" *78 Quarterly* no. 1 (1967): 10–17.

——— . "He's a Devil of a Joe." *Blues Unlimited* no. 146 (Autumn/Winter 1984): 16–20.

———. "Robert Johnson." *78 Quarterly* no. 4 (1989), 44.

Wardlow, Gayle and Randy Meadows. "Searching for Willie Brown." *Living Blues* no. 229 (February 2014), 66–69.

Waterman, Dick. "Finding 'Son' House: Step by Step, They Followed a Trail that led to Forgotten Blues Singer." *National Observer* (20 July 1964): 16.

———. "Obituary: Son House." *Living Blues* no.84 (January/February 1989): 48–50.

Welding, Pete. "I Sing For The People: An Interview With Howlin' Wolf." *Downbeat* 34, no.25 (14 December 1967): 20–23.

Wilson, Al. "Son House." *Broadside* (of Boston), 4, no. 3 (31 March 1965): [3–4]; 4, no. 4 (14 April 1965): [12–13]; 4, no. 5 (28 April 1965): [6]; 4, no. 6 (12 May 1965): [4]; 4, no. 7 (26 May 1965): [2]; 4, no. 8 (9 June 1965): [9]; 4, no. 9 (23 June 1965): [7]; 4, no. 10 (7 July 1965): [4]. Reprinted complete in *Blues Unlimited Collectors Classics* no.14 (Reprints volume 3) (October 1966), and as the booklet *Son House: An Analysis of his Music and a Biography* (Bexhill on Sea: Blues Unlimited, 1965).

### *Discographic Resources and Histories of Recording Firms*

Calt, Stephen, and Gayle Wardlow. "Paramount: Anatomy of a 'Race' Label, pt. 1" *78 Quarterly* no. 3 (1988): 9–23; "Pt. 2," *78 Quarterly* no. 4 (1989): 9–30; "Pt. 3: The Buying and Selling of Paramounts," *78 Quarterly* no. 5 (1990): 7–24; "Pt. 4: The Advent of Arthur Laibly," *78 Quarterly* no. 6 (1991): 8–26; "Pt. 5: Paramount's Decline and Fall," *78 Quarterly* no. 7 (1992): 7–29.

Dixon, Robert M. W., and John Godrich. *Recording the Blues.* London: Studio Vista, 1970.

Dixon, Robert M. W., John Godrich, and Howard Rye. *Blues and Gospel Records 1890–1943.* New York, London: Oxford University Press, 1997. Fourth edition. Previous editions were in 1963, 1969, and 1982.

Hilbert, Bob. "Paramounts in the Belfry. . . ." *78 Quarterly* no. 4 (1989): 70–76.

James, Steve. "Of Paramount Importance." *Acoustic Guitar* 15 (June 2005): 150.

Renard, Henry. "Letters from McKune." *78 Quarterly* no. 3 (1988): 54–62

*The Rise and Fall of Paramount Records.* Revenant Records and Third Man Records. 2013—2014. Two sets, each one containing two books, a pouch of facsimile documents, 6 LPs, and a USB drive containing 800 audio music tracks and related advertising artwork.

Van der Tuuk, Alex. *Paramount's Rise and Fall.* Denver: Mainspring Press, 2003. Revised and expanded edition, 2012

Van der Tuuk, Alex, and Guido van Rijn. *New York Recording Laboratories Series.* Overveen, The Netherlands: Agram Blues Books, 2011–2015. Five volumes.

Vreede, Max. *Paramount 12000/13000 Series.* London: Storyville, 1971.

Vreede, Max, and Guido van Rijn. "The Paramount L Master Series." *78 Quarterly* no. 9 (1995): 67–87.

Wheeler, Geoff *Jazz By Mail: Record Clubs and Record Labels, 1936–1958.* Manassas, VA: Hillbrook Press, 1999.

Whelan, Pete. "The Man Who Bought Paramount." *78 Quarterly* no.7 (1992): 30–42.

### *Contextual Resources*

Baker, Ray Stannard. *Following the Color Line.* New York: Doubleday and Page, 1908.

Barry, John M. *Rising Tide: the Great Mississippi Flood of 1927 and How It Changed America.* New York: Simon and Schuster, 1997.

Brandfon, Robert L. *Cotton Kingdom of the New South.* Cambridge, MA: Harvard University Press, 1967.

Broonzy, William. *Big Bill Blues: William Broonzy's Story.* Revised edition. New York: Oak Publications, 1964.

Brown, Henry Bates. *Cotton.* New York: McGraw Hill, 1938.

Bruce, Phillip. *The Rise of the New South.* Philadelphia: George Barrie and Sons, 1905.

Calt, Stephen. *Barrelhouse Words: A Blues Dictionary.* Urbana and Chicago: University of Illinois Press, 2009.

Cash, W. J., *The Mind of the South.* New York: Knopf Books, 1941.

Cobb, James C. *The Most Southern Place on Earth: The Mississippi Delta and the Roots of Regional Identity.* New York; London: Oxford University Press, 1992.

Cohn, David. *God Shakes Creation.* New York; London: Harper and Brothers, 1935.

Daniel, Pete. *Deep'n As It Comes: The Mississippi River Flood.* New York: Oxford University Press, 1971.

Darling, J. N. "The Yazoo Delta of Mississippi, and Location and Construction of its

Railroads." *Journal of the Western Society of Engineers* 7, no. 6 (November-December 1902): 560–573.

Davis, Allison, Burleigh B. Gardner, and Mary R. Gardner. *Deep South: A Social Anthropological Study of Caste and Class.* Chicago: University of Chicago Press, 1941.

Dean, Eddie. "Skip James' Hard Time Killing Floor Blues." *Washington (DC) City Paper*, 25 November 1994.

Eagle, Bob and Eric S. Leblanc. *Blues: A Regional Experience.* Santa Barbara, CA: Praeger, 2013.

"Eudora Welty and Walker Percy: The Southern Imagination." *Mississippi Quarterly* 26 (Fall 1973): 493–516.

Farmer, John Stephen, and William Ernest Henley. *Slang and its Analogues Past and Present* ([London:] for subscribers only, 1890–1904. 7 volumes.

Faulkner, William. *The Mansion.* New York: Random House, 1955.

Garon, Paul. "The Dirty Dozens." *Living Blues* no. 97 (May/June 1991): 33–35

Gioia, Joe. *The Guitar and the New World: A Fugitive History.* Albany: State University of New York, 2013.

Gordon, Robert and Bruce Nemerov, editors. *Lost Delta Found: Rediscovering the Fisk University-Library of Congress Coahoma County Study, 1941–1942.* Nashville: Vanderbilt University Press, 2005.

Grant, Richard. "Selling the Blues: To Draw Tourists, the Mississippi Delta Plays on its Musical Heritage." http://projects.aljazeera.com/2015/04/mississippi-blues/, accessed 21 April 2020.

Guralnick, Peter. *Feel Like Going Home: Portraits in Blues and Rock 'n' Roll.* New York: Outerbridge and Dienstfrey, 1971.

Gussow, Adam. *Beyond the Crossroads: The Devil and the Blues Tradition.* Chapel Hill: University of North Carolina Press, 2017.

Harrison, Tinsley Randolph, editor [et al.] *Principles of Internal Medicine*, 2nd edition. New York: Blakiston, 1954

Hart, Albert Bushnell. *The Southern South.* New York: Appleton and Co., 1910.

Herskovits, Melville J. *The Myth of the Negro Past*, reprinted edition (Boston: Beacon Press, 1958), 205.

Hubbard, W. L. *History of American Music* (*American History and Encyclopedia of Music*, volume 8). New York: Irving Squire, 1910.

Hudson, Arthur Palmer. *Specimens of Mississippi Folk-Lore.* Ann Arbor, MI: Edwards Brothers, 1928

Hurston, Zora Neale. *Mules and Men.* Philadelphia: Lippincott, 1935.

Johnson, Charles S. *Growing Up in the Black Belt.* Washington DC: American Council of Education, 1941.

Key, V. O., Jr, *Southern Politics in State and Nation.* New York: Random House, 1949.

King, Stephen A. *I'm Feeling The Blues Right Now: Blues Tourism and the Mississippi Delta.* Jackson: University Press of Mississippi, 2011.

Komara, Edward. “No Water Anywhere: The Drought Blues of Charlie Patton, Son House, and Skip James.” Unpublished paper, 1996. Read at the Delta Studies Symposium “The Blues II,” Arkansas State University, Jonesboro, April 19, 1996.

Lawson, R. A. *Jim Crow's Counterculture: The Blues and Black Southerners (1890–1945)*. Baton Rouge: Louisiana State University, 2010.

Leadbitter, Mike, editor. *Nothing But The Blues: An Illustrated Documentary.* London: Hanover Books, 1971.

Lomax, Alan. *Mister Jelly Roll.* New York: Grossett and Dunlap, 1950.

———. *The Land Where the Blues* Began. New York: Pantheon, 1993.

Lornell, Kip. “Living Blues Interview: J. B. Long.” *Living Blues* no. 24 (September/October 1976): 13–22.

Lynd, Robert Staughton and Helen Merrell Lynd. *Middletown: A Study in American Culture.* New York: Harcourt, Brace and World, 1929.

Martin, Jay. *Nathaniel West: The Art of His Life.* New York: Farrar, Strauss and Giroux, 1970.

Mathews, Mitford Macleod. *A Dictionary of Americanisms on Historical Principles.* Chicago: University of Chicago Press, 1951.

McCord, Charles H. *The American Negro as a Dependent, Defective, and Delinquent.* Nashville: Benson Printing Co., 1920.

McCormick, Mack. Notes and lyric transcripts for *“Ragtime Texas” Henry Thomas: Complete Recorded Works, 1927–1929, in Chronological Order*. Herwin H 209, 1975, 2 LP set.

McLean, Keith Somerville Dockery. *Wanderer from the Delta*. Xlibris Corporation, 2002

McNamara, Brooks. *Step Right Up.* Garden City, NY: Doubleday, 1976.

Mooney, C. P. J., editor, *The Mid-South and Its Builders.* Memphis, TN: Mid-South Biographic and Historical Association, 1920.

Moye, J. Todd. *Let the People Decide: Black Freedom and White Resistance Movements in Sunflower County, Mississippi, 1945–1986.* Chapel Hill: University of North Carolina Press, 2004.

Muir, Peter. *Long Lost Blues: Popular Blues in America, 1850–1920.* Urbana; Chicago: University of Illinois Press, 2010.

Nordhoff, Charles. *The Cotton States in the Spring and Summer of 1875.* New York: D. Appleton and Company, 1876.

Odum, Howard, and Guy Johnson. *The Negro and His Songs: a Study of Typical Negro Songs in the South.* Chapel Hill, NC: University of North Carolina Press, 1925. Reprinted Hatboro, PA: Folklore Associates, 1964.

Owsley, Frank Lawrence, Jr. *Plain Folk of the Old South.* Baton Rouge: Louisiana State University: 1949.

Partridge, Eric. *A Dictionary of Slang and Unconventional English,* 7th edition. New York: Macmillan, 1970.

Percy, William Alexander. *Lanterns on the Levee.* New York: Knopf, 1941.

Perrow, E. C. "Songs and Rhymes from the South." *The Journal of American Folklore* 26, issue no. 100 (April-June 1913): 123.

Puckett, Newbell Niles. *Folk Beliefs of the Southern Negro.* Chapel Hill: The University of North Carolina Press, 1926. Reprinted New York: Dover, 1969.

Reedy, William Marion. *The Hot Springs of Arkansas.* Missouri Pacific brochure, c. 1916.

*Relief Work in the Drought of 1930–31: Official Report of Operations of the American Red Cross.* American Red Cross no. 901 (October 1931).

Scott, Emmett. *Booker T. Washington: Builder of Civilization.* New York: Doubleday, 1916.

Southern, Eileen, editor. *Readings in Black American Music.* New York: W. W. Norton, 1971.

Stone, Alfred Holt. *Studies in the American Race Problem.* New York: Doubleday, Page and Co., 1908.

Swinnich, James W. *Living and Playing the Blues on Dockery Plantation—Farms.* Parker, CO: Outskirts Press, 2021.

Tackaberry, Andrew. *Famous Ghosts, Phantoms, and Poltergeists for the Millions.* New York: Bell Press, 1952.

Tracy, Steven C., editor, *John Henry: Roark Bradford's Novel and Play.* New York: Oxford University Press, 2008.

Wald, Elijah. *Escaping the Delta: Robert Johnson and the Invention of the Blues.* New York: Amistad, 2004.

——. *The Dozens: A History of Rap's Mama.* New York: Oxford University Press, 2012.

Warren, Harris. *Herbert Hoover and the Great Depression.* New York: Norton and Co., 1967.

Wentworth, Harold and Stuart Berg Flexner, editors. *Dictionary of American Slang.* New York: Thomas Y. Crowell and Company, 1960.

Wharton, Vernon Lane. *The Negro in Mississippi, 1895–1890.* Chapel Hill, NC: University of North Carolina Press,1947.

Wheeler, Mary. *Steamboatin' Days: Folk Songs of the River Packet Era.* Baton Rouge: Louisiana State University Press, 1944.

White, Calvin, Jr., *The Rise to Respectability: Race, Religion, and the Church of God in Christ.* Fayetteville: University of Arkansas Press, 2012.

White, Newman Ivey. *American Negro Folk-Songs.* Cambridge, MA: Harvard University Press, 1928. Reprinted Hatboro, PA: Folklore Associates, 1965.

Woodruff, Nan Elizabeth. As *Rare as Rain: Federal Relief in the Great Southern Drought of 1930–31.* Urbana: University of Illinois Press, 1985.

Work, John Wesley. *Folk Songs of the American Negro.* Nashville: Fisk, 1915.

Young, Melanie. "Where the Southern Cross the Dog." *Living Blues* 45 no. 5 (October 2014): 36–37.

# General Index

# Song Index